Politics of Land

Also available:

*Ralph Nader's Study Group
Report on Land Use
in California*

POLITICS
OF LAND

Robert C. Fellmeth, **Project Director**

Grossman Publishers New York 1973

All royalties from the sale of this book will be given to The
Center for Study of Responsive Law, the organization established by Ralph Nader to conduct research into abuses of the
public interest by business and governmental groups. Contributions to further this work are tax deductible and may be sent
to the Center at P.O. Box 19367, Washington, D.C. 20036.

This book is a condensation of the full, 1200-page report of
the Nader Study Group, *Power and Land in California,* prepared by the Center for Study of Responsive Law.

To the memories of
Michael J. Wollan and Edward Pachniak

Introduction by Ralph Nader

The bloom, it is increasingly said, is off California. The state is facing hard times compared with the economically golden fifties and sixties. In 1970, more people left California than came to live there—the first time this has happened in history. Rich in many natural resources and talented with diverse peoples, California seems bent on pulling itself down by its own bootstraps. The Gold Rush mentality continues unabated, digging deeper into the state's basic wealth with a greed, injustice, and disregard whose costs to the people of California are now unmistakably clear. Even so rich a state can only absorb such costs for so long before it becomes impossible to defer the reckoning.

Most of what people consider undesirable in California is similar to what is undesirable elsewhere in the country. What is unique about California is that it has less excuse to duplicate these ills, much less compound them. For California there was history to learn from, planning to benefit from, and abundant wealth to nourish the dreams of all those who trekked west or north to invoke its promises. But the promises, in their fullness, are fading before the pressures of corporate farming, minority-group isolation, pesticide profligacy, urban sprawl, mindless development spawned and exploited by speculators, the near certainty of catastropic earthquakes, bumper-to-bumper mobility, pollution, private seizure of public wealth, and the complicity of government and land interests. These and other ills have been tolerated and often embraced by Californians with little thought for the consequences, for there were always more resources to go around and other places to move to in the state.

This book studies California's land, its use and abuse by private and public powers, and the now all too visible effects on present and future generations—those forgotten beneficiaries of our contemporary trust. In our "paper economy" where symbols of wealth such as checks, credit cards, bills of lading, stock certificates, futures contracts, deeds, insurance policies, and financial instruments represent the "real wealth" of the nation, our attention is too easily diverted away from economic foundations. A goodly share of that "real wealth" is the land—what goes on over it, on it, under it, and through it. Too much analysis of economic activity is restricted to the symbols of wealth. As a result, the analysis has been highly abstract, excessively aggregate with its data, and devoid of focus on the powerful players as they jockey for control of this scarce and unique resource.

The approach taken by the authors of this book is that of a citizens' board of inquiry—searching out information that affects citizens and identifying the leverage points of accountability and potential change so that crime in the suites, corporate civil disorder, and a government policy of anarchy toward business lawbreakers are required to confront the organized wrath of a properly outraged populace. Diagnosis, analysis, and prescription are the elements of the study. But no study can supply the metabolism for its prescriptions. That can only come from those victimized by the destructive patterns described in such detail here. These abuses are endemic in a system where public and private power collude against the unorganized. For real change to occur, the responses must be enduring and systematic.

Underlying all the specific reform proposals which Mr. Fellmeth and his associates lay before the reader is the principle of accountability, a principle continually undermined by the institutions of corporatism and private government. The corporation, under present laws, can exercise with near impunity its lust for instant gratification, regardless of future costs to others or past frauds on innocent people. The reader may wish to reflect on how much of the unjust enrichment of corporations documented in the book is likely ever to be returned to the defrauded or recaptured by the government. Indeed, the laws as presently constituted and administered virtually guarantee that social myopia and profiteering are securely wedded; the bond is corporate irresponsibility and nonaccountability.

The agony that follows is not the concern of the company or of its managerial predators. They move on to their next plunder with their responsibilities either cancelled by the passage of time or assigned to their hapless customers or neighbors. If the heat of the law should become uncomfortable, there are always the last resorts of strategic bankruptcy, reorganization, or asset or stock sellout. In short, in a society that must increasingly pay attention to future impacts and longer-range costs, the legal permissiveness surrounding and shaping the corporate structure as a legal entity allows the seizure of the public's resources with an immediacy comparable to a croupier's grasp. It is doubtful whether the recommendations in this book can be made effective and durable, even given dedicated enforcement, if more basic legal changes are not made in the corporation's structure under state charter. These changes would include the mandatory public reporting of now hidden corporate information which significantly affects the public, such as that regarding pollution and landholdings, with data substantiating representations. They would also faciliate corporate compliance with the laws by designating compliance officials within the corporation, requiring verifiable records to be kept, and exposing these and other company officials to direct civil and criminal sanctions for violations of law as a more effective deterrent than civil sanctions applied merely to the impersonal undeterrable corporate shell. Laws permitting more expeditious citizen class actions will open up local initiatives outside regulatory frameworks for just recoveries. All of these changes are designed to link responsibility with power, preventing the corporate shell from being a buffer or a diffuser of responsibility and evading or eroding laws enacted for the protection of people.

The corporation's ability to separate power from responsibility or accountability received recognition as far back as the first half of the 19th century. The rapid growth of the railroad, timber, and oil companies was met by a countervailing force in the form of government regulation and the populist-progressive movement at the turn of the century. This force temporarily curbed some overt abuses but soon exhausted its energies. The burgeoning ability of the corporations to develop new practices and acquire new resources enabled them simply to circumvent and outstrip the reach of these reforms. The land interests in California, to a significant extent, have bought, intimidated, compromised, and supplied key officials in state and local government to the point where these interests govern the governors.

Californians can still repair much of the damage. Some

of the solutions are simple and old-fashioned. Requiring
the civil servant and legislator to relieve themselves of occupational and other significant conflicts of interest is a
preventive policy of continuing validity. Citizens injured
as a class or individually should have the right, remedy,
and legal representation to initiate sanction procedures
against the offending officials in these industry-indentured
agencies. Willful nonenforcement of laws, the calculated
deception of the public, the suppression of facts essential
to the public's evaluation of the agency's performance—
these are some grounds for such censure actions, for which
there should be orderly procedures. Irresponsible, corrupt,
or incompetent behavior by agency officials or civil servants
are predictable consequences of a structure of nonaccountability to the people they are commissioned to serve by
their oath of office.

As the following pages reveal, California was the obvious candidate for a study of land resource use. The state
is the leader in dollar volume of agricultural production,
yet is perhaps the most urban-suburbanized of all the states.
The geographical diversity of its deserts, mountains, valleys, and beaches provides the stage for equally diverse
land-use practices. The State has experienced an unprecedented development boom, causing a dramatic confronta-
tion of competing rights and mights at a pell-mell pace.
For California, the future is now. Although it has repeated
the errors of the East, it may still save what has not yet
been irrevocably lost. Further, California has the reputation of having the most "advanced" state government in
the nation, thus giving this book an understated relevance
to conditions in other states.

The Study Group was composed of twenty-five researchers who began work, under the direction of Robert Fellmeth, fifteen months ago. They included specialists in conservation, law, biology, economics, city planning, ecology,
and land development. The group made use of many
secondary sources, known and little known, but spent most
of its time in original research, interviewing literally hundreds of people engaged in the fields being studied: local
district attorneys, middle level agency staff, logging fore-
men, field testers, water pollution enforcement attorneys,
developers, corporate executives, affected or victimized
citizens, and many others. Oral and written information,
verified and integrated, is reflected in the following chap-

ters, which also contain relevant material from hitherto suppressed reports and memoranda withheld from, yet paid for by, the taxpayer. Special mention and gratitude should be extended to the ethical whistle-blowers who shared information with the Study Group because their allegiance to the laws and their sense of higher ethics superseded a subservience to illegally or unethically operating institutions which employed them.

What is happening to California is happening elsewhere, in Florida, the Southwest, the Northwest and other developing areas of our country. The utter disregard for the integrity of the land and its relationship to man inflicts special penalties on the young and the unborn. The uses of land resources throughout America must be brought under a working philosophy of trust, buttressed by fair, democratically enforced laws and farsighted planning. This same philosophy of trust inspired the conservationists' partial victory early in the century when the federal government secured and protected large portions of public lands and forests. The demands on our natural resources are now much greater and much more critical. And time is not so plentiful for the exercise of indifference.

It would be reassuring to view this book as one source of citizen movement for restoration of land resources to more just and rational uses. Certainly, there are groups and individuals who have long shared the concerns expressed here. They hail from diverse backgrounds, occupations, and philosophies, yet the conditions they decry suggest a common bond. Some of this unity of purpose was observed in Santa Barbara after the oil spills, where citizen commitment to the environment led to the partial cessation of destructive drilling and to the respect of Californians (except for some oil executives who still privately refer to residents as "Santa Barbarians"). It remains to be seen whether Californians can pioneer once again. This frontier will be a more difficult one than the first.

Ralph Nader
Washington, D.C.

The Task Force

Project Director
Robert C. Fellmeth

Contributors

Mike Berman	Tim McCarthy
Dean R. Brett	James F. McFeely
Geoffrey Carliner	Harry E. Miller
Chris Citron	Gary Mottola
Mary Claire King Clark	Doug Nelson
Jim Douglas	Richard Parker
Elaine C. Eff	Keith Roberts
Bernard Haeckel	Polly Roberts
Roger Haines	Diana Roose
Robert Eldridge Hicks	Kirk B. Roose
Lavell Jackson	Lew Sargentich
William Kinsey, Jr.	Richard B. Spohn

Staff

Candy McCarthy	Larry Luce
Maureen O'Connell	Janet Lund
Kenneth Blum	Alan J. Branco
	Yan B. Linhart

Production

Theodora Fine	Sherry Leibowitz
	Connie Jo Smith

Editorial Consultants

Peter Schuck	Julia Lockwood
Gregg Fawkes	Diana Roose

The work of this study group was made possible through the generosity of the Sierra Club Foundation and the Abelard Foundation. Special thanks are also due to Santa Clara University for use of facilities, to numerous whistleblowers, to Faye Hove, Pauline Koch, Steve and Tim, and to the many others who gave us their time and use of their homes and offices.

Foreword

Land is a unique resource. Its supply is limited. Once land has been developed, reconversion to agricultural use is costly; once a large lake has been polluted, it may remain dead for decades; once a twenty-square-mile airport has been constructed, it cannot be moved. Land use entails high external costs. Neighboring landholders, the environment, or future generations often bear the costs of a given land use while receiving little or none of the benefits. Land-use policies affect not just the land, but crops and timber growing on it, wildlife protected and nurtured by it, and the nature of commercial, industrial, residential, recreational, and other facilities constructed on it.

Our objective was to discover how this unique resource fares at the hands of public policy and private power in California. We were guided by one major economic premise which is best stated at the outset: Insofar as possible, those who benefit from the expenditure of public monies should generally pay the cost of providing that benefit and those who impose costs—whether long-range, speculative, or indirect—on others, should bear those costs. These principles cannot always be implemented nor can they always be counted on to effect a "proper" allocation of land or other resources. Yet to the extent that they operate, they are counsels of efficiency as well as equity.

We ask the following questions throughout this book: Are the costs to the public of private land-use practices charged to those who cause and profit from them? For example, are the costs of topsoil erosion and water pollution from shoddy logging practices charged to the logger? Does government effectively regulate or prohibit uses producing permanent, noncompensable damage or threat? For example, are precautions taken to prevent intense development in areas below weak dams near active earthquake faults?

Are tax systems allocating resources fairly and efficiently? For example, how is the property tax affecting sprawl, speculation, and resource allocation?

If the tax system provides special privileges and incentives, or there are direct subsidies, are they defensible? For example, do the matching fund systems for roads lead to profligate construction? Do tax breaks for oil firms via depletion allowances, royalty deductions, etc., unjustly enrich some and improperly allocate resources? Do price-support payments favor large corporate farmers or fulfill a legitimate purpose? Is underassessment of timberland justifiable—or overassessment of utilities, or special exemptions for homeowners and insurance firms?

Have public works been planned, constructed, and located efficiently to serve the interests of the public? For example, is the Palmdale Airport located and planned to minimize environmental harm, to coordinate with neighboring land-use schemes, to efficiently serve transportation needs?

Are those receiving the benefits of public works and expenditures paying for them? For example, are agricultural corporations that receive the benefits of water via massive projects paying the cost of providing those benefits?

And finally, has the state set up local fiscal and political structures properly responsive to these questions when the answers have been delegated to them? For example, is local government visible by geographic area and function? Is there competition between jurisdictions for revenue from higher-value property which compromises land use in the public interest?

Land use does not operate in a vacuum. Government has intervened on a massive scale to impose extremely complex and influential tax systems, rules of liability, regulatory schemes, and its own public works. We want to know the circumstances under which government has intervened—or not intervened—as well as the causes, effects, and nature of these public decisions. We have analyzed the nature and administration of current laws and regulatory schemes by the mix of jurisdictions at and below the state level, and present recommendations for reform. Suggestions for reform seek correction through the adjustment of self-regulating systems, so that they may properly function, rather than through the imposition of additional layers of bureaucracy dependent on the perpetuation of the problem they were designed to solve.

Although the scope of the Report is quite broad, there are inevitably some omissions. We focus primarily upon the state of California, and on the state and local government. Federal policies (as on taxation and environmental protection) are briefly discussed because of their enormous impact. Thus, we touch on the management and project responsibilities of federal government agencies with large landholdings in the State. Federal laws governing these agencies, as well as the actual operations of the agencies, are scrutinized, particularly with respect to the Bureau of Reclamation, the Forest Service, and the Bureau of Land Management. Areas excluded are Indian land use and federal housing programs for low income families.

In order to consider in some depth the nature of the political process dictating various policy decisions, we rely heavily upon a case-study approach. We tried to select case studies which were not atypical, although we often chose large projects because of their significance. Sometimes, as in the case of Santa Clara County in Chapter Nine, we chose the very best. For example, in Chapter Three we chose the Regional Water Quality Control Board that the State Board identified as the "best," and then analyzed a "discharger" that the Regional Board felt was "typical." Where there was any doubt about typicality, we conducted surveys to verify comparable conditions elsewhere, or selected enough case studies so that they would stand on their own.

During the course of our investigation, we received hundreds of letters from residents throughout California. Most of the writers were citizens who offered documentation of particular alleged abuses, frauds, and depredations in their locales. Many offered their homes for our use. Some wanted our assistance. There are striking parallels among the various allegations of land abuse communicated to us in letters and via phone over the past several years. We did not investigate or comment on these complaints. We chose our own case studies in order to select genuinely typical subjects.

Ordinary citizens, although organized in hundreds of stopgap environmental groups, are not represented with effective force at the state level where policy is set. So organized, they could perhaps constitute a potent political force to establish an honest and responsive political structure. Many of us are prepared to join in such an effort. All of us are aware that, at least for us, this book is not the culmination of our work, but the opening bell.

Robert C. Fellmeth
Sacramento, California

Contents

Part One

RESOURCES

1

Who Owns California

Land monopoly is not the only monopoly, but it is by far the greatest of monopolies—it is a perpetual monopoly, and it is the mother of all other forms of monopoly.

Winston Churchill

Any understanding of the politics of land in California must be based upon knowledge of the principal actors. Who owns the land? Who finances the land? Who uses the land? Who makes public policies affecting the land?

The interests of private landowners, financiers, and users are inextricably bound to government interests, since every policy decision that is made about land and its use involves governmental aid or acquiescence in one form or another. Government influences land-use decisions directly through enforcement of zoning codes and tax laws, through its own proprietary rights, and through massive public works, such as roads, airports, and water projects. Indirectly, government affects major land-use decisions by shaping the political and economic incentives of private owners. For example, a governmental policy encouraging small ownerships fosters the land-use decisions that flow from such a pattern of holdings: 100 people each owning 100 acres will use that 10,000 acres very differently than would a single owner, simply because their financial abilities and points of view differ from that of a single large owner. The government also shapes incentives by offering rewards or penalties for various types of land-use decisions. For instance, a policy of subsidizing irrigation water encourages agriculture; heavy tax assessments of open space near cities encourages development of that space; tax rules, such as rapid depreciation of "capital improvements" to land (charging the depreciation "expense" against current income), encourage speculation and development. Even the ground rules for the formation of local governments to which land regulation authority is delegated affect land-use patterns.

California covers 100,185,000 land acres [1] and contains 1,379,840 acres of inland water.[2] The various uses to which these 100 million land acres are put are presented in Table 1a.

Table 1a [3]
LAND AREAS BY MAJOR CLASS OF LAND
1964–65

Class of Land	No. of Acres
Total	100,185,000
Forest land	42,416,000
Commercial[a]	17,345,000
Public	9,253,000
Private	8,092,000
Productive–Reserved[b]	1,255,000
Unproductive[c]	23,816,000
Crop land[d]	11,815,000
Urban and suburban land[e]	2,200,000
Other land	43,754,000

[a] Forest land producing or capable of producing crops of industrial wood and not withdrawn from timber utilization by statute or administrative regulation.

[b] Productive public forest land withdrawn from timber utilization through statute or administrative regulation.

[c] Forest land incapable of yielding crops of industrial wood because of adverse site conditions.

[d] As reported by 1964 Census of Agriculture. Excludes land cultivated in developing improved pasture.

[e] Residential areas containing at least five homes, with a density of one home or more on each two acres; industrial and commercial development; and the actively occupied portions of military reservations—as determined by land and water use specialists of the Department of Water Resources.

The federal government has proprietary rights over 44.4% (44,394,000 acres) of California's land area, mostly desert or mountainous forest land in the northern and eastern parts of the state. Federal holdings have declined by 5.3% since 1961, when they constituted 49.7% (49,703,000 acres) of the state's land. The state itself owns 2,310,000 acres, and local governments another 2,050,000. Table 1b sets forth the amounts of California acreage controlled by various government subdivisions and their agencies in 1965 and 1969.[4]

Table 1b
GOVERNMENT OWNED LAND IN CALIFORNIA [a]

	1969	1965
Federal	44,394,000	45,076,000
Department of Agriculture		
U.S. Forest Service	19,971,000	19,971,000
Department of Interior		
Bureau of Indian Affairs	761,000	547,000
Bureau of Land Management	16,816,000	14,969,000
Bureau of Reclamation	1,089,000	1,105,000
Department of Fisheries and		
Wildlife	62,000	75,000
National Park Service	4,102,000	4,061,000
Department of Defense		
Army	1,058,000	1,062,000
Air Force	486,000	506,000
Navy	2,772,000	2,646,000
State	2,319,000	1,954,000
Resources Agency		
Department of Conservation		
Division of Forestry	75,000	74,000
Department of Fish and Game	117,000	115,000
Department of Parks and Recreation	811,000	697,000
State Reclamation Board	199,000	13,000
Department of Water Resources	119,000	56,000
Division of State Lands	609,000	634,000
State Comptroller (tax-deeded		
lands)	73,000	72,000
Business and Transportation		
Agency		
Department of Public Works	210,000	198,000
Counties	793,000	617,000
Cities (incorporated and excluding		
city-counties)	809,000	770,000
School Districts	25,000	78,000
Junior College Districts	7,000	7,000
Special Districts	418,000	467,000[b]
Total	48,765,765	48,969,000[3]

[a] Federal and State totals include small miscellaneous holdings of departments not included in breakdown.

[b] Includes:

Irrigation Districts	191,000
Reclamation Districts	24,000
Water Districts	
State	13,000
County	10,000
Municipal	26,000
L.A. Metropolitan	86,000
Water Conservation Districts	14,000

The 51.2 million acres that remain in private hands include most of California's coast and nearly all of her rich valleys.

Public knowledge of landowners' identities and the nature of their holdings is essential for several reasons. The most obvious threat posed by undisclosed landholdings is abuse of market power. A large landowner may be able to monopolize a particular market because he has the power to set prices on the products of his land; he may even be able to exercise control over an entire regional economy. Owning several thousand acres of developable land does constitute what Churchill calls "the mother of all other forms of monopoly." Once development is established, power over gas stations, retail stores, and countless other economic activities connected with the initial development can be exercised through land-lease arrangements; the greater the distance to alternate services, the greater the margin for excessive profit. And in California, owning even a small piece of land may confer a great deal of economic and political power: California is the foremost producer of many specialized crops, and ownership of several hundred acres of land having the rare soil and climatic qualities for production of a specialized crop means the power to set prices on that crop. Two basic conditions which qualify this power are the elasticity of demand for the commodity (as when above a given price consumers will substitute peas or broccoli for excessively priced asparagus), and the cost of transporting the commodity from distant points of production.

Public knowledge of landholdings is also essential for adequate government regulation. When the state grants monopoly power to utilities, it assumes responsibility for careful examination of costs and revenues—since increased costs are passed on to consumers as higher rates. Proper state regulation, therefore, entails detailed knowledge of the utilities' landholdings, and public disclosure of their finances, in order to facilitate public monitoring. This kind of information is also essential for state regulation of banks, savings and loan associations, and insurance companies, and for the enforcement of specific laws which limit or prohibit land ownership by these financial institutions. The proper administration of laws relating to agriculture, logging, grazing, and mining depends on knowledge of specific holdings. And the property interests of corporations involved in land development should be public information for proper real estate regulation and general public understanding of who owns the land through which publicly financed utilities and services are being extended.

However, in spite of these compelling reasons for public disclosure of land ownership, no statewide compilation of "who owns California" exists. The Public Utilities Commission keeps no formal records of land ownership by utilities. Banks, savings and loan associations, and insurance companies have formed holding companies which enable them to enter into direct land speculation, ownership, and development in spite of laws designed to prohibit such activity on the part of organized financial interests; the state departments designed to regulate these interests do not have adequate ownership information to deal with this twentieth-century loophole. Neither the California Department of Real Estate nor any other agency requires disclosure of the holdings of land development corporations. The State Department of Agriculture has no statewide list of large agricultural concerns. Neither the California Resources Agency nor any of its numerous commissions or departments could tell us who owns California (aside from government land), nor could the State Office of Planning or the State Board of Equalization.

The absence of land ownership records is not always mere oversight. The Department of Water Resources (DWR), in administering the State Water Project, was required to collect figures by 1968 on land ownership in excess of 160 acres for the areas to be served. Governor Brown had pledged, when he was promoting the Project, that such owners would be charged for the subsidy conferred by the Project. However, at the DWR office in Sacramento we found, instead of those figures, a series of memoranda from State Water Resources Director William R. Gianelli to the contracting water agencies. The memoranda, never made public, reveal that the 1968 date for submitting the figures was postponed; then Gianelli asked the contractors if they really wanted to disclose their holdings and to tell him at their next meeting. A final memo notes that the contractors indicated at the meeting that they did not want to supply the information. Gianelli agreed to drop the requirement. At present, therefore, the DWR does not appear to have specific land ownership information, and will not collect it in the future, much less

require payment for public subsidy—regardless of the
Governor's promises.

Even where information must exist, it is sometimes
suppressed. The U.S. Department of Agriculture will not
release the acreage figures for farms receiving federal subsidies. California Stabilization and Conservation Service
offices deny public access to this information, which forms
part of the basis for multimillion-dollar grants of public
money to California's large farmers. The defense of this
denial rests in the view that the information is somehow a
"trade secret."

The last serious attempt to determine who owns California was made in 1940, when a Congressional committee investigating free speech and the rights of labor
sought to compile a list. The committee came up with an
incomplete list of twenty-seven properties, omitting hundreds of owners.[5]

Thus, having found no statewide list of landowners, we
were obliged to compile our own from the offices of county
recorders and assessors, from surveys of the popular and
trade press,[6] financial directories,[7] county atlases, maps
and survey reports issued over the past decade,[8] and from
personal compilations of agricultural interests, union officials, and others.

The results of our survey are presented in Appendix 1-A.
They show that remarkably few corporations own much
of the state. Twenty-five landowners hold over 16% of
the state's privately held land. Including government land,
the top twenty-five landowners own 58% of California's
total land area.

Obtaining this information proved extremely difficult.
Assessors must collect information relating to all taxable
property in the county, but canvassing their offices is
problematical because, in addition to legal problems regarding right to inspection, there are fifty-eight counties in
California, and the filing system is complex, poorly organized, and has no index, thus proving useless for our purposes. Our survey of all fifty-eight of California's assessors
yielded eighteen replies; only seven of these could or
would supply the requested information—the names of the
twenty largest landowners in the county. The Santa Cruz
office gave a typical response, dated October 6, 1970: "A
few of the old-timers could guess at the top three or four
largest landowners but it would be just that, a guess."

Once we had identified large landowners, we wrote to them asking for acreage figures. Corporations generally refused to answer, and even some public utilities termed their acreage figures "confidential." When we rewrote our letter the results changed somewhat. The new version did ask about ownership; it asserted that we had discovered that *x* company had *y* acres and left two blanks at the bottom. One was to be checked if the number filled in was correct, another if incorrect, with the correct number supplied. If we thought we knew the acreage, we filled in our estimate. If we had no idea, we used the arbitrary figure of 28,000 acres. Interestingly enough, the opportunity to correct an apparent error brought in well over 100 replies (25% to 30% of those queried by this method). Nevertheless, some would check "incorrect" and mark "x" or "confidential" where the correct amount was to be supplied in our form. Most still would not answer despite the easy form and the self-addressed, stamped envelope. Even utilities (except for Pacific Gas and Electric) maintained a secrecy inappropriate to the nature of their public trust and functions. Following is the reply of Ross Workman, Financial Vice President of California-Pacific Utilities Company:

> Dear Mr. Fellmeth:
>   This is in reply to your form letter of August 3, 1970 inquiring about our ownership of some 28,000 acres of land used for "use and development." It is not altogether clear to me who you are or why you want this information.
>   Should I receive from you satisfactory answers to those questions, I will consider responding to your letter.

In spite of these difficulties, however, we were able to examine land-ownership concentration in a number of different counties, to do trend analyses in several counties for which we had older (map) data, and to examine concentration by land value as well as by acreage—to look not only at who owns the most land but at who owns the most valuable land.

Table 1c lists the twenty-five largest private landowners in the state, according to our survey results. Given California's size, wealth, and diversity, statewide concentration of ownership by acreage is remarkably high. If we include government, the top 25 owners hold at least 58% of the state. Table 1d analyzes concentration in greater depth and reveals that 257 entities own at least 25% of the privately owned land of the state. If we include government, even counting agencies as separate ownerships, 250 holders control almost two-thirds of the state's total land.

These figures, high as they are, understate the levels of concentration. First, although we believe that most of our acreage figures are accurate (about 5% to 10% of our figures are from data more than three years old and therefore not reliable or current), we could obtain no reliable acreage figures for many whom we know to be large landowners.

Table 1c

THE TOP TWENTY-FIVE PRIVATE LANDOWNERS IN CALIFORNIA
Total Private Land Acreage in State: 51,419,000

Owner	Number of Acres	Cumulative Percentage of Total Private Acreage
Southern Pacific Co.	2,411,000	4.7
Newhall Land and Farming Co.	1,590,000	7.9
Shasta Forest Co.	479,196	9.0
Tenneco, Inc.	362,843	9.7
Tejon Ranch Co.	348,000	10.4
Standard Oil of California	306,000	11.0
Boise Cascade Corp.	303,000	11.6
Georgia Pacific Corp.	278,000	
Pacific Gas & Electric	250,000	
Occidental Petroleum Co.	200,000	
Sunkist Corp.	192,000	
The Pacific Lumber Co.	171,062	
Fibreboard Corp.	155,000	
American Forest Products Corp.	150,000	
The Times-Mirror	145,000[a]	
Penn Central Co.	120,000	
Hammond Lumber Co.	119,840	
Kaiser Industries	111,000	
Masonite Corp.	110,000	
J. G. Boswell	108,000	
International Paper Co.	103,547	
Diamond International Corp.	100,000	
Vail	98,000	
Miller & Lux, Inc.	93,058	
Irvine Ranch Co.	91,600	16.2

[a] Some through partial interest and repeated elsewhere.

Table 1d
STATEWIDE LAND OWNERSHIP CONCENTRATION

Size and Type of Holding	No. of Owners	No. of Acres	Cumulative Percentage of Total Private Acreage
90,000 + acres			
Agric.	9	5,410,000	
Timber	12	2,305,000	
Dvpmt.	4	681,000	
Cumulative Total	25	8,396,000	16.2
40,000–90,000 acres			
Agric.	20	1,020,000	
Timber	7	478,000	
Dvpmt.	9	428,000	
Cumulative Total	61	10,322,000	20
20,000–40,000 acres			
Agric.	46	1,394,000	
Timber	4	122,000	
Dvpmt.	9	216,000	
Cumulative Total	110	12,054,000	23.4
10,000–20,000 acres			
Agric.	118	1,770,000	
Timber	8	121,000	
Dvpmt.	21	315,000	
Cumulative Total	257	14,260,000	27.7
5,000–10,000 acres			
Agric.	152	1,064,000	
Timber	5	33,000	
Dvpmt.	24	180,000	
Cumulative Total	438	15,537,000	30.1

Second, our figures are low because economic and political power concentration is more relevant by land category than by simple acreage. Although 110,000 acres do not constitute a dominant share of the state's land, if there are only 250,000 acres of white pine and the 110,000 acres are white-pine land, the share is quite significant. In Appendix 1A our division of owners into three categories by type of land is extremely rough, but it affords some opportunity to see how concentration increases when the land is divided into agricultural, timberland, and development groupings. Twenty firms, including Southern Pacific, own about 43% of the state's private timberland; the top twenty owners, including government, control 70% of all the commercially viable timberland in California.

In agriculture, a distinction must be made between the 11,815,000 acres of *cropland* and the 37,000,000 acres of "farmland," which includes private range and waste land. Taking cropland alone, we found that 29 concerns own 21% of this land, 75 own 27%, and 220 own 35%. A very recent survey confirms these concentration levels but suggests they may be understated. The survey, conducted by the Agricultural Extension Service of the University of California in cooperation with the Economic Research Service of the U.S. Department of Agriculture in 1969, examined the 2,566 corporations engaged in agricultural production in California and 6.1 million acres in corporate farms. The majority of this acreage is prime cropland and probably represents close to half of the prime cropland in the state. The study [9] reveals that as of 1969, forty-five corporate farms, representing less than one-tenth of one percent of the commercial farms in the state, controlled 3,714,000 acres or approximately 61% of the land covered by the survey. The survey also found that half of the acreage is controlled by large conglomerate corporations with other business enterprises, and often with additional farming operations in other states. At the same time, most of the corporations are closely held, controlled by another corporation or by fewer than four stockholders. (Evidently, we were not alone in having difficulty obtaining data, or in concluding that our findings understate the degree of concentration: fewer than half of the corporations in the 1969 survey returned their questionnaires; when the authors conducted a follow-up study of 164 nonresidents, they found a "significant difference between nonresidents and those who had answered the original request—nonresidents were significantly larger [owners] than the original respondents.") [10]

Third, our figures as clarified are further understated because they are statewide. Owning that 110,000 acres of white pine means more if the other 140,000 acres are in another part of the state, 500 miles away. Taking somewhat smaller areas, such as counties, gives a clearer picture of localized land-ownership concentration. Table 1e presents two typical counties. (Appendix 1B presents all eight rural counties and three urban counties for which we have data.) Generally, the top twenty landowners of rural counties (amounting to from one-fiftieth of one percent to just under one percent of the population) own from 25%

to 50% of the private land. If the government land is included the figure becomes 50% to 90%. In urban counties, the top twenty landowners (constituting from one two-hundredths of one percent of the population on down) own 15% to 30% of the private land. Breaking each of these counties down by land type would raise these levels still further.

Moreover, counties chosen for this analysis did *not* have the most concentrated private ownership. The state's largest landowners concentrate their ownership in Kern County (Kern County Land, et al.), San Bernardino County (Southern Pacific Land Co.), and other counties. Yet concentration is so high in the counties for which we had data as to suggest images of medieval baronies. When examining county maps plot by plot, land domination by small numbers of firms and individuals is most striking.

The trend in land ownership seems to be toward further

Table 1e

LAND OWNERSHIP CONCENTRATION BY SELECTED COUNTIES

Rural County of Sierra
   Total acreage: 612,480
   Total private acreage: 229,278

Owner	No. of Acres	Cumulative Percentage of Total Private Acreage
1. Fibreboard Corporation	28,978	12.7
2. Southern Pacific Land Co.	25,852	23.9
3. Ramelli, Donald	8,280	27.5
4. Russell, Daniel (director of So. Pac., & Tenneco)	7,893	34.3
5. Trosi, Frank C.	7,473	
6. Monarch Investment Company	5,717	
7. Sierraville Properties	4,520	
8. Webber, G. D. & E.	3,626	
9. Sierra Pacific Power	3,430	
10. Johnson, Clifton O.	2,942	
11. Roivley, Sterling H.	2,496	
12. Di Giorgio Lumber Company	2,176	
13. Yuba River Lumber Co.	2,101	
14. Graegle Land & Water	2,054	
15. Turner, Frank	1,937	
16. Genasci, A. R.	1,853	
17. Torri, Kenneth	1,800	
18. Vanetti, Alice	1,558	
19. McPherrin, Anastasia	1,482	↓
20. Pacific Gas & Electric	1,406	48.9

Table 1e (continued)

Rural County of Nevada
  Total acreage: 624,000
  Total private acreage: 438,483

Owner	No. of Acres	Cumulative Percentage of Total Private Acreage
1. Southern Pacific Land Co.	59,958	13.6
2. Pacific Gas & Electric	12,750	16.5
3. Taylor, A., et al.	9,418	18.5
4. May, W.	7,213	20.2
5. William Austin Co.	6,247	21.5
6. Fibreboard Corporation	5,357	
7. Johnson, D.	4,897	
8. San Juan Gold	3,995	
9. Sierra Pacific Power Co.	3,905	
10. Hoffert Co.	3,840	
11. Walton, J. E., et al.	3,590	
12. Boise Cascade Corporation	3,269	
13. Peacock, J. C.	3,021	
14. Viscia, A. A.	2,882	
15. Robinson, Guy	2,484	
16. Nicholls Estate Co.	2,441	
17. Spring Valley Land Co.	2,155	
18. Graham, R. K.	2,081	
19. McAllister, J., et al.	1,954	
20. Bancroft, J., et al.	1,818	32.5

concentration. Although homesteading and sales reduced California's land empires of the eighteenth and nineteenth centuries, a U-curve has formed as concentration has lately begun to enter another upswing. For the past three to four decades, diversified giants have been accumulating new territories. Increasingly, they own California.

Table 1f shows the trend of ownership in Modoc County, where there is much timberland and increasing development. The twelve years between 1958 and 1970 have seen a marked increase in concentration.

In agriculture, the U-curve trend is even more apparent than it is in timberland: the average acreage of agricultural landowners has been increasing steadily since 1930.

Almost by definition, highly concentrated ownership and control of land mean more political and economic power and greater ability to oppose contrary interests than do widely diffused ownership or control. Large landholders direct a greater portion of their earnings toward political

Table 1f
COUNTY OF MODOC
CONCENTRATION OF PRIVATE LAND OWNERSHIP BY ACREAGE,
1958 AND 1970

Owner	No. of Acres	Cumulative Percentage of Total Private Acreage
1958		
1. Shasta Forest Company	130,640	14.9
2. Weyerhaeuser Company	22,080	16.9
3. Roger Jessup Farms Company	18,500	19.0
4. Flourney Brothers	13,540	19.4
5. S. S. Jaksick	12,680	20.8
6. Citizen's National Trust & Savings Bank	11,600	
7. W. H. Hunt, Est. Co.	9,280	
8. George Dams	8,200	
9. Herbert E. Bell, Jr.	7,500	
10. Fee Ranch, Inc.	7,200	
11. H. C. Cattle Company	7,120	
12. Lloyd S. Whaley	7,000	
13. Stanley Johnson	5,000	
14. Johnson Stock Company	4,500	
15. Stephen Takacs	4,500	
16. North Fork Cattle Company	3,200	
17. David J. Bayne et al.	3,200	
18. N. H. Monroe	2,640	30.9
1970		
1. Shasta Forest Company	151,445	16.8
2. Weyerhaeuser Company	27,174	19.8
3. Grace, Willoughby T., et al.	25,045	22.6
4. Leisure Industries, Inc.	19,522	24.8
5. National Drilling Co., Inc.	15,365	26.5
6. Johnson Stock Company	13,002	
7. McKinley, William S. & John M.; Unruh, Ira E.	10,976	
8. Byrne, Robert A. & Elizabeth D.	9,208	
9. Bell, Herbert E. Jr. & Bernice	8,995	
10. Fee Rranch, Inc.	7,200	
11. Flournoy, Warren J. & Beverly R.	8,033	
12. Johnson, Stanley	7,127	
13. H. C. Cattle Company	6,965	
14. Rouse, Carlton O. & Ethel & Wilbur	6,838	
15. Eicholz, Robert E. & Alice J.	6,837	
16. Weber, John D. & Mary L.	6,619	
17. Hunt, W. H. Estate Company	6,264	
18. Flournoy, Robert L. & Lizette	5,777	38.3

Table 1g
AVERAGE SIZE OF CALIFORNIA FARMS

Year	Average Acreage
1920	250
1930	224
1940	230
1950	267
1954	307
1959	372
1964	458
1969	627

ends than do smaller holders. And the large owner's land-use decisions have a greater public impact, thus giving him greater bargaining power with officials. Above all, a few owners can unite in common cause (for example, to advocate the State Water Project) far more easily than can a diverse and heterogeneous multitude. The few, who own more and more of California's land, control their own political and economic destinies; the many are more subject both in economics and politics to the automatic regulation of competition.

Indefensible Ownership

Many of California's large land holdings were obtained fraudulently and are now being held illegally. There is no reason to assume that large landowners, who frequently control government policy, have clear rights to the land they allegedly own. The questions to be asked in each case are: How was the land acquired? On what basis is it held? Who should have it if not the present owners? Have they managed it responsibly or have they sacrificed future use for present profit? How are damages to be assessed?

The federal Homestead Act of 1862, designed to prevent land monopolies and to open the West to the small independent farmer and rancher, was undermined not only by federal grants to Southern Pacific and others but by the Mexican land-grant system as well.

The Mexican government broke up the early mission estates in 1833, granting over 26 million acres to some 800 families. The criteria for receipt of this land usually involved political, economic, or military "service" to the regime. From 1833 to 1870, the courts were clogged with property disputes involving these grants. In the 1870s a federal commission examined the grants and "approved" 588 of them, covering approximately 8.8 million acres. The federal examination of these grants was sketchy at best, but the grants form the basis for many of the top twenty-five landholdings in Table 1c. Tejon Ranch, Irvine Company, and Miller and Lux, among others, derived their holdings from this system. Not only the nature of the grants themselves but also (as with Southern Pacific) their unlawful sale, leasing, and use, pose serious legal questions that demand renewed and exhaustive investigation.

Of course, there are many examples of a ruthlessness which is not strictly illegal. Henry Miller, for example, creator of the once immense Miller and Lux holdings, became famous for his tactic of controlling water supplies and forcing dependent farmers to sell to him at a pittance of the land's irrigable market value (after they had cleared and cultivated the land) or face a devastating cut-off of water. He eventually acquired 150 miles of shoreline, or approximately one million acres of land, along the Kern and San Joaquin Rivers.[11]

The complexities of water and property law were not taught in the elementary schools where settler-victims were educated. Thus, Southern Pacific could advertise and promise to sell its land (according to the requirements of its grant) at $2.50 per acre and then lower the boom by demanding $25 to $40 per acre (fine-print charges, interest, etc.) after the land had been cleared, buildings erected, irrigation ditches dug, fences put up, and when the first crop was about to come in to pay for the land. If the higher figure were not forthcoming, public auction would provide it.[12]

But as often as not the law *was* violated—sometimes in a most explicit manner. For example, in 1850 land speculators pushed through the U.S. Congress a bill which granted all federally owned "swamp and overflow lands" within each state to that state. California then sold more than two million acres of what was designated swampland for $1.15 to $1.25 an acre. California has never had that much swampland. Two state surveyors who were authorized to designate tracts as "swampland" left office with 300,000 acres apiece. Horace Greeley wrote that much of the land with which he was personally acquainted was "so dry there was not enough muck to supply a single small frog." An investigating committee later adjudged the disposition of this land as "wholesale fraud." But the damage had been done. Henry Miller bought a great deal of this land. In fact, he hitched a small boat to a team of horses and had himself dragged through one tract so he could testify that it was swampland.[13]

William Carr, James Haggin, and Lloyd Tevis created much of the current Kern County Land Company through similar manipulation of the federal Desert Land Act in the mid-1870s. The law limited each entry to 640 acres. Carr acquired seventy thousand acres at a mere $1.25 per acre under the Act through "dummy" individuals. Despite later investigation disclosing fraud, Carr and his associates were allowed to keep the land after explaining that they had deceived officials because they were the only ones who had the resources to irrigate and make the land useful. After so improving it, they promised, they would sell it to the settlers who were supposed to receive it under the Act. However, they did not sell the land, and government is now providing the waterworks which will irrigate it and increase its value immensely (see Chapter 3).

Land was granted to the Southern Pacific Company from the public domain, "for the purpose of *aiding in the construction of* said railroad (western half of the transcontinental) and telegraph line, and to secure the safe and speedy transportation of the mails, troops, munitions of war, and public stores thereon . . . [emphasis added]."

Southern Pacific was given directly alternate sections of one square mile to a distance of 20 miles to either side of a line for a possible 128,000 acres (200 square miles) for each 10 miles of track. Southern Pacific got six and one-half million acres in all, according to Mr. J. P. Van Loben Sels, manager of the Natural Resources Division of the Southern Pacific. This is an area larger than the state of New Hampshire. The intent of the original grant was that the railroad sell the lands granted to help finance the railroad. The Act of July 1, 1862 provided:

> And all such lands, so granted by this section, which shall not be sold or disposed of by said company within three years after the entire road shall have been completed, shall be subject to settlement and preemption, like other lands, at a price not exceeding one dollar and twenty-five cents per acre, to be paid to said company.

This section of the Act has never been enforced or obeyed. Southern Pacific still holds almost two million acres of land. It has sold thousands of acres at well over $1.25 an acre. The line was completed over a century ago, and in fact portions of it are now being abandoned.

Perhaps the major purpose of the grant of sections on either side of the line was to "aid in the construction" of the railroad by giving "so much of the timber thereon as shall be required to construct said road over such . . . land. . . ." Southern Pacific is now the state's largest private tree farmer. It makes a third of the annual land-grant profit from the sale of standing timber to big timber corporations such as U.S. Plywood and Kimberly-Clark. Its forests, 475,000 acres in California, provide 100 million board feet a year. In the words of Kermit Cuff, presently chief forester for Southern Pacfic: "We are making more selling trees than we could ever make selling the land."

The Southern Pacific Company makes an annual net profit of approximately two million dollars on use of its lands that contain minerals. At any one time, it has approximately 200,000 acres leased out to concerns searching or drilling for gas and oil. The company carefully retained mineral rights when it sold much of its land grant in the past. The present arrangement exists despite the fact that the intent of the original grant was to except lands which contained minerals other than coal and iron. ("That all mineral lands shall be excepted from the operation of this act." ". . . The term 'mineral land' . . . shall not be construed to include coal and iron land.") Not a word is said about allowing the railroad to keep lands containing oil, yet Southern Pacific is running a profitable business centered around the presence of petroleum.

The Southern Pacific Company also leases land to farmers. It leases land to ranchers in the northern part of the state for grazing purposes. The parcels are large, approximately 3,000 to 5,000 acres in size. The railroad also leases areas for recreational purposes, usually to groups. It leases a small piece of land to Squaw Valley. It also rents to Alpine Meadows.

In addition to leasing its land-grant land for oil and mineral exploration, for agricultural use, for grazing purposes, and for timber, Southern Pacific is now opening up vast tracts for development—bulldozing lots for sale to speculators (see Chapter 4). Specific mineral, timber, and other uses of the land violate specific grant restrictions. And no present use seems to "aid in the construction of the railroad" which supposedly limits the grant. And, finally, land was not and has not been sold at $1.25 an acre within three years after the railroad's completion, as required by law.

Where common-law analogy and the terms of major laws and grants allow, land obtained fraudulently or used in violation of express conditions should *escheat* to the state. That is, the land should be forfeited or should revert to federal or state government. Most of the land of the Southern Pacific Company would have to escheat to the state, and serious inquiry would uncover other cases in which the owner remains accountable for continuing violation.

There are many cases of fraud, mismanagement, and public corruption that cannot be remedied by forfeiture. Henry Miller's famous "loans" to county assessors in return for low assessments do not violate a condition of his interest in the land, and therefore Miller cannot be required to pay the penalty of forfeiture. The body of this book will present scores of such extralegal activities; these can be dealt with only through acknowledgment of ownership and subsequent enforcement of the responsibilities that ownership entails. Throughout we emphasize prospective general social remedies (e.g., changes in rules of liability, tax systems, and subsidy programs); but it is also essential that private covenants, equitable servitudes, enabling acts for disposition of public land, and grant terms be reviewed, in order to pose fundamental questions about the right to ownership and present use.

Land Power

In addition to the present level and trends in land-ownership concentration described above, there are increasing interconnections between the many parties with interests in land use. Only a few of these pervasive links can be discussed here. They include the lending of money from one institution to another, holding company relations, trade associations, and interlocking directorates.

Rudolph A. Peterson, until recently president of Bank of America, is also on the boards of Dillingham Corporation (construction and development), Kaiser Industries,

Consolidated Food Corporation, the State Chamber of Commerce, and the Di Giorgio Corporation (grapes, wine, and food). Robert Di Giorgio, president of Di Giorgio Corporation, is on the board of Pacific Vegetable Oil Corporation, Union Oil Company of California, New York Fruit Auction Corporation, Philadelphia Fruit Exchange Incorporated, Pacific Telephone and Telegraph, Bank America Corporation, and Bank of America. Peter Cook of Pacific Telephone and Telegraph is on the boards of several large insurance companies, the Wells Fargo Bank, Western Pacific Railroad, and formerly the Kern County Land Company. With Wells Fargo Bank there is Ernest C. Arbuckle, also a member of the executive committee of Safeway stores. Safeway's board consists of men, including J. G. Boswell, who control approximately one million acres of California's richest agricultural land. And there is Edward Carter, Chairman of the Board of Regents of the University of California, who is a trustee of the Irvine Foundation, on the boards of Southern California Edison Company, Pacific Telephone and Telegraph, and United California Bank, and president of Broadway-Hale Stores.[14]

Despite antitrust laws, and in addition to extensive corporate interlock at the directorate level, those interests with stakes in privately profitable land use have organized trade associations as vehicles for cooperation to affect state and local land-use policies. Some have at times fixed prices and product characteristics, but their major efforts are directed at government policy. They channel campaign contributions. They hire lobbyists to maintain surveillance and provide information at hearings and for speeches by friendly politicians. They hire academicians and "experts." They constitute what is perhaps the most powerful political force in the state. Yet few Californians could name even two or three trade associations, much less identify their interests or operations.

The following chart lists many of the trade associations formed by California's various land interests: [15]

Agriculture
Agricultural Council of California
Associated Farmers of California, Inc.
California Agricultural Conference
California Farm Bureau Federation
California State Grange

California Cattlemen's Association
Western Dairyman's Association
Pacific Dairy and Poultry Association
Dairy Institute of California
Associated Produce Dealers and Brokers of Los Angeles
Timber
California Forest Protective Association
California Industrial Forest Consultants
Pesticides
(Various chemical associations)
California Agricultural Aircraft Association (sprayers)
Fertilizers
(Various chemical associations)
California Fertilizer Association
Finance
The American Insurance Association
Association of California Insurance Companies
California Association of Mutual Insurance Companies
Life Insurance Association of America
California Association of Thrift and Loan Companies
American Investment Company
California Loan and Finance Association
California Savings and Loan League
California Bankers Association
California Mortgage Bankers Association
Investment Bankers Association of America
Real Estate
The California Land Title Association
California Real Estate Association
Mortgage Brokers Institute
Building and Construction
Associated General Contractors of California
California Builders Council
California Conference of Mason Contractor Associations,
    Inc.
California State Builders Exchange
Construction Industry Legislative Council
Consulting Engineers Association of California
Engineering and Grading Contractors Associations
Parking and Highway Improvement Contractor Associa-
    tion, Inc.
State Building Builders Exchange Legislative Council
Trades Council of California
Parking Area Industry Education Fund

California Council of Air Conditioning and Refrigerator
  Contractor Association
Plumbing-Heating Association of Sheet Metal, Heating,
  and Air Conditioning Contractors
In addition to statewide associations, the construction
industry has also organized the following regional associa-
tions where there is now or is likely to be lucrative activity:
  Central Contra Costa Builders Exchange
  North Coast Builders Exchange
  Peninsula Builders Exchange, Inc.
  Builders Exchange of Santa Clara County
Even auxiliary land development services have organized:
  Land Surveyors
  California Land Surveyor Association
  Transporation
  California Trucking Association
  Highway Campers Association
  Motor Car Dealers of Southern California
  California Automotive Wholesalers Association
  Automobile Manufacturers Association
  California Railroad Association
  Public Utilities
  California Municipal Utilities Association
  Outdoor Advertising
  California Outdoor Advertising Association
  Pacific Outdoor Advertising Company
  Water Industry
  California Water Association
  Delta Water Agency
  Major Developers
  Western Developers Conference
Individual land-development (and related) corporations,
as well as major industries, are organized to exert political
influence. Among the land-related firms with major offices
and lobbyists operating regularly in Sacramento are:

Allstate Insurance Company, American Cement Corporation, Santa Fe Railway, Bank of America, Atlantic Richfield, Bethlehem Steel, Boise Cascade, Brunswick Drug
Company, California Portland Cement Company, California Western States Life Insurance Company, Du Pont
Company, Fireman's Friend American Insurance Company, Ford Motor Company, General Electric Company,
General Motors Corporation, General Telephone Company of California, Gulf Oil Corporation of California,

Humble Oil, Kaiser Industries, Leslie Salt Company, Liberty National Bank, Mobil Chemical Company, Mobil Oil, Monolith Portland Cement Company, Pacific Gas and Electric Company, Pacific Lighting Service and Supply Company, Pacific Telephone and Telegraph, Parke, Davis and Company, Phillips Petroleum Company, Standard Oil of California, Ken Ross and Company, San Diego Gas and Electric Company, Shell Oil Company, Signal Companies, Southern California Edison Company, Southern California Gas Company, Southern Counties Gas Company, Southern Pacific Company, Southwestern Portland Cement Company, State Farm Insurance Companies, Superior Oil Company, Tenneco Incorporated, TransAmerica Financial Corporation, Union Oil Company, United Air Lines, United Financial Corporation of California, West Coast Life Insurance Company.

Still, some associations and organizations represent broader interests than those listed above, including the Roadside Council, two homeowners' groups, several cities, some unions, and recently some student groups. These groups lobby in Sacramento, but their resources are extremely limited and most of them deal with land-use issues very rarely or only in specialized areas.

Two additional groups—the California Wildlife Federation (hunting and fishing groups) and the Planning and Conservation League—have a single lobbyist each (many of the industries and corporations listed above have two or three). Other "environmental" groups are often temporary, organized on a volunteer basis around a specific type of land abuse—usually when a specific area is threatened by a highway or other project where citizens are politically active. Among these groups, which have virtually no impact on state policy, are:

FOCUS, Friends of Newport Bay, International Society for the Protection of Mustangs and Burros, Torrey Pines Association, the Wilderness Society, Berkeley Hiking Club, Build the Earth, Committee for Green Foothills, People for Open Space, Save San Francisco Bay Association, Get Oil Out, Regional Parks Association, Save-the-Redwoods League, Zero Population Growth, Desert Protective Council, World Ecology Committee, Students Organizing for Survival, League to Save Lake Tahoe, Tri-County Conservation League, People against Pollution, Stanford Environmental Law Society, PLAN, SPUR, Citizens for Century III.

Although these groups receive more publicity than do the corporate organizations listed above, they lack the powerful trade associations' permanence, financial resources, clear and definable interest stake, sophistication, and simple presence in Sacramento. Local environmental groups can and do win some temporary local victories, stalling damaging development projects in specific areas; but they are not present when statewide policy is set. The more established environmental groups—the Sierra Club, Nature Conservancy, California Tomorrow, Friends of the Earth, and the National Audubon Society—are represented in Sacramento, if at all, by the single Planning and Conservation League lobbyist. The Sierra Club, however, has provided its own separate lobbyist for 1971–72, bringing the number of conservation lobbyists concerned with land use up to three. The land interests listed above have 235 lobbyists.

2

Agriculture

California produces 25% of the table foods in the United States and over 250 diverse crop and livestock commodities annually. Since 1947 it has yielded more in value of farm produce than any other state, exceeding $3.5 billion in 1964. Among the products for which California is the primary source are: almonds, apricots, artichokes, asparagus, avocados, lima beans, broccoli, Brussels sprouts, carrots, cauliflower, celery, cherries, cut flowers, dates, eggs, figs, garlic, grapes, lemons, lettuce, cantaloupes, nectarines, olives, onions, navel oranges, peaches, pears, chili peppers, persimmons, plums, pomegranates, spring potatoes, prunes, safflower, alfalfa, spinach, strawberries, sugar beets, tomatoes, turkeys, and walnuts. California's agricultural enterprise is thus critical not only to the economy of the state itself but to the entire nation.

Three major land-use issues presently concern California's and therefore America's agricultural future: (1) urban sprawl and land speculation in the heart of prime, irrigable farm land; (2) public subsidies provided to large private agricultural corporations on a massive and increasing scale; (3) destruction of the land through erosion and contamination by fertilizers and pesticides. There are many other critical agricultural issues which we cannot, unfortunately, cover in this work. The three we have chosen relate most directly to land-use policies; each poses a test of the political system's response—through tax, subsidy, and regulatory policies—to major social and economic problems.

Urban Sprawl and Disappearing Farm Land

"CALIFORNIA LAND IS RUNNING OUT!!!" cries the gaudy brochure of the land developer. Citing statistics on the rate of migration into California over the past few years, the developers' promotional literature evokes the spectre of a land-hungry mob scrambling for claims in the Golden State.

There is in fact a land rush on in California, but in recent years each new person added to the population of California has "fenced in" an average of only seven one-hundredths of an acre. The real race for California's territory is between land developers, urban and suburban interests, recreation enthusiasts, transportation engineers, and large corporate investors—all of whom are vying for that half of California's land that is privately owned. A very large part of this land, and the great bulk of the best land, is now planted with the crops and grazed by the livestock that make California the nation's richest agricultural state.

The Soil Conservation Service of the U.S. Department of Agriculture estimates that 17 to 18 million acres of land in California are suited for intensive agricultural use, with varying degrees of conservation management.[1] This is land in Classes I to IV of the Soil Conservation Service's land-use capability classification system (an eight-class system which rates land on the basis of such factors as slope, water-holding capacity, soil depth, and texture; Class I consists of soils with the greatest capacity for response to management and the fewest natural limitations on use). However, not all of these 17 to 18 million acres of prime agricultural land are available for farming. By 1942, 2 million acres of that land had already been put to other uses, and since 1942 the rate of withdrawal has been between 60 and 150 thousand acres each year. At the current rate of withdrawal, one-fourth of the California land suitable for intensive agricultural use will have been converted to nonagricultural land by 1975.[2]

Only a very small part of the post-World-War-II urban and industrial expansion in California has taken place on land in the Soil Conservation Service's Classes IV to VIII, none of which is suited for irrigation. By far the greatest part of the expansion has occurred on the three best land classes—especially on Class I, prime irrigable land. In 1960, Dr. J. H. Snyder, presently Chairman of the Department of Agricultural Economics at the University of California at Davis, estimated that the City of Los Angeles had occupied about 90% of the best agricultural land in the County of Los Angeles.

There are understandable reasons why cities have sprung up on prime irrigable land. Land classed as "prime" for agricultural purposes is generally flat, with good drainage, and is therefore ideal for the construction of buildings, transportation networks, communication systems, and sewage, gas, and water lines. Good weather for agriculture means pleasant weather for residents. Building costs are lower on prime agricultural flat land than in the moderate hills that are equally suitable for housing. Thus, in spite of the state's best long-range interests, prime irrigable land is buried under the cement, asphalt, and steel of urban and suburban development. In the 1940s, the Santa Clara Valley produced fruit from 100,000 acres of excellent land. By 1965, only 55,000 acres of fruit orchards were left in the Valley, and it was then projected that by 1977 only 35,000 acres would remain.

Nor is the trend subsiding. A recent report of the Soil Conservation Service, not yet published, projects that between 1967 and 1980 another two million acres of California land will have "gone under." And it is estimated that over one-fourth of this land will be the best irrigable land in the state. An examination of the trends in irrigated farmland for counties at the periphery of urban sprawl points out even more clearly what is happening to much of the best land:

Table 2a

| | Acres Irrigated | |
County	1954	1964
Los Angeles	147,288	78,813
Orange	101,140	54,893
San Bernardino	101,981	81,173
San Diego	62,779	52,436
Santa Barbara	68,984	65,079
Santa Clara	114,776	78,665
Ventura	112,306	103,161

Total loss 1954–64: 195,034

Not even the irrigated desert valleys are safe. In southern California the productive Coachella Valley is threatened with urbanization, and Antelope Valley developers are touting a potential "desert paradise" for resort and vacation homes.

There are those who argue that this loss of prime irrigable agricultural land to urbanization is not a grave problem. The national condition of market-glut in the food and fiber supply is well known. Surpluses in almost all crops, although not nearly as great as they were in the early 60s, are still the rule rather than the exception. Indeed, projecting ahead to 1985, it is difficult to envisage a significant agricultural shortage in this country. Farmers nationally are now tilling sixty million fewer acres than they did forty years ago, and population and productivity have risen rapidly during this period. About fifty-five million crop acres are currently idle in the nation under various federal government farm programs which directly cost $4 billion each year. There is no need for agricultural preserves, goes the argument.

There are, however, nearly four billion people in the world, many of whom are hungry. The U.S. will not be able to maintain forever its privileged position as consumer of 40% of the world's goods and services, with per capita food, power, and resource consumption and waste expulsion many times that of the rest of the world. And there are limits to productivity increases. Eventually, yield per acre will begin to level off. Eventually, the land upon which our homes sit may be needed to feed American mouths. Diminishing productive land acreage and population increases are so outstripping productivity gains that even if birth control is relatively successful, California will soon be an "import" state. That is, the richest agricultural state in the nation will require more food for its residents than it can produce.

And there are other reasons for concern over the loss of prime irrigable land in the Golden State. One is simple economic waste. The soil under freeways, airports, commercial buildings, and housing developments is lost to agriculture: the sheer weight of these public works crushes the soil beyond hope of reclamation for many years. Yet the value of agricultural land is not subtracted from its urban value when the net cost to society of urban development is reckoned.

If established agriculture must move in the face of development to areas less favorable to farming, the original farm investment must be duplicated, usually at inflated prices, and a higher annual expenditure for fertilizer and irrigation water will be needed to compensate for the inherently less productive land. The California State Division of Soil Conservation has estimated that the total of new capital investments required to replace the prime land lost to agricultural production in California is as much as $207 million a year.[3] With no simultaneous increase in prices received by the farmer for his products, the effect of the change in location is to make farming less profitable and therefore more hazardous. If prices to the farmer do rise, they may be passed on to urban consumers in the form of higher-priced food, which then must be considered a real cost of urbanization. And taxpayers must bear the enormous cost of massive public works bringing water to new farmland, as prime land served by existing projects is converted. Unfortunately, the current land market does not assess these costs under current tax and regulatory schemes.

Still another reason for concern with the loss of agricultural land is the loss of open space or greenbelt areas. The benefits of greenbelt land are significant, and not limited to people who live on the open sites. The social benefits of open space include: air "recharged" because of the presence of trees and green plants; underground water reservoirs recharged by rain water soaking into the unpaved ground; the creation and preservation of scenic areas; and the conservation of soil and water resources. Agricultural land serves all of these purposes while still producing food and other products for the general population. Virtually none of the social benefits of open space are reflected in the land market.[4]

Ironically, if the full social costs of urbanization *were* reckoned and charged to the developers, there would be no cost advantage in converting prime agricultural land to urban uses. As things now stand, however, the public pays the difference while the developers not only pass costs on to others, but are subsidized to develop land wastefully for private profit.

The farmer himself is frequently a casualty in the path of urban sprawl. For example, as farmland becomes suburb, the life style of the new suburbanite comes into conflict with the farmer's established practices: the farmer's use of fertilizers or pesticide sprays may be objectionable to neighboring homeowners; the burning of grain stubble after harvest may turn the suburban matron's clean white sheets into soot-covered rags. As a result, the farmer on the urban fringe is often forced to substitute a different, more expensive method for the offensive practice. His production costs rise, but since he still has to compete with farmers who haven't had to change methods, and since he alone cannot control prices, he makes a smaller profit.

Air pollution is another aspect of creeping urbanism that affects the farmer adversely. The total loss in crop yields experienced by the farmer as a result of air pollution is substantial but very difficult to measure. A recent study at the University of California at Riverside compared the yields of orange trees which were exposed to the normal air in that area with the yields of trees kept in plastic tents with artificially purified air. Although all the trees were grown in the same soils, with the same amounts of irrigation, pruning, etc., the trees exposed to the "normal" Riverside air yielded a crop only *one-half* that of the trees kept in the plastic tents.

But perhaps the single most important effect of metropolitan spread on the individual farmer is increased property taxes. These work to his disadvantage in two ways. First, as farmland is increasingly subdivided for suburban use, new services such as street lighting, sewers, and schools must be provided by local government. Tax income within the subdivision is rarely sufficient to pay for these facilities. Consequently, the local tax rate goes up to provide government with the necessary income, and the farmer—who owns a great deal more land than the suburbanite—has to pay for most of the new services in spite of the fact that he may neither need nor desire them.

And second, in addition to a rise in tax *rates,* the farmer is subject to a rise in the assessed valuation of his land. Zoning restrictions, requiring land to be assessed according to market value at highest and best use regardless of present use, are observed only in the breach (see Chapter 9 for a full discussion of state zoning laws). As cities spread out over agricultural land, developers and speculators want to buy up everything in the path of the spread. One will buy Farmer A's land at a price which reflects part of the value of the land for development purposes. This value is usually much higher than its value for agricultural purposes. Farmer B's land down the road will then be reappraised on the basis of the sale price of Farmer A's land, and probably that of Farmer C before him. In some cases, assessments of agricultural land have increased between 400% and 1600% in one year under this system of appraisal.

Thus, a farmer who would rather not sell his land for high capital gains—who would prefer to live and farm on the land, passing it on to his sons—often cannot afford to pay the increased property taxes out of his agricultural income. He is forced to sell his land to those developers or speculators willing to pay the price.

Solutions that Fail

The governments of California, both State and local, have at various times recognized the loss of prime land as a problem and have allegedly tried to solve it. Exclusive zoning for agriculture, a much heralded solution, was first tried in Santa Clara County. The case study which follows details that county's experience in trying to save its orchards and fields.

THE VALLEY OF THE HEART'S DELIGHT

In the first two decades of this century, the Santa Clara Valley was seized by a spirit of optimistic boosterism, first expressed, appropriately enough, by the manager of the San Jose Chamber of Commerce, Roscoe D. Wyatt. Envisioning his city as the future hub of a vast urban and agricultural complex, Wyatt in 1921 produced a motion picture to tell the rest of the world about the wonders of the Santa Clara Valley. The title of his film: "The Valley of the Heart's Delight."

In the middle of the nineteenth century, a Frenchman named Louis Pallier had realized that the climate and soil of the Valley would be ideal for the growing of prunes. By 1915 the Santa Clara Valley was producing more than one-third of the world's prunes, and substantial crops of apricots and walnuts as well. In 1921, the Valley seemed endless. Fertile orchards stretched as far as the eye could see, and here and there sleepy towns grew up around the canneries. But Roscoe Wyatt and others looked forward to the day when the valley would be a full industrial center.

Wyatt's glowing report to the world was intended to bring growth and prosperity to the Santa Clara Valley. Subsequent development surpassed anything Wyatt could have imagined. What he saw in 1921 was a trickle of newcomers to Santa Clara. What the Valley got in the years that followed was a flood. Table 2b presents a picture of the population progression from 1930 to 1970.

Table 2b [5]
POPULATION CHANGES IN SANTA CLARA COUNTY, 1930–1970

Year	Population	Increase in Percent
1930	145,118	—
1940	174,969	20.6
1950	290,547	66.1
1960	642,315	121.1
1970	1,057,000	64.6

Total increase 1930–1970: 628.4%

Santa Clara County had adopted a master plan in 1934 (it was the first county in the state to do so), but over the following twenty years the subdividers moved south from San Francisco and made a shambles of both the master plan and the county. Though by 1954 the subdividers had taken only a fraction of the land, they had taken it in small bits and pieces, creating a patchwork of farms and subdivisions.

A pattern that has since become all too familiar began to develop. The growing populations in the new subdivisions demanded that local governments supply them with the same services that were supplied to residents in dense urban areas. The suburb-dwellers were fruitful in their own fashion and swamped local school districts with thousands of new children. Farmers, while not contributing to the new service load, were being taxed to pay for it. And they were being taxed on rising assessed valuations. Pressures were also increasing on tax assessors to tax farmland on its market value rather than on its farm value.

Farmers worked together with the County Planning Commission to set up zoning ordinances, on the basis of then existing state enabling laws, with the objective of maintaining greenbelts. The chief objective of these land-policy measures was not the conservation of prime orchard land but rather an orderly transition from agricultural to urban land use. But even this humble goal was to be discarded as the land-grab picked up speed.

So determined were farmers to hold onto their land at this early stage that they got the state legislature to enact the specific "Green Belt Exclusion Law" in 1955 and the "Agricultural Assessment Law" in 1957. In the greenbelt zones there could be no subdivisions, no industry, no commerce—only farming. It was hoped that the assessors would thus find it easier to continue to value land only as farmland, since there would be no nonfarming activity to push up assessments. "Highest and best market value" was limited to agricultural use. It was also hoped that the new legislation would keep local municipalities from annexing farmland to build up broader tax bases.

The idea of exclusive zoning for agriculture began to spread, stimulated by increasing suburbanization around more and more California cities. Soon other counties began to experiment with exclusive zoning, until even such rural areas as the Salinas Valley were attempting to use this new tool to protect their highly specialized cropland. Exclusive zoning expanded within Santa Clara County. By 1958 some 40,000 acres had been so zoned. By 1960 the land area involved had increased to 70,000 acres. In a few years, word of the experiment spread and other parts of the country began to implement their own versions of exclusive zoning.

But while farming interests were busily seeking ways to preserve their land, the pressures to develop it were steadily increasing. With the introduction of assembly-line housing on a large scale, developers turned with renewed interest to the land that remained. In his book *The Last Landscape,* William H. Whyte describes what happened then:

> The agricultural zoning had saved large unbroken tracts, and large unbroken tracts were what developers now wanted most. They raised the offers—to $3,000 an acre, to $4,000, to $5,000. Farmers began to ponder. They had gotten themselves zoned; they could get themselves unzoned. They could, among other things, ask the nearest city to annex them. One by one they began to do so. The cities, which had detested the idea of exclusive agricultural zoning from the beginning, went to great lengths to oblige. If the farm was far away, they simply gerrymandered the

city boundaries to meet it, sometimes snaking out a strip along several miles of road to do it. By 1965 five thousand acres had been subtracted from the agricultural zones; by 1968 several thousand more.

Clearly, zoning did not prevent the loss of farmland to urbanization in the Santa Clara Valley—in large part because the farmers themselves favored the repeal of local zoning ordinances when large capital gains could be expected from urbanization.

THE AGRICULTURAL ASSESSMENT LAW OF 1957

The California State Legislature has always looked to the zoning powers of local governments to solve the problem of the continuing loss of agricultural land. In 1957, it wrote a provision into the California Revenue and Taxation Code which allowed county assessors to take into account zoning restrictions on a piece of land when appraising it. The provision was designed especially to afford tax relief to farmers whose land was zoned strictly for agricultural use. The theory was that the zoning restrictions on the use of the land would decrease the land's market value, for developers certainly would not offer a top dollar for land which the County Board of Supervisors had said could not be developed. Thus, with a lower market value for the farmer's land, there would be a lower appraisal and, therefore, lower property taxes. (As we have seen, however, property-tax pressure is only one of the forces compelling farmers to sell prime cropland.)

What the state legislators did not reckon with in 1957 was local zoning politics. Zoning decisions require supervisors to deny a specific and valuable favor (e.g., rezoning) on behalf of a general principle (such as maintaining agricultural land) which is compromised only a little by each exception. The principle is for the benefit of unborn generations or the very general, unknowing public. The favor is for an old friend or associate. The cumulative effect of exceptions for old friends is an ignored master plan, described in Chapter 9.

Zoning *is* an unstable method of restricting the uses of land, given the forces that control it. And the assessors in each county recognize this instability. Thus, when told by the California State Legislature in 1957 that they should take account of zoning restrictions when appraising land, county assessors for the most part said that zoning restrictions, since they were so easily changed, had little or no effect whatsoever on the value of a piece of property. What they did, then, was continue to appraise land just as they had before the law was passed.

THE WILLIAMSON ACT

The Land Conservation Act of 1965, or the Williamson Act, is an extraordinarily complex piece of legislation that was designed to preserve agricultural land and stop urban sprawl by relieving farmers of the economic pressure of ever-increasing property taxes. When it was introduced, the Act was heralded as the salvation of California's cropland and open-space land, and it has been touted and used as a model for other states. However, the Williamson Act has failed to conserve the state's prime agricultural acreage.

John Williamson, an assemblyman from agricultural Kern County and chairman of the Assembly Committee on Agriculture, is given credit for the bill, which came out of his committee in 1965 and was introduced under his name. (Williamson is now the executive director of the State Legislature's Joint Committee on Open Space Land.) But the actual drafting of the bill was done by a small group of men behind the scenes, including Don Collin, then director of research for the California Farm Bureau Federation. From the outset, established farming interests were heavily represented and involved in the formulation of the Williamson Act.

The original Act allowed but did not require counties to set aside lands which they wished to designate as "agricultural preserves." Within these preserves the Act called for a dual system of "contracts," which pertained only to prime agricultural land, and "agreements," which pertained to all lands, prime included, within the preserves. Under both "contracts" and "agreements" the landowner would promise to keep his land in its present state of use for a given number of years, in return for which he was to receive a break in the amount of taxes which he would have to pay on the land.

The idea behind the Williamson Act's binding restrictions, imposed by the voluntary entering of "contracts" or "agreements," was to avoid the zoning restriction farces discussed earlier. Land under these restrictions was supposed to drop in value on the market, for no developer would wish to pay development prices for land that could not be developed; with this drop in market value would come a drop in the appraised value of the land, and thus a drop in the taxes on the land—theoretically.

The system of "contracts" provided for by the Act was much more rigid than the system of "agreements." An owner placing his prime farm land under contract had to promise to keep the land in agricultural use for *at least ten years*. Each contract was automatically renewable each year, in the absence of notice that either the county or the landowner did not intend to renew it. Thus, each year the county and the landowner would enter into a new ten-year contract. Notice of nonrenewal meant that the contract would remain in effect for the nine years left in the term, with the property tax assessment gradually being increased each year until it reflected the market value of the land when the contract finally expired.

Notice of nonrenewal by one party was not the only means by which a contract could be ended, however. A contract was automatically voided if a government took over the land under its powers of eminent domain. And the Williamson Act provided for cancellation at the request of the landowner if the landowner could show that the ending of the contract was in the "best public interest" (not defined by the Act). Final cancellation could not come until it had been approved by the director of the State Department of Agriculture.

A further incentive to the farmer to place his land under contract was a provision allowing the county to pay the landowner annually five cents for each dollar of assessed value of the land under contract. This payment was waivable, however, and was rarely forthcoming. The county, too, was supposed to get some money out of the deal, for the state was annually to pay the county one dollar for each acre of county land under contract. This payment, along with the power to approve or deny cancellation of a contract, was about the extent of state involvement in the original Williamson Act.

"Agreements" were the other form of arrangement between county and landowner provided for under the 1965 Act. These could be made on any land within an established "agricultural preserve," including the prime land which was eligible to be placed under contract. Unlike owners of land under contract, owners of land placed under agreement were not to receive payments from the county. And the state was to have no control at all: "the length, terms, conditions, and restrictions of such agreements shall be determined by negotiation between the city or county and the landowner," read the Act.

Since neither the counties nor the landowners wanted the state involved in their transactions, and since the terms of the agreements were shorter and more flexible than those of the contracts, it is not surprising that most of the land placed under the original Williamson Act was done so by agreement. A 1969 report of the Joint Committee on Open Space Land showed that as of March 1, 1968, only two counties in California had even offered to enter into contracts with landowners: of the 2,061,968 acres of land under the Williamson Act at that date only 40,194 were under contract. By March 1, 1969, there were 4,252,157 acres in the program, of which only 572,611 acres—about thirteen percent—were prime agricultural land. And more than half of this acreage was located in a single county (Kern County) of the fifty-eight California counties.

Ironically, the state failed to fulfill even its minimum responsibilities as defined by the Act: final approval of contract cancellation (by the Director of Agriculture) and payment to counties of one dollar per acre under contract. Earl Coke, then Director of the State Department of Agriculture (now Governor Reagan's Secretary for Agriculture and Services and his Assistant for Cabinet Affairs), refused to ask for funds with which to reimburse those counties that had entered into contracts under the Williamson Act. The request, had it been made and granted, would have added only $40,000 to a $5 billion budget—less than one one-hundred-thousandth of the budget.

In return for entering into either a contract or an agreement, the farmer was to receive substantial property tax breaks under the Williamson Act. With a tax break and a promise, reasoned the Act's advocates, the farmer would be encouraged to keep his prime land in agricultural use. However, both the counties and the landowners had reservations about the tax break.

The counties would lose money in tax revenue even if the state did pay its dollar per acre for land under contract —which, as we have seen, it did not do. And many farmers were wary of the program because they were not sure how extensive the resultant tax break might be, and because it might keep them from selling out when they chose. The California State Constitution still required appraisal for property tax purposes on the basis of "highest and best use," or fair market value. Appraisers took some account of the Williamson Act restrictions, but there were no clear guidelines; over 50% of the landowners in seven counties reported that uncertainty about the effects of the Williamson Act on their property taxes kept them from entering the program.[6]

In 1966, the voters of California passed Proposition Three of the General Election ballot. Proposition Three, which is now Article XXVIII of the California Constitution, gave some teeth to the Williamson Act by providing for new tax assessment formulae. Land subject to an enforceable restriction—a contract, an agreement, a scenic restriction, or an open-space easement—was *not* to be appraised on the basis of its value on the land market (the traditional "highest and best use"). Rather, the land assessment was to be based on a formula according to the *income derived from the land in its present use*. In other words, agricultural land placed under the Williamson Act program was to be appraised for property-tax purposes on the basis of the agricultural income derived from that land, rather than on the basis of what others might be willing to pay for it.

Since prime agricultural land is making farm income, however, it still has relatively high taxes even under Proposition Three, whereas waste and range land, which makes little income, gets a more substantial tax break. Extremely low taxes on waste land encourage the cheap holding of this land for speculative gain, and actually *increase* pressure to develop prime farmland.

In 1969, the state legislature made several important amendments to the Williamson Act. State involvement was reduced to an absolute minimum: no payments were to be made to the counties from the state, and the Director of Agriculture no longer had to approve cancellations; the only function left to the state under the amended Williamson Act was annual reporting. And the distinction between contracts and agreements was removed: as the Act now reads, the only arrangement that can be made is a "contract," which is just like the old "agreement." (Although the new contract must promise to keep land in agricultural use for at least ten years, local governments may waive the requirement on an undefined showing of "public interest.")

The 1969 amendment also expanded the definition of "agricultural preserves" covered by the Williamson Act to include scenic highway corridors, wildlife habitat areas, salt ponds, managed wetland areas, and submerged areas.

Still another 1969 amendment concerns land located within one mile of any city's limits. A city now has the right to protest the signing of a contract between the county and the owner of any land within a mile of the city's limits —land which is most likely to lie in the path of the Great Bulldozer. This provision has discouraged many counties from entering into contracts with owners of land located close to the city, and thus removes from the protection of the Williamson Act land which is in the greatest need of it.

With the 1969 amendments, then, the Williamson Act became more comprehensive and less strict. The terms of a contract could be almost anything agreed upon by the county and the landowner, provided they lasted for at least ten years. And the state was not to be involved in the mechanics of the program.

With the cooperation of State Senator George Danielson (U.S. Representative Danielson as of 1971), we conducted in 1970 a special survey of all fifty-eight county assessors in order to examine the actual results of the Williamson Act. Appendix 2A presents a summary of the fifty-five counties that responded, as well as a sample of the detailed individual answers.

The survey demonstrates how thoroughly the Williamson Act has failed to preserve California's prime agricultural land. Twenty-one counties appear to have no land registered under the Act at all, although some of these are now in the process of negotiating contracts. The thirty-four counties with land under the Act have a total of 5,391,564 acres in contract. Of those 5.4 million acres, only 1,517,734 are "prime agricultural" land—less than 20% of the prime agricultural land in the state. Thus 6.5 of the 8 million acres of California's rich farmland remain unprotected by the Williamson Act.

And 70% of the land under contract is not prime cropland; it is low-grade land which *ought* to be used for development in place of the 80% of California's prime cropland which is now even more vulnerable than before because of the Act.

The beneficiaries of the land are not the small, independent, dedicated farmers forced to sell their land because of high taxes that the Act and its proponents envisioned. Our survey reveals that the ten largest beneficiaries of the Act in descending order of acreage are: Tejon Ranch Company, Kern County Land Company, Southern Pacific Land Company, Michigan-California Lumber Company, J. G. Boswell, American Forest Products, Standard Oil of California, Giffen Incorporated, Irvine Company, and Getty Oil Company. These ten account for over one-fifth of all land affected by the Act. Their land is assessed a whopping $50 million less because of the Act, costing taxpayers $4 to $5 million each year. Most of these corporations contributed to the public advertising for Proposition Three, which gives their land the special break under the Act.

And the Act has not succeeded in protecting prime agricultural land from sprawling urban and suburban development. Only 73,000 acres—1.3%—of land under the Act could be identified as within one mile of a city, and only part of that is prime agricultural land. From one to two miles out, another 68,000 acres are added, and from two to three miles out, another 108,000 acres. Within a three-mile radius of any city, there are only 249,000 acres— less than 5% of the land under contract. (Again, only part of this is prime agricultural land.)

The land under the Williamson Act as of 1971, then, is basically nonprime land located away from urbanizing areas. The Act does not preserve open spaces near urban centers. It does not stop or even affect sprawl, except insofar as it takes less productive land, on which there should be development, temporarily off the market, thus increasing pressures to develop prime and urban-periphery land. It does not provide relief for the farmer in the path of inefficient sprawl, since it does not give him a realistic incentive in the face of high capital gains from land sale. It in no way assesses the long-range social costs of the development of land which will be needed later for open spaces or food production. It deprives counties of needed revenue, causing local tax rates to rise. It deprives school districts of necessary funds because state aid is given on the basis of the district's assessed valuation per unit of daily pupil attendance. (City and county general funds now make up the difference, but that money comes from taxpayers' pockets.) It benefits only large corporations that do not have to contribute their fair share in taxes, and that serve no useful purpose in holding their waste land undeveloped. In essence, the Act seems to be a complicated system of tax evasion for the state's large landowners.

With no state supervision for effective planning, with all major decisions in the hands of county officials who are either landowners themselves or are influenced by them, with contractual promises lasting only ten years, and with easily won approval of contract cancellations after tax savings, the boondoggle is complete.

Our own survey of contract agreements in Santa Clara County shows that the beneficiaries are speculating corporations located away from cities—with the criteria for local approval of contracts precluding the inclusion of farmland in the path of development. Ironically, the type of land whose owner and location local governments refuse to protect, for the reason given ("too likely to be developed"), is precisely the land the Williamson Act was meant to protect.

Remedies

It would be a great mistake for California to rid itself of the Williamson Act, however, without putting something meaningful in its place. Agricultural land drain is a state-wide problem. Local governments simply cannot function effectively in this area without some guidance from those who have a broader view of the subject. State involvement in land-use planning is not only theoretically appropriate, it is a practical necessity in the face of local fragmentation, corruption, and competition for tax revenue.

A step in this direction would be the establishment of a meaningful state planning agency and a revamping of the tax system.

The land-use classification system of the U.S. Soil Conservation Service has been in existence for years but is seldom used in making statewide planning decisions. Soon the Soil Conservation Service will have classified nearly all of the open lands in the state according to best use on the basis of fairly sensible criteria. Those who know even a little about the classification system realize its merits as an aid in effective planning; nevertheless, it has received little notice and even less use.

But the state could do much more than supply information about social land values or future statewide planning needs. Some have suggested, for instance, that the state buy all or at least the most valuable land still in agricultural use and then lease it back on a long-term basis to individuals or corporations who wish to farm. Such a move would accomplish three things: it would assure the preservation of the state's agricultural economy; it would compensate owners whose land was purchased by the state and then restricted to agricultural use; and it would provide a revenue to the state (or county) in lieu of the property taxes no longer collectible from the land. It would also guarantee the state maximum use of taxpayer investment in irrigation facilities and water provision.

There are thirty-five million acres of land in California that are classified (loosely) as "agricultural," including hilly range land used for grazing livestock. About eight million of these are prime agricultural land. If one assumes that the average price of the prime land is near $1200 an acre,[7] with some variation, then the cost of purchasing *all* of the prime agricultural land in the state would be around $9.6 billion. Purchasing all thirty-five million acres would cost around $35 billion. Even the latter purchase is feasible since the return from lease charges could cover bond interest and indebtedness.

Others have suggested that the federal government buy agricultural land on a nationwide basis, and control it much as it controls valuable timberlands throughout the country.

For those who contend that land-use decisions are best made on the local level, the state could still play a big role. A state planning agency could be given the power to decide how much agricultural land in the state should be preserved and then set a preservation quota for each county in the state. It would then be up to local officials to decide which of the lands in their county would be preserved in light of the quota set for them.

And there are still other alternatives. The Williamson Act could be improved by establishing statewide guidelines, confining "contracts" to prime agricultural land, and assessing for all back taxes avoided if there is subsequent conversion to nonagricultural use. However, none of these reforms will work under a voluntary system. Farmers, particularly large corporate landowners, want freedom to sell with maximum tax breaks and to wait for the best deal—long-run public cost notwithstanding.

Another solution is presented at the end of Chapter 9. Briefly, it calls upon the state to utilize its police powers and zone, as "open space" or agricultural land, all land not now *in fact* developed. All other decisions would be made on the local level as they are now. But "home rule" would work because when a locality did decide to rezone land for development, the owner would have to pay the state a "zoning-up fee" equal to the increased value in the land provided by population and general public expenditures. Large landowners would no longer be able to manipulate and market public works and expenditures for private gain through land speculation because holding land for speculative gain would not pay. Sprawl would lessen. Land would be freed and its price would decline.

An addition to the zoning-up plan in Chapter 9 should guarantee that when new development does take place it does so on land with low environmental value, so as to reserve prime cropland and guarantee adequate reserves for future needs. Thus, the state should establish a schedule of "conversion fees," on the basis of the U.S. Soil Conservation Service land survey and/or other criteria, for each of at least the first three classes of prime land. Development of any of this land could be undertaken only after the payment of very high fees: land with low undeveloped social value would thus tend to be converted before prime agricultural land.

As a substitute for the zoning-up fee scheme, another tax policy change (also in conjunction with the conversion fees) would have a similar impact. Ending the current tax break for capital gains from sale of land would have the effect of reducing speculative holding. But to set an equitable tax policy, capital gains on land should be taxed at 40% to 50% *higher* than normal income is taxed, instead of at *half* the normal rate, as is presently the case. Much of what publicly financed works contribute to a property's value increase would thus be taxed. Any work or expense of the *landowner* which increases the value of the property would not be part of the capital gain, and would not be taxed at all. The effect of this system is to discourage the speculative holding of land off the market, thus diminishing sprawl, lowering the price of land, and lessening corruptive pressures for the location of public works. At the same time, the system would encourage improvements to the land from private effort.

Alternatively, the state could exercise its police power and exclusively zone all of this land as agricultural—with rezonings, or variances *unobtainable* and with local powers pre-empted. The state has this power, and it could be utilized without compensation.

Subsidies

The Labor Subsidy

Throughout the American Southwest, growers have for generations assured themselves of a cheap, abundant, and docile source of labor by importing large numbers of foreign workers, who depress wages and prevent American workers from obtaining jobs. Currently, hundreds of thousands of Mexican nationals are imported to provide special labor despite U.S. immigration laws. Of an estimated 486,000 professional farm workers in California, 59%, or 285,000, earned less than $1000 a year in a 1965 survey. Their median income from farm work was $763; their median income from all work was $1388.[8]

BRACEROS

During the labor shortage immediately after World War II, there was a large influx of "wetbacks"—Mexicans who entered the country illegally by wading across the Rio Grande or riding in on the buses of the growers' labor contractors. Instead of insisting that the Border Patrol do a better job of keeping the wetbacks out, the U.S. government decided to "legalize" some 55,800 wetbacks in 1947; an additional 19,000 Mexicans had already been brought into the country as "braceros," or emergency labor, after U.S. government agreements with Mexico in 1942 and 1944. In 1949, four-fifths of the 107,000 braceros for that year were legalized wetbacks. In 1950, even more wetbacks arrived, in addition to 67,000 legal braceros. During these years the U.S. immigration officers used to take captured wetbacks across the border, hand them special slips of paper, and allow them to step right back across the border to qualify as braceros.

In 1951, Congress codified the Mexican agreements into Public Law 78, authorizing the government to import braceros "a la carte" for growers who needed them. No other industry in the history of this country has enjoyed government-guaranteed-and-supplied cheap labor. Both government and growers justified the special favor as a kind of "foreign aid" to Mexico. PL 78, however, did contain a number of conditions. First, the Mexican government required a minimum wage of fifty cents per hour and certain minimum housing, clothing, transportation, and health-care standards. (As the braceros generally did not know their rights, and dared not complain for fear of deportation, growers freely defied these conditions.) Then, in order to protect domestic labor, the Labor Department was supposed to certify a shortage of domestic labor in a given area before Mexicans could be brought in, and to ensure that wages offered to Mexicans were at the prevailing level. This task fell to the California Farm Labor Service, a federally financed but state administered branch of the Department of Labor, created to help farm workers find jobs.

In 1959, the Department of Labor finally declared in a report, *The Mexican Farm Labor Problem,* that the program did indeed hurt domestic laborers, since the growers preferred to hire braceros: "Some employers of foreign labor make only token efforts to cooperate in obtaining domestic workers," says the report, and "under PL 78, foreign workers may be used for any commodity or product which the Secretary of Agriculture deems essential. . . . Since the inception of the law, however, the Secretary of Agriculture has not exercised his discretion to declare any commodities nonessential, even those which are in surplus and heavily subsidized. . . ."

As a result, when PL 78 came up for renewal in 1960, James P. Mitchell, then Secretary of Labor, came out for a minimal wage in agriculture and stated that PL 78 required "substantial amendment" to protect domestic labor. He stipulated by regulation that growers paying less than prevailing wages and maintaining substandard conditions would not be eligible for the program.

Led by the Farm Bureau Federation, the growers descended on Washington, demanding that the bracero program be returned to the Department of Agriculture, or at least that the Secretary of Agriculture be allowed a say in the determination of "shortage of domestic labor" and "prevailing wage." The Department of Agriculture and the Department of Labor eventually agreed on a "compromise": PL 78 was extended essentially unchanged. (Secretary Mitchell confessed in July 1960 that the toughest opponents he had ever faced were not big unions such as the Teamsters, but "big commercial farm groups, every time legislation is introduced that would stop the importation of migrant farm workers from foreign countries.")

But PL 78 did not last much longer. Congress, subjected to increasing attacks from liberals, labor organizations, and xenophobes, allowed the bracero program to expire in December 1964, almost twenty years after the war-induced labor shortage had ended. Finally the way was opened to labor organizing, and the California grape strike and boycott began promptly in the middle of 1965.

But the growers did not give up. Complaining about "food rotting in the fields," they invoked the 1952 McCarran-Walter Act, Public Law 414, providing for the contract importation of foreign labor to perform tasks which no Americans can do. (Usually the Act applies to foreign opera singers, actors, and other performers.) Yielding to the growers, the Department of Labor established a panel to investigate the problem: if braceros were needed, the Labor Department, through the Farm Labor Service, would import them, on condition that they be paid a minimum wage of $1.40 an hour.

The panel, made up of professors from the University of California, excused the growers' disregard for labor regulations as "oversight" and proceeded to certify a labor shortage for the strawberry harvest at Salinas; the government therefore sent in 2,500 Mexicans, all of whom were quickly returned because of a sudden "labor surplus" in the area. The panel found the largest strawberry grower employing local workers at eighty-two cents an hour, in contrast to the $1.40 required by the Labor Department.

In 1967, the Labor Department raised the required rate to $1.60 an hour. At the same time, the California Rural Legal Assistance (CRLA), an OEO-funded organization, successfully challenged the Labor Department's method of certifying domestic labor shortages, so that no further braceros have been admitted under PL 414 in California (though they continue to be admitted in Florida). The growers, therefore, have fallen back on three other cheap sources of labor: "greencard commuters," a resurgent flow of wetbacks, and the Farm Labor Service.

GREENCARD COMMUTERS—"LINGUISTIC JIGGERY-POKERY"

Until 1968, the United States had no quota on the number of immigrants admitted from the Western Hemisphere, and the current quota is fairly liberal. Consequently, a Mexican desiring admission need only get through some red tape, including proof of a job in the United States, to obtain an immigrant visa. In addition, as in the bracero programs, the Labor Department must certify a shortage of domestic labor in his particular category. Having obtained his visa, he then has four months in which to establish residence before the visa runs out. During this period or afterwards, *if he establishes residence,* he can receive a special form or "greencard" allowing him to visit Mexico and return without obtaining another visa. If he fails to establish residence, he theoretically cannot continue to use a greencard after four months.

In fact, the U.S. Immigration and Naturalization Service, a branch of the Justice Department, winks at the residence requirement. And certification of a labor shortage in the immigrant's category usually breaks down because of lack of communciation between the Immigration Service and the Labor Department. Thus, there are about 60,000 "greencard commuters" in California—men who once having obtained a greencard use it year after year to cross the border for temporary work in the United States, returning to Mexico nightly or in the off seasons. For these men, the greencard is simply a U.S. work permit. Since they have not in fact established residence, they pay no U.S. taxes, and cannot be drafted like real immigrants.

Domestic workers have brought a number of suits trying to make the Immigration and Naturalization Service enforce its own laws, and Congress has repeatedly tried to eliminate "greencard" abuse—so far in vain. After lengthy hearings before a subcommittee of the House Committee on the Judiciary in 1965, Congress again strengthened the law. Originally, only "aliens lawfully admitted for permanent residence" could obtain greencards to leave temporarily. But by what Sheldon Greene, CRLA counsel, terms "linguistic jiggery-pokery," the Immigration Service interpreted the regular entry of a *commuter* as the readmission of a returning *resident.*[9] The subcommittee therefore expressly limited greencards to the "returning *resident* immigrant," defined as "returning from a temporary visit abroad." The subcommittee also strengthened the certification requirements, so that while previously an immigrant could be admitted *unless* the Labor Department certified the domestic labor supply to be adequate in the immigrant's category, the Labor Department now has to affirm the labor supply to be *inadequate* before the immigrant can be admitted.

However, the Justice Department simply ignored the new amendments. The Immigration and Naturalization Service, while changing its regulations to exclude commuters (as opposed to immigrants who establish residence), in practice continued to allow the use of greencards as usual. Glen Pullin, Chief of the Investigation Section of the Immigration and Naturalization Service in San Francisco, explained the Service's failure to enforce the law as follows: "Well, that's the way we've always done it, and we aren't going to change unless the courts make us." The courts have not yet done so.*

The CRLA, on behalf of a large group of farmworkers, recently brought two cases challenging the right of growers to employ wetbacks knowingly. In the first case (*Pedro Hernandez and Julio Martinez Alvarado et al. v. Zuckerman Farms et al.*), the judge of the California Superior Court ordered the growers to show cause why they should not stop employing wetbacks, and why they should not request proper identification from proposed employees and present it to the court. Unfortunately, the decision in the second case has stopped action on the first. After finding a cause of action in the great harm to domestic labor caused by wetbacks, the judges in the second case ruled:

> Partial expropriation of the farm job market by illegal entrants represents an abject failure of national policy. Plaintiffs ascribe some part of that failure to agricultural employers who ignore the illegal status of newly arriving crop workers. In far greater measure, it must be ascribed to the self-imposed impotence of our national government.

* See *Gooch v. Clark,* brought in 1968, now pending before the U.S. Supreme Court, an attempt by the California Rural Legal Assistance to compel the Justice Department and the U.S. Immigration Service to enforce the 1965 law as written. The defense of the government has consisted primarily of the allegation that whatever the law may say and the government may refuse to do, the matter is "political" in nature (affecting foreign relations) and is "nonjusticiable," or beyond the jurisdiction of the courts to require enforcement of the law.

Both the Congress and agencies of the executive branch bear moral responsibility for the government's failure to protect the ill-paid and transitory job opportunities of American farmworkers from the competition of illegal entrants.[10]

But for all this rhetoric, the judges denied relief on the grounds that "it is more orderly, more effectual, less burdensome to the affected interests, that the national government redeem its commitment" by better financing the Border Patrol and changing the Social Security laws.

THE FARM LABOR SERVICE

As you drive into any city or town in California, you may notice a green and white sign saying, "Farm Labor Information," with an address. At that address will reside one of the forty-two local offices of another special subsidy to growers: the Farm Labor Service. As part of the Wagner-Peyser Act of 1933, "the first employee bill of rights," Congress established federally funded, federally regulated, state operated farm labor offices, "to ensure insofar as practicable that workers are placed on jobs which utilize their highest skills." [11] In 1969, the California Farm Labor Service had a budget of $3.5 million, 15% of all Federal Farm Labor Service funds, yet it made less than 10% of farm job replacements in the state.

The Farm Labor Service has long been a target of both labor organizers, who claim it serves only the growers, and of the growers themselves, who claim it serves them very inefficiently. During the bracero years, charges periodically reached the papers that the Service not only ignored domestic laborers in its haste to help the growers get braceros for cheap labor, but actively kept them from jobs. In early 1959, the *Los Angeles Times* carried a report of a march by angry workers on an Imperial Valley labor office. It turned out that the office had been directing workers to the Imperial Valley Farmers Association, which, to get rid of them, assigned them to impossibly remote farms.[12] The Farm Labor Service regularly allowed the Farmers Association to set the "prevailing wage" low enough to create a "labor shortage," justifying the importation of braceros.

When the Brown administration took office at the beginning of 1959, the Service reeked so badly that Brown ordered a full-scale investigation. In July William M.

Cunningham, assistant chief of the service, was peremp-
torily fired for receiving gifts of produce from farmers
and sending his employees on state time to pick up the
goods from various growers' associations and deliver them
to his and his friends' houses.

A day later, the Brown administration confirmed that the
Service had been placing Mexicans illegally in preference
to domestic workers, who were "deliberately horned off by
people . . . whose duty it is to assure them of their
rights." [13] In addition, many growers were pocketing the
$2.75 a day intended for the braceros' meals and insurance.
The big growers began to panic; a group of them gathered
in Los Angeles to initiate a million-dollar public relations
campaign in support of their use of braceros.

In March, 1970, the CRLA brought suit against the
Farm Labor Service and Secretary of Labor Schultz on
behalf of 250 farmworkers who remain anonymous for
fear of reprisals. The suit asks either that the Service observe its own rules, or that the Department of Labor close
the Service down for failing to serve its proper purpose.
Backed by an exhaustive volume of affidavits from farm
workers and Service employees, the suit charges the Service with collaborating with growers to keep wages down.

For example, the Service advertises for more workers
than are needed for a given job: Gilberto Valenzuela was
sent by the Farm Labor office in Calexico on the Mexican
border to a Green Giant packing house in Washington
State. The rates had been advertised as $25 to $30 a day,
with a $30 advance on arrival. When Mr. Valenzuela got
there, however, there were too many people, only two to
three hours of work a day, and no $30 advance. So he
worked his way home—only to find the Service still sending people to Green Giant.

The Farm Labor Service also, claims the CRLA suit,
regularly and illegally refers workers to growers offering
substantially less than the prevailing or minimum wage,
assigns them to jobs without giving them any choice, and
refers them to contractors who take a cut out of their
wages. It ignores state health regulations which require
inspection and verification of working conditions, and refuses to use sanctions against the growers even when it
knows of health violations. And it depresses farm wages
not only for the ten percent of workers who obtain their
jobs through the Service, but for all farm workers: as long

as growers knew they can get cheap labor from the Service during the crucial harvest weeks, they will not offer higher wages.

The Farm Labor Service, according to Frank Valenzuela, a former Service employee and former Mayor of Hollister, is a "grower-oriented, grower-dominated, and grower-staffed operation." (CRLA lawyers found one office entirely staffed with ranchers or their close relatives.) Valenzuela also stated:

> The Farm Labor offices do not even serve the best interests of many growers. Growers that provide prevailing wages and good working conditions do not need the services of the Farm Labor office and seldom call upon the Farm Labor offices.
>
> The growers that are most dependent upon the Farm Labor offices are those growers who offer poor working conditions and poor wages.
>
> In effect, the Farm Labor offices act as a form of subsidy to those growers who refuse to compete in the open market place.[14]

When the CRLA filed the suit making these charges in March, state "investigators" began showing up at the homes of the workers who had signed affidavits, trying to get them to sign statements of retraction. Before the CRLA lawyers obtained injunctions against this behavior (which violated California bar ethics), the "investigators" had made one man sign a partial retraction and severely intimidated a number of others.

On July 23, the Federal District Court ordered the Department of Labor and the Farm Labor Service to ensure that growers comply with sanitation laws, wage laws, and pesticide precautions. The judge also directed the Farm Labor offices to inform workers of all jobs available, together with rates of pay and conditions, and not to help contractors serving anonymous growers. Nonetheless, the thorough grower domination of the Service will make change slow, if not impossible. And even if the Service were to improve dramatically, the difference to workers would be small, without a reduction in greencard and wetback abuses.

The small farmer not using this subsidized labor is a major victim. According to the 1964 Farm Census, 60% of California's 81,000 farms have no hired labor. Only

7% of the state's large farms employ 75% of total farm labor—these are the beneficiaries of the labor subsidy.

Farm workers have fewer rights than any other segment of American labor, and consequently the growers who employ them have greater unchecked power than any other management group in the country. Not until 1955 did farm workers become eligible for Social Security, and only in 1966 did Congress amend the Fair Labor Standards acts to give them a minimum wage of $1.65 per hour—and neither provision has been adequately enforced. Farm workers are not eligible for state or federal unemployment insurance, although 41% of California's professional farm labor force suffers from unemployment for twenty-seven weeks or more a year: the most recent Senate vote to exclude farm labor took place on August 4, 1970. And although California farm workers do receive disability insurance as of 1959, they rarely get the payments to which they are entitled.

Because California's agricultural workers are affected by so many obstacles in the Farm Labor Service, as well as by the lack of right-to-unionize laws and Mexican competition, it took them five years and a national boycott to unionize the grape industry. A similar struggle is currently being waged to unionize the lettuce industry, and the federal government has joined the forces working against labor: during the grape strike, the Department of Defense purchased huge quantities of grapes for shipment to Vietnam. At present, the Defense Department is selectively purchasing Bud Antle lettuce, against which the pickers are striking, at 16.19 cents a pound, more than 3 cents above the national wholesale price of lettuce (12.9 cents a pound). The lettuce strike and boycott began in 1970, and Defense Department lettuce bought directly from Bud Antle rose from 9.9% in 1969 to 29.1% in the first quarter of 1971 (these figures do not include lettuce bought indirectly through wholesalers). Defense Department purchasing agents have allegedly been instructed to seek out Bud Antle lettuce at produce terminals. The union claims that the Department of Defense has purchased something like 60% of its lettuce from Bud Antle.

Thus the federal government—along with state and federal laws, policies, and practices—directly and indirectly subsidizes California's agricultural industries by depriving farm laborers of the rights and benefits to which other workers are entitled: rights to collective bargaining, federal unemployment and disability insurance, minimum wage, etc. Since over the years Congress has repeatedly yielded to grower pressure and denied farm workers these rights, the farm workers have now resorted to the courts. On the workers' behalf, the CRLA has brought suits claiming that the exclusion of farm workers from benefits available to all other laborers is unconstitutional. One case, challenging farm workers' exclusion from unemployment insurance, lost in the California courts. The U.S. Supreme Court refused a hearing, and also refused to hear a case on the federal minimum wage.

The Water Subsidy

California agriculture depends heavily on irrigation. The state will have 12.9 million acres of cropland and cropland pasture in 1975, 9.7 million acres (or about 75%) of which will be irrigated.

State and federal agencies subsidize California's agricultural water use in various ways, depending on the source: ground water, river water, or project water. They justify giving water away substantially below cost, at the expense of taxpayers and utility consumers, in terms of a "regional development" theory that a water subsidy will return many times its value by stimulating the local economy.

California's law of water "rights" and its philosophy that "water should be gratuity-free" underlie all the forms of subsidy. Individuals establish their "right" to the state's water simply by taking it, first come first served, and once they have a "right" to use a certain volume of water they can neither sell nor transfer it. Water obtained in this fashion tends to be wasted, since the holder of the free right does not necessarily put the water to as valuable a use as would someone who had paid for it. The water-rights system leads landowners to grab water resources and use them wastefully long in advance of need, in order to claim future rights, and benefits wealthy large landholders at the expense of their poorer neighbors since the rich can afford to grab water resources they do not need and sit on them, or use them to no benefit for a long time. Big landholders who can use the most "free" water get proportionally bigger subsidies—not only from the use of the water directly but from the increased value of their land due to the water.

GROUND WATER

Ground water normally comes free for the pumping, and growers all over the state depend on it. But when each individual grower pumps maximum amounts of water from the ground, the water table drops rapidly, greatly increasing everyone's pumping costs; and in coastal regions salt water starts seeping into the ground-water basin on the side next to the ocean. By 1968, an estimated 5,000 acre-feet of water had been rendered useless by salt in the Salinas Valley. An economist estimated that the cost of preventing this loss by rational pumping would have been only 15% to 20% of the cost of bringing in new water from elsewhere.[15] Growers seem incapable of solving this problem rationally. As one grower in the badly overdrafted Westlands Water District put it, "Each grower figures he can outlast the guy down the road. So they all keep pumping. The water table is 600 feet down now and going."

If the water table gets low enough, the growers may go to court to get their water rights adjudicated. In accordance with what is called the "doctrine of mutual prescription," the court will divide up the quantity of water that can safely be pumped between the growers in proportion to the amount they have been pumping. This solution makes sense only insofar as it saves the court and the growers endless haggling, for, of course, the water does not go to those who need it most (as determined by how much they would be willing to pay), but to those who have been pumping more powerful pumps, to those who may have been pumping extra amounts in anticipation of the adjudication, or to growers where the ground water is higher or otherwise more easily available. Since growers cannot sell water rights, those who have managed to hog disproportionate shares of the adjudicated water will use it wastefully, while the losers will complain of a water shortage and demand publicly subsidized imported water.

Finding outside water is extremely difficult, because water is also parceled up into rights which cannot be sold or transferred. Therefore, a district that needs water must report to giant water projects, such as the Central Valley Project and the current State Water Project, to bring water that has not yet been grabbed from a great distance and at great public cost.

LOCAL RIVER PROJECTS

Growers get river water by owning land on the river bank, which gives them "riparian rights." If growers having riparian rights take too much water, their rights may have to be adjudicated like those of growers overpumping an underground basin—with the same misallocations. Riparian rights give water to the land which needs it least, since the high water table next to rivers makes *groundwater* pumping especially cheap.

Growers can also gain "appropriative rights" to surface water by demonstrating to a court that they have put the water to "beneficial" use over some period.* Appropriative rights are ranked by seniority, first come first served. Since in a given region growers usually start developing slow-growing, high-value crops like citrus *later* than low-value, fast-growing crops like hay, the bulk of the water may thus remain frozen into low-value use. Appropriative rights also encourage rich growers to start using water at a loss long before they really need it in order to claim "beneficial" use when the court determines rights.

A 1968 study by economist Mason Gaffney of the Kaweah Water Conservation District presents evidence that this system of rights can produce enormous waste.

BIG WATER PROJECTS

In 1933, the state legislature authorized $170 million in state revenue bonds for a limited version of the Central Valley Project. Funding the project with state money rather than federal money available through the Bureau of Reclamation would allow large landowners to avoid the 160-acre limitation on the amount of land a single beneficiary of a federal water project could hold. Since it was the middle of the Depression, however, no one bought the bonds. California reluctantly turned to the Bureau of Reclamation, and in 1935, President Roosevelt made an allotment for the Central Valley Project available under the Emergency Relief Act. In 1937, the Central Valley Project

---

* Pumpers of ground water need not show "beneficial" use—indeed, in one case, described in Chapter 3, large companies simply sump water and return it to the ground, in order to claim it later.

received full authorization and funding of $12 million in the Federal Rivers and Harbors Act.

Unlike the current State Water Project (see Chapter 3), the Central Valley Project encountered no serious political opposition save that of Pacific Gas and Electric Company, which dislikes public power dams like those included in the Project.

However, economists such as Bain, Caves, Margolis, and others raised serious objections to the Project when it was authorized, and have continued to voice these objections. The pricing policies of the Bureau of Reclamation, they contended, encourage the use of far more water than is justified by the value of the crops produced; and the Bureau encourages waste by building Bureau-subsidized distribution systems which would be unnecessary, were water priced nearer its true cost and thus used more sparingly. Project facilities, claimed the economists, are far too large for their intended purpose; and the Bureau pays much closer attention to political than to economic considerations in routing its canals. The Bureau irrigates new land while the federal government pays farmers elsewhere *not* to grow crops, the economists have pointed out, and it values crops at their *supported* price in estimating the *benefits* of the project. Under these circumstances, the net effect of Bureau projects is to transfer crops from non-irrigated areas of the country to irrigated areas. California's cotton farmers have prospered at the expense of cotton farmers in the south.

And the Bureau cheated on its benefit-cost analyses. According to economists Bain, Caves, and Margolis, there are

> manifest biases tending to inflate the resultant benefit-cost ratios. For example, the feasibility report for the Sacramento Canals (several proposed gravity canals running south-west from the Sacramento River) estimates primary irrigation benefits of $15.71 per acre-foot of water, not counting substantial water transmission losses and not deducting for the costs of constructing local distribution systems. Judging from our own estimates of agricultural benefits to much more productive soils in the San Joaquin Valley . . . this estimate is overstated several times; indeed, local water users have been unwilling to commit themselves to pay the costs of distribution systems and a $2.75 charge for water. Similarly inflated figures appear . . . for . . . the Central Valley Project. . . .[16]

Earlier Bureau projects did not enjoy the advantage of any benefit-cost evaluations whatsoever. The basic Central Valley Project itself received evaluation only *after* its major features were under construction or completed.

Finally, the Bureau has inflated its benefit-cost ratio not only by omitting crucial costs and exaggerating benefits, but by excluding the cost of invested capital—the interest lost on the money invested. Thus, to make its calculations look good, the Bureau has assumed it could only get between 3% and 4% interest on its money, when in fact the federal government—which borrows for tax reasons at 3% to 4% below market rates—must now pay about 6%. For some aspects of its programs, it has even assumed 2% interest.

Using interest rates of 5% and 6%, Bain et al. arrived at their "best estimate" of the ratio of total benefits to total costs for the basic features of the Central Valley Project as so far constructed. At 5% interest, the ratio is 0.57 or 57 cents returned for every dollar invested. At 6% interest, the ratio is 0.47 or 47 cents for every dollar. Bain concludes about the Project:

> . . . the Central Valley Project is a nonfeasible project.
> . . . If the value of the surplus crops grown with Central Valley Project water is measured realistically from a national-welfare standpoint, the project is a loser at any faintly plausible interest rate.[17]

Today, not having learned anything from the Central Valley Project except that big growers detest the 160-acre limitation as much as ever, the state has embarked on the even larger State Water Project (See Chapter 3). As far as agriculture is concerned, the State Water Project will provide water to irrigate some 292,000 new acres and to irrigate fully 134,000 that were poorly watered, for a total of about 426,000 new acres in production by 1980; by 1990, the figure will have risen to about 453,000 acres. The economists are objecting as before, and again their objections are in vain.

A casual visitor to California's farmland can see other evidence of inefficient water use. Most California growers irrigate with ditches, although sprinkler irrigation, while more expensive in terms of equipment, requires about 20% less water. If these growers had to pay the $25 to $40 the water should cost per acre foot, instead of the $12 to $14 it costs as subsidized, they would use sprinklers. And since most California irrigation ditches, as well as some of the major canals, are unlined, they lose a great deal of water: the Coachella Valley Canal, by an estimate of the Bureau of Reclamation, loses approximately 300,000 acre-feet of water a year out of 1.2 million because it is not lined.

Almost 50% of California's irrigated land is used to grow low-value crops such as wheat, other feed grains, and hay, and as pasture land.

Table 2c

IRRIGATED LAND USE [a]

Crop	Million Acres	Percent	Low Value
Grains (except rice)[b]	1.475	20.8%	15.9%
Hay crops (mostly alfalfa)	1.18	16.6	16.6
Other field crops ex. seed	1.18	16.6	
Fruit trees & vines	1.18	16.6	
Vegetable crops	0.59	8.3	
Seed, silage, nursery, etc.	.295	4.2	
Irrigated pasture	1.2	16.9	16.9
Total	7.1	100.00%	49.4%

[a] Source: Adapted from table p. 2 of *Facts About California Agriculture,* 1968, University of California Extension Service.
[b] Rice is planted on 343,000 acres, or 4.8%.

Two economic studies by Bain, Caves, and Margolis in their exhaustive work on water use in northern California, confirm statistically the impression of waste given by the large proportion of low-value crops. In their first study, they examined the returns of investment in water of eighteen irrigation districts. They found that growers in fifteen of the districts were getting a return on their money between minus five percent and plus three percent a year. Since the same money invested elsewhere could earn the growers up to seven percent, the market interest rate, clearly they were wasting money. Bain concludes that these findings "suggest an excessive level of water usage" by the districts, due either to an "overallocation of scarce water to them," or an excessive use of free water with corresponding overinvestment in facilities to deliver the water.

In a second study of twenty-four irrigation districts, Bain compared the cost of water to the value of the crops produced. He found that over half of these districts grew a substantial quantity of crops not worth the cost of the water

the growers applied to grow them. In other words, because
the water was so cheap compared to other costs, growers
would unwittingly be using five dollars of water to get an
extra dollar's worth of crop.

There are simple solutions to California's environmental
and economic water-waste problems. Water, be it from the
ground, rivers, or projects, should be bought and sold at
full cost, allowing the market to ensure its efficient allocation. If water-project users will not buy water at cost, then
water projects should not be built. The fact that a maze of
private water holdings would distribute water less fairly and
efficiently than a central state administration makes state
ownership preferable. And in fact, by a statute passed in
1927, the state already holds rights to water not claimed
at that time. But even private ownership of water would
serve water users and state taxpayers better than the present
crazy quilt of "free" water and water "rights."

THE RESEARCH SUBSIDY

> . . . with few exceptions, growers aren't involved in their
> own research, relying instead on the university. And their
> contributions to the university are minimal. In [a typical
> year], the university's State Experiment Station spent more
> than $25 million. Of this, more than $17 million was state
> funds, and nearly $7 million Federal funds. Less than $1.5
> million was from industry.[18]

On a drive through the Central Valley of California in
the summer, a visitor will see the spectacular mechanical
tomato harvester in operation. Rotating circular blades cut
off tomato vines at the ground and dump them on a conveyor belt. The belt carries the vines to the top of the
machine where the tomatoes are shaken off. Then the
tomatoes move along conveyor belts on either side of the
machine, where workers standing in a row on a running
board pick out and throw away green or overripe tomatoes.
Finally, the remaining tomatoes cascade down a chute into
a row of heavy brown wooden cases, labelled "Hunt,"
"Heinz," "Campbell," or "Del Monte," according to their
destination. These tomatoes have been specially bred to
develop the tough skins that can take this kind of treatment.

The harvester, the tomato, and various sophisticated
tomato-production techniques, are the results of over ten

years of research during the 1950s at the University of California's Davis campus, where about $1.3 million of state and federal money was spent on the project. The Blackwelder Corporation and other private firms then built and marketed the machine for an additional $2 million. Today, the harvesting of virtually all processing tomatoes has been mechanized, saving the tomato industry an estimated $5.41 to $7.47 a ton.[20]

Two agricultural economists in the Giannini Foundation of Agricultural Economics, David Sekler and Andrew Schmitz, have published an article in which they try to calculate not only the monetary gain from this invention but its cost to displaced farm workers. According to their calculations, the harvester returns between 929% and 1,288% a year on the original investment of some $3.3 million—rather a high rate of return. (Dr. Sekler says very little of this gain is passed on to the consumer, and not much goes to the growers; rather, the big processors like Hunt get most of it.)[20] Sekler and Schmitz then go on to calculate that the gainers from the harvester could have paid the displaced workers partial or even full compensation and still come out ahead. But, of course, no compensation was ever paid.

Displacement of men by machines occurs throughout American industry. But most American industry is unionized—and one of the prime functions of a union is to extract compensation from employers for new laborsaving technology, either in the form of direct cash payments, or indirectly, in the form of featherbedding or make-work. As an example cited by Sekler and Schmitz, the International Longshoremen's and Warehousemen's Union receives approximately $3 million a year for the "men's share of the machine." Sekler and Schmitz calculate that were the tomato pickers compensated at the same rate (between 5% and 10% of the net savings from the new technology), they would receive between $2 and $4 million per year.

Much more important, however, is a point Sekler and Schmitz delicately refrain from discussing: that state and federal governments do not normally help industries develop and finance laborsaving technology. On the contrary: government responsibility generally is to help *increase* employment, not decrease it. Imagine the furor should the federal government grant General Motors money and skilled engineers to develop machinery that would eliminate employment for auto workers! Yet the state and federal governments routinely aid and even lead agribusiness in the elimination of employment for farm workers.

There are currently 674 projects in the Division of Agricultural Sciences at the University at Davis. Out of the entire list, only four projects can be said to benefit the general public directly: three studies of human nutrition, and one study of "insects affecting man and animals." Of the rest of the projects, a few are pure basic research, as on "the relation of protein structures to enzyme activity," while most are more or less directly applicable to improving the productivity of agriculture (e.g., "Codling Moth Population Management in the Orchard Ecosystem") and the profitability of agriculture-dependent industry (e.g., "Consumption and Use Patterns for Dairy Products and Their Substitutes"). Most of this research benefits only the large operator, despite the fact that 78% of California farmers have a *gross* income under $40,000 a year. And a large number of projects, like "Economics of Processing," benefit only the large, prosperous food and fiber processing industry.

The other half of the Division of Agricultural Sciences is the Extension Service. The Extension Service is a hybrid creature funded in part by the U.S. Department of Agriculture, the state of California, and the counties, and partly responsible to each. Thus, during the war years, Extension operated the bracero program. Today, Extension chiefly performs what it calls "adaptive research." That is, if the scientists at Davis come up with a new strain of wheat, the Extension agents will test it out on a number of "cooperative test plots" all over the state, furnished by friendly growers. Last year, Extension operated about 5,000 such plots statewide.

Members of the Extension Service, possibly even more than their research brothers, consider themselves primarily obligated to large commercial agriculture. About half their $13 million budget for 1970 went to promoting the two goals of "Production Capacity" and "Efficiency," followed by about 20% for 4-H Club work, 12% for "Plant and Animal Protection," 7% for "Resource Conservation, Use, and Development," 6% for "Family and Consumer Sciences," and 5% for "Marketing and Utilization." According to Dr. Win Lawson, Assistant State Director of Extension, Extension agents generally "work very closely with people who need information"; he cites as an example "the managers and research people on the big oil-company farms." Dr. Lawson considers Extension politically neutral. "We don't take sides with anybody, union or grower. We're just employees of the University of California. Our job is to 'find the truth and tell it'."

Of last year's $13 million budget, 27% came from the federal government, 56% from the state, and 17% from counties. Federal law requires the state only to match federal funds, but California has always been more generous. According to Dr. Lawson, "there have been occasional attempts in the legislature to cut funds for Extension, but outcry from the farmers always stops it. I guess they figure it's a good investment."

The University scientists and Extension agents serving agribusiness are fully conscious of this bias in their work; in fact, they take a certain pride in serving only the "best" farmers and agribusinessmen. They justify their bias very simply. First, the benefits of new technology eventually trickle down to the small farmers. Second, the public as a whole benefits from more, better, and cheaper food.

This argument may have been valid back in the days when the supply of nutritious food was adequate, but today American agriculture suffers from chronic overproduction. The only individuals who benefit from new technology are those who adopt it first, and they benefit at the expense of those who adopt it last. Thus, university research in increased productivity and mechanization benefits big farmers at the expense of small farmers and farm labor. Overproduction means that public money invested in increasing productivity not only goes to waste but generates a need for more expensive public programs to support the prices of overproduced goods. Finally, agriculture forms only a small part of American industry today; there is no compelling reason why its richer members should continue to benefit from such government largess.* The publicly supported universities should not be doing for agribusiness

---

* Research on biological control of insect and other plant pests should be an exception; not because failure to control the pests will result in any food shortages, but because until these pests can be controlled by their natural enemies, farmers will continue to spray with dangerous pesticides—to the disadvantage of the general public. Also, biological control research, unlike most of the practical research listed in the catalogue of projects, contributes substantially to the important science of ecology.

what other American industries have to do for themselves.

A few hints of change have whispered through the Division of Agricultural Sciences. A number of the younger men we talked to do not share, and even criticize, the "commercial" orientation of university research. Extension has begun to devote somewhat more attention to the needs of small farmers—to the extreme disgruntlement of more traditional members. For example, D. C. Alderman, Extension Pomologist at Davis, complained in an article in *Western Fruit Grower* (April 1969, p. 13): "Extension's role is changing in a way that may benefit the diligent commercial grower a lot less than it does the inefficient and often poor farmer." As he told a meeting of leading growers of fruit, grapes, and nuts, "efforts to solve the problems of the 'disadvantaged' in the rural areas would do little or nothing to solve the problems confronting commercial producers such as yourselves."

Income Maintenance Subsidies

Despite their traditional independence, farmers have a long history of organizing to demand government interference in the free market on their behalf, or to gain monopoly control over the market for some given commodity. In 1933, they finally found sufficient support in Congress to win passage of the Agricultural Adjustment Act, the first special government program to manage farm income, prices, and production. Although the programs enacted in 1933 were supposedly just "emergency" measures to protect the hard-hit farm population during the Depression, they have managed to survive fundamentally unchanged, though with enough encrustations to prevent laymen from understanding how they work.

There are two basic kinds of income programs: marketing order programs and commodity programs.

MARKETING ORDERS

Today, California has forty-four marketing orders—twenty-nine state, and fifteen federal—covering roughly two-thirds of its approximately $1.4 billion fruit and vegetable production. There are state orders for grapefruit, apples, peaches, pears, plums, prunes, avocados, figs, olives, bush berries, olallie berries, strawberries, raisins, wine, artichokes, Brussels sprouts, lettuce, and lima beans. There are federal orders for grapefruit, lemons, oranges, nectarines, peaches, pears, plums, dates, olives, Tokay grapes, raisins, almonds, walnuts, and potatoes. The overlap is only apparent, as federal and state orders may cover produce in different parts of the state or going to different markets. In addition to these fruits and vegetable orders, California has state and federal milk marketing orders supplementing federal milk price supports.

Present-day marketing orders under federal or state jurisdiction may regulate quality and quantity marketed, standardize packaging, collect marketing information, institute federal inspection, prohibit "unfair practices," and provide funds for advertising and research.

If growers and handlers of a crop in a given area think a marketing order might improve their income, they can get together, decide which provisions they want, and petition the Secretary of Agriculture or state chief of agriculture for a hearing. In practice, usually only an established agricultural association will have the legal manpower and inside knowledge of the USDA or State Department of Agriculture to draft a marketing order. After hearing the proponents and opponents (and there will be opponents, otherwise an order would be unnecessary) the USDA or State Department of Agriculture will approve or disapprove the proposed order. Next, at least two-thirds of production, and at least half the handlers, must vote approval. In practice, if a big growers' organization, like Sunkist for citrus or Sun-Maid for raisins, wants the order, the order will be approved since the head of the organization votes for the membership. An elected committee of growers will supervise the administration of the order, which will be financed by a per box or per ton charge on the crop. The USDA's Consumer and Marketing Service oversees the federal orders.

Under "quality" agreements, growers can sort their produce into a number of grades by size, maturity, and other characteristics. They can restrict the supply and hence increase the price by keeping "inferior" grades off the market altogether. For example, according to John Knechel, a Bank of America economist, the plum growers "had a fantastic crop this year. And there were an awful lot of plums that were falling through those grading screens that wouldn't have last year," thus reducing the supply of marketed plums. In addition, quality regulations enable growers to reduce foreign competition, as grades kept off the market as "inferior" *may not be imported*. For example, the California Almond Growers Exchange secured an order in 1949 solely to exclude foreign competition.

Growers can also regulate the quantity going to market, and twenty-one of California's forty-four marketing orders do so. Quality controls let growers divert "surpluses" into areas where they do not compete with the crop in its principal market. Orange producers divide up their oranges between the valuable fresh market and the less valuable orange juice and orange by-product markets. Milk producers divide milk between liquid milk and less profitable butter, cheese, ice cream, nonfat dry milk, glue, and other products. Raisin and almond producers divide up their raisins or almonds between the domestic and foreign markets, with domestic raisins or almonds going at a higher price. Growers parcel out their production among these markets so as to get the biggest total returns, and then prorate the increased profits among themselves in proportion to each one's production.

Two California industries, cling peaches and Brussels sprouts, have marketing orders allowing tighter control of production. The $50 million cling peach industry, which produces 58% of California's tonnage and 30% of national tonnage of canned fruit, has an order allowing production control by "green drop" (shaking green fruit off the trees), by destruction at the cannery, and by elimination of culls. For example, 17.5% of the 1962 crop of 794 thousand tons was destroyed: 59 thousand tons by "green drop," 39 thousand by cannery diversion, and 41 thousand as culls.[21]

As Dr. John Jamison points out, while the growers under such a marketing order may be able to drive the price up at first, they cannot prevent the ensuing increase in production. As a result, although agreement may limit the amount sold, the industry winds up with more and more overproduction. Each grower produces more crop because his share of profits will be determined by his production share of the total crop. This increases the cost of the restrictions, since more and more of the crop that costs money to grow is destroyed or screened. Thus, both costs and prices increase. The cling peach industry today suffers from chronic overproduction and such high prices that growers of average efficiency lose money. And a government study of marketing orders has found that marketing orders with quantity controls appear to hasten the consolidation or elimination of small handlers.[22]

In the marketing order programs, which apply to fruits and vegetables (with some exceptions) and to milk, the federal or state government allows producers of a crop to design their own regional cartels and helps them enforce the provisions, or "marketing orders," as they are called. Marketing orders allow grower associations to control the quality and quantity marketed, and to fund advertising and research. Of ninety marketing orders in effect in the United States in 1966, forty-four were in California.

The citrus industry still has a relatively large number of very small growers. According to the 1964 U.S. Census of Agriculture, 70% of citrus growers had farms of under 50 acres and grew citrus on a little over 4 acres on the average. Even the 447 biggest farms averaged only a bit over 100 acres each. One hundred acres is not as small as it looks, however, since an acre of producing citrus trees varies from $5,000 value for navel oranges to $6,400 for lemons. Thus, 160 acres of lemons is worth over $1 million.

Sunkist, which has between 75% and 80% of California-Arizona citrus, was founded in 1896 as the Southern California Fruit Growers Exchange, a cooperative of growers who banded together in self-defense because the marketing of oranges was "in the hands of five or six concerns."

Since its inception, Sunkist has tried to control the western citrus market and to use its near monopoly to increase profits. But by the early 1930s Sunkist began to feel the results of its policies in the form of increased competition; from better than 90% of lemons, its share dropped to 75%.

The 1933 California Pro-Rate Act, followed by the 1937 California Marketing Act, established that by vote of the majority of growers and handlers (packers, processors, shippers, etc.), the state government will enforce upon the "recalcitrant minority" the provisions desired by the majority. The control of marketing orders provided by the 1933 Agricultural Adjustment Act came as a welcome relief to Sunkist, which controlled more than the required 67% of growers and 51% of handlers (packers); Sunkist easily rammed through orange, lemon, and grapefruit marketing orders, imposing on the rest of the industry the same restraints it put on its own growers and packers. Congress and state legislatures have thus given to agriculture a privileged exception to U.S. antitrust laws.

COMMODITY PROGRAMS

Through commodity price support subsidies, the public pays farmers to keep their prices high so that the public can pay more for food, fibre, and cigarettes. According to the calculations of former Budget Director Charles Schultz, the annual cost of the farm subsidies currently exceeds $10 billion, or roughly the combined costs of all local state and federal welfare programs, including Medicaid, and is rapidly increasing.

The system works by what noted agricultural economist Marion Clawson has called the "trinity" of price supports, surplus storage, and production control: the government maintains an artificially high price by buying up extra production and putting it into storage. The surpluses are then either given away to the poor, or dumped abroad at artificially low prices. Meanwhile, since raising prices inevitably stimulates further increases in production, the government makes farmers reduce the acreage they have in use, in many cases actually paying them to do so.

Sugar Beets. In 1889, Claus Spreckels, a millionaire cane grower from Hawaii, established the first large sugar-beet processing plant at Watsonville, California. Aided by state tax exemptions for an "infant industry," he made an 80% profit the second year. After a brief price war with his eastern competitors, Spreckels merged with them to form the Sugar Trust, which in 1902 constructed the largest beet-processing factory in the world in Salinas. Soon California had a number of large beet processors. These processors paid small farmers to grow beets, and then set beet prices so low that the farmers had to forfeit their land.

In 1897, Congress passed the Dingley Tariff Act, which put an exorbitant tariff on foreign sugar. This tariff brought California growers an estimated $140 million annually. The Dingley Tariff remained in effect until 1934. After a series of bills and amendments, Congress passed the Sugar Act of 1948, which, with further amendments, forms the basis of today's sugar program.

The Sugar Act parcels out the domestic U.S. sugar "requirement" (the quantity that can be sold at the established price) between domestic and foreign sugar producers. Domestic producers provide a little less than two-thirds of the U.S. sugar "requirement," while some thirty foreign countries each receive a set percentage of the rest.

The Agricultural Stabilization and Conservation Service (ASCS) boasts that this quota system assures U.S. consumers of a steady supply of sugar at a stable price when the world sugar market suffers from violently fluctuating quantities and prices of sugar. But the sugar program also ensures that U.S. consumers pay more than double the average world price for sugar. For example, in 1964, sugar in New York cost less than three cents per pound before import duty, about six cents per pound after duty, about seven cents per pound after the U.S. excise tax of slightly more than half a cent per pound, and 12.8 cents per pound retail. These taxes fall most heavily on the poor, who spend the largest proportion of their income on food. In addition, the sugar program prevents many underdeveloped countries from *earning* far more than they get from us in foreign aid. Only domestic sugar producers and processors benefit—and benefit they do.

About half of U.S. sugar production comes from beets. California today ranks first in the nation in sugar-beet production with about 21% in 1967, down from about 29% in the 1950s. In the early 1960s sugar beets occupied about 287,000 acres and grossed around $75 million; the returns were down to about $54 million in 1967 because of damage by a pest, but have since risen again.

Big processors still have regional monopolies or oligopolies which they use to squeeze out small operators. The processors completely control the production of sugar beets, from selling beet seed to the growers to digging and hauling the beets eight months later. No grower can plant beets without a contract with one of the processors. Spreckels today has three processing plants, one on the southeast border of Monterey County next to Fresno County, one in San Joaquin County, and one in Northern California.

Sugar-beet growers in each processor's area in turn receive acreage allotments, called "farm proportionate shares," whenever overproduction seems likely. And sugar-beet growers receive incentive payments for their beets. These payments decline with the quality produced from $16 a ton down to $6 a ton for over 30,000 tons. The ASCS claims the program is very cheap, since the tariff on imported sugar and excise tax on both imported and domestic sugar brings considerably more into the U.S.

Treasury than the USDA pays out. By the same line of reasoning, the price support for wheat could be cheaper if financed by a tax on bread. The Sugar Act requires that the Agricultural Stabilization and Conservation Service, in establishing proportionate shares, protect the interests of small and new producers, tenants, and sharecroppers. In practice, however, the Act fails to protect these small growers. Growers in Fresno County, a major sugar-beet growing area, complained of Spreckels' arbitrary use of monopoly power. A grower can plant beets only with a Spreckels contract. Spreckels provides the best seed, harvests and hauls the beets, processes them, and pays the grower in proportion to sugar content of the beets. According to Tom Moody, sugar-beet specialist in the main ASCS office in Berkeley, Spreckels "has 100% discretion" as to who gets the contracts. Spreckels prefers to deal exclusively with large, "efficient" growers. Smaller growers do not receive the lucrative beet subsidies. And Spreckels' contracts make no date guarantee for the digging. Thus, Spreckels can and does leave the smaller growers until last, when the beets have deteriorated and the growers have lost the use of their fields.

The ASCS does not supervise or control the exercise of this kind of power. Spreckels continues to receive a liberal bounty from the U.S. government—a fixed share of the U.S. sugar market—and in turn decides which growers receive the further federal bounty of sugar payments of about $42 an acre.

Cotton. Cotton is one of the most important subsidized crops in California. In the early 1920s, growers discovered that California farms grew the best cotton with the highest yields; cotton planted in the Imperial Valley eventually reached phenomenal yields of five bales an acre. From 1,500 acres in 1921, cotton acreage grew to close to 600,000 acres in 1937, and roughly 775,000 acres today. (The national cotton allotment for 1970 is 17 million acres.)

Despite the importance of the industry, cotton in California survives chiefly by means of federal subsidies. These operate as follows:

To qualify for subsidies, a farmer must plant no more than his allotment, which is based on the average number of acres planted on his land from 1951 through 1953— during which time large landowners, such as Russell Giffen and J. G. Boswell, went on planting sprees.

Farmers who comply with the allotment requirements (the ASCS conducts spot checks) qualify to receive price support *loans* from the Commodity Credit Corporation (CCC) at about 20 cents per pound. They receive an additional 16.8 cents per pound, for the 65% of the acreage they are allowed to market domestically. Thus, growers receive about 37 cents per pound (20 plus 16.8) for the 65% of their cotton which must be sold domestically and 20 cents per pound on the rest. As a result, many growers plant only 65% of their allotment.

Since loans and payments are in proportion to amounts produced, big operators receive more per acre. For example, Russell Giffen has a yield of 1,620 pounds per acre or a little over three bales per acre. (One bale weighs 500 pounds.) At 16.8 cents per pound, he receives $272 per acre support payment on 65% of his allotment. The payment for yields of 600 pounds per acre would be about $100 per acre as opposed to Giffen's $272. Giffen received a little over $3 million total payment in 1970 on 65% of his allotment of 17,124 acres.

A certain planting technique adds to this disproportion. A number of years ago, University of California scientists invented "skip-row" planting, planting one or two rows and then skipping one or two, all the way across the field. Since the remaining plants get more light and fertilizer, they produce more heavily, so that only two-thirds as many plants will produce over 80% the yield of a full field. When skip-row planting began, the Agricultural Stabilization and Conservation Service of USDA counted an acre of skip-row planting as 80% of a regular acre of cotton in computing acreage allotments. But according to an official in the Fresno office of the ASCS, the big operators complained in Washington. Shortly thereafter, the ASCS began counting an acre of plant-two-skip-one acreage as equivalent to 67% of a regular acre. This means that a 100-acre allotment, which formerly was equivalent to 125 acres planted skip-row, now covers 150 acres skip-row, a 25-acre bonus. Now, more cotton can be grown by those who plant skip-row. But only the bigger growers can afford to put the extra land, machinery, and chemicals into skip-row planting. (Giffen gets his yields of 1,620 pounds per acre planting skip-row.) Thus, skip-row planting further increases the already disproportionate yields of the big growers.

For all the bonanzas to big operators, the cotton program has apparently backfired. Domestic cotton-support payments through 1965 went directly to cotton mills, which could then pay growers the high supported price. The CCC marketed surplus cotton abroad at very low prices. In 1965 the government decided to let the cotton mills buy cotton at the world price, so that support payments now go *directly* to the *growers*. In 1966 and 1967, the price of cotton rose sharply until it reached an average of forty-five cents per pound. Growers in the San Joaquin made a fortune, and big operators like Giffen expanded their holdings greatly, borrowing heavily from the banks.

Then in 1968, the price dropped suddenly to around twenty-two cents per pound. Banks began hauling in their credit; seven of the twenty largest subsidy recipients in Fresno County, including Russell Giffen's son, Price Giffen, filed bankruptcy. The CCC in California suddenly found itself with 100,000 bales of cotton. What had happened?

It seems the switch in payments from the mills to the growers sent the mills into a panic over cotton shortages, so they bid the price way up. Then, as a result of the high price, a large number of mills threw out their old cotton equipment and switched to new equipment for milling cheaper synthetics. Having now invested in new machinery, the mills will not switch back, and the domestic cotton demand has dropped permanently.

Appendix 2B explains briefly the concept of "parity," and the way in which federal commodity programs, price-support loans, direct payments, and production controls work. The direct payments alone to California growers in 1969 amounted to $11,533,000 for sugar-beet subsidy, $80,189,000 for cotton subsidy, $18,833,000 for various grain subsidies, and $4,139,000 for wool subsidy.

These production-control measures, despite their expense, have succeeded in reducing considerably the costly stored surpluses of the 1950s. But reducing production by reducing acreage does not work very well, since new technology keeps increasing the per acre productivity. In effect, price supports combined with acreage reductions encourage farmers to bring more resources into agriculture when agriculture already has a surplus of resources.

And, controlling production by reducing acreage proportionately favors large growers over small growers. During World War II and the Korean War, allotments were removed to encourage production. After the wars, only the big growers like Boswell and Giffen had the money and land to plant huge quantities of supported crops like cotton at a loss in order to have a large "base acreage" when the USDA reimposed allotments. Also, large growers can better afford to apply technology to their land to get higher and higher yields. As a result of *their* increased production, everybody's acreage allotment gets reduced. Eventually, the smaller growers wind up with too small an allotment to make a living.

The USDA's various support programs have succeeded moderately well in stabilizing prices and controlling production, though at a high and rapidly increasing cost; they have also succeeded in raising *average* farm income. Nonetheless, few farm economists can be found with a kind word for them. According to economist Marion Clawson, "these programs seem to have fallen into a rut from which the U.S. Department of Agriculture has been unable to extricate itself; their efficacy for their stated purposes is at least doubtful and they have grown increasingly expensive." Varden Fuller, Professor of Agricultural Economics at the University of California at Davis, terms the programs, simply, "perverse."

The Congressmen who carried the original Agricultural Adjustment Act through in 1933 on a wave of sympathy for the suffering farmers intended primarily to maintain farm income. However, they made one fatal mistake: they assumed that all farmers were poor. Since, of course, some farmers are not poor, and a few are very rich, a program which rewards production inevitably rewards the rich who produce the most. Yet the vast majority of farmers, who really *are* poor, get almost nothing—just enough to make them support the programs politically. As Charles M. Hardin at the University of California at Davis comments, "The windfalls of the wealthy may well be politically sustained by the pittances to the poor." [23]

The farm programs have also backfired in another, equally serious, way. The originators of the farm programs worried that the returns for a farmer's labor were disproportionately low compared to the returns from his land and equipment. In other words, if the farmer had invested his money in the stock market instead of land and equipment, and had taken a managerial job commensurate with his abilities outside agriculture, he would receive the same for his money but much more for his labor.

But instead of increasing the returns for the independent farmer's labor, the farm programs have done exactly the opposite: they have greatly increased the value of farm *land* at the expense of farm *labor*. Tying price supports to production automatically enhances the value of the means of production, particularly the land; when the government tries to control production further by reducing the land in cultivation, the price of the land goes up that much more. As Clawson puts it, "American farm policy for the past generation has been directed—often unconsciously—more towards farm property values than towards welfare of farm people." California has virtually the highest farmland prices in the nation, higher than could possibly be justified by the productivity of the land alone.

These inflated land values benefit the large landholders— big growers and big speculators—and people investing in land as a hedge against inflation, driving prices up even further. They hurt small farmers who try to make a go of it performing all or most of their own work. These farmers, if they are to survive and compete, must continually expand their operations by purchasing or renting more land and equipment; but inflated land values make expansion difficult, and of course the pressure for expansion also inflates land values. With higher land costs, the farmers receive proportionately smaller returns for their labor. The independent farmer does not feel the labor devaluation directly since he receives his income from both land equipment and labor all in one bundle. But farm workers do feel the pinch both in their miserably low wages and in the rush of technology to replace them.

The government farm income maintenance programs have aggravated the problems—farm poverty and proportionately low returns to labor—they were intended to solve, while making the relatively wealthy farmers richer, at considerable expense to the public.

Varden Fuller is quite blunt about what should be done about farm programs: "Stop messing with markets." He would simply phase out farm programs over a period of five to ten years. (The farm economy has become addicted to regular federal transfusions; a sudden withdrawal would be disastrous.) Marion Clawson suggests that in addition to abandoning price supports and production controls, the government could try, among other things, a system of pensioning small farmers to retire early on condition that they sell their land cheaply to the government. The government would then resell it cheaply to help remaining small farmers enlarge their operations. Such a scheme would reduce both the surplus of labor in agriculture and the inflated price of land. Several other alternatives have been suggested, and it is at least clear that the present price-support, production-control, storage programs have been disastrous and should be abandoned.

Taxes and Credit: Farmer Brown, Inc. vs. the Dun and Bradstreet Sodbusters

The large conglomerate farm, which operates farms in several states and engages in nonfarm enterprise as well, is the beneficiary not only of labor, water, research, and income-maintenance subsidies but also of economic favoritism in tax and credit rules and policies.

Some of the large conglomerate enterprises engaged in farming are: American Cyanamid, Bunge, CBK, Del Monte, Gates Rubber Company, Goodyear Rubber Company, Jewel Tea Company, Libby, McNeill & Libby, Massey-Ferguson, Minute Maid Groves, Oppenheimer Industries, Pacific-Gamble-Robinson Company, Pillsbury Company, Purex, Ralston Purina, Swift and Company, Tenneco, Textron, United Fruit, Standard Oil of California, and Southern Pacific Company.

TAX POLICIES

Federal and state tax policies encourage large corporations to go into farming. Substantial capital gains, favorable depreciation rates on equipment and machinery, and tax losses written off against nonfarm income are major benefits that return sizable tax savings to absentee investors and thereby permit them to operate with a cost structure entirely different from that of the small owner-operator (whether or not he is incorporated). The independent operator who earns a living entirely from farming is able to make some use of depreciation and capital gains provisions, but he is not likely to have taxable nonfarm income against which to offset farming losses.

In 1963, the Secretary of the Treasury told the House Ways and Means Committee that tax policies "create unfair competition for farmers who may be competitors and who do not pay costs and expenses out of tax dollars but who must make an economic profit in order to carry on their farming activities." (See Robert Dietsch, "The Merger Boom—Who Owns What?" *New Republic,* February 22, 1969, p. 15.)

Federal tax laws (duplicated by California tax laws) subsidize the entry of outside investors, usually large corporations, into farming. Conglomerate A, for example, buys 10,000 low-grade acres at $300 per acre (a $3 million expenditure). Conglomerate A invests $1 million each year for five years in irrigation and soil improvements on this low-grade land. It is able to deduct this $1 million each year from its profitable operations elsewhere—profitable operations that a smaller operation, Farmer Brown, Inc., does not have. With a 50% corporate tax rate, this means a $500,000 annual tax gain Conglomerate A would otherwise have to pay each year. Over five years the savings come to $2.5 million. Conglomerate A has managed a 31% return on total expenditures in tax savings alone over five years, and a 50% return on the improvement investment which is not available to Farmer Brown, Inc. In other words, although these improvements will certainly add value to its property, probably more value than the investment lost, Conglomerate A is taxed as if it had a net *loss* of $1 million per year on these investments. After five years, Conglomerate A will probably sell for over $8 million. The $5 million in improvements will actually have added at least that much to the value of that land; yet when Conglomerate A sells, it will not have to make up that $5 million in tax write-off from investments which were not losses, but gains.*

When Conglomerate A makes the sale, not only will it gain, but its gain will be taxed at the capital gains rate of 25%, half the tax rate for income. This is a break which both Farmer Brown, Inc. and Conglomerate A enjoy, but Conglomerate A can use it to greater advantage. Land to Conglomerate A is merely another corporate asset, to be disposed of when tax and investment demands dictate. Conglomerate A knows that it can invest in value-escalating farmland for speculative gain at an opportune time, given

---

* The capital gains law also has the effect of giving the investor a free loan, with the public footing the interest charges through tax deficiency. Conglomerate A can *use* the first $500,000 tax-saving amount for five years (until it sells the land) without paying any taxes on the gain. The next $500,000 (the second year) it uses for four years, etc.

the losses or needs of other enterprises. And as long as appreciable gains can be made from land sale, the corporation can and will accept a low rate of return on crop production. Farmer Brown, however, is attached to the land, without other enterprise, and dependent upon adequate rates of return from agricultural activity.

A third tax advantage lies in Conglomerate A's depreciation write-offs, flexibility, and operating cost write-offs. If Conglomerate A decides to plant tree crops (with the exception of citrus), it can deduct as operating costs all the expenses which go into caring for the trees until they are ready to bear. It can then sell this land after the trees are ready to bear fruit, just before harvest, when the value of the land has greatly appreciated. After sale, all of this appreciation can be considered a capital gain. That is, *expenses* are deducted from income, but the gains *from* these expenses are now not considered "income" but capital gains and taxed at half the rate income is taxed.*

The effect of this gimmick is such that a total stop had to be put to the practice in citrus orchards. As the Commerce Clearing House said in their *Explanation of the Tax Reform Act of 1969* (p. 198):

> The tax advantages of being able to deduct currently the costs of developing a citrus grove has apparently resulted in speculative plantings of orange groves, overproduction, and low selling prices. To remedy this, the new law re-

---

* The 1969 Tax Reform Act limited this loophole to some extent. For example, assume Conglomerate A spends $60,000 per year on its orchards and this is its only cost. It decides to sell the orchard after two years. At this time, assume that the orchard is worth $120,000 more than it was when the Conglomerate bought the land. Before the 1969 Act was passed, the entire $120,000 could be treated as capital gain; now the farmer must subtract $35,000 (*the amount of deductions in excess of $25,000*) from the $120,000 which previously could be treated as capital gain. (If the farmer took less than $60,000 per year in tax losses, then he will be able to subtract less of it from the $120,000 capital gain and more of it from "income.") That is, after $25,000 per year in "losses," any further "losses" (investment in land) will reduce the capital gain by that amount—acting as a capital loss. This is as it should be, but if the farmer had a profitable operation overall (i.e., if he did not lose any money in his farming operation), then the entire $120,000 could be treated as capital gain and the farmer would have succeeded in converting his capital development costs for the orchard into operating costs so that a greater percentage of the final selling price of the orchard will be taxed at the lower capital gain rate. Further, there are other holes in this "loophole-closing" measure.

quires capitalization of all amounts spent for purchase, planting, cultivation, maintenance or development of any citrus grove within four years after the trees are planted.

So far, no such protection has been given to the growers of other tree crops.

The tax loopholes and advantages enjoyed by Conglomerate A are not merely hypothetical. In 1966, 108 individuals with annual incomes of more than $1 million were involved in some phase of farming. Ninety-three of them, as did Governor Reagan, reported farming losses for income tax purposes.

LAND . . .

A trend that has paralleled the entry of corporations into agriculture has been, as noted in Chapter 1, the growth in average farm size and the concentration of farmland in fewer and fewer hands. Over the twenty-four year period from 1930–1954 (see Table 2d), the average size of farms in California increased only 37%; but over the shorter five-year period from 1954 to 1969, the average farm size jumped over 100%, from 307 acres in 1954 to 627 acres in 1969. This trend toward larger farm size has been stimulated by accelerated technological developments in crop mechanization. As farm wages rise, farmers are encouraged to substitute machinery for human labor. There is a direct, positive correlation between the horsepower (i.e., capacity) of a farm machine and the wages of the machine's operators. When wages go up, machines with greater capacity are purchased so that the expensive operator can get more work done. But with rapid technological change, the capacity of the machines soon outstrips the ability of the farm to use that capacity. The farm must therefore be expanded in order to utilize fully the machinery purchased originally to cut labor costs. The result of technological change in agriculture has been inexorable growth.

The total number of farms of all sizes in California has declined from 135,676 in 1930 to 80,846 in 1964. From 1930 to 1954, the total number of farms decreased by only 9%.

Over the period 1954–1964, farms under 10 acres declined by 53% and farms from 10 to 49 acres declined by 34%; by contrast, farms between 500 and 999 acres decreased in numbers by only 9%, and farms in the largest

Table 2d

AVERAGE SIZE AND LAND AREA OF CALIFORNIA FARMS
SELECTED YEARS, 1930–64 [a] (IN ACRES)

Year	Average Size of Farms	All Land in Farms	All Cropland Harvested	Irrigated [b] Land in Farms	Irrigated Cropland Harvested
1930	224	30,442,581	6,549,967	n.a. [c]	3,540,350 [d]
1940	230	30,524,324	6,932,355	4,276,554	3,732,215
1950	267	36,613,291	7,956,671	6,438,324	5,309,653
1954	307	37,794,780	8,326,331	7,048,049	5,948,068
1959	372	36,887,948	8,021,836	7,395,570	6,216,950
1964	458	36,996,327	7,837,133	7,584,363	6,421,974
1969	627	n.a.	n.a.	n.a.	n.a.

[a] U.S. Department of Commerce, Bureau of the Census, *1964 U.S. Census of Agriculture;* 1969 figure from *California Information Almanac,* Bank of America, 1969, p. 285.

[b] Includes both cropland and pasture.

[c] Not available.

[d] Includes some duplication where two or more crops were harvested from the same land.

size group decreased by only 8%. This great decline in the number of small farms and very small decrease in the number of large farms is perfectly compatible with the growth of a smaller number of extremely large farms.

Table 2e shows how the earning power of California's agriculture has changed along with the changes in the number of farms. If we consider the two periods 1954–1964 and 1955–1965 as roughly comparable, it is apparent that the increase of $1.06 billion in cash receipts over that period was paid out to a rapidly diminishing number of farms. Only two-thirds of the farms in existence in 1954 were still around to take advantage of greater earnings in 1964. By 1968, when California farm cash receipts were even higher, the realized gross income per farm in California was almost $71 thousand, more than four times the income of the national farm average.

> People talk of corporate farming being evil, and really that isn't the problem at all. It isn't corporation farming . . . it's a problem of sheer size. . . . The people who are trembling in their boots are the little people who don't have an opportunity to merge, grow, expand. Their farming venture is really in jeopardy because they can't compete.

Thus Walter Minger, a Bank of America credit officer. Among the most important advantages of sheer size, Minger

Table 2e

CASH RECEIPTS FOR CALIFORNIA FARMS,
BY SELECTED COMMODITY GROUPS, 1950–1968 [a]
(IN THOUSANDS OF DOLLARS)

Year	Total	Fruit and Nut Crops	Vegetable Crops	Livestock and Poultry	Government Payments	Forest, Nursery, and Greenhouse Products
1950	$2,315,267	524,656	270,052	847,220	13,641	54,021
1955	2,692,172	587,400	378,047	966,602	11,970	80,836
1960	3,210,879	614,529	407,600	1,245,120	21,913	105,728
1965	3,751,402	678,346	545,001	1,424,910	41,258	176,069
1968	4,374,785	849,380	774,642	1,604,851	100,731	206,711

[a] Source: Department of Agriculture, Bureau of Statistics.

went on to point out, are: bulk purchasing of all inputs, labor utilization, efficient-sized blocks of crops, volume enough to interest major buyers, greater sophistication in marketing, better leverage in the market place, greater diversity and hence less risk, more financial sophistication, better projections, and use of skilled management with great depth and a high degree of continuity.

How, then, can the small farmer afford not to expand? Given the present biases against small operators, he can't afford not to expand and he can't afford to expand.

. . . AND CREDIT

Mr. Minger continues:

> Some [small farmers] are going to have a credit squeeze, because the profit margins in farming are so poor. When you look at the capital requirements these fellows face— just to expand operations to keep efficient—with no margins to speak of, there is an inability to set up a financing plan that will repay these capital requirements. It's profits after taxes that repay debt and without the margins—without an adequate level of profits—you just can't take on a lot of term debt even though in your best interest you should do this to become more efficient, develop land, or get out from under a labor problem.

And an economist at Stanford University's Food Research Institute points out that ". . . farmers of 200 to 300 acres are losing their credit base because they are losing their land and, therefore, their ability to secure a loan."

Large conglomerate farms and small family farms operate in completely different capital markets. Traditionally, the local bank is the only source of credit for the small farmer, while outside corporate farms operate within a broader capital market—issuing securities and bonds as well as securing loans.

The Bank of America (B of A) is the single largest investor in California agriculture, and its 1,000 retail branch banks provide farmers and ranchers with some 850 million to a billion dollars a year in seasonal production credit. The B of A is further involved for well over a billion dollars seasonally in agribusiness.

As big corporations take over in agriculture, the structure of financial activity shifts. In Salinas, reports a Bank of America credit officer:

. . . we had two giants come in: United Fruit and Purex. They had bought up a total of, I think, seventeen grower-shippers of lettuce, celery, and onions. Our bank had commercial accounts with nine of these people and seasonal crop liens with more than half. And if it wasn't our bank, it was somebody else. They did their borrowing locally . . . they bought locally. But when these managements were centralized—United Fruit out of Boston, and Purex out of Los Angeles—the financial activities and hence most of the major purchasing was centralized in these areas. It had a dramatic effect on our Salinas branch.

B of A has a declining number of farm borrowers every year, but the totals keep going up so that the Bank is not losing gross business. B of A credit officers claim that even with a tight money market there is no finite limit to the amount they might want to put into agricultural financing. As to the criteria for selecting those farmers who receive credit: "What we want to finance are people who have capability, who have proven history, who have home (market) for product, where there is some reasonable expectation of repayment of a production loan. We're trying to identify those people who're going to be around in 1980."

Agricultural economists, however, dispute the B of A's claim that it is willing to provide unlimited credit to agriculture in the middle of a tight money market. The economists point out the obvious—that credit will go where the returns are the highest and where the risk is least. If a small farmer in the midst of an expansion program has one bad year, his credit will often be cut off. One of B of A's own economists indirectly verified this charge: "When they get in trouble, you have a carry-over for another year on their loan commitment. When do you shut it off? If you shut it off, you know they're sure to fail. If you don't shut it off, they may fail in even worse condition." It is no mere coincidence that the road to larger-sized farms has been paved with a rising number of farm bankruptcies.

Purex and other conglomerates, however, do not risk bankruptcy even if they have several bad years. Tax deductions and tax favoritism provide them with sufficient credit to be able to expand to optimum size at will. Thus, credit denial is self-justifying: noncorporate farms fail not only because of a lack of other enterprises to carry them, but because they lack credit to expand or adjust; they do not receive credit because they run the risk of failure.

The once minor involvement of the conglomerate corporation in farming is minor no longer. Corporations engaged in other business enterprises and controlled by unrelated individuals or other corporations now hold substantial acreage and account for substantial shares of crop and livestock production.* They own most of the land they farm, with much larger than average farms. They also average two to three managers per farm and employ about twice the employed labor per farm as the family or individual farming-only enterprise. The proportion of absentee owners continues to increase.

The small farmer is clearly no match for the huge corporate conglomerate. He is—for reasons of intentional and unintentional discrimination—unable to accumulate

---

* "A Statistical Profile of California Corporate Farms," December, 1970 (USDA), indicates that from one-fourth to one-third of cropland production from California's 57,289 total farms comes from 1,673 corporate farms. Corporate farms account for 35.6% of California's corn, 29.5% of all other grains, 32.5% of potatoes, 29.5% of sugar beets, 23.2% of strawberries, 38.4% of cotton, 29.9% of citrus, 24.2% of tomatoes, 62.3% of lettuce, 89.2% of melons, 34.6% of carrots, etc. These levels have steadily increased. Corporate farms now control 6.1 million acres, according to the Report. Forty-six percent of California's agricultural corporations operate farms in two states or more. Twenty-five percent operate them in four states or more. Twenty percent of the corporations do more than farm, and this twenty percent controls one half of the acreage held by corporate farms. 267,000 acres are held by corporations engaging in agribusiness on the side, averaging 2,453 acres per farm. Those engaged in other business unrelated to agriculture hold 2,384,000 acres and average 16,553 acres. Corporate farms engaged in just farming hold 2,866,000 acres, averaging 2,293 acres, and rent one half of their land. Those engaged in other business rent less than 15% of their land and own the remainder. Moreover, 39% of farming corporations are controlled by another corporation or by unrelated individuals ("other controlled"). Once again, this 39% nonfamily group is much larger in size, averaging 8,481 acres as opposed to 2,924 acres per family-controlled farm and 1,690 acres per individual-controlled farm. The "other controlled" farm accounts for about 40% of corporate crop production from fewer and larger farms. ("Other controlled" farms are larger for eighteen of the twenty-four crops surveyed.) "Other controlled" farms account for 34% of California's corporate farm cattle production, 64% of its beef cows, 55% of yearling cattle, and substantial percentages of milk cows, hogs, sows, broilers, hens, turkeys and sheep.

the resources of land and credit that would give him advantages equal to those of the corporate farmer.

A number of studies of crop-farming situations, however, indicate that, given nondiscriminatory financing and public policy (credit, opportunity to buy land, no volume discounts), the noncorporate farm and/or very small farm will produce as efficiently as the large corporate farm; that except for volume discounts, a well-organized two-man or three-man farm operating with modern technology can easily exhaust the technical economies; and that for certain types of farming even the one-man farm can achieve this same level of efficiency.

Certain basic requirements have to be met, however, before the family farmer can actually compete and therefore survive:

(1) Capital acquisition must be assured. Credit terms have to be liberalized and more provisions made for permanent financing. If noncorporate farms cannot meet economies of scale (e.g., supply volume discounts), either by expansion or cooperative efforts, they will suffer.

(2) Price discounts and services for inputs must be competitive. If small farms can't expand, they must form purchasing co-ops to match automatically large and credit-rich corporate farms.

(3) Selling prices must be competitive. Either "special arrangements" and tied markets must be eliminated and policed, or cooperatives will have to provide the same advantages for the smaller farmers.

(4) Tax disadvantages must be minimized. Institutions and governments must be made aware of the effects certain taxes have on relative competitive positions, and they must make the necessary changes.

Although this is not the place to draft specific legislation, we would offer the following general suggestions for possible reform.

The key to providing adequate land for acquisition by small farmers to achieve efficient economies lies in ending land-holding for speculative gain. The reforms (zoning-up fee) described above and in greater detail in Chapter 9 would make land a more fluid or adjustable commodity.

Second, the tax break given capital gains must be ended. At present capital-gains breaks encourage the removal of land from the market for speculative gain. The state must set the example and apply political pressure to the federal government for federal tax legislation. At the least, land should be exempt from capital gains breaks in the state tax system.

Third, means must be found to close loopholes which enable land-investment deductions from income, thus creating wealth taxed at a capital-gains rate. Further, for tax purposes, any agricultural enterprise could be mandatorily severable from òutside sources of income or expense.

Fourth, California could limit the amount of land a corporation may hold. Minnesota now restricts ownership of farmland by corporations to 5,000 acres, and North Dakota and Kansas also have partial restrictions on corporate ownership of land. Restriction to 5,000 acres would be defensible under current judicial interpretation. It would break up land empires which, above that size, certainly do not produce greatly increased efficiencies. It would bring more people into rural areas on a self-sufficient, nonemployee basis. It would undermine much of the basis for excessive special-interest domination of public policy concerning land. It would reduce the possibility of market abuse and monopoly power in the food industry.

Most credit-provision reforms would merely involve the active enforcement of *current* regulatory law; antitrust laws could be invoked to challenge many of the "special agreements" discriminating against the nonconglomerate farmer; bank laws could be enforced against illegal discriminatory practices. But where new legislation is needed, an analogy can be made with the "common carriage" notion in transportation. In transportation, certain nondiscriminatory policies have been arrived at through common-law tradition and there are critical parallels between the basic need by all businesses for transportation and a need today for credit. Since financial institutions are regulated, as is transportation, it is appropriate to consider imposing analogous "common *credit*" requirements on these institutions. Many small farmers and businessmen could not survive in the late nineteenth century because of railroad favoritism for large corporation traffic; today they cannot survive because of credit favoritism. Financial institutions could be required by law to adhere to standards comparable to common carriage: discrimination in the lending of money, or the terms therefor—whether on the basis of company size and business volume, bargaining power, or interlocking directorate relations—should be illegal.

If, in order to break the vicious circle of no credit-cash shortage-failure-no credit, the government wants to go further and remove risk as a criterion for credit extension, it might be necessary in return for the law to specify minimum standards to qualify for loans. A government failure-insurance fund might be necessary to recompensate or provide security to the institutions required to make more of what they consider "higher risk" loans.

This policy would aid not only the nonconglomerate farmer, but small business in general.

The Impact of Large Corporation Farming on the Quality of Rural Life

In its report on corporation farming, the Senate Subcommittee on Small Business has recently republished a study of two rural California communities conducted by Walter Goldschmidt, a renowned anthropologist, in Arvin and Dinuba, California. The purpose of the study was to determine whether industrialization of farming is a threat to the family farm as well as to the rural society founded upon the family farm. The study consisted of detailed analysis and comparison of the two communities: Dinuba, where agricultural operations were on a modest scale, and Arvin, where large factorylike techniques were practiced. Both communities lie in the fertile southern San Joaquin Valley.

The investigation revealed vast differences in the economic and social life in the two towns. Among the specific findings were:

(1) The small-farm community supported sixty-two separate business establishments compared to thirty-five in the large-farm community, a ratio of nearly two to one.

(2) People in the small-farm community had a better average standard of living than those living in the community of large farms.

(3) Less than one-third of the breadwinners in the small-farm community were agricultural wage laborers, while almost two-thirds were wage laborers in the large-farm community.

(4) Physical facilities for community living—sidewalks, paved streets, sewage and garbage disposal, and

other public services—were more prevalent and of superior quality in the small-farm community.

(5) The small-farm community had three times the number of parks and five times the number of schools than the large-farm community had.

(6) The small-farm community had more than twice the number of organizations for civic improvement and social recreation than its large-farm counterpart.

(7) The small-farm community supported two newspapers, each with many times the news space carried in the single paper of the industrialized farm community.

(8) Facilities for making decisions on community welfare through local popular elections were available to people in the small-farm community; in the large-farm community such decisions were in the hands of county officials.

The small-farm community is made up of middle-class persons with a high degree of stability in income and tenure, and a strong economic and social interest in their community. Differences in wealth among them are not great, and people associate freely in those organizations which serve the community. Where farms are large, on the other hand, the population consists of relatively few wealthy persons and large numbers whose only tie to the community is an uncertain and relatively low-income job. Differences in wealth are great among the residents of this town, and social contacts between them are rare.

Despite the fact that this study was made twenty-five years ago, the distinctions between the two towns still held when they were revisited in 1968.

Poisoning the Land

Air Pollution

California agriculture is both a contributor to and a victim of air pollution. It dumps literally tons of poisonous pesticides, herbicides, and fungicides into the environment every year. And agricultural burning is a major source of air pollution in the Central Valley and other farming centers: fumes from burning unharvested plant materials are high in organic pollutants and carbon monoxide.

The State Department of Agriculture conservatively

estimated air pollution damage (from nonagricultural sources) to California crops in 1969 at $44.5 million. This estimate does not include the crop destruction that occurs without visible evidence of damage when plants are exposed continuously to low concentrations of pollutants for long periods of time. Many agriculturalists believe a more accurate estimate of the damage to California crops is $100 million per year. The worst damage is to crops in the Los Angeles basin, although farms in the San Francisco Bay Area, the Sacramento Valley, and the San Joaquin Valley are also badly affected. Photochemical smog ruins a vast range of crops; few, if any, appear to be immune. Oranges and lemons, grapes, ornamental plants, beets, tomatoes, celery, alfalfa, and beans suffer the most severe losses.

SMOG

Two of the Los Angeles area's most famous products are oranges and smog, with the latter gaining the upper hand. The southern California citrus industry lost over $33 million in 1969 as a result of photochemical smog damage. Photochemical smog develops when automobile gases—chiefly unburned hydrocarbons, ozone, and oxides of nitrogen—are trapped over the ground by an atmospheric inversion layer and slowly stewed by the sun's ultraviolet light. The resulting chemical brew is whiskey-brown in color and causes all kinds of damage to plant and human life.

As mentioned above, scientists at the University of California's Statewide Air Pollution Research Center in Riverside found that navel orange trees grown in shelters filled with smoggy air yield less than half as much fruit as trees grown in shelters with filtered air. Lemon trees grown in "smog-ambient" air tents either fail to bloom at all or abort their fruit very early, yielding less than half the lemons grown in tents with filtered air.

Photochemical smog also ruins fruit quality. It destroys the leaves of lemon and orange trees so that photosynthesis and water use are not sufficient to supply the plants with food. As a result, the fruit on these trees is not as sweet and juicy as fruit on healthy trees.

Grapes and wine are reduced in both quality and quantity by air pollution from automobiles. Scientists at the Air Pollution Research Center found that smog reduces the yield of grapevines by as much as 60% and results in smaller vines, smaller grapes, less sugar in the grapes, and yellowed vine leaves. Zinfandel grapes grown in San Bernardino County for a year in filtered air average 17.8 pounds of grapes per vine, while vines grown for a year in smoggy air yielded only 6.9 pounds per vine.

Ethylene, a component of smog present in low concentrations throughout the Los Angeles basin and the Bay Area, is ruining both flowers and profits in part of California's $100 million-a-year flower industry. Carnation growers in the Los Angeles area have been forced to move in recent years to areas such as San Diego and Santa Barbara Counties in order to escape air pollution and inflated land taxes. Both air pollution and development are now spreading to these areas as well. Even Monterey County carnation growers are worried about abnormal plant growth. Studies of Monterey carnations in the smog-tested chambers at the University of California at Riverside confirmed that very low concentrations of ethylene harm the growth of stems and flowers. According to Dr. O. C. Taylor of the Statewide Air Pollution Research Center, "In concentrations such as those near freeways, [ethylene] is strong enough to harm nearly all plants. Tomatoes, peppers, almonds, roses, orchids, snapdragons, and carnations are all sensitive to ethylene injury." Smog damage to flowers has forced nurseries almost entirely out of metropolitan areas. Even small amounts of pollution are affecting the growth of many varieties of plant life in areas far from major freeways or population centers.

Agricultural geneticists have had some success in identifying and breeding smog-resistant varieties of tobacco and certain other crops. But this reasearch is slow, and even resistant plants cannot tolerate heavy smog damage. The ultimate solution to smog damage in agriculture must lie in stricter controls on the pollution-emission levels of automobiles and industry.

But on the question of increasing the power of the Air Resources Board to improve air quality by strengthening emission standards, California agriculture speaks softly or not at all. Our interviewers heard bureaucrats in the Agricultural Extension Service and the State Department of Agriculture make various excuses for industrial pollution: "We have to understand the economic considerations; some of the suggested standards are so rigid the Industry couldn't make a decent profit. . . ." "We need motor vehicle trans-

portation and highways for market. . . ." "Growers and
the agricultural chemical industry have a great deal in
common. They must stand or fall together."

LEAD POISONING—THE CASE OF BENICIA

Benicia, a small bay-front town near San Francisco, is
surrounded by lush, green, rolling hills. While the Spaniards
owned California, the Benicia-Vallejo area was ranch country, but in 1849 the U.S. Army established the Benicia
Barracks, which was maintained as an arsenal until 1964.
The area formerly occupied by the arsenal is now the
Benicia Industrial Park, and, since the army left, about
seventy companies employing about 2,000 people have
moved into the area. The largest of these is a Humble Oil
refinery. The American Smelting and Refining Company
has been located across the Carquinez Straits in Selby
since 1900.

Between June, 1969, and May, 1970, twelve of the
approximately thirty Appaloosa show horses pastured in a
170-acre field owned by Mr. and Mrs. B. G. Wesner died
of unknown causes. This field is directly across Highway
21 from the Humble Oil Refinery. Other ranchers in the
Glen Cove and Elliot Cove areas a few miles away have
lost approximately twenty-five horses during the past two
years. Dr. Humphrey Knight, a veterinarian at the University of California at Davis, determined that the animals died
of hemolytic anemia, which causes a drastic destruction of
red blood cells and thus insufficient delivery of oxygen to
the brain. For several months the Public Health Department, the University of California at Davis, Solano County,
and Humble Oil worked secretly in an attempt to determine the cause of the disease before the media discovered
the story. The proximity of the refinery, the fact that the
first of the Wesner horses died a few months after the
refinery went into operation, and the fact that the horses
recovered at Davis but were soon sick again after returning
to the Benicia pasture worried the Humble Oil public-
relations men. On February 11, 1970, the story appeared on
the front page of the *San Francisco Chronicle*.

On May 1, 1970, the California Department of Public
Health released its Interim Report on the "Study of
Benicia Horse Deaths." The study was conducted by Drs.
Fred Ottoboni and Ephraim Kahn of the Bureau of Occupa-
tional Health and Environmental Epidemiology. They stated

that "the information we have developed so far indicates that the Wesner horses and the Glen Cove-Elliot Cove horses died as a result of lead poisoning. The source of this lead appears to be pasture grass which is contaminated with lead. . . ."

The Public Health investigators found that lead poisoning was not new in the Benicia-Vallejo area. In 1904–05, horses died of lead poisoning; the source of the lead was the Selby Smelting and Lead Company, now owned by the American Smelting and Refining Company. In July, 1908, an injunction was issued in perpetuity enjoining the Selby Smelting and Lead Company from emitting sulfurous and other injurious and noxious gases and smoke from March through November of every year; this injunction was upheld by the California Supreme Court. (The District Attorney of Solano County has ignored the Public Health Department's request for information about the current status of the injunction.)

Horses are not the only animals to have been affected by lead in the area's pasture grass. Another rancher, Mr. Gomez, reported recent abnormal deaths in his sheep flock. His pasture is directly east of the Wesner pasture on which the horses died. Lead was present in abnormally high amounts in the tissues of the dead sheep and the blood of those sheep still living. The death rate of Mr. Gomez's sheep was again high in 1970. However, sheep are not as sensitive to lead as horses. Sixteen percent of Mr. Gomez's sheep were killed, but 40% of the horses on the Wesner pasture died, and 100% of the horses on the Klatt and Vail-Glen Cove pasture died.

Grass normally contains less than ten parts per million of lead. The grass samples tested by Public Health technicians contained from 150 to 350 parts per million.* FDA regulations set 3.5 and 7 parts per million as maximum lead concentrations in some agricultural commodities. Ideally, lead concentration would be 0.15 to 0.30 parts per million in human food and drink. About half of the lead contamination was on the surface of the grass, and therefore of recent origin. The other half was inside the grass, probably absorbed by the grass from soil and surface deposits. The investigators concluded that "the pastures are severely polluted with lead." Obviously. They found that

---

* Based on dry grass weight.

the area of lead contamination extends at least *five miles,* from Elliot Cove to the area east of Benicia. As a result of veterinary studies, they concluded that "grazing animals may be expected to show evidence of excessive lead absorption from such food supply—safe grass should probably contain no more than twenty parts per million lead." In addition to ranching, the contaminated area included fields growing hay and grain that are harvested. The California Department of Agriculture has been asked to investigate the level of contamination of the hay and grain. This might well prove to be a serious economic blow to farmers in the area.

The Public Health study listed six possible sources of lead in the area. They are: (1) the Carquinez and Benicia Bridges and the autos which use them (the bridges are painted with lead-bearing paint); (2) the U.S. Government's Reserve ship fleet located in Suisun Bay, opposite Benicia (also painted with lead-bearing paint and sandblasted regularly); (3) the American Smelting and Refining Company (the villain of the early 1900s and a probable source of current poisoning); (4) the Benicia Refinery of the Humble Oil and Refining Company; (5) Associated Metals Company (a metal scrap recovery operation which is located about a mile and a half from the Wesner pasture and which burns ten to twenty railroad boxcars covered with lead-bearing paint each week in the open air); and (6) the Waste Refinement Company (now defunct, but whose tetraethyl lead memorial remains). Any or all of the sources may have contributed to the deaths of the horses. The Public Health investigators found that the "Selby Smelter is probably responsible for the bulk of the lead contamination" that killed the Benicia horses. But the poisoning continues.

The Benicia area has no effective local or regional pollution control. The Benicia City Council regulates only under pressure and with restricted jurisdiction. The State Air Resources Board investigates only on a complaint basis. They haven't assigned blame in this case or made any efforts to shut down sources of pollution in the area. The Selby Smelter is under the jurisdiction of the Bay Area Air Pollution Control District since it is in Contra Costa County, but since the BAAPCD cannot regulate lead emission, and the effects of the emission are on animals across the county line, the BAAPCD has no jurisdiction on the affected areas. In addition, the BAAPCD report on emissions from the smelter will probably depend on data given by the smelter itself. In May, 1970, Milton Feldstein of the BAAPCD reported to a closed meeting of the Air Resources Board that, according to the industry, emission rates from the main stack of the Selby Smelter were 109 pounds of lead, 48 pounds of cadmium, and .1 pound of silver per day. Emissions from other stacks of the smelter were not reported. These rates were suppressed. According to recent work published in the *Journal of the American Medical Association*, airborne cadmium is correlated with certain types of heart disease. The State Public Health Department is now quietly "studying" the cadmium levels in urine of a sample of the Solano County population.

Dr. John Goldsmith is head of the Environmental Epidemiology Unit of State Public Health and an acknowledged international authority on the effects of pollution on human health. In the fall of 1969, before SPH began its investigation of the Benicia horse deaths, Dr. Goldsmith submitted an extremely well documented research proposal to the National Air Pollution Control Administration (NAPCA). He suggested testing for lead poisoning in children by measuring the level of a particular enzyme, (δ-amino levulinic dehydrase) in the urine. The test is easier than a blood test and large numbers of individuals could be screened for excessive lead exposure before deaths from lead poisoning occur.

NAPCA referred the proposal to its "Lead Liaison Committee," asking if any of its organizations were interested in pursuing the study. The Lead Liaison Committee of the NAPCA includes representatives of General Motors, International Lead Zinc Research Organization, Du Pont, Esso Research and Engineering (a subsidiary of Standard Oil of New Jersey), American Petroleum Institute, Ethyl Corporation, Mobil Oil, and the Lead Industries Association. Inviting the sources of pollution to measure the effects of pollution is like asking Richard Nixon to write a critique of his Supreme Court appointments. Needless to say, the proposal has been ignored.

Detailed discussion of federal and state weakness in the drafting of air pollution control laws is beyond the scope of this book.[24] Lead, cadmium, and other poisonous elements do not break down naturally—they remain in the air and on the land and build in concentration unless they are dispersed. They are extraordinarily dangerous poisons, affecting life even in very small quantities.

What is noteworthy about the Benicia example is that government nonfeasance prevails even in an area in which damage is dramatic, visible, and specific. Here there is information. Yet not only is nothing done but one of the guilty parties uses the area as an example of its environmental "achievements": Humble Oil Refinery officials point with pride to the $10 million Humble Oil purportedly spent to diminish the refinery's impact on the environment. An entire advertising campaign has been built on the company's "concern for the environment," complete with giggling girls and weekend fishermen testifying on TV that a Humble Oil Refinery can be a "good neighbor." But Humble's efforts didn't come close to eliminating pollution from their plant. According to the company's own estimate, the refinery spews twenty-four tons of pollutants into the air each day. (This total is less than that of other refineries, but it is hardly negligible). Its waste water processing systems have failed, and the refinery was found to violate the water quality standards set by the State Water Resources Quality Board. And Public Health investigators found that people working in the neighborhood of the refinery "are routinely disturbed and annoyed by odors emanating from the refinery."

These incidents are not a part of the "good neighbor" policy depicted by the company's advertising men. Deceptive and illegal PR campaigns are currently quite fashionable among the nation's major polluters. It costs millions of dollars to praise one's own nonexistent environmental concern in the mass media, millions that could be well spent in beginning to correct some of the companies' most offensive practices.

BIOCIDES

In the first six months of 1970, California farmers sprayed, poured, and dusted over seventy-one million pounds of poisons on over seven million acres of the state.[25] Advertised as killers of pests ranging from fungi and broad-leafed plants to mites, mosquitoes, and mice, these fungicides, herbicides, and insecticides have also killed and maimed birds, fish, and human beings. Because they are lethal to so many different living organisms, the proper term for these poisons as a class is biocides.

There are at least 900 chemical compounds used in the 60,000 brands of biocides available to the farmer or consumer. These compounds differ in regard to the pests which they are supposed to kill and the crops on which they can be applied, as well as the adverse effect they have on other living things. Among the most harmful biocides are the DDT family of compounds, organophosphate (or phosphate ester) and carbamate insecticides, arsenic and mercury biocides, the 2,4,5-T family of herbicides, and synthetic organic fungicides.

The best-known class of pesticides is chlorinated hydrocarbons, which include: DDT, DDD, aldrin, dieldrin, endrin, heptachlor, lindane, Thiodan, and toxaphene. Between January and June, 1970, over three million pounds of these pesticides were applied to a vast range of fruits, vegetables, and grains in California. Because of their chemical composition, chlorinated hydrocarbons require a very long time (possible fifty years or more) to break down into harmless chemicals. According to the report of the Human Relations Agency of the State Department of Public Health to the 1970 State Legislature on the effects of DDT use, "DDT is probably present in the air everywhere in California."

Chlorinated hydrocarbons pose a greater danger to wildlife than any other form of pesticide. In the first place, DDT concentrates as it progresses up the ecological food chain. When DDT is sprayed on agricultural lands, the runoff of irrigation water causes gross DDT pollution of the aquatic environment. The microscopic plants in water readily absorb and retain DDT. These tiny plants are eaten by many different kinds of small animals. Each small animal eats several times its weight in plants, and most of the DDT in the plants becomes stored in the fat tissues of the animal's body. Since the animal contains DDT absorbed by many plants, the concentration of DDT in its body is much higher than that in the plants which it eats. Small animals are eaten by larger ones, and these in turn by still larger animals. At each successive step in such a food chain, the DDT concentration increases. In water, DDT is present in a few parts per trillion. In marine plants, it is many parts per trillion. In smaller animals, it is measured in parts per billion. In larger animals, levels of DDT are measured in parts per million, a million times more concentrated than DDT in water.

At these DDT levels, life is in real trouble. Food and Drug regulations prohibit marketing of fish which contain more than five parts per million (ppm) of DDT and its residues. The jack mackerel, caught off the coast of southern California, has already passed this limit. DDT adversely affects marine plants, shellfish (shrimps, crabs, oysters, and clams), fish, birds, and man. The highest concentrations of DDT usually occur in the larger animals which feed on fish, such as pelicans and ospreys, and in the peregrine falcon, which preys mainly on fish-eating birds.

One of the clearest examples of poisoning by chlorinated hydrocarbon pesticides in California is the Clear Lake incident. Clear Lake was sprayed with DDT to control gnats in 1949, 1954, and 1957. Shortly after these treatments, levels of DDD (a breakdown product of DDT) in eight species of fish inhabiting the lake ranged from 5 ppm (the permissible limit for edible fish) to 133 ppm. The grebes (fish-eating birds) which inhabited the lake began to die, but the gnats soon began to thrive again.

Another dramatic example of the deadly effects of DDT on wildlife in California is the reproductive failure of the brown pelicans, which nest off the coast of southern California. Anacapa Island is the only nesting site used by large numbers of this species on the U.S. Pacific Coast. In 1968, pelicans made at least three attempts to nest on the island. Each time, the eggs were thin-shelled and broke before hatching. More than 600 adult pelicans in the colony produced only five young. In 1970, only one brown pelican hatched on the island. High residues of DDT and its by-products were found in the nesting birds and in collapsed eggs collected from the island. The bald eagle, osprey, Bermuda petrel, peregrine falcon, and other predatory birds suffer similar reproductive failure in other parts of the country. Eggs of the black-crowned night heron and snowy egret contain over 1000 ppm DDT, more than five times the residue level in brown pelican eggs.

The accumulation of chlorinated hydrocarbon pesticides in the bodies of animals may also impair coordination to such an extent that the animal is unable to obtain food or escape enemies.

People in the United States carry in their fatty tissues DDT levels averaging about 12 ppm. DDT is present in human breast milk; among California women it is at levels so high that under Federal Food and Drug Administration standards it could not be sold for human consumption. Little work has been done on the long-term effects of DDT on man. Recent clinical research shows a strong correlation between high DDT levels and encephalomalacia, cerebral hemorrhage, portal cirrhosis, and various forms of cancer. DDT and its derivatives can also induce cancer in tumor-susceptible mice.

Although DDT and the other chlorinated hydrocarbon pesticides have played an important role in the development of agriculture, they now pose a very real threat to important human food resources and to species of wildlife that are ecologically irreplaceable. In addition, DDT is less effective now than when it was first used, since nearly 150 species of insect pests have developed resistance to it. For these reasons, many biologists, physicians, and public health officials have recommended that DDT be banned. The California Director of Agriculture has responded to these recommendations by acting to phase out the use of DDT and DDD in the state within the next two years. But California will continue to feel the effects of DDT use in other parts of the United States and abroad; and the DDT used here, now and in the past, will remain in the environment for a very long time. Accumulation of DDT in the sea will surely continue as wind and water transfer the chemicals now in soils, lakes, and the atmosphere into ocean basins. Meanwhile, problems associated with the pesticides substituted for DDT and DDD are rapidly increasing.

Among the compounds most commonly used as alternatives to DDT are the organophosphate (or phosphate ester) pesticides: parathion, Guthion, ethion, malathion, Thimet, Phosdrin, demeton, and tetraethyl pyrophosphate (TEPP). Millions of pounds of these insecticides are sprayed on fruits, vegetables, cotton, ornamental plants, weeds, grains, pastures, and parks in California every year. The extraordinary toxicity of these poisons will be described in more detail below. They have caused more deaths and serious illnesses among humans than any of the previously mentioned poisons. The phosphate ester pesticides break down in the environment much more quickly than the chlorinated hydrocarbons; but since just a few drops of any of these poisons will kill a human being, they are much more dangerous to agricultural workers than DDT and its relatives.

Carbamates are also used as substitutes for chlorinated hydrocarbon pesticides. The carbamate Sevin has been used most commonly in California on cotton, beets, sugar beets, corn, and tomatoes. Sevin kills bees, and as a result threatens the livelihood of the orchard owners—whose fruit crop depends on how well the bees help pollinate his trees —and the beekeeper, who makes his living by renting his bees to orchardists. And recent studies have shown that Sevin induces bird deformations in experimental animals. The 1969 report of the Health, Education, and Welfare Commission on Pesticides and their Relationship to Environmental Health recommended that use of Sevin be "immediately restricted to prevent risk of human exposure."

Poisonous metal compounds, particularly arsenic and mercury compounds, are widely used in California as pesticides, herbicides, and fungicides. Arsenic probably kills more small children than any other biocide because of its wide and often careless use in homes and gardens. Very small doses of arsenic and mercury compounds cause chronic poisoning, with irreversible brain damage. Even smaller doses may cause birth defects in humans. Arsenic and mercury compounds constitute an immediate and major water pollution problem, but the chronic poisoning they cause may take two to six years to appear and then may not be diagnosed correctly.

Mercury compounds are very widely applied as a fungicide and herbicide in California on corn, barley, milo, wheat, safflower, and other grains. Mercury compounds are concentrated as they progress up the food chain like the chlorinated hydrocarbon pesticides, and are particularly hazardous to wildlife which eat contaminated grain seed. In addition, recent experiments indicate that mercury fungicides remain in plant leaves, roots, and fruit, later to be ingested by people.

The best-known herbicides are modified plant hormones, chief among which are 2,4-D (2,4-dichlorophenoxyacetic acid), 2,4,5-T (2,4,5-trichlorophenoxyacetic acid), and silvex, a close relative of 2,4,5-T. These herbicides are widely used in agriculture, in forestry, in home gardens, and as the principal defoliants in Indochina. About a million pounds of these herbicides were applied to California's agricultural land in the first half of 1970. Purified 2,4,5-T and several forms of 2,4-D, including the form most commonly used in weed control, are known to cause abnormally high fetal death rates and birth defects in experimental animals. Missing or abnormally small eyes, absence of the lower jaw, abnormal kidneys, and cleft palate are among the most frequent observed defects.

Biocides which cause defects in experimental animals may well cause abnormalities in unborn children as well.[26] The HEW report "Pesticides and their Relationship to Environmental Health" recommended that 2,4-D and 2,4,5-T be immediately restricted to decrease the level of human exposure. However, eight months after the published recommendation and four *years* after government tests first showed that 2,4-D and 2,4,5-T cause birth defects, no action has been taken to restrict human exposure to 2,4-D; the federal regulatory response for 2,4,5-T has been weak and ineffective. The state of California has done nothing at all.

The Dow Chemical Company's manufacturing process for 2,4,5-T introduces extremely toxic contaminants called dioxins, of which the worst is tetrachlorodioxin.[27] Very small quantities of dioxins can cause fetal deaths and bleeding in the stomachs and intestines of fetuses of experimental mammals. Even low levels of dioxin contamination in 2,4,5-T are hazardous to man and his environment. The burning of shrubs, brush, timber, or other materials exposed to 2,4,5-T and similar herbicides releases high concentrations of dioxins into the atmosphere.[28] Furthermore, the usual aerial applications of these herbicides present real drift hazards to agricultural and residential areas whose vegetation is not supposed to be destroyed. There are no available data on the persistence of dioxins in soil, water, crops, milk, and animal or human tissues. Nor are there data on the possible accumulation and transmission of dioxins in the food chain, although dioxins' heat stability, and their ability to dissolve in human fat, as well as the cumulative toxicity of dioxins in experimental animals, all make food-chain transmission more likely. Dr. Samuel Epstein, chief of the Laboratories of Environmental Toxicology and Carcinogenesis at the Children's Cancer Research Foundation in Boston, has written that "continued use of these herbicides in the environment constitutes a large-scale human experiment in teratogenicity (the

production of malformations in unborn children which
cause disability or death). . . . Such an experiment is unwarranted by any conceivable criteria in the face of the
unambiguous warnings sounded by available scientific
data."

Clearly, many of the pesticides, herbicides, and fungicides used by the hundreds of millions of pounds in California each year are hazardous to man and wildlife. But
how effective are they in killing the pests for which they
are intended? According to Dr. Robert Van den Bosch of
the University of California at Berkeley, it is a "sobering
reality that (1) today there are more insect pest species
than ever before, (2) over 200 of these pests have developed resistance to chemicals, (3) costs of pest control
have increased strikingly, and (4) pesticides have polluted
the biosphere."

There are two biological reasons why many pesticides
are not the solution to pest infestations of agricultural
crops.

First is the development of resistant pests. When a
biocide is sprayed on large numbers of pest insects, a few
survive because they have developed some resistance to
the effects of the poison. The resistant pests soon multiply
and in the next generation the pest population has a larger
proportion of resistant individuals. This process continues
over many generations so that after repeated pesticide
applications, the entire population of pest organisms is
resistant to the pesticide. The farmer therefore has to use
more and more pesticide with less and less effectiveness.
If he changes to a second pesticide, resistance to the new
chemical will usually develop even more quickly than it
did to the first.

The second biological problem results from the broad
range of toxicity of most pesticides. The sprays kill not
only the pest insect, but also most of the predators and
parasites that normally keep the pest population down.
Larger animals poisoned by the pesticide, such as fish and
birds, do not become resistant because their populations
are smaller and their generation times much longer than
those of the target insect. Consequently, few of the large
animals survive and many years pass before the bird or
fish populations develop the genes for DDT resistance.

The grower is eventually faced with increased numbers
of pest insects, which may well be resistant to his pesticide,

and no more predators or parasites to keep the pests in check by natural means. These two factors together create a "chemical treadmill" effect, or secondary pest outbreak, more devastating and difficult to control than the first. Shell Chemical Company advertisements quaintly refer to the secondary pest outbreaks as "migrations," and encourage the grower to apply more and more of their product. Secondary pest outbreaks are almost never migrations, but are instead the natural evolutionary result of too frequent use of a poison that kills too many different kinds of organisms.

Herbicides also cause outbreaks of insect pests that never before troubled a farmer. For example, herbicides have been used to clear brush, including wild blackberries, from vineyards in California. As a result, the grape leafhopper has become a major pest in California grapes: the destruction of wild blackberry bushes destroyed a blackberry leafhopper which served as food for a small wasp in the winter. This small wasp paralyzed grape leafhoppers during the summer months, providing a natural control on the number of grape leafhoppers. Because the wasps were wiped out when their winter food supply was destroyed, the grape leafhoppers infected the vineyards in larger numbers the following year.

Are massive applications of pesticides really necessary? After the 1968 cotton harvest, the cotton growers of Graham County, Arizona, discovered that together they had spent almost $200,000 on pesticides. They had used the multiple-treatment, mass-spraying method recommended by chemical companies and had killed not only the pink bollworm pest, but also its predators. Fed up, and in dire economic straits, nearly all the cotton growers in the county formed the Pink Bollworm Committee. They decided that in 1969 they would spray their crops only when a hazardous number of pink bollworms were present in their fields. They hired and trained high school students to scout their fields weekly and count the number of pink bollworms on cotton samples. In addition, instead of buying pesticides from the most persistent salesmen, the growers decided to buy pesticides in bulk from the lowest bidder. In 1969, the combined expense of all the members of the Pink Bollworm Committee on pesticides and the salaries and training of the students was $37,000, less than one-fifth the previous year's total. Their cotton yield increased.

POISONED FOOD

In order to check pesticide residues on food offered for sale in California, the State Department of Agriculture inspects fruit, produce, milk, and meat samples in growing areas and wholesale and retail outlets in the state. The federal Food and Drug Administration does the same thing for interstate traffic. Tolerances for pesticide residues in California are the same as those developed by the federal Food and Drug Administration. These tolerance levels do not protect the public, because they are based on inadequate scientific information and enforcement is virtually non-existent.[29]

Complete elimination of pesticide residues in food is not practical, but that fact should not be used to excuse unsafe practices. The FDA and California set pesticide tolerances on vegetables, fruit, meats, and other foods individually. They do not seriously consider how much residue a person will ingest if he eats several of these foods at one meal, or if there is chemical residue in the water he drinks and the air he breathes.

In all probability, the sum of all the ingested "insignificant" residues is not significant at all, although the long-term effects of residues, individually and in various combinations, are unknown. Studying the effects of combinations of chemicals is particularly important since two or more compounds may cause more harm together than their individual effects would indicate—as when one takes sleeping pills and alcohol at the same time. The tolerance levels themselves are suspect, since the research to establish tolerance levels is usually conducted by the pesticide manufacturer and is so limited that the danger to humans is not clearly determined.

A more conservative tolerance-setting program by the FDA or the California Department of Agriculture could be a strong motivation for the development and use of alternative means of pest control. However, the FDA, and thus the California Department of Agriculture, is in fact raising the allowable tolerances of pesticide residues on food rather than lowering them. The original FDA pesticide tolerances for many foods (e.g., DDT level in milk fed to babies) was zero. Now that improved measurement techniques have indicated that pesticide residues do indeed exist, the FDA, instead of using this new information to enforce the zero tolerance more effectively, is raising the allowable tolerance to conform with the observed residue levels! In the meantime, the FDA and the California Department of Agriculture are not enforcing those zero tolerances which remain. Instead, the two agencies have established "action levels." While the public is told that many chemicals are not tolerated at all on food, in fact no action is taken against the grower or distributor unless the residues exceed the "action levels" of 0.05 to 0.3 parts per million. These levels *are* very low, but the long-term effects of continuous ingestion of "negligible" amounts of combinations of pesticides are unknown. And the public has a right to know that pesticide residues may be present on the food they buy: "action levels" within the FDA and the California Department of Agriculture may deceive the consumer, especially as they are constantly being raised.

From our investigation and conversations with California Department of Agriculture pesticide-residue specialists, we believe that most of the inspectors in the Field Crops and Agricultural Chemicals Division are hard-working men, trying to keep food safe from pesticide contamination. However, there are so few of these officials, particularly as a result of the state budget cutbacks in the last two years, that their program cannot possibly be effective. Each of the permanent-residue analysis laboratories, in San Francisco, Sacramento, Fresno, and Los Angeles, is staffed at any one time by only one inspector and a few laboratory assistants. In addition to sampling wholesale markets every morning, and testing water, soil, and suspected crop samples for pesticide contamination, these overworked inspectors must also regulate licensing for commercial pesticide applicators, feed restrictions, fertilizer use, etc. At the time of one of our visits, officials of the Field Crops and Agricultural Chemicals Division were investigating an incident in which a commercial applicator sprayed dimethoate and Cygon on children playing in a school yard during recess in Bakersfield, another incident in which parathion was sprayed on workers in the field, and still another in which sulfur was sprayed on a large group of striking farm workers on a road near Modesto. Confronted daily with incidents like these, the Department of Agriculture inspectors cannot possibly devote adequate time to pesticide-residue analysis. The recent cuts in state support for the pesticide-residue program have increased the chances of contaminated food escaping inspection entirely.

One of the severest handicaps facing the pesticide-residue inspectors, particularly in view of the understaffing problem, is their inability to hold a food shipment suspected of contamination from sale for more than twenty-four hours. The closest lab for analysis of the suspected food may be over a hundred miles from the packing shed. The inspector is somehow supposed to sample the shipment, return it— possibly over 100 miles through heavy southern-California traffic—to the laboratory, measure the level of pesticide residues present, analyze the results, and return to the packing shed to withdraw the shipment from sale, all within twenty-four hours.

If pesticide contamination of foodstuffs is found to be over the "action level," the investigator will usually take no action against the grower on his first offense. Repeated offenses lead to fines, rarely more than several hundred dollars. However, because of the overwhelming chance of escaping inspection entirely, the grower has little incentive from this inspection program to apply pesticides sparingly or use alternative pest control means.

HUMAN CASUALTIES

California agricultural workers suffer the highest occupational disease rate in the state; the risk of illness or death for these workers is over 50% higher than for workers in the second most hazardous industry and is about three times as high as the average rate for all industries. The most formidable of all occupational hazards threatening farm laborers are probably heat stroke and pesticide poisoning.

The pesticides, or more properly, biocides, which have claimed the largest number of human victims are the highly toxic phosphate esters, closely related to compounds developed by the Nazis for use as nerve gases during World War II: parathion, Guthion, ethion, malathion, Thimet, Phosdrin, demeton, and tetraethyl pyrophosphate (TEPP).

Phosphate esters poison people in the same way that they kill insects. The compounds inhibit cholinesterase, an enzyme in nerve cells. As a result of this inhibition, acetylcholine, another chemical found at nerve endings, is not destroyed after it acts. The excess acetylcholine makes the nervous system run wild. An insect goes into uncontrollable spasms and tremors, and then dies. A human being is affected by nausea, vomiting, muscle cramps, headache, giddiness, blurred vision, sweating, difficult breathing, pinpoint pupils, muscle twitching, and so on, then loses consciousness and soon dies unless *large* doses of atropine antidote are administered.

A very small amount of concentrated phosphate ester poison will kill a human being. Three to nine drops of parathion swallowed or thirteen drops absorbed through the skin are fatal. TEPP is the most deadly of all phosphate esters. One drop in the mouth or on the skin will kill an adult.

Case 1.[30] A 28-year-old worker with no record of occupational exposure to pesticides was employed as a sprayer by a licensed agricultural pest-control operator. He began his employment by applying parathion, TEPP, and Phosdrin under the direction of a more experienced sprayer. After one safety meeting at the company headquarters and three weeks of employment, he was assigned his first job alone at a ranch in the adjoining county where he was to spray a mixture of Phosdrin, parathion and TDE (a mixture of chlorinated hydrocarbons) on lettuce. His employer did not place him under medical supervision as required by the California Division of Industrial Safety's Agricultural Safety Orders, did not make sure he got baseline cholinesterase tests, and made no advance arrangements with a physician to take care of any poisoning emergency which might arise.

He began to spray forty acres of lettuce at the ranch at about 9:30 P.M. He was last seen alive at midnight by an irrigator who said he had by then sprayed half the field. He was expected to complete his job about 2 A.M. It was a cool, cloudy evening and he had no illumination except the headlights of his vehicle. The ground-spraying apparatus included a closed system for mixing the parathion and TDE. However, the Phosdrin, a 50% concentrate, was poured manually from a five-gallon can into a tank on the truck. The sprayer apparently spilled some of the poison on himself while pouring it. He then finished the job, secured his equipment on the truck and began to vomit. He tumbled out of the truck about 2:30 A.M., landing face down in the ditch. At 8:00 A.M. he was found by the ranch owner, who described him as possibly still alive and frothing at the mouth. He was pronounced dead on arrival at the hospital. Postmortem tests showed that cell, plasma, and brain cholinesterase levels were all close to zero, confirming the diagnosis of phosphate ester poisoning.

Case 2. In 1963, ninety-four California peach harvesters were poisoned by parathion residues on the foliage of the orchards in which they worked. By law, there is a waiting period between pesticide application and crop harvesting so that the poison will have deteriorated to the point where residues on the food are within safe limits. Apparently, in this case, the law was obeyed. Nevertheless, the workers got sick. Medical tests indicated that the probable cause of the illness was a poison in the spray residue which is a product of parathion but is even more toxic than parathion itself.

Case 3. Two farm laborers, 16 and 21 years old, were hired to apply a phosphate ester and sulfur pesticide mixture to strawberries. (Five drops of this phosphate ester poison ingested orally or six drops on the skin will kill an adult.) The workers began work at 7:30 A.M., using knapsacks to carry the pesticide dust. By noon, the 21-year-old worker became ill and began vomiting. After a while, he felt better and drove home. Fortunately, he did not have an auto accident: victims of phosphate ester poisoning often do have accidents with moving machinery. The 16-year-old began vomiting at 4:00 P.M. and went home. At 8:00 P.M., he complained of weakness and giddiness and was taken to a physician's office. His clothing was covered with sulfur, so the physician called the Poison Information Center to ask about sulfur, which is far less harmful than phosphate ester compounds. The doctor gave the boy a prescription and sent him home. By 9:30 P.M., the boy was much sicker and was taken to the local hospital, along with the label from the pesticide container he had used. Once again the boy was sent home, although he was unable to walk! At 7:30 A.M., the boy was found dying in his bed, still in his contaminated clothes. He died in the ambulance on the way to the hospital. The 21-year-old worker reported the next day for a cholinesterase test which confirmed that he had also been poisoned by a phosphate ester chemical. Getting sick early and going home probably saved his life.

Case 4. In 1970, sixteen farm workers in Tulare County were poisoned while working in orange groves that had been sprayed a few days previously with parathion, Guthion, and ethion. The interval between application of pesticides and the harvest of edible crops is subject to state regulations and is based on the time required in a typical year for the pesticide residue on an edible crop to fall below the legal tolerance for market sale. It has been assumed that, by the time the phosphate ester levels are below tolerance on the crop, the orchards will be safe for the farm workers.

However, the interval between the time of spraying and time the workers reentered the groves was not sufficient to allow breakdown of the phosphate esters in a dry season. The leaves in this orchard were so heavily contaminated that 2,500 other orange pickers in the area had been warned to stay out of the groves for thirty days after spraying. There was no attempt to withhold the oranges from sale: State Director of Agriculture Jerry Fielder said that the leaves of the orange trees were heavily contaminated, but the oranges themselves were perfectly safe to eat.

Case 5. A young Mexican laborer was employed to process edible nuts. He assisted in fumigating infested nuts under tarps, using methyl bromide. He became ill rather suddenly at home and died a few hours after being admitted to the hospital. The physicians could not determine the cause of his illness until after the young man died, and health department officials tested his body for chemical poisoning and investigated the history of his repeated exposure to methyl bromide. Methyl bromide, an "insidious poison" (according to the Merck Index) used as a fumigant, causes more deaths in California than any other pesticide except parathion. High concentrations of methyl bromide kill by destroying the lungs, but even low concentrations cause depression and sensory and psychic disturbances. Methyl bromide is all the more dangerous because it has no unpleasant odor. The State Department of Public Health has studied workers exposed to methyl bromide. Their report, part of Contract Report Number 19, California Community Studies on Pesticides, should be made available publicly and appropriate restrictive measures should be taken against this poison.

All of these deaths were preventable, and we could cite many more cases of serious illness and deaths resulting from the careless use of pesticides. Every year the California Department of Public Health adds to its already bulging file of pesticide victims. And thousands of cases of chronic illness among farm workers exposed to agricultural chemicals go unreported.

There are at least two clinics in the Central Valley where farm workers and their children can get competent and inexpensive medical care. The Salud health clinic in Woodville, Tulare County, run by Dr. David Brooks, and Dr. Lee Mizrahi's community health clinic in Earlimart, Tulare County, provide general medical and pediatric care, emergency care for pesticide poisoning and other occupational sicknesses and injuries, treatment for drug addiction, screening for phosphate ester poisoning in adults and children by measuring cholinesterase levels in the blood, and various other special services that farm workers and their families require. The fees at the Salud health clinic range from $1 to $6 a visit, depending on the number of children in a family, and all members of the staff, from doctors to the janitors, receive the same $250 monthly salary.

In view of the unique services and character of these clinics, it is particularly revealing—and discouraging—to learn that Dr. Brooks has been barred from both the hospitals in the Tulare area. Three years ago he was expelled from the Tulare County Hospital and, just this summer, the Board of Directors of the Tulare District Hospital expelled him from their staff. The issue is apparently not professional competence, for Dr. Brooks is recognized throughout the state as a pioneer in community health treatment, but antipathy toward the Salud clinic on the part of most of the 140 or so other doctors in Tulare County. Dr. Brooks will continue his clinic, but he no longer has any institutions at which he can treat his 15,000 clinic patients when they require hospital care.

California officials boast that the rate of illness and injury caused by pesticides is two cases per 1,000 agricultural workers per year. This rate is based on the number of claims made for Workmen's Compensation Insurance, a medical insurance program for which farm workers are legally eligible. However, a study sponsored by the California Department of Public Health in Tulare County in 1969 reveals that the true rate of illness among farm workers due to pesticide poisoning is 250 cases per 1,000 workers per year, 125 times the official figure. Even this rate includes only those workers who actually visit a physician with their symptoms. The Public Health Department investigators found that nearly 90% of the farm workers they talked to experienced one or more symptoms commonly associated with pesticide poisoning. These reports have been suppressed.[31] As one worker put it, "Anybody who works in grape who tells you that he hasn't ever been affected by lime sulfur is either a superman or a liar."

There are reasons why farm workers rarely seek medical help for their chronic but not incapacitating sicknesses, and often fail to see physicians even when they are seriously ill. The nearest doctor or hospital may be twenty miles away. Even if the farm worker owns a car, he can't afford to take time off from work to make the trip, wait for a long period in a crowded office, and return. Most farm workers have not been informed of their right to receive Workmen's Compensation, and even those who are aware of the program usually cannot cope with the red tape necessary to file a claim. The language barrier reduces claims even further: roughly 75% of California farm workers speak only Spanish and are unfamiliar with U.S. law, while virtually all representatives of growers, employment offices, and welfare departments speak English exclusively. Physicians and their office staffs often don't bother to ask whether a sickness was work-connected, both because compensation cases require more paper work than private cases, and because the doctor's fee is usually lower under the Workmen's Compensation system. Consequently, most workers pay for medical care for pesticide injuries themselves, in cash, and visit physicians only when their symptoms become very serious indeed.

At a San Francisco hearing of the U.S. House of Representatives Select Subcommittee on Labor, on November 22, 1969, Elton Gebhardt, the Legislative Director of the California Farm Bureau Federation, proudly lauded the safety-consciousness and responsibility of California farmers. As "evidence" he noted that $13,500,000 has been returned to agricultural employers from the California Farm Bureau Federation's Workmen's Compensation Insurance Program, because farm workers' claims for medical payments fell far short of the anticipated levels. Yet illnesses caused by pesticides are almost epidemic in some of California's richest breadbaskets. The surplus in the Workmen's Compensation Insurance Fund results not from the care and responsibility of the growers, but from the failure of growers, contractors, physicians, welfare workers, and nearly all other representatives of the "Establishment" to inform the farm workers about the program, and their strong tendency to discourage in various ways those workers who have heard of the program from using it.

REGULATING POISON

Testifying at the same hearings, Jerry W. Fielder, Director of the California Department of Agriculture, stated: "Through the years California farmers have supported legislation and regulations that provide the most comprehensive control over the sale and use of pesticides of anywhere in the world. . . . Agricultural producers . . . are most cooperative in the regulation and control of pesticide uses, and are strong proponents of the principle of 'safety first.' "

Before an insecticide, herbicide, fungicide, or other biocide may be legally used in California, it must be registered by both the U.S. Department of Agriculture Pesticides Regulation Division and the California State Department of Agriculture. For all practical purposes, the California Department of Agriculture simply rubber-stamps chemicals registered by the federal agency. The tests for safety to wildlife and effectiveness of the chemical involved are performed *by the industry* for both the federal and state registration procedures.

Even with new legislative directives enacted in 1969 for stricter control, the State Department of Agriculture fails to regulate the pesticide industry. There are only three specialists reviewing thousands of registration applications for poisons. The entire registration program is funded on less than $40,000 and is strictly a paperwork, red-tape operation. The Department fails to ask for adequate manpower and simply ignores new directives designed to protect the environment. It registers virtually upon request. Except for a possibly effective DDT limitation, even the thirty-five pesticides now classified as "injurious" are not restricted in amount or location in any meaningful way. About one-fifth of all pesticides in California are mislabeled, according to a survey cited by the state's Legislative Analyst. Sanctions here are not used and violations of the law are not declining, according to Analyst Post.

One reason the pesticide registration program is doomed to impotence is the same reason that less than $40,000 is spent on registration application review and $298,000 spent to enforce "labelling and quality control": industry directly finances the program. The program is dependent upon a special fund fed from "registration fees" collected for the approval of a pesticide (which encourages approval). The Legislative Analyst quietly remarks:

> When a governmental regulatory service is financed through special funding, as opposed to General Fund financing, there is a natural tendency for the groups supplying the funds to view the expenditure of the funds in a proprietary manner and to attempt to influence the program objectives for which the money is spent. The State employees who are paid with the funds are naturally aware of the source of the funds.

The job of enforcing state regulations on local pesticide use falls to the Agricultural Commissioner in each county, who is appointed by his County Board of Supervisors. Agricultural Commissioner jobs tend to be political plums, and the Boards of Supervisors in the agricultural counties are made up primarily of the large growers and of those who work for the agricultural industry in the towns.

Even if willing to enforce the law, the County Agricultural Commissioner has very limited resources, and so must take the grower's word for what he has been applying to his crops, the times at which he has sprayed, and the amount of chemical he used. But growers do not necessarily keep accurate records: one told a visiting biologist that he doesn't keep records of the spraying activities on his farm because "the Agricultural Commissioner would look at it and we'd be out of business." Even with limited resources, however, the County Agricultural Commissioner could check on growers who receive permits to buy tremendous amounts of a particular injurious pesticide, and investigate when and where the chemical is used. But even when violations are detected, enforcement of the weak state laws and regulations is nil. The Commissioner is likely to be engaging in similar operations on his own farm.

There is a cozy community of agricultural interests in California: the Department of Agriculture is considered "an agriculture-oriented agency"; growers communicate freely and in a friendly manner with their County Agricultural Commissioner; the various County Agricultural Commissioners communicate well with the California State Department of Agriculture; and the State Department of Agriculture is in close touch with the USDA. But this comfortable system omits the majority of people who work within the state's agricultural structure: there is no viable system of communication between the County Agricultural Commissioners and the 700,000 farm workers in the State.

The institutionalization of preferential access for big agriculture to Department decision-making is guaranteed through the California State Board of Agriculture. This board, established in 1929, is empowered to confer with and advise the Director of Agriculture, the Governor, and the Director of the State Department of Employment on farm labor. Boards such as this have great informal power. They have access to information and personal contact at the middle levels of the bureaucracy. They are able to help formulate public policy when it is most malleable, at initial stages.

The Board consists of 13 members appointed by the Governor. Two, by law, must be from the Agricultural Sciences Division of the University of California and the agriculture department of a State college, respectively. The other 11 are all growers. See Appendix 2C for their biographies and current conflicts. There is no representation given to farm laborers, consumers, or other groups. The head is also president of the Farm Bureau Federation.

INTEGRATED CONTROL

The ultimate solution to the problem of pest control in California agriculture is the "integrated control" approach. Integrated control involves chemical pesticides when absolutely necessary to prevent severe crop damage; that is, when the numbers of pests actually reach troublesome levels. These pesticides could be more ecologically selective than those now in use: they could kill only the target pest insect and not harm other beneficial insects, such as the predators and parasites of the pests, and the pollinators (including honeybees); nor should they harm decomposing microorganisms, wildlife, or man. Such specific pesticides are more costly to develop than the existing broad-spectrum biocides, but because of their ecological selectivity, they can be used in much smaller quantities, can control target pests more effectively, and would cause fewer secondary pest problems; and they are less conducive to the development of resistance in the pest species than those poisons now in use. In sum, they are less costly to the user in the long run, and are much less hazardous to man and the general environment.

The key to the integrated-control approach is "biological control"—control of pests by their natural enemies or through male-sterilization techniques. Imported insect pests, which usually cause the worst problems, can be almost completely eradicated by importing and releasing their natural predators, parasites, and diseases. Similarly, weeds can be brought under control by introducing insects that eat only these weeds. Over 100 formerly major insect and plant pests have been partially or completely controlled by natural means.

For example, scale insects on citrus fruits in California are being controlled by introducing the natural parasites of these pests. And a new strain of the bacterium *Bacillus thuringiensis* has been developed which is 96% to 100% effective against the cabbage looper, a leaf-eating insect that harms cabbage, lettuce, and other leafy crops. The bacterial product presents no known hazards to higher forms of life or to beneficial species of insects.

The development of biological control methods requires sophisticated techniques and ecological training, as well as the motivation to replace hazardous chemicals with the more effective biological approach. Research on biological control is therefore carried out almost entirely within university agricultural research stations, on extremely limited budgets. Naturally, chemical companies are not interested in the biological approach, since their profits from the introduction of natural enemies of pest species will be low. Biological control works, and when a pest is controlled, the chemical company loses a customer.

There are a number of other components in an effective integrated pest-control program. Crop-protection researchers have developed pest-resistant plant varieties. A grower can prune diseased plant parts or remove diseased plants entirely if the outbreak is not yet severe. Heat treatment of seeds, bulbs, etc., will destroy pest organisms. In many cases, the farmer can plant seed crops in disease-free areas and time plantings to avoid infection or infestation. Alternating strips of different crops reduces the opportunity for pests to overtake an entire field. Crop rotation helps prevent pest multiplication over several years in one area.

In the Central Valley, a few trained biologists have established small, independent advisory firms to work with farmers on their problems of pest control. They emphasize biological and other nonchemical control approaches. Their firms are highly successful, but from economic, ecological, and public-health viewpoints have only a small effect compared to the massive advertising and sales campaigns conducted by the chemical industry. Most growers do not seek alternatives to the traditional use of biocides until they are backed to the wall by economic disaster. Unfortunately, only economic and ecological chaos may finally force California agriculture to adopt more sophisticated pest-control methods.

3

Water

Pollution

California's water is one of its principal attractions. The famous swimming beaches in the southern part of the state, Yosemite Falls, the lakes and rushing wild rivers of Northern California, Lake Tahoe, and San Francisco Bay are lures to fishermen, sunbathers, boaters, swimmers, beachcombers, and people who simply enjoy being by the water. Californians have fought for years to maintain and improve their water resources.

We therefore expected to find strong, independent state agencies to protect the public's interest in clean, good water, and powerful water pollution control laws to back them up. We had heard glowing reports, particularly about the new Porter-Cologne Water Quality Control Act passed by the Legislature in 1969. Governor Reagan called it the "toughest water quality control law in history." [1] Knowledgeable conservationists, including the Sierra Club, had told us that the State Water Resources Control Board, the prime agency responsible for pollution control, was a tough agency. The Federal Water Pollution Control Administration—now the Federal Water Quality Administration (FWQA)—virtually ignored California because of the reputation of this Act.

The Law

The forerunner and model for California's present water pollution control scheme was the Dickey Water Pollution Act of 1949, which removed the State Department of Public Health from most pollution law enforcement. According to Frank Stead, then head of Public Health's Environmental Sanitation Division, industry wanted enforcement taken out of Public Health's hands because the Department had been independent of industry pressure and had been "too tough" in its enforcement procedures. A member of the State Water Resources Control Board concurs, saying that "the Dickey Act was written to protect industry."

The Dickey Act had two new major features which were outstanding among all its other flaws: a regional board system responsible for pollution prevention and control, composed of representatives of "dischargers," and an arsenal of enforcement procedures which a Study Panel, set up in 1969 to revise the Dickey Act, declared "totally inadequate."

The Study Panel, set up by the State Water Resources Control Board in response to mounting public pressure and the threat of federal intervention to protect the quality of California's water, was also composed of representatives of those most responsible for water pollution.* The industrial polluters had four major points of interest in the law's revision: (1) they wanted the regional board structure to stay basically the same; (2) they wanted to keep the "orange crate" policy, in which only the result of waste disposal, not the method, was to be regulated (you could filter your sewage through an orange crate so long as it met standards afterwards); (3) they wanted opportunities to fight board orders; and (4) they wanted to insert the word "reasonable" into the law everywhere. These four points were prerequisite to their support of the bill. Seasoned legislative aides felt that the industrial interests' support was so essential to passage of the bill that all of these concessions had to be made.

---

* Burt Smith, chairman of the Study Panel's Subcommittee for Organization and Administration, was the founder of Western Water News, the newsletter of the Irrigation Districts Association. He has recently been appointed by Governor Reagan as one of the new "public" members of a regional board, although present law requires that public members be *not* specifically associated with any of several interests, including irrigated agriculture. Jerome Gilbert, vice-chairman of the Study Panel and chairman of its crucial Subcommittee on Definitions and Policy, is a past section head of the Irrigation Districts Association. Mr. Gilbert is now executive officer of the State Water Resources Control Board. Norman Hume, chairman of the Intergovernmental Relations Subcommittee, is an ex-director of the Los Angeles Bureau of Sanitation which disposes of Los Angeles' sewage, and is now head of the State Board's Committee on Water Quality.

Regional Boards. The Porter-Cologne Act as passed did not change the basic regional board structure. The Dickey Act had provided for five interest-group members, one recreation and wildlife member, and one public-at-large representative; to these the Porter-Cologne Act added two more public members who are required to have "special competence in areas related to water quality." The regional boards now consist of the following members, appointed by the governor:

> One person associated with water supply, conservation, and production;
> One person associated with irrigated agriculture;
> One person associated with industrial water use;
> One person associated with municipal government;
> One person associated with county government;
> One person from a responsible nongovernmental organization associated with recreation, fish, or wildlife;
> Three persons not specifically associated with any of the foregoing categories, two of whom shall have special competence in areas related to water quality problems.[2]

Although the law includes a "conflict of interest" provision which requires that a board member disqualify himself from participation in any decision in which he himself is personally interested,[3] the structure of the boards in effect guarantees that anyone regulated by a board will be heard by a colleague who may be counted on to "understand" his problems. Clearly, polluting interest groups have the same right to be heard as anyone else; but the appropriate form for their participation is in public hearings and in generally bringing their cause before the board, not in sitting as board members to weigh those arguments.

"Orange Crates." The Porter-Cologne Act kept the "orange crate" provision—that pollution regulations not specify the design, location, type of construction, or manner in which clean water should be maintained.[4] This provision could theoretically encourage efficiency and innovation in treating waste products. However, in practice it serves to restrict the regional boards' investigative powers: all they can do to determine water quality is sample water. While it is the quality of water that is ultimately to be protected, the power to declare certain waste treatment facilities inadequate *per se* would be a useful administrative time-saver, according to experts. If treatment facilities are obviously

inadequate, the burden of proof in water-quality preservation shifts to the polluter.

The individuals who wrote the Porter-Cologne Act were well aware that the orange-crate provision would ensure case-by-case enforcement of board pollution limits, involving complicated technical questions of the extent of water-quality degradation, rather than across-the-board mass enforcement relying on the simpler issue of whether or not facilities are adequate.

To The Bitter End. The Porter-Cologne Act provides for a unique system of appeals from regional board actions: a full hearing of every issue, and what amounts to a de novo review of a regional board's action or inaction at the State Board level and then at the judicial review level.[5] That is, it provides for a complete retrial from scratch at each of three levels *before* judicial review for errors. Procedures under the Act were written, according to a State Board member, "so that the polluters would have the ability to fight an order [to stop polluting] to the bitter end." The appeal provisions are designed to tie the agency up in lengthy legal proceedings, and act mainly to the advantage of those with economic stakes in pollution. It takes a great deal of money and interest to pursue an appeal through this extraordinary three-tiered process in which the case must be made completely anew at each level. Several state and regional board members have said that powerful economic interests such as agriculture—shielded by the resources of the Irrigation Districts Association—and oil—protected by the Western Oil and Gas Association and large individual companies—could not be regulated by the boards to prevent water pollution, because these interests had the attorneys and finances and technical staffs to sustain time-consuming prizefights with the agency in three rings.

"Reasonable." The fourth concession made to polluters in the Porter-Cologne Act was the insertion of the word "reasonable" at key points in the law. This adjective limits the definition of pollution, the power of the regional board to plan the water quality of its region, the board's ability to prescribe limits on discharges, and the quality of water to be sought in the state.[6] For example, each regional board must determine water-quality objectives that "will ensure the *reasonable* protection of beneficial uses" of its water (emphasis added).[7] "Reasonable protection" of the beneficial uses of water, especially when "economic considera-

tions" are explicitly recognized as an element of reasonableness, implies a vague compromise between private gain of polluters and the protection of the public good. One State Board member admitted that his job was not to provide good-quality water, but to provide reasonable-quality water.

It may be true, as one member of the State Board argued, that a court would read "reasonable" into the Act even if it weren't written there. Even so, the function of "reasonable" at the judicial stage is quite different from its function as a guide to the board's discretion.

In the contexts of an old law which was a clear compromise with polluting interests, and a regional board structure built to include polluters, the use and placement of the modifier "reasonable" indicates a legislative intent to give the boards great discretion in compromising the principle of clean water for the sake of polluter convenience.

The Porter-Cologne Act was written primarily by polluters. After it was drafted by Study Panel subcommittees in which industrial polluter groups were dominant or present, and strengthened slightly by the Panel itself, the bill was heard in four committees of the legislature: the Assembly and Senate Water Committees, the Assembly Ways and Means Committee, and the Senate Finance Committee. The only changes made were in the two finance committees, which effectively weakened the bill by making specific exceptions to some of its provisions.

Assemblyman Carley Porter's Water Committee was committed to the bill as it was written by the Study Panel. Senator Gordon Cologne's Water Committee passed the bill without opposition or amendment. Cologne himself is an active attorney in the firm of Cologne, Erwin, McIntosh, and Angle, whose clients include three sanitary districts, one city, and the I.K.I. Farms.[8]

Porter had assembled a formidable list of organizations to support his bill, including not only the Irrigation Districts Association, the League of California Cities, the State Chamber of Commerce, and the California Supervisors Association, but also the Planning and Conservation League, the Sierra Club, the League of Women Voters, and the Save the American River Association.[9] The support of these latter organizations must be seen in the context of "political reality" in California. Big polluters have enough power in the legislature so that even slight attempts to strengthen water-quality laws prior to the Porter-Cologne Act were, in the words of a legislative aide, "popped off one by one" by the polluters. "Beggars can't be choosers" we were told, and these good-government and conservation groups were allegedly faced with the choice of going along with the polluters' bill or missing their only chance to strengthen water-quality control in California.

The only attempt to strengthen the bill was made on the floor of the Assembly. Conservationists proposed an amendment to strengthen the conflict-of-interest provision to keep employees of, and individuals with financial interests in, dischargers of waste off the boards. In exchange for the cooperation of interest groups in passing the Porter-Cologne Act, the Study Panel members and the bill's sponsors used their influence to protect the bill from this strengthening amendment. The bill passed unanimously without the amendment, having been, in the words of the Assembly Water Committee secretary, "well greased."

Supporters of the Porter-Cologne Act had then to convince the public and the federal government that the new law was a strong step forward, while simultaneously convincing the polluters that it would not "rock the boat." They succeeded. Many Californians, even strong conservationists, feel that the Porter-Cologne Act is adequately tough on pollution; the federal agency in charge of water pollution, the Federal Water Quality Administration, has developed an informal policy of noninterference with California's water polluters, allegedly because the state seems to be doing such a good job on its own.[10] And industrial polluters were placated as the provisions of the Act were seriously qualified—not in the published version but in Assembly and Senate Water Committee Reports of "legislative intent." For example, the Porter-Cologne Act provides for a $6,000 fine per day for violating an order to cease polluting,[11] but Porter's Water Committee report, printed in the obscure Assembly Journal of May 5, 1969, on page 2677, contains the following comment: "It is not expected that this section [the fine] will be used except with discretion, and when administrative remedies have been ineffective." Furthermore, the new law deleted references to waste disposal as a beneficial use of water, one of the major express recognitions that California's waters were useful as sewers; however, in "small print" of the official legislative intent it was noted that: "Waste disposal and assimilation are not included in the definition of 'beneficial uses,' but they are recognized as part of the necessary facts of life. . . ." [12] The legislature didn't intend to stop using water as a sewer; it merely intended to stop talking about it. The Porter-Cologne Act would have looked quite different if its covert provisions, which guide actual enforcement and judicial interpretation, had been apparent.

THE STATE AGENCY

Weakened as the Porter-Cologne Act is, with a strong and independent State Board and diligent regional boards to administer it, the waters of California could be reasonably protected from pollution.

The State Board has five members, all of whom serve full time and are appointed by the governor. We assumed that in consonance with his proclaimed "continuing commitment to an all-out war against the debauching of our environment," and the need for the most independent and strongest possible generals to shape the battle tactics under the new law, the governor would appoint strong and qualified advocates of the public's interest in clean water.

A major function of the State Board under the Porter-Cologne Act is to formulate statewide policy for water quality. To set rational priorities for quality control, the Board must have an accurate and complete picture of water conditions in the state. The State Board allocates money to the regional boards, presumably in accordance with the seriousness of the problems facing each board. We assumed that the State Board would have information about water quality throughout the state and would have devised some system of evaluating the relative seriousness of water quality problems.

We were wrong. The State Board and its staff have no systematic information on which to base intelligent judgments about California's pollution problems.

To get some idea of where industrial pollution is most serious in California, we asked for the total amount of industrial waste water in California to compare with local figures. One engineer on the staff guessed that the total would be about 200 million gallons per day; another guessed 300 million. Bewildered by the huge discrepancy, we asked how the figures had been arrived at, and found that the basic figure both men had relied on was 100 million gallons per day, the amount of industrial waste water recently attributed to the San Francisco Bay Delta. One engineer had multiplied by two, the other by three, in guessing the statewide figure. Since the regional boards have data on most industrial waste dischargers in their areas, simple addition would produce a passable statewide estimate if the State Board were interested in having one.

State Board members believe that it is misleading to make comparisons between local cases of pollution. The Board's executive officer stated that weighing the seriousness of San Francisco's pollution against San Diego's pollution would be "like comparing apples and oranges."

Since the Board doesn't seek statewide objective data, and since it does not have priorities for action based on comparison of conditions, its action is reduced to what one staff member characterized as "putting out fires." It relies heavily on citizen complaints and the visible effects of pollution to guide its actions. Rational priorities based on a statewide picture of water quality would have two advantages: the Board would avoid arbitrary enforcement on problems which might not be the most serious, and by knowing the extent of its problems it would tell the public and the legislature how much additional support is needed.

Another way in which the State Board minimizes its own powers is by not demanding of the Department of Fish and Game that it enforce Section 5650 of the Fish and Game Code strongly. Section 5650 is important because it is an all-embracing statute making pollution a criminal misdemeanor. It has obvious advantages over the cumbersome cease-and-desist order as an enforcement tool. It can be used for a first-time spill as deterrence. And conviction carries with it the stigma of criminality. The final report of the Study Panel for the Porter-Cologne Act suggests that it would be bad to have on the books a statute under which State Board-sanctioned "reasonable" pollution would be criminal.

ENFORCEMENT

Board members' speeches exude pride and accomplishment. Every speech made since the Porter-Cologne Act became effective has implied that California's waters are improving. Win Adams, in a typical speech made before California's State Chamber of Commerce four months after the Act went into effect, said: "We are on the threshold of achieving our goal—clean waters for California." [13] Kerry W. Mulligan, Chairman of the State Board, reported with pride to the State Legislature that "there have been more legal actions taken in the first four and one-half months under the Porter-Cologne Water Quality Control Act than had taken place in the entire history of the Dickey Act." [14]

Using performance under the Dickey Act as a standard by which to measure performance under the Porter-Cologne Act is hardly meaningful since the Dickey Act was found to be "totally inadequate" in its enforcement provisions. A more meaningful evaluation of enforcement under the new law would be a comparison between the number of orders to cease polluting issued and the number of violators of the Board's pollution standards. According to the State Board's official report to the legislature, in the first five and one-half months of the Porter-Cologne Act the State Board issued only seven cease-and-desist orders. During this same period our best estimate is that there were at least hundreds, and probably thousands, of violations. The Board, however, claims to have no information compiled on numbers of violations.

We were told that the State Board had acted against the city of San Francisco because it was known as the biggest polluter of the Bay. The Board could tell us of no systematic process by which they had come to this conclusion, no comparisons of amounts by which dischargers were violating their requirements, and no formal comparison of the long-range ecological effects of various pollutants.

In theory, once a violator is discovered, the enforcement process goes into action. If a polluter goes over the pollution limits set by a regional board, the regional or state board can order him to cease exceeding the limit. If the limits are still being violated after either board orders a stop, the board can then ask a court for an injunction to stop violating its cease-and-desist order, or can ask the court for imposition of a $6,000 fine for every day that the polluter violated the board's order.

In fact, however, regional and state boards issue "timetable" cease-and-desist orders: the polluter has a schedule to stop polluting, ranging from weeks to years, and no fine or injunction can be sought by the board unless the polluter breaks the schedule, even if (as is often the case) during the allotted time the polluter is exceeding the limits set by the board. Useful enforcement of the law is thus negated, since all deterrent effect is lost.

The San Francisco Regional Board's attitude toward compliance with the time schedule is even more startling than the timetable "license to pollute for a while." Policy statement 69-17 formulated by this board suggests that most violators of time schedules should not be taken to court unless they miss the cut-off date by more than three months! Thus the board issues a "license to pollute for a while plus ninety days."

Reasonable discretion might include a timetable when a board suddenly lowered permissible pollution levels or when there was no warning, so that a waste discharger suddenly became a violator through no fault of his own. However, the State Board told us that many dischargers start out in compliance, then slip into violation by increased gallonage, or sloppy operation, or aging equipment. In using the "timetable" cease-and-desist orders in these cases, the board is giving away its right to seek a fine against a polluter. And in fact, as this Report is written, not a single penny of the famous $6,000 fines have been collected.*

Polluters know that they need not stop polluting excessively until the day, if it ever comes, that they finally get taken to court.

The state and regional boards thus fail to use the deterrent powers given to them by law. And in fact they appear uninterested in the concept of deterrence. "What purpose would be served," asked a State Board member appointed because of his legal background, "by us going in for a $6,000 per day fine after the problem had been solved? It would just take our staff time away from more pressing problems." Given the water-quality situation in California, with hundreds of violators and only enough regulatory staff to take a few cases at a time, it is imperative that those few who can be caught be made uncomfortable enough to dis-

---

* Three weeks after receiving a preliminary copy of our Report, and four days before its announced date for public release, the Board announced, amidst much hoopla in Sacramento, a $12,000 fine against U.S. Steel for pollution. U.S. Steel had been violating the law since the middle 1960s, dumping tons of contaminants each week into San Francisco Bay. The out-of-court agreement was actually a "contribution" enabling U.S. Steel to deduct it as a normal business expense. And they were given permission to violate some standards through 1974.

courage them and others from risking the same treatment in the future.

Another major deterrent which the boards have failed to use is public opinion. We were told over and over by staff and board members that public opinion is one of the strongest prods of polluters. To mobilize this citizen lobby on water, the State Board should be educating the public about water pollution and its causes and culprits. Instead, it is dispersing whatever public lobby it may have by systematic misrepresentation of the extent of pollution, and by misrepresentation of the facts which relate pollution to the public's interest.

A proper public understanding of the pollution problem requires data about its basic causes. The State Board consistently understates the role of industry in pollution. Ronald Robie, a Board member, has stated: "The key to water quality improvement is greatly increased expenditures on facilities by local governments, which are the major dischargers in terms of volume in California." [15] He lists percentages as follows:

Region	Municipal	Industrial
San Francisco Bay and Delta	90%	10%
San Diego	95%	5%
Central Valley	80%	20%

His "municipal," however, includes all the domestic and industrial wastes flowing into a municipal sewage system. The Board told us that about 70% of California's industrial dischargers are hooked into municipal systems. But it keeps no information on how much of the state's wastes are produced by *all* industries, including both "industrial" wastes and those lumped in with "municipal."

Suppose that 70% of industrial dischargers which feeds into municipal systems account for an arbitrary one-quarter of the discharge by volume put into San Francisco's municipal sewers, then, using Robie's figures above, one-third of the area's pollution is caused by industry, and undoubtedly the more toxic and hard-to-treat third.

When we asked what a citizen might do to help clean up the water, the State Board staff told us to "support bond issues." They mention nothing about the expensive subsidy of industry through municipal plants.

Regional boards also minimize citizen participation and

information. The Los Angeles Regional Board staff, we are told, has refused to provide before its meetings its full agenda to the *Los Angeles Times,* the largest newspaper in the region. Mrs. Ellen Stern Harris, a former member of the Board, said that the staff systematically fails to keep board members up-to-date on water-quality problems of particular interest to them. Mrs. Harris, probably the most aggressive public member on any of the boards, has had to consult with the Attorney General's office to protect her right to be informed by the staff. Far from welcoming active board participation and education in water quality, the staff has tried to put a damper on this likely source of public input.

A TYPICAL BOARD AND A TYPICAL DISCHARGER

At the suggestion of the State Board, we examined the operations of the San Francisco Regional Board. The only atypical feature of the San Francisco Board is its explicit system of rating pollution violators in order of the magnitude of their guilt, reducing to writing what presumably takes place less explicitly at other regional boards. This above-the-table operation made the San Francisco Board a fortunate choice for study.

The typical waste discharger in the San Francisco region is not on file with the Board. Of over a thousand waste dischargers in the region, fewer than 350 have obeyed the law to file a report of their pollution.[16] Although the Board may be correct in asserting that the 350 on file are the major polluters, no routine sampling is done to check that the 650 others are not harming the water.

We asked the Board's staff to trace the story of a typical discharger subject to pollution limits set by the Board. They offered us the Union Oil Company's refinery at Rodeo as a "typical discharger—not too good, not too bad."

Union's pollution limits were set by the Board in 1968. The technical details were well done: characteristics of the waste flows were required to be given as an average value, an index of how much variation takes place, and a maximum figure; uneven flows were to be sampled so as to get a true picture of the amounts of pollution.

Despite its technical thoroughness, however, the Board did not sound the alarm at the first appearance of illegal and dangerous pollution. In the summer of 1970, mercury residues were found in fish caught in the Delta area.[17]

Mercury lodges in the human brain and destroys cells there.[18] We asked the San Francisco Board about mercury in the water, and were told that the Regional Board was not set up to handle such unknown threats.

The uses for which nearby San Pablo Bay water is to be protected are listed by the Regional Board,[19] and include swimming, fishing, and recreation. The Board has a general policy for Bay waters,[20] so it sets pollution limits for both the waters near the Union refinery and for the actual wastes coming out of its pipes.[21] We were told at first in our questioning at the state board level that once the standards for a body of water are set numerically (for example, a limit of two milligrams of nitrogen per liter of water in the Bay), it is a straightforward engineering problem to take into account how much nitrogen can be present in the discharge as it leaves the pipe to insure that the body of water meets the Board's standards. However, Dr. Teng-Chung Wu, head of San Francisco's Surveillance Section and a Ph.D. in Sanitary Engineering, probably the most technically competent man in the area, told us that the Bay standards and the pipe standard bear no logical relation in a majority of cases. A logical engineering conclusion based on a model of the body of water is usually replaced by what are really "performance" standards. Performance standards are the pollution limits which a refinery, for example, can "reasonably be expected" to meet. The specific pipe standards are in most cases, then, arbitrary and related to the antipollution efforts (expenditures) of the "state of the antipollution art." Dr. Wu showed us that of Union Oil's five pipe standards, three bore no engineering relationship to the standards desired for the water of the Bay.

A more serious trouble-spot appears in the Bay water standards which Union Oil must protect. What the Board calls a "dilution zone" is the amount of space in the water the Board gives a discharger to dilute his pollution before it is measured and compared with Bay standards. There is necessarily a zone around the pipe where Bay standards are not going to be met. The extent of that zone is of great importance, since it measures the amount of the public's water which is to be given over to Union Oil Company to pollute freely. Union Oil's refinery has in effect been given a license to add turbidity and color to the water anywhere within 100 feet of each of two pipes; [22] to create deposits on the bottom of the Bay anywhere within 100 feet of each of two pipes;[23] to create growths of algae sufficient to look or smell bad anywhere within 100 feet of each of two pipes.[24] For some pollution parameters, Union's refinery has been given a total of one-half acre of Bay water to pollute freely without the Board's attention.

Along with its pollution limits, the Union refinery was given a self-monitoring program to follow,[25] requiring that periodic samples of water be taken and the results sent to the Board every three months. The bacterial content of one waste flow was to be checked twice a week. Typical sampling frequencies were weekly and quarterly, some twice a year. Every discharger was to sign its reports under penalty of perjury.

The Union refinery's reports appear complete. Since January, 1970, Union has violated the bacterial standard at least sixteen times, by its own admission. The refinery was guilty of overloading the water with toxic materials in three-fourths of the samples taken from January through March. (Union's toxicity was tested by killing test fish with the wastes from its pipes.) Union Oil, a "typical" discharger, reported [26] letting oil get out with its wastes in four of ten samples during January and February. An "iridescent film" of oil was spotted on the waters of the Bay twice in January—once 100 to 200 feet in radius, and the other time a quarter of a mile wide. Outside the limits of the refinery's 100-foot permissible pollution zone, it polluted with caustic materials in January. A person rowing along the shore by the refinery in January or May would be greeted by an illegal "ammonia odor," in Union's words. The San Francisco Regional Board considered this to be a "middling" performance by a typical discharger, and did nothing.

The San Francisco Board's rating system institutionalizes the Board's incredibly slow response to water pollution. Each year a rating number given to each polluter reflects the percentage of time during the preceding year he polluted excessively, the seriousness of his pollution, and the location and amount of his discharge. The staff prepares a list of all the excessive polluters. The Board has a policy of scrutinizing the top 15% with an eye toward issuing cease-and-desist orders to stop the pollution.

In 1969, Union Oil won the fourth-place polluter's medal among the top twelve on the list of about eighty violators.[27] Union's record over the whole year 1969 was astounding. From March through September, the refinery violated its requirements concerning toxicity, odor, acidity, dissolved oxygen, suspended matter, and land disposal. It was legal only with respect to its requirements concerning chromium, grease, settleable matter, and dissolved sulfide and undissociated hydrogen sulfide. Six requirements were not conclusively checked at all.[28]

Not until early 1970 were Union's illegal pollution activities brought to the attention of the Board, and then only because Union was among the twelve most illegal. Union responded with a flurry of action. A Union representative called the Board, saying that the company was "disturbed" about the press coverage resulting from the previous Board meeting.[29] They were quite surprised to be number four on the list because they "felt they had been *violating only a very few requirements*"[30] (emphasis added).

Union launched an attack on two fronts. First, they sent technical people in to "discuss the calculation of position on the priority list,"[31] to scrutinize the reports of violations in detail, and to make arguments about such questions as how many observations constitute a violation. Second, they arranged a meeting with the executive officer of the Regional Board to "meet our new refinery manager,"[32] and sent many letters to improve communications with the Board's staff. As a result of this two-pronged attack, the staff issued a memo saying that reevaluation indicated that many of the items noted as violations should have been shown as "not checked." The entries in Union's self-monitoring report had been "vague" and did not support a determination that the requirements had been met or not met. The staff concluded that, by not counting these vague reports as violations, Union would be dropped from number four on the list to number twenty-one.[33] The Board, in effect, concurred, and Union Oil was no longer in the "dirtiest dozen." By pointing out their own reports had been too vague to be reliable, Union was off the hook, with one more job of refining well done.

Union's near brush with the Board in early 1970 was the result of a full year of unlawful dumping of wastes. *No action has been taken against Union's refinery for its chronic pollution.* The San Francisco Regional Board members' conflicts of interest are just what the Porter-Cologne

Act would lead one to expect. The industrial representative is a public-relations man with Pacific Gas and Electric; a fellow board member notes that "PG&E is involved with almost every discharger." One public member is a real estate developer. Two local governmental officials are on the Board, and a Board member claims they are susceptible to local pressures from their industry constituents.[34] The wildlife and recreation representative on the Board, James McCormick, told us how the Board deliberates: "The most important thing we have to do is to be *reasonable, economically feasible*. All the representatives can come to a reasonable solution to a problem usually. We each argue the matter from the standpoints of the groups we represent, but then when it is time to vote we all take off those hats and put on the hat of all the people. The dischargers are always wanting to take us out to lunch . . . [and] a lot of the other members accept the invitations. There is a lot of conflict of interest pressure on individuals, but usually they can resist it."

So little money is being appropriated for water pollution surveillance and enforcement by the Reagan administration that only harsh, selective prosecution can have any deterrent effect. Jerome Gilbert, executive officer of the State Water Resources Control Board, estimated that the initial $500,000 appropriated for implementation of the Act was one-quarter to one-fifth the amount necessary to enforce the law effectively. The 1970 appropriation is approximately $900,000 for surveillance enforcement. The 1971 request is $1,000,000, still under one-half the monies needed to enforce the law in 1967–68. Mr. Gilbert's assessments of need were probably grossly underestimated three years ago. The people of California can afford more than a nickel each to clean up and preserve their water. The enforcers must request as much as they need—which they have not done.

Agriculture

The Central Valley Regional Water Quality Control Board is responsible for controlling water pollution in most of the agricultural areas of California's Central Valley. Agriculture was logically to be that board's main concern. McKee and Wolf, authors of *Water Quality Criteria,* California's handbook on water pollution, mentioned in a discussion of California's regional water-pollution problems that the "industrialized San Francisco Bay area is as different from the San Joaquin Valley as New York Harbor is from central Texas." It's often said that the San Joaquin River is an "agricultural sewer."

When we had visited the Central Valley Regional Board to ask what was being done about agricultural pollution, George Schmidt, the Board's senior engineer, admitted that it was a "tremendous problem," but apologized that he couldn't give us any information about it, since "agriculture is the subject we're least up on."

The Board's staff estimates that it has jurisdiction over approximately 4,000 agricultural waste dischargers, an estimate taken from the number of farms in the region. This figure represents over one-third of all the waste dischargers in the Central Valley Region, probably the largest single source of water pollution to be regulated by the Board. However, the Board is making no attempt even to discover what kinds of pesticides, fertilizers, and other agricultural pollutants are going into its waters. It has neither asked for reports on present agricultural seepage and runoff nor established pollution limits for any major agricultural operations. It has made virtually no attempt to understand or control the worst agricultural pollutants in its region.

The only agricultural establishments which the Board has attempted to regulate are a few chicken and dairy farms. According to a senior staff engineer, residents complained so loudly about the stench that the Board established limits on the disposal of manure and other discharges into waterways.

Most pollution which results from farming is not noticeable by visible or odorous signs. How would the public know to be alarmed about deadly but invisible levels of mercury in the fish we eat? Or about the levels of nitrates in our drinking water? It is the responsibility of a water quality agency to act to *prevent* pollution before it becomes a public nuisance.

In cases where agricultural waste waters seep into underground basins, it is doubly important that preventive rather than curative measures be taken. Ground water travels through underground aquifers in unpredictable ways and at unpredictable speeds. Once it becomes contaminated, there is almost no way of knowing where it will turn up next. And once contaminated, ground water takes decades to purify itself. Since Californians rely on ground water as a major source of drinking water (half of all water used in California is from wells), this resource must be protected from degradation by agricultural pollution. The Central Valley Board at the very least should be required to monitor its waters for agricultural pollutants, and to require that *all* agricultural waste creators submit reports of their wastes. The Board currently has no such policy.

A clue to the reason for this failure to check agricultural pollution lies in the history of the Porter-Cologne Act. When the provisions of the Act were being negotiated, the agricultural representatives on the Study Panel and on its subcommittees were particularly interested in preserving their right to add whatever they wanted to their irrigation waters without fear of reprisal or regulation. They fought hard, says Jerome Gilbert, who was vice-chairman of the Study Panel, to prevent the regional boards from taking jurisdiction over water on private lands and so to keep it immune from state regulation.

The Act as passed didn't give agriculture this exemption, but buried in an obscure Assembly Water Committee Report was a passage (*Assembly Journal,* May 5, 1969, p. 2679) that eased the anxiety of the agricultural lobby. It suggested that agriculture's water pollution had not been regulated in the past and shouldn't be in the future:

> Although farmers as well as other persons are theoretically required by sections 13054 and 13054.1 of the present Water Code to file reports of waste discharges with the regional boards, it has not been the general practice of the regional boards to request such reports or to issue waste discharge requirements covering agricultural operations and other land use, except in cases such as feeder lots of dairies, involving substantial discharges of waste.

It would be more effective, felt the Act's originators, to establish regional planning for agricultural land use which would take into account the effects upon water quality of the use of irrigation, pesticides, and fertilizers, and of other practices. They felt that particularly those waste waters which seep into the ground water, coming from a diffuse source rather than from an identifiable pipe, might be hard to regulate by traditional "pipe-oriented" waste discharge requirements. It was understood that nothing would be done until statewide study of agricultural practices and their effects had been made, and then only a broad statement of recommended policy on land use would be issued.

The Central Valley Regional Board, following these guidelines, has simply refused to regulate agriculture. It has not even bothered to waive its powers toward any of the estimated four thousand agricultural waste dischargers within its jurisdiction. The Board's staff tells us that no current effort is being made to establish regional plans for agricultural land use. They foresee no such plans in the near future. Agriculture has an effective immunity from *all* regulation.

The Central Valley Board does determine waste-disposal practices in refuse dumps where seepage could threaten to contaminate underlying ground water. And it has begun to regulate aspects of water quality that previously were considered strictly land management. For example, it has notified every city and county planning commission in the Central Valley that tentative subdivision maps must be submitted for review. The Central Valley Board has the authority, and the means, to limit the use of dangerous agricultural chemicals (such as high-nitrate fertilizers) in critical areas and to require certain agricultural land and water management practices (such as adequate drainage facilities) now, rather than several years hence. When asked why the Board had not taken any such action, the executive officer replied, "We never thought of it."

Fully one-third of the members of the Central Valley Board have direct personal and professional interests in agriculture. The representative of irrigated agriculture owns a farm northwest of Fresno. The board member representing "water supply" is a specialist in irrigation and drainage employed by Westland Water District, which represents some of the largest and most powerful corporate farms in the Central Valley and is a member agency of the Irrigation Districts Association. The Board's "industrial" representative is a retired employee of a food processing company. An agricultural polluter is therefore likely to be heard by a jury of sympathetic colleagues.

The State Board has not attempted to stimulate control of agricultural pollution by its regional boards, nor has it taken action to regulate agriculture itself. Paul Bonderson, a twenty-year veteran of water-quality management in California, and apparently the man most responsible for the State Board's water quality policy in its day-to-day operations, claims that the only action needed in the case of agricultural pollution is *education:* no stronger sanctions are needed to convince California's farming industry to adopt more environmentally useful habits. "Educating" polluters to accept their environmental responsibilities has been tried in California and elsewhere. It has failed.

And Bonderson made it clear that even if "educating" polluters were proven ineffective, agriculture would not be subject to regulation. "Agriculture," he aphorized, "is a sacred cow." Unfortunately, it is also the most dangerous and important source of water contamination in the state.

Nitrates and Drinking Water—Delano. While the state and regional water quality control boards have responsibility for protecting all uses of water, including drinking, from pollution, the State Department of Public Health has become the main guardian of the public's drinking-water supply. In 1949, when the state and regional boards were created under the Dickey Act to regulate water pollution, the Department of Public Health was given responsibility to deal with "contamination," which had been defined as an "impairment of the quality of the waters of the state by sewage or other waste to a degree which creates an actual hazard to the public health through poisoning or through the spread of disease." [35] Public Health has an arsenal of weapons, including peremptory orders, injunctions, quarantine orders, and revocation of water-supply permits, to abate conditions of contamination.

In February of 1967, water users of Delano received letters from their city manager telling them that the public water supply of Delano was no longer considered safe for infants to drink.[36] Nitrates in the water drawn from the city's wells had exceeded the U.S. Public Health Service standard of forty-five parts per million.[37] In fact, three of the city's wells had nitrate levels which were more than double the federal standard. The U.S. Public Health Service drinking water standards recommended that where nitrates exceed forty-five parts per million, the public should be warned of the potential danger of using the water for infant feeding. Such a warning would allow parents to substitute bottled water for the hazardous tap water. The city of Delano, finding that its water supply was degraded to such an extent, had taken the federal precaution.

U.S. Public Health Service has determined that beyond the forty-five parts per million level, there is danger that the nitrates in the water might cause the occasionally fatal disease methemoglobinemia. Nitrate itself is no more harmful than many other common substances found in drinking water. But its chemical cousin, nitrite, can be extremely dangerous because of its ability to bind itself to hemoglobin in the blood, preventing red blood cells from carrying oxygen to body tissues. Some bacteria sometimes found in the digestive tracts of small babies convert nitrate to nitrite, with resulting depletion of the oxygen in the blood. This produces a smothering effect, much like the breathing of carbon monoxide, resulting in labored breathing and sometimes suffocation. Methemoglobinemia is sometimes called infant cyanosis, or the "blue baby" disease.

At the time that the residents of Delano first heard of this danger in their drinking water, the city manager's letter suggested that nitrates in Delano's water supply could have built up from the use of fertilizers in the agricultural areas surrounding the city. The technical director of the laboratory which had done the city's water analysis also felt definitely that "the sources of the nitrates is due to the ammonia gas being used for fertilizer." [38]

Nitrate is an important constituent of commercial fertilizers. California uses more nitrogen fertilizers than all other states combined. Three years ago, California farmers used a total of 2,166,700 *tons* of fertilizer to increase their crop production.[39] Farmers have a clear economic interest in the continued use of fertilizers, since everything used in agriculture has risen in price in this country except fertilizer, which has actually fallen in price.[40] Nitrates from fertilizers reach ground water through leaching as irrigation water applied at the surface percolates down through the soil.

In 1968, the Department of Water Resources made an exhaustive investigation of the Delano situation.[41] It found that in the Delano area rates of fertilizer application as high as 1,000 pounds per acre had been reported to the Kern County Farm Advisor's office. If the agricultural waste waters collected in the area were allowed to continue to seep into the ground water of the San Joaquin Valley, this report predicted, the concentrations of nitrates in the water supplies could be expected to approach ninety parts per million, double the recommended U.S. Public Health standard for safe drinking water.

Even more alarming was the report's finding that nitrate levels had been steadily increasing, not only in Delano but in the ground water reserves underlying large areas across the state. The study closed with the strong recommendation that "the most important task presently remaining is the determination of the significance of nitrate levels with respect to public health."

The State Public Health Department, faced with a situation in which nitrate levels over wide areas of the state had exceeded permissible limits, and with no very desirable general solution to the problem at hand, abdicated its responsibility during the study period entirely. The Department decided not to follow the federal standard on nitrates. (It isn't required to follow it; the federal standard applies only to interstate carriers.) According to an internal policy memorandum [42] issued in March, 1967, and still in effect, the public is *no longer to be told* when nitrate levels pass safe limits. Only the local health officer and the water company are to be notified. When the level reaches ninety parts per million, twice the federal limit, local health officers in the state are to advise the physicians in the community of the hazard and begin "investigating" the water supply that exceeded it. The public is still not to be notified.

State Public Health's Bureau of Sanitary Engineering, headed by Henry Ongerth, is in charge of protecting the state's infants from the nitrate hazard in drinking water. The Bureau is supposed to enforce drinking-water standards set by physicians. However, H. B. Foster, Ongerth's predecessor, had chosen to disregard the federal nitrate standard which had been carefully set by a physician committee. Today, State Public Health has no standing committee of physicians acquainted with the nitrate problem, even after the 1968 study indicated that it was a statewide problem and would increase.

The reasons given by State Public Health for overruling the federal standards for nitrates are unclear. In its 1967 memorandum establishing the new policy, it was noted that "the widespread occurrence of well water with nitrate levels exceeding these standards *has not been shown* to produce methemoglobinemia in California residents" (emphasis added). Infant cyanosis, or methemoglobinemia, has been tied to nitrates in drinking water in the United States since 1945. In July, 1950, an article called "Methemoglobinemia and Minnesota Well Supplies," in the *Journal of the American Water Works Association,* described 139 cases of the disease identified since 1947, of which 14 had been fatal; all were attributed to contaminated farm well water.

In 1951 an eighteen-state survey was conducted, and 278 cases of methemoglobinemia were reported. In 39 cases, the children had died. "In all of these cases the concentration of nitrates in water supplies was in excess of forty-five parts per million."

That cases of methemoglobinemia have not been reported in California may be because methemoglobinemia is not listed as a reportable disease in the state. (In fact, we were told by a State Public Health official that *no* pollution-related diseases are reportable in California.) Doctors who diagnose the illness are not required to tell Public Health about it. Even if the disease were reportable, however, its symptoms might be confused with other common infant diseases. Public Health recognizes this: a current study is attempting to determine whether there are symptoms of methemoglobinemia which might be missed by a routine medical examination—but even if the disease were accurately diagnosed and reportable, it might still not come to the attention of Public Health. Recently, State Senator Walter Stiern, who represents the agricultural community around Bakersfield, told the Senate Agriculture Committee that doctors "in small communities [such as Delano] are under pressure of growers" and that the "social climate" weakens enforcement of health laws.[43]

Since the 1967 State Public Health memo, the citizens of Delano have not been told of the potential hazards of their drinking water, which has continued to show levels of nitrates above the forty-five parts per million level and occasionally more than ninety parts per million. In June of 1969, Delano's city manager asked the Public Health Department for advice about Delano's responsibility to warn its water users, as it had done in 1967, of the possible dangers of the high nitrate content of the city's water supply. This time State Public Health [44] advised that the city had no legal responsibility to inform its citizens of the danger. It suggested, however, that as elected officials the City Council might feel duty bound to make the information available to Delano's citizens. Reflecting Public Health's apparent lack of concern, and allowed to follow its inclinations, the City Council decided not to advise its citizens about their dangerous drinking water. The city manager, Gerald Minford, defended the Council's actions. "Public Health tells us that no deaths from nitrate poisoning have been caused by water from public water supplies. Of course there's a slight chance the water may be hazardous, but we're willing to take the risk." Minford is willing to risk the health of other people in Delano—but he mentioned to us that his own family drinks bottled water.

Local doctors and health officers have been left with the responsibility for the health of these babies; but doctors do not systematically inform their patients of the nitrate situation, and the local public health clinics do not offer information or issue warnings about drinking water to new mothers.

The one avenue through which many mothers in Delano are getting some information about the hazards of their drinking water is a study currently being conducted by the State Department of Public Health in Delano, to try to determine once and for all whether nitrates cause methemoglobinemia in infants. We visited the special clinics where most of the study is being done. New mothers bring their babies to special clinics in Delano's community center twice a month; each baby's blood is sampled and questions are asked about his diet and health. The drinking water in the home and the baby's formula are also sampled. All this data will be compared with similar data from control families in Berkeley to determine whether there are relationships between methemoglobinemia and nitrates. The nurse reassures the mothers that if she notices anything unusual about the baby's appearance or his blood's methemoglobin level, she will be sure to let the mother know. She asks the mothers whether they know of the nitrate situation; they often shake their heads, no. Many of these women do not read the papers and do not understand why they are being asked to come to the clinic. They have been drinking water from the faucet for years. Often they ask what kind of water they should be using for their babies, whether they should use bottled water to be safe. This is the one piece of advice the investigators refuse to give. To do so would be to destroy the scientific basis of the study. How could you study effects of nitrates on babies, they explained, if no babies were drinking the questionable water?

Recently the State Department of Public Health was given an opportunity to reverse its 1967 policy. Senate Bill 787 was introduced on March 30, 1970, by State Senator Anthony Bielenson, on the suggestion of David Stanton, Deputy Attorney General in Los Angeles. The bill provided that the mandatory drinking water standards of federal Public Health Service would apply in California. In the event of noncompliance with these federal standards by water suppliers, the bill provided for both public notice and reasonable enforcement measures. When a local water supply fell below federal standards, the public would be informed by newspaper advertisement. The advertisement, four columns wide by four inches high, would continue in the newspaper each day until the water became once again acceptable. Should the supply continue to be substandard for ninety days, and the water supplier fail to submit a plan for compliance, the State Department of Public Health would be required to issue a cease-and-desist order to compel the supplier to stop sale of water. Continued sale of unacceptable water by a supplier would be a misdemeanor.

Public Health's Bureau of Sanitary Engineering approved of the bill; public awareness of, and pressure to solve, the nitrate problem was increasing. But Senate Bill 787 met a great deal of opposition in its first hearing, before the Committee on Health and Welfare. Every one of the state's large water suppliers opposed it, including San Diego, Los Angeles, San Francisco, East Bay Municipal Utility District, and the Metropolitan Water District of Southern California. Also in opposition was the Irrigation Districts Association, a lobbying organization representing irrigated and fertilized agriculture in California. Ongerth summarized "the facts of life here. . . . If a bill comes up affecting water suppliers, they will work to defeat it or modify it. In this case they wanted no bill at all."

Senator Bielenson's administrative assistant met with Ongerth and another sanitary engineer from a water supply company to formulate amendments that would be acceptable to the water-supplier opposition. The resulting amendments emasculated the bill. Its main reason for existence, the provision that the federal health standards would apply in California, was deleted, leaving only the old, weaker state standards. Bielenson's aide reports that Ongerth himself suggested this deletion, explaining that there had been a few cases where the U.S. Public Health Service standards had been restrictively high. In the amended bill there is to be no public notice or adequate enforcement even when the relaxed state standards are not met by a water supplier. Notice is to go only to the water company's customers; and the State Department of Public Health is to have no power to stop sale of water. (It "may" seek a cease-and-desist order only to stop new connections from being made to the system.) Finally, the misdemeanor provision was eliminated, so that there is less chance of any penalty for a supplier who ignores such a mild order.

The amended Senate Bill 787 is essentially what the water suppliers wanted—"no bill at all."

Public Health alone represents the public's interest in safe water. In Delano nearly everyone looks to Public Health for the answers. The City Council uses Public Health's policy as justification for its own inaction. Local doctors depend on Public Health to determine sound medical policy in this complex and confusing situation. The public has the right not only to know the quality of its drinking water but also to be warned of its hazards.

When Ongerth was asked why he bothered to work on and approve the amendments that resulted in the "non-bill," he said he thought some legislation would be better than none at all. "We were concerned with the art of the feasible, not what we would like to have." The State Department of Public Health was *not* in fact forced to arbitrate and compromise between public and private interests, yet it deferred without objection to the interests who are supplying and threatening to contaminate the water.

Public Health defines its jurisdiction so narrowly that in most cases it is restricted to dealing solely with the health aspects of water degradation. For example, Public Health has not attempted to look into the *sources* of ground-water contamination in Delano. The state and regional boards are more properly equipped to attack a problem of water pollution via its sources. In fact, a vigilant regional board acting to protect its domestic water uses would immediately go into action whenever a public health notice were given concerning waters within its jurisdiction.

The Central Valley Regional Board has made no attempt to do anything about the rising nitrate levels in the ground water near Delano. The Board's executive officer admits that the problem is a serious one, and that fertilizer is the main source of dangerous nitrate levels in Delano, "but," he said, "we can't go around attacking an entire industry, putting regulations on each individual farmer."

Obviously, the Board would not be obliged to crack

down on every individual farm simultaneously. A logical approach would be to require each agricultural operation to submit information regarding its fertilizer and water management use immediately, and then begin by regulating the largest contributors to the local problems.

One Board staff member told us, however, that "agriculture sure wouldn't appreciate it if we came messing around in their affairs." And according to a State Board member, "the Irrigation Districts Association would tangle us up in court for years if we tried to take them on." The fact that agricultural pollution, in this case as in others, had not been controlled is a tribute to the strength of the agricultural lobbies in Sacramento.

When the Central Valley Board did ask for money several years ago to begin a study of the Delano situation, they were told by the State Board that there was no money available for a study, and they have not repeated their request. At the State Board level, Paul Bonderson agreed that the ground water in Delano is in serious trouble but dismissed the problem as too undefined at the present, and excused the Central Valley Board by saying, "They're doing more important things. You can only do so much."

In October, 1968, the City Council of Delano, in a formal resolution, asked the State Board to institute the necessary investigations to establish controls on the source of nitrates in its ground water. The Board did nothing. "We didn't really take the feelings of the local people into account. Maybe we should have," explained Bonderson. If the problem ever got to a point of crisis, he continued, if, for instance, many babies died, the Board might take action. Meanwhile, he didn't see that any further investigation was necessary. In other words, a citizen must die and his death must be proven attributable to the contamination before water pollution is considered critical enough to be prevented.

Even if the State Board did feel that the situation were critical enough to warrant serious action, said Bonderson, it couldn't take action on the basis of its current information about the sources of nitrates in the Delano area. He added that the Department of Water Resources was looking into sources, and that the State Board was relying on them for new information instead of studying the problem. A check at the Environmental Quality branch of the Department of Water Resources revealed that *no* significant investigation of sources of nitrates was being done and that no follow-up on the Department's 1968 Delano nitrate investigation was planned, since it had been determined that fertilizers were the main source of the problem in that area and the Department had observed no significant changes since then.

Blame for the continuing policies of inaction toward one of California's largest sources of water pollution belongs at the doorsteps of:

—the State Department of Public Health which, although it is meant to be an independent, scientific body protecting the public's health and safety, has preserved irresponsible public policies and lenient drinking water standards.

—the State Legislature, which obscured from public view its promises to protect agricultural polluters, and the Porter-Cologne Act which treats wastes from houseboats in detail and does not touch California's multibillion-dollar agricultural industry.

—the agricultural lobby, which insisted on the protection supplied by the Porter-Cologne Act's provisions of "unofficial legislation," and which opposes every attempt to regulate the industry without regard for the public's water.

—agricultural water suppliers in the state, who are violating the law by not filing reports of their waste-water seepage and runoff.

—the Central Valley Regional Water Quality Control Board, which has done nothing to protect water from degradation by agriculture, has not regulated agricultural pollution, and has obscured its decision to abdicate responsibility for agricultural pollution.

—the State Water Resources Control Board, which realizes the inadequacy of the decisions of the regional boards and has done nothing to correct them, and has moreover worked with agriculture and the fertilizer industry against legislative efforts to control agricultural water pollution.

The problems of pollution by irrigated agriculture in California will be magnified in the future, particularly if the State Water Plan opens up vast new lands to irrigation. It is especially important, therefore, that action be taken immediately to prevent expansion of already existing agricultural pollution problems.

Federal enforcement officials have noticed the increasingly apparent failure of the Porter-Cologne Act, and are reportedly anxious to begin remedial action. Governor Reagan of California, however, who has staked his prestige on the publicly acknowledged success of the Act, has written President Nixon to request that the federal government "lay off" California. Federal prosecution would of course expose the law's profound deficiencies. The letter from Governor Reagan requestiong federal deference is now in the office of federal Far Western Regional (Water Pollution Control) Director Paul DeFalco.

THERMAL AND RADIATION POLLUTION

"Thermal pollution" occurs in natural water bodies when water is taken from these bodies for industrial cooling and then returned at a higher temperature. The power industry has attempted to minimize the danger of thermal pollution, referring to it euphemistically as "thermal enrichment" or "thermal enhancement." In 1968, the Subcommittee on Air and Water Pollution of the U.S. Senate Committee on Public Works held extensive hearings on the subject of thermal pollution. The chairman of the Subcommittee, Senator Edmund Muskie of Maine, noted that one of "several important problems" that the scientific testimony revealed was that "waste heat discharges can seriously and adversely affect the ecological balance of the receiving waters and, though much remains to be learned about these effects, a sufficient body of evidence exists to establish standards and require control." [45] The then Secretary of the Interior Stuart Udall referred to thermal pollution as "one of the most critical environmental problems facing this Nation" [46] in his statement to the Subcommittee.

It is clear that increased temperature in a natural water body causes profound changes in the water ecology. The extent of the change will, of course, depend on a number of factors: the amount of the temperature change, its duration, and the sensitivity of the various organisms in the particular ecosystem to temperature changes. Small or temporary changes may have little effect; and more substantial changes may in some instances "improve" the ecology of the water body by increasing the supply of a desirable species such as a sport fish. However, substantial changes are far more likely to be harmful, and unchecked thermal pollution will lead ultimately to ecological disaster.

Among the specific effects of increased water temperatures are the following:

—For every increase of 18°F in temperature, the rate of a chemical reaction in an organism or in an environment doubles.

—Temperature increase reduces the quantity of dissolved oxygen in the water, which reduces the ability of the water to sustain life. Increased temperature may also lead to increased evaporation, which increases the salinity of the water, which in turn reduces the ability of water to hold dissolved oxygen.

—Use of cooling water for industrial purposes results in the elimination of certain small organisms from the water actually used for the cooling. Particularly in inland bodies, this may have a devastating cumulative effect.

—Although nuclear power plants reduce air pollution, they may increase thermal pollution because they are less efficient than conventionally powered plants and thus produce more waste heat.

Pacific Gas & Electric's propaganda states that "steam-electric power plants, the primary source of your electricity, must be located with access to large bodies of water for cooling." The company further notes that "some have questioned the effect of warmer water on marine life. Our scientific studies in this field over 19 years have shown there is no harmful effect on aquatic life due to exposure to this slightly and temporarily warmed water." Nothing is said about substantially and permanently warmed water.

PG&E's "studies" are not respected among biologists in the Department of Interior's Fish and Wildlife Service, who describe them as "P.R. documents" and "bogus studies." PG&E has studied neither the long-term effects of thermal pollution nor the effects of warm water on sensitive invertebrates.

In a statement to the U.S. Senate Subcommittee, Albert H. Stevenson, Assistant Surgeon General and Chief Engineer, U.S. Public Health Service, indicated that the claims of the utilities were fallacious:

> *Actually,* thermal pollution of waterways can produce a variety of adverse effects, particularly from the standpoint of aquatic life. The quantity of oxygen that can be dissolved in water decreases as water temperatures increase. Conversely, the growth of biological organisms is stimulated by such increases. Thus, an increase in water temperature can not only bring about adverse effects on fish life, but also major changes in the entire aquatic ecological system as well.

. . . More significantly, from the standpoint of human health, thermal discharges into marine waters may create health hazards as a result of the ingestion of shellfish harvested from such waters. Recent measurements taken in Puget Sound, for example, indicate that during the summer a temperature increase as small as 1° F can "trigger" a rapid increase in the growth of plankton organisms which are toxic to humans.[47]

The utilities use natural cooling water because it lowers the cost of producing power. They do not include the environmental costs of thermal pollution in their tabulations.

Feasible alternatives to the use of once-through cooling include cooling towers or cooling ponds. The former involves cycling water through a tower, a process which facilitates the exchange of heat with the atmosphere, after which the water is recycled to cool the plant. The latter involves constructing a pond from which the heated water can exchange heat with the atmosphere. The expected additional cost to the consumer of power produced using a cooling tower or some similar method has been estimated at one to two percent in a study done by the Northwest Water Laboratory of the Federal Water Pollution Control Administration.

PG&E has refused to install the cooling towers that public utilities such as the Sacramento Municipal Utility District (SMUD) are installing. SMUD's cooling towers at its Rancho Seco nuclear plant are going up even though SMUD's utility rates are lower than PG&E's.

By far the most troubling kind of nuclear power pollution, however, is radiological. Many waste radionuclides have a long half-life and take years to deactivate or decay: cobalt 60 takes 5 years; strontium 90 takes 27 years; cesium 137, 30 years; carbon 14, over 5,000 years; plutonium 239, over 23,000 years. Radiation is cumulative; in effect it becomes increasingly concentrated as it ascends the food chain, and is very difficult to detect.

This last feature is especially important. The symptoms of radiation poisoning are varied and often indirect. Different isotopes collect in different parts of the body: krypton 85 dissolves in fatty tissue, iodine 131 collects in the thyroid gland, strontium 90 in the bones, and cesium 137 in the muscles. Depending upon the absorption of a specific kind of isotope, radiation levels can cause great harm to specific organs and body parts without being detected.

Because of the food chain effect, even low levels of emission are dangerous. A study of the Columbia River found little radioactivity in the water, but 2,000 times more radioactivity in river plankton than in the water, 15 to 40,000 times as much in fish and ducks feeding on the plankton, and one million times as much in the egg yolks of water birds.[48]

Little is known about the effects of current high levels of radiation on ocean plankton which provide most of our oxygen, or on animals further up the food chain. Practically nothing is known of the effects of low-level exposure, or genetic effects. And the level of *observable* damage varies by isotope type, organ, and individual.

Nevertheless, the government regulates radiation by specifying a crude "maximum permissible dose" which an "individual" can receive from any "single" radioactive source without suffering readily observable harmful effects. Maximum levels vary, depending upon the isotope and exposure to *other* sources. When a given level of radiation is reached, changes, malfunctions, and finally severe damage begin.[49] Until regulators view each individual as possessing an exhaustible *budget* for different types of radiation from numerous sources, and until more is known about effects, radiation emissions should be avoided whenever possible.

The federal government has exacerbated the hazards by granting automatic license to power plants with only cursory review of structural safeguards, by approving sites within range of large cities despite the possibility of disaster, and by directly subsidizing the use of atomic energy. It has contributed billions to civilian reactor research and development (more than double industry expenditure); it has contributed to reactor construction costs, waived lease charges on fuel for the first five years, reprocessed irradiated fuel at government expense, purchased reactor by-products (plutonium) at high prices for weapons purposes, and indemnified the plants from major liability for damage to third parties in the event of a "major reactor accident."

Fish and Wildlife Kills. Between 1965 and 1968, approximately 2,340,000 fish were counted dead in 352 separate "kills" in California;[50] those counted were only part of the total number of dead fish.

The most deadly sources of pollution known to be killing fish as of 1969 are unaffected by the Porter-Cologne
Act. Nationally, the leading cause is agricultural pollution:
fertilizer and pesticide runoff. Next is major public works,
particularly highway and building construction, airport
and service station operations, and mosquito control. Third
is oil spills, and fourth is industrial waste. Municipal sewage
is now fifth, although in 1968 it was the leading killer [51]—
not that municipal sewage has declined, but the others have
increased.

Federal regulations limit DDT in fish to five parts per
million (ppm). Leon Woods, chemist for the Department
of Fish and Game, has recently verified residues of *100*
parts per million in fish caught off Los Angeles and Santa
Monica. The livers of Santa Monica fish contained *1,026*
ppm of DDT, the highest concentration of DDT ever
found in fish in any U.S. coastal waters.

Ninety sea lions were washed up dead on the beaches
of northern California in late 1970. Dr. John Phillips of
the Hopkins Marine Station reported an *average* of 1,200
to 1,500 ppm of DDT in the blubber. One reading reached
3,900 ppm. The state is now banning DDT, but its enforcement procedures are questionable; and because of the
persistence of DDT already released, the ban may have
come too late. What has been sprayed is not disappearing
but moving inexorably up the food chain, increasing in
concentration.

Dr. Henry Schroeder of Dartmouth's medical school
believes that lethal metals are the most dangerous pollutants
of all. He names cadmium, lead, nickel, carbonyl, beryllium
and antimony; add to these selenium, chromium, cobalt,
zinc, mercury and arsenic. Like DDT, these substances do
not deteriorate, and they concentrate as they rise up the
food chain, often collecting in specific organs. According
to Dr. Schroeder, cadmium's effect is to replace zinc in
the human body. Since zinc is needed to break down fats,
the system can't digest these materials and they accumulate
in the circulatory system. The result is hypertension, or
high blood pressure, and heart disease.

Concern about these elements is not academic. Two
San Francisco scientists, Dr. Rolf Woldseth and Dr. David
Porter, have found mercury, arsenic and selenium in cans
of Pacific Ocean tuna picked off the shelf. Their measurements indicate 5,000 times the concentration of arsenic and

selenium found in sea water. FDA findings of mercury in swordfish well above the federal guidelines of 0.5 ppm also apply to Californians. Ephraim Kahn, a California public health doctor, found similar levels above the 0.5 federal limit in striped bass and channel catfish. He also warned, in October of 1970, of mercury in trout, smallmouth and largemouth bass, and white catfish. Contaminated fish were found in a wide area, including San Francisco Bay and Delta, up to the mouths of the Sacramento and San Joaquin rivers. Fifty fish-eating seals caught off the West Coast had thirty ppm of mercury in their livers.

Dr. T. J. Chow of the Scripps Institute of Oceanography at La Jolla reports twenty-two ppm of lead in the livers of twenty-five sea bass caught off the Los Angeles coast. Fish near the coast had twice the lead content of those caught 200 miles offshore. Dr. Chow's tests of sediment from the Santa Barbara Channel floor reveal a drastically increasing buildup of the same lead used in gasoline, increasing as gasoline consumption has increased.

Even when sources are apparent, action for prevention or curtailment is not vigorous. Fish and Game biologists discovered that crabs had been dying by the thousands from the dumping of toxic industrial wastes in the Gulf of the Farallons. Harvests in 1970 were one-sixth as large as previous harvests, and biologists clearly established the correlation between the wastes and the death of crab larvae. The state's strictest board, the San Francisco Water Quality Control Board, merely issued warnings. The Army Corps of Engineers was given until June 30 "to *report on whether* its dumping or dredge tailings at sea pollute the water (emphasis added)." The Oakland Scavenger Company and Standard Oil of California were given approximately one year to set up new equipment. U.S. Steel was given six months.

Appendix 3A reproduces the State Department of Fish and Game's internal compilation of known wildlife kills for 1969. Several points are worth considering in examining the table: the variety of contaminants causing death; the fact that many of the contaminants are indirect (caused by construction or other erosion- and siltation-producing activities) or are agricultural poisons; and the widespread nature of the kills throughout California, not just in one or two problem areas. Kills listed on the table are only those counted, reported, and verified—a small portion of the total.

The State Department of Fish and Game appears to be interested primarily in game. Kills of nongame animals are rarely noted on the table. And those kills which are marked with an "X" were not reported to federal water pollution authorities as required by agreement. And examination of the Department's internal statistics on enforcement activity reveals a total of five enforcement actions (complaints filed) covering the seventy-eight incidents. Of these five, two offenders were let off with a warning, two are still pending, and one received a $50 fine. In *Outdoor California* (March–April 1970, page 16), however, the Department refers to its "crack Water Projects Branch" and notes that for past kills "legal action was initiated . . . in virtually all these cases."

Recommendations

To clean up and stop the pollution of California's waters, a rigorous and comprehensive statewide program should be prescribed. Each regional board could take one major polluter and, after a short warning period, crack down with every tool at its disposal—meetings, hearings, cease-and-desist orders (plus building bans if applicable), cleanup and abatement orders, and collection of the full $6,000 per day fine if the orders are violated.

There must no longer be safety in numbers for polluters. Regional and state boards must establish rational priorities for enforcement, and adhere to them regardless of pressure from violators.

Into every self-monitoring program should be written the provision that waste dischargers must report any violation of pollution limits immediately. No vigilant board should wait three months, as in the case of Union Oil's violations, to learn that pollution is taking place.

Every board should issue cease-and-desist orders in every case of violation unless it gives general public notice of its specific reasons for refusing to do so. No cease-and-desist order should include a timetable without prior approval of the State Board and the attorney general. As soon as a cease-and-desist order is violated, it should be reported to the attorney general for imposition of a fine.

The executive officer of each board should be authorized

to issue immediate cleanup orders without waiting for board approval. He should be required to issue a cleanup order upon learning of a violation unless he certifies to the board that the order is inappropriate.

The boards should use every means at their disposal to publish the identities of polluters and to educate the public about the causes of pollution. They could, for example, request newspapers that run a daily crime count to include a daily pollution count. The boards should warn communities to charge the costs of waste treatment equitably to those who produce wastes.

More basically, conflict-of-interest prohibitions should be put into effect immediately. All state and regional board members with financial or other interests in corporations that are responsible for water pollution should resign. The "category" structure of regional boards should be altered.

Until it is clear that regional boards are adequately protecting public waters, the State Board should demand enough information in each case to enable it to take immediate action should the regional boards fail.

The State Board should take immediate action to strengthen the provisions of the Porter-Cologne Act. The Act must include some provision like the Fish and Game Code's §5650 which the attorney general or local D.A. can use against polluters, with part of the fine or damages collected available as a bounty to complaining witnesses. Other steps must be taken to maximize citizen participation and education. California corporation law should be amended to require a corporation's annual report to display, along with its financial liabilities, its environmental liabilities—the convictions (and nolo contendere pleas) received and the violations of the Porter-Cologne Act perpetrated in that year.

The full cost of regional and state boards, including research costs, must be charged to polluters through a license fee for discharging wastes, and an initial fee. Past costs of regulation must be repaid by waste dischargers (perhaps into a fund to be allocated to the attorney general for prosecution of polluters). The burden of showing that he will not cause long- or short-range damage to the public resource must be borne by a potential discharger. Upon discharging, he must be bonded, as are others in possession of public property.

The State Board must antecede federal efforts to require as a condition for grants not only an equitable assessment of sewer costs in a municipal sewer system, but also a refund to taxpayers and domestic sewer users from industries that might have profited by "sewer subsidies" in the past. This refund might come as lower-than-equitable sewer charges on previously overcharged domestic users.

Thermal pollution must be curtailed. Special sanctions and standards must be provided for the single event problem, e.g., the oil spill. Given the federal administration's deference to California control and given its discouragement of action under the Federal Refuse Act,* aggressive state action is needed.

The State Department of Public Health should take immediate steps to adopt federal standards for drinking water, and should be required to give adequate public notice whenever a state drinking water supply falls below those standards. Moreover, the Department should exercise its powers to prevent the sale of contaminated drinking water which endangers the public's health.

The state legislature should enact whatever measures are necessary to provide strict control of agricultural waste waters, to obtain precise data about the causes and extent of agricultural pollution, and to publish the identities of the largest agricultural polluters in the state.

Agricultural operations which discharge their wastes into the waters of the state must be required immediately to abide by the law. They should be made to submit reports about the amount and type of polluting materials contained in their agricultural drainage waters. Steps should be taken immediately by the Central Valley Regional Board, with the full help and cooperation of the State Board, to set specific standards for the quality of agricultural waste waters, including consideration of both ground and surface waters which will ultimately be affected by those wastes. The regional and state boards should move immediately with every legal method at their disposal to enforce those water-quality standards. The use of potentially dangerous

* The Refuse Act establishes a cause of action for any pollution of "navigable" water, now broadly defined, unless licensed permission has been obtained from the Army Corps of Engineers; the Nixon Administration has begun a program to grant thousands of licenses permitting pollution, which may emasculate the law.

chemicals, such as nitrates or pesticides, should be prohibited entirely until the effects of these substances are demonstrated to be harmless in the long and short run.

Distribution

The great wonder-working wizard, Irrigation, took possession of the land, millions of dollars worth of capital were invested. . . . The ignorant herder was crowded aside by the intelligent farmer; gentle women and laughing children made the country smile. All over the plain pet cows were seen staked out in front of rosy cottages, and it seemed as though the great magician Irrigation had suddenly transformed the dreary, lonely waste of arid sand into one vast garden of happy homes.

—*1886 Speech to the Irrigation Convention, San Francisco*

Much of California is desert. Since land without water is virtually useless, water actually creates land value. An eminent water lawyer writes, "Because water has been the key to Western economy, control of water resources has been in many ways the keystone of Western politics." [52] Water development in California is a vast, multibillion-dollar enterprise.

The State Department of Water Resources (DWR), which builds water projects and collects facts about water, estimated that California used about thirty-two million acre-feet (maf) [53] of water in 1960. About nine maf were recycled, so Californians depleted streams and underground basins of twenty-three maf. About half of this was pumped from underground water basins, the rest coming from surface-stream flows via a vast network of dams and canals.

The total amount of water available vastly exceeds present and projected use. The DWR estimates that seventy-two maf run off in surface streams alone each year, while underground basins store five hundred maf or more. But the areas which use the most water lie in the southern part of the state, while most of the water flow occurs in the north. The historic pattern of water development, and the legal rules governing it, have cemented ineffi-

Table 3a
MAJOR WATER PROJECTS IN CALIFORNIA

Total state water use (est. 1960): 32 maf
Agricultural use: 28.5 maf
Groundwater used: 15 maf

Name and Principal Present Components	Agency	Completed?	Size
All-American Canal Includes Coachella Valley Branch	BOR	yes	4 maf
Colorado River Aqueduct	MWD	yes	1.2
Owens River Aqueduct Includes first barrel, completed in 1924, and second, completed in 1970	LADWE	yes	.47
Hetch Hetchy Aqueduct Includes O'Shaughnessy Dam, Cherry Valley Reservoir, Hetch Hetchy Aqueduct	SFWD		.29
Mokeluanne Aqueduct Includes Comanche and Pardee Reservoirs	EBMUD		.3
Central Valley Project Dams: Shasta,* Trinity, Keswick,* Friant,* Folsom, Nimbus, San Luis. Total 1969 storage of CVP reservoirs was 8.8 maf. Aqueducts: Contra Costa,* Delta-Mendota,* American River, Friant-Kern,* Madera,* Mendota Pool, Sacramento River, Corning Canal, Sly Park Unit, San Luis Canal, Trinity.	BOR	no (started 1936)	4.95
State Water Project Oroville Dam, California Aqueduct, North Bay, South Bay, and Coastal Aqueduct, San Luis dam shared with CVP.	DWR	no (started 1960)	4.23
Total			15.34 maf

* = original CVP units

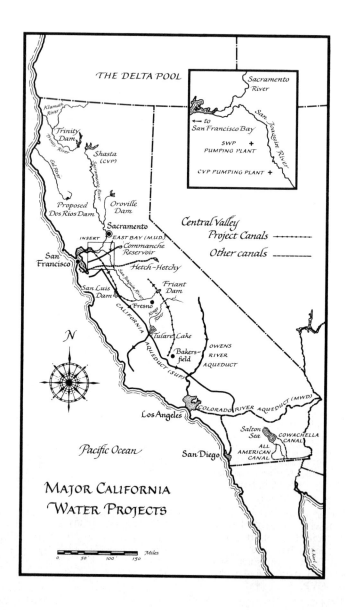

THE DELTA POOL

Sacramento River

to San Francisco Bay

SWP PUMPING PLANT +

CVP PUMPING PLANT +

San Joaquin River

Klamath River

Trinity Dam

Trinity River

Shasta (CVP)

Sacramento River

Cal River

Proposed Dos Rios Dam

Oroville Dam

Sacramento

East Bay (MUD)

Commanche Reservoir

San Francisco

Hetch–Hetchy

San Joaquin River

San Luis Dam

Friant Dam

Fresno

Kings River

Tulare Lake

Bakers–field

Owens River Aqueduct

Central Valley Project Canals - - - - -

Other canals - - - - - -

California Aqueduct (SWP)

N

Colorado River Aqueduct (MWD)

Los Angeles

Salton Sea

Cowachella Canal

All American Canal

San Diego

Pacific Ocean

Major California Water Projects

Miles

0   50   100   150

A. Karl

ciencies into place, creating even more need for transporting water than would otherwise exist. Consequently, the state has seen an ever-increasing surge of water development, starting in the nineteenth century with purely local systems, and expanding in the twentieth century to vast schemes for importing water from distant rivers. The major water importation systems currently account for about eleven of the fifteen maf annually diverted from surface streams by Californians.

The State Water Project

Five hundred dollars per man, woman, and child in California buys the state a giant plumbing system to transfer fresh water from San Francisco Bay and north coastal rivers to the south. This scheme, the California State Water Project, benefits a few corporate farms in the San Joaquin Valley, a handful of landowners, speculators, developers, and water-using industries in southern California—and the Project's builders. Economists who have analyzed the Project claim that it will return barely fifty cents in benefit for each dollar of cost. The Project also threatens to destroy the San Francisco Bay Delta estuary—the largest in California, and one of the most important breeding and feeding grounds for fish and fowl on the West Coast—as well as the wild nature of California's last free-flowing rivers. The actions which could trigger the Project's severest environmental damage have yet to be taken, but the Project has already cost the people of California billions of unnecessary dollars and has set in motion forces that are driving thousands of small farmers from the land.

The State Water Project, like other vast governmental and corporate projects (the ABM, the Vietnam War, various highway systems, the SST), is highly technical and completely dependent on the advice of trained experts. But the making and selling of the State Water Project show that their celebrated "objective expertise" was mythical.

The California Water Project consists of: a dam at Oroville, to stop the frequent floods on the Feather River and to impound a million acre-feet which would otherwise flow out to sea each year; the Delta Pumping Works, to pump fresh water from the San Francisco Bay Delta into the California Aqueduct; the Aqueduct itself, a concrete-lined ditch running from Tracy, in the Delta, along the San Joaquin Valley's West Side to the Tehachapi Mountains 200 miles south; the San Luis reservoir on the West Side near Los Banos; Tehachapi Pumping Plant, to pump the water 2000 feet up and over the mountains. It also includes a network of canals feeding all this water into various areas and cities en route (Sonoma and Napa County north of the Bay, Alameda and Santa Clara Counties south of it, Santa Barbara, Los Angeles, San Diego, and the Mojave Desert southeast to Barstow)—and a drain, to take waste water from the San Joaquin Valley back to the Bay and out to sea. These works deliver fresh water, which has flowed down the Sacramento River and its tributaries to the Delta, to thirty-two local water agencies which have contracted to buy it.

Californians never voted for the present Project. The Burns-Porter Act, which the legislature passed and Governor Brown signed in 1959, did not authorize it. The $1.75 billion general obligation water bond which the voters approved in 1960 was not meant to finance it. And the voters who in June, 1970, agreed to raise the permissible interest rate so the rest of the loan could be obtained on today's market did not vote for this Project.

Californians actually voted for a $2 billion project, although the real cost, as the experts knew, will be closer to $10 billion. The Project was supposed to save southern California from a rapidly approaching water famine, according to the experts; but in fact no shortage of cheaper, local sources is likely until at least 1990, by which time alternative sources would probably be able to satisfy increased needs. The experts also claimed that the Project would cost taxpayers virtually nothing. In reality, however, they will pay about half its cost as power users and as federal, state, and local property taxpayers—without counting the cost of generally higher bond interest rates owing to the Project's erosion of California's credit.[54] The experts proved equally deceptive about the Project's benefits and about its costs.

THE COST SHELL GAME

The agency which created, promoted, and now constructs the Water Project, California's Department of Water Resources, claimed in 1960 that the Project would cost $2 billion, a figure presently adjusted to $2.8 billion. One reason for the claim was that when Governor Edmund G. Brown took office in January, 1959, his political instincts told him that the voters of California wouldn't accept anything costing more than $2 billion. According to his Special Water Assistant, Ralph Brody, the Governor told the Department of Water Resources to present a specific project at that cost. As an analyst for the Senate Water Committee later pointed out, the Project submitted by the DWR was trimmed to an acceptable figure only by ignoring the quarter of a billion dollars which the DWR had calculated for inflation. Harvey Banks, Director of the DWR at the time, claims that this omission was by Governor Brown's orders.

Another omission which slims down the Project's apparent cost is the proposed Eel River Development, which the DWR presently estimates will cost $680 million in State money. Since the costs of other projected but as yet unauthorized units *are* included, there is no justification for the Eel River omission.

However, the DWR's major deception in the area of cost estimates is its claim that "Project customers will repay about 90% of the total project costs." That claim is false as it stands, and false in its implications. As it stands, the statement ignores the fact that state taxpayers will pay a large portion of the Project's cost. It is axiomatic that the largest expense in any major construction project is neither the labor nor the materials, but the cost of the money needed to finance it. That is why, for example, housing construction drops when interest rates rise, and vice versa. But California will make an interest-free loan to the Water Project of $1.1 billion from Tidelands oil and gas revenues. Since the Project doesn't pay interest on the loan, the taxpayers do: the Tidelands money, and the interest it could earn, are lost for schools and various social programs. More than $2 billion in extra taxes will be required to make up for all of the interest given to the Project over the years.

And to the untutored eye, "Project customers" reads like "water users," especially since the DWR uses the statement to rebut charges that taxpayers will pay for the project. In fact, however, Project "customers" are not water users: they are purchasers of electric power (who will pay about 10% of the costs) and thirty-two water agencies, many of which are supported by local property taxes. The Metropolitan Water District of Southern California, which will buy about half the Project's water, presently pays more than half its water costs from property taxes. The Kern County Water Agency, which will buy about a third of the Project water, was formed expressly to let its agricultural water users draw on the Bakersfield tax base, and it expects to meet one-third of its payments through property taxes. All told, taxpayers and power users will pay between 49% and 65% of Project costs, depending on the future taxing policies of local water agencies—not quite what is suggested when the DWR says Project customers will pay 90% of the costs.

Table 3b
DEPARTMENT OF WATER RESOURCES INFORMATION

DWR Says:	*DWR Data Says:*
Cost: $2.8 Billion	$8 to 11 Billion
State Pays: $280 Million	$2.38 Billion
Other Taxpayers: Pay: $74 Million (Federal Flood Control)	$3 Billion
Benefits: $2 per $1 of cost	$.59 per $1 of cost
Environmental Effects:	Disaster for S.F. Bay and North Coast
Improvement of water quality, more recreation	

THE WATER-FAMINE HOAX

In 1904, some San Fernando Valley landowners (including the Chandlers, owners of the *Los Angeles Times;* W. C. Mulholland, Los Angeles' "expert" water engineer; and the mayor of Los Angeles) aroused great public concern by predicting an imminent "water famine," and thereby obtained money to build the Owens River Aqueduct. At that time, Los Angeles had water for several times its population. But by pointing to the self-evident desert conditions of southern California, Mulholland and the city's sympathetic newspapers prevailed. Carey McWilliams, lawyer, former California Commissioner of Labor, editor of *The Nation,* and author, described the situation in his book *California: The Great Exception:*

> . . . Owens Valley [was] far removed from the watershed of Los Angeles . . . [and] the project was brought off by fraud and violence and ruined a once prosperous farming community. For many years Owens Valley water was used, not to supply domestic needs in Los Angeles, but to irri-

gate farm lands in the San Fernando Valley, to the
$50,000,000 enrichment of the plotters and schemers who
had gobbled up thousands of acres of unimproved land.
Moreover, to induce the residents of Los Angeles to bond
themselves to the tune of $25,000,000 an artificial water
famine had been created. . . .

It is important to note the 'spring' or mechanism of this
plot: the use of an artificially created urban water famine
as a cover for a trans-mountain raid on water put to use,
during the interval when population expectation had not
been realized, to irrigate farm lands in Southern California. . . .[55]

Since the actual need for that water didn't materialize
until several decades later, Los Angeles couldn't sell its
new supply, and had virtually to give it away—to large
landowners in the San Fernando Valley.

In 1928, Los Angelenos and their neighbors again
learned that a "water famine" was imminent. The solution, their experts said, was Colorado River water, and
the experts—this time the Metropolitan Water District
(MWD) of southern California—assured the public that
it would be using 400 cubic feet per second (cfs) in 1940.

Despite the lack of serious economic study of the [Colo-
rado River] aqueduct, the MWD was able to gain public
approval of a $220,000,000 bond issue. . . . The elec-
torate did not realize how expensive the Colorado water
was to be. Project publicity stressed the point that the
aqueduct would be largely self-supporting from the sale
of water.[56]

The Colorado River Aqueduct was completed in 1941.
Instead of selling 400 cfs in its first year, as the engineers
had predicted, the District sold 20; instead of 1,000 cfs by
1950, the District sold 500, mostly below cost. By 1969,
the original members of the MWD still took only 370 cfs.
Instead of the Aqueduct's being self-supporting from the
sale of water, the District's taxpayers shelled out $254
million between 1929 and 1956. During the same period,
water users paid only $30 million. In other words, for
each acre-foot of water delivered, the recipients paid
$13.63, while the taxpayers paid $115.37.[57]

The taxpayers who footed most of this bill lived in Los
Angeles. Since Los Angeles had developed its own water
supplies from the Owens Valley, however, it didn't use
much of the Colorado River water. According to Los

Angeles City Councilman Ernani Bernardi, from 1941 to 1965 Los Angeles bought only 825,357 acre-feet, while San Diego bought 2,266,868 acre-feet and Orange County acquired 1,890,010 acre-feet. That is, between 1941 and 1959, San Diego and Orange County accounted for fully 40% of the District's water sales. But Los Angeles' purchases cost $272.10 per acre-foot, while San Diego's cost only $34.06, and Orange County paid $26.21 per acre-foot. As the Councilman added, these have been "staggering and unreasonable" subsidies, which didn't even go mainly to residents, but to ranches and industry.

What worked twice worked again in 1959, only this time the flimflam came from the Department of Water Resources, and this time the experts should have known better.

The Department calculated the water available to southern California, and it calculated the area's "requirements." But in calculating the water available, the Department took absolutely no account of various existing sources: recycled waste water, estimated at the time to be worth 200,000 acre-feet a year (and now admitted by the DWR itself to be worth 600,000 acre-feet!); ground-water reserves beyond the amount replenished each year (100 million acre-feet, by latest estimate); and more efficient canals (a Bureau of Reclamation spokesman estimated that lining just one canal in southern California would save 300,000 acre-feet per year on the purchase of water being used for agriculture). This omission, according to the Bain, Caves, and Margolis economic study of *Northern California's Water Industry,* "resulted at the extreme in valuing Project-supplied urban water in a desert area at $150 per acre-foot . . . when abundant irrigation water in the area could be transferred to urban use at . . . cost of no more than $30 per acre-foot without significantly affecting the supply of irrigation water." Nor did the Department consider that desalinization might be available at tolerable cost by 1990.

The Department's estimates are based on what economists sardonically call the "requirements" philosophy: the Department determines how much water will be needed without referring to price. "Requirements" for 1990 are calculated by projecting present numbers of users and amounts of use to 1990, even though water in 1990 will cost much more and people will presumably buy less. But the Department's experts assume that the same pattern of use will prevail—that people will want just as much ninety-dollar water as they now want twenty-dollar water. (Another economist, Professor Jack Hershleifer of UCLA, comments, "There is a shortage of new Cadillacs at a price of $500, except that desires for Cadillacs are usually not dignified by the term 'needs' or 'requirements'.") Even the Department itself, in a suppressed 1968 report, has admitted that price will significantly affect demand— so significantly, in fact, that the DWR's own report concludes the project was started at least ten years too soon. But they knew that in 1960, too.

While the Project was being formulated and considered, the DWR used a whole covey of "independent consultants" to check its work and convince the skeptical. But on examination, these consultants prove nearly as dishonest as the Department. Most, in fact, disapprove of the Project; but with the bright exception of one member of one team of consultants, Professor Adolph Ackerman, they kept their reservations quiet, and allowed the public to gain from their reports the false impression that they approved. The most remarkable example of expert equivocation is the Charles T. Main Company, an eastern engineering firm. After Ackerman's objections aroused concern, the Department hired Main to evaluate the Project's "economic feasibility"—whether its benefits would outweigh the costs. Main released its report just before the public voted on the Project in 1960. The *Los Angeles Times,* a Project promoter, stated in a headline: PROJECT GETS SOUND RATING; the *San Francisco Chronicle,* an opponent, said the opposite: STATE WATER PLAN CALLED IMPOSSIBLE. What happened was that Main said both. The firm's report declared, in clear and forthright terms, that "on the basis of the previously cited definition of economic feasibility, the project . . . could pay back all costs. . . ." The *Los Angeles Times,* the DWR, and the Project's other supporters seized upon that statement. But Main had defined "economic feasibility" in a very strange way, to mean whether or not the state could raise the money. By this definition, it might be "economically feasible" to throw a billion silver dollars into San Francisco Bay—but that isn't what Main was asked, and that isn't what everyone understood by "economic feasibility" when the report was issued. The rest of Main's jargon-infested report goes on to say, in effect, that anyone would be crazy to build such a project.[58] But reporters, politicians, and the general public don't usually wade through fine print.

Harvey Banks did concede that the consultants had been deceptive, but he noted that Charles T. Main had never done a water project before. It perhaps epitomizes the state of engineering standards that Mr. Banks could say, when we asked him why the DWR thought benefits of the Project would outweigh costs, "You tell me what benefit-cost ratio you want, and I'll get it for you, without straining my conscience."

THE RICH GET WATER AND THE POOR GET SOAKED

Legally, the Project is a scheme for selling water. The state sells it to thirty-two local water agencies, who in turn retail it to farmers, residents, factories, hotels, etc., or sell it to smaller water agencies. While many people ultimately receive this water, the only ones who actually benefit from the State Water Project are those who receive substantially more or substantially cheaper water than they would get without the Project. The average resident in southern California does not stand to benefit from the Project. He uses, at most, one-fifth of an acre-foot per year—a lot of water, but still too little to be affected by the Project. There is enough water for him in the foreseeable future without the Project; and even if his only supply would be desalinized water costing $150 an acre-foot, the extra cost over the Project's $60 per acre-foot water would be only $18 per year. If he owns a $10,000 house, he pays that amount in taxes to the Metropolitan Water District anyway.

The major beneficiaries of the Water Project are the corporate farms of the San Joaquin Valley. More than half of all the water delivered by the Project between 1970 and 1990 will go to the San Joaquin Valley. In 1959 the California Labor Federation and the Young Democrats mapped the Valley lands that are eligible to receive Project water, and found that 64% of these lands are owned by about 100 persons! Of the remaining land within the Project service area, a substantial amount belongs to local governments.

Kern County will receive the largest share of San Joaquin Valley Water. Seventy-eight percent of the Kern County land that will receive state water belongs to people

Table 3c

LAND OWNERSHIP IN THE SAN JOAQUIN VALLEY
AREAS SERVED BY THE STATE WATER PROJECT [a]

Owner	Acreage	% of Total
Tenneco, Inc. (Kern County Land Co.)	348,026.46	8.7
Standard Oil of California	218,485.48	5.5
Other Oil Companies	264,678.64	6.6
Southern Pacific RR	201,851.75	5.1
Tejon Ranch [b]	168,531.07	4.2
Boston Ranch (J. G. Boswell)	37,555.58	0.9
TOTAL owned by approximately fifteen firms:	1,238,228.98	31.0
Other private holdings over 1000 acres/person:	1,323,821.57	33.1
	2,562,050.55	64.1
U.S. Government	192,762.13	4.8
Owners of less than 1000 acres/person, including city, county, and State:	1,240,648.24	31.1

[a] Table from Ballis, "Land Ownership in the San Joaquin Valley," 105 Cong. Record, Pt. 6, p. 7677 (1959).

[b] Does not include acreage owned by Tejon Ranch in Southern California.

or interests that own more than 160 acres each. These large landowners hatched the whole idea for the Project, and provided the major lobbying muscle which pushed it through. Much of their land, prior to the Project, lay fallow; the huge federal Central Valley Project supplied farms to the north and east of them, but did not reach the southwestern section of the San Joaquin Valley. Moreover, what ground water they had was rapidly receding as a result of overuse. To farm or otherwise develop their land, these owners had to import water. The most logical alternative, of course, was to extend the Central Valley Project. This would provide water and also the huge federal subsidy that goes with Bureau of Reclamation irrigation projects. Unfortunately for the landowners, however, reclamation water comes with a condition attached, based on a long-standing federal policy of encouraging small farms and limiting the amount of irrigation subsidy any one farmer may receive. This condition, the 160-acre limitation, requires anyone receiving reclamation water on more than 160 acres to sell that "excess" land within ten years, at pre-water-subsidy prices. The large landowners would have none of that, of course, and fought for many years to have the legislature repeal the limitation or the courts nullify it. According to most observers, it was the failure to achieve these objectives that finally made them turn to the state. California, of course, has no 160-acre limitation policies.

So the Water Project brings the San Joaquin owners the water they badly need without imposing conditions on its use, and with a considerable subsidy.

For example: Kern County has contracted to buy a maximum of 1.15 million acre-feet of water per year from the state. The state has set the price of this contract water to cover all costs of constructing the system and delivering the water to Kern County—that is, all costs allocated to "water users." At present, the state charges Kern County an average of $21 per acre-foot. But this charge does not include costs borne by those who buy electric power from the Project, nor the real but unstated costs assumed by the state through its interest-free loan to the Project. It probably costs California closer to $35 an acre-foot to deliver water to Kern County, so the landowners receive a subsidy of $14 per acre-foot.

Kern County has also established the Kern County Water Agency, with the sole function of buying the water and selling it to local water districts. This intermediary exists to help pay for the water through a countywide property tax. Taxes in Kern County now pay approximately $6 towards every acre-foot the Agency buys, raising the total direct subsidy for contract water going to Kern County's landowners to $20 an acre-foot.

But between now and 1990, Kern County expects to receive more water than it has firmly contracted for. The additional water is known as "surplus" water, for which the state charges merely the cost of transportation—$4 an acre-foot in Kern County. Obviously, whatever "surplus" water Kern County can obtain amounts to a tremendous windfall. If, as now predicted, it receives nearly as much "surplus" water as contract water, the average price of its water will be lowered from $21 per acre-foot to $12.50 per acre-foot.

The DWR justifies its giveaway rates for "surplus" water on the ground that delivery is unreliable, since it cannot guarantee the water's availability after the contractual obligations have been met in a drought year. That makes sense, until one notices that the Project's contractual obligations are so low that plentiful "surplus" water will be available in any years except one as dry as the driest year ever recorded in California, which came after a seven-year drought. Even then, "surplus" should be available until the year's supplies reach their maxiumum contractual level in 1990.

In addition to the tax and "surplus" water subsidies, large landowners receive yet another bonus from the State Water Project: increases in land value. In California, land without water is worthless. Water can raise prices $1,000 an acre or more. A study made in 1968, before water deliveries had begun, showed that an isolated tract of Kern County land rose by over $100 an acre in assessed valuation, merely in anticipation of water coming to nearby acreage. Should the Water Project ultimately increase land values in the Service Area by $300 an acre—a conservative guess—the big landowners will have received a capital gain of $780,000,000, taxable at a lower rate than ordinary income, such as wages.

Incidentally, it is interesting to note that the farmers bagging these huge subsidies feed at the trough of public welfare elsewhere. J. G. Boswell, owner of the huge Boston Ranch, received over $5 million in 1970 from the Federal Government in crop subsidies. Boswell is the nation's leader in income received for not growing crops, but the other State Water Project beneficiaries are right up there with him. Both Tenneco and the Tejon Ranch, for example, received several hundred thousand dollars too.

SOUTHERN CALIFORNIA: WHY?

At first glance, southern California's eagerness for the State Water Project seems hard to understand. Its agriculture does not need state water. Its residents do not need state water. Even the local real-estate interests—the builders, dealers, and speculators—gain nothing from state water, since cheaper local sources will sustain any foreseeable demand for development. With adequate local water for a significant period of time, southern California's best strategy would be to wait for desalinization.

But closer examination yields explanations for the southland's fervor on behalf of the Water Project. Most southern Californians, including most builders, developers, and speculators, know no more about the area's water needs than any ordinary citizen. The experts all told them the Project was desperately needed, so they supported it. The Metropolitan Water District of southern California, which supplies water to more than ten million people, should theoretically have been a source of alternative expertise for southern Californians. But the powerful MWD has contracted to buy half the Project's deliveries, and has embarked on a billion-dollar building program of its own to distribute the water, and consequently has a very solid self-interest in seeing the Project come to fruition. To the general public, the District's promise to buy all that water, shortly before the bond referendum, looked like proof of the claim that the Project was needed, and that water users would pay for it. After all, here was a water agency making a huge commitment. In fulfillment of the promoters' repeated claims, it looked as if water users were committing themselves to paying for most of the Project. In reality, of course, the District is not a water user, and its commitment meant nothing except that its engineers had failed again. But the public didn't know that, and the District did not hasten to enlighten them. Nor did the Chamber of Commerce's Water Committee. Nor did the Los Angeles Department of Water and Power.

Another fact that explains the southland's acceptance of the Project is that a few very important interests stand to benefit a great deal from it. Among these are the owners of Los Angeles' two major newspapers, the *Times* and the *Herald-Examiner* (owned by the Chandlers and Hearst, respectively). The Chandlers own 20% of the huge Tejon Ranch, a major State Water Project beneficiary; Hearst owns extensive ranch land in southern California. Therefore Los Angeles residents have been subjected to a barrage of propaganda on behalf of the Project, stressing the need for water in Los Angeles.

The Project also changes the pattern of development within southern California; it enables new towns to spring up on interior sites that, were it not for the Project, would remain desolate. Naturally, the owners of these sites strongly favored the Project—which will visit its bounty on virtually all the major landholdings in the southern part of the state: the Irvine Ranch, Newhall Ranch, Tejon Ranch, Rancho California, and others.

In southern California the "surplus" water ploy takes a slightly different twist than it does statewide, since the Project itself will deliver comparatively little real "surplus" water. The MWD, however, creates "surplus" water of its own. Quite simply, the District has contracted to buy far more water from the state than it can sell at full price.

Having placed itself in this ridiculous position, the only "rational" solution will be to sell what it can at full price, and sell the rest—the "surplus"—for whatever it can get. This, of course, is precisely what Los Angeles had to do with the Owens River Aqueduct, and the MWD itself has had to do with the Colorado River Aqueduct.

There is an upper limit to how much water most users will take, even if they get it free. Thus, the only real customer for the MWD's "surplus" water are water districts with a storage capacity—primarily those overlying depleted ground-water basins—known as Water Replenishment Districts. Whereas the MWD intends to sell state water for $60 an acre-foot to agencies that supply the water directly to their customers, it will sell "replenishment" water for only $30 an acre-foot, plus the nominal cost of pumping it out of the ground again. The people living within a regular water district, such as those served by the Los Angeles Department of Water and Power, will be paying $60 an acre-foot, plus substantial additional fees for distribution costs—all told, in Los Angeles, about $120 per acre-foot.

The lucky people living in Water Replenishment Districts happen to be the largest water users in Southern California: various private water companies, and the biggest industries. Table 3d is based on a survey of two Replenishment Districts in Los Angeles.

Table 3d
SUBSIDIES TO SOME LOS ANGELES-AREA WATER USERS

Firm	Water Pumped per year (acre-feet)	Water Project Subsidy per year
Container Corp. of America	1,323 x $80 =	$105,840
Fibreboard Paper Products Co.	1,521	121,680
Firestone Tire & Rubber	1,536	122,880
Flintkote Co.	2,567	200,560
U.S. Steel	1,791	143,280
Gulf Oil Co.	1,795	143,600
Richfield Oil Corp.	4,428	354,240
Shell Oil Co.	4,516	361,280
Union Oil Co.	2,670	213,600
Texaco	3,432	274,560
Standard Oil Co.	4,542	363,360

The subsidy calculation is based simply on the difference (about $80 per acre-foot) between what these firms pay for their water and what the rest of Los Angeles pays. Only the availability of Project water to supply their ground-water basin keeps them from rapidly depleting it and turning to direct deliveries for a supply. The subsidy calculation does *not* include another very real subsidy many of these firms are receiving: the MWD property-tax subsidy. Presently, the District meets half its water payments through funds raised from property taxes. To the extent that a firm uses a larger share of the water than it pays in taxes, it receives a tax subsidy—and most heavy water users would fall into that category.

The industries do not receive the full benefit of these phenomenal subsidies. Long before they would have to pay an extra $100,000 a year or more for water, they would convert to recycling processes consuming vastly less fresh water—processes available to virtually all the industries cited. The $363,360 subsidy to Standard Oil merely saves Standard the cost of such conversion—a saving of perhaps $30,000 a year. Thus, these subsidies are not only outrageously large, they are outrageously inefficient. The same holds true for the subsidies being supplied through the Water Project to the farmers in the San Joaquin Valley. The total actual benefit those farmers receive can be measured by the amount their land increases in value—perhaps $780 million. But the cost to the state of supplying that benefit, the amount of subsidy it provides by picking up the difference between the real cost and the actual price paid, is several times $780 million.

There are other consequences of providing these enormous subsidies. First, the big farmers are prime customers of the world's largest bank, the Bank of America. Insofar as the state subsidy enables them to extend their business, they borrow more money (for crops and equipment) from the bank, and extend the bank's near-monopoly hold over California agriculture yet further. Second, even with the huge subsidies, state water is so expensive that the only profitable crops these farmers can grow are presently high-priced "specialty" crops—fruits, nuts, etc. The farmers who now grow these crops are mostly small farmers, who must gain enough income from 160 acres to support themselves. When the San Joaquin agribusinesses weigh in with their crops in the next few years, prices will plummet, and it is presently expected that thousands of these small farmers will be driven from the land. This has nothing to do with their efficiency, which rivals that of agribusiness in all areas except the ability to obtain credit from the Bank of America and subsidies from the U.S. government.

THE FUTURE

The Project's past is a story of injustice and special-interest favoritism, of outrageous costs and slim benefits. But Water Project construction so far has had little adverse effect on the environment—except for possible destruction of the salmon run up the Feather River. Plans for the future, however, threaten environmental disaster. Conservationists who remained silent in 1960 have since become the leaders in opposition to the Project.

There are four related federal and state project proposals for the future, none of which has yet been authorized, and all of which can and should be stopped. All relate to the Delta pool—to which fresh water flows down the Sacramento River, and from which both the DWR and the Federal Bureau of Reclamation pump it into their respective canals for transport further south.

Project Number One, the U.S. Bureau of Reclamation's project, called the East Side Division of the Central Valley Project, would use up present Sacramento River supplies to irrigate yet more land in the San Joaquin Valley. That makes it necessary to augment the Sacramento's flow (Project Number Two) by diverting into it the nearest as yet untapped river, the Eel—a wild river flowing through redwood country to the sea. One of the reasons the San Joaquin Valley wants so much water is that irrigation deposits salts and eventually ruins the soil unless farmers "flush out" the salts with even more water. The Valley needs a sewer for the "flushed" salts, pesticides, and other assorted poisons (Project Number Three). As presently planned, however, this drain will dump its waste into the Delta, thus polluting the source of San Joaquin Valley irrigation water. Even without the drain, however, engineers have found that the pumps for the state and federal irrigation plans will be so powerful that long before they reach full capacity they will be sucking up saline water from the Bay. For these reasons, the Bureau of the DWR proposes to build a huge *Peripheral Canal* (Project Number Four) to circumvent the Delta altogether and take all the unpolluted water they need directly from the Sacramento River. Without so large a canal, it would be impossible to build the East Side Division, and unnecessary to attack the Eel. With the canal, the engineers can suck up ever-increasing amounts of water until they have drained the Eel, the Klamath, the Trinity, and even the Columbia Rivers.

These projects also threaten the Delta and San Francisco Bay itself. The Bay and Delta form one of the major estuary ecosystems on the West Coast, supporting millions of transient and resident birds and providing spawning or maturing ground for innumerable fish and other water animals. Ecologists present conflicting views on the effects of these projects, depending on who pays them, but only those hired by the state or the Bureau show anything other than grave concern.

The Peripheral Canal cannot proceed unless three bodies decide in favor of it. Governor Reagan is already on record as favoring it. The Bureau of Reclamation must gain approval from the President's Office of Management and Budget before submitting it to Congress. The OMB has been known to oppose faulty projects, but it also gives in to special interest pressure in its low-visibility deliberations. The decision-maker most subject to present influence is the U.S. Congress, which must authorize the Canal and approve funds for it. Congressman Jerome Waldie of Contra Costa County has been leading the fight against the Canal in the House of Representatives; both of California's senators remain officially uncommitted.

The East Side Division, which would be the immediate trigger for "development" of California's north coastal rivers, has not yet received even the governor's approval. In fact, important Californians concerned with water, such as Secretary of Resources Norman Livermore and former Director of the DWR Harvey Banks, have expressed opposition to it, so there remains a substantial chance that Governor Reagan will veto it. Should he approve, the proposal would have to receive approval from both the President's Office of Management and Budget and Congress itself.

The Eel River decision has an interesting history. In 1968 the Army Corps of Engineers proposed a dam on the Eel at Dos Rios. The dam would have some minor flood-control function—the basis for the Army's interest—but would serve mainly to collect the Eel's water so it could be tunneled through the mountains to the Sacramento. The Corps's plans found some angry conservationists waiting.

They didn't like turning one of California's last wild rivers into a dead and turbid lake, destroying one of the few remaining salmon and steelhead runs in the state, drowning a beautiful valley, and displacing its Indian inhabitants in violation of their treaty. The Corps compounded its difficulty by presenting a particularly stupid and dishonest "evaluation" in support of its proposal, which was demolished by Harrison Brown and other economists sought out by the conservationists. The Corps also showed remarkable callousness to the Indians, proposing to trade them worthless mountainside land for their Round Valley farms. As if all that were not enough, the Department of Water Resources chipped in with some transparently dishonest estimates of water "requirements" in southern California, which it used to justify the development. The estimates were proved transparently dishonest by the conservationists, who had obtained a suppressed report which had been prepared two months earlier by the Department's southern California staff, and which showed requirements far lower than what the Department was asserting. Although the Department attempted to discredit it (and reprimanded its authors), the report obviously played a role in Governor Reagan's decision to call for additional studies.

While those additional studies, completed in 1969 by the DWR, again recommended Dos Rios, the Department has since issued its Bulletin 160-70, surveying and predicting all of California's water demands and supplies for the next fifty years. This document is vastly superior to any study the Department has previously produced. It draws upon revised population estimates and the more sophisticated analysis of the suppressed 1968 document to conclude that southern California won't need any more water for at least ten more years, thus pushing the Eel River decision back several years and relieving at least the immediate pressure for development. The Report's conclusion may have a similar effect on the Peripheral Canal, although the DWR and the Bureau of Reclamation won't admit that. Time is probably working against them, and if they don't get the Peripheral Canal soon, they may never get it.

The Drain (Project Number Three), once also a hot issue, has subsided for the present because Valley farmers appear unwilling to pay for it until their land becomes more obviously polluted. Some sort of drain will eventually be needed, but the solution to that problem will probably be to remove the salts and poisons in a treatment plant before returning the water to the Delta. The legislature and the governor will make the primary decisions about the Drain, although the state's water pollution standards, and their enforcement by the Water Resources Control Board may become important as well.

The State Water Project can and should be stopped at the Peripheral Canal. The DWR expects huge additional costs to be met not out of Project revenues or bond issues but out of the public treasury, through a $680 million interest-free loan, now projected for use on Dos Rios. By stopping the Project now, the state can save itself the interest on that money—well over a billion dollars. The state's present financial squeeze seems to be due largely to the Project.

What of southern California's water "needs"? They should, at the very least, be recalculated with sound economic techniques. Bulletin 160-70 is a start. All indications presently suggest that real "needs" can be met through available water in the south, at a cost comparable to that of Dos Rios or other State Water Project increments.

The prospects for stopping the State Water Project seem excellent. The Peripheral Canal, the East Side Division, and Dos Rios or its equivalent must all receive Congressional approval, and Congress has shown itself increasingly responsive to environmental considerations. Congressman Jerome Waldie has submitted positive legislation to give wild-river status to the Eel, Trinity, and Klamath rivers. Should Waldie's bill pass, the Project could not draw upon their waters and would be effectively blocked. In addition, various individuals are trying to stop the Project through lawsuits. Efforts on the state level may have a chance once the facts about this Project penetrate the smog of deception which the DWR pours forth. Most politicians who favor the Project sincerely believe it is good; some, at least, can be persuaded otherwise.

As this study should make clear, the chief losers from the Project are southern Californians, who must pay for it. Efforts by the Project's opponents to make this a battle of North versus South only obscure that point, and of course place a majority of the state's voters firmly on the Project's side. But if the Project doesn't stop now, its continuation will have not only regional factionalism on its side, but economic as well. For once the basic pipeline from north to south exists, it may well prove cheaper to meet additional demands by damming another river than to initiate a whole new water supply system such as desalinization. The state has full plans for this further growth, outlined in a document entitled the California Water Plan. It will take all the remaining rivers of the North Coast—the Klamath, the Trinity, the Van Duzen, the Mad, and the rest of the Eel— with unforeseeable effects on the climate, the beaches, the redwoods, the fish, and other wildlife.

United States Bureau of Reclamation

SENATOR MORSE: As one pauses in this debate to refresh his memory in regard to some of the great scandals in the field of natural resources in our history, and when one thinks of the oil scandals and the oil 'steals,' the Teapot Dome, the great land frauds, the various types of 'steals' of which the powerful economic vested interests of the country have been guilty throughout our history, I should like to ask the Senator from Illinois if he thinks I am too far wrong when I suggest that today we raise the question of whether [San Luis] is going to represent a great water 'steal'?

SENATOR DOUGLAS: Mr. President, I try to be very guarded in the language I use. I will say that if this bill passes in its present form, it will be a public catastrophe.

SENATOR MORSE: Mine is mild compared with that language, I wish to say. But let the record show that I think that if our amendment is not adopted, the bill will be a water 'steal'. . . .

SENATOR DOUGLAS: Mr. President, I would not reprove the Senator from Oregon if he were to use such words; I would say that, on the whole, he was a man of restrained speech.

—From the United States Senate debates over the San Luis reclamation bill.[59]

The Bureau of Reclamation delivers nearly one quarter of all the water used in the state. Its major operations, outlined in Table 3a, include the All-American Canal, serving the Imperial and Coachella Valleys, and the Central Valley Project. These two alone deliver nearly 8 maf a year (compared to the 4.2 maf deliveries from the State Water Project) and smaller projects deliver another million or so. The Bureau, as of 1968, had authorized, proposed, or under construction further projects "costing" $2.8 billion by 1990.

One of them is the San Luis dam and canal, located near Los Banos on the west side of the San Joaquin Valley, which the Bureau shares with the State Water Project. San Luis also includes a federally administered and serviced distribution system in the area, under federal administration and service, consisting of the Westlands Water District; it also includes a drainage system required to flush away the salt brought in by the distribution system. The Bureau operates San Luis as a unit of its Central Valley Project.

The present Westlands Water District is 190,000 acres larger than was originally contemplated. It was joined in 1964 by an adjacent unit which had hoped until then to receive water from the State Water Project. When the Bureau prepared its feasibility report on the San Luis project in 1955, it surveyed the ownership of the original 440,000-acre District. It reported that a grand total of 130 people and corporations owned 363,000 or 83%, of the acres. Of these, sixty-six owned 323,000 acres, or 74%, and four owned 144,000 acres, or nearly one-third of the whole District.[60] It was for these 130 that Congress in 1959 approved the $480 million San Luis project. The loan to each privileged farmer was almost $4 million.

The federal expenditure of $480 million naturally increases land values. Sales figures in Westlands show an appreciation of about $300 an acre, conferring a windfall of more than $23 million on the Southern Pacific Company; $13,500,000 for Russell Giffen; nearly $7 million for Boswell's Boston Ranch; and over $9 million for the Anderson, Clayton Company. The total District's land values have increased over $150 million.

While the increase of land value is one measure of the benefit, the amount of annual water subsidy itself is another. Adjacent lands receiving state water pay, on the average, about $10 more per acre-foot, or $24 per acre-foot. As demonstrated elsewhere, state deliveries receive a large subsidy from power users and taxpayers, in this case approximately $9 per acre-foot.[61] So the total federal subsidy on Westlands water equals about $19 per acre-foot, or $19 million for the District's annual one-maf supply.[62] Huge as these subsidies are, the reader may have noticed that they don't approach the $480 million being spent by the federal government: the recipients of water subsidies almost never benefit by as much as the taxpayers spend. San Luis is a rich people's welfare program: the government spends about $480 million to enrich seventy-six landlords by about $150 million. That's a waste of $330 million.

The most extraordinary feature of this boondoggle is that it will go far to destroy the benefits which earlier phases of the federal government's Central Valley Project brought to small farmers in other parts of the Valley.

According to a 1968 statement, the District expects to use San Luis water to increase production of the following crops:

—Cotton (mostly skip-row), from 130,464 to 152,000 acres—a price-supported crop because of present over-production.

—Sugar beets, 6,107 acres to 39,000 acres—likewise a price-supported crop because of cheaper foreign competition and domestic overproduction.

—Fruit trees, from 680 acres to 50,000 acres—a high-valued crop with limited production, grown mainly by small farmers. The vast new acreages will drive prices to cost or below until those farmers least able to last without profits—the small farmers—are forced out.

—Alfalfa hay, from 8,461 acres to 30,000—the only projected crop increase that won't harm either taxpayers or other farmers.

When Congress passed the San Luis bill, Senator Russell of Georgia added an amendment seeking to prevent San Luis from adding to farm surpluses. His amendment forbids the use of San Luis water to grow any more price-supported crops (such as cotton or sugar-beets) than were already growing in Westlands, unless the allotments were increased. The big farmers readily accepted the amendment, because it was essentially meaningless. They could grow the price-supported crops with other water, freed for that purpose by the San Luis supply; moreover, by transferring their allotments from other places to Westlands, they would technically stay within previous acreage limits, while in fact the more fertile Westlands soil and better climate would increase production considerably.

The Bureau argues, and Congress assumed, that in fact San Luis does not benefit the seventy-six Westlands landowners, at least not on more than 160 acres of their land. This claim has its origins in the famous 160-acre limitation, which applies to the federal service area of San Luis. The

160 acre limitation provides that federal water shall not be delivered to more than 160 acres owned by any one person, and if it is, the "excess lands" which receive it must be sold, within ten years, to small landowners *for a price which does not reflect the existence of the federal project*. In short, the Bureau argues, the 160-acre limitation will spread the San Luis benefits to many by breaking up the present large holdings and selling the land at low (pre-subsidy) prices, so that the new purchasers will be the ones to gain from the increase in land values.

However, even if the law proceeded properly, the large landowners could receive the $19 per acre-foot subsidy for ten years before having to sell. Southlake Farms, for example, owned by Producers Cotton Oil Company, and controlled in 1959 by the then "President" of Westlands, J. E. O'Neill, owns about 10,000 acres and will receive during those ten years an annual subsidy of $570,000. No wonder Harry Horton, a lawyer for big southern California grower interests, stated:

> I will give you my own opinion of Jack O'Neill's willingness to sign the 160 acre limitation. He thinks if he gets water for ten years on there without having to sell, he can make enough money out of it so he can afford to sell the land at any old price.[63]

But Jack O'Neill's successors don't have to sell their excess land at "any old price." The Bureau's assessment policies see to that. In one example, given by a Westlands realtor, Jack Molsbergen, the Bureau approved the sale of land for $425 an acre. Its appraised value at the time of sale was $450, but the Bureau considered that $25 worth of value came from the San Luis project, and in conformity with the law requiring sale at pre-water prices, marked the land down to $425. In other words, by the *Bureau's own straight-faced estimate,* the United States was spending approximately $1,000 an acre to confer benefits which it valued at $25 an acre.

The Bureau's $25 figure was as phony as a water engineer's cost estimates: anyone selling for $425 an acre receives over 90% of the land value added by the project. In 1960, the land cost $150 an acre and its value was declining rapidly as ground-water levels plummeted from overpumping. Westlands was "mining" 900,000 acre-feet a year from a basin with an estimated replenishable yield of

190,000 acre-feet, dropping pumping levels ten feet a year. The San Luis project is the only change throughout Westlands since 1960 that could possibly affect land values. Even adding a factor for inflation, based on the average increase of all farms during the period, yields a price of only $190 an acre by the time of its sale in 1968. But with the water levels dropping, it probably wouldn't have been worth $100 an acre without the project.

Unfortunately, the Bureau's conclusion that the land without San Luis would be worth only $25 less than the land with it was not an isolated aberration. The Bureau actually has an appraisal technique, applied as a matter of policy and promulgated from Washington, which guarantees a similar conclusion for every sale of excess land. The Bureau's trick is to compare land receiving project water with nearby land not receiving the water, claiming that the difference in sales price (about $25 an acre) represents the project's value to the land. But San Luis has helped nonproject land in the area a great deal, replenishing their fast dwindling ground-water supply, by appreciating its value and by relieving the general demand for its water. The Bureau's assessment technique is illegal, permitting O'Neill and associates to cash in on the full unearned increment in land value created by San Luis, contrary to federal law.

But because the fraudulent assessment technique of the Bureau puts the post-subsidy land value in the "pre-subsidy assessment" for sales purposes, no one wants to buy. So the landowners, some of whom (like Southern Pacific) never wanted to sell in the first place, get to keep their land and the subsidies that go with it, while theoretically complying with the 160-acre limitation as the Bureau applies it.

The Bureau's projects and policies lead to further problems within California. Not the least of these is the need for additional water projects created because the Bureau uses so much so inefficiently. Bureau projects use too much water not only because of the interest-free subsidy, but because Bureau policies lead to rates below even the amount required to return the interest-free loan! If the Bureau didn't scoop up water with such projects, state or local agencies could use it. Almost certainly they would use it more efficiently, too, since they have neither the built-in distorter of interest-free federal money nor the ability to price water below the amount required for full repayment.

The further projects which they must build prove expensive, environmentally destructive, and progressively less efficient. The latter problem arises from the simple fact that the good dam sites have all been taken, many by the Bureau which uses their capacity so wastefully. The most outstanding single example of a project required because of Bureau overuse is the State Water Project. The SWP would not exist if southern California were not deceitfully convinced of the need for northern water. Southern California, with an aqueduct already tapping the Colorado River, may need more water (obtainable from southern sources) only because unjustifiable Bureau projects on the Colorado have reduced or will in the future reduce its flow to less than southern California needs. The future expansion of the SWP also hinges on Bureau inefficiency. Briefly, the SWP will need to build new water-supply systems on the North Coast rivers only if the Bureau expands its demand for Sacramento River water. The Bureau's demand will expand only if its underpricing policies continue.

The environmental effects of Bureau projects and projects made necessary by Bureau projects have become increasingly serious as they cut into a rapidly dwindling supply of wildlife, wildlife habitats, and wilderness. Unlike the state, which at least provides some funding to mitigate the environmental effects of its projects, the Bureau's appropriations contain no such allowances. Further, perhaps by happenstance, the Bureau has in the past constructed, and plans in the future to construct, many of the dams most destructive of wildlife and natural environment. Under current conditions, with these commodities turned precious through scarcity, their irrevocable destruction for the sake of projects which lack even economic justification seems puzzling. Yet the Bureau marches on.

How does the Bureau obtain political approval for its projects? It begins by shaping them according to "the expressed preferences of would-be local beneficiaries," with the result that projects are designed to produce "those classes of benefits destined for groups with active political organizations and spokesmen." [64] In the past, these local groups have never had trouble gaining state approval for the Bureau project: noted economists Bain et al. explain that "a general inclination of legislatures to subsidize agriculture should be mentioned as an obvious reason . . . as should the equally general faith within California in the efficacy of water supply projects to promote general economic (especially urban) growth." [65] From the state, a project goes to Congress where "support is likely to emerge from a process of vote-trading in a legislative logrolling process, and to depend on many things in addition to an evaluation of the project's consequences for the national welfare." [66] The Bureau has achieved a remarkable record through its careful solicitation of good local relations: "All California water projects thoroughly studied by the Bureau or the Corps [of Engineers, which follows similar procedures] and supported by local interests have ultimately received congressional approval and appropriations. The differences from case to case lie mainly in the time required . . . and, to a lesser degree, the compromises necessary along the way." [67]

While this review of the Bureau's operations has been comparatively brief, the Bureau has received a great deal of detailed criticism in economic and other literature. The Bureau, having outgrown the original social justification for what is now an economically unwarranted existence, must now fight and scrape with every trick at the command of its professional policy-makers to continue. These tricks are considerable: its engineers and economists falsify their data and results in many ways. As Bain and others note, the Bureau's formal criteria are "broadly reasonable"; the fault lies in the numbers it fits into the equations. The Bureau's lawyers are masterful politicians, gauging and playing on local, state, and congressional sentiment. Of course, they could not succeed if the pattern of interests and decision-making did not so permit, but they do. A Bureau project helps one area in a striking and obvious way; it hurts others only indirectly and subtly, but massively. Projects are ideal for logrolling: divisible, local, and eminently tradable.

The Bureau should be disbanded, at least in California. Its administrative and enforcement functions could be taken over by other agencies, state or federal. There is nothing the Bureau can build or operate in California in the foreseeable future which can bring anything but harm to the state—socially, economically, and environmentally. It has overseen the transfer of California's richest farmlands from small holders to large, in direct violation of its mandate and the laws designed to ensure that mandate's enforcement.

4

Wild Areas,
I: Commercial Threats

Private Recreational Development

Over half a million acres of California's mountain and desert land have been committed to recreational "development"—mostly in the past decade. Most of the northern coast of California up into Mendocino County is now subdivided for second-home recreation, and the southern half of the state is keeping pace. Over 100,00 acres of land per year are currently being committed to development.

In the far north of California, large Siskiyou County (population 35,400, with 240-person increase per year) has seen more than seventy subdivisions put up for sale since 1964. In Nevada County (population 26,500), where subdivisions cover over 50,000 acres, if the increase in lots over the past five years continues at a similar rate, by 1975 every square foot of privately held land in the county will have been subdivided into suburban-style lots. In new Sierra County (population 2,500), several of the subdivisions now underway cover more than 10,000 acres and will accommodate 25,000 persons each. As Appendices to Chapter 1 suggest, the situation is similar in Mendocino, Sonoma, Tuolumne, Placer, San Bernardino, Calaveras, Mariposa, El Dorado, and other counties. A single proposed development in Shasta County would house the county's entire population. Within the last twenty years, 21,048 lots have been offered for sale in Madera County. This would house Madera's entire population many times over. As with Shasta and most of the counties here listed, existing lots (if used for living quarters) could accommodate the established growth rate for the next 100 to 300 years.

However, there is little actual building. In the case of Madera County cited above, the 21,048 lots bulldozed over the past twenty years have supported a total of 100 houses. The other counties have similar records, with a consistent rate of "buildup" (construction) of between 0% and 1% per year.

To illustrate the buildup rate, we surveyed the rate of construction on Boise Cascade developments. They are typical of the rest of the recreational subdivisions in the state (at Lake Tahoe there are more than 20,000 bulldozed lots with no homes on them).

Leaving out Lake Arrowhead and Incline Village, which are located at two of the choicest recreational areas in the state and which were developed before Boise Cascade acquired them, and Lake of the Pines, where the rate of construction has been slightly higher than average, there are a total of approximately 100 houses on the over 84,000 acres of land in B.C.'s eighteen developments—many of them models or the residences of B.C. representatives.

"This type of development is the number-one environmental problem in California," says State Engineer Glen Browning, who supervises public-health water and sewer inspection in northern and central California. "Speculative subdivisions irreversibly change land-use patterns and, in some counties, subdivisions have already outstripped water supplies."

For the past five years the State Department of Public Health has been suppressing, in violation of the California Records Act, the results of major surveys of recreational development impacts. Fifteen northern counties were exhaustively surveyed, and the information gathered was compiled in a document entitled "Contract Services Public Health Program Evaluation." The cover is stamped "For Departmental Use Only."

The summary states the results in as positive terms as is possible, given the findings:

1. *Water Supplies*

62% of large Public Water Supplies and 33% of small Public Water Supplies meet USPHS Standards.

2. *Sewage Disposal*

Approximately one-half of the population is served by community sewage systems. Only 48% of these systems meet Water Pollution Board criteria. There are 62 central sewage areas in the 15 counties representing areas that could benefit from new Community sewage systems.

3. *Solid Waste Disposal*

64% of dumps are satisfactorily maintained.

4. *Recreational Sanitation*

Over 10 million people use recreation in the Contract Counties each year. One-fourth of the water supplies serving recreation areas is considered substandard or unsafe.

5. *Swimming Pool Sanitation*

Less than 50% of swimming pools constructed prior to 1960 meet state swimming pool standards but 90% of those constructed since the Act went into effect do meet these standards.

Little has been done to safeguard natural bathing places.

6. *Institutional Sanitation*

Over 80% of schools have safe water and approved sewage disposal systems but only 57% meet all the standards for health and safety.

7. *Land Development*

In a two-year period of time, 221 subdivisions have been developed in the 15 Contract Counties with a total of 8,600 developed lots. During the same time a large number of lots have been developed without formal approval of the health department with a failure rate three times as high as approved lots.

Few counties have developed a county Master Plan or plan for water, sewage and refuse.

Since this summary, development has more than tripled in these counties and the rate of deterioration has surpassed the rate of development. Yet the future promises no release of the full data, let alone action to remedy the situation.

The state's Environmental Quality Study Council, strictly an advisory body, issued a "memorandum of facts" on July 29, 1970, listing their findings concerning some of the developments. The Council focused especially on Nevada County:

—At Lake of the Pines in Nevada County the developers bought land at $873.30 per acre and sold it one year later for from $12,000 to $36,000 per acre.
— . . . 33% of the [developer's funds go] into high pressure advertising.
—Serious degradation to the natural land and water en-

vironment will occur including direct impacts upon public
health, wildlife, and alternate land uses:

a) Impacts regarding water supply and waste-water disposal.
b) Impacts upon wildlife natural food and shelter.
c) Impacts related to transportation requirements.

—An estimated 160 miles of streams (37% of the stream
mileage within Nevada County) have already been damaged by siltation, stream-bank alterations and domestic
waste discharges resulting from subdivision development.

—Much of the land occupied by subdivisions within
Nevada County is located in the pine-chaparral or wood-
land-chaparral habitat zones, both of which are particularly important to deer and upland game species. Hunting opportunities have already been sharply curtailed on
much of this land and the value of the land for wildlife
is expected to diminish steadily as more homes are constructed. Some of the land now being subdivided is deer
winter range which is already in critically short supply.

—Poorly designed subdivision roads are one of the biggest sources of silt pollution in Nevada County. For example, eroding road fills within a recent subdivision have
discharged so much sediment into a downstream creek
that salmon spawning gravels in the Yuba River will be
severely damaged if the erosion is not arrested. The Yuba
River salmon fishery is worth about $600,000 annually.

—Auburn Lake Trails in El Dorado County has a planned
density of from 1,700 to 2,300 units but has a questionable water supply that currently does not adequately serve
a town of less than 1,000 people.

—In Humboldt County at Shelter Cove the vital utilities
(roads, drainage, etc.) all required replacement by the
county as soon as all the lots were sold. Total cost to
county—$2 million.

—Since 1964, some 23,000 lots have been formed or are
in the process of being formed within Nevada County subdivisions. An additional 13,000 to 18,000 new lots have
been formed since 1964 through property splits. Formal
subdivision lots occupy about 22,000 acres of land. In
addition, lots formed through property splits cover an
estimated 26,000 to 36,000 acres. Thus, there are between
48,000 and 58,000 acres of land in Nevada County occupied by some type of subdivision. The lots formed during the last six years are already capable of accommodating 110,000 to 125,000 new residents. If the present
trend of new lot formation continues at the same rate for
the next three decades, the county will have 170,000 lots
capable of accommodating 510,000 people.

—The Nevada County District Attorney recently reported

that only 159 homes have been built on the 8,500 lots formed within large subdivisions since 1964. Many of these unoccupied lots still retain their original ground cover.

—In Fresno County 11,540 acres with 2,130 lots are being installed, and plans for another 7,475 acres are tentatively approved.

—Boise Cascade has pending or in process developments of 2,000 acres in El Dorado County, 8,500 acres in Tulare County, 15,000 acres in Tuolumne County and 9,000 acres at Incline Village, as well as other projects in southern California and throughout the country.

—The subdivision questionnaire as issued by the State Department of Real Estate does not, for the most part, apply to the problems, and most of the control over environmental factors is relegated to the local agencies.

—County ordinances often do not have the provisions necessary to control the actions of the developer.

THE RECREATIONAL DEVELOPMENT PROCESS

Although Boise Cascade's property division was started only four years ago, today it is one of the two largest development firms in the world, and has been redubbed Boise Cascade Recreational Communities, Inc., with over thirty projects in over a dozen states. Nineteen of these projects were originated by other entrepreneurial concerns which B.C. subsequently acquired while the projects were in various stages of becoming. When B.C.'s Lake Wildwood's lots had all been sold, the sales manager wired headquarters: "Mission accomplished. Wildwood is dead. Where do you want us next?"

Environmental concern is an extension of B.C.'s sales or public relations. Following is a Boise Cascade interoffice memo. The emphasis is theirs.

INTER-OFFICE MEMO
Recreation Communities Group   Boise Casade

To _____

From _____

Subject   Thoughts on organizing publicity for maximum returns

Date _____ 1970

_____, to get the maximum exposure possible in publicity, I would like to suggest the following plan of attack.

From my previous memo (attached) it's a fair bet that in '71 we will get good *national exposure in the big publications.*

We will get a sprinkling of *small publications,* too, maybe 15 or so.

Now comes the part where we show our "smarts" or we go the hit-and-miss way.

With available manpower, myself and an Indian, not too many more stories can be done than the above in '70 and '71. (As you know, if you do a "big" story you spend 50 hours—or more—phoning, writing memos, researching, getting preliminary pics, traveling, etc. And if you do a *small magazine* story where I do the writing, for, say, a cement magazine (and have to become an instant cement expert), it's another 50 man-hours or so of production time).

But there is *one way* you can pick up *reams* of publicity till we have it coming out of our ears—and favorable publicity, too. That is to organize a *program.*

Please read carefully the attached story on ecology by Joanne Woodward.

It's the *now* way of thinking—the *now* journalism— *what editors want!*

I'm suggest [*sic*] we immediately start at all our projects (we could have a test case of one), giving all the project employees one morning a week off (but paying them their regular salary):

    a. to pick up litter on main street of, say, Auburn, Calif.

    b. another day to pick up litter at town park.

    c. another day to take paint (we contribute) and paint a town eyesore ala Groveland, Calif.

By doing this, every week we *create* favorable news, that the media can cover and they do the writing and take pics.

    a. They photograph our project manager pinning arm bands we've designed on our employees that say "Litterbug vigilante" (or some cute name). The mayor looks on and comments. All good story stuff!

    b. Another time our B.C. vigilantes talk to the school kids and do-good clubs. *More coverage.*

    c. Another time our B.C. vigilantes bring townspeople to project to show them how we're reseeding and re-sodding. More coverage by local press.

Local press would love us because we'd be furnishing them with *people*-type news, lots of names, about the most vital *issue of our day—pollution.*

Our stance would be our projects have "good housekeeping" and we want to help other people have good housekeeping in their town in a pollution-periled world.

If question is raised about any of our questionable practices, we say we're correcting them as fast as possible.

National publicity will naturally come about as publications like to get a *local* story with broad appeal. Subtly we'll get plenty of publicity, too, on your projects in each of these seemingly local-town stories.

Time-saving (and thus *money-saving*) to us, these stories could be handled by *brief invitations* to local press. What they dig up and write about we can use for background material to give a *Life, Look,* or *Time.* Also, trade magazines.

The *most vital issue* today is ecology. I feel we're missing the boat trying to publicize *recreation per se* when people want to read about pollution and ecology. They can learn about our communities' recreation *seeded* into stories on ecology.

There are many, many fresh angles for feature articles: "How an employee picks up *litter* for a morning and finds he's *trimmer* than an hour's jogging." This to me is more relevant than trying to do a story on historical features near a project—it's livelier, more an *in-demand* story. It is a *now approach.*

And with our present work force we could have more of these stories published than the historical type.

A few figures on production time—to prove my thesis of why our strategy should be to publicize our project employees as "litter vigilantes."

Writing or supplying information for *magazines,* as opposed to newspaper stories, is really *time-consuming.*

I have kept a time-sheet on hours involved in the following: *Fore Magazine*—for researching; writing; collecting, identifying and captioning pictures; typing; and checking our story _____ 54 hours

Selecting slides, getting duplicates, writing text for your slide presentation _____16 hours

Writing and typing this memo _____ 7 hours

total 77 hours

The basic work week of _____ and me is 80 hours. All I can put in in overtime (the spirit is willing but the flesh gets sleepy) is about 20 hours. In other words, a two-man work week is about 100 hours for this department.

This is why I strongly recommend a *vigilantes litterbug* project.

Also: it makes sense because we may be concentrating in the future more heavily on other forms of developments than our present communities. And we can continue this "employees as vigilantes" concept in publicity whatever our recreation vehicle is.

The fall-out publicity for all of Boise Cascade would be *enormous!*

"Look at Hawaii—what was it before the United States took it over?" This remark by an eager salesman of B.C.'s Lake Don Pedro illustrates land developers' sense of mission as they go into a specific area to get yet another project under way. Typically, the developer sends out his scouts into an area not zoned, or into one not zoned for density development, to insure that the land is relatively cheap. While attempting to conceal his intentions, the agent proceeds to buy up options on all the land needed, offering the owner a small sum. If the project goes through, the owner will get quite a high price for it. A holdout is told that he is threatening his neighbors, that without him the subdivision won't go through, and that even if it did, his taxes would be prohibitive. This tactic usually works. However, we came across one successful holdout to the B.C. rush, an owner with a 200-acre parcel who wanted to hold onto his house and 12 surrounding acres. He was permitted to retain this portion, under the assumption that he could later be bought out. Having started at $500 an acre, the ante was ultimately raised to $100,000 for his small remaining piece, with the tax threat if he persisted. It is critical for the developer to acquire *all* of the land in an area. The immense profits desired are possible only with monopoly control of the supply.

In the initial phase of maneuvering, the developer has to obtain a water source for the projected subdivision. B.C. approached this problem in a creative way at its Tuolumne County Lake Don Pedro development. B.C. waited until contracts were out for the new Don Pedro Dam and then purchased 1,000 acres that were to lie beneath the reservoir. It then offered to sell the land back "dirt cheap" for water rights in the reservoir for its project of 8,000 lots. Presumably, the reservoir is part of a $100 million *public* investment on the part of the city of San Francisco and the Modesto and Turlock irrigation districts. The cost of the B.C. adjacent land was about $200 per acre; the lots are now selling for the equivalent of approximately $7,000 per acre, and B.C. stands to gross as much as $40 million from the project. The water sought would, of course, greatly enhance the sale of the lots, but the new Don Pedro Board of Review declined the swap, leaving B.C. high and dry. Eventually B.C. had to purchase water from another reservoir in another county several miles distant. This water will service lots on the east side of

Lake Don Pedro, and the system must be self-supporting within ten years; yet only 30% of the lots will be hooked up to the system by 1980, so 30% of the lot owners will pay 100% of the operation cost of the system. Lot owners on the west side of the lake will have to dig wells at about $1,200 a try, and hope for the best, with no guarantee on the quantity, quality, or availability of water. B.C. is still trying to pressure the Review Board into giving them water from the lake, using Tuolumne County officials as go-betweens, and have told the Board they will not discuss the sale of land needed for the reservoir without discussing the water issue. Yet a Don Pedro salesman recently told a prospective buyer that there was "no problem" with water.

Rural Sonoma County is located on the northern point of San Francisco Bay. It has no commercial shipping facilities and no direct hookup with a transcontinental railroad. The next major metropolitan area, Portland, Oregon, is 600 miles to the north. The only city in the county large enough to support an influx of industry is Santa Rosa, scenic but located in a natural basin that would trap smog and industrial waste. The population of this beautiful coastal county has increased by almost 25,000 in the last decade to around 204,000.

Since 1965, the Sonoma County government has re-zoned and approved subdivisions along its coast with a total capacity of over 30,000 living units, presumably to increase their tax base.

Sea Ranch, a subdivision of Oceanic Properties, which sits on ten miles of the Sonoma Coast, initiated a sales program in the summer of 1965. The development was hailed by planners and the developer's "experts" as particularly "innovative": it was to be esthetically consistent with the environment, and would maintain a "visual corridor" to permit a view of the ocean. These lots would go like hot cakes.

Sales in 1965 totaled 40. In 1966 they totaled 166; in 1967, 363; in 1968, 402; in 1969, 296; in 1970 (first two quarters), 131. In the first five *years* of sales, total deeds recorded numbered 1,398, only 28% of their 5,000 "hot cakes." The sales peaked out in the third quarter of 1968 and then went downhill. The "visual corridor" has been preserved because few lots have been sold and because only about one in twenty lots sold has a house on it.

It is clear that developers have a substantial interest in: (1) achieving tax breaks by keeping land in agricultural zoning or under Williamson Act exemption until conversion; (2) marketing public expenditures for private gain (exclusive or peremptory use of public-works benefits— water, highway, etc.); (3) transferring expenses onto future lot owners through high water costs, bond-interest burdens, or the depletion of some resource; (4) controlling the land supply in a large area to preclude market under-cutting for enormous profits (buying all land in an area, inhibiting resale until developers have sold their holdings); and (5) purchasing the most beautiful land possible for ease of promotion and sales.

To these ends, the developer can commit vast resources. Currently, the trend is toward larger subdivisions and greater population density. The average lot is from one-fourth to one-half of an acre in size, with prices averaging about $5,000 per lot, or $20,000 per acre. The developer will pay an average of about $200 per acre. Some sales go as high as $50,000 per acre. The usual investment formula, according to representatives of these promotional developers, is one-third for land acquisition and all improvements, including engineering, streets, water supply, sewers if required, country clubs, artificial lakes, and the like; one-third for advertising, promotion, and sales; and one-third *profit*. And some do far better than that. The promoter-developer doesn't really invest the first third, and the second third is often in the form of sales commissions. The return on actual capital invested can be and has been often 1,000%.

With profits like this there is little hesitancy to commit money to these projects, and great reason to exert maximum influence to overcome local planning barriers.

Once the options are all in for the purchase of the land, the developer then moves into more serious planning and preparations, investing in necessary preliminary engineering, drawing of maps, borrowing of money, and preparing the local community. First, there are discreet inquiries into whether the local business community wants such a development, usually coupled with glowing gold-mine estimates of the trade that will accrue to them. Then comes the persuasion of the planning commission and board of supervisors. Working staff of the planning department may hesitate in considering whether or not the subdivision is wanted in the community.

Even given the opposition of planning staff and a fair hearing, the developers have the advantages in terms of information. The current practice is to set up their own "environmental" studies to prove (*after* the substantive corporate decisions have been made) that the project is needed to "save" the environment. To determine independently what the impact will be, the local planners would have to determine the environmental consequences of an 8,000-acre subdivision: whether a specific area is appropriate for urbanization; what types of uses can be made of the area; the capability of the land in terms of soil conditions and geological and hydrological factors to accept and dispose of waste or to support permanent structures; the impact on erosion control, fire, drainage, and flood problems; adequacy of water resources to support the subdivision; sewage control systems in a wild land area; the form of government, be it a service area, a district, or incorporation, which would be appropriate to insure the installation and ongoing maintenance of needed improvements; wildlife and atmospheric factors; and general questions on the rights of citizens of the state and nation when access to public-recreation land is restricted through the location of the subdivision. The local planning staff is no match for the professional "experts" brought in by the developer to downgrade any objections they may be able to come up with in the maximum proposal-review period of fifty days allotted under the State Map Act.

The most important overt pitch of the developer is the expanded tax-revenue base which he will provide if increased revenue exceeds increased public expenses resulting from the new service demands.* Preliminary studies show that people who do build on these "recreational community" lots plan to live there the year round, yet adequate social planning and the full range of necessary urban services are frequently not provided by the initial developer. A few county officials are beginning to have doubts about

---

* That is, there must be economies of scale in the expansion or extension of services the developments require—or they must require fewer kinds of services and less county expense.

the economies promised by the new subdivisions. One calls the promises of expanded revenue "a snare and a delusion." He cites not only his own county's subdivisions, but numerous others throughout northern California, including one where there is a 28% delinquency rate in tax payments coupled with a $2 million bill for repairs in roads, drainage, sewage, etc., installed by the promoters, to be paid by county taxpayers. The subdivision was approved and initiated in 1965. Another county assessor believes that a county never "reaches a break-even point on subdivisions because they are tax users as well as tax producers," and finds that only in the first couple of years do they return "slightly" more in tax income than they cost the county for services. The service most frequently demanded in these isolated areas is schooling. The costs of education in the assessor's own county are $518 per year for an elementary school pupil and $845 for a high school student. A $40,000 home would produce for all purposes only $1,000 of taxes per year—most of which would go to schooling—and he simply does not believe there will be many $40,000 homes built. If the middle-class buyer is forced to struggle with the exorbitant costs of the lots, up to $25,000 per one-half acre, a $40,000 house is likely to be out of the question.

In the past it was thought that requiring expensive "improvements" would slow down unneeded development. It is now clear that there is a seller's market at almost any price in times of inflation, particularly when people are convinced that the safest investment is real estate. The more the consumer is "protected" by the requirements for sewers, water systems, long-lasting streets, etc., the more irreversibly the land is converted to development. When population growth forces California to seek proper development, the best of the land will be committed to inefficient, scattered land use.

During a Board of Supervisors' meeting in Sonoma County on July 7, 1970, Supervisor George De Long proposed that a "percentage of completion" clause be added to any agreement with American Leisure Land Company regarding their subdivision request, noting that "many counties in California have been subject to unnatural exploitation, at the expense of the county." Supervisor De Long added that "the land itself and the area around it become nothing more than a prostitute. All you see are real estate offices with flags flapping in the breeze and a few weeds." He asked that 50% of the houses be completed in five years. "If their intentions are honorable, the County can benefit. If not, Jenner could turn into a blighted area."

Chairman Robert Theiller, a former real-estate operator, objected that Mr. De Long's plan would create "difficulties." "Looking at it from years of experience in the real estate business, if you made development contingent upon performance, you may hinder the developer's ability to find investors. No one will invest millions of dollars in what may end up as a sheep ranch."

Supervisor De Long asked, "Whose interest are we championing? The people of Sonoma County, or the ability of the investors to get money? We owe more allegiance to the 204,000 people in this County than to eight or ten people in American Leisure Lands and their financial backers in Eastern cities. . . . If this overburdens Mr. Commings [President of American Leisure Lands] he should say so. If he can't live with this condition, it's all the more reason to impose it."

De Long's proposal was voted down four to one, and the ordinance permitting the subdivision to proceed was approved four to one, with Supervisor De Long dissenting.

In addition to a widened tax base, another tool of persuasion by the developer is the promise of personal pecuniary reward. In Riverside County a large corporate developer recently purchased a ranch in the Garner Valley, a few miles southeast of Idylwild in the San Jacinto Mountains, with a plan for a $50 million, 3,911-lot second home resort subdivision of 10,000 people, with a 140-acre artificial lake (to be closed to the public) and a private eighteen-hole golf course. Original proposals to the county government had been turned down, in part because of objections by the Park Commission and the Planning Director that there was a potentially serious pollution problem because of a unique temperature inversion layer which traps smog. There was legislation pending in the Congress calling for the purchase of the Valley as an addition to the San Bernardino National Forest. And there was opposition from several local citizen groups, including the San Jacinto Mountain Conservation League and the Supervisors.

On July 20, 1971, the Supervisors suddenly reintroduced the question and OK'd the rezoning which would allow development. On the motion of the developer's attorney, no representatives of the Forest Service or the conservationist groups were allowed to testify. One of the Supervisors who switched his vote on the rezoning was previously a vocal opponent who had claimed that if the federal government bought the land and set up a campground, there would be more pollution than would come from development, and in any event he "could not accept" the Forest Service report and studies done by scientists at the University of California at Riverside regarding the air-pollution problems. After the meeting he reportedly assaulted the treasurer of the Conservation League. Subsequent investigation revealed that of the three supervisors who voted for the rezoning, one who was running for reelection to the Board had received $2,500, or 42% of all his campaign funds from the developer; another, running for the Republican nomination to the State Assembly, $750, or 10% of his funds; and a third, the previously vocal opponent of the project, $3,500, or 25%, in his campaign to win the Republican nomination to the U.S. House of Representatives. The money came from the developer through its attorney, in the form of cashier's checks. It is reported that the San Jacinto Mountain Conservation League will seek a grand jury investigation of the matter.

Developers use many techniques to persuade local politicians and officials. One local D.A. was hired by Boise Cascade to handle a water problem in a neighboring county. A county planning director was hired off the public payroll by B.C. midway through a development project. The mayor of a North Coast city is also B.C.'s public relations man for the area, while two of the five-man city council work for B.C. and a third depends upon it for his business. In another area, the B.C. task force patronized the hotel and restaurant of one of the county supervisors, who also received free advertisement in the company newspaper. In another county, the head of a project that had been purchased by B.C. saw fit to take out a $40,000 life-insurance policy from an obscure mid-Western company, through its local agent, one of the county supervisors, while another supervisor was awarded a sizable campaign contribution and yet another was graced by the project's purchase of three automobiles from his local dealership. In another case, a planner is doing master plans for both a developer and for the local public regional planning agency; in another county, a member of the Planning Commission is a licensed B.C. salesman; and in another an engineer who does design work for developments in the area also is a member of the Planning Commission. In one case, the subdivider willingly paid a county official for "overtime" which he had accrued. Trips are a common ploy, and B.C. made a plane available for one former County Supervisor running for statewide office.

The law firm of former Governor Edmund G. "Pat" Brown represents several large developers, including Boise Cascade. Jesse Unruh, 1970 Democratic gubernatorial and "populist" candidate, represents the most notorious developer in the state—"Nat" Mendelsohn, in an effort to bulldoze 25,000 acres of Shasta County mountain land for speculative lot sales.

Once the political problems are worked out, the developer files the necessary information with the State Real Estate Board, secures their go-ahead, and gets local county approval on his project maps and plot. (He is not supposed to engage in any promotional activities prior to the issuance of the state's "public report." We came across several instances which seem a lot like promotion, including the introductory free dinner which B.C. is staging to promote its Lake Wildwood West.) The sell is generally anywhere from gross to subtle—from advertisements showing topless stars pointing to idealized drawings of a lake, with the caption "Get a Lot—While You're Young," to a full-page photograph of Yosemite Falls, with the caption "They Couldn't Give It Away," as a come-on for a B.C. project twenty-six miles distant. The pitch is always recreation-oriented, with additional investment promises. The "lifetime dream," the "little plot of paradise" in "California-land-which-is-going-fast-and-becoming-more-valuable-all-the-time," on which the buyer can always make "a killing" in the future, is adorned with promotional gimmicks that include free dinners, aerial views, free weekends in nearby motels, VIP admission cards, and the promise of being able to flee from the pressure, people, and "problems" of the urban scene. Boise Cascade salesmen pass out a typical "land-is-going" leaflet with the following message:

101,000,000 ACRES

        80%   Government
        10%   Churches, Fellowship, Groups
         5%   Greenbelt, Agriculture
        2.5% Already Developed
        ───────────────────────
        97.5% GONE

        2.5% Left For Development
        2.5% ÷ 20,000,000 People =
        ¼ ACRE PER CALIFORNIAN
        —TODAY—
WHAT'S GOING TO HAPPEN IN 1980?
WHEN WE HAVE 30,000,000 CALIFORNIANS?

Specific advertisements are glowing—and often false. Lots in a subdivision in a "virgin redwood forest opened to the public for the first time," for which the salesman promised the developer would pay "everything," turned out to be a nightmare of costs for the buyer, including a $2,000 lien on his property to pay off $4.5 million of special assessment bonds, liability for a special tax levy of up to ten cents per $100 of assessed value to cover defaults on any lot in the subdivision, another tax to pay off $250,000 in bonds for water and sewage, another not specified and unlimited tax to meet the possible liability of $4 million in general-obligation bonds which could be issued without a vote of the lot owners, and a fifth possible levy to maintain improvements which would be constructed by the project Improvements District.

The State Attorney General's office recently sent a discreet inquiry to B.C. regarding certain assertions it was using in its promotional literature concerning land values. Three months later, B.C. was able to respond about the sources and bases for their claim, documenting only two of eight assertions. One of these was based on an article in *House Beautiful*, written by a "building and real estate consultant"; the other was based on fancy use of outdated statistics of the State Board of Equalization. Three of the assertions were admitted as being false. A sixth was based on an alleged Ford Foundation study which B.C. was unable to identify after three months. A seventh was based on a quote from *Time* magazine, which B.C. had as yet been unable to run down, and the eighth was supposed to have come from the *Wall Street Journal,* but B.C. did not know where. Independently, the investigator from the Attorney

General's office had asked the *Journal* to verify the statement, and the reply came back categorically negative.

Another developer's ads stated that there would be no assessment bonds and that all improvements would be installed and paid for; at the same time, he was planning a $950,000 water district to be paid for by assessing each lot owner approximately $30 to $40 per year for twenty-five years. The state public report said on one page that the buyers must pay for the water system, and on the next that the developer would install it at his own cost. Salesmen testified in the prosecution trial for misleading advertising brought by the local D.A. that buyers weren't always given the report until after they signed for the lot, but if there were questions asked, the latter statement was the answer offered by the salesmen. The developer's project manager privately was insisting that there was no false advertising, since the water system would be paid for *not* by assessments, but by a "fixed lien." Apparently he realized that such arcane legal niceties probably would fail to stimulate a mountain-county jury *or* judge, and so the company pleaded nolo contendere and agreed to put in the water system itself, at a cost of over $980,000. The project manager was put on a two-year suspended sentence, which was later dismissed. When B.C. bought out this development company, the project manager went along with the deal and became a B.C. vice-president. The comment of the prosecuting D.A. in reference to this case and the public report is informative:

> "It's confusing and misleading. The [State] Real Estate Division acts like they're up there to protect the developers instead of regulate them. If a real estate salesman made statements as misleading as those contained in the public report, he would find himself subject to criminal prosecution."

Lake Earl

Just north of Crescent City lies Lake Earl, a fertile, shallow, 5,000-acre saline lake formed by feeder streams and high-tide inundations from the Pacific Ocean. Despite its large size, it is not well suited for boating because of its shallowness and dense plant growth. The plants are essential to the ecology of the lake in providing cover for waterfowl and feeding areas for fish. In September of 1969, the waterfowl population, not including shore birds, was in excess of 12,000, and has been known to be as high as 40,000. Cutthroat trout, silver salmon, sturgeon, and several species of estuarine fishes are also found in the lake, although angling is limited because of legal and physical access. Visitors to Lake Earl find woods and marshes, bush country, deep grasses, beaches, polished rocks, grass-covered dunes, rolling hummocks of shrub, open swales, tiny lagoons and swamp areas, masses of wild roses and other flowers, flat stretches and hillocks crossed by deer and raccoon tracks, and much evidence of Indian campsites in shells, flints, firestones, arrowpoints, and broken bone splinters.

A recreational subdivision of 1,500 lots was put in on the lake, and was at the time of its promotion one of the fastest-selling in the state. There have been no houses built, primarily because provision for sewage was not provided initially, and it is unclear whether the development was sold pursuant to an appropriate permit from the California Department of Real Estate.

In the mid-sixties, a local rancher and real estate speculator named Bliss was involved in a land-acquisition effort all around the lake, picking up approximately 15,000 acres for an average of $100 per acre. He purchased one ranch through a third party, because the owner was loath to let him have the property. He also claimed title to the bed of the lake, although litigation with the state regarding this title has been in the courts for years. Lacking the capital to develop the land himself, he entered into an agreement with an outfit called New Life Crusade (NLC), a Southern Baptist Church organization operating out of Los Angeles and described as a church-related Indiana-based corporation whose "chief purpose is the propagation of religious faith." A reliable confidential informant having access to the financial records of New Life Crusade says that the organization is involved in many land and securities transactions. Under the agreement, Bliss was to acquire all property in the areas needed for successful development, using New Life Crusade money, and was to retain an interest in the profits realized by later resale and development. For 7,300 acres of his property he received $1.5 million and a 25% interest in future profits.

Acting as NLC's agent, he has been able to keep the tax assessments on the land at the level it was when he purchased it. The County Assessor was asked why the land had not been reassessed as subdivided property; he answered: "I've tried to get the Supervisors to raise it, but Bliss has so many friends we didn't get anywhere."

In May of 1969, NLC transferred the property to the Los Angeles Church Loan Company (LACLC), apparently affiliated with the Southern Baptist Group located in Atlanta, Georgia. It was incorporated in 1966, but was inactive until 1969, and had no prior earnings record nor capacity to meet dividends. The address reported for the LACLC is a three-story building which, like NLC, has no listing in the directory, although there is a listing for "Los Angeles Southern Baptist," with three names listed, none of which has been identified as being affiliated with either group. The head of NLC was one of the nine original directors of LACLC, and in their behalf stated that they had acquired the Lake Earl property for "capital gains purposes" and that they proposed to develop the entire property into small lots having fishing and boating rights upon the lake. The reason for the transfer is not altogether clear, though one likely explanation is that the transfer was handled as a loan so as not to result in taxable gain (or threat to tax exemption) for NLC. In any event, the property was transferred to LACLC, which gave a $1,060,000 promissory note (secured by first deed of trust) to Bliss, and a $440,000 promissory note (secured by second deed of trust) to NLC. LACLC is working with the original speculating rancher under the same terms as NLC. Financing for the development was to be raised through the issuance of church bonds, and the LACLC board of directors authorized the issuance of $2 million in bonds; a permit to issue the bonds was filed in mid-1969. However, this idea has been formally abandoned.

LACLC then contracted with "Orange County VTN," a large planning and development firm, for the development of the property under the name of "Bliss Properties Development Company." VTN apparently agreed to pay $1,800 per acre for the land used in development, and has acquired from LACLC a total of 2,800 acres for promissory notes in the amount of $2,800,000. Thus, it appears that LACLC has abandoned the idea of developing the property itself, using proceeds from the sale of bonds, and is now selling the land to the development company as it is to be developed. However, it may still intend to develop the remaining portion itself, using payments on the $2.8

million note to pay off interest on bonds issued at some future date. As yet, no hard cash seems to have changed hands. Unless some equity money or institutional financing is forthcoming, there will probably be loan defaults and the whole structure may collapse.

Yet things are rolling along. VTN has already engaged in preliminary engineering work on the project, and has flown a team of engineers up to the lake. Their plans are to subdivide the property into less-than-one-acre lots, giving unlimited fishing and hunting rights on the lake with the lots. They speak of 15,000 lots to be available on one portion of the overall potential acreage of anywhere from 7,300 to 15,000 acres, including a golf course, industrial development, and shopping centers. Conservation groups, federal and state agencies, especially the California Department of Fish and Game, agree that development of the Lake Earl area would be disastrous to its vegetation and wildlife. "Any major disruption of the vegetation," claims the Department's Regional Manager, would result in mass movement of sand, the creation of drainage problems, and a "general deterioration of the environmental and aesthetic values of the area." The U.S. Department of the Interior gave the area high priority as a possible National Wildlife Refuge. The lake was being considered for inclusion in the state's Protected Waterways Program.

The Nature Conservancy has attempted to purchase the property around Lake Earl from LACLC for about twice the amount the church group paid to Bliss, but the LACLC rejected the offer, offering only 7,000 acres for sale at more than $7 million for the package, which is approximately ten times what Bliss initially paid for the land.

Morrison Creek

The Morrison Creek Stream Group Basin consists of some 192 square miles in south-central Sacramento County. The upper portion of the basin is rapidly becoming urbanized, but the valuable lower portion is still undeveloped. In the southwestern Beach Lake-Stone Lake area, one finds a series of natural valley lakes connected with tree-lined waterways and surrounded by rare permanent marshland, lush meadows, and agricultural cropland. These resources provide valuable wildlife habitat, natural drainage, and outdoor recreation. Once common in the Central Valley, such natural areas are fast disappearing under the onslaught of developers.

The Beach-Stone Lakes area serves as valuable habitat for such resident game birds as pheasant and quail. It is the home of more than 100 species of nongame birds including the relatively rare white-tailed kite and the sandhill crane. Many of these native species require substantial contiguous habitat area. They are joined by a variety of valuable fur-bearing mammals, including muskrat, weasel, mink, raccoon, beaver, gray fox, and one of the largest populations of river otter in the Sacramento Valley.

In the late 1950s, the city of Sacramento was pushing out beyond its southern borders into this area despite certain flood and drainage problems. An early subdivision had brought the problems to the attention of the county, which began to require subsequent developers to dike off and drain their properties. Proposals were eventually made to create a master drainage plan for the entire area, and the Army Corps of Engineers met with various neighborhood and civic groups to discuss the possibility of a Corps drainage study and project. Planning and construction-prevention facilities before development would save time and money in the future. The Corps proceeded to secure Congressional authority in mid-1963 to conduct a study of flood control for the Morrison Creek Basin.

At about this same time the McKeon Construction Company, a large land developer and builder in the Sacramento area, acquired the large Elliott Ranch in the Beach Lake and Stone Lake area, a key portion of the area that would be benefited by the Corps project. With a volume of $65.5 million in construction in 1969, the McKeon Company is ranked by *Professional Builder* magazine as twenty-fifth in the top 252 construction companies in the country, described as "the fastest growing building company on the North American continent." One of McKeon's specialties, "fourplex" dwelling units, which he has peppered all over the Sacramento area, are said by the magazine to be "the hottest sales success on the West Coast."

The Elliott Ranch had been used primarily for grazing, but was taxed as potential subdivision land subsequent to purchase. In 1965, McKeon was able to convince the County Board of Supervisors, sitting as the Board of Tax

Appeal, to reclassify the land as a long-term, exclusively agricultural area, under a county agricultural preserve plan. He thus secured a zoning classification which permitted only one house per eighty acres, declared the land floodable, and secured a sizable tax assessment cut on the land. This reclassification was in keeping with the 1965 Sacramento County General Plan, which designated the area on which the ranch was situated as a permanent, exclusive agricultural-recreation reserve. At the time, the topography and drainage of the area made it unsuited for development, but quite valuable as open space and as a wildlife-recreational area. In spite of this designation by the County General Plan and by the Board of Supervisors, the federal Corps of Engineers in its study and proposal of March, 1969, projected urban development into the area, saying the staff recognized the need for urban growth and had chosen this site because it was nearest to Sacramento. A 1968 report by the Sacramento Regional Area Planning Commission (published during the period of the Corps's study) pointed out that within the presently urbanized portion of the Sacramento region there was already enough vacant land to accommodate all anticipated growth through 1990. Approximately 60,000 acres that had been bypassed by urban development had little or no potential for agriculture or wildlife and should be utilized as urban tax-producing properties in place of the agricultural areas currently being destroyed. Nevertheless, the Corps justified its intentions on the basis of a letter written to the Corps by one of the County Supervisors, without the knowledge, approval, or concurrence of either the Board of Supervisors or the County Planning Commission, stating that it was "the intent of Sacramento County to zone lands in the Beach-Stone Lakes area to permit recreation-oriented urban development." The Corps apparently did not recognize that such major alterations of the General Plan could only be made by the entire Board of Supervisors, after full and adequate public hearing.

In any event, the Corps in March of 1969 revealed its plan for a $55.6 million project providing flood control and drainage facilities for about 190 square miles of land, including such structures as an 11,000 acre-foot reservoir and extensive levee and channel improvements. The Corps announced that the project had a benefit-cost ratio of 1.3 to 1. One-third of the project benefits would be drawn from flood-control measures in the creek channels in the urbanizing northern part of the basin, the remaining two-thirds from drainage and reclamation of the sloughs and marshlands in the Beach-Stone Lakes area in the southern part of the project.* The project was at this point supported by the Bureau of Reclamation, the State Department of Water Resources, the County Board of Supervisors, and the Sacramento City Council. Opposition came from the California Wildlife Federation, the Audubon Society, and the Sierra Club. The State Department of Fish and Game also expressed concern over the "lack of any provision to replace wildlife value in the area."

The criticism of the conservationists centered on the destruction of the "most productive wildlife habitats remaining in the Central Valley," the conflict with the County Master Plan and the Regional Planning Commission, and the use of land enhancement to justify costs when this meant a windfall, at great public expense, to "a handful of large property owners, speculators and landgrabbers," a windfall to the tune of $57 million to "these lucky property owners." Benefits from "land enhancement" represented *two-thirds* of the projected benefits of the Corps project. The Corps estimated that the land values of certain areas of "reclamation" would increase from an average of $620 to $6,200 per acre. By far the largest property concerned was the developer-owner of the former Elliott Ranch, the McKeon Construction Company.

The conservationists hit hard at this "land-enhancement" justification, and at the failure of the payment method to require the landholder who would profit so greatly to pay an equitable share of those project costs. Of the $55.6 million in construction costs, local government, the state, and Sacramento County would have to pay approximately $125.8 million. The county would have to pay all maintenance costs, more than half a million annually in perpetuity. Around this time, a bill was introduced into the State Senate which would limit the state share to costs associated

---

* The Corps "creates" benefits by pointing to the flood protection that a dam will provide to flood-plain residents. This justifies the project, which then encourages more development in the flood plain, which then requires more flood protection, which then requires more dams, and so on. By this logic, the *highest* benefit-cost ratio can be obtained by developing precisely those areas *most* susceptible to floods.

with flood control, rather than land-enhancement features of such projects. The conservationists supported the bill, hailing the fact that it would shift costs from the state to the local interests, and went beyond the bill to comment that at the local level it should be specially created local improvement districts, and not an entire county, which should have to assess and raise the local contributions to pay for such land-enhancement costs. This would shift the cost from the general taxpaying public to those in the area who would directly benefit. Opposed to the bill was the powerful County Supervisors Association of California, which had been instrumental in securing the establishment of the partnership formula whereby the state would pick up, out of State General Fund monies, the nonfederal share of flood-control project costs. The chairman of the association was a close friend of Mr. McKeon. The bill was defeated. In the 1970 session, a similar bill was introduced in the Senate, this time limiting the state's share to one-half of land enhancement costs of flood control projects. This bill was also defeated.

The local Corps hesitated, and in December of 1969 it proposed an alternative: the floodable parts of the Elliott Ranch would continue to flood, and the land would be left in its present state with much of the recreational, wildlife, ecological, and aesthetic values intact.

However, McKeon was not taking any chances. Faced with the possibility of having much of his land purchased in fee by the state, at a value determined by its zoned use as agricultural-recreation, he began asserting that nobody would come up with the money for "the frills" planned in the Corps's project. He noted that the county was considering the possibility of requiring that lands placed under exclusive agricultural zoning in order to obtain lower tax assessments—as his was—be left in those zones for a minimum of twenty years. Stating that he did not want to be so "locked in," he undertook to get out of the tax-break zoning. He applied to the County Planning Commission to change zones to one which would permit him to build one dwelling structure on every two acres of land, as opposed to the one-per-eighty-acres of the tax-break zoning. His architects then revealed his plan for the area, which included high-density apartment complexes, condominiums, shopping centers, and the like. The Planning Commission turned down the plan on the grounds that it was opposed to the

Master Plan of the County and of the Regional Area Planning Commission, that built in a flood-prone area it would endanger residents as well as the Corps flood-control project. Rezoning would have raised the cost of the land to the state nearly tenfold, making implementation of the whole Corps project completely impractical.

Yet three members of the Sacramento County Board of Supervisors overrode the Planning Commission on appeal, granting the rezoning of the Elliott Ranch. The action was taken without hearing the Planning Commission report that rejected the rezoning, without an explanation of the rejection by the Planning Director, and without the voices of community opponents, including the Sierra Club, the Audubon Society, and the California Wildlife Federation. Two of the three Supervisors voting with McKeon were lame ducks. The Planning Commission voted to go on record in opposition (three yeas, one nay, and one abstention) to the Supervisors' actions and argued for a public hearing. Said one of the Planning Commissioners:

> By four to one this Commission denied the application. What discourages me is the democratic process that did not occur [at the Supervisors' meeting]. The staff was not even consulted. I get the feeling it was a complete railroad. It's very discouraging. The rezoning is a rollback of AG [exclusive agricultural] zoning and it destroys the Morrison Creek drainage plan. The public didn't even get a chance to be heard.

If the Corps project *is* authorized, and monies appropriated for it, the developer stands to make a 1,000% profit. If it is not authorized, he will be able to develop the land into high-density proportions, probably with the usual "recreational-community" tag. Only the people of the area in legitimate need of flood control, the people of the state suffering from tax burdens, and the wildlife retreating before urbanization stand to lose.

Access

Of the 1,072 miles of California coast, only 356 miles are publicly owned and accessible for recreation. Another 55 miles are publicly owned for exclusive uses (military bases). Of the 1,072 miles, only 290 are beaches suitable for swimming. Only 90 of these miles are publicly owned, and most of this (53 miles) is held in military bases.

Sea Ranch

In California, all tidelands from the mean high tide line (the "driftwood line") on out are state property. The problem is how to get to these tidelands when most or all of the property fronting on them is in private hands.

The California State Constitution provides as follows in Article XV, Section 2:

> Section 2—People Shall Always Have Access to Navigable Waters
>
> No individual, partnership, or corporation claiming or possessing the frontage or tidal lands of a harbor, bay, inlet, estuary, or other navigable water in this State, shall be permitted to exclude the right of way to such water whenever it is required for any public purpose, nor to destroy or obstruct free navigation of such water; and the Legislature shall enact such laws as will give *the most liberal construction* to this provision, so that *access to the navigable waters of this State shall be always attainable for the people therof* [emphasis added].

Although this provision would appear to be a clear mandate for access to public tidelands, the details for providing access have never been spelled out by the legislature and the section has never been implemented. The phrase "right of way" is susceptible to interpretation as requiring an easement through private property, but there are no cases or statutes on point.

Private owners of land fronting on state-owned tidelands have always been able to deny access across their property. The Sea Ranch, a second-home development fronting on between 10.5 and 14 miles of coast (depending on whose figures one accepts) in Sonoma County, is distinctive because a lack of access touched off a battle whose repercussions are still being felt.

Oceanic Properties, a subsidiary of Castle & Cooke, bought the land—approximately 5,200 acres—in mid-1964. The original use permit granted by the county for the development of the first third of the subdivision stated that the developers would submit plans for "designated area or areas for the purpose of public access to the ocean. . . ." No access was provided, however, during the development of the first third of Sea Ranch.

In January of 1968, Sea Ranch officials met over lunch with four of the five members of the Sonoma County Board of Supervisors. Although California's Brown Act prohibits the transaction of public business in private, two of the Supervisors told reporters that they had reached a "general agreement" with the Sea Ranch officials as to a development plan, and that the agreement covered the question of access. The two other Supervisors present, apparently more familiar with the Brown Act, denied this. One stated that no general agreement had been reached regarding Sea Ranch's development plan; the other denied the existence of a plan.

Sea Ranch's plan for implementing the original promise to provide access was to offer approximately 100 acres at the end of the ranch to the county for development as a park. In return, the 10.5 to 14 miles of coast within the development would be allowed to remain totally private and inaccessible to the public. The lure of exclusivity was one of Sea Ranch's main selling points:

> You'll find relief here from the daily crush of people. The Sea Ranch is a private development, for the exclusive use of Sea Ranch residents and their guests. Access is guarded by a full-time security patrol.[1]

The County Planning Department recommended accepting Sea Ranch's offer, rejecting contentions that Sea Ranch had implicitly agreed to provide further access. Already citizens were becoming aroused over the prospective blocking of access through the development. By March, 1968, the County Planning Commission had received 1,700 letters on the subject, 1,400 of which opposed the Sea Ranch proposal. Nevertheless, the Planning Commission followed the recommendation of its Planning Department and approved the Sea Ranch proposal, passing it on to the County Board of Supervisors.

In early April, opponents of the plan filed an appeal with the Sonoma County Board of Supervisors opposing the grant of the use permit to Sea Ranch by the Planning Department. The Supervisors rejected this appeal by a vote of 4-1.

In May, opponents of Sea Ranch's proposal founded Citizens Organized to Acquire Access to State Tidelands (COAAST) and announced their intention to gather signatures to get a referendum concerning access on the ballot— to establish a county policy on access. Briefly, the proposed policy would have required the designation of "public access corridors to publicly owned tidelands" as a condition to

approval of development of coastal lands "for more intensive non-agricultural use." The corridors would be required
to be placed in "natural terrain features" (arroyos, ravines,
etc.) in a manner that would allow access to all publicly
owned tidelands; the petition specified that in any case the
corridors should be no further than one mile apart. The
policy would apply to Sea Ranch since its use permit provided that any county policy on access adapted within one
year would apply retroactively.

The Supervisors were upset by this attempt to take the
issue to the people. One called the initiative "the stupidest
thing I ever heard of." Another characterized it as "sub-
version."

During the course of the signature campaign by
COAAST, the Supervisors publicly hinted that they might
begin legal action to keep the initiative off the ballot, but by
the middle of August, COAAST had gathered 9,158 valid
signatures (only 6,342 were needed).

The Supervisors, however, still had one card up their
sleeve. On September 3, they announced their refusal to
place the initiative on the ballot. This decision, they stated,
was based on the County Counsel's finding that the initiative was "not a proper subject for an initiative petition."
With the election barely two months away (COAAST
wished to have the referendum on the regular November
ballot to avoid the expense of a special election), COAAST
was forced to seek court action. COAAST was able to
appeal directly to the California Supreme Court and in less
than two weeks obtain a decree that the referendum was
appropriate for initiative and must be placed on the ballot.

The initiative then became known as Proposition B.
Immediately after the court order, Joseph McClelland,
director of the Sea Ranch project, announced the formation
of an organization to fight Proposition B. The organization
was named Citizens Committee for Preservation of Property and Conservation Together, or PPACT.

For the next month and a half, the citizens of Sonoma
County were subjected to a barrage of propaganda from
PPACT. An estimated $50,000 was spent by Oceanic
Properties during this period for advertising, including full-
page ads in all the local newspapers, numerous television
commercials, letters to all those who had signed the original
petition, and a PPACT beach party with free refreshments.
COAAST, on the other hand, forced to rely on volunteer

action, spent approximately $2,300. The local newspapers eventually opposed Proposition B. One editorial in the Sebastopol *Times* attributed the support for Proposition B to that favorite whipping boy of our times, "a vociferous group of students and their professors."

Three basic arguments were used against Proposition B in paid advertising by PPACT, in newspaper editorials, and on the ballot itself (each side was allowed space on the ballot to present its case). The first argument was that the proposed access policy would create a burden on the taxpayers because of the cost of acquiring the access corridors (although compensation would not be required if the dedication of such corridors were required as a condition to the granting of a zoning change or use permit as the proposed policy specified).

The second argument was that there was little beach available along the Sea Ranch coast, it being mostly steep cliffs, and that therefore the policy would in effect create "alleys to nowhere." However, a county planning report had estimated that there were six usable beaches in the developed one-third of Sea Ranch alone. Furthermore, the Sea Ranch advertisements in the San Francisco papers attempted to give the potential buyer an entirely different picture than the PPACT ads gave the Sonoma County voter:

> "Great white beaches and coves to explore. . . ."
> ". . . the loveliest stretch of unspoiled north coast."
> ". . . every Sea Ranch resident will have *free and equal access to the shore* [emphasis added]."

Cartoons appearing in the local PPACT ads and in newspaper editorials depicted a distraught family in a car filled with beach paraphernalia peering over a steep cliff at the end of one such "alley."

The third argument stated that there were two studies in the state legislature regarding access to and acquisition of beaches; "definitive legislation" was expected by mid-1968, and therefore any "hasty" action now might frustrate these studies. What could be more "hasty" and likely to frustrate these studies than the approval of private control over 10.5 to 14 miles of state-owned tidelands is difficult to imagine. Furthermore, there was no real indication that the two studies would lead to definitive legislation any more than had past studies. The only significant coastal legislation that has been passed since 1968 is a bill inspired by the Sea Ranch debacle.

The week of the election, a full-page ad by PPACT appeared in a number of newspapers. The ad carried the headline, "Look Who's NO on 'B'." Among those prominently listed as being anti-B was Assemblyman Willie Brown; the next day he retracted his statement and explained that he had been misinformed on the issue. Leading the list of those claimed to be anti-B were N. B. Livermore, Jr., State Secretary for Resources, and William P. Mott, Jr., director of the State Department of Parks and Recreation. Actually Livermore and Mott never took a position on Proposition B, choosing to skirt the issue and release a highly equivocal joint statement supporting access and calling for more planning. The statement was an attempt to please everyone; it was used misleadingly by PPACT, which quoted only the part that made Livermore and Mott appear to be against Proposition B. (Although Livermore was unwilling to take a stand at the time and in fact became an unwitting ally of PPACT, he was quick to bemoan the loss of access at Sea Ranch after the fact. In May of this year, a magazine article portraying Livermore as the "Protector of the Environment" quoted him as follows on the subject of coastal access: "No real estate development such as Sea Ranch which takes 12 miles of ocean front should be permitted unless it provides for public use.")

A twenty to one expenditure advantage for PPACT, misleading advertising, and the appeal of a "we're for access too (but not this way)" argument resulted in a narrow (approximately 55% to 45%) defeat for Proposition B. The county then accepted Sea Ranch's original offer and approved development of the remaining land therein with no access. Today, access to all the tidelands on which Sea Ranch fronts is denied to the public. Sonoma County eventually established a policy on coastal access, but not in time to apply it to Sea Ranch. PPACT was never heard from again and, needless to say, 1969 did not bring the promised definitive coastal legislation. Nor for that mattter did 1970 or 1971 or 1972.

The only significant legislative development of the past two years concerning the coast is a bill originally inspired by the loss of access at Sea Ranch. In February of 1968,

Assemblyman John Dunlap (D-Napa) introduced an access bill and a resolution requesting that the Sonoma County Board of Supervisors not act without requiring access. Both the bill and the resolution were defeated. At the meeting of the Assembly Subcommittee on Conservation and Beaches at which these measures were considered, both the president of Sea Ranch and an attorney for Oceanic Properties appeared to testify against the bill and the resolution. The attorney opposed the resolution on the grounds that the Sea Ranch development was an "accomplished fact," a rather tenuous argument considering that at that time (April 1968) the grant of Sea Ranch's use permit was not final and no construction had begun on the remaining two-thirds of the development. Assemblyman Dunlap persisted and introduced substantially the same beach-access bill in 1969, where it again was killed in the Senate Business and Professions Committee, a common graveyard for bills passed by the Assembly.

However, in 1970, on his third attempt, Assemblyman Dunlap gained passage of his access bill. The bill, labelled AB 493, prohibits any city or county from approving a subdivision map for a subdivision fronting on the ocean if it does not provide or have available reasonable public access. Access must be by fee or easement from public highways to land below the ordinary high-water mark on any ocean coastline.

One limitation of the bill is that it does nothing to provide access through now existing subdivisions. Thus, developments such as Sea Ranch may continue to exclude the public from state-owned tidelands.

To examine the extent to which this prospective law (and prospective planning) has been rendered moot by previous commitment, we surveyed a portion of California's North Coast. We took a fifty-mile stretch of coastline well north of San Francisco. Starting at Dillon Beach in north Marin County we surveyed up through almost all of Sonoma County to just north of Del Mar Point. The coast appears as follows as one moves northward:

1. Three and one-half miles of recreational second-home development one to two miles into shore
2. Three-fourths of a mile undeveloped
3. One and one-half miles of recreational second-home development one mile into shore

4. One-half mile undeveloped
5. Fifteen miles of recreational second-home development three-fourths of a mile into shore
6. Four miles undeveloped *
7. Three-fourths of a mile recreational second-home development one mile into shore
8. One mile undeveloped
9. Six miles recreational second-home development one to three miles into shore
10. Seven miles undeveloped
11. Three miles recreational second-home development one to three miles into shore
12. Three miles undeveloped
13. Three miles recreational second-home development one mile into shore
14. Five miles undeveloped
15. Ten and one-half miles recreational second-home development one mile into shore.

Although the survey area was picked arbitrarily, only 21.25 miles of the 50-mile stretch is undeveloped, and only one of the undeveloped portions is publicly owned. All but one of these developed stretches has been begun *since* 1965. Two of the largest stretches (10 and 14 above) are owned by elderly persons whose heirs have told us they intend to sell to prospective developers—second-home recreational.

Dunlap's bill makes no specific requirements, but uses the word "reasonable" in several places, leaving the city or county to determine what is reasonable. Dunlap's original approach was to require access at least every 2.5 miles, but the opposition of powerful development interests made passage of such a bill impossible.

Recognizing that commercial threats to California's coast required special protection, the State Office of Planning began studies in 1963. In late 1964, a California Advisory Commission on Ocean Resources (originally called CACOR, and later CACOR-I) was appointed. This body held six meetings over the course of two years and made numerous recommendations, none of which it had the power to implement. The result of this Commission was the subsequent appointment of a second such Commission

---

* This is Bodega Head, and the total coastline mileage expands to eight miles if one includes the irregular extension out into the ocean.

(CACOR-II) which held three meetings during 1967. Pointing to administrative fragmentation, their prime recommendation was the formation of an Interagency Council for Ocean Resources (ICOR), chaired by the Lieutenant Governor and consisting of the top official in each state agency concerned with marine and coastal affairs. This would create a responsive body to which recommendations could be passed.

As well as being the last year of the CACORs, 1967 marked the completion of a legislative study on marine and coastal problems.[2] The report of the Subcommittee on Marine Resources noted the need for a "comprehensive State policy and program" and recommended the formation of two bodies to meet this need: an Interagency Council on Ocean Resources (the same ICOR recommended by the CACORs) and an advisory commission (strikingly similar to the two CACORs).

Late in 1967, these recommendations were implemented in part through the Marine Resources Conservation and Development Act of 1967. This Act called upon the Governor to develop the California Comprehensive Ocean Area Plan (COAP) in order to accomplish "the policy of the State of California to develop, encourage, and maintain a comprehensive, coordinate state plan for the orderly, long-range conservation and development of marine and coastal resources which will insure their wise multiple use in the total public interest." Although the Act did not specify who (other than the Governor) would create the plan, it did create the California Advisory Commission on Marine and Coastal Resources (CMC) to review the COAP and to make recommendations and changes in the plan if needed. The CMC was in effect the successor to the CACORs. The sum of $60,000 was requested to be divided between the CMC and the agencies which were to initiate the development of the COAP. This sum was subsequently reduced to $35,000 by Governor Reagan, indicating the degree of priority that coastal planning enjoys in Sacramento.

Furthermore, this thirty-five-man advisory committee (CMC) includes representatives of Chevron Oil, Lockheed Aircraft, Ralston Purina, PG&E, Dillingham Corporation, Kaiser Refractories, General Motors, North American Rockwell, Todd Shipyards, and Bechtel. There was only one ecologist.

The ICOR, established in 1967 by an executive order,

was charged with designing and producing the plan that the CMC was to review. Almost two years passed before any work on the plan began. Not only was the CMC not appointed until the spring of 1968, but the ICOR was almost totally inactive during and immediately after the 1968 election because of the activities of its members and the change in Lieutenant Governors (chairmen of ICOR). In an attempt to alleviate the additional problem of a shortage of funds, the also meagerly-budgeted CMC loaned the ICOR its staff and funds during a part of this period of almost two years. The situation deteriorated to the point where in 1969, the Legislative Analyst recommended the CMC on the grounds that it wasn't accomplishing anything.*

On the point of dissolution in 1969, the CMC was able to convince the Legislative Analyst to reverse his position, with the result that separate staffs and funds for the CMC and ICOR were approved by the legislature. The ICOR was somewhat reactivated, relying in part on work done by an interim Ocean Area Task Force of the Resources Agency.

Under the Governor's Reorganization Act #2, the ICOR has been transferred from the Lieutenant Governor's office to the newly created Department of Navigation and Ocean Development (NOD). Governor Reagan wants NOD to be the agency charged with the implementation of the Comprehensive Ocean Area Plan (COAP). However, as presently constituted, NOD does not have authority over a number of areas essential to overall responsibility for the coastline, including fish and wildlife (presently under the auspices of the Department of Fish and Game), mineral resources (the State Lands Commission), and state-owned lands in the coastal areas (also under the State Lands Commission). Furthermore, many conservationists feel that NOD, formerly the Department of Harbors and Watercraft, is too oriented toward development and steeped with conflict of interest to consider adequately the need for conservation in coastal areas. None of Governor Reagan's original appointees to the NOD Commission (which is advisory to the Department) were conservationists; included among the

* Originally the CMC was expected to have a comprehensive report ready for the 1969 legislative session. Instead, it issued an apologia for not having been able to get anything started.

seven, however, were representatives from such corporations as PG&E and General Motors.

One might well wonder whether any significant legislation or policy changes have or will result from this bowl of bureaucratic alphabet soup—CACOR-I, CACOR-II, CMC, ICOR, COAP, NOD, etc. The ICOR itself has noted the possibility that its 1972 report may be only "an outline or design of a project still to be done." In fact, it can hardly hope to be more without some new legislation either creating an agency with strong powers over the coastline or by delegating these powers to a currently operating agency.

Thus far, legislative attempts in this direction have met with no success. SB 371 in the Senate and AB 640 and AB 730 in the Assembly—legislative attempts to create a commission with real control over the coast—never got off the ground. These bills would have given such a commission the power to halt, pending the implementation of a state planning mechanism, any development that would cause irreversible damage to an area of the coast. Needless to say, this concept is not well received by the land development interests; these groups quite naturally prefer commissions whose only duty is to "study" the problem and recommend the formation of new groups to do the same.

One bill, AB 2131, was passed by the Assembly and died in the Senate Government Operations Committee. This mild bill would merely have declared legislative intent and the terms of control over coastal development. It was probably invalid and unworkable (vague, and without separate financing, meaningful sanctions, standards, or even jurisdiction). It even called for a considerable degree of local control, the developer's best friend.

In the meantime, the uncontrolled building of private subdivisions and marinas, drilling for offshore oil, construction of power plants, building of highways, etc., seem destined to continue, with access loss, degradation, and cost borne by the public.

Endangered Wildlife

Future development portends the destruction of the last remaining breeding or feeding grounds for many species—upon which other species depend for survival.

A detailed study of one area affected by development

was released on February 4, 1971. It was conducted by the Tahoe Regional Planning Agency. It revealed the following dangers to wildlife in the Tahoe basin: land grading, paving, surface-soil compaction, land clearing, noise, movement, climate, insects and disease, use of chemicals, and controlled burning. Among those species that have not adapted to these changes nearby are: three species of deer; the mountain lion; the black bear; raccoon, fox, weasel, wolverine, marten, beaver and mink; waterfowl, including ducks, geese, coot, snipe, and heron; upland game birds, including quail, grouse, dove, and pigeon. Most disturbing of all, the Agency predicted the "imminent extinction" of eleven species: fisher, marten, wolverine, pileated woodpecker, golden and bald eagles, prairie and peregrine falcons, osprey, Washoe chipmunk and spotted rat.

At present, twenty-four native California animals are on the federal endangered-species list. One hundred and twenty-nine wildlife forms are believed to be in dangerously short supply in California.

The federal government has regulatory jurisdiction for migratory waterfowl and the bald eagle only. Otherwise, the regulation and protection of California's game and nongame species rests with the state. Naturally, federal and local policies pertaining to land acquisition and use will indirectly affect wildlife, but four state regulatory agencies are directly charged with their protection: the State Fish and Game Commission, the Department of Fish and Game, the Wildlife Conservation Board, and the Marine Resources Committee.

The Fish and Game Commission consists of five members appointed by the governor. It is established by Article IV, section 20 of the State Constitution. Its policies guide the Department of 1,300 employees. The powers of the Commission are delegated specifically by the legislature pursuant to § 20 and are contained in the Fish and Game Code.

Although the Department administers several specific funds and bonds,* it is primarily a special fund-financed agency through the Fish and Game Preservation Fund. In 1970–71, the Department spent $22,018,553; $17,389,806 was from this Fund, while another $2,187,825 came from

* E.g., Wildlife Restoration Fund, State Recreation and Fish and Wildlife Enhancement Bond Act of 1970, etc.

federal funds. The source of the Preservation Fund and the lifeblood of the agency is the sale of hunting and fishing licenses, court fines (e.g., for fishing without a license), and commercial fish taxes. The special funding source gives the Department an automatic bias which precludes its preserving wildlife in any balanced manner. Its bias is reflected in its legal authority, manpower allocation, operations, and appointees to the guiding Commission. Over one-fifth (270) of the employees are fish and game wardens. Thus, more inspectors are on the job collecting $5 fines for the Department than the State Water Quality Control Board has policing water pollution throughout the state. The majority of the rest are involved in breeding stock and hatchery operations to maintain an adequate supply of animals and fish favored by sportsmen.

The bland *California Journal* recently remarked: "Historically, sportsmen have been California's most vocal wildlife management constituency, a situation undoubtedly reflective of the fact that sportsmen pay the major portion of the bill for the State's wildlife management functions." These sportsmen's groups are organized in the California Wildlife Federation, which includes fourteen different specific organizations and many clubs.

Control is exercised not only through lobbying and financing but through direct participation as decision-makers. Although the Department's director, Ray Arnett, is the former public-relations man for Richfield Oil Company, the *California Journal* notes that "the active decision-makers, legislators, and members of the Fish and Game Commission are frequently sportsmen themselves. . . . The hunting and fishing clubs have carefully preserved a decision-making structure which encourages legislative intervention whenever a public agency's actions fall short of achieving uniform acceptance."

The bias of the Department of Fish and Game (DFG) is reflected not only in ignoring nongame animals or general environment but in direct policies towards predators. Hence, March of 1971 saw the DFG authorize liberal hunting of the mountain lion. The mountain lion (or puma or cougar) is down to an estimated 600 in number. DFG policy and state law generally allow unlimited hunting of "predators." But the 1969 legislature had reclassified the mountain lion as a game animal so that its hunting could be restricted. The Department responded by opening a five-month hunting season on the endangered species. The effect of the mountain lion's elimination is not only more licenses and more hunting of the animal itself, but fewer predators and more deer for hunters to kill "in order to preserve the ecology of the species because of the lack of natural predators." The Department did ban certain areas from hunting, but Department staff admit that these provisions are designed to head off a bill to ban lion hunting and to forbid the use of dogs in lion hunting. After the bill's defeat, these restricted areas can be opened up.

The major agency charged with wildlife protection is a sports agency financially dependent upon and controlled by sports interests demanding lots of game fish, game birds, and game animals. There is little sympathy for fish species that don't make the reels whine, or for nature's predators. Indeed, there is a strong interest in eliminating predators. Without them, sportsmen can claim that killing is needed "for the good of the animal" to prevent overpopulation, exhaustion of food supply, and then mass starvation. The answer, however, is not forced hunting but the protection and resupply of nature's own predators.

The emphasis of the Department has not even been on maintaining a healthy environment for game species. The approach is on massive breeding in hopes that many will survive to reach man's hooks and bullets. There are some exceptions to this emphasis, but their nature illustrates the imbalance. The two major exceptions include $66,000 being spent for research into toxicity and biostimulation (from the Water Resources Control Board), and $103,000 to study trout genetics, shellfish laboratory staffing, *and* "pesticides in marine species." This is well under one percent of the Department's budget. The Department had been conducting a Delta Fish and Wildlife Protective Study, financed by the Department of Water Resources. Theoretically, the Department must also abide by the Environmental Quality Act of 1970 and prepare impact reports on its own projects. But the Department's studies are generally conducted when there is a highly visible die-off of or danger to a sport or commercial animal. These studies are strictly "advisory," whether commissioned by the Department of Water Resources or the Public Utilities Commission.

In July of 1968 the Department of Fish and Game did start a program to determine the fate of the 129 endangered wildlife forms, many of them nongame animals—and some of them even predators. The federal government provides some funds. Nevertheless, all 1970–71 expenditures totalled $82,000, less than one-half of one percent of the total Department budget. Even as a public-relations gesture, the program's future is uncertain. The *California Journal* remarks: ". . . the long-term political future of this program may be dependent upon the development of a reliable source of non-sport funding."

The third and fourth state government agencies theoretically responsible directly for wildlife health are the Wildlife Conservation Board and the Marine Resources Committee—both extremely minor forces. The Board has a total budget for 1971–72 of $121,951. The Committee has $227,400. The Board's functions are specialized and even more sports-oriented than those of the Department of Fish and Game. The Board is to "acquire areas to sustain wildlife, provide recreation and furnish public access to lands or waters for fishing, hunting and shooting." The Legislative Analyst comments: "Most of the money expended by the board, although nominally General Fund money, has gone for the direct benefit of hunters and fishermen."

The Marine Resources Committee is even less "environment-oriented." Its purpose is to finance "research in the development of commercial fisheries. . . ." Moreover, of its nine members appointed by the governor, five *must* be engaged in the canning or "reduction" of fish. Once again, taxpayers are subsidizing private interests.

5

Wild Areas,
II: Industrial Threats

Logging

Of California's 100 million acres, 42 million are forest land. Sixteen different species of pine grow in California, including: bristlecone pines, some specimens of which are the oldest living organisms known; Torrey pines, which number only in the thousands; and Monterey, ponderosa, sugar, Jeffrey, and Coulter pines. Living along with the pines in "mixed" forests are white firs, red firs, Santa Lucia firs, and Douglas firs. The largest natural stands of coast redwood and giant sequoia in the world are in California. Cedars, junipers, spruces, hemlocks, willows, poplars, maples, alders, birch, cypress, and oaks grow in considerable abundance and variety within the state.

More than half of the state's forest land—some twenty-five million acres—is valuable primarily as park or wilderness land. The other seventeen million acres are valuable as *commercial* forest land. On a map, California's commercial forest lands form a giant arch over the northern half of the state. Following the Pacific Coast northward, the belt begins in the second-growth redwood forests of the Santa Cruz mountains just below San Francisco. Above the Bay Area, the North Coastal region, consisting of northern Sonoma, Mendocino, Humboldt, and Del Norte counties, contains the most productive forest land in the state, perhaps in the world. In this area, generous rainfall, a mild, steady climate, and rich soil combine to produce extensive stands of valuable timber, mostly coast redwood and Douglas fir.

Along the northern border of the state is an area of dense pine and fir forests, which extends down the state's eastern border along the lower elevations of the Sierra Nevada. California produces more lumber than any state in the nation except Oregon and Washington.

Slightly over half of California's 17 million acres of commercial forest land is publicly owned. The remaining 8.2 million acres—including virtually all of the rich redwood and Douglas fir stands of the North Coastal region—are owned privately.

Damage

A great deal of public attention has recently been directed at the damage done to forests by the logging industry. But unfortunately, the bulk of public criticism has centered around a single issue—"clear-cutting" *vs.* selective logging—instead of larger ecological considerations.

"Clear-cutting" removes all the trees from a given area, leaving the desolate vista of charred stumps and gashed soil that is photographed by conservationists and news media to illustrate the evils of logging. Clear-cutting does denude and deface the land, but ugliness is not a critical factor in the delicate ecological balance, and although the question is in dispute, many believe that clear-cutting is necessary for certain species of trees. Redwoods and Douglas firs need a great deal of light and may not grow when shaded by an overstory; their seeds germinate only in "mineral soil" —soil that has been somewhat disturbed. Clear-cutting—logging or burning all the trees in a Douglas fir or redwood grove, leaving only a few seed trees to start the next generation—may facilitate the survival of these species.

Selective logging, on the other hand, is clearly appropriate for shade-tolerant trees such as grand fir, white fir, and hemlock, and involves cutting only a few of the largest and most (commercially) valuable trees.

Categorical criticism of any and all clear-cutting, although popular with emotional conservationists, is simplistic, gives the loggers an excuse for righteous indignation, and deflects public attention from the more substantial harm that is being done by the logging industry. The real issues are: the clearing of more trees than is necessary even for the most shade-sensitive species; logging practices, both in clear-cut and selectively logged areas, which fail to take ecological considerations into account; and inadequate or nonexistent attempts to regenerate logged areas.

Good forest growth requires about five feet of topsoil, but logging practices frequently speed up the process of erosion.* For example, logs hauled to a landing along tractor skid trails can gouge through rich topsoil, making regeneration of the forest difficult or impossible. Tractors tear up the earth until loosened soil slides down the trails and large areas of land are eroded. Heavy logging near streams causes a great deal of topsoil to run off into the water, filling the streams with sediment.

Dr. James Wallis has discovered that "northern California's mountains are eroding at a prodigious rate . . . greatly in excess of the rate of new soil formation." Dr. Wallis found the cause to be logging and road construction. University of California Professor of Geology Clyde Wahrhaftig found, in studying sediment discharge data from the Eel and Mad rivers, that soil is being destroyed 10 to 100 times faster than it can regenerate in the north coast ranges.**

Fish are also dying as a result of shoddy forest practices. Walter T. Shannon, former director of the State Department of Fish and Game, asserts that logging operations are clogging streams throughout much of northern California with silt and debris, making the beds useless for spawning fish and causing a significant drop in the fish population of these streams. Mr. Shannon also claims that stripping stream banks of their shade trees has caused the water temperature of the streams to rise to levels intolerable to fish.

There are a few basic principles that should apply to all logging practices in order to prevent excessive erosion, among them: keeping the number of skid trails to an

* A statewide soil conservation policy is essential for the preservation and continued usefulness of the state's soil resources. The ranks of the State Division of Soil Conservation within the Department of Conservation were recently decimated, however (the number of authorized staff positions was cut from thirty-four to fourteen), and by 1972, according to the office of the Legislative Analyst, there will be no Division of Soil Conservation at all.

** John Callaghan of the California Forest Protective Association (the commercial loggers) has criticized those studies which conclude that logging has significantly increased erosion on the North Coast. Mr. Callaghan asserts that much of the erodable material in the Eel and Mad River drainage basins is not soil, but rather "pulverized rock."

absolute minimum; sloping skid trails to follow the natural contours of the land; using light, rubber-tired equipment; prohibiting tractors on steep hillsides where soil is unstable; preserving buffer strips on which no tree is felled and no equipment operated along both sides of streams to prevent runoff of loose topsoil into the streams; and minimal bulldozing and careful grading of roads in forest areas. Clearcutting, when necessary, should be confined to small areas (twenty-five acres or less). The trees and vegetation which remain when an area is *selectively* logged help to prevent soil erosion and, by absorbing water from the denuded soil, to control water runoff; when selective cutting is done, the decision to cut particular trees must take into account the makeup of the next generation of trees.

These, then, are some of the principles of a properly conducted logging operation. Some California companies are making conscientious efforts to improve their logging practices along these lines: Simpson Timber Company, for example, is beginning to use light, rubber-tired equipment and cable-logging techniques on some of the steep hillsides. But for the most part loggers ignore these principles and continue to destroy the resource on which they depend. Even the areas logged by Simpson, which is interested in long-range forest management and has a reputation as one of the more careful logging operators, are disturbed on a massive scale and made vulnerable to erosion for years.

Reforestation

Unlike many other natural resources, forests are renewable. The lumber industry in California uses virgin forest exclusively. Since this resource is rapidly running out, the industry will soon have to rely on second-growth timber in reforested areas of managed woodland. It is clearly in the industry's long-range best interests to reforest a logged area, to establish and care for second-growth forests.

For proper regeneration, second-growth trees must be adequate in number and of good timber quality. These two standards can easily be met by reseeding or replanting after logging with trees of good genetic parentage. Yet although this principle has been applied with great success elsewhere in the United States and Europe, it has been neglected by most companies in California.

Simpson Timber Company has been working closely with University of California forest geneticists to obtain better methods of reproduction in second-growth forests. Under the direction of Chief Forester Herb Peterson, Simpson is also attempting an extensive, and rather expensive, reclamation of lands which have been overrun by commercially valueless hardwood stands. This reclamation involves a controlled burn of the hardwood stand, cultivation of the land, and planting and seeding with appropriate softwood species. Such efforts substantially reduce the threat of a future timber shortage, but they are exceptional by California standards.

The Masonite Corporation, a large forest-products company which owns 80,000 acres of Mendocino County, is probably typical of the larger landholders in placing low priority on reforestation. On a recently logged area of Masonite property now undergoing "reforestation," the seed used to regenerate the forest was from a species (Oregon Douglas fir) that is not native to the area and that, according to experts, does very poorly even with careful attention as far south as Mendocino. But Douglas fir seed is cheap, and the company is not generous with reforestation funds. Most of the seed failed to germinate; the surviving seedlings may not make it through another year.

In 1970 the Tree Improvement Committee of the Society of American Foresters, the professional forestry association, recommended that the "California Forest Protective Association" sponsor a study of the feasibility of using genetic methods to improve reforestation practices on privately held land in the state. In California's new "environment" parlance, the "Forest Protective Association" is the association of major timber-growing companies, the commercial loggers. The total cost of the study was to be $10,000—a fraction of the larger members' advertising budgets in the area of environmental self-applause. Each firm's share would be much less. Two companies—Soper-Wheeler and Simpson—were willing to sponsor the study; the rest refused.

Regulation

THE FOREST PRACTICE ACT

Until the 1940s, there was no governmental regulation of forest lands in California. Many companies in search of quick profit devastated the land and failed to provide for even token regeneration. The lumber baron ideology was perhaps stated most succinctly by an early forester named C. A. Schenck: "That kind of forestry is best which pays best."

The lumber industry feared that the federal government would initiate strict regulation of forest practices if it were not headed off by cooperative industry-government "regulation" at the state level. As a result, the lumber industry and the state legislature initiated discussions that led to the Forest Practice Act of 1945, the most important law concerning forest use in California.

The objective of the Act, as set forth in the Public Resources Code, is "to encourage, promote, and require such development, use and management of forests and timberlands as will maintain the continuous production of forest products to the end that adequate supplies of forest products are assured for the needs of the people and industries." In the eyes of the industry, this objective is a limited one indeed. The Northern California Section of the Society of American Foresters stated in a recent report that "many people have thought of the Forest Practice Act as a way of preserving aesthetic values, preventing stream and watershed damage, and protecting fish and recreation resources. The fact is that the Forest Practice Act does not authorize regulation of private cutting practices to achieve these ends, except insofar as they may be produced as a by-product of rules aimed at maintaining the productivity of timberlands." Further, the Act does not specifically call for sustained-yield forestry, i.e., for a balance between the amount of timber cut and new trees regenerated.

"California's forestry practice law [is] a generally weak statute affording little environmental protection [and] designed chiefly to protect the interests of the timber industry," reported *Science* magazine on December 25, 1970. The timber industry itself is supposed to set up the regulations under which it will operate. The Act is administered by the State Division of Forestry under the direction of the Board of Forestry. This Board consists of eight members, all of whom are appointed by the governor. By law, three Board members represent the timber industry directly, one represents agriculture, one grazing, one the water interests, and two the general public. At least six of the eight Board members, then, represent commercial pro-logging interests.

The Board of Forestry does not have the power to establish the actual rules that regulate the logging practices of the timber companies. That task is delegated to four Forest Practice Committees, made up of four timber operators and owners, a State Division of Forestry representative, and two public members, all appointed by the governor.

For timber operators in their respective regions, the Forest Practice Committees propose minimum regulations which will insure continued productivity of the forest resource in that region. Before these rules are adopted as law, however, they must be approved by two-thirds of the private timberland owners voting in the district. Then the State Board of Forestry must approve the rules. Clearly the industry has almost complete control of its own regulation, and the appointive jobs can be handed out to deserving allies.

Since it was passed, the Forest Practice Act has been the subject of heated controversy between conservation groups and the timber industry. It has been attacked by the Sierra Club and by conservation-minded foresters on three principal grounds. First, its objectives are far too narrow to allow for the proper management of California's forest environment. Second, the rules established by the Forest Practice Committees are inadequate, since they are too general and too vague to provide adequate protection for the total forest resource. Third, enforcement of the Act by the State Division of Forestry has been ineffective.

Conservationists have fought to expand the scope of the Act explicitly to include consideration of recreational interests, comprehensive watershed protection (including prevention of soil erosion and excessive sedimentation of streams and rivers), maintenance of aesthetic values, and protection of fish and wildlife. But the timber industry has fought expansion of the Act. Industry spokesmen argue that the ill effects of logging on the forest environment have been grossly exaggerated by the conservationists. They also feel that it is unfair for the state to regulate only logging practices while ignoring other industries that are potentially harmful to the forest resource, such as mining, grazing, and highway construction. And they don't wish to see the timber industry burdened with the additional costs of increased regulation.

In 1966–1967, the Assembly Subcommittee on Forest Practices and Watershed Management conducted an extensive investigation of "Man's Effect on California's Watersheds," reviewing the effectiveness of the erosion control provisions of the Forest Practice Act. After hearing evidence on both sides of the issue, the Subcommittee issued the following warning:

> The basic state policy governing forest practices on private lands should be broadened and strengthened. To ignore by maintenance of the status quo the possibility of major damage to many vital watershed resources would be a serious gamble, especially when a relatively simple elevation in the overall standards of forest practices would go far toward minimizing these long-term consequences.

To date, this warning has not been heeded. The California legislature, under intense pressure from the state's timber industry, failed to enact any of the legislation introduced as a result of the Subcommittee's report. In John Callaghan's California Forest Protective Association, the industry has an adept and effective Sacramento lobby. Primarily through the efforts of Callaghan and his organization, the industry has prevented broadening the interpretation of the objectives of the Forest Practice Act, and has fought off most legislation which would strengthen forest regulation.

Despite the opposition of the Board of Forestry, the State Forester, and the California Forest Protective Association, however, one amendment to the Forest Practice Act that was of tremendous potential benefit to Santa Clara, San Mateo, and Marin County citizens did slip through the 1970 legislature. These three counties, in the southern part of the Redwood Forest District, now have the power to adopt comprehensive logging-control ordinances stronger than the Forest Practice Act rules. Citizens' complaints to county officials about soil erosion, water pollution, spoiled scenery and recreation areas, and even fire hazards, together with the potency of the environmental protection movement in the Bay Area, led to limited success in the public interest. However, these are primarily urban-suburban counties and small in area.

The vagueness of the Forest Practice Rules makes enforcement difficult, if not impossible. For example, the Forest Practice Rules of the Redwood Forest District provide the following rules for erosion protection:

> Tractor roads, tractor skid trails, logging truck roads, and firebreaks shall be so laid out, constructed, used and left

after logging that water flow on or from them shall not at any time create or contribute to *excessive erosion* of the soils [emphasis added].

And,

. . . timber operators will use *due diligence* to prevent unnecessary gouging or cutting of stream banks and beds during the conduct of timber operations [emphasis added].

To prevent the cutting of stream banks, the rules specify that timber operators may not use:

beds of streams or portions of beds of streams which carry running water throughout the year as roadways, logging skid trails or log landings *where such use will cause excessive disturbance of the soil* [emphasis added].

Such terms as "excessive erosion," "due diligence," and "excessive disturbance" can hardly be considered definite or explicit regulations. Because they are difficult to interpret, they are difficult for State Division of Forestry inspectors to enforce and easy for timber operators to ignore.

The Forest Practice Act's rules providing for regeneration are somewhat more explicit, but many foresters believe they are silviculturally inadequate. The Redwood Rules attempt to insure regeneration by requiring timber operators to leave standing a certain number of trees per acre (usually four) as a seed source. But often this measure alone will not insure adequate restocking. The seed requirement is useless for trees which bear no seed, such as the redwoods found in Mendocino County. The Forest Practice Act requires timber operators merely to make an effort at restocking. They don't have to succeed. They don't even have to try very hard.

An increasing number of California foresters, led by Dean John Zivnuska of the School of Forestry at the University of California, have urged that the rules for regeneration should prescribe objectives instead of practices. Under this plan, timber operators could use any methods they desired, but before beginning a logging operation they would be required to post performance bonds. If, after several years, cutover lands failed to meet stocking requirements, these bonds would be forfeited. The state could then use the forfeited funds to seed or plant the unstocked lands.

Perhaps most alarming about the Forest Practice Act's application is the exception granted to anyone who expresses a bona fide *intent* to use the land for nonforest purposes.

Such an "intent" confers absolute freedom to cut, drag, and decimate without control.

Rigorous enforcement of the vague forest practice rules that do exist, however, could help save California's forest resource. Legal sanctions against timber operators caught and prosecuted for violating the rules are strong. Section 4595 of the Public Resources Code allows the State Forester to suspend or revoke the permit of any operator who fails or refuses to comply with the rules. Sections 4612–4613 provide for the issuance of a restraining order or an injunction "to enjoin the violation or threatened violation of the rules." Sections 4615–4618 allow the Division of Forestry to spend up to $40 per acre to correct rules violations, and to recover these expenses from the owner or operator, or both.

But since its passage the Forest Practice Act has been poorly enforced. The enforcement procedure is cumbersome and time-consuming, and the state's failure to fund the State Division of Forestry adequately has reduced the number of inspectors to eight for the 8.2 million acres of privately owned timber land in the state.

Attorney David Pesonen, in testimony before the Assembly Forest Practices and Watershed Management Subcommittee, stated:

> It has been estimated by experienced enforcement personnel that an adequate level of compliance with the existing forest practice rules would require at least four inspections per season. Yet the average number of inspections over the last few years has been only about 1.4 per operator per season. (In fact, the average number of inspections per *operation* is less than one.) . . . There seems little room for argument that the gross level of inspection effort is far below the minimum necessary for an acceptable level of compliance. . . . It seems quite fair to say that the Forest Practice Act has received little attention in the field.

U.S. FOREST SERVICE

The Forest Practice Act pertains only to privately owned timber land in California. The U.S. Forest Service controls the amount and location of logging in the National Forests of California, some of the most beautiful and productive forests in the state. Industry foresters admit that the Forest Service spends more time and effort on erosion control, reforestation, and other aspects of ecologically sound forest management than the industry, since "they can afford to— the federal government subsidizes them." The Forest Service has also written a firm set of guidelines regulating the number of trees to be left, particular trees to be spared, areas to be logged, and so on, which apply to any logging operation in the National Forests.

However, it is almost impossible for the Forest Service to enforce its logging-practice rules. The Forest Service is *required* to contract logging rights to the highest bidder, regardless of his past record of logging practices. The only way for the Forest Service to enforce its regulations, there- fore, is to harass the logging operator at the site.

Three things are necessary for meaningful preservation of long-term forest resources: precise and strict standards, adequate manpower, and sanctions. The sanctions must cost the loggers more than they benefit from violating the law in order to have any deterrent effect. The state has strong (theoretical) sanctions, and the federal government has precise standards; but neither has adequate manpower, and nobody has all three of the prerequisites for effective regulation.

The Merger Menace

In 1968 and 1969, forty companies in the California forest industry were involved in mergers. Often these mergers involved the absorption of a small, long-term-management- oriented timber company by one of the few huge land- development conglomerates. William H. Holmes, the presi- dent of one small timber company in northern California, attributes the current frenzy to combine to "chain-letter" momentum on the stock market.*

Mr. Holmes uses a hypothetical example, appropriately

---

* The tax system also favors the large conglomerate. The Depart- ment of Treasury has calculated in 1972 that capital gains loopholes (income made growing timber is taxed at half the rate of normal income) subsidizes the timber industry by $130 million per year. This tax gift, surviving the 1969 Tax Reform Act intact, accrues "to large corporations," according to Emil Sunley of Treasury. The sub- sidy favors conglomerates since it operates as with agriculture, described above. Sunley calculates that about half of the subsidy goes to "just five corporations."

And the capital gains break, in addition to systematically low property assessment and taxation of timberland in California, which is acknowledged in correspondence to the Project from the State Board of Equalization, subsidizes and stimulates logging and its products over other building materials.

called "Georgia-Cascade." Georgia-Cascade is committed to a 25% annual increase in earnings. It is a glamorous market stock selling at thirty times earnings. It can, simply through mergers, maintain this earnings growth and justify continued market prices of thirty times earnings.

Assume G-C has one million shares outstanding, with earnings at one million dollars, or $1 per share. At thirty times earnings it is selling at $30. It spots Company X, also with one million shares outstanding, also earning $1 per share. But X is a plodding, steady firm and is selling at a mere $10 per share (ten times earnings). G-C offers *$15* a share for X's stock—a nice profit for X. And G-C offers to pay in stock that is guaranteed to rise another 33% within a year.

G-C then issues another 500,000 shares of its stock, worth $30 per share, or $15 million ($15 for each X share), to X's shareholders to pay for their stock. Now the new corporation has *1,500,000* shares outstanding—but its earnings are now $1.33 per share (the 1,500,000 shares divided into the combined $2 million in earnings). Presto, G-C has achieved a 33% increase in earnings. Investors see this and the stock shoots up more, staying at thirty times the new earnings. Then the cycle begins again.

The critical problem in terms of timber policy is the plundering of corporation X's forest reserves. Mr. Holmes writes:

> Let's assume that [Corporation X] had reasonable timber reserves which it was cutting conservatively to make them last as long as possible. With this policy they were making their regular annual one million dollar profit. However, let's assume that G-C wants to show even higher per-share earnings than were generated by the simple merger. It can do this quite simply by doubling the cut of [Corporation X] timber, so that instead of that company producing one million dollars in earnings, it will produce two million dollars. Added to G-C's original one million, this will give a total of three million dollars profit for the 1,500,000 shares outstanding, or a whopping $2.00 per share.
>
> So by the process of merging and a partial liquidation, G-C has apparently doubled their earnings per share. Stock analysts are ecstatic, and G-C stock climbs to thirty times $2.00, or $60 per share. All this in spite of the fact that there has been no real increase whatsoever in true earnings.[1]

The fluidity and ease of buying and selling makes this plundering easy. The catch, as Mr. Holmes remarks,

> is that it can't go on forever. As G-C gets bigger and bigger, each acquisition has less and less chain-letter effect. Also, the competition for companies to acquire has been such that new ones with the proper qualifications are getting hard to find. In addition, showing liquidation as earnings has a limit, and in the timber business overcutting has a way of catching up. The whole process will eventually slow down and when it does, look out.[2]

Mining

California produces an enormous volume and variety of mineral commodities. Of the eighty major minerals and mineral products that contribute approximately $2 million annually to the state's economy, liquid fuels (natural gas and petroleum) are the most valuable, constituting 65% of the state's mineral income. Most of the remaining 35% of California's mineral income comes from cement, sand, gravel, and boron. In addition, California yields substantial amounts of iron ore (Eagle Mountain mine in Riverside County), tungsten (especially in the Bishop and Atolia areas) and most of the mercury produced in the United States (New Idria deposit in San Benito County). Quantities of industrial minerals such as diatomite (Santa Barbara and Monterey counties), gypsum (Imperial, Kings, Kern, and Riverside counties), and fifteen extremely valuable "rare earth" minerals (San Bernardino County) are also mined. Less substantial deposits of the following principal minerals have been mined: asbestos, barite, borates, chromite, copper, dolomite, iodine, lead, magnesite, manganese, soda ash, sulfur, talc, potash, perlite, pumice, pyrite, salt, silver, zinc, some remaining gold, and the clay and limestone used for cement. A survey of data and maps from the Division of Mines and Geology of the Department of Conservation within the Resources Agency reveals deposits of at least one of thirty-two principal mineral commodities in fifty-five of California's fifty-eight counties. Only Modoc, Lassen, and Merced are without substantial deposits.

The mining and refining of many of these minerals involves soil erosion, spills, by-product water pollution, and other disturbances of wild areas related to road construction, timber clearance, etc. If these "costs," which are now borne by government and future generations, were reflected in the cost of the mining operation, they would be minimized. For instance, if a manufacturer can use either of two minerals in a process, assessing him for the indirect and future costs will cause him to choose the mineral causing the least environmental damage. Or, if there are two possible ways to mine a given mineral, assessing him for the cost will encourage him to use the less damaging method. In some areas, the costs may be so great or so difficult to measure that outright prohibition will be necessary.

However, government regulation of mining does not provide these prohibitions or assess these costs, but instead subsidizes inefficient, wasteful, and environmentally destructive practices.

Federal Regulation

The most important set of laws regulating mineral development are federal, since most of the California land subject to mining and drilling is owned by the federal government. Mineral development is divided under federal laws into four categories for special treatment.

LOCATABLE MINERALS

The first category of minerals is "locatable resources," defined as hard-rock metallic ores such as gold, copper, and silver. This mining is regulated by the Mineral Location Law of 1872.

A great deal of prospecting has been done under the aegis of the 1872 law, since the metals covered by it are valuable. The law was passed when Congress was attempting to encourage the development and settling of the West, when prospectors with picks and shovels did most of the exploration and could not do major damage. A law designed 100 years ago to make exploitation of natural resources as easy and attractive as possible is clearly obsolete; yet it remains in effect in 1972.

Essentially, the law permits anyone to do whatever he wants with mineral land. ALL PUBLIC LANDS are open for exploration and claim unless specifically withdrawn or reserved. Once a mineral deposit has been discovered, the land is subject to patent for surface and subsurface rights, and the issuance of a patent is mandatory once minimum legal requirements are met. The law contains no provisions to protect against land abuse or assess its cost, and places no limitations on prospecting.

Mining claims under the 1872 law have unlimited life: the claim-holder is required only to perform $100 worth of work on the claim each year, and this requirement is not enforced. A prospector must dig a ten-foot "discovery hole" but does not have to repair surface damage. Only one restriction is placed on the owner of an unpatented claim: he must use the land for mining purposes only (i.e., he cannot gratuitously burn down a forest, but he can do anything he likes as part of his mining operation). There are no restrictions at all on a patented claim. And a claimant is entitled to unlimited free access to his land—he cannot be charged for a road he has used to develop and maintain his claim.*

Three major attempts have been made to modify the federal mining law—in 1955, 1964, and 1969—but these have had little or no effect on locatable mineral resource land. Costs incurred under the law are borne by the public through taxes, lost park land, and environmental damage. The law even provides ample opportunity for private appropriation of federal land for nonmineral uses or for excessive profit.

California's Central Valley Water Quality Control Board is well aware of the devastation that can come from one mine. The old Walker Mine in Plumas County has been polluting Dollie and Little Grizzly creeks for well over twenty years. The mine was closed down in 1941, but it is still devastating the area. Before the copper mine, the creeks in the area were considered among the best trout fisheries in the state. There were meadows with sweet grass and grazing deer. Tailings heavily laden with copper and azurite have turned the area into a lifeless gravel wasteland. The Forest Service is unable to grow trees in the meadows around Little Grizzly Creek. Clear-cut logging in the area has added to the pollutive flow in recent years, and additional streams, including Indian Creek, are now seriously threat-

---

* "The result of this statute," comments Boalt Law School Professor Ira Heyman in his unreleased draft report to the Public Land Law Review Commission, "is that a small claim (insignificant perhaps in its own environmental impact) may thus permit many miles of road to be constructed as a matter of right causing major impacts in terms of visual scarring of the landscape, erosion, and disturbance of streams and drainage ways." [p. IV–19]

ened. The state has known about the pollution since 1950 when an investigative team discovered that water seeping from one of the mine's ventilator shafts was responsible for the pollution of twelve miles of watershed. The pollution is worse twenty years later, with runoff so toxic that not even low forms of life can survive in the area. The mining laws (and the water-quality laws) offer little comfort, despite the fact that pollution could be stopped by plugging the mine openings with concrete.

The failure to regulate or monitor the effects of mineral development is not just academic: there are 250,000 mining claims under the 1872 law in southern California alone, many with the ten-foot bulldozed gouge and their perpetual stake to surface use, timber, roads, and access, whether the claim contains valuable minerals or not.

In April of 1971, the U.S. Geological Survey published a ninety-page technical report based on the most extensive research to date on the effects of strip mining. U.S. Gypsum is planning to conduct substantial open-pit mining right in Los Padres National Forest near Ojai. There is little to stop them.

The Geological Survey Report includes an eleven-year field study of a twenty-five-square-mile creek basin in southern Kentucky. It is entitled, "Influences of Strip Mining on the Hydrological Environment of Parts of Beaver Creek Basin." The Report concluded that small-scale strip mining within the study area killed or reduced fish in streams by filling the water with acid and mineral poisons, brought down hundreds of thousands of tons of channel-clogging silt, and killed or stunted trees. It adds that devastation is likely to continue unchecked for an "indetermined" period of years as nature attempts to rebalance. The Report notes, "The killing of aquatic vegetation has resulted in an unstable stream substrate. Aquatic life will not return to these streams until the stream habitat has been restored. . . . During the six-year period following the cessation of mining, no repopulation of aquatic fauna was observed on Cane Beach and only limited repopulation was observed in Hughes Fork." John J. Musser, a Geological Survey hydrologist, admitted that the study, one of the few and certainly the most extensive in this area so far, is a portrait of a "disaster."

Mining interests have not encouraged objective study into the effects of strip mining and have consistently claimed that "properly reclaimed" strip-mine land is actually "better" than it was before the mining. There has been no evidence to substantiate these dubious claims. In any event, the Geological Survey has reported that only 58,000 of 1,800,000 strip-mined acres have been restored nationwide.

LEASABLE RESOURCES

The second category of mineral operation is "leasable resources," which include oil, gas, and nonfuel minerals such as sulfur and phosphate. Two laws regulate these minerals: the Minerals Leasing Act of 1920 and the Minerals Leasing Act for Acquired Lands of 1947.

Leasable resources are theoretically amenable to greater control than are locatable resources. Prospecting permits are usually issued to control exploration. Lease provisions can directly prohibit damaging practices or assess their social cost. Special regulations for transfer lands and land reclamation are possible. And environmental regulations enacted in 1969 apply to leasable resources.

The question, then, to be asked about regulation of leasable resources is: what use is being made of what appear to be substantial supervisory powers?

The Bureau of Land Management (BLM) has primary authority to issue permits and formulate leases. Specific lease forms vary, but they all contain common provisions which indicate how the law has been enforced. First, for nonfuel minerals such as sulfur, phosphates, or the sodium salts, the lease forms for the Mineral Leasing Act of 1920 apply. The lessee must agree to prevent operations from *unnecessarily* causing soil erosion, water pollution, or vegetation damage. The lessee *may* be required to fill excavations, and restore the land. These provisions to prevent contamination, erosion, or conversion of the land are extremely qualified and vague. Specific attention is given only to minor matters (e.g., "that no rubbish burning be done without the consent of the authorized officer"). The burden is on the agency to intervene in specific cases— although it has neither the expertise nor the manpower to do so—rather than on the mining operation to obtain permission under specific criteria or conditions. Thus, the lessee is required to do all things *reasonably necessary* to prevent scarring and erosion, pollution, and watershed damage.

Oil and gas restrictions can be imposed at the initial

stage through the oil and gas exploration permits or through the denial of specific terms of a lease agreement. Exploration permits urge that "due care be exercised . . . that existing roads and trails be used *wherever possible,* and that if new trails or roads are made, care should be taken to follow natural contours of the lands *where feasible* (emphasis added). These provisions do little to safeguard the environment. The exploration permit does provide a mechanism for reclamation. But here the burden is on BLM's district manager to specify the conditions under which the Permit shall be issued. No bond is required nor is any burden placed on the explorer. As for implementing restrictions, Professor Heyman notes that "given the lack of funds and manpower available to the BLM, the degree to which the BLM can enforce these terms and conditions is an open question."

The primary BLM lease form itself specifies certain measures for environmental protection covering all federal land. If there is another dominant use on land that is officially "segregated" for that use, operations must not conflict with that use. Since segregation is extremely rare, and since mining is not viewed as an activity which conflicts with most dominant uses, this provision is no barrier to mining. Once again, the lessee must not "unnecessarily" cause soil erosion, damage forest and timber, pollute air and water, damage range improvements, or damage fossils. The lessee is to restore the surface to its former condition "so far as it can reasonably be done." The form does expressly require the driller to fill pits and excavation and remove debris. This is the extent of environmental control for general drilling.

In addition to the lease, there are separate regulations governing actual oil and gas operations on federal land, administered under the director of the U.S. Geological Survey. Enforcement is delegated out to regional oil and gas supervisors. Authority here is limited to the prohibition of stream or underground water pollution or "unnecessary" damage to the surface of leased lands.

The word "unnecessary" that modifies all the damage mentioned in these prohibitions is critical. A method is unnecessary if it results in less efficient mineral extraction by the industry. Contamination and environmental damage may add to industry's efficiency. Current regulations and lease provisions (the strongest set of laws governing mining and drilling in operation) simply give the mine lessee a blank check to damage the land for his own profits.

SALABLE RESOURCES

The third category of mineral extraction consists of "salable resources"—sand, gravel, stone, and pumice— subject to the Minerals Disposal Act of 1947. These minerals are regulated by contracts of sale. The stone or pumice in an area is simply sold to the purchaser, who is required to remove it. How he removes it can be affected by the terms of the contract of sale. The contracts do include provisions for environmental protections, as authorized by BLM staff. The terms will vary according to conditions. Generally, the purchaser must remove with "due regard" to bank and road maintenance. He must dispose of his refuse and downed timber and make the area safe and sanitary. He must avoid disturbing watershed, and "where possible" avoid "unnecessary" disturbance to underground aquifers. He must refill holes and excavations. These general provisions are quite limited in scope and occasionally qualified. Little is said about erosion, clearing, access (road construction), water pollution, or wildlife-habitat disturbance. Sanctions are unclear, since bonds are rare and the purchaser has his mineral when the violation is likely to occur or be discovered.

OUTER CONTINENTAL SHELF RESOURCES

The fourth mineral extraction category—mineral operations on the outer continental shelf—is regulated by the Outer Continental Shelf Lands Act of 1953.* The chief minerals involved are oil, gas, and sulfur, and the three methods of extraction are drill hole (oil and liquid minerals), dredging (for deposits along the surface), and underground mining (vein deposits). Drilling is the most dangerous and the most common form of mineral extraction in California's shelf.

The Outer Continental Shelf Lands Act gives the Secretary of the Interior the authority to grant mineral leases and rights of way for pipelines, and to attach appropriate restrictions and safeguards to these grants. In the past, the Department of the Interior has delegated responsibility for

---

* The state owns and controls the tidewater within three miles of the shore. From there the federal government claims jurisdiction (as of 1954) to the shelf edge.

supervising these operations under its regulations to the U.S. Geological Survey.

Although the role of the new Environmental Protection Agency in this area has yet to be determined, regulations have recently been put into effect in the interests of environmental protection: the director of the BLM, within the Department of the Interior, is supposed to evaluate the effect of leasing on the entire environment; public meetings give private organizations and individuals a voice in the leasing process; if the harm to be caused by extraction is thought to outweigh the gains to be made by drilling, the President may withdraw unleased lands from disposition; if an extraction threatens to cause irreparable harm to aquatic life, property, other valuable mineral deposits, or the environment, the district supervisor of the Geological Survey can suspend the operation.

In practice, however, the regulations provide little environmental protection. The President has only once withdrawn a piece of land from disposition. Once the lease is granted the rights of the lessee are practically illimitable. Virtually all dealings between the lessee and the Geological Survey and between the Survey and the BLM and other agencies are kept absolutely secret, including the lessee's plans for minimizing pollution. The significance of the public hearings is lessened by the fact that no member of the public can get information from which to make cogent comments. In the past the Geological Survey has not conducted the independent investigation required by law but has relied on geological data submitted by oil companies after routinely granting exploration permits. Depending upon industry information means that oil firms are able to control estimates of likely reserves of oil or gas, and thus to pay more or less what they wish to pay, particularly when there is no competitive bidding for rights. Finally, sanctions are vague and weak, despite enormous damage: leaks and spills must be reported; pollution which threatens life or property is to be removed at the expense of the lessee. The lessee's liability even for direct damage to third parties is unclear.

Events in Santa Barbara between 1967 and 1969 have illustrated the failure of regulatory policy with regard to offshore drilling. The Santa Barbara Channel consists of extremely porous and permeable sands. In many locations only several hundred feet of sand lie between the ocean bottom and large deposits of oil. There is no cap of rock to hold the oil firmly underground, and the area is criss-crossed with faults. In 1965, the Supreme Court declared that water beyond the three-mile limit was under federal jurisdiction.

The Johnson administration was in the midst of the Vietnam War and trying to show a balanced budget. Issuing drilling leases was a quick way to pick up revenue, and in February of 1968, $603 million was collected for leases to 71 tracts covering 363,000 acres. The Administration refused the requests of Santa Barbara citizens for careful geological study and suppressed efforts by the Solicitor of the Department of Interior to require the Geological Survey to make the independent analysis required by law. Pages 143 to 158 in James Ridgeway's recent *The Politics of Ecology* document what happened:

> By January 1969, the United States Geological Survey had approved five development wells on Platform A, which was operated by Union Oil. For each of these wells, Union obtained from the Geological Survey regional supervisor a variance on the usual well-casing requirements. The company obtained permission to set one string of conductor casings to only fifteen feet below the ocean bottom, as opposed to the usual Survey requirement of at least 500 feet. More important, a smaller surface casing went to only 238 feet below the floor as opposed to the 861-foot minimum requirement of the Survey.

On February 4, 1969, the ocean floor buckled in a massive blowout which spilled oil over 100 miles of beach. Estimates of the gallonage that escaped ranged from 2 million to 3.5 million. The damage to the ocean floor, aquatic life, and other wildlife is incalculable. Subsequent drilling permits were requested to "relieve the pressure." The County of Santa Barbara objected to new permits and asked for public hearings, but the Army Corps of Engineers, with jurisdiction over harbors, issued the permits with the Department of the Interior's acquiescence and without hearings. Two and one-half months later, one of the new platforms belonging to Sun Oil began to cause major leaks. When the well was shut down temporarily, pressure once again built up and once more oil began to gush from beneath the ocean floor. By the end of 1969, another twenty miles of beach were polluted.

The political outrage engendered by these events led

Secretary of the Interior Walter J. Hickel to propose temporary absolute liability for oil blowout, spillage, and other damage. In April of 1969, Pauley Petroleum, a lessee in the channel, sued the federal government to enjoin the new liability rules. Pauley (and others) had no intention of taking responsibility for the damage they were likely to cause; they had been aware of the risks all along, and so, they allege, had the federal government. The hazards connected with drilling in the Santa Barbara Channel area were so great, claims the Pauley complaint, that

> . . . when the United States solicited bids and substantial cash bonuses for oil and gas leases under the waters of the Santa Barbara Channel, it knew or should have known, as plaintiffs did, that no operator could guarantee that, even with the greatest degree of care, its exploration and production in the area would be free of well blowouts or of other events which would give rise to the unintended discharge of oil into the surrounding waters.

The Santa Barbara blowout has resulted in a state moratorium on new offshore drilling and in the cancellation of numerous leases by the Department of the Interior. In April of 1971, thirty-five of the original seventy-one leases were canceled at a single stroke. Presumably, the government will have to return much or all of the $603 million it collected. Neither the government nor the oil companies *like* spills, but both appear willing to run extremely close risks as long as they don't have to pay for their errors. The state is now talking of opening up drilling again, and has granted lease rights for tideland drilling off Orange County. The Department of the Interior may be politically unable to take the extreme chances it would otherwise take with public assets in Santa Barbara for a while, but as long as the above procedures continue, and as long as oil-company desires have great influence in Washington, repetitions of the Santa Barbara incident are likely to occur. Surveys indicate that Hickel's new safety regulations are being violated everywhere.

State Regulation

The state interest in mineral extraction is represented by three bodies: the State Lands Division, the Division of Oil and Gas, and the Division of Mines and Geology. All of these bodies are under the jurisdiction of the Department of Conservation within the Resources Agency.

STATE LANDS COMMISSION AND DIVISION

The State Lands Commission and Division is the most important of the three entities in terms of mineral extraction. The Commission has numerous responsibilities in the management of tidelands and submerged lands, swamp and overflow lands, and the beds of navigable rivers. It has the authority to provide for the extraction of minerals, including oil and gas, from all lands in its custody. The Commission itself consists of the Lieutenant Governor, the State Controller, and the Director of Finance; the Division provides the staff.

Total state revenue from oil and gas and other leasing operations on state lands is estimated at $38,798,000 for 1971–72. Most of this revenue comes from the Wilmington oil field off Long Beach, the single largest source of oil currently being tapped in California and the only important mineral extraction under the regulation of the Commission and Division. The field lies under sovereign state tidelands. About 95% of the field is administered for the state by the city of Long Beach, which collects revenues to pay for administrative and subsidence costs and has been given approximately $184 million (over 30%) of the state's share of the revenues. The state collects directly the remaining $425 million, or 69.8%, from the total reserves in the field.

Under Chapter 138 of the Statutes of 1964 (First Session), Long Beach is allowed to use this revenue for improvements within the harbor district or adjacent to Long Beach tidelands, and for small boat harbors, a maritime museum, or beaches on or adjacent to Long Beach tidelands or Alamitos Beach Park Lands. Any capital expenditure by Long Beach in excess of $50,000 is to be submitted to the State Lands Commission, which can object to it within sixty days if it is not permitted by Chapter 138. The Commission remains responsible under the law for the general supervision of the terms of the trust and of the drilling operation.

In 1967, Long Beach acquired the British ocean liner *Queen Mary*. Local promoters and prospective concessionaires developed this project and touted the ship as the location of a "maritime museum."

After receiving notice of the proposed expenditure, the State Lands Commission asked the Attorney General for an opinion of the project relative to Chapter 138. The

Attorney General stated that use of the ship as a maritime museum was permissible but that no trust revenues could be spent for conversion or improvement of any commercial area. The original proposal envisioned a $9 million land-based museum and private contributions of $2 million for exhibits. Total expenditures of trust revenue as of the middle of 1970 amounted to $25,667,000, much of which was spent on hotels, restaurants, parking lots, and numerous other commercial facilities. Total costs exceed $57.7 million, not including extensive supporting facilities such as bridges, roads, and utilities provided by local government.

The Commission's response has been abject acquiescence for four years and through seven expenditure proposals. To the last three proposals—for a total of $33,343,395 for berth, parking, and "supportive" facilities—the Commission has responded with what it calls "conditional nonobjection." Rather than object as specified under Chapter 138, the Commission "reserves the right" to object to future expenditures if they do not conform to Chapter 138. "The Commission," comments the Legislative Analyst on page 423 of his 1971 Analysis of the Budget,

> has permitted the city to spend its tideland revenues as the city proposes, while simultaneously stating that it is controlling the expenditures. As a practical matter the commission is not now limiting or objecting to any city expenditures on the Queen Mary even though the general impression is given that the commission is exercising control.

Analyst Post points out that the threat to review or disapprove future expenditures after all the expenditures have been made is a questionable check at best. The State Lands Division has calculated, according to criteria most generous to the city of Long Beach, that 30% of the $22 million spent thus far for acquisition and conversion is allocable to *commercial* (i.e., illegal under Chapter 138) enterprise—a fact which the Commission suppressed in its 1970 Report to the legislature. The figures "were not final," rationalized the Commission, but the legislature is entitled to what information is available on the expenditure of state land lease revenues for illegal purposes, even if it is only a preliminary estimate. Analyst Post comments on page 425:

During all these events, the commission did not inform the Legislature fully of its problem. . . . Instead it indicated that "the issue is one of basic policy considerations between the state and its grantee that can only be decided properly within the legislative province. . . ."

Of course the legislature had already set forth its policy with clarity in Chapter 138. The Commission and only the Commission was responsible for enforcing this policy and it alone was in a position to provide information for a change in state policy if such a change was called for. It did neither.

STATE OIL AND GAS DIVISION AND COMMISSIONS

The Division of Oil and Gas, together with the District Oil and Gas Commissions, is the next entity concerned with mineral extraction at the state level. The chief function of the Division is to carry out the Oil, Gas, and Geothermal Protection Program. The stated purposes of the Program are to protect these assets from damage or waste and provide for greater "recovery." The only environmental concerns explicitly stated in the Division's mandate are to protect waters penetrated by wells and to prevent damage resulting from subsidence.

Although reasonable governmental policy would require that individuals with public responsibilities have no financial connection with the industries regulated, a majority (five members) of the powerful Oil and Gas Commissions *must* be from the oil and gas industry. The entire Division is financed directly through "special fund" revenues. Staff salaries are paid out of funds from charges on operators of producing oil, gas, and geothermal wells through the Petroleum and Gas Fund and the Subsidence Abatement Fund. Thus the Oil and Gas Division represents industry interests in both its manpower and financing.

In 1970, the Division began incursions into Land Division territory, proposing $50,317 to establish an "offshore" regulatory unit. This would cover the tidelands under the jurisdiction of Lands. The new unit would be responsible for regulating the drilling operations on state-owned tidelands by private operators who would finance and man it. The Legislative Analyst, on page 794 of his 1970 Analysis of the Budget Bill, reminded the legislators:

The Division of Oil and Gas is a special fund agency, supported by charges on the operators of producing oil and gas wells. The State Lands Division is a General Fund agency representing the state's general interest and protection of that general interest in the state-owned lands. The proposal advanced in the budget is to have a special fund agency reviewing and acting in a control capacity over a General Fund agency.

It is not clear what would happen if the State Lands Division did not agree with the actions of the Division of Oil and Gas. It is possible that the State Lands Division would then have to appeal to the District Oil and Gas Commissioners for settlement of the dispute. The District Oil and Gas Commissioners by statute are representatives of the oil and gas industry. The conflicts of interest are apparent.

But the offshore regulatory unit was funded by the legislature anyway.

California gives larger subsidies to oil development than any other state in the nation. The state has no severance tax, and its oil depletion allowance is even higher than the federal level. Oil firms are allowed to deduct oil and gas royalties paid on their properties in figuring property tax. Since property tax is a tax on value of land, not on income, allowing such deductions has no economic rationale. The royalty deduction was signed by the governor against the recommendations of the governor's own staff.

The total cost of these tax breaks runs into the tens of millions. As Professor Stanley Surrey of Harvard has pointed out, special breaks of this kind must be made up in higher taxes applied under the same laws to other interests not similarly exempt. They constitute a gift or welfare payment to the industry.

The oil industry in California has been characterized with some accuracy by Jesse Unruh, the 1970 Democratic gubernatorial candidate, as the most powerful and arrogant political force in the state.

6

Public Land

On Labor Day of 1970, Californians were told by state officials via television simply to "stay home," not to go near state parks. Those who do not stay home even on less crowded weekends often arrive from crowded cities to camp within twenty feet of another family after surviving bumper-to-bumper traffic to get into the "preserved wilds." The larger parks are now taking reservations weeks in advance. From July 1968 to June 1969, 219,000 persons were turned away from state parks and beaches during the day. Another 148,000 were turned away overnight.[1]

Hundreds of separate agencies administer recreation facilities in California, including more than 16 federal, 13 state, 58 county, and 401 city agencies, and more than 650 special districts. There are no unified federal or state policies to guide those who must decide what land will be developed for recreation.

According to our survey, all of California's city-owned land for parks and recreation, beaches, green strips, ball parks, water and pools (not including reservoirs), and open space amounts to 55,381 acres, or 22% of the land area of city-owned roads (246,699 acres).

All the county-owned land for parks, fairgrounds, open greenbelt space, recreation, beach, stream, and even grazing land comes to 46,344 acres statewide—or about 800 acres for each of the state's fifty-eight counties. Since the counties average one and three-quarter *million* acres in size, their trivial commitment to recreation land use is apparent. These same counties own eight times this amount (356,969 acres) for county roads.

Of these 46,344 acres, 40,218 are owned by just twelve

counties.* The other forty-six counties are reserving a grand total of 6,126 acres for these purposes, averaging 133 acres per county. These same forty-six counties are willing to purchase in fee and process for county-owned roads 236,438 acres, or about *twenty-five times* as much land as for parks, open space, etc., although the costs and legal procedures are similar. This figure excludes state and city-owned roads.

Refining the totals further, we find that 17,455 acres of open-space land are in just the two counties of Los Angeles and Santa Clara.

Local communities have not only failed to add to park and open space reservoirs in the face of rising population and demand, but often fail to preserve what was established years ago. Oakland's Lake Merritt is an example. One part of the park is now a freeway and another is now a large parking lot. Only an aroused public prevented the Council from allowing a hotel to displace another part.

State Government (Department of Parks and Recreation)

The use of the state park system is growing faster than California's population. In the past twenty years, while the population has doubled, park attendance has increased more than ten times. Last year, attendance at state parks swelled by 20.5%, with 44 million visitor-days of use, in comparison to 36.5 million the previous year. The major factors accounting for this increase are found in the State Department of Parks and Recreation's TIM formula—time, income, and mobility. In the period between 1968 and 1988, participation in outdoor recreation by Californians is expected to increase 87%, from 2.3 billion "activity occasions" (or participation days) in 1968 to more than 4.3 billion in 1988.

According to the latest Department of Parks and Recreation statistics available—they are nearly two years out of date—the system consists of 796,441.1 acres. There are fifty state parks, fifteen scenic or scientific reserves, thirty-

* Contra Costa, Kern, Los Angeles, Monterey, Sacramento, San Bernardino, San Francisco, San Diego, San Mateo, Santa Clara, Stanislaus, Ventura.

two historical units, twenty-eight state recreation areas, seventy-one state beaches, and nine unclassified areas. The system includes 8,137.54 acres operated under interagency agreement or permit, and 41,461.43 acres operated under lease. The state-owned lands represent an investment of $131,183,246 including $93,156,229 in state funds. These lands today have an estimated market value in excess of $800 million. In the system are also 101 miles of ocean and bay frontage, 82 miles of major river frontage, and 259 miles of lake and reservoir shorelines.

Peak usage is the months of July and August. It is estimated that 83,900 additional picnic units, 65,000 additional boat-access parking spaces, 1,399 additional boat-launching lanes and 4,720 additional miles of riding and hiking trails must be constructed by all recreation suppliers to meet the 1980 demands in California. The price tag on providing these facilities is approximately $950 million at today's costs—not including the price of additional recreation lands needed, or the cost of providing beach parking, marinas, ski-lifts, and other facilities. In fact, to meet imminent needs at present costs would require expenditures in the billions.

Resources

No matter how park lands are acquired by the state, whether by negotiated purchase, eminent domain, transfer, gifts, or less-than-fee ownership, money is required. Financing comes primarily from three sources: bond acts, the General Fund, and other funds such as the Tidelands Oil and Gas Fund, the Land and Water Conservation Program, and several other state and federal sources The state also receives substantial revenues from fees and concessions, amounting to approximately 50% of the cost of *operating* individual units of the state park system, and some 30% of the gross support expenditures of the system.

The grand total of acreage acquired by the Department from all sources between 1963 and 1969 equals 13,539 acres. About half of this is the Point Mugu Park, which is scheduled for recreational development.

The Department and the governor have made grand claims about parkland acquisition, increased funding, and future projects. During the past year, the Department was preparing plans on nineteen projects for its 1970–71 capital-outlay program. It anticipated receiving approximately

$9,055,000 in General Fund development appropriations and $350,000 in Harbors and Watercraft Revolving Fund money as set forth in the Department's five-year plan. However, the budgeted 1970–71 capital-outlay program consists of only $3,261,000 for major development projects and a few minor projects; and in fact there is only one major project financed in the budget—the redevelopment of the San Clemente State Beach just south of President Nixon's western villa.

Thus, after only minor additions in recent years, the state came to a virtual halt in 1970–71. The 1971–72 budget shows no increase.* The Legislative Analyst notes that, "in view of the shortages of General Fund money for the current *and* budget years, the major portion of the department's capital-outlay program and its associated planning effort involves financing from . . . two bond sources (emphasis added)." [2]

These sources are the $250 million 1964 bond authorized by Chapter 1690, statutes of 1963, and the $54 million authorized in 1970 by Chapter 782 (Recreation and Fish and Wildlife Enhancement Bond Act). In addition, there are several minor bond bases, such as the Clean Water Bond Fund. But these latter are limited to State Water Project recreation onshore facilities and sewerage projects respectively. The 1964 bond authorization reserves the major portion for acquisition of new park land. And another large portion is granted to local governments for their needs.

If General Fund commitment is nonexistent, bond financing is academic. To date, the state has been able to sell only about $75 million of the bonds. As for contribution to local governments, there is "a reduction of approximately $4,400,000 in grants to local agencies from the 1964 Bond Act because the funds have been exhausted." [3]

The consistent cutoff of general funds and the exhaustion of bond resources was brought home last year when the state had to turn down a gift of 390 acres of redwoods. The priceless tract was offered by the Georgia Pacific Company and constituted one of the largest gifts of this type in conservation history. It was accepted by Nature Conservancy, a private group dedicated to acquiring land of

---

* Although the totals are the same for the two years, when analyzed in detail there is an increase comparable to the rate of inflation.

particular value or beauty and deeding it to the state. The group held the tract for eighteen months and incurred an $8,000 tax bill while it waited for the state to move. The Department refused to pay the $8,000 tax bill, arguing somehow that this should "not be passed on to the state." The Department pleaded a lack of resources as well. The state lost a $6 million tract for refusal or inability to pay the $8,000 tax bill.

In addition to a lack of real commitment, there has been a failure to advocate changes which would make spending more effective. Chapter 9 discusses the tax and public-works subsidies which encourage useless speculative holding of land. Speculative holding removes acreage from the market, raising the price for government purchase of what is left. Time and again government pays between 50 and 100 times the assessed valuation—with no tax recapture. Finally, there has been little use of less-than-fee acquisition, police-power application, or more imaginative and frugal methods of open space preservation.

Administration and Coordination

California at one time was looked to as a model of planning. And indeed, several comprehensive studies in the early sixties were used as prototypes by the Bureau of Outdoor Recreation of the U.S. Department of the Interior. Currently, State Parks and Recreation is involved in meeting BOR's demands in the designing of the State Comprehensive Outdoor Recreation Plan as a condition to receiving federal financial assistance. But the Department of Parks and Recreation is having difficulty simply compiling the total recreation demand and supply from the fragmented and often competitive recreation agencies.

In 1970, the Legislative Analyst declared that the Department's program budget was unsatisfactory "both as a departmental management tool and as the basis for legislative review and control of the department's funding." Firm management decisions were lacking regarding programs, policies, and priorities, which should be reflected in the budget. Also lacking was any "reasonable narrative discussion" to substantiate the funds requested. The Legislative Analyst underscored the lack of success he has had in securing such justification and back-up data from Parks and Recreation.[4] Except for the governor's line-item budget,

Department budget plans for 1971–72 are the same: "The budget does not provide much useful information for analysis. . . ." [5]

But the budget did reveal that "the department has been unable to carry out the scheduled planning for the capital-outlay projects in the 1971–72 *and 1972–73* budgets or even to construct most of the projects for which it had appropriations." [6] Thus, for the third consecutive year we are to see not only the usual failure to acquire land as demand increases, but a halt to acquisition altogether.

Improper priorities and lack of coordination with other bodies are evident as the Department fails to spend for or develop judicious or important projects because of planning errors. Some examples follow:

1. The recreation plans for Perris Reservoir included great expenditures for a "wave machine" for surfing, convention facilities, and extensive concessionaire facilities. Whatever the questionable priorities the expenditures evince, given the Pacific Ocean's surf and considering other needs, the Department failed to take into account the fact that the Metropolitan Water District holds an option to enlarge the reservoir, and this might flood many of these structures. The entire plan is now being "reevaluated" after this was discovered—and after considerable preparatory expense.

2. The Department proposed to spend $750,000 to improve building for concessionaires in the Pico-Garnier Building at the Pueblo de Los Angeles. "The historical significance of this development is debatable and has caused considerable controversy in Los Angeles." [7]

3. "The proposed extensive development of concessionaire and other facilities at the Point Mugu Project has been the subject of much controversy. . . ." [8]

4. The Department is preparing for a massive swimming complex at Cuyamaca State Park, at a cost of $660,000. At the same time, the Parks and Recreation Commission adopted the following policy:

> Developments within state parks shall be for the purpose of making the areas available for public enjoyment in a manner consistent with the preservation of natural, scenic, and ecological values for present and future generations. . . . Recreational developments that conflict with the public's enjoyment of the natural values inherent in the re-

source and/or which are attractions in themselves, such as playgrounds, golf courses, *swimming pools,* ski facilities and other such developments which are best provided within state recreation areas, are not to be encouraged within state parks.[9]

Even less in keeping with this policy are plans for Point Mugu State Park. Point Mugu has a beautiful high valley and a deep canyon with sycamore trees and a rocky beach. Into these 6,450 rare open acres the Department proposes not only the usual trails and picnic tables, but: a hotel, a hostel, an inn, restaurants, a general store, a gift shop, a laundry, a gas station, motorcycle trails, rifle and archery ranges, a swimming pool, horse stables, a conference center, a golf course, and a model-airplane flying field. The golf course, model-airplane flying field, inn, restaurants, shops, and rifle range have recently been deleted after public outcry.

This kind of development, on a smaller scale, is taking place throughout the state park system.

The Legislative Analyst has identified other questionable expenditures, including the San Francisco Maritime State Historic Park disposal, Castaic Reservoir development, Carpinteria State Beach facilities, and the $3,000,000 commitment to the San Clemente project near the President's western villa. Most of the Department's operations are considered questionable or wasteful by the Legislative Analyst.

The Department has consistently failed to consider the environmental effects of its projects. The State Environmental Quality Act of 1970 requires a detailed statement on the environmental impact of any project which "could have a significant effect on the environment of the state." Nevertheless, the Department has failed to provide such statements.

In light of the Department's record, we were not surprised to find them suspicious of our study. We were refused an interview with the Department Director, Mr. Mott. Mr. Mott's assistant did see us, asking whether we were "gainfully employed, paid for doing this work, represented any town or civic body, etc." We then requested from him basic information about the members of the State Parks and Recreation Commission—information which was clearly public and "had" to be released to us under the California Public Records Act. This information had been requested at two other offices, Information and Personnel, and we had finally been given, after a two-day wait, a list of the members of the *Underwater* Park Commission. Mott's assistant refused to give us a list of the members and their backgrounds, saying that it was not available to the public. If we wanted the information, he said, we would have to take it from him orally. He then proceeded to expound on the "conservationist" spirit of each member.

We were told that no one in Parks and Recreation could give us any figures on projects funded, budgetary levels, and the Department's progress in meeting its projected acquisition and development plans. No one would admit that there was a gap between projected expenditures and actual funding, even though it was a matter of public record and confirmed by the Legislative Analyst. Secrecy and reticence are especially problematic in the Department of Parks and Recreation, which is the only focal point for public pressure to acquire and preserve on a large scale wild areas and park land.

Federal Government

With the U.S. government owning more than 44% of California, federal agencies are crucial to the state's recreational needs. Over half of this land, more than 25,000,000 acres, is available for recreational use.* The land is in four national parks, eighteen national forests, and eight monuments. As with the 800,000-acre state park system, and 100,000 acres of local parks, acquisition has rarely proceeded as fast as state population, much less than demand, and now has slowed to a virtual halt. And there is a movement to give much federal land into private hands.

The maze of federal-agency jurisdictions administering federal land confounds the uninitiated. Three Cabinet departments are primarily involved: Interior, with the Bureau of Outdoor Recreation, Bureau of Reclamation, Bureau of Land Management, National Park Service, and Fish and Wildlife Service; Defense, with the Army Corps of Engineers and numerous military plants, bases, and reservations; and Agriculture, with the Forest Service and Soil Conservation Service. The Federal Power Commission also has the power to make crucial decisions affecting recreation and the

---

* Another one million acres is in military reservations.

landscape. With the exception of the Bureau of Outdoor Recreation (BOR), these agencies were formed long before the boom of current recreation needs.

The Bureau of Outdoor Recreation is a comparatively new agency formed in 1962 to develop and maintain a nationwide outdoor recreation plan, keep a national resources inventory, lead and assist other agencies in dealing with national recreational resources, and administer the grant programs of the Land and Water Conservation Fund. The master plan is already two years late in being finalized. Although Congress has given BOR the responsibility to develop the master plan, it has not given it the power to make other federal agencies follow the plan. Nor does it have the power to use the plan to coordinate one agency's recreation function with another's. And other agencies resent BOR intrusion as one more layer of bureaucratic oppression made up, as one National Park Service official put it, of "a lot of rejects and retreads from elsewhere" in the federal bureaucracy.

Nevertheless, BOR does represent a very important new force for sound federal recreation planning. And it has some incentive powers to induce state and local planning. Specifically, under the Land and Water Conservation Fund Act of 1965, BOR has the power to allocate funds to state and local agencies on a fifty-fifty matching basis for projects conforming to the state's outdoor recreation plan.

The failure to add land to federal, state, or local systems has not dramatically increased the numbers turned away from parks. In fact, although these numbers are quite high, they were even higher five years ago because the intensely developed systems are now accommodating more people. More people are being jammed together in adjoining camp-sites, larger parking lots, etc.

But even with denser use, these facilities are reaching their limits—and their long-run value and health is often threatened. State Park and Recreation Information System surveys by the State Department of Parks and Recreation traces the supply of facilities within mileage distances of zero to one, one to two, etc., from urban centers, and estimates demand accordingly. Stanford Research Institute studies indicate a 30% rise in demand over the next ten years. Judging from prior projections, this is probably an understatement. The National Park Service's Branch of

Table 6a

ESTIMATES OF POTENTIAL DEMAND FOR RECREATION IN
PARTICIPATION DAYS [a]
(1960, 1970, 1980)

Activity	Participation Days (*millions*)		
	1960	*1970*	*1980*
Passive outdoor pursuits			
Walking for pleasure	11.3	13.9	19.6
Driving for pleasure	19.5	24.9	34.8
Sightseeing	5.9	7.9	11.1
Picnicking	4.0	5.4	7.1
Attending outdoor sports events	3.8	5.2	7.1
Nature walks	2.6	3.1	4.5
Attending outdoor concerts, dramas	0.2	0.3	0.4
Subtotal	47.3	60.7	84.6
Physically active recreation			
Games and sports	11.8	18.1	24.8
Bicycling	6.0	8.8	12.9
Horseback riding	3.3	4.2	5.5
Subtotal	21.1	31.1	43.2
Water sports			
Swimming	4.4	6.6	9.2
Sailing and canoeing	0.2	0.3	0.4
Other boating	1.5	2.0	3.0
Water skiing	0.6	1.0	1.3
Subtotal	6.7	9.9	13.9
Winter sports			
Sledding [b]	0.2	0.2	0.3
Ice-skating [b]	c	c	c
Skiing [b]	0.1	0.1	0.1
Subtotal	0.3	0.3	0.4
Back-country recreation			
Fishing	4.6	7.1	9.0
Hunting	3.9	4.7	5.9
Camping	1.9	3.5	4.5
Hiking	0.5	1.0	1.0
Mountain climbing	0.1	0.1	0.1
Subtotal	11.0	16.4	20.5
Miscellaneous [b]	0.5	0.7	1.0
Grand total	86.9	119.1	163.6

[a] Includes all California counties except Humboldt, Monterey, Sonoma, Stanislaus, Tulare, and Ventura. Projections are generally higher for the excluded counties.

[b] Estimates based on extremely small per capita estimates that may include error.

[c] Less than 50,000 participation days.

Source: Stanford Research Institute, based on data obtained from the Outdoor Recreation Resources Review Commission and the California Department of Parks and Recreation.

Statistics Analysis has issued a ten-year forecast of public use. It anticipates small increases or static demand for four parks (including Yosemite). But it sees between 20% and 35% increase in use of Death Valley, Channel Islands, Joshua Tree, Kings Canyon, Lava Beds, Muir Woods, and Sequoia Parks. It predicts a 50% increase for Devils Post-pile and over 100% for Whiskeytown and Point Reyes. All areas not now overcrowded soon will be.

Despite projection, the federal government has reduced the Park Service's meager inholding-acquisition program. Monies budgeted for purchasing privately owned areas in the national park system were cut from $8 million to $1.7 million.* One million of the $1.7 million was a Rockefeller contribution earmarked for inholdings in Grand Teton Park outside California. The $200 million appropriated for the Land and Water Fund in 1968 was cut to $154 million in 1969 and to $124 million in 1970 by the President. Acquisitions are at a standstill.

The National Park Service is unable to coordinate with the Bureau of Outdoor Recreation. Forest Service is not in the Department of the Interior, but in the Department of Agriculture. And there is little coordination with the state. Thus, the Park Service merely plans for its own sites incrementally, making its own projections for each of its facilities.

The primary responsibility of the U.S. Forest Service is to conserve publicly owned timber resources. However, the demand boom has increasingly forced the Service into recreation. The Forest Service, with almost twenty million acres in California, maintains more than 16,000 campsites and 1,200 picnic sites, in addition to winter-sports areas, resorts, and pack stations operated under permit by private concessionaires. The Forest Service is continually under tremendous pressure to open up more of its land for ski developments. Its projections for recreational demand have been consistently too conservative, and it cooperates with the state even less than the Park Service. At one point, the state was seeking land for park purposes at the Pfeiffer-Big Sur State Park, while the Forest Service was proposing to trade 800 acres of Big Sur beach property to private owners for lands in the Los Padres National Forest.

* The estimated cost of acquiring all private inholdings in the natural areas of the nationwide park system is now $114 million—a cost increase of 93% over the last six years.

To keep portions of its holdings unspoiled, the Forest Service has established three special classifications of forest land: wilderness, wild, and primitive. Restrictions on both public and private use are well established for all three. Congress sanctioned the designations in the Wilderness Act of 1964, over the strong opposition of timber, mining, and grazing interests. Seventeen areas covering 1.7 million acres have been given these classifications in California.

The sympathies of the Forest Service seem to lie with the commercial loggers. Nonenforcement of standards regarding erosion or sustained yield is not the extent of their involvement. For example, the Sierra Club proposed in March of 1968 that 171,500 acres in remote Siskiyou County be designated wilderness. The Forest Service conducted an investigation and issued a preliminary report entitled *Multiple Use Plan Review—Siskiyou Study Area* in December of 1968. The purpose was to catalogue the resources and gauge their importance. Following analysis of these measurements, a decision was to be made.

The "preliminary study" by the Forest Service appears objective, but close analysis reveals it to contain many statistical presumptions of doubtful veracity. These presumptions consistently favor the logging "use" for the area as opposed to wilderness use.

First, without study of any kind, the Forest Service suggests that classifying the area as wilderness may be *detrimental* to wildlife because it would "eliminate the creation of additional game range through timber harvesting. It would also eliminate the possibility of any stream channel clearing for fish passage." The impression given is that the fish are clamoring for river clearing and dredging and game for clear-cutting so they can have room to "spread out." The Forest Service then adds that "There are no known animal species which would be endangered by any of the management alternatives under consideration." Nowhere in this Report is there any environmental survey justifying these judgments. The environmental analysis consists of listing the more apparent and larger animals observed by various people in the area (weasels, badgers, etc.). Not only is there no basis for concluding the above, but what evidence there is indicates quite the opposite. Elsewhere in the Report, it is noted that fish are plentiful and that wildlife is served by more than adequate forage distributed over the entire area. Further, as to assurances against damage from logging, the Report notes in passing that much of the soil is extremely unstable.

Gordon Robinson, a former logger who is intimately familiar with the area and who studied the Report, remarks:

> Resistance to the Siskiyou Wilderness Study Area proposal seems to come entirely from spokesmen for forest industry. One observes that they are constantly putting pressure on the U.S. Forest Service to relax timber management standards by a variety of rationalizations aimed at promoting the single use of wood production. Their aim is to coerce the Forest Service to mass produce low quality wood at the expense of other wild land values. In this case, they would have the Forest Service ignore watershed values and sustained timber growing capacity, for surely erosion of unstable soils will result in lessening of its growth capacity. They would ignore the habitat for fish that would be greatly endangered by accelerated erosion. They would ignore the great biological and scenic values unique to the area.[10]

Probably more disturbing than all this is the deliberate game-playing on the other side of the ledger. Comfortably situated in their arena of empirical expertise, Forest Service economists calculated the benefits from logging. Part of this calculation was the yield in board feet. Timber expert Robinson, however, revealed that the yield estimates are based on figures which do not apply to the study area for numerous reasons, including failure to consider trees not merchantable, utilization practice, or the fact that "at least half the timber . . . is marginal and the rest is located on unstable to highly unstable soils." The Forest Service failed to take into account their own vague admission about erosion. Robinson quotes from an industry source concerning much of the area:

> Approximately 80 percent of the commercial forest land in that working circle involves topography too steep for tractor logging without causing excessive erosion. Logging by clear-cut blocks and highline is required on all slopes over 30 percent. This limits logging . . . to stands of moderate or better densities.

If the loggers are prohibited from these steep areas, they still gain some timber in other areas if the wilderness area loses or is reduced. If they are not prohibited, they do not bear the cost of their erosion.

The Report continues. It then uses the highly inflated board-foot-yield estimate and applies a formula to it to compute the benefit to the area in terms of employment from logging. Not only is the original figure inflated but the employment-benefit formula is patently absurd. The Forest Service asserts that the annual cut of "22.5 million" board feet will provide 1,995 jobs when employment in dependent service industries is added. If we apply this formula to Siskiyou and to the forested neighboring counties, we discover that Del Norte County's annual cut (300 million board feet) gives it 26,610 jobs. Unfortunately, there are only 5,900 people employed in *any* occupation in the entire county, according to the California State Department of Employment. In fact, there are only 16,600 people in the county. Siskiyou County (485 million board feet) would yield 43,020 jobs. Siskiyou has 13,775 employed persons in all occupations and 35,400 people. Humboldt County (1,300 million board feet) indicates 115,310 employees benefited by the Forest Service formula. Humboldt only has 35,700 employed persons and a total population of 101,000.

A major stumbling block to sound forest management in California is the existence of large areas of checkerboard land ownership, encompassing tens of thousands of square miles. In these areas, every alternate square mile is under Forest Service ownership, while the remaining lands are in private hands—a holdover from the federal land giveaway patterns to railroads in the nineteenth century. It is Forest Service policy to consolidate these holdings by trading lands with private owners. As Congress has not furnished the necessary funds to purchase the private lands,* the ultimate fate of all lands, public and private, within the checkerboard areas, is going to be determined largely by private owners.

The Bureau of Land Management has jurisdiction over fifteen million acres—over one-seventh of California. It is a catchall agency responsible for managing or disposing of vast stretches of desert and mountain terrain. It is currently making a comprehensive inventory of its lands. It is author-

---

* The Forest Service lacks the authority to purchase private inholdings or to regulate land uses on the inholdings. Only by difficult "land exchanges" can the Forest Service consolidate its twenty million acres riddled with private inholdings, and then only by agreement.

ized under the Classification and Multiple Use Act of 1964 to offer for sale those lands classified for recreational use. Thousands of twentieth-century homesteaders have taken advantage of the Bureau of Land Management's traditional land-giveaway policies. Large areas in San Bernardino and Imperial counties were blemished under the Small Tract Act of 1938, which permitted the Bureau of Land Management to sell or lease two-and-one-half- or five-acre parcels of desolate, windswept land for a token sum to anyone who would put a small building on them. When the buyers' dreams of weekend hideaways or get-rich-quick investments didn't materialize, the land often reverted back to the Bureau of Land Management. The desert was cluttered with 75,000 "jackrabbit" homesteads, many of them littered with refuse and deteriorating shacks.*

The Bureau administers a variety of commercial uses of its land, including mining, oil exploration, grazing, and logging. Regulations prohibit logging along main roads, streets, and lake shores of Bureau land leased to timber companies. Within limitations of its budget, the Bureau replants trees on cut-over or burned-over land. However, Congress has never provided the Bureau with sufficient funds to manage these lands or to dispose of them in a rational manner. The Bureau is further handicapped by lack of a trained staff in land-use planning, by anomalous land laws which are often contradictory, and by conflicting pressures from private interests. Mining claims, for example, are often used for homesites, hunting sites, motels, service stations, and farms—everything but serious prospecting.

The Army Corps of Engineers builds harbors, improves navigation, and erects flood-control installations; it is also responsible, under the law, for recreation development in projects it constructs. Its fifteen reservoirs in California

---

* The Small Tract Act was amended in 1961 and the Bureau of Land Management is required to work closely with local agencies to prevent shoddy, scattered, and uneconomic growth, but the damage has been done. The Bureau of Land Management is slowly moving from a custodial office to a resource and development agency. Its land is available under the 1964 Act to state and local agencies at $2.50 an acre for recreational use. To prevent resale of this acreage to private development, the Bureau has authority to repossess if the original recreation purpose, as shown in a local or regional plan, is not carried out. One of the largest recreational projects the Bureau proposes to develop on its own is the Kings Range conservation area south of Eureka. This is a 53,000-acre preserve, more than half of which is administered by the Bureau.

attracted eleven million visitors in 1966. But the Corps has persisted in encouraging local agencies to take over the operation and maintenance of its recreational facilities, in spite of the fact that the local agencies cannot afford to maintain regional facilities on county budgets. Development of recreation sometimes runs into direct conflict with other functions of the Corps. In the Sacramento River Delta the Corps has spent nearly $3 million annually in repair of flood-control levees, but the banks of the river have been scarred by stripping off the vegetation, and the area's potential for fishing, swimming, and picnics has been destroyed.

The Bureau of Reclamation was established to construct, operate, and maintain irrigation systems for reclamation of the West's arid lands. And it has drifted into the recreation business. However, the Bureau often delegates planning, development, and management of recreation sites to other federal, state, or local agencies. For example, recreation at the Bureau's Shasta and Trinity dams has been turned over to the U.S. Forest Service. At the new Whiskeytown Reservoir, the National Park Service has inherited the recreation functions from the Bureau.

The Bureau is discussed elsewhere, especially in Chapter 3, and is the subject of a separate study made by a Nader investigative team and to be released in 1972.* Other federal agencies affecting recreation and wild area preservation include the Federal Water Pollution Control Administration and the Fish and Wildlife Service in the Department of the Interior. Both of these, but especially the former, defer regulation to state bodies because of California's public relations regulatory image. The FWPCA is also the object of a detailed Washington, D.C., investigation, *Water Wasteland* (Grossman, 1971).

Special Problems

Acquisition

Government failure to buy in the face of land appreciation will make the cost prohibitive for future generations. The leading 1965 *Urban Metropolitan Open Space Study,* con-

---

* There is also a special study of the U.S. Forest Service. No material from the detailed Washington, D.C., investigations has been duplicated herein.

ducted by Eckbo, Dean, Austin, and Williams for the State Office of Planning, identified 1,973,156 acres available for proposed and needed acquisition. The Study identified about 60% of this acreage as appropriate for less-than-fee acquisition. Over one-third was subject to high encroachment (immediately threatened) in 1965. The cost in 1965 dollars for acquisition, 60% less than fee, was estimated at $3,125,987,781. Because this amount was not spent, the cost is estimated to be $4,135,526,459 in 1970. The estimated cost of acquiring private inholdings has risen at three times this rate. Cutbacks by local, state and federal jurisdictions as described above, when massive purchase is now feasible and necessary, appear to be false economies.

Consolidation of Inholdings

After acquisition, a second major problem is the mutually profitable exchange of land with other government units, and the often related need to consolidate lands for park purposes (e.g., purchase of privately owned inholdings).

The acquisition of privately owned inholdings within park lands is a major consolidation problem. It is now the practice to use the checkerboard pattern of private inholdings as a major selling point when speculating on these lands. Anza-Borrego State Park has such an inholding.

The Anza-Borrego Committee of the Desert Protective Council is a nonprofit conservationist group which raises funds to purchase private lands within the park to preserve them and eventually deed them to the state. In March of 1970, this group noticed a sign offering for sale some 800 acres of land within the Park boundaries near Hawk Canyon—land it had hoped to purchase. Investigating the offer, the group learned that the state had known of the offer of sale but had chosen to do nothing about it, primarily because of money. The group then initiated a title search of the property. They discovered that the property was listed as 640 acres, and that the current owners of the property were five employees of the San Diego County Assessor's office. One of these public servants confided that the parcel had never been surveyed, and that its boundaries actually included about 822 acres, which made their purchase a "good bargain." These five county employees had purchased the parcel as a quarter section (640 acres) for $16,000, or $25 per acre, out of an estate, knowing from their access to records and experience with land maps that the parcel was considerably larger. The price they paid was claimed to be the fair market value of the land at the time, that is, $25 per acre. The county records indicate that the land is currently appraised as 640 acres, at a fair market value of $21,000. Six months after the purchase, one of the five sold his interest in the land for a 50% profit, which would mean that the property ought now to be assessed at $24,000. It also indicates that the five did indeed make a fine bargain when they purchased the property only six months earlier. Having made a very good deal by virtue of their positions as public employees, the group then offered the entire property (as the approximately 800 acres it was) at $125 per acre. And yet the land is only being appraised at $32.80 per acre! There have as yet been no takers for their offer.

The upshot is that if the state or a conservationist group now seeks to purchase the property to complete the park, the price they will have to pay will be anywhere from 50% to 500% greater than that paid initially by the speculating public servants. Our title search indicated that two of the five have been involved in a number of other land deals in the county, including at least one with the county.

Preservation

After acquiring and consolidating, government must then preserve its land from direct conversion, from commercial conversion of private inholdings it has failed to consolidate, and from disposal.

The prime danger of direct conversion comes from the state's own highway programs, which will consume two million acres by 1980. Freeway construction threatens three parks in California's north coast and several in the south. The Division of highways proposes to place a freeway over Goleta Slough in Santa Barbara, one through Tamalpais State Park, and has even proposed an eight-lane freeway through San Francisco's famous Golden Gate Park. The Golden Gate Highway now bisects Plumas National Forest. Environmentalist Sam Wood writes: "During the next ten years, freeways are expected to occupy 1,000 acres of California parks. This destruction will permit a total savings of between ten to fifteen miles out of 12,400 miles of freeway planned for 1980.[11] That was in November of 1964. In the seven years since, the 1,000 acres have been converted and many more thousands are threatened.

One way to preserve areas from human damage is through

explicit restrictions of land under government control. The federal government theoretically created such a system when it passed the Wilderness Act of 1964.* Forest Service has classified seventeen areas as wilderness within the seventeen National Forests in California. They cover 1.7 million acres. The Fish and Wildlife Service has declared additional areas as wildlife refuges. California's Protected Waterways Act and the federal Scenic Rivers Act of 1968 theoretically protect rivers.

The acreage in wilderness may seem impressive, but the sight of litter, debris, and crowds quickly dispels optimism. The National Park Service is more or less ignoring the Act as applied to Parks, and meeting the excessive demand with more intense development to handle more people.

The Park Service tends to define away its areas through "threshold zones" and "enclaves." The "threshold zone" is the area along the edge of a road which the Park Service claims is not within "wilderness" designations (thus allowing concessionaires, etc.). On occasion, the Park Service will declare the "zone" to extend out from the road as much as two miles. The "enclave" idea is the creation through wilderness areas of circles one-eighth of a mile in circumference, with toilets, bunkhouse hostels, restaurants—perhaps a few hot dog stands.

The Park Service is even talking about "motor vehicle" trails—twelve-foot-wide roads for low-speed driving. This allows a "wilderness experience by automobile."

Mineral King

The overdevelopment of private inholdings which government has failed to consolidate into parks or refuges is a problem for all jurisdictions, exemplified by the Disney development in Mineral King.

The Mineral King area is the popular name for the 15,000-acre Sequoia National Game Refuge of the Sequoia National Forest. Located fifty-five miles east of Visalia, it is an enclave bounded on three sides by Sequoia National Park, and is both geographically and ecologically part of the park. It is within the same watershed and possesses the same

---

* The purpose of the Wilderness Act was to enable the designation of land areas, by a specified process, for preservation in various natural states. The "wilderness" category allows the most absolute preservation of land. Man is permitted in these areas, but no roads or structures are there to greet him, and he may leave nothing behind.

flora and fauna. The area is classic high-Sierra near-wilderness, with Mineral King Valley the focal point of a region of high peaks and mountain bowls studded with Sierra lakes and meadows. Five major streams tumble down into the valley, each watering splendid little mountain gardens of flowers, from white orchids to sneezeweed, and groves of aspen and cottonwood in the valley meadows. The ecology of the area is extremely fragile, given the high elevations (8,000 to 12,000 feet), thin soils, and a short growing season. Mineral King Valley is a key part of the Game Refuge, since it is the only area of lush vegetation and is the summer range of deer and other animals. The Game Refuge was created by a direct act of Congress in 1926, and there is currently pending legislation before Congress to incorporate it into the Sequoia National Park.

Interest in developing the area as a winter sports site originated in the 1930s, and studies were made which identified the skiing potential of the valley and the surrounding high country. Seeing that a ski area could be developed, the Forest Service issued in 1949 a prospectus seeking private capital to do the job. The scope of the projected development at that time would be modest by today's standards, calling for about $200,000, but there were no takers because of the lack of an adequate all-weather highway into the valley. In 1965, another prospectus was issued, this time outlining a winter sports development to cost approximately $3 million, with a condition imposed on the eventual permittee that he secure construction of the highway before the permit would be issued. Of the six qualifying bids, four were relatively modest, and two called for $35–40 million developments. The $35 million development proposal of Walt Disney Productions was selected, and a three-year permit for further study was issued late in 1965. The Forest Service's prospectus called for four ski lifts, a parking capacity of 1,200 automobiles, and resort accommodations for 100 overnight visitors. Disney's accepted proposal was for an alpine village with a system of twenty-two to twenty-seven ski lifts, an eight- to ten-story parking structure for 3,600 vehicles, including buses, resort accommodations for 3,300 visitors—plus extensive accommodations for nearly 1,000 employees, in addition to extensive complementary developments in the form of administrative offices, restaurants, shops, a hospital, a heliport, a convention center, a theater, an arena complex, an equestrian center, swimming and skating facilities, a cog-assisted railroad, stream control features, avalanche dams, and so forth. Such development would also require water-storage facilities, sewage-treatment plants, and local power generation or power transmission through lines which would run across Sequoia National Park. The resort development will cover over 300 acres, and year-round use will affect over 13,000 acres. The concentration of persons and vehicles anticipated is double that presently found in crowded Yosemite Valley, yet the area is nearly 4,000 feet higher and much more fragile than Yosemite.

In the development proposal there is envisioned "grooming and manicuring of most slopes," which will require "extensive bulldozing and blasting in most lower areas and extensive rock removal at higher elevations." The Forest Service recognized "a need for land modification, earth moving, and possibly stream channel changing beyond what we might normally permit . . . a great deal of earth and debris moving. . . . By accepting the development proposal, we have also accepted that some effect on fishery values, streamflow, vegetation, soil, and other resources must be provided for." This was Mr. W. S. Davis, the Chief of the Forest Service Division of Recreation speaking.

Disney indicated that future efforts would be "dedicated to making Mineral King grow to meet the ever-increasing public need. I guess you might say that it won't ever be finished." Whether it will ever be constructed will depend on the outcome of litigation brought by the Sierra Club to stop the project and currently in the federal courts.

All of this development will be in a game refuge established by the Congress of the United States for the protection of the land and "the game animals which may be thereon." The Secretary of Agriculture was left with the power to authorize only uses "consistent with the purposes for which said game refuge is established." Yet there is no evidence of an attempt by the Forest Service of the Department of Agriculture to determine whether or not the proposed development was a use consistent with the national game refuge.

An official from the California Fish and Game Commission stated that although his department had made no specific studies on the matter, "we can say . . . that in an extensive development such as the Disney proposal, considerable wildlife habitat would be lost and wildlife would suffer from human encroachment." The Forest Service's own Range and Wildlife management section agreed, after making an examination of the preliminary site studies proposed, and stated that "the extent and nature of the proposed alteration of the basin is unacceptable to us—the damages extend beyond the effects on fish and wildlife and these alone are critical." However, the views of Range and Wildlife within the Forest Service were not solicited until several weeks before the press conference announcing Forest Service acceptance of the proposal. Most in Range and Wildlife believe that their "views" were solicited to defuse any charges of environmental unconcern—i.e., as public relations. The reply from the Forest Service to its own section's surprising disapproval came some six days before the press conference from the Director of Wildlife Management, who prefaced his brief memorandum with the introduction, "After one quick review of the Mineral King Master Plan, I have a few comments to offer. . . ." The memo dealt with the need to surface horse trails, a question on the capacity of the soil to handle the project's sewage and whether it should be piped out of the valley, and a conclusion in which the Wildlife Management Director hoped "that we study the impacts of this concession for a long time before permitting another one." Apparently, the only studies done related to snow, weather, and development. No ecological studies were made, nor any kind of biological survey of the area, to determine what species were present, with what kind of distribution and numbers, and what the total impact would be on the animal populations or on the plant life. No attempts were made to identify how fragile the margins of life in the basin might be, or the needs of the delicate habitat. In reference to the summer range needs of migratory deer herds, the suggestion was made that deer numbers should be reduced to "minimize problems of conflict." Certainly eliminating wildlife would solve the problem of threats to them posed by the development.

In 1939, under Reorganization Act II, certain conservation functions were transferred from the Department of Agriculture to the Department of the Interior. The Department of the Interior, here through the National Park Service, has the duty specified by this Act to enforce basic conservation functions, including the enforcement of "*any* Act of Congress for the protection, preservation or restoration of game and other wildlife and animals." The Secretary of the Interior has made *no* investigation and has made no findings on the issue of whether Disney's plans will have a deleterious effect on wildlife, game, and migratory birds.

At the time the preliminary permit for study was issued, in late 1965, no agreements had been reached with the National Park Service concerning the key question of highway construction into Mineral King nor on any other items dealing with the impact which the proposed development might have on Sequoia National Park, although the plan clearly would require access across the park. Late in 1967, the California State Highway Commission approved a high-speed highway following the route of the old road, and committed $22,000,000 of state funds for the construction of this road into the resort, to be coupled with $3,000,000 from the U.S. Economic Development Administration. It is interesting to note that this road was placed in the state highway system in July of 1965, as intended access to the Mineral King development, several months before any one of the bids was accepted by the Forest Service. No legislative hearings were held on this addition, and it was accomplished by means of a rider on another bill, and by maneuverings by the president pro tem of the Senate. The central 9.2 miles of the proposed routing is within Sequoia National Park, yet the highway was not proposed by the Park Service. The road will cut a new swath across the park, including structures, cuts and fills, and, contrary to statutory and regulatory requirements, will in no way conserve scenery or natural and historic objects and wildlife, nor provide for their enjoyment in a manner "as will leave them unimpaired for the enjoyment of future generations." The politics of this road and its immense public subsidization for private profits are detailed as a separate case study in Chapter 10. The road will cost taxpayers several dollars per car and will probably have to be widened to four lanes —Disney pays nothing for it.

The Department of the Interior also proposed to permit the construction of a 66,000-volt power line across the National Park in order to enable Disney to obtain electric power necessary for the project—even though 16 U.S.C. 45(c) applies specifically to Sequoia National Park and provides that no permit for transmission lines or for the transmission of power within the park limits shall be granted or made without specific authority of Congress.

Congress has set an 80-acre limit on the area on which resorts may be developed under lease on National Forest land, for a lease of forty years. The Mineral King developments will cover some 300 acres, and will be permitted to construct lifts and trails throughout about 13,000 acres. The Forest Service intends to lease the excess acreage on an annually revocable year-to-year lease basis. The statutes enabling the Service to let such leases state quite explicitly that the construction of hotels, resorts, and any other structures or facilities is permitted only on land "not exceeding 80 acres." It is clear that this statute is not being observed, and that the two types of permits, the thirty-year and the year-to-year, are so inextricably intertwined that it would be inconceivable that the Service could revoke the latter at any time during the duration of the former.

Congress has never expressly authorized the "revocable" permits. The Department of Agriculture claims authorization for them only under its general power to regulate the forest lands or "to preserve the forests thereon from destruction," and under an Attorney General's Opinion of 1928. That opinion narrowly restricts their use, including requiring that the permitted use will not permanently damage or destroy the land for government use. It is highly questionable whether so-called "revocable" permits in the present use meet the strict requirements laid down by the attorney general. The extent of the investment of Disney, in excess of $35 million, suggests that the Service will have some difficulty enforcing the thirty-year limitation at the point of its expiration. What is contemplated is a grant of 13,000 acres for a period of thirty years, an arrangement violating the spirit and letter of the law.

There have been no hearings by any federal, state, or local agency with responsibilities in the matter, either on the question of whether the development should take place or regarding its myriad details. Nor has either of the two key federal departments of Agriculture or the Interior provided any formal administrative remedy or review procedures for the action, in spite of numerous requests by various groups, and in spite of laws and regulations requiring such review procedures.

Individual giveaways by legislative pork barrel are also a threat. On June 5, 1969, Senator Murphy quietly introduced Senate Bill 2329: "Be it enacted . . . that the United States of America does hereby relinquish and quitclaim unto Chaplin E. Collins, Esquire, and Security Title Insurance Company of California, . . . any right, title and interest it might claim . . . to . . . certain real property. . . ." The bill then lists over 1,200 full sections and additional partial sections. At 640 acres each, this is a gift of over *750,000* acres. A quitclaim grant would cede *any* claim the government might have to this land. All of this land is clearly within the ownership of the federal government under the management and jurisdiction of the Department of the Interior. The former Senator's claim that the bill was a routine favor to allow Congressional review of a private claim is belied by two facts. First, the normal procedure to accomplish this is to refer such cases to the Court of Claims, which Senator Murphy had done on numerous previous occasions. Second, the Senator refused to reveal the identity of the actual claimant behind the title insurance dummy. How a person is going to argue his right to federal land before Congress or elsewhere without identifying himself is unclear.

Lake Berryessa

Lake Berryessa is a creation of the Solano Project, a Bureau of Reclamation project authorized in 1948 and constructed in the 1950s to provide for flood control, and to supply water for irrigated, municipal, and industrial portions of Solano County. Impounded by Monticello Dam, the lake inundates Berryessa Valley, measures twenty-two and a half by three miles, and has a storage capacity of 1,600,000 acre-feet, making it the second largest in the state. The total federal ownership is approximately 26,250 acres, of which 19,250 is water surface area at maximum water level; 7,000 acres lie above the maximum pool to form the perimeter of the immediate project area. At this maximum level, the lake has a shoreline length of approximately 170 miles.

The lake area is also a valuable asset as a wildlife habitat and as open space and grazing lands; it is surrounded by scenic hills covered with verdant woodlands and brush which contribute to the lake's function of watershed collection. Located approximately seventy miles from San Francisco and fifty miles from Sacramento, Lake Berryessa would provide unlimited recreational opportunities for the growing urban populations, especially for one-day and weekend trips.

Because of very stringent policies of land acquisition and

maintenance around federal water projects during the Eisenhower administration, the authority under which the dam and lake were created did not provide for recreation. Then, as now, the Bureau of Reclamation was not seen as being in the recreation business, and it was expected that some other public body would assume responsibility for developing the recreational potential of the area. Soon after construction was completed, the public began using the area, producing problems of sanitation, safety, pollution, traffic, and the like. Need for some sort of responsible administration in the area was recognized. The National Park Service was cool to the idea of assuming this responsibility, because of its low-profile emphasis on recreation at the time and because of budgetary pressures. Similarly, the then State Division of Beaches and Parks had its own budget limitations and resented having such a responsibility thrust upon it by the federal government without benefit of previous planning.

The Bureau was forced to turn to Napa County. The county was averse to the idea of assuming the administrative responsibilities alone, but agreed to do so if Yolo and Solano counties helped shoulder the burden. An arrangement was worked out in mid-1958, followed in early 1962 by another agreement, the controlling document to this time. Under it, the federal government transferred to the county (while recognizing the primary jurisdiction of the federal government over the project area) responsibility for the development, administration, and maintenance of the recreational and other land uses involved. The county would be permitted to lease various lands to private concessions for recreational purposes for a period of thirty years, plus two ten-year options to renew.

In 1959, the National Park Service had prepared a comprehensive multi-use Public Use Plan for the Lake Berryessa federal lands, and the agreement stipulated that the county and the concessions were to use the plan as a guide in developing the area. The emphasis in the plan was on day and weekend use, with facilities for camping and *very* few facilities for temporary mobile-home trailer parking. All licenses, permits, and contracts let by the county were to be approved by the federal government before issuance. The concessionaires were to agree to develop the area leased to them in accordance with the use designation given that area in the Public Use Plan. The federal government has a ninety-day termination right which may be exercised for certain reasons, including the failure of the county to comply with the agreement.

All plans and specifications of all improvements were to be approved in advance by the county and the County Park Director, and they were to be subject to approval by the Bureau of Reclamation if necessary. All such development was also to be in compliance with county requirements. A land management plan was developed by the county and approved by the Bureau.

Sophisticated plans and the review by local and federal bodies seemed to guarantee the responsible addition of an invaluable and much needed public asset. Checks for protection of the environment were plentiful. People envisioned a sparkling lake, with public access for fishing and boating, picnic facilities, and sophisticated sewage and water-quality controls.

In the early 1960s, the county noted that it might not follow the Public Use Plan too closely, since it needed to develop overnight accommodations to create a vacation area as well as a day-use area. A policy-making Park Commission was created and a park director appointed, along with ancillary staff, to be in charge of administration of the area. They were directly responsible to the County Board of Supervisors.

At the time the county picked up the recreational management responsibility under the above arrangements, it pleaded limited financial resources and anticipated heavy usage by noncounty residents to justify relying on revenue-producing concession operations for development of "most" public-use facilities to be provided during the "initial" years of operation. It was then hoped that the county would accrue funds through the concessionaires and use them to develop additional public-use facilities.*

A decade has passed. "The lakeline area has become a private residential area instead of a public recreational area as intended in the 1959 public use plan," says a County Planning Department report. The Department has recog-

---

* The concessions pay the county 3% of their gross receipts plus a possessory interest tax, which in 1969 amounted to $127,000. The east shore of the lake was precluded from development and is used today for private grazing purposes. These private lands on the east shore above the lakeline are serviced by a federally constructed and maintained road, for reasons that are unclear.

nized that neither the county nor the concessionaires has followed the Public Use Plan, that the concessions have developed into private areas with quasi-permanent mobile homes strung along miles of the shoreline for profits, and that the private sublessees and concessionaires have been "slow" to meet their "legal and moral obligations" to provide safe swimming areas, beaches, lifeguard service, inexpensive picnic areas, campsites, and other such public facilities. Federally owned lakeline has been ingeniously turned into a private mobile-home residential area. "Campers" come and stay for years, constructing permanent "mobile" homes and claiming the land as private domain. There are seven concessions and approximately 1,600 permanent "mobile" homes. There is now only one "public" area free of the exorbitant rates charged in the resorts. The only facilities provided—a few trash barrels and two chemical toilets—are in one wholly unimproved area. There is no water provided, no picnic tables or barbeque facilities, no parking facilities for the public other than an extended shoulder of the public highway, no lifeguard services (there have been eighty drownings up to 1970), very little in the way of shade, and no landscaping whatsoever.

A warning sign identifies the area as "Bureau of Reclamation Land" and announces "camping only in authorized resort areas." Within walking distance down the highway is a chained-off road with a large "Do Not Enter" sign, which leads down to a delightfully landscaped, watered area with flowers and picnic and barbeque facilities and a lawn being watered almost continuously. This is the county's "Park Headquarters," which serves as an occasional gathering place for county employees' outings to the lake. The public is not admitted to this oasis, but can gain limited access to the resort areas for fees far in excess of any public recreational area elsewhere in California. One can occasionally find a picnic table and extremely limited camping facilities. These expensive "public" provisions are consistently in the least desirable areas. Tents are pitched out on the asphalt or on dusty parking lots, next to boat trailers, truck-campers, and automobiles.

The emphasis is on the "mobile" homes which range from spacious three-bedroom, two-bath sixty- by twenty-foot doubles with redwood siding to smaller, less affluent boxes. Most of the trailers are surrounded by landscaping, permanent decks, concrete driveways, and patios installed by the "tenants," as well as by fences down to the lake shore and private docks. Sea walls spread along the shore, some to protect against high lake waters, others to terrace the steep slopes for sundecks, gardens, and cabanas. There are vegetable gardens and chicken coops. A General Motors vice-president has one of the nicest of these residences, a trailer-house that would in no way suggest that it might be a trailer except for two trailer hitches behind some high flowers, and ancient license plates.

One resort was peppered with signs boldly announcing: "Private Property—$100 Reward—Arrest and Conviction of Anyone Molesting or Trespassing."

New bids for concessions have been precluded: one new-comer was told outright that the present concessionaires had been assured that they would suffer no competition. When a resident asked to see the Lake Berryessa Land Management Plan in order to establish his grounds for a possible complaint against a resort owner, he was told that the only way he could see it would be "by a court order." He was eventually able to secure a copy by writing to the Department of the Interior in Washington, D.C.

The owners have managed to get their resorts exempted from a recent moratorium on all mobile-home park development in Napa County, pending a study and introduction of regulation ordinances—in spite of the fact that they could reasonably be viewed as the worst offenders, by any norms, of mobile-home abuse, specifically with regard to density and setbacks.

In addition to the private appropriation of public land and aesthetic and recreational loss, there is also a serious problem at Lake Berryessa with sanitation and water pollution. There has been a long history of sewage-treatment deficiencies at most concessions. The installations are poorly designed and constructed and are inadequate to handle the peak loads of the summer months. The common method of disposal is by "spray evaporation" on hillside areas; the sewage is of course carried off into the lake by rain runoff. Recently, the County's Department of Public Health designed facilities for three of the resorts at no cost to the resorts, and yet not one of them used this design, apparently because of the cost of the recommended facility.

Sewage-retention ponds are used for the disposal of chemical toilet waste, and the lake is rapidly approaching a lifeless, eutrophic state. Human waste is sometimes dumped directly into the lake and its feeder streams. At some of the resorts there are neither fencing nor posting to keep hikers and children from nearing the sewage ponds or spray areas, and no storage or power supply to prevent overflows during power shutdowns.

Other sources of pollution include the heavy development of trailer homesites on steep slopes, causing soil erosion and siltation pollution. There are also existing and abandoned road and gravel operations (necessary for road-building and construction materials) which have already destroyed the spawning grounds of steelhead trout in one of the tributary creeks.

The County Department of Public Health has submitted many reports on existing deficiencies and recommendations of proposed projects with noticeable deficiencies. These reports and recommendations have been ignored or overridden by public officials, including the Director of the Lake Berryessa Park Commission. The Health Department does not appear to have this difficulty in enforcing sewage ordinances on private lands.

Recently a number of concerned property owners outside the lakeline have organized themselves to effect some changes on the federal lands, especially with regard to access to the lake, planning for the area, and the murky politics which they feel to be pervasive. Several business people who had joined or shown sympathy were promptly threatened with a boycott of their goods or services by all of the resorts unless they desisted. Similar threats and pressures have been brought to bear on local businessmen and shopkeepers who had advertised in a new local weekly newspaper that has assumed a critical editorial posture regarding the conditions at the lake. The threats seem to have been almost completely effective.

The Bureau of Reclamation does not govern, it defers to the county. Remarked one top official: "They've got the contract, let 'em administer it. . . . At least there's something there." One official in the Sacramento Bureau Office, whose efforts to alter the Berryessa situation have been rejected by his superiors, admitted that the Bureau had abdicated its responsibility there, banking on empty promises from the concessionaires and the county that the public interests would soon be better served. Yet when his superior was asked about the need for improved public-use areas, he replied, "The county says they don't have the money for expanded facilities." Upon receiving complaints about conditions at the lake, the Bureau asks the county to investigate the matter and furnish a report, and then answers the complaints on the basis of the county's response.

That the county does not take the Bureau seriously is not surprising. A review of the Bureau's confidential files and the lake area indicates that, repeatedly, areas within the resorts which had been promised as public day-use and camping areas had in short order ended up packed with mobile homes. In response to Bureau "encouragement" that the county provide for short-term public users, the county consistently replied that it did not want to get into the camping and day-use business and thus compete with the concessions, and that the "concessionaires would provide" for those persons desiring such facilities. They never have, to the mildly expressed consternation of the Bureau.

It is curious that the Bureau has not seen fit to encourage the county to take one simple step toward remedying their alleged shortage of cash with which to develop public-use facilities—by increasing the 3% franchise tax on the resorts. This suggestion was made in an internal memorandum at one time, and it was pointed out that doubling or even tripling the tax would be consistent with what is done in other comparable areas and arrangements. Concessionaires at state parks pay a 10% tax on gross receipts.

The National Park Service is also supposed to review the Berryessa situation, but it too pleads inadequate staffing. "We've never had the staff to keep on top of all this crap that is going on," complained a key Park Service official. "It's the way the whole goddamn government works; it's a quagmire and you can't get a damned thing done. I even laid out a trailer park for them and they just laughed at me. I'm so damned frustrated about the whole damn thing that I'm speechless. We've got so much else to do—even though nobody listens to us—that I just decided it was a dog, a dead dog, and we might as well forget it. To hell with it. Sacramento defaults on their arguments, then makes new ones, and all we can do is concur in them. It's a real dead dog—you'd need a federal employee living there fulltime and then they'd probably still ignore us. The thing has so deteriorated I don't know what to do."

In mid-June of 1970, Mike Morford, a hopeful and courageous biologist in the Fish and Wildlife Service of the Department of the Interior stationed in Sacramento, sent a memo to then Secretary Hickel under the Department's new "Early Environmental Warning System." In it he detailed some of the more glaring and "self-evident" abuses at Lake Berryessa. His opening remarks included the statement that "the recreation developments appear to be geared to benefit a very few with apparent disregard for the needs of the general public." A responding memo from the regional director of the Bureau of Reclamation was basically an apologia for the concessions, although acknowledging that there had been some "growing pains" and that there was a need for further expansion of the facilities. He insisted that "we have continuously worked with the County and the concessionaires toward the development of additional facilities for the 'short-time' recreationist." He further stated that "there are *no areas* [emphasis his] which are given over to the exclusive use of individuals or groups." One wonders if he had ever been to Lake Berryessa.

The regional coordinator of the Department of the Interior forwarded the two memos to Washington with an accompanying memo of his own, which identified them as describing "a rather messy and complicated situation." He extended the Department's thanks to the Fish and Wildlife biologist "for his diligent effort and for calling the Lake Berryessa situation to the attention of the Department." He went on: "I plan no further action at this level on the problem unless you provide instructions for such action." The matter still stands, despite increased discussion and planning, as it has for almost a decade. The deterioration and need for public recreation increases.

The Lake Berryessa fiasco initially grew out of inadequate policies of land acquisition and maintenance. According to federal officials, the same thing has happened at numerous other federal multipurpose water resource projects. Under Public Law 89–72, passed in 1965, the federal government can still enter into the same sort of agreements with "local bodies" as were made at Berryessa. In the federal water development agencies, the pressures are still to seek a local agency to manage the recreation facilities, and the projects are most often found in poor, rural counties which see in the given reservoir a cash register for the county or for themselves, rather than an opportunity for recreation for all people in the region.

Upper Newport Bay

According to the *National Estuary Study,* "Upper Newport Bay is the last major baylike body of water remaining in a fairly pristine condition along 400 miles of coast between Morro Bay and Estero de Punta Banda in Mexico." Located in Orange County, it is the third largest natural bay in southern California. Lower Newport Bay has been fully developed into a marina-residential complex and is, as the California Department of Fish and Game has noted in a classic understatement, now "of little value to wildlife."

In 1919, the state of California granted by statute tidelands and submerged lands bordering upon Newport Bay to Orange County to be held in trust, with the understanding that a public harbor would be developed. In 1957 the governor signed a bill authorizing the exchange of state tidelands in Orange County for privately owned lands, subject to the approval of the State Lands Commission (since state-owned tidelands were involved). This so-called Enabling Act, State Statute 2044, required that the State Lands Commission make certain findings prior to approval of any such exchange. Section 3 states

> that the lands located in the area commonly known as Upper Newport Bay which are to be exchanged are no longer useful for navigation, commerce, and fishing, and that the lands to be received in exchange are at least of equal value thereof.

In 1963, the Irvine Company, the county's largest landowner, offered to give up some uplands and an island (totaling 292.7 acres) in exchange for 151.8 acres of filled tidelands in the Upper Bay. After several modifications, the proposal that finally emerged involved Irvine's giving up 447 acres of islands and uplands, and in exchange receiving 157 acres of filled tidelands. This plan was submitted by the Orange County Harbor District to the county's Board of Supervisors, who approved the land-exchange plan in 1964. In January of 1965, the county and Irvine signed a "Dredging and Land Fill Agreement" * and a separate "Agreement" spelling out the terms of the land exchange.

The plan still had to be approved by the State Lands Commission (among others). In August, 1966, the Commission voted to withhold approval of the exchange, stating that it did not appear to be in the greatest "statewide interest" because "the project would create commercial areas completely privately controlled which could add to the preponderant private domination of the bay." The Commission suggested that alternative solutions for the bay's development be explored.

In 1967, with a new administration in power, the new Commission completely reversed itself and approved the exchange on the same terms. This approval was given despite the opposition of many local residents and conservationists. The minutes of the meeting reveal no significant change in facts to warrant reversal, nor does it appear that the parties involved made any real effort to devise alternative plans.

As for the required finding of "equal value," the Commission accepted the findings of an independent appraiser showing an $8 million advantage to the county. The appraiser found that the filled tidelands that Irvine was to receive had a value of $11 million (based on per-acre evaluation). The appraiser stated that the county would receive lands worth $19 million, of which the three islands in the bay constituted $14 million. The accuracy of these findings has been severely criticized by many, including the current County Assessor. The value of the islands under this estimate, for example, is over *100 times* their recent assessed valuation.

The tidelands to be received by Irvine were evaluated on a per-acre basis. Another method, probably the more realistic one, evaluates shoreline ownership on a lineal-footage basis. After the trade, Irvine will hold title to filled tidelands with about 30,000 to 35,000 feet of natural shore. By "fingering" (i.e., creating artificial inlets and peninsulas

---

* This Agreement contained a provision that any of the parties could withdraw if certain conditions had not been met within a three-year period from the date of signing. One of these conditions was approval of new harbor lines by the Army Corps of Engineers. This was not done within three years.

to increase shore length), this figure may be increased to about 75,000 feet. Land in similar residential developments has been selling for in the neighborhood of $2,500 or more per lineal foot of shoreline. By these figures, Irvine stands to receive property worth as much as $200 million for its possibly overvalued $19 million "equal exchange."

Even accepting the $11 million figure, there is a serious flaw in the State Lands Commission's finding of equal value. The three islands to be given to the county are valued at $14 million. This figure is based on the assumption that the islands can be developed for residential purposes, a questionable assumption given the propensity for flooding. However, under the terms of the exchange, the islands are to be *dredged* and used to fill the estuary which Irvine is to receive—and the county and Irvine are to share the expense of this dredging. Thus, the county will actually end up with no islands. The county actually does receive title to the islands, but with the proviso that they be dredged. There appears to be some confusion about the value to the county of islands that the county must wipe out, partially at its own cost, to then give back as earth-fill to Irvine.

As for the other necessary finding that the estuary is no longer useful for fishing, commerce, or navigation, it appears that this finding was never actually made. What the Commission did find, however, was the following:

> That the lands that are to be filled and conveyed to the Irvine Company by the County of Orange, pursuant to the exchange and in accordance with the application filed with the State Lands Commission, at the time of said conveyance, will be no longer useful for navigation, commerce, and fishing.

This result is achieved by structuring the agreement in such a way that the estuary is to be *filled first* (i.e., *before* Irvine receives title thereto). Therefore, at the time of conveyance the estuary will no longer be useful (since it will be filled). Thus, in effect, the county is agreeing to fill the tidelands and destroy their estuary usefulness—thus justifying the exchange.

We sought to understand how Irvine could justify this. During an interview with William R. Mason, president of the company, and two other executives, which lasted over two hours, we asked about this agreement to "give" the county the islands with the requirement that they be dredged (at partial county cost), to be given back as earth to Irvine.* What was Irvine "exchanging" for this last piece of substantial southern California estuary? President Mason said, "I never can understand why people can't understand that." He then drew us a picture of the bay, and explained that all Irvine was doing was taking land they already owned (the islands) and moving it. Thus, they would end up with the same land they started with, but with it around the bay instead of in the middle. He seemed really convinced that this made sense.

After the land exchange had been approved by the State Lands Commission, a "friendly" suit was brought by the Auditor of Orange County against Irvine. The purpose of this suit was to establish the legality of the trade in order to finalize Irvine's title to the tidelands and to satisfy the title insurance companies. Much to the surprise of Irvine and the county, a group of local citizens sought and gained the right to intervene on behalf of the county—that is, in opposition to the trade. Led by Newport Beach residents J. Frank Robinson and his wife Frances, who have fought the trade for years (often alone), the intervenors have waged a vigorous court battle in opposition to the exchange. They are now represented by Phil Berry, president of the Sierra Club. The State Attorney General's Office, as counsel for the State Lands Commission, is arguing in favor of the exchange.

One of the major hurdles that the intervenors faced is the ruling by the trial judge that the State Lands Commission was acting in a quasi-legislative role rather than in a quasi-judicial one in approving the exchange. This means that it is necessary for the intervenors to show not merely that the Commission acted unwisely but that it acted arbitrarily and capriciously. Thus, they conceivably could lose—not because the trade is found to be in the public interest, but because the actions of the State Lands Commission are not found to be sufficiently egregious.

The intervenors did manage to introduce quite a bit of evidence pertaining to the potential ecological effects of

* This interview occurred at 3 P.M., August 14, 1970 in the Irvine offices at Newport Center. The company rather clumsily attempted to conceal a tape recorder behind the president's desk. There is therefore available, we have been told, a full transcript. Any requests for it should be made to Irvine Corporation, Newport Center.

the proposed development. This evidence included portions from the *National Estuary Study* and a report on Upper Newport Bay done by the State Department of Fish and Game. This evidence concerned the water-cleansing features of the estuary; the necessary fish- and wildlife-nurturing qualities; uniqueness; and the loss of most of California's estuaries, with the threat of pollution damage to those remaining. This information went unexamined by the Harbor District (party to the agreement). The harbor manager formally stated before the Orange County Supervisors that a great deal of study would be made "*once* the land exchange has been consummated" (emphasis added).

The intervenors established that the dredging and fill would estroy the estuarine environment. Dredging to ten feet would "eliminate practically all the shallows," thereby cancelling any sewage-treatment function (which requires a wide expanse of shallow water as in the original estuary). This would worsen pollution in the Lower Bay (already becoming severe) quite apart from pollution from the resulting development itself. The boat-launching facilities, flood-control entrance, and two marinas would contribute additional pollution. There would be a loss of sport fishing with reduction of numerous species, including croakers, bass, and opaleyes. Sand dabs and clams in the Upper Bay would be eliminated altogether. Commercial fishing would also suffer. Citing one expert witness: "The destruction of natural resource values related to commercial and sports fisheries is predicted to be 80%." Dead-end areas such as the marine stadium and rowing course would deteriorate. The former "would tend to become a stagnant pool of green scum. . . ." Swimming in Upper Newport Bay would be impossible at times during the year. According to the Department of Parks and Recreation, the effect would be analogous to what has happened to Copta Slough and Brannon Island. Loss of the area will endanger birds using this critical part of the Pacific flyway, which the United States is bound to protect by international agreement. Invertebrates in the mud flats would be eliminated, and sixty species of native birds would no longer be able to survive.

The public has quite a current stake in this area. There is much fishing and boating, including sailboating, kayaking, and canoeing. It is the last large area in southern California for clamming.

The proposed exchange would result in an arrangement involving water-skiing, power boating, and a private club to replace this—with minimal public access to what is left of the Upper Bay.* The State Lands Commission considered virtually none of this evidence and made no detailed environmental study itself.

The position of Irvine was elucidated by President Mason at the interview cited above. On the one hand, Irvine contends that the exchange was all "the county's idea." They were just "helping out" the county. As for ecology not being considered, this "was the fault of the public agencies."

Yet Irvine still wishes to project itself as a white-hatted environmentalist firm. The home office is decorated with sculpture depicting various kinds of wildlife, and Irvine executives are capable of eloquent speeches concerning company philosophy. On the other hand, how to explain Upper Newport Bay—public agency malfeasance or not? There seemed to be two responses. First, the president referred to the Upper Bay as "a great big mudhole," and denigrated studies (e.g., by the State Department of Fish and Game) asserting the bay to be of critical importance. Moreover, President Mason stated that members of the Irvine Company were disturbed over the current concern for ecology because they're for ecology and they're afraid that this concern for ecology will lead to a reaction against ecology which will be bad for ecology and they don't want a reaction against ecology and therefore there shouldn't be so much concern for it!

The Orange County Superior Court Judge issued a forty-one-page memorandum opinion favoring the trade.*

---

* Of 3,000 boat berths, 200 would exist in public ownership. The lineal shoreline open to the public is now 43,600 feet. It will be about 13,000 feet. There will be less access to this smaller footage.

* The opinion can be obtained from the Orange County Superior Court, Case No. M-1105.

7

The General Overseers

Over the past five years a new kind of government unit has appeared in California—the "general protector of the environment."

At the state level there are currently three general-purpose "environmentalist" bodies and innumerable supplementary "declaratory" bills and public reports. The federal government has three new units of similar design, several declaratory bills, and even more public reports.

State

The Resources Agency

The California Resources Agency was created to "coordinate" state environmental agencies and give ecological concerns a powerful voice in state affairs. However, there are strong indications that the Agency is, as an Agency official put it, "a tiny ship of political patronage floating atop a sea of bureaucracy."

There are sixty-six boards and commissions under the Agency's "coordination," having a total of 10,000 employees and spending billions of dollars each year. The departments under the Agency (see Table 7a) are powerful and experienced bureaucracies. Only a sizable organization could supervise and coordinate all of these departments; however, the Resources Agency consists of but five individuals, including its director or "Secretary," Norman B. ("Ike") Livermore. One of the Agency members (Federal Projects Coordinator) communicates with the federal government about the impacts of federal projects on California's resources. Another (Special Assistant) deals with the legislature on bills affecting resources. A third (Assistant to the

Secretary) does research work for Livermore—for instance, on regional solutions to metropolitan problems—and "some work on the budget." Thus, only Livermore and the Assistant Secretary are left to supervise 10,000 bureaucrats on sixty-six boards and commissions.

The Agency knows little about the departments it "coordinates." ("We stay out of the Departments," says Secretary Livermore; "We read their quarterly reports," says Assistant-to-the-Secretary Hill), and can't possibly keep track of them: Livermore told us that the Water Quality Control Act of 1969 (the Porter-Cologne Act) was "bitterly opposed" by polluters, when in fact it was written and supported by them.

We were told quite openly by Secretary Livermore that the purpose of having a Resources Agency was to present a "united front" among the departments and boards. The governor's policies are supposed to "funnel down" to the departments through the Agency; the Agency controls the public-relations efforts, legislative testimonies, and contacts of the boards and commissions; it issues highly laudatory publicity for the Reagan administration.

Controlling, or, as one water pollution control official termed it, "gagging" the departments under the Agency, is done in two ways. First, when there is a conflict between two departments, Livermore "persuades" the departments to come to agreement, to "iron out their differences out of the public view," as the Secretary puts it. Thus, where the public could be educated and involved by hearing two sides of a question, the Resources Agency makes sure that only one is heard. "It is bad bureaucracy," says Livermore, "to have your departments bickering in public." That some differences of opinion have been aired publicly, as in the case of Dos Rios Dam and some other water project cases, is attributable primarily to the weakness of the Agency.

The main threat used to persuade the departments not to "bicker in public" is the budget cut. The Agency sets the shares of the various departments in the next year's budget, and the Secretary admitted that "next to persuasion, the budgetary power is our number-two tool."

The second control is applied by not permitting departments to deal directly with the legislature. The State Water Resources Control Board, for example, cannot support or oppose legislation without first submitting its position to the Agency and the governor. If it is so bold as to place its

Table 7a

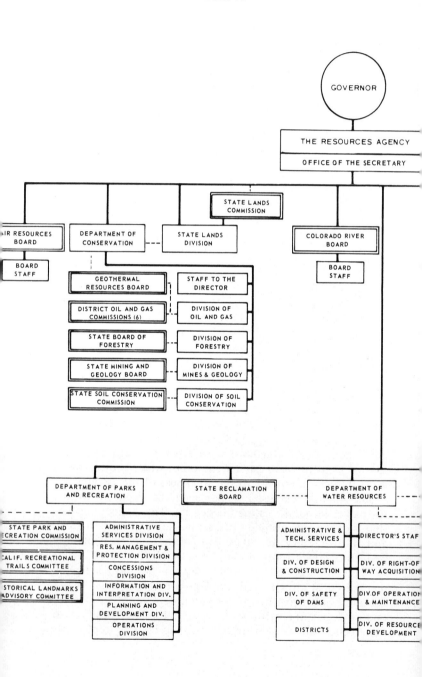

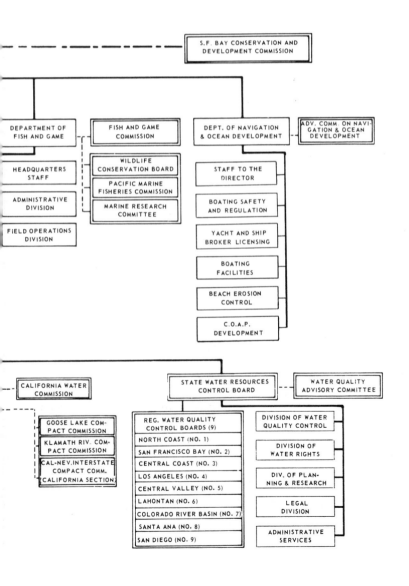

professional judgment on water quality first, it "gets its knuckles rapped," according to Livermore. The State Water Resources Control Board's positions on legislation are extraordinarily similar to those of the governor.

A united front is also maintained by firing dissenters. Livermore says that "we had to get rid of a few because they were out of line with the governor's policies against 'high spending'." When we inquired about what they had done to exhibit their philosophies of "high spending," Livermore said that they had gone before the legislature and testified that problems in their area were serious and that consequently more money was needed.

The Agency puts out an avalanche of self-congratulatory prose, detailing the accomplishments of the Reagan administration from the acquisition of five acres to an increase in fines for littering to numerous label shufflings. None of these measures threatens any problem with solution or any campaign contributor with economic loss.

Livermore's interest in boosting the administration is more than organization allegiance. He is deeply involved in the lumber industry; he also gave $1,200 to Reagan's 1970 *primary* campaign (see Chapter 12), and was appointed by the governor.

Ford B. Ford, the Assistant Secretary, was appointed by Livermore; A. Alan Hill, the Assistant to the Secretary, was appointed, he says, after "working for four years for the Republican Party." John Tooker, the Special Assistant, was also appointed. Only Paul Clifton, the Projects Coordinator, is under civil service, and in a special civil service category which makes him partly appointive. Hill told us that the civil service law, which allows each agency one non-civil-service appointment, has been "skirted" in the Resources Agency by "borrowing" the non-civil-service appointments of the Departments of Water Resources and Parks and Recreation, thus giving the Agency three appointments to make instead of one. "What we need in the Agency," Hill remarked to us, "is 500 appointments. We need more *patronage*."

The State Office of Planning

The Office of Planning was established in 1959 within the Department of Finance to prepare a state development plan. This "plan" was finally published in 1968, after six years and an outlay of $4 million in state and federal funds. About half of this money went to hire outside consultants to prepare studies on population and economic forecasting, land use, transportation problems and projection, resource management, welfare and employment programs, etc.

What the Office produced in 1968 was not a plan but a report about a series of plans that were never made public and are now generally outdated. It calls for bits and pieces of planning to be undertaken some time in the future. It makes no conclusions about what lands should be used for what specific purposes. It supports "completion and maintenance of a statewide inventory of open space." It proposes that the word "conservation" be dropped or replaced by "resource management." The Office itself does not have the authority to execute whatever plans it might have developed. Thus the responsibility for most of the state's planning remains fragmented at the department level.

The Reagan administration was enthusiastic about the "non-plan," and parried criticisms by claiming that it was not intended as a physical planning document. It was, stated then Director of Finance Caspar Weinberger, in whose purview lay the Office of Planning, a "combination of relevant information and processes directed toward identifying goals and marshalling the resources necessary to solve the problems which face the people of California now and for many years into the future. . . ."

According to Mr. Weinberger, the many state agencies "along with 59 counties, over 400 cities, and almost 3700 special districts" with varying responsibilities make state "blueprinting . . . patently absurd." It is precisely these conditions that make it patently absurd not to have a state "blueprint." Throughout our months of investigation, the most consistently voiced criticism of state planning was the lack of a comprehensive land-use policy. The State Commissioner of Real Estate, numerous county officials, local people in mountain counties, conservationists, and developers said that what was needed to save California was some sort of coherent statement about how and where the state would grow. Even the most vocal adherents of the "local control" philosophy that pervades California called for guidance in their decision-making.

The state does in fact intervene in local land-use decisions—in providing the structural and revenue setting for local government, and in its own numerous public works. The question therefore is not *whether* but *how* it is going to "interfere" with local home rule: will the state represent the interests of the larger public and then provide a setting for visible, responsive, noncorrupt home rule where local government prerogative is appropriate?

Probably not in the foreseeable future. The "plan" says that the Office of Planning is to concern itself with "updating information, improvement of interprogram relationships, and improvement of intergovernmental relationships."

Governor Reagan recently transferred the responsibility for environmental policy and planning coordination to the "State Environmental Policy Committee," whose stated purpose is "to catalogue all State projects affecting the environment, maintain and coordinate such projects, eliminate duplication and conflict . . . and to consolidate the development of a long-range program of California's environmental goals, and the criteria for priorities." The State Office of Planning is now an office within the governor's office; it is called the "Office of Planning and Research" and is staffed by eight persons. It is no longer independent. Its function is purely decorative.

Environmental Quality Study Council

The Environmental Quality Study Council, established in 1968, consists of the Secretary of the Resources Agency, the Secretary of the Business and Transportation Agency, the chairman of the State Water Resources Control Board, the chairman of the State Air Resources Board, seven public members, and four legislators.

The Council studies problems, issues reports and warnings, and holds hearings, but its powers are strictly "advisory." The Legislative Analyst has remarked that "the Council cannot fulfill even its advisory role. . . . As a result of a delay in getting organized and various recent problems such as a staffing change, the Council has as yet had no observable impact on environmental problems." [1] The Council has *not* succeeded in changing state policies or obtaining meaningful power, but has investigated and publicized environmental problems, helped defeat local projects threatening the environment, and forced various officials to take public stands on issues they might otherwise have avoided.

One major piece of "general" environmental legislation has been passed in California, the Environmental Quality Act of 1970. It is generally a "declaratory" act expressing concern, but does *require* government agencies to "consider alternatives to proposed actions affecting the environment." But the Act gives environmental groups no sound basis for action to implement the "policy." Its requirements are only to "study."

The specific recommendations of the better environmental study groups, including the "Environmental Bill of Rights" Report of the Assembly Select Committee on Environmental Quality, the Environmental Quality Study Council's "recommendations," and the specifics in the Office of Planning output, have been ignored with very few exceptions.

Several recent proposals have been made for new or additional "super bodies." Assemblyman Edwin Z'berg has introduced a major bill to create a body with substantial authority over the coast and to consolidate water and air quality control functions. Another proposal would create a Land Quality Control Board analogous to the Water Board to control pesticides, erosion, etc. A third would create an "Environmental Quality Board" which would have the power to overrule projects of other government agencies. Many of these ideas have been proposed before. Those that survive, if recent history is our guide, will serve public-relations needs. There is no constituency in Sacramento monitoring the legislative or executive branches on behalf of the general public interest, the environment, or the future. Even if one or all of these measures were to pass without weakening compromise, there would still be conflict-of-interest problems in appointments and in performance, no sanctions or power to make the necessary structural changes, and massive staffing deficiencies. No "general purpose" state overseer for environmental protection has so far overcome these obstacles.

Federal

At the federal level, there are three new agencies: the Environmental Protection Agency, the Council on Environmental Quality, and the National Oceanographic and Atmospheric Administration.

The Environmental Protection Agency (EPA) is supposed to enforce antipollution standards, administer financial grants, conduct research, and help "develop a national environment policy." It has assumed under its jurisdiction the antipollution functions formerly scattered among the Department of the Interior, HEW, the Department of Agriculture, and the Atomic Energy Commission.

The EPA has shown some signs of sincere commitment and vigor in its first months of operation. Its positions on auto-exhaust emission standards, the Florida and Southwest canals, and other issues indicate that more than a label-shuffling has occurred. But the agency suppressed a devastating report on nationwide lead contamination until it was released in May of 1971 by a member of our group. And it has yet to have any substantial impact on water pollution and most other serious environmental problems.[2]

The President's wide-ranging environmental message of February 10, 1970, which promised concern for and solution to every environmental problem imaginable—garbage, water and air quality, noise, land use, etc.—has (not surprisingly) not been translated into action: paltry sums for enforcement, sanctionless laws, and some agency reshuffling are about the extent of the Nixon administration's implementation program.

And the federal government, like the state of California, expresses its official legislative concern by requiring agencies merely to review the environmental impacts of their projects and consider alternatives. Reports are far more numerous on the federal level than they are in California. With regard to the ocean alone, we have *From Sea to Shining Sea,* by the President's Council on Recreation and Natural Beauty; *Our Nation and the Sea,* by the Commission on Marine Science; Engineering and Resources; the *National Estuary Study* cited in Chapter 6; and others. But the most important report is *One Third of the Nation's Land,* by the Public Land Law Review Commission.

This Report is particularly important to California since it covers suggested policies for the 44% of California that is federal land. And it illustrates the extremely limited public-relations role played by the new general environmental overseer agencies.

The Report's 137 recommendations are largely unrelated to the forty contracted studies that were conducted by independent experts without financial ties to industry interests. For example, a draft study by Professors Heyman, Twiss, and Rabin emphasizes the nonenforcement and inadequacies of the law for the protection of the forest environment, and catalogues the damage caused by the logging industry. Nonetheless, the Report recommends that timber production be the "dominant use" wherever "public lands are highly productive for timber use"—i.e., wherever the loggers want to cut (Recommendation 28); that "sustained yield" requirements be relaxed (Recommendation 31), allowing loggers to cut and run; that "there should be an accelerated program of timber access road construction" (Recommendation 33). Only in the final recommendation in the chapter on Timber Resources is the environment mentioned: "Controls . . . to minimize adverse impacts on the environment on and off the public lands must be imposed" (Recommendation 36). Professors Heyman and Twiss are cited as the Report concludes ". . . that even greater efforts be made in the future," but the Report does not mention any of their specific discussions or suggestions.

The Report follows this pattern throughout—vague gestures in the direction of ecological principles followed by specific, concrete recommendations for exploitation without concern for environmental consequences.

The standards set forth in the Report involve finding a "dominant use" for land and then allowing all subsidiary activities that do not interfere with the dominant use to continue. Wilderness and game preservation are nowhere defined as dominant uses.

Since the Public Law Review Commission's Advisory Council is made up of industry executives (from the American Mining Congress, National Coal Association, Jefferson Plywood Company, Getty Oil Company, Weyerhaeuser Company [loggers], Southern California Edison, True Oil Company—over half of the Council's members work for interests with profit stakes in public land disposition), it is not surprising that all of the dominant uses involve economic gains. Virtually all restrictions are removed on logging, grazing, mining, drilling, etc. Hunting is permitted everywhere under any circumstances unless specifically prohibited by statute. Disposal of land is encouraged wherever economic profit is to be had. The Report recommends that:

> —"Mining operations should not be unreasonably impeded by regulations pertaining to wilderness areas." Current mining acreage limits (to minimize damage) should be expanded immensely to allow for unhampered strip mining.

For example, "a mine having 500 acres of mining claims may require 5,000 acres of surface plant facilities and waste disposal areas."

—Grazing permittees who are privileged to use federal grass for token payments are to be "compensated" when permits are removed; land investments that benefit grazing interests should "come wholly from the general fund of the United States"; and lands used for grazing should be sold "with grazing permittees given a preference to buy them" to "place the management and use of the forage resource in the hands of those who normally manage productive resources in a free enterprise economy, and thus provide an incentive for the investment needed to make those lands fully productive."

—Claimants to federal water are to be compensated for their claims, although federal pre-emption supersedes any pretended rights under state laws. Why claimants to invalid rights should be compensated is unclear.

—The 160-acre limit should be ended and large landowners should receive disproportionate subsidies from federal water projects.

The "environment," however, receives more verbal attention than any other subject in the Report. Thousands of sentences proclaim respect, honor, and love for the land: "Federal statutory guidelines [should] . . . be established to assure that Federal public lands are managed in a manner that not only will not endanger the quality of the environment, but will, where feasible, enhance [it]. . . . Environmental quality should be recognized by law as an important objective. . . ." (Recommendation 16) "Congress should provide for greater use of studies of environmental impacts. . . ." (Recommendation 20), etc. Meanwhile, the land interests continue to take all the soil, minerals, grass, and timber they please, incurring costs that others must bear.

Part Two

DEVELOPMENT

New Development

The important fact about new development is that it is new. Once the roads, drainage, sewers, utilities, and so on are in, however mistaken the arrangements may be, change becomes difficult. It is at this initial stage that planning should take place.

The issues raised by new developments include: avoidance of bulldozing where there is no demand for houses; coordination of large new development with public works and service needs; proper location of development on secure and safe ground; equitable financing; and honest sale. In each of these areas the present market may allow the initial developer to profit by passing costs on to future lot owners.

Either by adjusting the market on a rule of liability or by regulatory control, these costs are supposed to be assessed or prevented. Those private parties with a stake in keeping the profits and passing costs on to unknowing future residents are listed in Appendix 1A. The new land speculator is increasingly likely to be a large conglomerate favored in his activities with subsidies and tax breaks. He is aided by a financial industry of insurance, banking, and savings and loan firms which often have large stakes in the immediate profit of the speculator and initial developer through loans, policies, and direct investment and ownership (See Appendix 1D).

Restrictions and "Coordinative" Planning: Antelope Valley

The development of Antelope Valley reveals the following great forces of development: the growth ethic, speculative profit from a major public work, and the fragmentation and perceived tax revenue needs of local government.

Even a casual reader of the Los Angeles newspapers knows that "Great Things" are happening up in the Antelope Valley, thousands of square miles of very thinly populated desert lying, at its nearest point, thirty-five miles north of the city center. Few Los Angeles residents have ever been there. For most, the Valley exists only in the propaganda of the landowners and realtors. These prototypical land promoters fill the papers with predictions of fantastic emerald cities and spaceports coming to the Valley. One large land owner, Calindel Enterprises Company, makes the expansion of the Los Angeles metropolitan area into the Valley seem inevitable:

> We were talking about Orange County when most of it was still orange groves and a few sleepy towns. Just as Beverly Hills replaced bean fields and Anaheim shouldered aside orange groves, so is the Antelope Valley pushing aside alfalfa ranches to make way for the most courageous land boom in California's history.

Under a photo of a vast expanse of vacant land, Calindel says, "This ad will become a valuable souvenir. The Antelope Valley will never look the same again!" A competitor, Continental Development Corporation, shuns fancy productions, and gets right down to the business at hand: "Looking for Something Just for the Profit in It? (Look at Land!)"

On paper, the Antelope Valley does appear to be in the path of progress, and thus to offer an obvious get-rich-quick opportunity. However, the history of land promotion in the Valley must at least give pause. Vast and flat though the land is, it is not the sort of lush farmland that has been transformed into suburbs around Los Angeles up to now. Its expanse of sand, its few Joshua trees, and its stifling heat and aridity are not enticing. As early as the 1880s, land promoters placed oranges on the spines of the Joshua trees to lure the nearsighted investor. And land promoters have had to deal with the natural barrier, a rugged range of mountains, separating the Valley from the Los Angeles suburban area.

Until World War II, despite a few minor booms and busts in the land market, the Antelope Valley was populated by only a few thousand people living in two or three sleepy little towns. With the advent of World War II, the Air Force came to wake up the Valley. Edwards Air Force Base, near the town of Lancaster, became an important facility; and the small airport in the town of Palmdale, built under a W.P.A. program in the 1930s, was leased by the federal government for one dollar.

Two events coincided in the early 1950s to focus the attention of land promoters on the Valley. Most important was the decision of major aircraft companies to locate plants around the Palmdale airfield. This first influx of business investment naturally brought new families to the Palmdale area, more than tripling the population (to 83,000 in the southern portion of the Valley) by 1960.

The second important event of the early 1950s was the creation in the Valley of a highly vocal group of local boosters. The first stage in the promotion of the Valley ran from 1951 to 1957. During this period the local boosters mobilized and formed an image of the southern part of the Valley to sell to the world. The City of Palmdale in 1952 was only beginning to install the first curbs, sidewalks, and blacktop on its main street; but its spokesmen predicted that "in the next few years" the town's population was destined to increase as much as 1,000%—from 3,000 to 30,000. The projection made little sense, yet the future was made to look rosy enough for one local subdivider to buy or option more than $800,000 worth of acreage in the Palmdale area zoned for business, hotels, motels and residences. Palmdale is "so located," he said, that "in a comparatively short time" it will be "a large population center."

When, in 1953, the first aircraft plant went into operation, the public-relations campaign of the local boosters shifted into high gear. Cliff Rawson, former manager of the Home Builders Institute and for sixteen years an employee of the Los Angeles Chamber of Commerce, came to Palmdale as manager of the Chamber of Commerce there. Soon, the small town began to be referred to in the press as "the Jet City" and the "next important economic boom area." "Here we have 1,000,000 acres of land," Rawson said, "with opportunity posted on every one of them." To supplement his predictions of growth and prosperity, Rawson moved to endorse a revision of the area's zoning law. Though by 1954 Palmdale was just installing its first traffic light, it prevailed upon the County Planning Commission to zone 180 acres for manufacturing enterprise, 211 for other businesses and 6,746 acres for residence. That the zoning pattern responded to no realistic demand made no difference; the commercial zoning was intended largely as enticement and a means of boosting the price of vacant land. Indeed, the zoning of desolate acreage became so important to local landowners that fisticuffs actually broke out at one County Supervisors' meeting considering the zoning law, as a local subdivider struck a supervisor. The subdivider wanted his land zoned commercial.

By 1954, modest growth was becoming a reality. Palmdale's population had increased to 6,000, not the 1,000% increment predicted, but a respectable 100%. During one seven-week period, the Chamber of Commerce proudly announced, $4 million worth of building permits were issued. And, by 1956, two multimillion-dollar business and residential developments were in the works. Finally, Los Angeles businessmen and developers were beginning to take notice. Cliff Rawson was invited to speak before the Los Angeles Chamber of Commerce, and he chose to emphasize the Valley's environmental pleasures as well as business opportunities. Already, with only a few aircraft companies in the area, land prices had soared far above their 1950 level.

In 1957, the bottom fell out of the Antelope Valley boom. After the national nervous breakdown over the flight of Sputnik, the federal government decided to reallocate much of its money from aircraft to missiles; and the Valley aircraft industry suffered accordingly. A newspaper report describes the effect on "Jet City":

> Thousands of jobs were lost. Tracts of unsold houses stood empty except for rattlesnakes and rabbits. Banks and savings and loan companies refused to lend a dime on Palmdale property. Businesses folded. Palmdale experienced a classic Southern California 'bust.'

The only victim of the "bust" not mentioned in that account is the small investor, lured into buying Valley land by the confident boosterism of the land promoters and his own avarice.

While the small investor was likely to have been ruined by the 1957 bust, the promoters arose to fight another day. The scale and energy of their campaigns increased exponentially.

It was clear that the best card, and indeed the only card,

in Palmdale's hand was its airport, known as Air Force Plant 42. Around the airport was a 17,000-acre buffer strip which the Air Force had insisted not be zoned for residential use. The purpose of the Air Force's coming to Palmdale in the first place had been to get away from the complaints of citizens in the Los Angeles area about the noise emanating from the Burbank air facilities and others nearby. There was no reason, however, why these 17,000 acres could not be used for industry. Accordingly, the local promoters led a successful effort after the "bust" to rezone the entire buffer zone for industrial use. It would be the largest single industrial park in the country, they said. In December of 1957, their newly formed organization, the Antelope Valley Progress Association, sponsored a "Welcome to Industry Day." It was a gala occasion. The fact that people and business were fleeing rather than coming to the area and that no industry had expressed much interest in moving into the wilds of the Antelope Valley did not dampen the enthusiasm of the day. The governor and the area's U.S. Representative were there, as were Miss Antelope Valley Industry and Miss Goodwill Ambassador to Industry. The day of speechmaking, terming the Valley the "biggest industrial Empire in the West," was topped by a sonic boom and the dropping of a bomb in the buffer zone to make the first excavation for the industrial park. The bomb crater was apparently never used; but it *was* the first time a great concentration of heavy industry had been bombed before it existed.

If they were to make the big time, local promoters knew they must sell to Los Angeles magnates the idea of the Valley as future industrial empire. Accordingly, Rawson (now executive director of the Valley Progress Association) journeyed to Los Angeles to deliver a "State of the Valley Address" at a luncheon of business leaders. By 1965, he said, the Valley would have a population of 500,000! Nevertheless, the Palmdale boosters did not put all their eggs in the Los Angeles business-community basket. In the late 1950s, there began a long series of trips to Washington, D.C. It was reported in early 1958 that "Cliff Rawson is heading for Washington to try to . . . garner for the valley a big slice of the stepped up missile program." Apparently a trip to Washington requires greater growth projections than a trip to Los Angeles. Rawson's mission, the newspaper said, was "to speed up the growth of the

Antelope Valley from its present 90,000 to the 1 million predicted by 1968."

Industrial zoning and extravagant claims were only two of the strings in the promoters' bow in the late 1950s. In 1958, they mobilized 500 supporters from the Valley to protest a regulation proposed by the County Regional Planning Commission "to control so-called 'bootleg sub-dividing' of property." Any development was better than no development, so far as land prices were concerned.

With the advent of the 1960s, it could be said that the promoters had got the Valley moving again. The most significant development of this period was the successful campaign to install the boosters as the duly elected "representatives" in the town of Palmdale, rather than as the merely self-proclaimed ambassadors to industry. In 1962, Palmdale was incorporated as a self-governing city. In several elections before 1962, incorporation was beaten; but the promoters kept altering the boundaries of the proposed city—cutting out areas whose residents preferred to be governed by the county—until they achieved a majority. At least two of the five-man City Council had substantial investments in Palmdale land. The mayor was Larry Chimbole, a hardware-store proprietor, who had been hard hit in the 1957 "bust," but who "worked his way free" somehow and became prominent in the local Rotary and Kiwanis clubs. "Economic development is my bag," he has said.

The city fathers' plans for Palmdale are illustrated by the attitude of Chris Rope, the City Administrator. "An area is rural simply because no one wants to do anything with it," he told us. We asked him if he didn't agree that uncontrolled land speculation might be harmful. "Oh, I don't think it's ever bad," he responded.

The Council's primary function, besides affording the promoters a cloak of legitimacy, is to approve zoning changes—the role played by the less cooperative County Regional Planning Commission before Palmdale's incorporation. Unlike most cities, Palmdale does not rely upon trained planners. Instead, its City Councilmen also sit as Planning Commissioners. To avoid difficult technical issues, they follow one simple rule of thumb: whenever there is any doubt, support the landowner seeking a zone change or exception. Even a local realtor admits that the result has been "a good bit of spot zoning." "Three members [of the Council] automatically say yes [to a zone change], because they want to see it developed," he comments. Trailer parks are as welcome as apartment complexes, and minimum common open space regulations for apartments are often waived by the Council, as are minimum lot-size requirements. Even though in 1968 the Council commissioned for the city a new overall land-use plan which allowed for even more industrial and commercial use of the vacant land, it has few qualms about making exceptions to that plan.

Well stocked with dreams, projections, and zoning gimmicks, all that the Antelope Valley boosters still lacked was a good reason for industry to come up to the desert. The aridity of the area, and its isolation behind a range of mountains were unfortunate obstacles, and there was nothing to attract industry to the Valley. The boosters tended to attack the secondary problem first. The water shortage, they said, would be solved by the new Feather River water project which would be sending millions of gallons of water "right through" the Valley by 1970. This claim, emblazoned on almost every realtor's brochure and every press release, was literally true. The water would be going "right through" the Valley—and right on to Los Angeles and Orange County, with very little allocated for use in the desert. The boosters' solution to the mountain barrier was perhaps even more ingenious, but no less wildly unrealistic. The Valley, they declared, was about to become the great civil defense retreat for southern California; in case of nuclear attack, hundreds of thousands of people would have to rush up to the desert. To accommodate this sudden influx of people, the boosters proposed a multi-million-dollar tunnel cut through the mountain range. Local realtors went so far as to draw this Jules Verne sort of tunnel on their promotional maps of the region. Needless to say, actual construction of the tunnel was not seriously considered outside of the Antelope Valley.

The lack of a basic incentive for industrialization of the Valley, however, was the principal stumbling block. Without any real prospect of employment, people would not move to the Valley to fill the mobile-home "parks" and closely packed subdivisions for which zoning exceptions and changes had been granted. Accordingly, many residential developments approved by the City Council were never built. By the late sixties, for example, 786 mobile-home spaces had been authorized, but only 248 actually constructed. In the words of one local realtor, zoning exceptions and changes came to be made for "a higher and better use." A commercially zoned piece of desert could sell for more than a residentially zoned lot. Such land speculation without real prospect of development dominated until 1968.

Suddenly, in 1968, lightning struck in Palmdale. It was announced in June that a new Lockheed plant was about to be built, which would employ thousands of workers. The excitement of the land promoters, reflected in the *Los Angeles Times,* was boundless:

> When ground is broken for Lockheed's new $30 million . . . facility in Palmdale, the shovelful of earth moved by dignitaries will symbolize one of the most dramatic real estate movements in recent Southland history. [It] touched off a veritable earthquake of escalating real estate values throughout the surrounding area . . . a high-rocketing bombshell in the Antelope Valley real estate market . . . Some nearby land actually doubled in value overnight.

Lockheed's announcement was the first event in a decade corroborating the boosters' claims that Valley land prices were rising and that now was the time to buy.

Then, in August, the Los Angeles Department of Airports announced that it planned to build a huge intercontinental civilian airport in Palmdale, one of the largest and most expensive airports in the world, billed as the "SST Airport of the Future."

The decision hit the area with the effect of the first circus ever to come to town. "Hold on to your hats, folks!" editorialized a local newspaper. "You're going to take a fantastic ride into the expanding future of this area . . . and it should be a lot of fun!"

Land near the proposed airport site was said to increase in value by 100% in twenty-four hours and over 1,000% in a matter of months. While only $1 million worth of building permits were issued in Palmdale in 1967 before the great announcements, $23 million worth were issued in 1968 and about $50 million worth in 1969. Quite clearly, the second Antelope Valley land boom was off and running.

Much of the credit for the airport decision must go to the local Valley boosters, who had persevered and paved the way. Speaking at a Los Angeles meeting of developers, an official of the State Department of Highways noted that "this meeting is one more indication that the Antelope Valley is one of the most promotion-minded parts of California—or maybe the world." (Unfortunately, the representatives from Palmdale, the future transport center of Southern California, were unable to attend the meeting because of a "heavy rainstorm that hit Southern California that day, closing off roads between the Antelope Valley and Los Angeles.") Yet even the Valley promoters recognize the facts of life when matters of ultimate political and economic power are at stake. According to the *Los Angeles Times:*

> Naturally in public the local boosters take much of the credit for making these things happen, pointing out how hard they have worked, how diligently they have organized, how they have wept and fasted, wept and prayed to publish Palmdale's virtues to the world. But *sotto voce,* over lunch at Howard Johnson's (itself a harbinger of future blessings) they will confess that somebody up there in L.A.'s power elite must have taken a fancy to Palmdale.

The Los Angeles City Planning Commission

The Department of Airports is technically a part of the city government of Los Angeles, subordinate to elected officials and coordinate with other city departments. The other city department with a broad interest in the location of the new intercontinental airport was, of course, the City Planning Commission. One might have expected the Commission to play an important role in the decision to locate the airport in the Antelope Valley, evaluating the environmental and developmental impacts of various alternative sites, imposing guidelines, and bringing the broader public interest into the councils of the Department of Airports.

The Commission played no role whatsoever in the airport decision. Not only was it never invited to do so, it was not even advised of what was going on by the Department of Airports. Nor did it make a concerted effort to participate in the decision-making process. Its maps, charts, and graphs, all paid for with taxpayers' money, remained in a limbo of idle speculation.

The Planning Commission had had extensive experience with the problems of the community around Los Angeles International Airport for many years, and no doubt would have had some suggestions to avoid the creation of another intense community-airport conflict. Its data on the historical trends of growth in the Los Angeles area would no doubt have been helpful. And its knowledge of techniques of regulating land development might well have been brought into the discussion. More important than what little expertise the Commission might have brought to the airport decision, however, was its responsibility to articulate and press the interest of the city in ensuring that a new airport would not somehow harm the already choked and sprawling community.

After the decision to build in the Valley was made, the Commission had its golden chance to intervene. In late 1968, the Department of Airports was required by law to pay formal obeisance to its technical master, the elected City Council of Los Angeles. To issue airport revenue bonds and to acquire land for the new facility, the Department needed Council approval. And the Council, in turn, sent the proposal to the Planning Commission for comment and recommendation. Under the city charter, the Commission has fifty days to consider such a proposal.

There is some dispute over what the Commission did at this crucial juncture. But the facts seem to be these: The Department of Airports immediately applied great pressure to ensure that the Commission's review would be as cursory as possible. It went so far as to request formally that consideration be "rushed"—apparently giving no good reason for haste. Statements about escalating land prices were all that was offered to the Commission, and it asked for no more. Dutifully, it rushed the airport consideration through in twenty-three days.

Twenty-three days might well have been enough time for the drafting of a detailed analysis of the airport decision, based on the reams of documents and transit plans already compiled. However, the Commission simply went through a motion or two and meekly approved the airport decision in a one-page letter to the City Council and a three-page staff report. The staff did no more than to review a fact sheet, a map, and some photographs sent over by the Department of Airports.

The staff report concludes:

Los Angeles International Airport will reach a passenger-flight saturation point between 1973 and 1976. An intercontinental airport will be needed to accommodate the future supersonic transport and service the regional satellite airports.

The Palmdale site offers 17,000 acres in Los Angeles County and is one of few areas where there is enough undeveloped level acreage to permit the development of an intercontinental airport.

The staff is of the opinion that the proposed airport use would be in harmony with existing and proposed land uses in the area and is needed to serve the future airport needs of the Los Angeles City and County areas. Therefore, approval of this condemnation ordinance is recommended.

On December 19, 1968, the Planning Commissioners unanimously approved the staff's recommendation. And soon thereafter the City Council did the same.

The County Regional Planning Commission

Palmdale and most of the western Antelope Valley lie within Los Angeles County, the domain of the Regional Planning Commission. The RPC, more than any of the other planning agencies under consideration, has a direct interest in the fate of that great expanse of open space. In 1961, it issued its first general plan for the county and devoted major attention to the Valley. But it was not even consulted by the Department of Airports about an action that would undoubtedly upset land-use plans in the county area. Said O. K. Christensen, staff director of RPC, "We had absolutely nothing to do with the site selection for the Palmdale Airport." When asked why, he answered: "Ask the Department of Airports."

Like the City Planning Commission, however, the RPC did have a later opportunity to block or alter the airport decision. And, again, it made not the slightest effort to take advantage of that opportunity. In May of 1969 the Department of Airports was obliged to go to the RPC for a ruling that building of the Palmdale Airport would not be "inconsistent with regional planning." This request for RPC review and approval was a prerequisite to a grant of funds for land acquisition from the federal Department of Housing and Urban Development.

In its 1961 general plan, the RPC had envisioned the Antelope Valley as a slowly developing preserve of open land. There had been no consideration of locating a million-passenger-per-week airport in the Valley. Thus, a thorough and probing review of the county's resources and competing needs would seem to have been in order. Surely, the RPC had the staff with which to begin such an effort. With extensive experience studying the Valley area, it was in a position to go behind the airport decision and bring considerations to bear that had as yet remained totally unarticulated.

Instead of twenty-three days, the RPC took almost six months before affirming that the Palmdale Airport was not "inconsistent with regional planning." However, no more extensive study had been conducted than by the City Planners. The documents submitted by the Department of Airports were practically the sole basis of decision.

One of the staff members involved told us that he and his associate made "some cursory" examination of Palmdale itself, finding the air warm and dry and the land flat. When asked why they made no in-depth study even of weather conditions for flying in the Valley, he said: "Some of these things are so evident to us. Such as weather." He told us quite frankly that he never felt "much urgency" in his task, since the airport would not be operational until the 1980s and, by then, something could be done to correct any technical problems that might turn up. It was not his job, he felt, to look too hard to turn them up himself. "Obviously, in planning," he said, "we're always a little bit behind." Planning *behind*, of course, is not planning at all.

The document that finally came out of the six-month RPC review of the airport decision was in the form of a two-page letter to Clifton Moore, General Manager of the Department of Airports. It included such "findings" as the following:

> The need for a major air terminal to serve the expanding commercial aviation needs of the Southern California region is unquestioned and the North Los Angeles County area offers outstanding locational and weather characteristics for such a facility.

The letter concludes: "The Commission wishes you every success in the development and operation of the major air terminal facility."

When we questioned the staff director of the RPC and

his deputy about the failings of their review and approval, they seemed uncomfortable. They pointed out that whatever mistakes may have been made up to now can be corrected since the county, the Department of Airports, and the city of Palmdale entered into a joint agreement to sponsor a spectacularly expensive planning study designed to adjust to the airport decision. Who is to conduct that study and administer the federal funds required for it? None other than the RPC.

The Southern California Association of Governments

In a real sense, the building of Palmdale Airport and the urbanization of the Antelope Valley are regional as well as county and city problems. The airport is intended to serve a large part of southern California, and thus an evaluation of the need for such a facility must consider the demands and resources of cities and counties other than Los Angeles. Recognizing all of these facts, the fledgling Southern California Association of Governments (SCAG) commenced a large-scale Regional Airport System Study in early 1968, well before the Department of Airports announced its decision. An association of ninety-seven cities and six counties, SCAG could have claimed a right to be heard before any new airports were constructed.

SCAG was not consulted despite its expensive study then in process of regional air transportation.

However, the Department was forced to come to SCAG for review and approval four months after its decision had been announced. As the regional planning agency, SCAG approval is a necessary part of any application for federal funding of advance land acquisition. Thus, in December of 1968, the SCAG staff undertook an evaluation of the airport decision in connection with the Department's applications for FAA and HUD money. Here, surely, was an opportunity to bring to bear the broad resource allocation and cost-benefit considerations particularly appropriate to a regional association.

And, again, the opportunity was squandered. Like the City and County Planning Commissions, SCAG accepted the "fact" sheet and other meager data submitted by the Department of Airports as essentially the sole basis of evaluation. In this case, some small effort was made to press the Department for any less conclusive analyses it might have, but even this hesitant request was rebuffed.

Needless to say at this point, no studies of environmental impact or resource allocation were supplied by the Department or conducted by SCAG. The focus, as in the other cases, was on the technical attributes of the Palmdale site with the overriding need for a new airport simply assumed. On February 3 and 25 respectively, SCAG gave its formal approval, announcing that the airport decision was "not inconsistent with regional planning." Its staff report in both instances was barely a page long. Giving an account of the matters brought under consideration, the report stated that:

> Discussion [by the SCAG Council of Airport Administrators] included questions regarding the relationship of the proposed facility to comprehensive planning, to air traffic, ground access, drainage problems, cross traffic within the Valley, impact upon the community, noise and the need for coordination between jurisdictions and agencies of interest.

According to SCAG staff members the references to "comprehensive planning" and "community impact" in the staff report were more public-relations gambits than accurate reflections of the review and approval process. One SCAG planner involved told us that he felt the airport decision was "just wrong enough to be a disaster," but that SCAG's role had been to "gussy it up to make it look right."

Like the City and County Planning Commissions, SCAG did urge that a *post hoc* planning effort be undertaken to facilitate accommodation to the airport decision. In particular, SCAG was anxious that its high-priced Regional Airport System Study not be brushed completely under the carpet. This Study, instead of concentrating on broad issues of resource allocation and the costs (as well as benefits) of newer and bigger airports, deals primarily with technical matters such as coordination of growing air traffic. The man in charge of the study is William Pereira, a private planner who has also served in the same capacity for the Department of Airports.

If SCAG's Airport Systems Study suggests its complete commitment to the essentials of the growth ethic that led to the airport decision in the first place, its Regional Policy Plan suggests the hopelessness of relying on SCAG to control the urbanization pressures that that decision has set in motion. The Plan is, of course, replete with stacks of computer print-outs and explanatory policy statements. But its method is no more than prediction, the familiar tool of the land promoter. Projecting present growth trends into the distant future, the computer print-outs are meant to advise the constituent governments of the problems that they will face and of the alternatives for dealing with them. Yet the alternatives fed into the computers are framed in a vague and useless form. No tough crackdown on the urbanizing of remaining open space is suggested, and ecological factors do not figure in the study at all.

Prior performance of local government indicates that land-use controls will be so inadequate that even maximum land values will not be achieved. But the wealthy and politically powerful speculators will have sold out before mixed zoning of industrial, apartment, and commercial uses results in reduced property value for homeowners. Future residents will be left with the legacy of quick profits for a few: sprawl; extended and expensive services (sewage, police and fire coverage, utilities, roads); scattered and ugly development; clogged roads; inadequate building setbacks for future transport expansion (road widening); lack of meaningful open space (e.g., urban parks); and so on. With little likelihood of meaningful, initial controls for these purposes, it was futile indeed to expect these agencies to consider the total development burden (cost of services, roads, etc.) which must be met by future airport-connected residents if the airport were constructed in *alternate* locations.

In many California counties, there are no meaningful controls or restrictions on new development at all. Antelope Valley is under the jurisdiction of California's most sophisticated and powerful planning forces. A nearby city with manpower and experience is involved, as are county and even regional planning agencies. And, usually, new public projects do not *require* approval by all surrounding planning units.

Location, Finance, Sale

Proper Location

We have discussed above the unnecessary location of new development on land which has irreplaceable agricultural or wild-area value. Another factor to be considered in the proper location of new communities is *land stability*. As Californians have learned at great cost, developers often think nothing of selling land for speculation or construction on unstable hillsides, slide areas, faults, or on land fill which subsides. The developer is gone by the time damage costs have to be paid.

Oceana Marin Development Corporation is marketing a second-home recreational subdivision at Dillon Beach in Marin County. When we visited lot 109, selling for $35,000, the ground was giving way under our feet and some of it was rolling down into the ocean. The developer on the site assured us that it wasn't serious and that given the proper foundations, we could build on this lot with confidence.

Following our visit to Oceana Marin we discovered a geologic report on the area that had been completed just three months earlier. The survey, conducted by Dr. Clyde Wahrhaftig, of the Department of Geology and Geophysics, University of California at Berkeley, and Salem Rice, of the California Division of Mines and Geology, San Francisco, California, reports that:

> The coast of Marin County north of Dillon Beach (Oceana Marin Property) is underlain largely by unstable masses of relatively impermeable crushed sandstone and shale, and is subject to very active landsliding. Retreat of the bluff top at the head of the landslides may average a foot or more a year, and cannot practically be controlled by riprapping at the base of the bluff. Soils formed from this material have a high content of swelling clays and will present serious foundation problems aside from the landslides . . . Already, only two months after the winter rains, the ground is seamed with open cracks. One can expect the foundation problems associated with swelling changes in any construction in the area.
>
> Geologic considerations based on our survey suggest the very strong likelihood that the planned urban development will be unsuccessful . . . that some of the proposed buldings and roads will eventually slide down the bluff toward the sea, much as happened at Portuguese Bend in Los Angeles County. The sewage-disposal plant, if disrupted by sliding, may pose a threat of epidemic requiring the area to be condemned and access prohibited.

Shelter Cove, a major development, is another example of location on dangerously unstable ground. Lots are placed on sixty-foot fills carved out of a mountainside. The State Department of Real Estate has warned that there is earthquake hazard in the area due to an active fault. Not even a token environmental study of Shelter Cove was conducted.

Earthquake danger is a special problem for California's new developments. According to the 1970 progress report of the Joint Committee on Seismic Safety, "California is one of the most seismically active regions in the world and is also becoming extensively populated with little or no regard for seismic danger." But although the existence of risk and the likelihood of enormous damage are indisputable, people tend fatalistically to accept the possibility of an earthquake as an "act of God."

Earthquakes *are* impossible to stop and difficult to predict with precision, but ameliorative measures can be undertaken. In California, these measures could save thousands, perhaps millions of lives in the event of a major quake. The governor of California remarked in the wake of the 1970 tremors that earthquake safety "is a top priority. Nothing has been left undone." In fact, little has been done by the state to minimize earthquake damage. The state exercises no control over development location, and provides no incentives to locate development away from hazardous areas. The Joint Committee on Seismic Safety in the legislature is "studying" the issue and is supposed to issue a full report in 1974; the report is not a serious attempt to deal with the problem—one-half of its small budget ($80,000 per year) is spent on typists, a building, a receptionist, and "staff travel"; the staff consists of two people.

The little that has been done to reduce the threat of earthquake damage—primarily the updating of construction standards—was done before the Reagan administration took office. The standards established are of dubious efficacy. The enforcement and implementation of building codes are far from satisfactory.

The two most important state laws designed to prevent earthquake damage provide for standards for school and dam construction. The Field Act, passed in 1933, requires minimal earthquake safety standards for school buildings. All schools must meet these weak standards by 1975 or be closed. As of 1971, 1,777 school buildings (pre-1933 buildings) do not meet the standards and enforcement of the law is nil. The legislature has not provided funds and local bond issues have failed. Fortunately, earthquakes have thus far been moderate and have generally occurred when children were not in school.

The dam safety law, passed in 1929, raises problems of retroactivity and jurisdiction. Section 6025 and 6026 of the California Water Code provide for exclusive state regulation of dams above a certain size: 225 dams qualify for state regulation. Fifty-five of these were completed prior to the 1929 law, and although some subsequent alterations were made, structural weaknesses remain. Cities and counties may adopt ordinances covering the smaller dams and reservoirs not within state jurisdiction. Only a handful of local jurisdictions have even passed, much less enforced, dam construction ordinances.

As for the efficacy of the standards, not much is known because not much is known about the effects of quakes on dam integrity. For six years, thirty seismologists and staff members studied seismic hazards related to the massive California Water Project. The Reagan administration has reduced this group to four. Major research on earthquake problems has been conducted by the University of California Departments of Geology and Geophysics, an Earthquake Engineering Research Institute, and Seismographic stations; but University budget cuts over the past several years have brought this research to a virtual halt.

Because of the lack of theoretical information for more useful codes, the cutback on surveillance of California Water Plan earthquake protection, the many dams built before protective legislation was passed, and the lack of any local controls over most of the "smaller" facilities, a major earthquake could prove disastrous from dam danger alone. The Report of the National Earthquake Information Center of the Commerce Department's new National Oceanic and Atmospheric Administration (January 29, 1971) describes the 1966 social service building in Santa Rosa:

> Practically every reinforced concrete column was cracked and several exterior beams were cracked on the main floor. This is not at all reassuring when extrapolated to reinforced concrete high-rise frame construction.
> There is an increasing number of high-rise reinforced frame structures being built throughout metropolitan San Francisco, Los Angeles and other Western cities.

The Report added that "the collapse of one or more of them in a great earthquake would not be a surprise."

Certainly it is going to be difficult to prevent all damage or loss of life in a major quake. But a coordinated calculation of risks can minimize the damage. High-rise structures can be prohibited in particularly vulnerable areas, height limits or additional strength requirements can be imposed, and conversion fees or bonds can be imposed to encourage development of less vulnerable areas first. New developments beneath weak dams can be prohibited or discouraged. Although retroactivity is difficult when applying construction standards, a reasonable "nonconforming use" period could be imposed. The Field Act gave schools more than forty years to comply, allowing amortization of loss and discouraging reinvestment in dangerous structures.

But the state has refused to research and set strict building standards for earthquake safety, and has not prohibited high-rise construction in especially dangerous areas.[1]

Nature issued a strong warning to California in February of 1971: tremors hit outlying areas of Los Angeles. Several multistoried buildings collapsed, killing scores of people. Estimates of property damage went as high as $1 billion. The Van Norman dam strained and threatened 80,000 people with inundation. Fortunately, the quake was moderate, with a reading of about 6.6 on the Richter scale, and was centered far to the edge of the Los Angeles sprawl. Scientists studying the quake estimate that, given present land-use practices, a million or more people will die in the event of a major quake during working hours.

Foster City Finance

In 1959, T. Jack Foster, a self-made millionaire real-estate entrepreneur, thought of a way to make $40 million on a $1 million investment. He would develop a planned community of 35,000 people on 2,600 acres of marshy pasture land and salt flats on the edge of San Francisco Bay just east of the town of San Mateo, and finance the project with tax-exempt public bonds. While he collected the profits from the huge increase in land values that would result from the dredging and filling paid for by the bonds, the bonds would be paid off by the people who eventually moved into his "Island of Blue Lagoons." The cost of filling and improving the land would not be included in the purchase price of the houses, but would come through enormous property taxes later.

A. O. Champlin, an accountant whom Foster allegedly induced to come to California from Oklahoma on the promise of $1 million in fees if the deal were successful, believes that the idea of having the project financed by municipal bonds never occurred to the previous owner, the Leslie Salt Company. Without the many advantages of this type of financing, the development was not at all attractive.

ECONOMICS

At a meeting in late 1959, Foster, Richard Grant of Leslie Salt, and accountant Champlin drew up plans for the Estero Municipal Improvement District. Ernest Wilson, Jones, Morton, & Lynch (bond attorneys) drew up a bill to create the District. The idea came, claims Champlin, from a somewhat similar improvement district a few miles to the north.

Special improvement districts began as a means of providing unincorporated areas with some of the services provided by cities, without forcing them to become cities. If an area needed sewers, or water, or streets, it could form a special improvement district which could provide the desired service, issue municipal bonds, and tax the property-owners of the district in some way according to benefits received.

During the 1950s, with Wilson and his firm leading the way, large property-owners discovered that they could finance improvements in their land at municipal bond rates, and for municipal bond maturities. Instead of having to finance their operations with ninety-day commercial credit, or even with two- or three-year long-term bank loans at or above the prime rate, they could issue improvement district bonds with up to forty-year maturities, and at interest rates several points below the prime rate. The long maturity meant that the principal did not have to be paid for many years. Thus, by using the tax exemption designed for municipalities, Wilson's clients, including Foster, could finance their properties with publicly subsidized bonds.

Foster was also able to capitalize interest. The first bonds were issued around 1962 and interest came due six months later. To avoid paying interest while he held the property, Foster paid most of the interest with the proceeds of *later* bonds. The plan was to float more and more bonds not only for development, but to pay interest due on other bonds until he had sold off most of the property for huge capital gains. Then the new property-owners could begin paying interest on the debt. While Foster held property and was liable for the interest, he preferred to pay it with more debt. This was legal because of a provision in the enabling act providing that interest could be capitalized throughout the life of the project, and for twelve months after its completion. Foster planned his project to last for a decade or more.

Not only did Foster have an interest subsidy, avoid taxes, and get new homeowners to assume much of the risk and pay off the debt; according to accountant Champlin and others, Foster also sold the District land for parks, had the District pay his dredging company for dredging and filling the land, and got the District to pay many of his own expenses.

For thirty-five acres of land sold to the District for parks, public safety buildings, and municipal service areas, "sales proceeds received by Foster" totaled $515,000, or $14,700 per acre. Foster bought the 2,600 acres from Leslie for about $8,000 an acre, so he made a tidy profit. Foster also sold land to the State Highway Department, the San Mateo City School District, and the San Mateo Union High School District for $23,000, $26,000 and $14,000 per acre respectively.

Since Foster virtually *was* the District he was able to have it pay many of his expenses. These expenses included not only District necessities such as streets, sewers, water, parks, playgrounds, small-craft harbors, fire protection, underground utilities, and police services. They also include: "preliminary title search for the acquisition of the Leslie Salt Company and Schilling Estate properties on Brewer Island" before the District was even formed, for $2,400 (so that Foster could buy the land, not so the Estero District could buy it); $113,000 for "preparation of the General Plan and report" presumably for Foster City, the Island of Blue Lagoons, including market research and fancy brochures for Foster's sales endeavor; $30,000 paid to Richard H. Grant for "services relating to reclamation and issuance of bonds" in April, 1961; checks to George A. McQueen for "public relations services and expenses" in February 1962 [2]; $1,100 to "establish the new property line between the land of T. Jack Foster and the State of

California and prepare the required legal descriptions for
the exchange of lands," January through April 1961; etc.

POLITICS

Foster controlled the District because in elections the
rule was not one man, one vote, but one dollar of assessed
value of land, one vote. "Land" does not include personal
property or improvements. People were *taxed* on the value
of their land plus improvements, but under the law which
created Estero District, they could only *vote* according to
their raw land. Of course, Foster owned all of the land in
the beginning, and still, when the population of Foster
City is over 8,000, he owns more land than all the others
combined. And since the assessor was his employee, Foster
had control over the elections and the District.

H. L. Hunt might support voting based on wealth, but
Governor Pat Brown had misgivings. He hesitated for almost a month, and almost vetoed the bill creating the
Estero District. But the San Mateo Board of Supervisors
had unanimously endorsed it, and both houses of the legislature had passed it unanimously. With such strong support for a bill which looked toward the fourteenth century
for its inspiration, Brown finally felt compelled to sign it,
and he did so on May 11, 1960.

Accountant Champlin has brought suit against Foster for,
inter alia, the reimbursement of several thousand dollars
which Champlin paid for insurance commissions to the
insurance firm of powerful State Senator Hugh Burns.
Champlin claims that it was a business expense made on
behalf of Foster to influence 1968 legislation which threatened Foster's control of the District.

THE ATTORNEY GENERAL'S REPORT

The response of public agencies to development schemes
such as Foster's can be inferred from the following excerpts
of a suppressed report written by staff of the Attorney
General's office:

REAL ESTATE DEVELOPMENT SPECULATIONS
ASSISTED BY TAX EXEMPT BOND FINANCING

In a series of reports to the California Legislature, the
Attorney General over the last 7 years has presented examples of promotional subdivisions where the off-site
improvements had been financed by assessment districts
formed at the request of the developer.

These districts illustrated a number of serious problems that did not occur in non-developer controlled districts. Specific problems included:

(1) Over burdening the land with debt so that sale or further improvement was not economically feasible;

(2) Construction of faulty improvements;

(3) Opportunities for self-dealing by the developer whereby funds were diverted;

(4) Exposing the local jurisdiction to liability on unpaid assessment liens;

(5) Subsidization by developer to conceal the true tax burden;

(6) Improvements created before need and deterioration before use;

(7) Default in the lands and consequent credit impairment and loss of investor confidence.

Although the Legislature tightened the laws over the objections of bond counsel and assessment bond sales firms, abuses still exist in counties that provide inadequate supervision or are susceptible to collusive practices between the developer and public officials. . . .

Our earlier investigations presented numerous examples and included the formation and initial operations of a resort improvement district and a municipal improvement district created and manipulated by land developers. The present status of these districts, now that their problems are manifest, reinforces the basis of our concern. It is clearly evident that a promotional district creates a disservice to its residents, to the community in which it is located and saddles the area with obligations that cannot be alleviated even when the residents are able to seize control from the developer.

California has no system whereby all land development bonds are reported to the state. Only a few issues are reviewed by the California District Securities Commission. Most issues are known only to the authorizing city, county or district. Consequently, there is no central source to determine the number of districts, the total amount of bonds or the defaults which occur. The full impact of the issuance of bonds to aid land developers cannot be determined at this time.

And, from the same report concerning Foster City:

Foster City [Estero Municipal Improvement District] is a 2,600 acre land reclamation and planned community development in San Mateo County. The district has issued and sold over $64 million in bonds to finance land reclamation, off-site improvements, a sanitation and drainage system and various civic improvements. Although pro-

jected as a balanced community, little business development has occurred and population growth is about 50%
the originally projected growth rate. The subdivider subsidizes the development by overassessing his property, sells
district assets to meet operating expenses and issues bonds
to pay current bond interest expenses. Despite this effort, the combined county and district tax rate is $17
which is $7 to $8 per hundred higher than adjacent subdivisions.

Residents of the area have been seriously disturbed by
the voting procedure of the special district whereby the
developer has been able to control the district and utilize
it to obtain the funds he needs to effect the development
of his land.

At present the outstanding debt is *258%* of the county's
assessed value. It appears that the market for Foster City
bonds has been saturated and no funds are available to
complete the reclamation and development project. As the
tax burden shifts from the developer, who now pays 67%
of the tax bill, to the homeowners and as a higher proportion of bond amortization occurs as well as the inability of the district to sell more bonds to pay current
interest, the district's taxes will become increasingly op-
pressive to the residents.

Foster City represents the type of "tax trap" that can
occur in a metropolitan area, when a developer is able to
avoid the costs of development by transferring the burden to the new residents who must discharge the debt
created by the developer's use of tax-exempt bond financing.

Selling California City

While eager land promoters in the Palmdale area of the
Antelope Valley were busy dreaming up fantastic schemes
to lure industry and spark a land boom, promoters in the
Eastern Valley were using an old but effective technique
commonly known as "the big lie." They took a vast expanse
of arid desert and called it a booming city—a boundless
opportunity for fun and profit, not in the future but right
now. Luring countless innocents from all over the country
and the world to invest in this wasteland, developer
N. K. Mendelsohn has collected, as of January 26, 1969,
$102,000,000. California City is a perfect example of
development fraud and the official nonfeasance that sanctions it.

An official investigative Report by the Attorney General
of California in 1969 thoroughly documented the history

and fraudulence of the California City development. The Report has been suppressed and its recommendations ignored. When we obtained a full copy of the Report in late 1970, we were told by our source that there were only three official copies in existence. Deputy Attorney General Charles O'Brien told reporter Ron Taylor of the *Fresno Bee* that the "investigation was as yet incomplete." The development is ten years old, and the investigation at least five years old. Nothing whatsoever has been done to "complete" the investigation for two and a half years.

Following are excerpts from the Report, with our comments and abridgments in brackets:

California City is probably the largest desert land promotion ever offered to a "land-investment" hungry public. It consists of 100,000 acres subdivided into 90,000 stake marked parcels linked by dusty roads to form the third largest city in California. Located on the Mojave Desert in eastern Kern County, for twelve years this development has been controlled by an investment group headed by N.K. Mendelsohn. The developer has transformed uneconomic farmland acquired at $109 an acre into a "planned city" with lots that the development company sells for $9,000. Lots being sold today are without utilities or water or any paved road linking them to a one block group of stores located ten to twenty miles away in the extreme southwest corner of the development. To date, the developer has sold 32,000 parcels at a total sales price of $102,000,000 to purchasers throughout the U.S., Germany and the Philippines.

Although the developer has attempted to attract industry and provides recreational and community facilities (using over $6 million in public financing) there is no significant industrial development and the population of 896 is almost entirely dependent upon the developer for employment or income.

To prospective land buyers, California City is represented as a safe, secure real estate investment in a community with "abundant water." These representations are false. Purchasers desiring to sell, find no ready market of buyers. Instead when they are fortunate enough to resell they usually take a loss. Mendelsohn's claim that an underground lake exists beneath California City is equally spurious.

. . . [T]his is no ordinary real estate sales scheme— Mendelsohn isn't trying to sell "land" and the public isn't really buying the "land." They are engaged in a grand illusion of creating wealth. Mendelsohn has a dream and the buyers believe the developer's dream is capable of providing them with a pot of gold.

The art of creating gold from base metals has long eluded our grasp, but N.K. Mendelsohn has perfected the art of turning desert dust into gold—but only for himself. . . .

A. GENERAL INFORMATION

. . . The more developed portions of California City are about fifteen miles northeast of the town of Mojave, sixty miles southeast of the City of Bakersfield, and 110 miles northeast of the City of Los Angeles.

. . . The Mojave Desert . . . is semi-arid with very little natural vegetation other than bushes and other desert growth. The elevation ranges from 2,400 to 3,500 feet above sea level and has characteristic desert temperatures and periods of high winds.

Public roads connect California City with Highways 14 and 58. There is no public air, rail or bus transportation; however a private airport is owned and maintained by the developer.

The most recent census determined that there were 302 occupied dwelling units. In addition, there is a small commercial and business area.

When California City became incorporated in December 1965 additional control of local affairs passed into the hands of individuals favorably oriented toward the needs of the developer. Several employees of the developer who reside in California City are active in city and district affairs. An employee of the developer has served as a member of the City Council since the incorporation of the City and is presently Mayor. . . . A recent survey of employees in the area indicates that of the 238 residents now employed, 141 either work for the developer or are employed in the nineteen local businesses heavily dependent upon the developer's promotional activities. . . .

The City and the district have incurred heavy debt to finance offsite improvements, and promotional and recreational facilities desired by the developer.* As of September 30, 1968, California City had a direct and overlapping debt of over $6,227,000 or a ratio to assessed valuation of 42.21%.

*These facilities were acquired by the Community Services District which issued general obligation bonds ** and used much of the proceeds to reimburse the developer for his costs* [emphasis added].

---

* [The developer constructed a man-made lake, par-three golf course, tennis courts, and three picnic grounds.]
** [As of July 1968, $3,700,000 in bonds had been issued.]

[The City has now determined to defer water, drainage, and road construction until "a need should arise." This is ironic in light of the developer's claims in 1959 that by 1970 there would be one million people in California City, and directly contradicts improvement claims made to purchasers.]

The City has also accepted for maintenance 485 miles of either paved, graded or compacted roads that provide access to the subdivisions. These roads are in generally poor condition, are rutted and pitted and are a source of constant concern to the residents of the City. If these roads were constructed to county standards and maintained, the cost would be substantial, and most counties and cities would require that the developer assume a principal share.

The City Planning Commission has superseded the County in the enforcement of the master zoning plan for California City. The general plan of development was prepared by the community planning and consulting firm of Smith and Williams, South Pasadena, California and was adopted as a zoning plan by ordinance of the City of California City on January 25, 1968.

Many purchasers are under the illusion that they have acquired valuable property rights in specially zoned areas [i.e., commercial, industrial] in the master planned community. However, the City can at any time change the zoning to meet the needs of the community and the community's developer.

Another important area of City control involves the issuance of building permits and construction inspection standards. Although California City emphasizes the aspect of the planned community, and provides an architectural review board, there is no requirement that lot buyers must construct improvements within a reasonable time. This has resulted in less than one percent of the subdivided parcels being improved and even the most developed tracts near the community center reflect the spotty development with large empty gaps between houses.

It has been alleged that construction materials used in housing construction by the developers are inferior, yet receive City approval. The exterior siding material now used by the developer's construction company is Homasote, which is manufactured from repulped newspaper. Its use as an exterior sheathing material is not permitted in California's major cities, (Los Angeles and San Francisco) and the State Division of Building Standards thought that its use in California had passed with the end of war housing projects. This material has a tendency to absorb water and decompose; in addition better and more attractive siding products are readily available.

In the twelve years of its development California City has become the third largest city in California [in geographic size] but it is mainly inhabited by cactus, snakes, and employees of the developer.

1. Industrial and Commercial Development

The establishment of business and industry in the California City area is of major importance to the overall growth and development of the community. Under the general plan of development adopted by the City of California City, substantial areas have been zoned for commercial and industrial use. The California City Companies have offered land in the California City area at or below cost to prospective businesses. To date the Companies' efforts have not attracted significant businesses.

Industrial and commercial development within the City of California City presently consists solely of the California City Airport and a few service businesses. The service businesses are a motel, restaurant, and food market owned by the developer but independently operated, and a service station and a few other retail stores neither owned nor operated by the developer. The nearest other shopping facilities are in the town of Mojave. The California City Airport, which is owned by the developer, consists of a small terminal and hanger facilities and a 4,200-foot surfaced and lighted runway. There are no scheduled flights to the airport.

In 1965, the developer leased from Kern County for a term of fifty years approximately 550 acres of land, which although not used for aeronautical purposes are located at the general aviation airport in the town of Mojave. The developer sought to develop the leased land as an industrial park. To date there has been no significant development of the industrial park facility.

2. Housing

The California City developer sells and constructs houses in the California City area. As of January 26, 1969, there were approximately 350 finished single-family houses in California City, about 90% of which were constructed and sold by the developer. Approximately 25% of the houses in California City are occupied by employees of the developer and their families.

The selling price of the developer's houses, independent of the lot, has been between $9,650 and $15,000.

These prices have been approximately the same as the costs of construction.

3. Utilities

Telephone service is provided to the City of California City by the California Interstate Telephone Company. Electricity is available from Southern California Edison Company. The cost of obtaining electric or telephone service is borne entirely by the individual landowner, and in portions of the development located a substantial distance from existing service lines the cost of obtaining either service at the present time is prohibitive. The California City Companies usually advance the deposit required to obtain electric service for developed subdivisions. No natural gas facilities are presently available within the City of California City. However, butane or bottled gas is available from individual suppliers and is widely used within the City.

Sewer service is not now available. The proposed facility . . . and sewer lines would serve the developer's commercial areas, the school, and the proposed civic center. Most of the present residents would not be served.

Water service is provided to existing developed areas by the District. It is *not* available to most subdivision tracts.

4. Other Public Services

Residents of the City of California City are provided police protection under the direction of the Kern County Sheriff. Fire protection is currently provided by a unit of the Kern County Fire Department located approximately fifteen miles from the more developed portions of California City and by a volunteer fire crew and one truck located in the westerly portion of the City of California City. In November, 1968, the City of California City sold general obligation bonds in the aggregate amount of $175,000, the proceeds of which will be used to construct and equip a fire station for the City of California City.

California City is served by the Mojave Unified School District, which provides elementary and secondary school facilities to residents. There is one elementary school located in California City. Free bus transportation to residents of California City is provided by the school district where necessary.

5. California City as a Desert Community

An editorial in the *California City Chronicle* of March 19, 1964, summed up the advantages and disadvantages of living in a desert community:

Residents of California City are troubled by the absence of a medical center, the rutted, washboard roads, and the absence of a sewer system. To the residents, these improvements are priority items, but the developer who resides in Santa Monica proposed to build a "million dollar city hall" instead.

When citizens question the developer's actions he publicly labels them as "cynics and Doubting Thomases" with "scornful" and "negative" attitudes.

Nevertheless, because of the developer's subsidization of the community and his dominant influence in community affairs, for the foreseeable future the desires of the developer will receive priority over the needs of the community.

C. SALES OPERATION

The developer, N.K. Mendelsohn, through his wholly owned company, the California City Development Company, operates a sophisticated land sales program.

The Company's sales program is conducted principally through company operated sales offices which promote only sales of the Companies' land. There are twenty-four such sales offices primarily serving, and located in, the States of California, Colorado, Illinois, Texas and Washington. During the fiscal year ended July 31, 1968, these offices accounted for approximately 96% of total sales. The Companies also have other selling arrangements with sales representatives located in Hawaii, Germany, Mexico and the Philippines and with independent real estate brokers and agents. The Companies estimate that approximately 75% to 80% of total sales of land in California City have been made to California residents.

Because of the extensive nature of the Companies' sales program and the relatively low cost of the Companies' land, *sales and administrative expenses,* including sales commissions and overrides . . . *have substantially exceeded the cost* (including capitalized interest, taxes and provisions for improvements) *of land* sold in California City [emphasis added].

Generally neither the Companies nor their sales representatives resell land on behalf of individual lot purchasers. . . .

1. Terms of Sales

Substantially all of the California City Companies' land sales in California City are made under installment land contracts with current minimum down payments of five percent of the purchase price. The balance of the purchase price and interest (which is charged on the unpaid balance at rates which have ranged from a low of six percent per annum to the current rate of seven percent per annum) are payable in equal monthly installments over periods ranging between seven and one-half and ten years. No investigation is made of the credit standing of land purchasers.

In most instances record title to land sold under an installment contract is not conveyed to a purchaser until he completes payment for his land.

* * *

If a purchaser defaults on his contract obligations, the Company terminates the purchaser's rights under the contract and retains all sums. Land repossessed by the Companies upon contract termination is restored to inventory for sale to other purchasers.

2. Sales Summary

Of the original 83,701 acres of land owned by the California City Companies, 49,033 acres had been sold as of January 26, 1969, consisting of approximately 24,622 acres in subdivided lots, approximately 14,971 acres in twenty-acre parcels and approximately 9,440 acres in 160-acre parcels. Approximately 2,844 acres have been deeded to City of California City.

D. SALES REPRESENTATIONS BY THE DEVELOPER

Sales materials published by the company stress "abundant water" and investors were asked about two specific representations. Fifty-three percent had been informed there was an underground lake capable of meeting future water needs; 61% had been informed that Feather River water would be available.

When queried about representations by the Company about business and industry, 44% of the investors had been informed that major industries have purchased land in California City; 43% had been informed that major businesses have purchased sites in California City; 61% had been informed there was an international airport (Kern #7) adjacent to California City; and 23% had been informed a state college will be built in California City.

1. Representations Concerning Water

. . . No natural watercourses exist [on California City's 100,000 acres] and the only nearby lakes are alkali flats. In order to merchandise parcels of this dry, untimbered desert, N.K. Mendelsohn has created for the prospective buyer an illusion of abundant water. The green, central park with its plastic bottomed lake and the artificial waterfall are used to visually accompany the developer's representations:

> "In addition to plentiful water, California City has hundreds of miles of streets and water mains."

". . . the land is beautifully flat . . . has abundant water."

In addition the developer has represented that the city's existing wells are capable of producing 15 million gallons a day, or enough water to serve a population of 75,000. The developer has also specified that Feather River water was being brought to California City.

Since an abundant supply of water is a prerequisite to population growth and industrial development, N.K. Mendelsohn has sought new sources of water for the complex of cities he has planned.

To this end he has engaged drillers and engineers to test novel theories of locating water supplies in addition to the limited ground water in the basin.

Mendelsohn commissioned one engineer, Olindo Angelillo to examine the terrain and geologic formations in the belief that the deep rock, thousands of feet beneath the desert, held an untapped supply of water. The theory that Angelillo was to confirm was that the run-off of mountain rains in the Sierra Nevada Mountains permeated the soil and was transmitted hundreds of miles beneath the earth's surface via a system of earth faults. Conceptually, these faults in the earth formed a continuous passage for water that could be tapped by deep drilling.

After a period of study, O.R. Angelillo announced that he had discovered a fault, which he named the Mendelsohn Fault, which connected with existing faults (the Garlock, San Andreas, and Lockhart) and which piped millions of acre feet of water into rock aquifers beneath California City. This discovery was announced to the world—and especially to prospective investors by N.K. Mendelsohn.

The claims of Mendelsohn-Angelillo concerning the vast lake in the Mojave were carefully examined by the State Department of Water Resources and found to be spurious.

Because the State Director of Water Resources found these claims to be contrary to the public interest and welfare, he took the unusual step of announcing publicly that he was opening his files on the developer's experts and issued a comprehensive report in 1960 after an earlier report in 1954. The Department of Water Resources concluded:

It is the opinion of the Department of Water Resources that there is no factual basis for suppositions and implications to the effect that "primary water" is a potential source of water supply. To our knowledge there is no scientific evidence that would support such suppositions. On the contrary, there is a convincing body of scientific knowledge which contradicts the contentions of proponents of "primary water," "deep-seated rock fissure aquifers" and related postulations that these constitute major sources of water supply.

The Department of Water Resources report also contained opinions from the leading geologists, geochemists and seismologists to this effect.

Dr. Charles Richter of Caltech commented that Angelillo's connecting fault theory which would permit transmission of ground water over very large distances ". . . is bound to appear to any disinterested man with scientific training as utterly fantastic nonsense."

At the time of the preparation of the report, the developer's engineer, Angelillo, on a pretext arranged a dinner with leading scientific personnel and Mr. Mendelsohn. One of the invitees, Dr. Hugo Benioff, Professor of Seismology at Caltech recalled the event:

Q. Now at this dinner, was there any discussion about the Angelillo theory of movement of water through the fault systems in California.

A. I—it came up in some manner there. As a matter of fact, I didn't know what my relationship to the whole thing was in the first place; but I found that there was a commercial venture of some sort going on in which we were involved in the way that—I am saying "we"— Richter and a few others—

Q. In a way that you—I didn't understand that.

A. Well, we apparently were involved in some form of commercial venture which I had no inkling of from all the times I talked to Mr. Angelillo. And as we got talking there, it occurred—we found that we were apparently there to confirm Mr. Angelillo's hypothesis as to the transmission of water in faults. And if my memory does not fail me, all but one of the scientists there were very unhappy with this conclusion.

Q. Did they express this unhappiness?

A. I am sure that some of us, if not all, did at that time.

Q. Did they express this to Mr. Mendelsohn and Mr. Angelillo?

A. Well, they were at the meeting and they must have heard it.

Q. Who was the one scientist who did not express his displeasure?

A. Pierce.

Q. What is his work?

A. I don't know his work. He is a Southern California man, but I am not familiar with it.

Q. Do you know what the field of work is?

A. I think it's entomology.

Q. What is entomology?

A. The study of insects, I suppose.

Q. Does the study of insects affect the flow of water in rock fissures as you understood the Angelillo theory, Doctor?

A. I think not.

Another invitee, Professor Percy B. Rowe, an expert hydrologist at the University of Arizona stated:

THE WITNESS: It was a very impressive affair. We were wined and dined. We were introduced to the other members of the place and at the end of this meeting Angelillo took the floor. He had previously introduced the various guests to each other, particularly the more important ones that he had, and then he talked about this crash program, that a large part of these guests had been contacted or involved somewhere in this program and described what he intended to do. He gave as the objective of this program that he wanted to develop and to get support, and implied government support, although he did not give a positive answer in this, in order to carry out a crash program to determine the source and the transmission of waters from the mountain areas through faults and cracks to the valley.

He implied that such a program would not only be of service to California, to the nation throughout the southwest, but to semi-arid areas throughout the world.

He implied that one of the things he was going to do was to sink a shaft or well through the outer crust of the earth for the purpose of studying the geophysics of this. I think this is pretty well the subject of his talk.

He gave some of his background. He indicated some of the support that he had in Europe. He indicated that the Pope had given his blessings and indicated the need for such a study. He had not at this time I believe connected himself as an employee of any organization.

Q. BY MR. TOBIN: Now, after this statement was made was there any discussion among the persons present?

A. Yes, he asked for questions. He got a few and then began to call on people that had discussions there. Most of them were very cautious or critical, somewhat skeptical of the program.

When it came to my part of the thing, I challenged the use or the application of his deep shaft or well as having any relation to the water problems with the hydrology of the desert. . . .

I think that one of [the] geologists indicated that due to the geophysics of the outer crust of the area you would not put the well in the Mojave anywhere.

You would put it somewhere out in the ocean and the discussion continued more or less in this vein with these people.

Q. Was there any discussion at that meeting relating to the sufficiency of information regarding the east side of the Sierra Nevada Mountains or some suggestion that there was a large unaccounted flow of water on that east slope?

A. I believe this is brought out. It had been brought out in other contacts and I think it was brought out on this evening and I think the general consensus of opinion, and I believe I expressed it, that there was not adequate data available to indicate any excess of unappropriated water or water beyond the consumptive use of the area; that this information just was not existent, to my knowledge, at least.

Q. Now, was Mr. Mendelsohn introduced to the people?

A. Yes.

Q. How was Mr. Mendelsohn introduced to the people present?

A. I don't remember the exact title, but he was introduced as interested in the program for the development of water for California City. This was brought out.

In direct opposition to these comments, Mr. Mendelsohn states:

"I satisfied myself that none of them had any contrary or negative attitude."

        ※   ※   ※

When Mr. Mendelsohn, who describes himself as a ". . . kind of geologist for my own purposes as a businessman" was questioned concerning his investigation into Mr. Angelillo's background he stated:

Q. At the time Mr. Angelillo undertook this study for you did you know what his educational background was?

A. Only in a general way. I knew that he was a licensed engineer in the State of California.

Q. Did you know then what degrees he held?

A. No.

Q. Did you make any attempts to find out?

A. No.

It is difficult to understand why an experienced developer, demographer and Columbia University teacher such as Mr. Mendelsohn rejected the opinion of experts and placed reliance on an unscientific study prepared by a high school dropout with no professional qualification or recognition. Mr. Angelillo's own conduct and claim to have located water on the moon would give any reasonable man some pause.

The empirical evidence also completely confirms the falsity of the Mendelsohn-Angelillo representations of deep rock fissure water.

[Mendelsohn also teamed up with a man named Stephan Riess who claimed to be able to locate water in deep rock aquifers and to have located seventy gushing wells of "primary" or "juvenile" water. Mendelsohn hired Riess and they formed a company to locate deep rock water. In 1959 the State Department of Water Resources studied the wells drilled by Stephan Riess (without Riess's cooperation) and found that the seventy wells produced zero to ninety gallons per minute instead of the 500–3,000 gallons per minute claimed by Riess. And Dr. Samuel Epstein, Professor of Geochemistry at the California Institute of Technology, reported that the waters were *precipitation* waters and not the "primary" water claimed by Riess. Undaunted, Mendelsohn financed a Riess project in Israel to locate water in the desert, which also failed, and then commissioned him to drill for deep rock aquifers in the vicinity of Galileo Hill, where experts have confirmed that no appreciable amounts of water are to be found; Mendelsohn paid Riess with development company and city funds.]

The developer has continually represented that California City would receive Feather River water. A developer-issued press release quoted in *Today in California,* April 1968, states: "By 1971, Feather River water will be available."

However, this representation was false.

Although California City was originally eligible for a share of Feather River water by virtue of being a member of the Antelope Valley-East Kern Water Agency, after a year's discussion and study by the developer and the city council, at the personal request of the developer, N.K. Mendelsohn and other owners of property in California City, the city in 1967 withdrew from the Antelope Valley-East Kern Water Agency and became ineligible to receive Feather River water. Mr. Mendelsohn personally appeared before the Kern County Local Agency Formation Commission on September 12, 1967 to make this request.

2. *Representations Concerning Industry, Growth and Investment Potential*

The sales program developed to sell California City has one focal point—the desire of a prospective purchaser to make a secure and profitable investment. All sales techniques and sales devices emphasize this as the primary point. Every piece of literature freely uses the word "investment."

To reinforce the investment potential, the Companies emphasize the anticipated future growth of the area and the existing and future industrial complex. One brochure used in the sales pitch states:

> At this time, let's talk about the industrial potential. Let me turn to this section of the brochure which illustrates not only how the area is growing industrially, but shows the many industries already there. For example, on this map, No. 1 is Kern County Airport No. 7. This is one of the larger jet airports in Southern California which also features a huge industrial park of its own. California City has a fifty year lease on 549 acres of it including 500,000 square feet of industrial buildings available for income industry. Some of this has already been leased to such firms as Power Line Erector, Inc., the United States Post Office, and Bakman Moving and Storage. Numbers 2 and 3 designate the California Portland Cement Company and the Monolith Company. They represent a $50 million investment and an annual payroll of $4,300,000. Number 4 is the Texas Aluminum Co. And, by the way, we own the land, built the plant for Texas Aluminum and leased it back to them for ninety-nine years.
>
> Number 5 is the Purdy Company, which is a railroad reclamation plant. Number 6 is the United Carbon Corporation. Number 7 is Great Lakes Carbon Company. Number 8 is the marshalling yards at Mojave Junction, which is the railroad center of the Antelope Valley for both the Southern Pacific and Santa Fe railroads. [etc.]. . . .

The developer's representations over the last ten years bear faint semblance with an unbiased observer's comparisons with the facts. *There is no projected college despite . . . inferences the developer has sought to create.** A similar misleading statement involves the developer's claim to have poured $22 million into the city's development.

Instead millions of dollars of construction were furnished by the proceeds of municipal bonds which are *continuing obligations of the city, the district and lot owners* [emphasis added].

When forced to make a full disclosure of the true facts the developer admits: "Relatively few people are presently

---

* [The old tactic of offering land and asking state authorities for "consideration" of a site was used to obtain a reply. The reply, naturally said they would "consider" it—and is used to convey the impression of imminent ground-breaking.]

permanent residents . . . and there has been very little commercial or industrial development to date."

Similarly [a] claim concerning the financial community's approbation of California City doesn't quite square with the developer's admission that ". . . institutional loans for the construction of houses in California City have not been available."

[The developer argues that the area's desirable "moderate" climate will draw industry, commerce, and people to California City. Despite his constant remonstrations against calling the area a "desert," that is exactly what it is, with fierce, constant winds and temperatures ranging from about 100° during the day to 60° at night. Table 8a is a synopsis of temperatures in the "City" for a two-month period in 1964.]

Population Growth

The developer's representation that "From 1960–1970 a new population the size of Chicago will flow into Southern California" and a master plan contemplating hundreds of thousands raises some justifiable expectation on the part of a land buyer that California will have a mushrooming growth. Yet the developer carefully omits to disclose to prospective purchasers the county planning commission's population forecast or the pre-incorporation study by J.B. Hanauer:

County		Hanauer	
1960	600	1965–66	1,000
1965	950	1966–67	1,150
1970	1,200	1967–68	1,300
1975	1,500	1968–69	1,500
1980	1,850	1969–70	1,750
1985	2,250	1970–71	2,000
		1974–75	3,000
		1979–80	5,000

Similarly, nowhere in the developer's literature does he mention the most recent census taken by the State of California at California City's request that gave California City a population of 896.

Perhaps the most informative population forecast was the developer's own.

In proceedings initiated by the developer to de-annex California City from the Antelope Valley-East Kern Water Agency, the developer estimated a maximum population in 1990 of 10,000 and claimed that there was no need for water to support a greater population.

[*Table 8a*
TEMPERATURES IN CALIFORNIA CITY,
JULY 13–SEPTEMBER 20, 1964

Date	Max. Temp.	Min. Temp.	Date	Max. Temp.	Min. Temp.
July			August		
13, 1964	108	72	17, 1964	102	55
14	104	66	18	99	70
15	98	67	19	101	67
16	97	62	20	98	62
17	101	62	21	99	61
18	103	63	22	103	60
19	104	66	23	105	66
20	103	60	24	104	65
21	99	61	25	103	69
22	103	64	26	97	79
23	104	65	27	98	73
24	108	69	28	95	65
25	103	68	29	93	57
26	97	73	30	91	54
27	98	70	August 31–September 6 not		
28	103	67	available		
29	105	65	September 7,		
30	102	67	1964	91	47
31	98	66	8	90	49
August			9	94	50
1, 1964	94	65	10	96	55
2	95	56	11	98	58
3	99	58	12	99	61
4	101	68	13	95	62
5	101	70	14	91	56
6	100	77	15	95	53
7	104	70	16	95	55
8	106	68	17	92	53
9	105	69	18	88	55
10	106	76	19	90	57
11	103	71	20	93	50
12	102	65			
13	100	63			
14	96	58			
15	94	60			
16	98	52			

Source: California City Chronicle.]

Business Development

Instead of a booming industrial city, California City has no industry. The 1968 business assessment roll of $261,650 is made up largely of data processing equipment used by the *developer* to process investors' installment payments. [Table 8b] indicated that the *improvements* on the land total less than $30,000.

It is significant (and the developer omits this fact) that

[*Table 8b*

CALIFORNIA CITY BUSINESS ASSESSMENT—1968

Business	Improvements	Personal Property	Tax
Joshua Aviation	$ 9,000	$ 360	$ 192.63
McIntire & Quires	3,400		69.97
" "		3,080	63.38
Calif. City Devel. Co.		8,320	171.23
Calif. City Enterprises		6,400	131.71
James Cobble (Jim's TV)		560	11.52
(9325 Aspen Ave.—Bankruptcy)			
E. Town Co.		1,160	23.87
Edwards Town Inc.		1,200	24.69
" " "		2,480	51.04
" " "		7,160	147.35
Xerox		18,400	378.69
Mort M. Boone		12,560	258.49
8835 Bay Ave., Cal. City			
Challenge Cream & Butter			
Assn.		1,160	23.87
Philco Ford (TV in motel)		1,360	27.99
" " (TV in East Lake			
apts.)		2,400	49.39
Pitney Bowes		240	4.93
Morgan Trammell (golf pro)		3,320	68.32
Ivan Manger	40	120	3.29
Wm. H. Bell (airplane)		10,000	150.00
Joshua Aviation Inc. (Airport)		8,990	134.85
John Kostopolulos (Airport)		1,100	16.50
Fred Loeffler (Airport)		5,600	84.00
Calif. Gas Service (tanks)		4,000	83.32
Amos Hamady (music)		1,720	35.39
Cal. Pacific Leasing		11,600	238.73
Paul Love (Cal. City Conc.)	1,280	16,080	357.28
Auto-Chlor		200	4.11
I.B.M.	13,720	99,960	2,057.27
Irwin Peoples, 8872 Holly		640	13.05
Eliz. King (Desert			
Specialties)		1,160	23.87
Painter (Hi Desert Cache)	40	9,720	200.87
Galileo Electronics, Inc.		600	12.34
Lawrence (Cruley's Mkg.)		5,480	112.78
Loma Brock (10200 Adler)		200	
Atlantic Richfield	560		11.52
		$247,330	
		14,320	
		$261,650]	

although for the five-year period 1964–1969 Kern County businesses grew by 2.6%, *an actual decline* took place in the six communities adjacent to California City. If this is the path of growth, the signs seem to point the wrong way.

*   *   *

A survey of employed principal wage-earners in 1968 showed that of the 268 responding, employment was in:

California City	141
Edwards Air Force Base	56
Mojave	21
Boron	8
Lancaster	3
Other	9
Retired	30

It is significant that of the 11 closest major industries cited by the developer in his sales literature, (and there are only 11 in over 1,000 square miles), less than one percent of their employees chose to live in California City. . . .

. . . Among the various services and businesses not available are:

1. Doctor
2. Dentist
3. Drugstore
4. Clinic
5. Hospital
6. Furniture store
7. Drapery/yardage store
8. Chain Supermarket
9. Taxi service
10. Shoe repair service
11. Laundry/cleaners
12. Department store
13. Travel service
14. Stock broker
15. Veterinarian
16. Mortician
17. Bowling alley
18. Movie theater
19. Accountants
20. Lawyers (during week)
21. Bookstore
22. Liquor store
23. Tailor
24. Shoe store
25. Clothing store
26. High School
27. Intermediate School
28. College
29. Bakery
30. Standard Oil Station
31. Union Oil Station
32. Texaco Station

33. Shell Oil Station
34. Mobil Oil Station

The developer claims that California City is "without question, the largest planned development in the history of the United States . . . it is also the best planned development. . . ."

Since the developer had had ten years of prosperous sales activity, his results indicate his inability to produce a well-balanced community providing elementary community services. Instead, California City is a series of unpaved streets to nowhere; over 30,000 subdivided parcels but less than 350 homes; a massive public debt; unfulfilled promises of water and streets and a community that is rejected by both industry and local residents as unsuitable.

3. Investment Potential

Although California City's developer asserts that raw land is an investment and not a speculation, his views enjoy little company. In an article entitled *Use, Development, or Speculation of Real Estate,* Max J. Derbes, Jr., M.A.I., states that speculative property is: "Property which is not typically held for present use, development or income. . . ."

Derbes also discusses the "created markets":

Created markets occur where the individual promoter attempts the marketing of speculative lands, usually as a "paper subdivision." High-pressure salesmanship promotions, low down payments, and even misrepresentation may cause values and activity to rise beyond reason in particular areas while similar properties remain at a low level. Free barbecues, gaudy advertising, and the "Hollywood-type" build-up get the people out, and the promoter does the rest. The buyer motivation tapped by such activities is the prospect of enhancement coupled with the capital gain aspect of the tax law. So long as there are a few illustrative cases of people actually profiting from such purchases, there will be fuel for such promoters to fire the imaginations of the gullible public. Never mentioned by those promoters are the legions of people who have lost heavily in unwarranted speculations.

California City's land prices are controlled by the developer who unilaterally can change the sales price to be charged by his sales force. Thus land that he acquired at $109 an acre can be sold if he chooses at $2,490 for a quarter acre or $9,000 for a 2.5-acre parcel. These values that the developer has created do exist. As Derbes describes it, "the value of truly speculative property is real today in the sense that it exists in the minds of typical purchasers and vendors."

It is this value that the Kern County assessor has recognized in establishing market values upon which to predicate his assessments.

But does this value exist today in a free market when land at California City is offered for resale?

*   *   *

The Rigged Resale Market

In 1965, Frank Davis, the vice-president of the California City Development Company in a sworn statement presented to prospective land investors, listed thirty-five purchasers of resold lots. In every case the resale prices two to five years later were one to five thousand dollars higher than the price of the property on original sale. This presentation created the impression that California City Property was a profitable investment. However, a check of the property records involved indicates that these "resales" were not transfers from the original owners who deeded to a new investor. Instead they were sales by the company of lots *the company had reacquired at the company's rigged market price*. Our investigation has concluded that *none* of the original purchasers effected a sale whereby they made one penny of profit [emphasis added].

The Open Resale Market

The record of sales during the period March 1968 to March 1969 is the best evidence of land values and profit potential of California City land.

All sales in two tracts, numbers 2066 and 2067 were analyzed [see Table 8c]. These tracts were selected as they are in the most developed area in California City, front on the only major road, the Randsburg-Mojave Road, and are closest to the commercial area. The two tracts have 1,225 parcels, paved roads and water mains, and sewer extensions. A total of twenty unimproved parcels were conveyed in arm's length transactions. Each lot listed on the following schedule shows the original cost, the investor's holding costs (taxes, interest paid, sales expense), the sales price and the cash profit.

These facts are the best proof of the true potential in California City. The individuals above who effected resales are fortunate; many others who have offered their property for resale have been unable to find buyers. The developer will not repurchase the property (at the value he places on it) and imposes strict requirements before he will accept a listing on the property.

An accurate analysis of the profitability of the above land purchases would be incomplete unless some analysis were made of the earnings that the purchaser would have

Table 8c

LOT SALES IN TRACTS 2066 AND 2067

Lot	Tract	Purchase Date	Original Price	Interest Charges	Taxes Paid	Commissions, Fees, etc.	Total Investment	Sales Data Date	Sales Data Price	Profit or (Loss)
51	2066	1/59	$ 990		$200.42		$1,190.42	12/68	$1,000	$(190.42)
129	2066	10/58	990	$160	213.40		1,363.40	9/68	1,000	(363.40)
272	2066	58	990	160	202.58		1,352.58	9/68	2,000	647.42
225	2066	10/58	990	160	213.40		1,363.40	9/68	1,000	(363.40)
73	2067	6/58	1,090	220	202.46	$342.70	1,855.16	11/68	1,800	(55.16)
119	2067	5/61	1,000		196.10			4/68 Donated to a missionary		
5	2067	6/58	1,390		209.47			1/69 Traded for property		
232	2067	12/58	4,014	a	328.71	195.00	4,537.71	10/68	1,500	(3,037.89)
242	2067	9/61	990		163.32	530.20	1,683.52	9/68	1,990	306.48
491}492}	2067	5/68	1,980	95	395.64		2,470.64	3/68	2,000	(470.84)

								5/68	2,000	886.54
									Trade—No cash involved	
289	2067	6/65	1,020		93.46		1,113.46			
212	2067	8/64	Trade		104.32					
584	2067	2/62	1,080		185.35		1,265.35	1/69	500	(765.35)
165}										
166}	2067	6/58	1,980	288	389.02		2,657.02	3/68	2,000	(657.02)
599	2067	11/58	1,090	220	192.92	60.00	1,562.92	11/68	1,500	(62.92)
736	2067	3/60	1,490	b	193.35		1,683.35	9/68	1,490	(193.35)
802	2067	8/58	1,040		221.34		1,261.34	1/69	1,750	488.66
249	2066	6/58	1,390		204.57		1,594.57	4/68	1,000	(594.57)
										$(4,425.22)

a Paid interest on balance for 26 months and then paid off balance to receive a discount. The purchase price as shown includes interest paid and the discount received.

b Paid interest on contract for approximately two years then paid off the balance to receive a discount. It is estimated that the interest paid and the discount received were approximately equal.

Note: Of the fifteen sales listed in the schedule for which a gain or loss could be determined, the purchaser on the average lost $295.01. The average time the lot was owned was a little over 9 years on these fifteen lots.

received if he had invested his funds in an alternative investment.

If the buyer of a $2,000 lot had placed $2,000 in a savings and loan account on July 1, 1960, today that account would have grown to $3,042.37.

Thus the investor in California City can expect not only an out-of-pocket loss but also the loss of an additional 5% a year interest on his invested capital.

E. CALIFORNIA CITY: CONCLUSIONS AND RECOMMENDATIONS

A person who buys a parcel of land in California City is engaged in a highly speculative venture where the only substantial land sale profits have and will continue to be made by the developer. The primary tax incentives to real estate investment [accelerated depreciation, prepaid interest] are clearly not available and the special lower tax rates on capital gains presupposes a profit.

A land buyer is acquiring a parcel of semi-arid desert land, indistinguishable physically from 30,000 parcels already sold and hundreds of thousands of other parcels available in the surrounding 1,000 square miles of undeveloped land.

In addition, he is assuming a share of tax indebtedness that is the highest of any city in California and receiving in return the fewest amenities possible under existing law.

Chances are approximately 1 in 5 that the buyer will awake to his folly and abandon the lot before he completes his purchase. If he completes his payments and receives a deed he will be in competition to sell his lot with the developer. According to the latest resale survey, the average investor will suffer a financial loss.

The future holds no promise either in this planned city. In ten years of development, no significant industrial or commercial development has occurred. The prospects are not bright when distant communities are easily able to absorb the normal growth for years to come and offer advantages that industry seeks.

The hot, dusty desert winds and absence of essential health services make the area unsuitable as a popular retirement community and the failure to provide a future water supply assures that other more foresighted areas will develop first.

A number of California City land buyers have sought advice of legal counsel and have initiated legal actions to recover their funds. Our investigation substantiates the basic merit of their contentions as to the absence of value in the property which they were sold. The allegation of fraud and misrepresentation is subject to their individual proofs, but the hiatus between the developer's representations and the facts as disclosed in this report are all too obvious.

It is therefore recommended that a series of legal actions be initiated by the Attorney General.

1. Consideration should be given to either intervening in the class action initiated by the California City litigants or the State should initiate an equitable action pursuant to Civil Code section 3369 to obtain restitution for the injured parties.

2. In addition, the State should obtain an injunction against further sales by the California City Development Company to halt unfair and deceptive business practices.

3. The State should also seek civil damages from the developer and responsible corporate entities based upon the sale of real property through false and misleading advertising.

These legal actions * are aimed at the investor's economic loss and obviously will do nothing to halt premature subdivisions, their speculative sale, or the use of municipal bond financing in conjunction therewith. In the speculative subdivision, the land is immediately divided into disparate ownerships that make future residential construction and development uneconomic. Valuable farm land is destroyed as an economic unit and replaced with mazes of unused streets, and deteriorating utility lines.

[End of excerpts from the Attorney General's Report. None of this material has until now been made available to the public, and none of the recommendations has been implemented.]

California City is a particularly stark study of government failure. The recent ouster of developer Mendelsohn and acquisition by Great Western Cities do not presage any change in fraudulent promotion for the coming decade. Recent sales pitches are concentrating on "master plan" and "environmental impact" rhetoric. In private, there is no pretense about such concerns. Great Western is engaging in speculation promotion, adding new deceptions to an already long list.

Yet only in longevity and size is California City unique. Thousands have lost their life savings. Many more will suffer before current law is enforced or new laws passed.

Mr. Mendelsohn is now seeking approval from the Shasta County Board of Supervisors for "Battle Creek

---

* [The recommendations fail to suggest criminal sanctions against the developer.]

Four views of California City. Above left, the land. Above right, "California City International Airport" with part of runway and scrapped planes. Lower left, the 10-button instru-

ment panel in the control tower. Lower right, the "Industrial Park"—decomposing Marine barracks.

Park" development in wild, mountainous Shasta County. The development will cover 25,000 acres. The eroded land of Shasta, land purchasers, and future generations will pay an even higher price for Battle Creek Park than the hapless purchasers of California City have paid.

Law and Regulation

The two basic state laws governing subdivision, both part of the Business and Professions Code, are the Subdivided Lands Act and the Subdivision Map Act. Subdivision laws do not exist where they are badly needed; where they do exist they are not enforced.

Subdivided Lands Act

The Subdivided Lands Act is administered by the Department of Real Estate, under the control of a Commissioner. Its objective is to protect purchasers from fraud or deceit in real estate transactions. Even within the confines of this limited purpose, the law is primarily one of *disclosure*. That is, the law compels the submission of specific information concerning the development to the Commissioner. A public report is then compiled, a copy of which must be given to each prospective purchaser. Only after the Commissioner has issued this report can the subdivider sell any lots. Thus, the potential power of the law is twofold: encouraging customer knowledge about possible disadvantages of a real estate investment, and refusal to issue a report. The Real Estate Division also tests, grants, and revokes brokerage licenses, audits brokers, and "regulates" some offerings of real estate securities and real estate syndicate securities.

The criteria for report approval include basic information about service costs and burdens, investment disadvantages, the completion of promised improvements by the developer, compliance with the Map Act, etc. The report and approval for sales can be denied unless certain information is provided and unless the purchaser is likely to get what he is promised.

There is a great deal this law does not do. It gives no one authority to determine what land is to be subdivided when. There is virtually no control over the environmental impact of a development, no state minimal control in terms of restrictions or quality, no power to prevent sales after a subdivision map has been filed, no requirement to install minimal services or to guarantee sales or minimal construction before the countryside is carved up so speculators can buy leveled plots; there is no requirement to demonstrate economic feasibility, no effective restriction on misuse of public bond-financing by developers using "dummy" special districts, no assessment by the state of the long-term social costs involved in the development of types of land which are rare or will be needed in the future, no absolute ban on development near faults or on insecure land. The developer is free, as far as the state is concerned, to do whatever he pleases with the land before the report is issued, except sell it.

The law has no practical methods of detection or sanction. Information is provided by the developer with little verification or investigation. Many frauds are not brought to the Commissioner for inquiry since they either allege the imminent appearance of outside public works and facilities (colleges, highways, water, airports, etc.) or involve complicated future financial burdens on purchasers at a later time. In both cases the purchaser does not learn of the fraud until very late. And even if the fraud is discovered early it is still *after* issuance of the report—the nonrelease of which is the Commissioner's only effective sanction.

The law does say that it is illegal to "materially change the setup of such offering without first notifying the Real Estate Division." But there is no guidance or background on what constitutes a "material change." Does the failure of a promised airport to appear constitute such a change? What about an alleged "delay" in an airport decision? Even if the law is interpreted strictly, the sanction for noncompliance is merely the issuance of a "desist and refrain order." Since the order constitutes neither a penalty nor a fine, and since penalties will only accrue when the order has been violated, developers feel free to lie and ignore regulations until they get this useful warning.

As weak as the law is, it is not applied by the Commissioner with any vigor at all. Over the fiscal year 1970, there have been 1,885 filings and notices of intention to subdivide; 1,849 final reports have been issued. The small difference does not signify all denials, but notices awaiting approval. There were but eighty-one desist and refrain orders over the past fiscal year, most on very specific matters. There has been only one major instance of penalty levy in recent years. Meanwhile, California City and dozens like it proceed without restriction—in the face of 4,268 acknowledged complaints received by the State Department of Real Estate over the same fiscal year. Nor is this non-feasance excused by lack of resources. The Commissioner is fond of stating publicly that manpower is quite adequate.

Customer knowledge about the possible disadvantages of a real-estate investment is, in spite of the Act's "disclosure" function, kept to an absolute minimum. The Attorney General's Report describes California City's marketing techniques:

> The basic supposition that an informed buyer is a pro-tected buyer overlooks the basic facts of salesmanship and the interest of the state in eliminating speculative land sales. . . .
>
> The salesman is cautioned against fully disclosing to the buyer relevant information. The salesman's manual states:
>
>> DO NOT be trapped by the customer into describing the improvement.
>> Never call the Mojave, the Mojave *Desert*. Call it the Antelope Valley.
>> Special Note:
>> Referring again to the question of "Mojave," and "Mojave Desert." Because people get their idea of the kind of land represented by the words "Mojave" and "Desert" from their early school geography book, it is better to *never* use either word. Always refer to our part of Southwest California as "Antelope Valley."
>
> The Division of Real Estate public report is a six-page mimeographed legal length document. The developer often places his own "Declaration of Protective Covenants," a legal length, single-page document, over the face of the report and staples it on top of it. Together they represent a formidable collection of verbiage that would discourage even an attorney from analysis, let alone comprehension.
>
> The key sales incentive—the value of California City as an investment is never discussed in the public report.

Subdivision Map Act

The other major law regulating subdivisions is the Sub-division Map Act, which places responsibility for subdivision regulation with local units of government. It requires local units to have supplemental local subdivision ordinances. The purpose of the law is to: (1) guarantee that developments are coordinated with community or county plans, and (2) insure that public areas (e.g., streets) will be improved and not become a burden on taxpayers.

The Subdivision Map Act in fact represents a major abdication of state government. It has no specific standards. The requirement of local subdivision ordinances is a mere formality. Virtually no new development in California is planned by anyone but the developer. In many localities, initial ordinances are so liberal and exceptions to them so commonplace that they are meaningless. Since local communities everywhere are in competition with each other for tax revenue from property (and sales), meaningful planning without state intervention or statewide reform is impossible (see Chapter 9).

Government Nonfeasance

If the failure of the Subdivided Lands Act is so apparent, and if the need for new legislation is so great, why haven't state agencies in the area pressed for the corrective and punitive legislation that is implicit in our criticism and spelled out in Chapter 9 below? The impotence of the Environmental Quality Study Council and the State Office of Planning are discussed elsewhere, but what about the Department of Real Estate? It would seem to have a positive duty to seek corrective legislation aggressively.

The Department of Real Estate has not been completely inactive. The public reports, although of little practical effect, have improved in their coverage since 1963 when they were little more than reiteration of developer advertising. The Department is experimenting with pictures and is moving to put in one place in the report all of the various costs to the purchaser. These are laudable but hardly revolutionary reforms.

Within the framework of its own executive powers the Department fails to make the fundamental and important computation of the number of lots actually built upon— and fails to submit and pursue corrective legislation. The prize law of the Department of Real Estate is AB 1214, introduced in 1969. It creates certain reporting requirements about defaulting purchasers and requires financing for promised improvements in so-called "land projects." It also permits a purchaser to rescind a purchase within two days after reading (i.e., signing a receipt for) the public report covering that development.

But the Department has failed to meet the real problems surrounding new development in any meaningful way. In fact, it has refused to support legislative proposals that might have some impact (such as SB 395, directed at the premature subdivision problem). It has authored no legislation since 1969 and has failed to support or take a stand on most of the real estate and land-use legislation recently considered.

Part of the Department's nonfeasance can be traced to natural bureaucratic conservatism. But only part. The Department is run by a Commissioner who is required to come from the real estate field, at least five years of experience as a broker are prerequisite for the office of Commissioner, although sensible regulatory policy would *prohibit* rather than *require* supervision by an individual so obviously linked with the interests he regulates. The Commissioner is at least required to relinquish his broker's license when he accepts office, but the seven members of the advisory Real Estate Commission are not. Each of them, with the exception of two "public" members added by AB 1214, also needs at least five years of experience as a real estate broker and does *not* have to relinquish his license. Of the majority group of members with real estate backgrounds, five of the past seven have served as president of the California Real Estate Association. And the relinquishing of the Commissioner's broker license while he holds office is apparently temporary: the last three Commissioners have gone into land development enterprise immediately after leaving public office.

Several simple reforms suggest themselves in this area of developmental abuse: a requirement that need for the final product of land development projects be demonstrated and guaranteed; the assessment of fees for residential or commercial conversion of land with an external "social value" (coast, wild, agricultural) to encourage development elsewhere first; an absolute ban on development until minimal research is conducted guaranteeing proper ground; state legislation abolishing the "holder in due course doctrine" enabling developers to hide behind banks and commit fraud without remedy; the abolition of independent special district units of "government," with state approval of all local bond issues required; stricter performance bonds required of developers for project completion; and vigorous prosecution of fraud for deterrent effect, including new legislation providing for citizen-initiated treble damage suits, and for unlimited fines and imprisonment for public prosecution.

9

The Mechanics of
Urban Expansion

A Walking Tour Through San Jose

Coming by car on the Nimitz Freeway (Interstate 280, California 17) take the Stevens Creek Boulevard exit and park right next to the intersection in the parking lot of the Valley Fair Shopping Center. If you have no car, it is more difficult: try to hitchhike or take one of the ancient yellow buses of the private San Jose City Lines that leave every hour or so from downtown.

In terms of sales per square foot, the Valley Fair Shopping Center, with Macy's department store, is the most intensive commercial area not only of the city of San Jose but of the whole metropolitan area ($73.50 per square foot as compared to $43.86 in downtown San Jose). You leave Valley Fair and walk west on Stevens Creek Boulevard. It is a stately boulevard, with three full lanes on each side plus additional turn lanes. Sometimes, when the air is not too polluted, you can still see the green Santa Cruz Mountains ahead. Progress has come rapidly to metropolitan San Jose: not twenty years ago the boulevard was a narrow county road, leading through pear and prune orchards to little, unincorporated farm towns. You cross North Redwood Avenue and you see a green sign on the sidewalk saying: "Santa Clara, The Mission City, population 8,000." Right behind this sign begins another large shopping center with parking space on grade level for some 4,000 cars. It is Stevens Creek Plaza, and the principal tenant is the Emporium Department Store. Turn right on

Winchester Boulevard and walk north some 800 feet: you will see a store on the right hand side, the Emporium Tire Center. Walk in and ask the salesman what city he is in. He told us Santa Clara, but he was wrong; his store is in San Jose. There is an invisible city line crossing the vast parking lot between the Emporium Department Store and the Emporium Tire Center.

Across Winchester Boulevard there is a farmhouse with a sign saying: "Deciduous Fruit Field Station, Division of Agricultural Sciences, University of California, San Jose." When we asked a gentleman there in which city he was, he answered, "San Jose." He, too, was wrong: this house is in an unincorporated county area. The street in between, on the other hand, is within the jurisdiction of Santa Clara City. Since maintaining a street without getting any taxes from the properties on *either* side of the street is no attractive deal for a city, there is no sidewalk on the western side of Winchester Boulevard in this section.

If you are walking on the left hand side of Winchester, you will enter Santa Clara, The Mission City. But this time you won't find any written sign. The San Jose sidewalk simply ends and another sidewalk—the Santa Clara one, which is much wider—begins about eight feet further to the left. There is hardly any connection between the two. If you look back on this detail you will notice that the boulevard is much wider in Santa Clara and that there are reflectors and warning signs to prevent cars from crashing against the "city limit." On the Santa Clara side of Winchester Boulevard at this spot the address is Number 100, a large three-story office building named the "Winchester Mall." The store right across the street in San Jose, Dunn-Edwards, Paint & Wallpaper, has the address 690 Winchester Boulevard; and as you walk farther north, the San Jose numbers *increase* and the Santa Clara numbers *decrease*. There is no way of telling whether a given number is in San Jose or Santa Clara without doing some research. You turn left on Pruneridge Avenue and now everything, the street *and* the properties on either side of it, is within the jurisdiction of the Mission City—but only for about 500 feet. For as you pass Jack LaLanne's European Health Spa, a colorful marvel of strip architecture with little white pseudo-Greek sculptures and a fancy, meandered cornice, you will find yourself on a street that belongs to San Jose but with a church that belongs to the City of Santa Clara on your right and a little residential neighborhood on your left that is unincorporated county land. You pass the 250 feet of county area and turn left on Crestview Drive. Here you are in San Jose. Enjoy the peace and order of this neighborhood. At the end of Crestview turn right on Forest Avenue; after some 200 feet you will run into a fence that is there to protect an unincorporated orchard. You walk along this fence; here the boundary between San Jose and unincorporated county area lies in the axis of the street.

After 500 feet you come to another three-jurisdictions corner: the intersection of Westridge Drive and Forest Avenue. There are *three* independent house-numbering systems on Westridge Drive.

You turn left on Douglane Avenue and follow it to the end of the block. Two single commercial lots belong to Santa Clara in the midst of this unincorporated residential neighborhood.

You pass some 200 feet of Santa Clara, cross Stevens Creek Boulevard and walk on the San Jose side back to your car. You have crossed municipal boundaries about twenty times during this thirty-minute walk but you have seen only one written sign telling you that you entered another city. People often don't know what city they live or work in, because there is no clear, easy way of finding out. People usually know their mailing address, but this knowledge can well be misleading as far as municipal boundaries are concerned: the two zip-code areas you have walked through on your tour are San Jose, California 95128, and San Jose, California 95117. Thus, many residences and businesses you have passed have a San Jose address although they are within the city limits of Santa Clara or in an unincorporated county area.

In this confusing context, it is hard if not impossible for people to identify themselves with any given political entity. No one really knows who is responsible for municipal affairs in a given area.

According to current definitions, California has approximately fourteen Standard Metropolitan Statistical Areas (SMSAs) involving some twenty-two counties, as follows:

Metropolitan area	*County*
Anaheim–Santa Ana–Garden Grove	Orange
Bakersfield	Kern
Fresno	Fresno
Los Angeles–Long Beach	Los Angeles
Oxnard–Ventura	Ventura
Sacramento	Placer, Sacramento, and Yolo
San Bernardino–Riverside–Ontario	San Bernardino and Riverside
San Diego	San Diego
San Francisco–Oakland	Alameda, Contra Costa, Marin, San Francisco, and San Mateo
San Jose	Santa Clara
Santa Barbara	Santa Barbara
Stockton	San Joaquin
Vallejo–Napa	Napa and Solano
Salinas–Monterey	Monterey

The map on page 000 depicts the location of these areas. They cover 43.8% of the land area of California and include 90.5% of the population.

All of these counties, with the exception of Riverside, devote a substantial part of their land area to a rapidly expanding urban-suburban complex. Each of the twelve most urban counties has a population of more than 300,000.* Each has the resources and the potential mechanisms for land-use control in the *public interest*. Unlike the new developments discussed in Chapter 8, here there is already a sophisticated local government structure which has been delegated most of the land-use control function by the state.

After an area has been carelessly built up, damage is undone at great cost, but failure to undo it results in continuous urban-suburban expansion ad infinitum along the same lines. The outward growth of currently built-up areas seems to be of greater consequence to the living environments of more people than initial new development in virgin territory.

We have chosen Santa Clara County in the San Francisco Bay area for case study. Santa Clara is a typical urban-suburban area. It has one major-sized city, San Jose, with

---

* With over 90% of its population in urban-suburban communities, California is now the most "urban" state in the United States.

numerous small to medium-sized towns, many of the suburban bedroom variety. It has a typical industry-residential
mix and some surviving agricultural activity.

Santa Clara County has been California's strongest hope
for planning in the public interest. It has a relatively active
citizenry, and a relatively unfragmented, visible government.
It has a highly touted general plan and reputedly one of the
finest county planning staffs in the nation. It issues a constant stream of press releases, plans, and promises. It has
the attention of the most active regional planning bodies in
the state—about a dozen of them. And it has secured more
open space, fought commercial overzoning, and integrated
its poor with more vigor and greater success than any other
developed county.

The Economic Setting: Fragmentation

State and local taxes provide the revenue for services and
public works which affect land use. Most taxes and local
government planning incentives influence economic and
development pressures by their very imposition. Property
taxes especially affect the economics of land use.

Property Tax

Property tax accounts for approximately 44% of all state
and local tax revenues in California. Including grants and
subventions, it amounts to about 38% of county revenues,
34% of city revenues, 38% of special district revenues, and
54% of school district revenues (as of 1966–67).

Perhaps the single most important tool of local power is
local taxation. And the most traditional source of local
revenue is the property tax. In general, each unit of local
government finances at least part of its budget by levying its
own separate property tax as a percentage of the value of
real property within its jurisdiction. Thus, a typical tax bill
will include a county tax rate, a city tax rate, a bundle of
school district tax rates, and a bundle of special district tax
rates. Each jurisdiction sets its own rate. Altogether, there
may be twenty different rates that, in urban California
today, add up to thirteen percent or more of assessed value
of real property. A tax code area is an area with one unique
package of local revenues. Santa Clara County, for example, is divided into nearly 1,500 different such tax code
areas, as the different boundaries of the county and its
cities and districts crisscross into 1,500 combinations.

The particular tax rates of the city and districts in which one's property lies are applied to the assessed value of one's real property. Increasing an area's "tax base," or the value or amount of a community's taxable land assets, by attracting new business or development to previously low-value land, is a much more politically palatable way of raising revenue than increasing tax rates or the assessments on existing properties.

The state constitution provides, briefly, that all property "subject to taxation shall be assessed for taxation at its full cash value" (Article XI). Section 401 of the Revenue and Taxation Code makes clear that "full cash value" is the same as market value, i.e., best use, not value according to present use. Later, Article XIII was added to provide that full cash judgment should be made in relation to uses "as provided by law"—to give zoning designations teeth, or to prevent assessors from assessing agricultural or other land high because it *could* be developed when legal restrictions prevent the owner from doing so. Effective land restrictions, such as Williamson Act contracts (see Chapter 2), lower the market value of land.

Although each taxing jurisdiction sets its own rate, nearly all assessment of property value against which the various tax rates (expressed as dollars per $100 of assessed value) are applied is done by a county assessor.* The county assessors are elected, on a nonpartisan basis, for four-year terms.

In fact, in California *no* land is assessed at full market value. Sacramento Assessor Irene Hickman tried to follow the explicit constitutional directive and was reversed by the State Supreme Court on the grounds that no one had assessed at full market value for many years. In 1966, the legislature directed that all counties at least assess at the same percentage of fair market value for the sake of uniformity. A 1967 survey found the state average to be around 23.2%. The assessors were legally obliged to increase gradually to 25% by 1971.

Why are assessments at 23% to 25% of a property's actual market value? Because of what can only be described as a political shell game. You have a house and lot which are worth $40,000. You pay taxes at about 3%, or $1,200.

---

* Most cities have transferred the authority and responsibility to assess, collect, and sell property for tax payment to the county, as per provisions of the government Code.

But if you are told that your house is assessed at $10,000 when you know full well that you could sell for $40,000, you tend to feel better about it. Of course, you are actually now paying at 12%, (still $1,200) but the psychology is very effective. It provides a variable that can be manipulated for the benefit of specific groups.* Hence, even if homeowner A pays the same tax rate as corporate speculator B, who may be a campaign contributor to the assessor, A may have his property assessed at 30% of its market value while B is assessed at 15%. If A wishes to appeal, he has not only to prove that his property is valued at more than its market value, he must prove that his assessment is at a higher percentage of market value than the percentage of the *average property in the county.*

The current assessment-property-tax system critically influences new development around and within the urban-suburban complex without reference to any conscious planning. Most of the present assessment patterns do not appear as planning decisions, yet have enormous ramifications as such. For example, the assessor will want to determine "fair market value" of land on the urban periphery. The land might be zoned agricultural, but the prevalent ease of changing a zoning designation leads him to ignore the zoning and tax on the basis of "best use," often urban. High taxes then make agriculture impossible on this land and help to fulfill the assessor's prophecy, long before the land is optimally ready for development.

But if the assessor values agricultural land around the urban periphery very low because it is zoned agricultural, speculators then buy the land and hold it cheaply with its trivial property tax. Developers offer to buy, but the speculators refuse to sell, forcing developers to skip out several miles past these lands on the urban periphery to agricultural land in the hands of farmers who will sell. City services, drainage, sewage, utilities, roads, etc., are then extended through the vacant strip or ring around the urban periphery to the new development. Then the speculator begins to sell, piece by piece, exploiting the development on both his sides and the city services running through or adjacent to his property for immense profits. Since zoning up from agricultural to commercial or industrial will add

* The Advisory Commission on Intergovernmental Relations has found that the frequency and degree of inequalities in assessments increase as assessments are put at a low percentage of market value.

to the assessment and local tax base, there is no *actual* difficulty in obtaining the rezoning (or annexation if needed), even with an honest local government. Of course, by this time the assessor raises the assessment because of the imminent new use. The speculator has by then sold and departed with huge profits.

Taxes are presently set so as to discourage optimum use of land in the public interest by taxing structures, fixtures, and improvements on the land. It is possible to justify an ad valorem rate on raw land since its value increases primarily from public works and social expenditures unrelated to any work output from the owner.* The National Commission on Urban Problems (the "Douglas Commission") notes that since

> such values result largely from social and governmental factors, rather than from actions by the property owners, it is entirely proper for government to capture through taxation a significant part of the economic benefits that flow in the first instance to private landowners.[1]

The Douglas Commission summarizes the long-range differences in the effects of structure versus raw land tax: "A tax that also hits structural values . . . [adds] to the cost of construction and property maintenance, tends to defer real investment in housing and other structural improvements, while [a tax upon land values] tends primarily to reduce the market value (cost) of land." [2]**

* The notion that "speculation" fulfills a needed function in a free-market society, as with the stock market, does not apply to land. With stock (and other) investment, one is providing capital and a measure of value for the performance of those firms in which one invests. With land, one bets that someone *else* will do something which will increase value.

** The impact of removing taxes on structures can be imputed from the leading study of property tax by Richard Netzer. Professor Netzer points out that the taxes on the value of bare land rest on the owners of the sites when the tax is imposed: "The tax cannot be shifted because shifting is possible . . . only if the supply of sites is reduced. But the supply of land is, for all practical purposes, perfectly inelastic." [3] So "collectively, landowners cannot reduce the stock of land: if individual landowners wish to liquidate in the face of higher taxes, they must sell the sites to other owners." [4] Since the *supply* cannot be *reduced* for price equilibrium, the end result of higher taxes on bare land is that "land prices will fall," i.e. "the taxes will be capitalized. Land rents before taxes are unchanged, but because of higher taxes, after-tax returns are lower, and investors offer less for land." [5]

The effects of current official policy to tax structures along with land encourages owners of urban and urban fringe land to hold it vacant, thus adding to sprawl as urban land goes unused for development or useful open-space purposes.

But let us accept the current notion that real property is all the same, whether structure or land, and that uniform tax rates should be applied to all real property, assessed at market value.* Even accepting this, there is gross under-taxation of raw land and excessive taxation of structures. The Douglas Commission estimates that nationally, the effective rate of land taxation was 1.24%, while structures were taxed at 1.86%.[6] One major reason for this estimate is the appraisal lag. About every three years a property is reappraised in California. In the intervening years between each appraisal, land value increases while buildings depreciate. Hence, land valued at $10,000 that rises to $11,000 the next year (a modest rise for California) will pay the rate applied to the $10,000. The owner, hence, pays less tax relative to actual current value. Meanwhile, a building of $30,000 may depreciate to $29,000. But the owner will have to pay the rate as applied to $30,000. Hence, he pays more than he should. In a state like California, where land values are increasing most dramatically (ten to twenty percent per year in many areas), the disparity is especially great—much greater than the Douglas Commission's estimate for the entire nation.

We are able to obtain as yet unreleased computer data compiled by the California Statewide Homeowner's Association. The Association went to the recorder of two urban counties, Alameda and San Diego. They recorded the parcel identification, location, name of buyer, and actual sale price (market value) of all land sold during 1969 on computer tapes, together with the actual assessed value of the raw land and of the improvements. (In California, the two increments must be separately listed.)

* We would favor the complete exemption of structural values on grounds of both equity and policy in favor of pure site-value taxation, but there are intermediate alternatives. The "Pittsburgh Plan" taxes structures at one-half the rate of raw land. Using this device as a transition to complete site-value taxation might be advisable because it minimizes displacement caused by sudden policy change. This, of course, assumes the continuation of property tax in any form, which we would end altogether.

In the San Diego County survey, which covered 18,419 parcels, raw land is not only undertaxed because it appreciates between appraisals, but is underassessed at the time of appraisal. These parcels were appraised approximately the same year they were sold. Of the 200 properties assessed the lowest relative to sale price, all were appraised at less than one-third of what the sale price would indicate is correct. Of these parcels, 162 were vacant land with no improvements at all. Only 3 of the 38 with any improvements had substantial improvements.* Of the 200 most overassessed properties at the other end of the spectrum, appraisals all exceeded the proper measure by twenty percent or more. Among these, were only 55 parcels with no improvements. And of the 145 with improvements, 86 were substantial, relatively valuable structures. The distribution indicates *current under*assessment of raw land and/or *over*assessment of structures. The results from Alameda County are the same.

One cause of current underassessment is the tendency of appraisers to underappraise land with no or cheap structures because it does not seem to be producing income, and also because commercial and industrial firms pack as much of their total property value into the building assessment as possible in order to maximize the amount they can depreciate for federal income tax purposes. In most property tax jurisdictions, the assessor lacks the staff or ability or desire to render an accurate assessment of large commercial or industrial properties, so he accepts the firm's own figures at face value. The firm will then use the property tax assessment, which it made, to justify to the IRS the allocation between land and buildings.

Sprawl, speculation, and unjust enrichment are further subsidized by the federal tax system, which taxes capital gains at one-half the rate it taxes so-called ordinary income.** This encourages speculative holding of land and

* Our measure of "substantial improvements" is a value placed on the improvement greater than the value placed on the raw land for a given property.
** The rationalization for this is that profits from the sale of real property gather gradually over many years. Forcing a seller to take all of his gain in the one year he sells would push him suddenly into a high bracket. The present tax system allows him to spread his gains over a number of years through "income averaging" and remain in a lower bracket.

jacks up profits. The basis for the capital gains changes
when there is a death, but no federal income tax is paid: If
Uncle John buys land at $10 an acre and dies with the land
worth $500, leaving it to little Billy, the "basis" changes
from $10 to $500; Billy only has to pay taxes on the gain
past $500. No one taxes the $490 profits that accrued. The
Douglas Commission estimates that one-third of the gain
on real estate capital profits escapes taxation through this
dodge.

California is genuinely advanced in its efforts to create
assessment parity among its fifty-eight counties. The State
Board of Equalization makes major efforts to minimize
assessment discrimination between counties, but discrimination *within* counties is a different matter.*

Taking the San Diego data above, we surveyed all 18,419
parcels. All assessments are supposed to be between 23%
and 25% of market value. Variation beyond this is illegal.
In fact, 1,139 parcels are assessed above 25% of market
value and 7,675 are assessed below 20%. Assessments are
strung out from 0.1% of the market sale up to 30%. Most
of the variation, understandably, is on the low side. *Less
than one-third* of the assessments are within the liberal
range of 23% to 25% (approximately 5,500 of the
18,419).

We tried to identify the owners of the 100 most underassessed (taxed) parcels and the 100 most overassessed in
San Diego County. There were approximately five times
more corporations, mostly insurance companies, savings and
loan companies, and large developers,** in the undertaxed
group than in the overtaxed group. Most of the overassessed corporations are retail establishments.

---

* The Board has three major functions: (1) helping in intra-
county equalization, primarily through technical aid to county assessors; (2) intercounty and state-county equalization of assessments; and (3) the direct assessment of railroad and public utility
property for purposes of local taxation. The Property Tax Department has three divisions, each responsible for one of those three
tasks. The State Board consists of four members elected from four
districts and the State Controller.

** Including: Hugas Corporation, Calpor Building Company,
H&R Investments, Irado Corporation, Lago Calavera Limited,
Southeastern California, Bonita Glen Development, S&A Investment, Spaulding Materials and Concrete, Rhodes Realty, H&M Investments, Big Golden State Corporation, et al.

These assessments were all made just *after* the sales. With the evidence of the actual sales before them, assessors chose their own version of market value, on a large scale. There is evidence of systematic favoritism for certain types of properties owned by corporations which provide the brunt of campaign contributions for the nonpartisan office of assessor throughout the state.

The International Association of Assessment Officers has a massive 1971 "Education Fund," the main financiers of which are: Du Pont Corporation, Bendix Corporation, Hilton Hotels, Sears Roebuck, General Foods, Celanese Corporation, Minnesota Mining and Manufacturing, May Department Stores, NL Industries, Montgomery Ward, Union Carbide, Continental Oil, Olin Matheson, Mobil Oil, Texaco, Gulf Corporation, Humble Oil, Atlantic Richfield, and Boise Cascade.

The homeowner deduction of $750 on assessed valuation is peculiar and costly. The current administration has made the cynical judgment that, since the property tax is visible to the homeowner, he is more angry about paying it than the renter who pays it indirectly. Present policy in effect hands to homeowners an $80 check merely because they own their homes. Because assessments are only at one-quarter or less of the actual value of a property, the $750 translates into a $3,000 actual reduction. The total loss in assessed valuation from the homeowner exemption for the state amounted to almost two billion dollars ($1,909,789,-000) in 1969, and lowered total assessed valuation approximately four percent. This reduction in tax base was made up for by increases in tax rates. Hence, the effect of this exemption is further to shift an inequitable property tax burden onto renters. In the language of California politics, this is property tax "reform." Further "reform" is promised as Governor Reagan's tax program, offered in an election year, would widen the disparity even more.

The tenor of tax "reform" movements is often entirely unrelated to equity or good economics. Another example is the governor's 15% exemption on business inventories, which reduced the assessed valuation of the state total by $475,340,000 in 1969.

Other "special exemptions" include certain oil company

land values,* insurance company deductions,** etc. which fail to contribute millions of dollars others must pay.

Past history indicates that genuine efforts to remove privileged exemptions or increase equity will be greeted with a massive public campaign, financed by the special interests concerned, against what is invariably called the imminent "tax trap."

Governor Reagan sold his own land for just under $2 million. It was assessed at less than one-eighth of that amount. The governor was either overpaid for the property by the large corporate purchase or he paid insufficient taxes. Under current law, he will not be assessed for this back tax debt; it is not deferred.

Clearer yet are the statistics concerning government purchase and sale of land. Time and again, the assessments indicate excessive payment by government for land, and government sale of land at absurdly low levels. Perhaps the city of San Diego might be able to explain why a piece of property that is assessed at $120 (parcel no. 371–030–12) was purchased by the city for $25,750. The assessment was less than one-half of one percent of the bought value. It would seem that the private seller was either undertaxed to the tune of $2,500 each year, or was given a gift of $25,000. Or why Salt Point Ranch was purchased as a State Park the year before at $2,193,000. The 3,182 acres had been assessed at $32,430. The project was able to collect some forty examples of public purchase at less than one-tenth of assessed valuation. Utilities, which provide much of the state's critical revenue and are assessed separately by the state, are overassessed (taxed). The State Board of Equalization, in a letter to an associate, admits that state-assessed property has been assessed at between 30% and 35% of market value. If unpopular taxes are

* Under pressure from the Western Oil and Gas Association and the numerous oil companies with individual lobbyists, the state has deducted oil company royalty payments from the assessments of oil-lease value on government land. Since this is a *value* tax (not income) the deduction is not defensible, but nonetheless costs others almost $3 million each year.

** Insurance companies are allowed under Article XIII §14 4/5 of the California Constitution to deduct home office property taxes from their gross premium state taxes. The premium tax is passed onto the consumer; the deduction amounts to approximately a $10-million gain each year for the firms.

hidden, they will not arouse opposition. The public pays the burden of this overassessment, through increased utility bills. Needless to say, communities where utilities choose to locate are satisfied, since the region's utility ratepayers are subsidizing their local government. There has been long-standing and admitted *under*assessment of timberland, to the benefit of Southern Pacific and other large landowners.

All of these inequities and favors may cost more indirectly than directly. Tax privileges give people an incentive to locate or build where they might not otherwise. Location or use B may mean $400 a year more in transportation or city service or development costs over location or use A. But if a person is taxed $500 less with B, he will choose B. So the community spends $500 to give him an inefficient $100 break. The full extent of these kinds of misallocations is unknown. They are hard to measure and there has been no attempt to do so.

Since local governments assess and collect property taxes, they seek valuable land and land uses which produce large tax revenues (assuming that the additional revenues will exceed costs of local services required by the new land or use).

Cities compete by annexing land merely because it may be valuable. The State Planning Office notes a few results of this competition:

> "defensive" fringe incorporations to avoid supposedly higher central city tax rates, annexations which skip over lands with low tax potential, and strangely shaped communities lacking both identity and balance.[7]

Cities also compete by "zoning up" land already within the jurisdiction to attract developers. Zoning for industrial, commercial, and low-density, single-family residential use is favored. Low-cost housing for larger families is avoided. Large tracts are reserved for the welcome influx of development—much more land than the community will ever see used for the zoned purpose. And other uses are precluded. So development that does come is scattered inefficiently through large areas that lie largely empty or are misused. Since neighboring jurisdictions are forced to compete and reciprocate, the results complement the annexation patterns: contradictory land uses scatter throughout an area. Commercial zoning in long strips along roads becomes the rule.

Cities compete by offering tax concessions and low rates —an often self-defeating practice, since an increased tax base is the motive for attracting development. Concessions are often hidden in the form of special low sewage rates and use of municipal systems.

Rarely do communities consider the desirability of predicting development so that presently existing services can operate at full capacity (and efficiency). Rarely is the fact of competitive response from neighboring communities considered. Yet intensive development does not automatically mean low tax rates. Contra Costa County, for example, is among the most industrialized counties in the state, yet it has the state's second highest tax rate. Contra Costa provides no special open spaces, roads, schools, sewage, or other services to its residents.

But to the extent the "zone-up-for-more-revenue-and-hence-better-services" theory is believed, it destroys building restrictions, density plans, codes, etc., in the effort to entice the developer on his terms.*

Many communities unable to attract developers are deprived of revenue and services. For example, in Santa Clara County, the per capita assessed valuation of the communities of Campbell and Gilroy is less than half the amount for Los Altos Hills. But service needs are not twice as great in comparably populated Los Altos Hills. There are examples within the state of areas with twenty times the assessed valuation of other communities with comparable needs.

Sales Tax

In addition to property taxes, municipalities and counties have other sources of local revenue, such as licenses, fines, service charges, grants from other agencies, "special assessments" (charging owners of specific properties for benefits by specific public improvements, usually confined to side-

---

* The fluidity of property taxes as a percentage of total local revenue testifies to the vigor and reality of competition. For example, from 1959 to 1969, Cupertino moved from 4% to 15% reliance on property taxes for all local revenue. Los Altos increased from 11% to 35%. In the same county over this period, Santa Clara dropped from 44% to 26% of its local revenue from property taxes and Milpitas dropped from 51% to 32%.

walks, street paving, and sewer lines, where benefits can be relatively reasonably allocated between properties; nationally, only 2% of local revenues derive from this source, far less than in the early 1900s), and other local taxes. The single most important of these is the local share of the state's sales tax, which generally provides from 15% to 30% of city revenue.

The sales tax is collected from whoever buys in a given city, whether or not he lives or works there. The tax cannot be adjusted to the requirements of the municipal budget as flexibly as the property tax. The rate is fixed by state law—one cent per dollar sale (of a larger state rate) for the municipality.

More important than proper balance between property and sales taxes is the *way* the sales tax is administered. Collection by each local unit of government means competition for additional revenue commercial enterprise can bring.

There are wide variations both between communities and over a period of time. From 1959 to 1969 Cupertino successfully increased the sales tax share of local revenues from 15% to 23%, while San Jose lost stores and shoppers and had to raise more in property taxes as its sales tax share of local revenue declined from 26% to 16%. And cities like Campbell and Los Gatos collect three times more of their local revenue from sales tax than does Milpitas, with few stores. There is displacement as commercial enterprise is suddenly bid for to fill a large revenue need. There are specialized communities, some highly commercial, some with virtually no commercial property. And there is, among many neighboring communities, vigorous competition to attract commercial enterprise. This means commercial overzoning, strip zoning along thoroughfares, and no sign restrictions to attract the business. Since all of the communities do the same to attract commerce, no one individual community gains more business by it, and all lose a great deal.

The Legal-Political Setting: Fragmentation

The evolution of local government in the United States is unique. Traditionally hostile toward strong government,

Americans were reluctant to form organized units of government at all unless the need was clear. To the extent that a need was clear, local control was ideologically preferable. The Constitution limited the federal government to specifically enumerated functions and the remaining powers were delegated to the states. Since few local government needs were strongly felt at the time, the Constitution did not set out any structure or basis for local government. Local government authority depended upon delegation of power from sovereign states.

As needs for local services (sewage, roads, water, schools, etc.) became clear, the state was left with the choice of performing the function itself or of creating a local governmental unit to do so. New units of local government were created, as were new positions and powers, with those pressuring for the new local government often assuming privileged posts. Over time, the incremental addition of different types of local governments, school districts, water districts, towns and counties, resulted in a system far different from the single, multipurpose European local government. Since the American units were formed separately, each chose its own system of boundaries, its own rules of governance, its own election procedures. Most of the governments possessed important powers over planning and land development.

The Units of Local Government

While elective local governments in most other parts of the world are one-layer multipurpose governments integrated in a hierarchy of levels (state or province and central or federal), in the United States there are four different layers of overlying *local* governments in one urban area: county governments, municipal governments, school boards, and elective boards of special districts. The National Commission on Urban Problems (the "Douglas Commission") devoted a good part of its efforts to investigating the complexity of this system, particularly in metropolitan areas. The Commission's final report states:

> In most instances there is no direct relationship of boundaries between the several types of local governments in Standard Metropolitan Statistical Areas (SMSA's). For example, less than one-fifth of the 5,033 school districts and only thirteen percent of the 7,062 special districts within metropolitan areas correspond geographically to

the area of a particular municipality, township, or county. . . .

Local government arrangements found in most SMSA's are the product of historical tradition and patchwork changes. In very few cases do they reflect any concerted attempt to develop a comprehensive pattern of local government designed to deal effectively with modern conditions of metropolitan life.[8]

In California, there is an additional ingredient to this fragmented setup: local elections are nonpartisan by law—so there is no organized party to reorganize or coordinate the Balkanized system.

Municipalities—cities, towns, and villages—were set up to provide for the public-service needs of closely settled local areas: fire protection, sewerage, water supply, refuse collection, public health and hospital services, and the like. Special districts make up the most recent and rapidly increasing class of local governments. Their growth has been stimulated by various factors, including state limitations upon the financial powers of counties and municipalities, and in some instances, other geographic or structural limitations of those governments. Although most special districts are relatively small, some have extensive territory; of the 7,062 such units in SMSAs, 323 are countrywide and 527 operate in two or more counties . . .[9]

Santa Clara County

Santa Clara County has seventy-two local governments, including (in addition to the county): fifteen municipalities, thirty-seven school districts, and nineteen special districts with elected boards. It has twenty-five special districts that have appointed boards or are governed by the County Board of Supervisors. The number of special districts in most other metropolitan counties of California by far exceeds the number in Santa Clara County. If it is true that local government in Santa Clara County is too fragmented to permit the kind of broad citizen participation that is necessary for a system of democratic home rule, then one can infer how great the need for local governmental reform must be in counties such as Los Angeles, where there are 342 special districts.

It is not difficult to imagine the confusion which confronts the voter in all these overlapping jurisdictions. The electorate of Santa Clara County is presently broken into eighty different voter combinations for elections to the following fourteen different categories of local governments:

1. County Board of Supervisors
2. Municipal governments
3. Elementary school districts
4. High school districts
5. Junior college districts
6. Special water conservation districts
7. Special fire districts
8. Special soil conservation districts
9. Special water districts
10. Special sanitary districts
11. Special park districts
12. Special hospital districts
13. Special cemetery districts
14. Special memorial districts

Each voter in the county is eligible to vote for at least four local governments: The County Board of Supervisors, the board of a junior college district, the board of a unified school district, and the board of one special district (the countywide Santa Clara County Flood Control and Water District). If he lives in an incorporated area, he can also vote for a city government; if he lives in a nonunified school district, he can vote for the board of an elementary school district in addition to a high school district board; and if he lives within the jurisdiction of one of the other eight kinds of special districts, he can vote for that board, too.

In fact, very few people actually take part in all these elections, and very few people have even a basic understanding of what these elections are all about, as indicated by: (1) the notoriously low voter turnout in local elections (with the exception, perhaps, of bond issue elections in recent years), and (2) the outcome of a pilot voter survey that was carried out as part of this project.

According to the preliminary count of the 1970 U.S. census, the total population of Santa Clara County is 1,057,032 persons. The county's age pyramid indicates that roughly 62% of all inhabitants are of voting age.[10] This means that there are about 634,000 people of voting age living in the county. The percentage of those who have bothered to register for local elections is not more than about 60%. According to the registrar of voters, the actual turnout of voters in local elections is often not higher than 20% of the registered voters, meaning that not more than 12% of the electorate actually participates in the determination of which candidate will make decisions in local government. That is, a disciplined voter group of about 6% of the electorate will be able to see their representatives on the boards. A special interest organization with several thousand or even several hundred members can (and often does) easily prove the difference in such a setting.

In the summer of 1970 we took a poll with a questionnaire designed to test the basic knowledge of voting jurisdiction that is necessary to an understanding of specific governmental units. It was intended to cover all the local jurisdictions of government. Most of the questions were self-explanatory and could be answered yes or no.

We administered the questionnaire to a sample of the registered voters of the county, since this group had openly expressed some interest in government in general.

Only a single individual, a man from the small town of Gilroy, answered all the questions correctly. *Fifty-seven percent* of those living in unincorporated areas did not realize that they lived in unincorporated areas and were under direct county jurisdiction. They named the city designation for their mail as their political jurisdiction.

Only 12% knew that Santa Clara County was governed by a Board of Supervisors. None of those respondents who knew that they lived in unincorporated areas knew what kind of elected government they had, nor did they know the name of any of the supervisors although they all answered that they had voted in the last supervisorial election.

Of those who live in cities and are not governed *directly* by the county, only 15% knew the name of the supervisor in their district. Yet about 45% of the city people claimed they had voted in the last supervisorial elections.

Of those living within the political jurisdictions of the twelve cities, 26% knew both the form of elected government and the name of one member of the city council.

Another 6% knew only the type of government and another 10% knew only the name of one council member. Yet 56% stated that they had voted in the previous council elections, which in most cases were held in April, 1970.

Forty-two percent of those who lived in cities correctly

identified the services that their city provided for them (they were specifically asked in yes or no fashion if their city provided police, fire, sewer, water, electricity, gas and library services).

In the school district section, only 5% correctly identified both their school district and one school board member. Thirty-five percent correctly identified the school districts but did not know the names of any of the board members. Several people stated that they were not interested in school boards because they did not have any school-age children.

None of the respondents knew that they lived within the jurisdiction of the Santa Clara County Flood Control and Water District, which covers the whole county area and which carries out many public projects.

In other words, government is invisible, its functions unclear, its officers unaccountable. Incumbents are rarely defeated in Santa Clara County.

Adding to the confusion of numerous overlapping political units are their boundaries. Even within the framework of the single major local government, the city shape often precludes a sense of community. When one lives in San Jose, the nearest substantial section of the city may be ten miles away. Reproduced below is the current outline of San Jose. There is no coastline, nor are there other cities or topographical features which account for the shape, built up through random annexation of land over the past two decades.

San Jose's geographical fragmentation is more bizarre than most, often seeping around three and one-half sides of neighboring cities and forcing them into undesirable shapes. But San Jose's methods and purposes are not atypical. The story of annexation has been researched by a Stanford University study group on a foundation grant to study San Jose land-use practices. Their report, given to us in its extensive preliminary draft, substantiates our findings concerning annexation.

Briefly, annexation is not viewed as a part of orderly expansion but as a competitive game for the acquisition, on behalf of resident developers, of all potentially valuable land. This means extending snaking corridors of the city along highways or rivers or into rich valleys. It means extending out to the sea. The expansion mania occurs not merely because the city government is influenced by the

San Jose

developers, but because of the economic myth that getting good land within city limits guarantees a large and secure tax base for the future and enables the city to plan without interference from conflicting land uses in other nearby cities.

Those who promulgate annexation rarely consider costs, partly because they often bear a disproportionately small part of those costs. There is the cost in taxes of unnecessary extension of city services miles farther than is economically feasible (cheap offer of city services is often the promise given to induce approval of annexation into the city by those under county supervision). The people paying for these generous and expensive services, the present residents of San Jose, are nowhere directly represented in the annexation process. Even if they were aware of the cause of skyrocketing local taxes, they would be hard pressed to stop annexation, which takes the form of hundreds of decisions, each adding small acreage to the city.

San Jose's tactics to spread itself all over the region are remarkable. They include: attempting to bankrupt three county sanitation districts; bypassing legal restrictions requiring an election within an "inhabited" zone by taking parcels which included less than twelve persons each (legally "*un*inhabited"); and loopholing the limit on "road strip" annexation (which prohibits annexation in one 200-foot-wide strip more than 300 feet long without permission of all cities within three miles) by annexing a strip 250 to 400 feet wide *for seven miles* out along Monterey Road. San Jose is not always successful. Milpitas, for example, was able to gobble up the Ford plant before San Jose could do so.

The county, perhaps seeing that things were getting out of hand, began to take some action after twenty years of benign observation. The Local Agency Formation Commission (LAFCO) was formed in 1963. Although most county LAFCOs have done little, Santa Clara's moved with lightning speed, and after seven years has come up with guidelines for annexation approval. The 1970 principles governing LAFCO judgment include disapproval of leapfrog and strip annexation, disapproval of annexation of territories for their high assessed values, encouragement of development of vacant and underutilized land within cities before annexation, and encouragement of "spheres of influence" annexation with prezoning of and planning for land that is within each city's "sphere of influence" by that city.*

A survey of annexation decisions by LAFCO in a sample (in 1968, after five years of operation) reveals an approval rate somewhat in excess of 98%; 114 of 116 annexations had been approved. If annexation expansion has slowed over the past five years, it is because San Jose has reached other boundaries or low-value land in every direction but east. San Jose is still extending east more or less at will, but the major emphasis of San Jose's present annexation is now on "filling in some gaps."

Compounding the geographic fragmentation of the community is the fact that annexation agreements are made with pledges of city services to the great profit of land speculators and developers. These public works compel planning decisions, but they are not made by, or with reference to, the Planning Department or the General Plan. Often, they are not made according to any public works plan (Capital Improvements Program) of even the Public Works Department. They are made substantially by the City Manager, creating a third completely independent internal "planning" force within the city. This planning fragmentation parallels political and geographic fragmentation.

The functions of the county and municipal governments are regulated by general law or by charter. In Santa Clara County, the county and fifteen cities are chartered. The actual range of services provided by the cities varies greatly. Table 9a, "Important Public Services by City in Santa Clara County," shows that some cities do not provide any of the basic services listed, but leave the county, special districts, and private companies to do the job. On the other hand, one city, Palo Alto, provides a full range of municipal services, including gas and electricity.

* Criteria for annexation are as follows:
1. Proponents must clearly demonstrate the need for municipal services and the city to which the territory is being annexed must be capable of meeting these municipal needs.
2. The proposed annexation must result in a logical and reasonable expansion of the annexing city.
3. The proposed annexation must consider the general plans of the city and the county.
4. The proposed annexation must not represent an attempt by the city to annex only revenue-producing property.

Table 9a
IMPORTANT PUBLIC SERVICES BY CITY IN SANTA CLARA COUNTY, 1970

City	Police	Fire Protection	Sewer	Water	Gas	Electricity	Library	Number of Full-time Employees
Campbell	city	city	county [a]	private [b]	PG&E	PG&E	county	106
Cupertino	county	county [c]	sp. dis. [d] & city	private [e]	PG&E	PG&E	joint	65
							city-county	
Gilroy	city	city	city	city	PG&E	PG&E	county	72
Los Altos	city	city	city [f]	private [g]	PG&E	PG&E	county	108
Los Altos Hills	county	county [h]	mix [i]	mix [j]	PG&E	PG&E	county	7
Los Gatos	city	county [c]	county [a]	private [k]	PG&E	PG&E	city	91
Milpitas	city	city	sp. dis. city [l]	city	PG&E	PG&E	county	150
Monte Sereno	county	county	county [a]	private [k]	PG&E	PG&E	county	2
Morgan Hill	city	city	city	city	PG&E	PG&E	county	35

Mountain View	city	city	city	city ᵐ	PG&E	PG&E	city	363
Palo Alto	city	city	city	city	city	city	city	689
San Jose	city	city	city	prvate ⁿ	PG&E	PG&E	city	2,427
Santa Clara	city	city	city	city	PG&E	city	city	639
Saratoga	county	sp. dis.°	mix ᵖ	private ᵠ	PG&E	PG&E	city	29
Sunnyvale	city	city	city	city ᵠ	PG&E	PG&E	city	452

ᵃ County Sanitation District 4
ᵇ San Jose Water Comp., San Jose Water Corps
ᶜ Central Fire Protection Distr.
ᵈ Cupertino Sanitary District
ᵉ California Water Service Company
ᶠ San Jose Water Works in eastern part of city, rest served by city in process of building joint plant: Los Altos-Mountain View-Palo Alto
ᵍ North Los Altos Water Company and California Water Service Comp.
ʰ Los Altos Fire Protection D.

ⁱ ⅔ of area septic tanks, ⅙ served by city of Los Altos, ⅙ served by city of Palo Alto
ʲ ⅔ of area special district: Purissima Hills Water District: ⅓ private: Cal. Water Works
ᵏ San Jose Water Works
ˡ Milpitas Sanitary D.
ᵐ California Water Works serves small part
ⁿ San Jose Water Works, small part served by city
ᵒ Saratoga Fire Prot. District
ᵖ Part of area county San. Distr. and part of area Cupertino Sanitary District
ᵠ ¾ city; ¼ Cal. Water Works

The county government has an intricate double relationship to the municipalities: it is a surrogate municipal government for the unincorporated areas; and it carries out a wide range of "countywide" functions delegated to it by the cities, such as countywide tax assessment, welfare, public health, and a spectacular county expressway program.

While the functions and powers of school districts are standardized by statute, special districts display a wide array of sometimes unique legal assignments. For example, the powers and functions of one of the county's special water districts are:

> To furnish water for present and future use; to acquire water rights; store and conserve water; salvage storm and sewage water; generate and sell incidental hydroelectric power; operate sewer facilities; operate irrigation works or power development with the U.S. Government; provide recreation facilities; own fire-fighting equipment; reclaim lands; sell or lease mineral oil rights. General Obligation bonds permitted. Ad valorem tax permitted on all property.

This water district, with all its powers, comprises about thirteen acres and furnishes water to about 110 customers from the Los Gatos Creek. It is easy to see how planning and land use are affected by these services and the governmental units providing them. Even more apparent from the definition of powers above, is the ease of private, incremental planning by organized interest which can take place through a "legitimate" governmental unit. The location, operation, and financing of schools, sewage, etc., although not formal "planning," affect land-use patterns directly and distort rational planning decisions.

Thus we have some services provided by cities, some provided by special districts, some by private industry, and some by the county. Not only does this confusion make government response to broad public needs less likely, it means costly duplication of facilities, inefficiency, and a lack of coordination.

Those services and public works that are provided by the cities themselves within their own jurisdiction offer the greatest hope for internal order. But even *here* there is haphazard planning.

San Jose is a good example. It is the city within Santa Clara County with the least excuse for failure to coordinate itself with the county and other cities and, even less of an excuse to mess up its own public services. The city itself provides everything except water, gas, and electricity—with P.G. & E. supplying the last two. Furthermore, it has a strong planning department; supposedly vigorous citizen participation through the 100-man "Goals for San Jose" group whose official report was adopted; a formal Capital Improvements Program; and a general plan described as one of "the best."

In San Jose, decisions are made by the Public Works Department without meaningful reference to the Planning Department or the General Plan.

> Public Works looks on the Capital Improvements Program as its bailiwick, and the only bow it makes to the General Plan is to glance at the General Plan map to see if development is called for in the relevant area anytime between now and 2010 A.D. If it is (and the General Plan calls for development virtually everywhere, even in the Eastern foothills), then the project is deemed to be in compliance . . .[11]

The basis for the independent Public Works Department decisions is described by the Stanford study group:

> The fact is that the Public Works Department 'plans' its projects largely by responding to the requests of individual developers, or its prediction of such requests. Thus a major part of the city's planning is simply dictated by a small group of private individuals, whose major concern is confessedly the maximization of their own profits.

The only coordinative entity left is the Planning Department. The 1970 Public Works Department Capital Improvement Program was not even seen by the Planning Department until one week before presentation to the Planning Commission.

As dismal a picture as San Jose presents, it is superior to the rest of California. Intracity coordination between public works and services departments is nonexistent in most cities. In fact, planning within individual *departments* is not always evident. A large citizens' group (FOCUS), surveyed the twenty-two Los Angeles city departments directly owning and regulating public land. It asked each about the size and location of public holdings. Seventeen departments answered and only three could identify the nature and location of land under their own jurisdiction.

The structure of the state's public works activities is perhaps even less coordinated. At the state level, there are separate and completely uncoordinated agencies regulating agricultural services, highways, water, etc. Each of these agencies responds to its own organized constituency with little reference to anything or anyone else.

In summary, there is little public works coordination within local city governments, within counties or regions, between local, county and state governments, or within the state. This fragmentation minimizes the visibility and accountability of government, protecting government from the judgment of the general public. Planning decisions and future development are dictated in large measure by preceding public works: buildings, schools, roads, utilities, and sewage.

Local Zoning:
The Basic Planning Device

The Douglas Commission counted some 76,000 elective officials of governing local bodies in the 228 SMSAs of the United States. There would be no reason to run for these unpaid offices if there were not some real power connected with them. Apart from the power implicit in taxation and public-works control, there is the related power of direct land-use control.

There have been restrictions on the free use of private property in British and consequently in American law since long before the modern concept of land-use controls in the form of building codes, zoning, and subdivision ordinances emerged. Since the turn of the century, four major types of regulatory instruments regarding construction and development have evolved in the United States, in addition to a large number of supplementary standards, codes, and regulations. All four are under the control of local government. The first two, building codes and housing codes, regulate primarily new construction and existing structures, respectively. The third, the subdivision control, is discussed above in Chapter 8.

In the beginning of the twentieth century, the concept of zoning emerged as the primary tool of local land-use control.* In the United States, zoning is a procedure, carried out by county and municipal governments on the basis of state enabling legislation and local ordinances, by which the land within a given jurisdiction is divided into districts or zones, each of which is subject to a set of specified restrictions. The restrictions affect such things as: (1) whether the land in a given district can be used for a particular kind of residential, commercial, industrial, or other purpose; (2) the height and bulk of structures; (3) which part of a lot may be built upon and which must be left as open space; (4) minimum lot and sometimes minimum house sizes; and (5) the permitted density of use. Zoning operates by restricting, not by prescribing, development.

In 1926, the U.S. Supreme Court upheld the constitutionality of comprehensive zoning as a valid exercise of state "police power." Only "clearly arbitrary and unreasonable" [12] zoning decisions will be reversed under a broad mandate. The Supreme Court has interfered to reverse a zoning decision only once since then.[13] California has followed the national pattern, delegating virtually unhampered powers to local legislative bodies.

In the United States, urban planning became a function of local government in the twenties when Herbert Hoover's Department of Commerce issued two important acts for enabling legislation: the *Standard State Zoning Enabling Act,* 1924, and the *Standard City Planning Enabling Act,* 1927. The recommended and generally adopted model was that local government appoint a citizens commission, the city planning commission, in order to provide protection for professional planners "from the wrath of the public on the one hand, and contamination of politics on the other," as Samuel E. Wood has put it in an article written against this institution.[14]

The professional planning staff (the city or county planning department) usually reports to both the city or county planning commission and the head of the ad-

---

* Other functions of urban planning, aside from zoning, include research and a number of more discretionary activities covering a broad spectrum. Among these activities in the Santa Clara County Planning Department are: a campaign for low income housing; efforts to set up a housing development corporation; conservation of the bay lands and the foothills; efforts to get satisfactory coastline legislation; and an ongoing land-use inventory system.

ministration (mayor, city manager, or county executive). The principal task of the staff is to provide recommendations for adoption by the commission and the city council or county board.

The planning commission, with attendant variance boards, provides yet another opportunity for preventing effective public scrutiny of specific decisions.

Planning commissions are appointive bodies and thus avoid the embarrassment of possible direct electoral challenge. An electoral challenge to a supervisor because a board of which he is a member appointed someone making poor decisions has little emotional impact. And appeal to a board of supervisors is relatively meaningless. Many of the most damaging decisions offend not a particular party, but the general public interest: the environment, or future users of the land. There is no one to represent this interest unless a public entity aggressively seeks to do so. And appeals are likely to be expensive and time-consuming.

The planning commission was supposed to be able to protect professional planners from corruptive politics or opportunistic organized interests, and its low visibility was considered ideal. It has, however, failed to serve this purpose.

First, supervisors have appointed their friends to commission positions—often those friends who have contributed to campaign coffers—and therefore, planning commissions are stacked with developers and land speculators.

Second, it has been easy to convince commissions, particularly as fellow businessmen and often as personal friends, that development is good, since it increases the tax base. Relatively subtle but critical questions concerning city-service costs incurred by the new development, city-service economies of scale, and so on, are rarely studied. Instead, sessions are often devoted entirely to considering very specific requests. Each individual request compromises the general interest very little. What difference does one gas station make, or even one small industrial park? Variances or exceptions to the current ordinance, special-use permits, or nonconforming use-allowances set decision-making in this incremental framework. At the end of several years, the cumulative result of these decisions is a land-use pattern determined not by plan or law, but by the sum total of individual requests.

Third, the structure of planning commissions leaves

them very susceptible to payoffs and corruption (see below).

Environmentalist Samuel E. Wood has suggested the abolition of the commissions.

Santa Clara County

Interviews with planning department personnel in the county and cities of Santa Clara revealed the same frustration that caused Karl Belser, former Santa Clara County Planning Director, to leave his job. One of the most esteemed men in his profession, Mr. Belser retired "early" from his post because he

> is consistently countermanded in his recommendations by elected officials and seldom receives a word of support as he bloodies his head ramming it against the stone wall of political expediency day after day. . . .
>
> The hypocrisy permeating the entire process is so gross that it is a shocking experience to witness an official decision based on principle alone. . . . All this planning money is expended ostensibly in the quest for a more ideal urban living situation. The public pays for it, but in place of the "Golden Ring" it deserves, it gets Joe Blatz's service station exactly where everyone agrees it should not be. That is, everyone except Joe.[15]

Planning commission session agendas, selected at random, indicate an enormous number of petty individual appeals dominating commission activity. The cumulative effect of these decisions is thought by planners to be devastating to long-range coordinated planning in the public interest. In the County Commission, 44% of these applications are approved, 40% delayed, and 16% disapproved. One-third of these approvals overrule the county's own Land Development Commission. Most contradict General Plan schemes.*

---

* The City of San Jose's Planning Department approves from 8% to 15% of "variance" and 60% of "exception" applications from the current plan and ordinance. Further, the Commission overrules the Department on approximately one-third of the applications that are turned down and appealed. And San Jose is more likely to refuse variances and exceptions than most California cities. Variances and exceptions, in any event, are only sought in extraordinary cases since rezonings allow more development options, are permanent, and are granted virtually upon request. Nevertheless, the "findings of fact" usually required by zoning ordinances for such approvals are rarely demanded. In terms of rezoning applications,

As shown earlier, in Santa Clara County there is a county government and fifteen municipal governments. Consequently, there are sixteen different sets of zoning and subdivision regulations. Each one of these consists of a different set of zoning symbols and a different set of permitted and prohibited uses, and different bulk, height, and setback restrictions for the respective zoning district identified by each zoning symbol. Assuming an average of about 30 different zoning districts per ordinance, there would be close to 500 different zoning districts in the county; since there are many so-called combination districts, this estimate is likely to be conservative.

Sometimes two ordinances will have the same zoning symbol. In such cases, particular caution is needed, since the same symbol in one jurisdiction might have substantially different implications in the other jurisdiction.* The list of discrepancies between restrictions uses in the sixteen zoning ordinances of this single county could go on ad infinitum. There is no one language or consistent set of definitions that would permit a straightforward analysis of the underlying zoning policies.

In 1966, the Santa Clara County Association of Planning Officials (SCCAPO) worked out a system of standardized zoning symbols, but only one city in the county bothered to translate its symbols into this standardized system.

The three land-use inventories of the County Planning Department, taken with the aid of federal funds in 1962, '65, and '67, still represent the only roughly accurate breakdown of total incorporated and unincorporated land by zoning category and by actual use.

Those who have the zoning power—the local govern-

57% (50 of 88) of those non-conforming to the General Plan were approved by the City Council in 1969–70; 53% of all rezoning applications approved were non-conforming.

* E.g., both the county zoning ordinance and the San Jose zoning ordinance have a "C-1" commercial district. In the unincorporated area of the county, the uses permitted in a "C-1" district include: "one-family, two-family and multiple dwellings and groups or combinations thereof. . . . Drinking establishments such as cocktail lounges and bars. . . . Self-service automobile washing facilities." In San Jose, the "C-1" district does not permit "one-family dwellings, two-family dwellings, and multiple family dwellings." Cocktail lounges, bars, nightclubs, and "washing of motor vehicles" are "expressly prohibited" in San Jose's "C-1" district.

ments—do not maintain accurate, updated, quantitative inventories of what they are doing. If one of the objectives of zoning is to achieve a sound balance of land uses in a community, then those who make the day-to-day zoning decisions should be expected to know how much land there is in each zoning category, how much of this land is vacant, and what kind of balance the community desires. Often the only way to find out how much land is actually in a given zoning category is to take the zoning map and figure out the areas of all the parcels in that category and then add the hundreds or thousands of them up. Each city zones and plans without knowledge of what its neighbors are specifically doing or what it has already done. Unless county plans currently in progress for an inventory work out, it is difficult or impossible for the "planners" of California to know even how much land they have already zoned commercial, industrial, etc., *or* how the land is actually being used.

The General Plan

Since its very beginnings in the 1920s, zoning was supposed to be done "in accordance with a comprehensive plan." But what constituted a comprehensive plan was never really specified in most early legislation, and after the experience of the Slum Clearance Program of the Housing Act of 1937 and the Urban Redevelopment Program of the Housing Act of 1949 had seemed to confirm the contention that isolated project planning was not enough, the Workable Program of the Housing Act of 1954 made comprehensive planning for the first time a federal requirement. The Workable Program provision required that a local community, in order to receive federal renewal funds, had to prove to have developed the following: (1) appropriate building and housing codes; (2) a comprehensive plan; (3) neighborhood analysis to determine problem areas; (4) an administrative organization capable of carrying out renewal; (5) financial resources to support the locality's share of the program; (6) local citizen participation in developing and executing the renewal program; and (7) housing resources for those displaced by the renewal process. Thus, the desire of municipalities to receive substantial federal funds from this act and its subsequent amendments was the first real incentive to carry out some comprehensive planning. In California, a comprehensive or general plan was also made a requirement by state legislation. The federal government not only required comprehensive planning but also paid for it: Section 701 of the Housing Act of 1954 provided planning grants.

The purpose of the general plan requirement was to prevent the incremental breakdown of community land-use goals. The plan would contain economic, topographical, environmental, and aesthetic input. It would spell out long-range coordinated development. Community services would be extended to take advantage of efficient economies of scale. Boundaries would be compact for a sense of cultural and political community. Open spaces would be carefully set aside. Density would be controlled. Commercial and industrial development would not be scattered throughout the city. Transportation would be efficient. Land suited to a unique use, particularly agricultural and wild areas, would be given priority for that use in the long-range interest of future inhabitants of the wider area.

In Santa Clara County, all municipalities have adopted a general plan since this legislation, and some have amended it. Most of the plans are simply public relations documents drawn to meet the literal requirements of federal law. In Cupertino, a 600-page detailed zoning ordinance has been "based" on one page of very general growth forecasts for the region, one-half page of objectives, and thirteen vague recommendations (e.g. that "the General Plan . . . be officially adopted . . .," or that "the City of Cupertino . . . should act early . . . to promote green belts and open spaces," etc.). The input into this "mammoth" study consists of a six-column, twenty-two line table showing some present neighborhood densities, and a six-inch-square storm-drain map. The muddled one-page General Plan map barely includes Cupertino; 70% of the map shows San Jose, Saratoga, and even Palo Alto. Cupertino is a splotch in the upper right-hand side, with some various shadings representing various broad kinds of uses assigned to vague, undefined areas. The only specific, identifiable entities are a proposed civic center, the town center, and someone's "auto sales and service" establishment.

The Cupertino plan was passed in February, 1964, and has not been amended since. Even its twenty-two-line density table is out of date, as population has more than doubled since that time.

In most respects, the government of Cupertino deserves commendation. It wanted to comply with the law, so it hired some consultants to provide general-plan paperwork. Many cities are not quite so responsible. Many have Cupertino's 600-page zoning ordinance *and* 100-page general plans, filled with tables and graphs and pictures and detailed commentary on each past or future public works project. Of these, former County Planning Director Belser remarks: "No one really expects the hundreds of thousands of dollars invested in pompous plans to materialize into anything other than a warped and distorted result with great advantages to powerful special interests." [16]

The average age of a Santa Clara County general plan, including all revisions and amendments, exceeds four years. Most plans are out of date and obsolete. Those that have been revised have generally merely been changed to conform to nonconforming uses. In 1970, one hundred *specific* amendments to the San Jose General Plan were made, all confirming nonconforming special-interest exceptions previously granted. The City Council was told by its attorney that it must accept all of the proposed amendments or none of them.

San Jose's plan would be the most likely to affect land-use decisions. It is quite long, as recent as most, with a relatively detailed layout and statement of purpose. Furthermore, it was prepared by the city's own professional planning department, considered one of the better in the state.

Interviews with San Jose officials, and empirical observation of City Development and Planning Commission decisions relative to the plan, indicate that the city is overwhelmed by organized pressures and that only the professional Planning Department adheres to the plan.

San Jose's first plan, published in 1960, was similar to Cupertino's. It consisted of some utility and road flow charts and summary statements of noble intent. Like Cupertino's plan, it was designed to meet the stated requirement for federal money.

A variety of forces, including some public clamor, demanded a real plan. In 1966 San Jose then adapted a precise new plan—too precise, in spite of the fact that its target date was 2010! The Stanford group remarks:

The General Plan is too specific to be a reasonable guide for city development. Its specificity leads to more rapid outdating, and thus provides an easy justification for ignoring the plan when making zoning decisions.[17]

City officials describe the plan as "too inflexible," and it has been totally ignored. Only four copies of the plan are known to be in existence. A condensed version, consisting of the usual pieties and a color-coded map of basic use categories is the version usually "used" by the city officials when planning "in accordance with the General Plan." The supply of condensed versions ran out in 1970. The Stanford group notes:

> The 1970 revision is no more than an updating to make the plan reflect the as-built conditions and non-conforming uses that had occurred despite the existence of the 1966 plan. [This] . . . speaks eloquently of the lack of serious planning in San Jose.[18]

The fact that San Jose continues to grow at an extraordinary rate makes the failure to plan all the more disturbing. The San Jose city government has been told time and again about the need for meaningful planning and rational criteria. In 1963–64 the American Society of Planning Officials conducted a study of San Jose planning. Although failing to treat the underlying political fragmentation we have emphasized, the criticisms and commentary paralleled many of the Stanford group complaints described above, and stressed the need for long-range policy guidance from the City Council, and Council support of the resultant implementation plans.

San Jose has responded at a public-relations level. A "San Jose Goals" committee consisting of "100 diverse citizens" prepared a report which the Council adopted years later, in 1970. The purpose of this report in the eyes of the American Society of Planning Officials was to hammer out clear-cut community growth decisions. All parties, such as developers, real estate and financial institutions, and community groups, were to fight it out in hearings, with the Council choosing the future San Jose—in *specific* terms (*precise* density goals, open space targets, recreational facility plans, transportation commitments, and so on). Instead, the document is the typical list of vague pieties. It was passed unanimously by the Council. Says the Stanford group: "It [the 'Goals for San Jose' Report] never even addresses itself to the question of whether San Jose shall put any limitation on either its pattern or rate of growth." [19]

State and Area Planning

The actual guidelines for local land-use decisions are a set of assumptions: More people mean a better community (particularly in single-family residential dwellings); more industry means better schools and services; annexation is necessary to claim future income-producing land for city expansion; city planning mechanisms should take precedence over those of the county; present local control is democratic; and so on. Former County Planning Director Belser calls these ideas "a primitive mythology regarding the urbanizing process." [20]

But even the established planning order is aware of the need for some planning above the city level, if only to coordinate for maximum revenue production. To this end, innumerable "coordinative" county and regional organizations have been created. There is the San Francisco Bay Area Council (nine counties), the Inter-City Council (Santa Clara), the Planning Policy Committee, the Santa Clara County Association of Planning Officers, the Association of Bay Area Governments, the Local Agency Formation Commission, Bay Conservation and Development Commission, etc. A Joint Cities-County Planning Council has just been proposed. In addition, of course, there are less general coordinative bodies, such as the Bay Area Air Pollution Control District, the Bay Area Rapid Transit District, and so on. It has been suggested that there is now a need for a coordinative body to coordinate the other coordinative bodies.

The purpose of centralizing planning decisions in a body with authority over numerous local jurisdictions is threefold. First, it is to enable tax revenues to be used for services and schools throughout an area—to guarantee equality of opportunity and comparable minimum services (sewage, water, etc.) regardless of the tax base.

Second, it is to prevent destructive competition between communities. For example, when each community sacrifices open-space land for industrial development, it is making an incremental gain: it is increasing its tax base. But when communities cumulatively follow this practice, relying on open spaces in other jurisdictions, the number of open spaces diminishes unbeknownst to all. The same is true with sprawling annexation. There will be an increase in the tax base for the entity annexing valuable land, but the total cost of services in an area is much increased by the long extension of sewers and streets and utilities from one city when other cities could more efficiently service the area.

Third, planning is centralized in order to coordinate boundaries where there is a need for interconnection through several local jurisdictions, or economies of scale for services.

Despite the existence of county and regional planning organizations and despite the existence of a State Office of Planning, there is no centralized or even coordinative planning in California. The regional organizations, at best, collect and disseminate information concerning economic and population trends, area-wide traffic and housing needs, and other factors. In several areas, they have served as forums for the resolution of squabbles between various planning entities.

But there is no single, visible entity with responsibility for eliminating the diseconomies and absurdities of local planning interaction. Voluntary seminar groups will not do it. It requires a change in the present incentive arrangements guiding intercity competition and some pre-emptive planning authority at an area-wide level.

The state itself has the responsibility to specify minimal information-gathering requirements in the formulation of general plans and standards of adherence to those plans. What the state has done in terms of planning can be surmised from the size of the State Office of Planning—two persons. The state has swallowed whole the "home rule ethic." The *1968 California State Development Plan Program,* described above, is the major state planning instrument thus far. Its definition of the "State Planning Function" consists of:

> 1) The provision of general intelligence . . . 2) Development planning and programming . . . (From this analysis will flow recommendations regarding future policies and programs, their relationship to overall State objectives, and recommendations as to priorities and schedules) . . . 3) The coordination of plans and programs for . . . departments and agencies of State government . . . (The

information gathered under the intelligence activities indicated above will facilitate evaluations . . .) 4) Improving intergovernmental relations. . . .

The State Office of Planning, although recognizing the current fragmentation and conflicting interests of local jurisdictions, states that two measures will solve all problems. "Local units" are to be: (1) informed as to what the state resource management policy is, and (2) shown that the best interest of the state and the particular area require them to adopt overall state policy.[21]

But the state created the present economic (tax), geographic, political, planning and public works fragmentation. While mouthing the ethic of "local control" of land-use decisions,[22] it has created a system of low visibility, democratically not accountable and destructively competing.

"Planning" as it exists is "project planning"[23] on works designed to serve specific interests. Former Santa Clara County Planning Director Belser remarked:

> Federal, state and local levels engage in madly competitive programs, all trying their very best to undermine the work of others. . . . The San Francisco Bay Area has federal, State, and local planning on such a broad scale that it is difficult to conceive—special planning for roads, water resources, air pollution, rapid transit, bridges, ports, etc., ad nauseam. . . .
> But in spite of all this planning for conservation and orderly development, the bay is being filled in, air and water are being polluted, hillsides are being mutilated and prime cropland is being paved over. Public and private efforts to halt this kind of defacement of the natural environment are to no avail.[24]

Attempts at even minimal political reform or meaningful statewide guidance are killed. Even the nonpartisan and bland *California Journal,* which reports on legislative activity, admitted the fate of any legislative challenge in its review of environmental legislation in 1970:

> Planning and Land Use. Most of the program introduced by the Assembly Select Committee on Environmental Quality concentrated on planning and land use (p. 187). Several of these measures passed the Assembly with difficulty, and only five relatively noncontroversial bills reached the Governor's desk following a Senate blitz dur-

ing the last two weeks of the session. Local opposition from both governmental and private sources had substantial influence upon the death of a number of proposals for state or regional participation in local planning decisions.*

The Consequences of Fragmentation

Santa Clara County has reserved more land for open space, parks, and related purposes than most in California. But state trends are reflected in Santa Clara County. Table 9b shows recent acreages for developed land by category and for land reserved for open space. At the bottom, urban, regional and total county open-space acreage is given per 1,000 population. The county had thirty acres per 1,000 people in 1960. It is already below twenty and falling. Urban parks are practically nonexistent, with less than one acre per 1,000 people. This ratio is also falling, as is absolute acreage devoted to urban parks. As the trend makes clear, land use for development is increasing along with population. Projections to 1975 and beyond hint only at further acceleration of development.

There has been little city or county action for reservation of adequate open spaces. As annexation continues and county open-space land is swallowed up, the entire county will begin to approach the ratio of .85 acre per 1,000 population of the urban category. In 1950, fifty-one square miles (32,640 acres) of the county were incorporated. In 1969, 280 square miles (179,000 acres) were controlled by cities. Sometime in the late 1980s, there will be few large tracts of land left to reserve. Meanwhile, urban residents live in a concrete environment that is expanding to make occasional escape more difficult.

---

* *California Journal*, August 1970, p. 229. The Journal commented regarding some of the defeated legislation: "Jesse Unruh's proposal to set up a powerful State Environmental Quality Control Board (AB 2050) was killed in committee in the Assembly. The Select Committee's Environmental Bill of Rights (ACA 55, Milias) which would have clarified the Legislature's power relative to local governments, was an obvious casualty. A continuing debate over the locus of power in Bay Area planning bodies caused the defeat of one Knox proposal for a modified form of regional government (AB 2310) and the abandonment by the author of another (AB 2345) to establish statewide regional planning bodies. A third (AB 1155) successfully required LAFCO decisions to be consistent with local general plans, and traded control over new services offered by special districts for potential membership on the local commission."

Table 9b
SANTA CLARA COUNTY POPULATION, DEVELOPED AREAS,
AND OPEN-SPACE TRENDS

	1965–66	1967–68	% Change Per Annum
POPULATION	919,700	1,008,000	+4.3%
DEVELOPED AREAS [a]	98,177	105,460	+3.7%
Resid. Acreage	45,965	48,391	
Industrial Acreage	2,144	2,450	
Manuf. Acreage	3,833	4,281	
Trans. Acreage	30,829	33,264	
Commercial Acreage	4,022	4,474	
Public Buildings	11,484	12,600	
OPEN SPACES [b]	19,190	19,371	+0.4%
Urban Parks	873	862	
Regional Parks	17,326	17,357	
Playgrounds, etc.	991	1,152	
RATIOS			
Acreage/1,000 Population for Urban Parks [c]	.95	.85	−5.2%
Acreage/1,000 Population for Metropolitan or Regional Parks	17.7	16.2	−4.2%
Acreage/1,000 Population for Total Public Open Spaces	20.9	19.2	−4.1%

[a] Vacant urban and agricultural land is excluded.

[b] Does not include cemeteries, "commercial" or so-called "nonprofit" open spaces.

[c] Adding on all nonschool playing fields, playgrounds, and neighborhood parks does not raise the urban park figure above 1.5 acres/1,000. These acreages are included in the total open-space figures.

Newly developing urban areas will *not* make up for the lack of public open spaces by guaranteeing large "yards" for everyone. The average lot size in Santa Clara County is under one-quarter acre for "suburban" extensions from the urban complex. The residents of Santa Clara County generally live in a congested, intensely built-up environment with small yards and little open green area, although Santa Clara County is one of the three or four best of California's fifteen most urban counties in both large yard size and open space preservation.

Strip Zoning

Santa Clara County and its cities have zoned 6,333 acres commercial—5,401 by the county's fifteen cities, 932 by the county itself. Of the 6,333 acres, a total of 1,983 are currently being used for commercial purposes. The ratio for incorporated and unincorporated areas is similar. Most of the land—2,862 scattered acres of it—is vacant.

Approximately 19,000 vacant acres now stand in highly *urban* areas of the county. This is more than twenty times the acreage of urban parks. It is almost double all land currently in use for commercial, manufacturing, and industrial purposes, and for dwellings for two, three, four, five or more families throughout the entire county. And because of the pattern, this latter development *is* "throughout the entire county." This vacant acreage could accommodate, at present rates, the rapid single-family residential development in the county for the next eight years.

The cost in terms of unnecessary land use is apparent, and there is also a loss of potential open spaces for public use. Other costs range from the need for more transportation because of checkerboard land use and hence more land for streets, parking lots, etc., to scattering of commercial and industrial facilities.

The motive for the overzoning is to attract maximum business to the community involved. Since each community is in competition, each wants to maintain a wide spectrum of attractive sites for anyone who wants to locate. The basis for this competition is increased local tax revenue for local services and schools.

Increased property tax, however, has not been the main inducement for attracting commercial enterprise. Rather, it is increased *sales* in the community that increase local revenue (through the sales tax kickback) more than anything. Value of surrounding property does not always increase *with commercial proliferation*. People do not especially like to live next door to the local A & W Rootbeer hangout.

Perhaps symptomatic of local solicitude for commercial revenue is the strip zoning prevalent throughout California. Major thoroughfares are ideal for commercial enterprise. Communities in competition with each other zone in strips along most of their major thoroughfares to attract business.

And local communities generally fail to restrict the characteristics of signs. Signs get larger and larger, colors get wilder, lights get brighter. Soon the buildings themselves are designed to get attention. A hamburger stand might be housed in a building shaped like a giant pink shoe, with someone dressed as a little old lady standing out front.

At night the signs are illuminated, most of them twirling,

turning, and flashing, often accompanied with "nervous" signs in the shape of an arrow flashing a combination of six different-colored lights each second. Every escalation along the strip must be matched.

This competitive advertising is wasteful as well as aesthetically offensive. Businesses are not "clustered" in available centers for easy pedestrian access after parking. Everyone must have parking facilities to satisfy possible store capacity. More total land must be concretized for parking and more will be empty of cars than if stores were clustered with one lot serving them all. And every twenty feet there is a possible entrance or exit from the main thoroughfare. Instead of one or two signal-controlled exits to a cluster of stores set back from the main thoroughfare by access roads, there is constant darting in and out of traffic. The maze of flashing, turning lights and signs makes it difficult to see traffic signs and signals. In some areas, it is generally difficult to see a red stoplight until one is directly on top of it—if then. Needless to say, traffic records show extraordinary accident rates along these roads.

In 1965, 2,125 acres, or 52.8%, of the commercially used land in the county was strip developed. These are the county's own figures and are low; they do not include banks, offices, and clinics.

The most recent figures, from 1967, show strip-zoned land use reaching an all-time high: 2,401 acres, now 53.7% of all commercially used land in the county. The average yearly *increase* in such use is 140 acres (amounting to a strip along a road fifty-five yards deep for *seventy miles*).

The Poor: Snob Zoning

Land policies play perhaps the major role in the various kinds of discrimination which inhibit fluid movement in our society and belie the Horatio Alger myth. The property tax, as presently administered, is among the most regressive of taxes in this regard. The poor are taxed a larger percentage of their income than are the rich; Appendix 9A describes how the current method of property taxation places a disproportionate burden on the poor.

Snob zoning and housing patterns isolate the poor geographically, culturally, economically, and socially. Once isolated, they find themselves concentrated in an environment with high unemployment, drug addiction, crime, and disease. Such environments tend to be self-perpetuating.

Boundaries for financing special services and education are drawn around the areas where the poor have been forced to concentrate. Education and services must be financed from the property and sales tax resources of the poor community, thus touching off a spiral of regressivity (see below). Land's role in diminishing equality of opportunity is not altogether related to discrimination by race; it is related to impediments for the poor generally.

After World War II, FHA policies permitting racial covenants helped exclude blacks from many suburbs; discrimination was permitted until recently in off-base military housing financed by public-housing allowances; and so on. More recently, two different kinds of forces have inhibited the dispersal of the poor. First, forces of urban renewal together with low-income housing policies have concentrated the poor where they are. Freeways have cut off many poor areas. Lack of mass transit has impeded movement, since the poor own fewer cars than the rich. In California, this disparity is most striking. The renewal process itself often results in the destruction of desperately needed low-income housing—in one case for a baseball stadium. The displaced poor are often not relocated. When they are relocated it is generally back into what remains of the ghetto, which increases crowding. Low-income housing is virtually nonexistent in the suburbs—partially because of a state constitutional provision requiring a majority vote of approval in a community before the construction of low-income housing. Practically every low-income project thus far approved has been for the elderly.

The second force is now the subject of a test case concerning Union City, California—snob zoning. Snob zoning is usually accomplished through a combination of extremely strict housing codes, large minimum lot sizes, and large minimum square-footage requirements per residence. The correlation between lots per acre and racial and poverty indexes is striking. Although there is only token black population throughout Santa Clara County, about 9.2% of the populace are Mexican-American. Saratoga, a typical "rich" district, averages two lots per acre—or large lots; it has about a one-percent population of Mexican-Americans, little unemployment, and high average incomes. Gilroy, a typical "poorer" district, however, averages *4.9* lots per acre. Gilroy has a 31% Mexican-American population, much lower average income, and almost *eight times* the unemployment of Saratoga. Gilroy also has a much higher percentage of renters. The same trends hold true with the other districts of the county. Montebello and Orchard, "rich" districts, can be compared to poorer Alum Rock and Mount Pleasant in the same manner with the same results. Minimum lot size standards usually correspond to the existing housing pattern, with one-half-acre minimums in places like Montebello and Orchard, one-fifth or one-quarter or lower minimum lot requirements in Gilroy, Alum Rock, and Mount Pleasant.

A major problem adding to the isolation of California's poor is the failure to balance living and employment opportunities, because of the growth of "special purpose" communities of all kinds. The city areas of San Francisco-Oakland-Berkeley hold only 32% of the Bay area's population, but 45% of the jobs. It is estimated that in 1990 San Francisco will have 11% of the population and 23% of the jobs. And San Francisco is losing manufacturing jobs and gaining employment in finance and related fields. The influx of unskilled and minority workers to the cities and the corresponding flight of middle-class whites (and jobs) to suburbs means that *both* groups now commute—in opposite directions. Lack of public transit in the suburbs has been a cause of the segregation that now makes freeways more necessary. But only half of all Negro households own automobiles. The Bay Area Transportation Study Committee (BATSC) projects that present trends will result in "continued growth of commuter transport needs on the part of both races due to racial separation. Rather than requiring balanced development in both cities and suburbs, we spend billions on transportation systems that are too expensive for the poor to use. Rather than make the cities more livable, we make them more accessible to suburban commuters. Rather than disperse a variety of income groups we have concentrated them in areas where they cannot work."

A second critical problem in the isolation of the poor is education. The single most significant share of the property tax, on an average about two-thirds, goes to the local school districts. Public school systems in California are financed on the basis of a basic aid per student (correctly: per "Average Daily Allowance" or ADA) plus as much property tax as the district is willing or able to pay for adequate education. If a district has less than $13,000 assessed valuation per ADA, the state will pay additional subsidy on a sliding scale.

Assessed valuation has absolutely nothing to do with the number of students requiring adequate education. In Santa Clara County, for example, there are some school districts with wealthy estates or with lots of industry. These districts have high-value property and hence high assessed valuation. But they have few students. In those districts, rich parents pay less for an excellent school system than poor parents have to pay in poor districts for poor school systems.

As Table 9c shows, there is a tiny school district in Cupertino named "Montebello Elementary School District"; it has few students, and consequently its assessed valuation per ADA is roughly thirty times higher than San Jose's Mount Pleasant Elementary School District. Correspondingly, the tax rate in Mount Pleasant is about 43% higher than in Montebello. So Montebello inhabitants pay a 43% lower tax for their school system, but they can spend 3.7 times more on instruction per student than Mount Pleasant inhabitants.

The elementary school *tax rate* of the residents in another tiny school district named "Orchard Elementary" in the northern part of San Jose (ADA in 1968–69: 216 students) is only *half* the rate of Mount Pleasant, although the amount of money expended per student in Orchard is considerably higher and the median salary of the teachers in this district is the highest in the county. The district consists mainly of industry which greatly adds to the tax base but not to the number of students. The children of the workers of that industry, who live in poorer areas, do not have any educational benefits from the wealth of the industries.

The solution to the snob zoning-financial squeeze dilemma rests with varying combinations of change: the abolition of the property tax (see Appendix 9A for reforms of tax as applied); the collection of sales tax (and property tax if still collected) by the state, with revenue-sharing to counties according to a mechanical area-population formula; the transferral of all independent school districts (and other special districts) to county or state jurisdiction; the allocation of school and other essential service expenditures by each county on the basis of need.

To end snob zoning, every community should provide

Table 9c

A COMPARISON OF TWO RICH AND
TWO POOR SCHOOL DISTRICTS IN SANTA CLARA COUNTY

Elementary School District	Instruction/ADA 1968–69 ($)	Total Exp./ADA 1968–69 ($)	Assessed Val. per ADA 1968–69	% of Tax Rate
Montebello	1,475.22	2,081.78	133,391.11	2.556
Orchard	552.97	862.03	127,265.32	1.840
Alum Rock	484.39	611.56	5,057.57	3.688
Mount Pleasant	397.00	514.20	4,874.44	3.662

Source: "A Report of Certified Salaries and Related Information in Santa Clara County School Districts 1969–70," prepared by John Satterstrom, Office of Education, Santa Clara County, January, 1970

at least 15% of its housing for low-income residents—
with low income carefully defined, and with state incentives
for compliance. If rewards are ineffective, sanctions may be
necessary.

Service Costs

High service costs are another consequence of the failure
to coordinate planning between neighboring jurisdictions.

> [Fragmented] development has been actively fostered by
> San Jose's policy of extending services to developers at
> the time or prior to the time of annexation and charging
> them no special assessment for this extension on the as-
> sumption that the cost would be amortized by the later
> development and hookup of the intervening areas. In a
> great many cases this intervening area has not filled in
> and the costs remain with the city.[25]

San Jose meets these costs through a $1.40 per $100
assessed value city property tax and numerous general obligation bond issues. Since the costs of subsidizing extraordinary speculator and developer profits continually increase,
so must tax revenue. But raising the $1.40 rate is politically
dangerous. Hence, it is necessary to increase the tax base.
Hence, it is necessary to attract more development. Someone in the near future is going to have to pay. When
bonds fall due, when the city reaches physical limits and
the tax base cannot be jacked up with more development,
the burden will be heavy. But it is not the speculators or
developers who will pay. They passed these costs on to the
future occupiers of the land they briefly held. They won't
pay the tax now or later.

The shape of San Jose itself, together with the rapidly
increasing local tax revenue need, indicates the unnecessary
and high cost of city services. Some of the excess cost is
borne by all of California's rate payers through higher rates
paid PG&E and Pacific Telephone. Some is absorbed by the
county. Excess police, fire, and sewage costs are the chief
culprits accounting for the rise in local tax need.

San Jose was told in 1957 by the State Water Quality
Control Board that more than primary sewage treatment
was necessary to meet state quality standards. More facilities were added but secondary treatment was still insufficient to meet state standards. The State Board issued a
cease-and-desist order in 1960 to San Jose to either con-

struct new facilities or stop all new construction. San Jose then acted. A $22 million bond issue was passed and a new giant plant constructed for primary and secondary treatment. This plant is now working at capacity and major expansion will soon be needed.

In addition to increasing plan needs, sewage lines (as with utilities and roads) must be extended out ten to fifteen miles to service a blob of development at the end of one of San Jose's tentacles.

The new size and population of San Jose does not make police protection efficient either. Here, however, the city has not taken action. There has been only a small enlargement of the police force since 1950. As a result, the present police-to-population ratio in San Jose is 1.2 to 1,000, compared to 2.8 to 1,000 in San Francisco and 3.2 to 1,000 in Oakland. (These latter cities have not been expanding geographically as have San Jose or Los Angeles.) The shape of San Jose makes it difficult to patrol. As a result, most police activity is confined to answering calls.

Fragmentation makes California susceptible to more than the usual amount of inefficiency from failure to coordinate. The Stanford study remarks:

> There have been instances of fires in these areas to which as many as four different municipality fire departments responded, all stopping at their boundary lines watching the fire burn until the county fire equipment arrived from a much greater distance.[26]

Solutions

It is of little use to suggest, as many do, that councils "formulate decent plans based on community goals and then carry them out." This is tantamount to telling a heroin addict that he should really stop because he is not contributing to society and is destroying himself. The addict doesn't care.

The effective general plan, the preservation of open space, and a pleasant environment cannot be created by suggesting that it happen. They are the *effect,* the natural result, of a sound economic and political system.

For minimal restructuring there must be:

(1) The complete restructuring of local government, creating visible, elected officials heading a multipurpose

government based on natural community boundaries, for *real* home rule by viable, responsive political units.* This means the end of school and independent special districts. It means fewer elected local officials with clearer responsibilities. It means new and permanent state-drawn boundaries for cities.

(2) An economic incentive plan which does not subsidize speculative land investment and encourage "zoning-up" ** by local communities in competition with each other for tax revenue.

The following system would properly assess costs. First, the state declares all land that is not being used intensively to be present open-space land—whatever master plan or zoning designation it might have.*** The state formulates a standard coding system for land classification which can be restricted in greater detail by local communities, but which serves as a minimum guide. Each category (e.g. single-family residential, apartment, retail commercial, etc.) will have minimum requirements in terms of city services and public works: utilities, roads or mass transit, sewers, and so on. These services must be provided by private or public utility, the developer or the city before the zoning change is obtained or within a specified period afterwards. The state is then constitutionally precluded from "zoning-up" any land under any circumstances. Local communities retain that function.

Second, when there is an application for any new development (i.e. to zone up from "open space"), there will be a "zoning-up" fee charged. It will be equal to the increase in value of the land due to the zoning change and the utilities, services, and public investments entailed in the zoning change. This fee will be payable to the state. It would generally be a *substantial* fee.

Assuming property taxes are not abolished, they should gradually be based on "site value" considerations alone. All property tax (as well as sales tax) would be collected by the state to increase uniformity. The local governments

* This might mean either allocating all land between the cities within each county and giving them school and special district functions, or perhaps devolving *all* government functions into revitalized county governments with new boundaries.

** That is, zoning from open space or agricultural to residential, commercial, or industrial development.

*** Land presently being used would be declared zoned for the use to which it is presently being put.

would then receive all of this money back according to a mechanical population-land area formula.

An alternative to this is the capital-gains reform mentioned in Chapter 2. It would require federal reform as well as state reform and would not give teeth to the zoning scheme, but it would be administratively more efficient and have similar effects.

(3) A state offer of special incentives for certain kinds of construction. Underground parking facilities at a city's perimeter, an efficient mass-transit system, low-income housing, acquisition of park land, etc., would receive additional state aid. But any aid received from the state would be conditioned upon the existence of an acceptable local general plan. The acceptability of the general plan will depend on the existence of certain minimum studies required (traffic and population projections, commercial and open-space needs, density, sign and height plans, coordination with surrounding jurisdictions, etc.). The results of the studies and of the plan will not be relevant to state acceptance, but there must be minimum resources devoted to study and there must be minimum adherence to the plan.

No extensions or rezonings would be allowed by state law. State law would allow exceptions or variance grants only upon specific findings of need, with minimum criteria provided in state law. General plans may be changed, but only after repetition of required studies and only at five-year intervals.

The end result of this system would be to insulate from planning decisions, extensive pressures, or incentives for zoning-up, and from either corruptive pressures from speculators or economic pressures for increased local revenues vis-a-vis neighbors. All zoning-up would occur only when the local community would need more commercial, industrial, or similar concerns. Schools and local services would be of comparable quality throughout the state. Since it would not pay as much to hold vacant land for speculative gain, park land would be easier for the cities to buy and sprawl would lessen. Revenue would not decrease in most areas, with zoning-up fees a substantial addition to general tax revenues.

The system would avoid the many pitfalls of the only serious proposal in this area yet advanced: for the state to recompense local governments for not zoning-up certain land. This proposal of payment by the state for *not* zoning

for the speculator or developer is administratively un-
manageable,* and would be ineffective even where applied.**

Retroactive remedies are difficult in this area. In fact,
one of the major virtues of our proposed system is the fact
that it chooses *now* as a starting point for ending unjust
enrichment. In most cases of past damage, the land speculators are out of the market with their loot. Taxing present
occupants of the land would make the victims pay the price.

Yet past damage must be rectified. The solution lies
with the new general plans. At the outset, the state declaration will make all zoning correspond to actual use. Yet
few proper general plans will want to maintain the arbitrary
errors of the past indefinitely. Therefore the new general
plans must be drawn with nonconforming uses of various
categories allowed for a specific number of years. This
would make gradual amortization of losses possible and
prevent reinvestment. The system described above would
give new general plans teeth and create land-use policies
set naturally according to community need.***

In order to permit local democracy to function, a city
must be small enough to permit active participation by all
its inhabitants, and it must be large enough to combine a
viable range of human activities and talents that are needed
in dealing with day-to-day local problems. Thus, "city" is a
political and not merely a physical concept. But in order
to be able to participate actively in the local democratic
process, people obviously have to be able concretely to
identify a city. And this has something to do with physical
urban structure. The human mind seems to associate a
place with its most outstanding characteristics, characteristics that can be perceived and grasped with our senses
and that provide meaningful, consistent cues for orientation.
When there was no talking and writing about the "urban
crisis," cities used to have such characteristics. They were

---

* For example, determining what land is to be subsidized would
mean the same unjust enrichment-politics scheme currently intact.

** Although it would somewhat lessen local revenue incentive to
zone up, it would not end unjust enrichment by speculators who
stand to profit and who could still "influence" individual local governments.

*** A.B. 1056 (Z'berg), introduced in 1971, incorporates some of
these principles in a system of environmental quality boards, an
Environmental Quality Citizens Council, and a system of conservation and development plans.

bounded and distinguishable from their surroundings and from other cities. They had centers that were often clearly visible, that meant something in terms of the city, and that therefore often had symbolic meaning for the whole place.

To be sure, the cities in our sprawling metropolitan areas are also bounded. But their city limits have often become something so confusing, arbitrary, and abstract that they do not mean very much. They cause confusion even when they become important—as in the case of some emergency such as fire or crime or accident, when one has to try to find out which fire station, police department, or hospital is responsible for dealing with a case.

Our cities also have centers, but as demonstrated with the example of the metropolitan center of San Jose, the most viable functional centers sometimes are municipal peripheries, located across the boundaries of several political jurisdictions. A Balkanized fringe center, such as the commercial core of metropolitan San Jose, also becomes a symbol, but a symbol for the weakening of local democracy rather than for its strength.

Thus, we can observe the closing of a vicious circle: the weakness of the political city has brought about what might be called the degeneration of the physical urban structure; the degenerated physical city, in turn, is further weakening the political city. To reverse this circle, more than symptom therapy is needed. We have to make sure that our political city can properly function; if we are serious about local democracy, then we will have to reform our cities both with regard to their presently incomprehensible layers of different local government and to their degenerated physical structure. This is to say that the limits and the centers of urban units should be newly determined on the basis of actual activities and comprehensibility. Unless it is possible to reunify the old central core, new boundaries should be drawn around what are really satellite cities, so that the new centers can begin to create new balanced communities.

10

Transportation: The Highway Complex

Transportation facilities and urban development are interdependent. Projected transportation facilities dramatically affect economic incentives and location choices, creating a demand for new development. The new development then appears to justify the projected road or airport.

Transportation also affects the *nature* of development. Different modes take up different quantities of land, affect the environment in varying degrees, compel vertical or sprawling development, and operate at disparate levels of cost efficiency, safety, speed, and resource depletion.

The automobile is an extremely flexible and enormously popular means of transportation. California has made extensive commitments to roads, to oil, and to auto production. The state's land-use patterns have created a need for the auto system, and a sudden, massive change to another mode would be extremely costly. But most of the costs of the auto-highway system itself have been hidden through so many indirect payments and public subsidies that the economics of the system are not accurately reflected in market dynamics. Current discrimination adds to the economic and political power of a highly organized auto-truck-oil-highway complex.

Freeway Mania

There are approximately twelve million motor vehicles and motorcycles registered in California as of 1971. There are actually more vehicles registered than there are licensed drivers to operate them. Eleven million additional vehicles, many of them registered in other states, enter the state each year through California's eighteen quarantine stations.

As of 1969, there were 158,159 miles [1] of federal, state, county, and city highways and roads in California, much of it multilaned. California's roads could encircle the entire earth six times with numerous lanes.

The average California family has two vehicles. The monthly cost of two automobiles is about $166:

Depreciation and Interest	$40
Fuel	$40
Upkeep	$15
Insurance	$46
Tax	$25
Total	$166 per month

One-seventh of the cost is hidden and subsidized through government protection and tax breaks. This total does not include any repair bills, hospital bills, or lawyers' fees in case of accident. It does not include the deceptively high "incidental" expenses (e.g., parking) which vary by family. Economists have concluded that many Californians pay more for their automobile transportation than for their housing.

Even the ascertainable costs of this economic commitment have been carefully hidden in the form of massive subsidies and indirect or invisible expenses.

—*Tax expenditures.* The taxpayer's annual bill is as high as it is because the oil and auto industries do not have to pay their share of taxes. The government subsidizes those industries by excusing them from tax liability. The oil import quota alone costs each California family approximately $100 per year. Statewide, the consumer cost is nearly $.75 billion. Oil depletion allowances, and other federal, state, and even local tax breaks account for about another half billion dollars. Gas is exempt from sales tax. Auto rights of way are purchased, maintained, and policed by government. (Railroads, however, have to pay enormous property taxes on their rights-of-way and properties because they are not publicly owned.) The total tax and market control subsidy of the auto and oil industries is near $1.4 billion per year.

—*Land-use costs.* The automobile directly uses up between 25% (Berkeley) and 60% (Los Angeles) of the land area of California's major cities. Lots, streets, driveways, service stations, etc., account for over ten times as much concrete area per automobile as cities and counties provide in all parks, playgrounds, etc., per person. This immense cost is reflected in rents and mortgage payments, since less land for other use means higher prices. Indirectly, the automobile stimulates sprawl and the inefficient use of the land it does not itself require.

—*Displacement costs*. The cost of displacing homes, businesses, and even communities in the continuous process of freeway construction is inestimable, but substantial. These costs fall disproportionately and often arbitrarily on the politically impotent.

—*Environmental costs*. It is impossible to put a price on the environmental costs of road construction: included are pollution from erosion and runoff, changes made in drainage patterns, the isolation of timid wildlife, and so on. Those who construct the roads and profit from their location do not pay the environmental costs which they impose. Vehicles, too, impose enormous social and physical costs by means of air pollution. The automobile is the major cause of air pollution in California; it pollutes more than any other mode or vehicle per passenger-mile [2]—and because of the sprawl it stimulates, it requires more passenger-miles, meaning more pollution and more direct transportation cost. Lead, carbon monoxide, nitrogen oxides, particulates, sulfur oxides, carbon dioxide, and organic compounds are major pollutants. Lung cancer, emphysema, and cardiovascular disease are increasingly attributed to auto pollution by statistical and laboratory research. More recent research is indicating that rubber particulate pollution from tires is dangerous and asbestos pollution from brake linings may be among the most carcinogenic substances known.* Auto pollution also corrodes metal and weakens fabrics. The damage to agriculture is estimated at $100 million per year (see Chapter 2). The harm to wild-area vegetation is inestimable (see Chapter 4).

—*Natural resource exhaustion*. Natural resource exhaustion is a future cost incurred by relying on a system that permanently consumes more metal and fuel per passenger-mile than any other except the airplane and helicopter. Many metals are now reaching points of predictable depletion. Lead, tungsten, zinc, tin, and copper are

---

* See J. Esposito, et al., *Vanishing Air* (Grossman, 1970).

already nearing a critical stage.** For autos and trucks 8,596,855,909 gallons of fuel and 494,041,066 gallons of diesel fuel were pumped in California in 1968.

—*Direct death and injury*. The auto is the least safe of all transportation modes, accounting for more than 4,000 deaths and 150,000 reported injuries each year in California. Since 1961 as many Californians have been killed in motor-vehicle accidents as Americans have been killed in Vietnam.

Table 10a

MODE EFFICIENCY COMPARISON

AUTO: A transportation corridor one highway lane (12 feet) wide can carry a maximum of 3,600 passengers per hour.[a]
BUS: Half-filled buses can carry 60,000 people per hour—17 times as many as the car.[b]
TRAIN: Half-filled trains will transport 42,000 passengers per hour —12 times the number handled by the auto.[c]
BICYCLE: A highway lane can comfortably hold two bicycle lanes, allowing passage of 10,600 people per hour—almost 3 times as many as cars.[d]
WALKING: A path the width of a highway lane can accommodate 6,300 walkers per hour—1.7 as many as automobile passengers.[e]

Mode	Number of Passengers per Hour	Efficiency Relative to Auto
Auto	3,600	1
Bus	60,000	17
Train	42,000	12
Bicycle	10,000	2.8
Walking	6,300	1.7

[a] Sixty-five m.p.h., 140-foot spacing (recommended for this speed), 1.5 people per car (the average number from many studies).
[b] Sixty-five m.p.h., 140-foot spacing.
[c] One per minute. The right-of-way for a train track is about the same width as a highway lane.
[d] Fifteen m.p.h., 10-foot spacing.
[e] Three m.p.h., 4 columns of walkers, 10-foot spacing.
Source: Ken Cantor, *Environmental Handbook*, p. 200.

Many of these hazards and expenditures could be minimized within the present system. A safe, pollution-free (e.g., external combustion or electric) vehicle could be developed. Noise could be reduced, road construction assessed the cost of damage caused, and so forth. Tax and

** See P. Ehrlich's well-documented *Population, Resources, Environment* (Freeman, 1970), p. 60. The world's total known reserve of crude oil, natural gas, uranium, gold, silver, and platinum (as well as those above) will be depleted within fifty years or less.

public policy changes could assess the cost of recovery for an automobile at time of sale. Auto companies could be required to provide minimal insurance for their cars, introducing an incentive to produce safer cars.

However, the present "system" is not only extraordinarily costly in both environmental and financial terms—it is also highly inefficient and not adequate to solve the congestion problems of an increasing population. Professor Kenneth E. F. Watt, a systems ecologist from the University of California at Davis, draws from a study by a reputable systems analyst, Professor R. J. Smeed, to point out that while freeways add to the increasing population in a given area, they *cannot* be expanded to satisfy the newly created need as that population grows.

The Stranglehold

The auto-freeway complex of trade associations has used various methods to promote its mode in the face of the relative desirability of other modes and/or the lack of necessity for roads. The associations lobby extensively, contributing to campaigns and employing administrative, legislative, and local officials as clients or executives. They spend fortunes in advertising to influence public electoral decisions. They have created a system of subsidies and competitive incentives which induce local and state governments to favor construction. And the auto-freeway complex takes advantage of the motivations of landowners and speculators who stand to profit privately from these public works.

"Conventional urban transit lost its market to the automobile because it lacked the speed, convenience, and flexibility of the car." [3] This statement, made in 1970 by the Automotive Manufacturers Association, neglects to add that automobile and allied interests have played a direct role in assuring that mass transit would lack that speed, convenience, and flexibility. Automobile, oil, truck, and road construction interests have lobbied since the 1920s against public mass transit and for public subsidy of their own operations in California. They have engaged in direct and illegal conspiracy to purchase rail-transit systems and destroy them. Using a dummy corporation, they persuaded governments that private mass transit could survive, that public investment was unnecessary. They then purchased rail transit systems and proceeded to tear up rail lines in city after city, destroying the basis for modern mass-transit right-of-way. They substituted buses for trains, not only to guarantee the death of a competitive system but also to give General Motors and allied corporations a market for bus vehicles, parts, and fuel. These companies, of course, stood behind the "dummy," a corporation called National City Lines.

National City Lines, now a very successful trucking firm, was incorporated in Delaware, in February of 1936, "to acquire securities of companies owning and operating motor bus lines." [4] By April 1, 1939, it controlled twenty-nine local operating companies in ten states.[5] Sometime during 1938, National approached General Motors, seeking investment funds to purchase streetcar lines which could be converted to buses. General Motors agreed, on condition that National buy buses exclusively from General Motors.[6] Similarly illegal agreements were reached by National and *its* subsidiary, Pacific City Lines, with Firestone Tire and Rubber Company for tires, with Phillips Petroleum Company for gasoline and oil in the Midwest, with Standard Oil Company of California for gasoline and oil on the West Coast, and with Mack Manufacturing Company for buses.[7] It was further agreed that National and Pacific would not sell any operating company without requiring the new owner to assume the same obligation to purchase exclusively from these suppliers.[8]

In accord with these agreements, GM, Firestone, Phillips, Standard, and Mack purchased over $9 million worth of preferred stock in National and its subsidiaries, at prices in excess of prevailing market prices. The money was used by National and Pacific to acquire control of or a substantial financial interest in various transportation companies throughout the United States.[9]

By April, 1947, National, Pacific, and another subsidiary formed in 1943, American City Lines, had expanded their ownership or control to forty-six transportation systems located in forty-five cities in sixteen states. Included among these were ten in California: Sacramento, Eureka, Fresno, Glendale, Pasadena, San Jose, Stockton, Los Angeles, Oakland, and Long Beach. The value of products sold to National, Pacific, and American by the suppliers in 1946 was over $11 million; for the period from 1937 to 1947, over $37 million.[10]

By late 1944, American City Lines had acquired a controlling interest in the Los Angeles Railway Corporation.[11] Almost immediately its name was changed to Los Angeles Transit Lines, and it was announced that a program for conversion to buses had been in effect since 1940.[12] Valuable rights-of-way were sold and the rails removed.

National's subsidiary, Pacific City Lines, was headquartered in Oakland, and, in May of 1946, it was announced that it had purchased a controlling interest (84,257 shares) in Railway Equipment and Realty Company, owner of Oakland's Key System transit line.[13] Jesse L. Haugh, Chairman of the Board of Pacific, was named president of Key, and immediately announced: "We plan to remove all tracks from Oakland streets except those used by transbay lines as rapidly as possible, replacing street cars with trackless trolleys and gasoline-powered busses." [14]

On April 9 and 10, 1947, the United States Department of Justice finally intervened, filing civil and criminal antitrust actions against all parties to the agreements, in Federal District Court in Los Angeles. The cases were transferred to Chicago, where National's home office was located. In March of 1949, a jury found National, Pacific, GM, Firestone, Phillips, Standard, and Mack guilty of criminal conspiracy in violation of the Sherman Act, 15 U.S.C.A.2.[15]

The defendants were convicted of one of two counts and fines totalling $36,007 were assessed.[16] The jury found there was a conspiracy to acquire a monopoly of the sales to local transportation companies but no conspiracy to restrain trade by securing control of those transportation systems.[17] The conviction was unanimously affirmed in *United States v. National City Lines,*[18] and the U.S. Supreme Court denied certiorari.[19]

Despite this and other court decisions, National continued to convert from rail to bus transit. The last streetcar ran in Oakland on November 28, 1948.[20] Repeated requests were made to the Public Utilities Commission to substitute buses for trains on the ground that the cost of maintaining the trains and their rights-of-way was too great. Preparations were made as early as 1945 for scrapping San Francisco-Oakland Bay Bridge trains in favor of buses.[21] National ran parallel buses on the Bay Bridge; trains were limited to 37.5 miles per hour for "safety" reasons. Newspapers at the time charged that Key was permitting the deliberate deterioration of its train system to the advantage of its buses. It was also noted that "Key System's drive to remove the rails comes at a time when the BART Commission is deep in plans to construct a $1 billion bay area rapid transit system which could use the tracks." [22] On April 20, 1958, the last train made the trip to San Francisco. On October 1, 1960, National sold the assets of an all-bus Key System to Alameda-Contra Costa Transit Districts for $7,500,000 cash.[23]

Los Angeles Transit Lines was sold on March 3, 1958, to the Los Angeles Metropolitan Transit Authority for $21,604,000.[24]

The 1960s saw National divest itself of the rest of its California transit companies. San Jose and Stockton City Lines were sold in 1962, and Glendale City Lines was dissolved. Glendale ceased operations in 1964, and its assets were sold. Pasadena City Lines was sold in 1963 for $237,486, as was the Long Beach bus system for $900,000.[25] In 1968, urban passenger transportation provided only 13% of National's consolidated revenues, the remainder coming from general commodity trucking (52%), specialized motor-carrier operations (19%), automotive parts manufacturing and distribution (12%), and automotive equipment leasing (4%). Its automobile hauling subsidiaries carry automobiles, auto bodies and related parts, primarily for Buick and Oldsmobile divisions of General Motors, and Ford Division of Ford Motor Company.[26]

There has clearly been a long and close relationship between National City Lines and these automobile interests. The real beneficiary of this relationship was not National, but General Motors and the other suppliers. They, of course, gained directly from sales to National's companies, and indirectly from increased sales of automobiles as transit service in private hands degenerated. The historian of Los Angeles' Pacific Electric Railroad noted in 1962, "The unprofitable situation of commuter traffic was obvious for at least forty years. If a state authority had been created as late as 1945 to utilize public funds to maintain the Red Car right-of-ways and purchase modern equipment, millions of dollars spent on freeway construction might have been saved." [27] Instead, in 1945 and earlier, National was able to convince a willing public that private transit was viable and grabbed up failing transit lines at a great discount. National paid only $3 million for 64% of Key System's stock, although total value of the property was estimated in Oakland financial quarters at about $20 million.[28] By thus distorting National's financial ability by $9 million in inflated stock purchases, General Motors and others were able to forestall the advent of public transit for the crucial ten years following World War II, in which the automobile became king and California embarked on a tremendous freeway construction program. As long as transit was in private hands, the question of subsidizing it rather than the automble never received serious attention.

The most recent test of the auto-freeway-oil-construction complex's growing collusiveness and effectiveness was its campaign to defeat Proposition 18. The California Constitution specifically limits all state fuel tax revenue to expenditures for road construction. Proposition 18 in 1970 would have allowed local communities who receive a share of this revenue by formula to use up to 25% of it to finance mass transit or air pollution control projects. A local vote would be required to free even these limited funds. It is not only good law but good economics to include in the price of the fuel the cost of cleaning up its effects on the environment and alleviating traffic congestion.

Proposition 18 was backed by virtually every public-interest organization in the state. Opposing it were those directly making money from highway construction, including trucking, automobile, construction, and oil associations. The State Chamber of Commerce, dominated by oil firms, opposed Proposition 18 but many city and local Chambers of Commerce endorsed it. Auto Association of America members filed suit against the Association for its expenditure of members' monies against the Proposition. But the real battle was not with endorsements, where Proposition 18 won handily—it was before the electorate. Preliminary polls showed Proposition 18 winning by a two-to-one margin or more. The margin rose to three to one when pollsters outlined the issues and provisions of the measure.

However, the oil and construction interests launched a massive public-relations campaign; billboards appeared all over the state, exhorting in stark yellow letters:

"MORE TAXES? NO! NO. 18."

Proposition 18 had of course nothing whatsoever to do with the tax rate, but the claim was augmented by a series of distorted and contrived ads alleging that road construction funds were depleted (they weren't), that gas-tax money could *already* be used for air-pollution control if the state legislature so decided (the same interests argued before the legislature that it lacked such authority), that motor vehicle registration money was already being used for these purposes (not in the amounts affected by this legislation), that it would mean coerced mass transit (untrue—only by local vote), that mass transit "never cured congestion." Massive television ads proclaimed that roads would deteriorate (also untrue considering that road *maintenance* money is unaffected by Proposition 18. Only a portion of new construction money is diverted upon local vote).

The final vote was 54% no to 46% yes. (The advocates had a budget of $22,721, about 6% of the $348,785 spent by the opposition.) After stretching the truth before millions, the opponents of Proposition 18 also violated the contribution-reporting laws of California. Three large oil companies contributed to the "Californians Against Street and Road Tax Trap" a total of $90,000 by anonymous cashier's checks. The complicated process of getting special cashier's checks casts some doubt on one firm's claim that the failure to report their identity before the election was the result of a "bookkeeping error." Indeed, only imminent prosecution by new California Secretary of State Brown has elicited their identities after the election.

Congestion

Despite favoritism for and subsidies to the auto-highway complex, traffic congestion is pervasive on California's highways. The history of the proposed Southern Crossing, which would be the fifth east-west bridge across San Francisco Bay, reflects the state's unwillingness to deal with this fundamental problem.

Preliminary studies for the Southern Crossing were conducted in January, 1947. Since then there have been no fewer than twenty major studies, as financial and political expediency dictated shifts in routes and plans.[29]

In 1953, Senator Richard Dolwig sponsored legislation directing the construction of the bridge between Army Street in San Francisco and Bay Farm Island in Alameda County. The project was dropped in 1958 for lack of sufficient toll revenues. Financing continues to be a major problem, particularly as the proposed cost of the bridge

and approaches is now almost half a billion dollars—
enough to extend the Bay Area Rapid Transit System to
San Jose on both sides of the Bay. The present route
recommended by the Division of Bay Toll Crossing in 1966
represents a compromise which pleases nearly all parties.
It extends from India Basin (just north of San Francisco's
Hunter's Point) to Alameda and Bay Farm Island.

On the Alameda side, it is proposed that there be a
toll plaza in the Bay, and that the bridge then split into
a "Y," with one leg going across Alameda through a tube
under the Oakland estuary to link up with the Grove-
Shafter Freeway in Oakland. This plan satisfies downtown
Oakland interests and the Port of Oakland which has built
a huge container ship facility and is planning new docks in
the area; without the Southern Crossing, Oakland's ambitious plans to lure automobiles into the core area would
have little chance for success.

The bridge is a key link in a future freeway program
of enormous magnitude.[30] The 1969 Bay Area Transportation Study Commission (BATSC) describes this program
in exhaustive detail and predicts that if the issue of land-use
planning is not faced by 1990 there will be *1,386* miles of
freeway in the Bay Area, including the Southern Crossing
and: [31]

—Route 1 along the coast, from the Santa Cruz County
line to the Sonoma County line.

—Route 13 along Berkeley's Ashby Avenue from a new
freeway (Route 61) in the Bay to Route 24 at the Calde-
cott Tunnel.

—Route 13 along Oakland's Hegenberger Road from
new Route 61 at the Oakland airport to the MacArthur
Freeway (Route 580).

—Route 25 near Walnut Creek's Ignacio Valley Road
from Route 680 to Antioch (Route 4).

—Route 61 along the eastern shoreline of San Francisco
Bay from the Dumbarton Bridge to the Southern Crossing
in the Bay off Alameda, then to Alameda, and through a
tube under the Oakland Estuary to West Oakland (this
will make a total of ten highway tunnels under the Estuary,
counting two presently existing and four proposed for the
Southern Crossing); then out into the Bay again off
Berkeley, and finally meeting the Eastshore Freeway
(Route 17) in Albany.

—Route 77 through the Oakland hills from Park Boulevard at the MacArthur Freeway through Shepherd Canyon to Moraga, and along St. Mary's Road and Pleasant Hill Road to Concord.

—Route 85 through San Jose from Mountain View to Coyote.

—Route 87 from San Jose in the Bay east of 101 to San Francisco, completing a *third* "inner" ring of parallel freeways around the Bay.

—Route 480 in San Francisco, continuing the Embarcadero Freeway from Broadway to the Golden Gate Bridge.

Yet all this costly freeway construction will not, according to the BATSC, ease congestion. Every existing freeway will be intolerably congested, with over 15,000 vehicles per lane each weekday.

The Southern Crossing and its attendant additions are justified on the basis of development projections which assume the existence of the bridge. Hence the bridge, like the freeway complex, justifies itself by attracting development and traffic flow which make it "necessary." There are several alternatives to freeways. One immediate boost to transit would be the abolition of bus fares, and free service on the Bay Area (rail) Rapid Transit. The $5 million spent on fare-collecting equipment would thus be saved.[32] Legislation along these lines, proposed in January, 1970, by Senator Lewis F. Sherman (R-Berkeley), was unsuccessful because it was to be financed by a doubling of Bay Bridge tolls. A much more modest proposal to provide an exclusive bus lane through congestion at the toll plaza was put into effect on April 15, 1970, with great success.

Senator Sherman recently polled his constitutents on the Southern Crossing. Twenty-five thousand responded to the poll, "the greatest response to a single-issue questionnaire in legislative history": 5,000 favored immediate construction; 10,500 wanted it stopped immediately; and 10,200 favored further study, deferring final decision until 1971.

Efforts were made in the 1970 session to stop the Southern Crossing outright. The "ban-the-span" bill, SB 331, authored by Senator Alfred E. Alquist (D-San Jose), was killed after spokesmen for the Toll Bridge Authority promised to make a complete reevaluation of the project and conduct hearings in the Bay Area.[33] Assembly Concurrent Resolution Number 26, by Assemblyman Robert W. Crown (D-Alameda), calling for restudy by the Authority, was

subsequently passed, but planning and right-of-way acquisition for the bridge continued.*

Road Selection

The Coyote Canyon County Road

Landowners and speculators who stand to reap a great increase in land value from publicly funded road projects
generally favor road construction regardless of need or
damage.

We have selected a county road as a case study, since
there are presently 70,821 miles of county roads in the
state.

The plan for a county road through Coyote Canyon
was originally adopted for the San Diego County Master
Plan in 1958, but the idea has been alive for at least twenty
years. It was originally proposed as part of a larger complex of roads running through the desert—most of which
have already been constructed. With a population of approximately 1,100 people, Borrego Springs is presently accessible via paved highway from five directions.

The Coyote Canyon road would run from Borrego
Springs through a "window" of private property within the
boundaries of the State Park, across miles of parklands
known as Coyote Canyon, to the county line, which is also
the boundary for the State Park. From there, Riverside
County would assume responsibility for construction of the
road to the town of Anza.

Coyote Canyon is a small but unique section of California's largest State Park. It contains the only spring-fed
stream in the Park that flows above ground all year long.
The area is thus alive with flora and fauna that are not to

* With the passage of AB 363, signed by the governor on September 15, 1969, the BATS Commission has now developed into a
nineteen-member Metropolitan Transportation Commission. The
Commission is directed to adopt a regional transportation plan by
June 30, 1973. In doing so, it is to consider the "regional, economic
and social impact of existing and future regional transportation systems upon various facets of the region, including, but not limited to,
housing, employment, recreation, environment, land-use policies and
the economically disadvantaged." [34] Once the plan is adopted, no
project can be initiated without the approval of the Commission.
Unfortunately, however, the Southern Crossing is exempt under a
specific provision,[35] and the California Highway Commission is
allowed to deviate from the plan where there is "an overriding
Statewide interest." [36]

be found in the rest of the desert. While the Canyon is presently inaccessible except by backpack or four-wheel drive vehicle, 15,000 to 20,000 people trek their way in each year to enjoy its natural beauty.

Coyote Canyon is also one of the last habitats of the bighorn sheep, a species that has been officially designated as "endangered." Only about 3,900 desert bighorn still inhabit the Golden State, and many linger in Sheep Canyon on the western slope of Coyote Canyon. Their water supply—Coyote Creek—is located on the eastern slope of the Canyon, and the proposed highway will cut them off from their only source of water in the summer. Proponents of the road generally agree that the sheep will not cross the paved road, but argue that underpasses can be built to accommodate them. However, these wild sheep are extremely timid, and flee at the sight of man; experts say that they can spot the wave of a hand at a mile and a half, and that they will never come near the road to use an underpass. Nor will they migrate to another water hole if isolated from Coyote Creek. Studies indicate that the bighorn generally live and die within twenty miles of their birthplaces. And one biologist noted that they need greater protection than other animals because they are not prolific: ewes bear only one lamb at a time and don't reproduce every year. A study by the State Fish and Game Department, "Report on the Status of Bighorn Sheep," recently recommended that the Department "take a firm stand against construction of a highway in the proposed [Coyote Canyon] location."

The most popular argument for the road is that it is necessary to transport agricultural produce to the markets in Los Angeles. Proponents argue that the road will cut travel from Borrego Springs to Hemet by thirty miles.

That argument has a number of drawbacks. First, while it may be true that the length of the road is thirty miles shorter than the present route, travel time will be reduced by only about fifteen minutes because the new county road is only two lanes wide and it will be constructed with substantially inferior alignment. Even discounting these drawbacks, no more than half an hour could be saved if the produce trucks travel the speed limit.

Second, the 1969 agricultural production figures for the area which the road would serve are: two bales of cotton, one green crop from a ten-acre field of alfalfa, yield from approximately 100 acres of citrus groves, and a negligible number of gladiolus bulbs. It seems that discussion of a road began in the early 1950s when Borrego Springs was a producer of grapes and vegetables. But today, virtually all of that land has been plowed under by "new development." The DiGiorgio family for example—once one of the largest grape producers in the state, and holders of thousands of acres in the Borrego area—has now divested itself of all agricultural interests and become a huge land-development corporation.

Proponents also argue that "the people" want the road. The shallowness of this argument became apparent during an interview with Assemblyman John Stull, the "representative" of the greater part of San Diego County, including Borrego Springs. Following the State Parks Commission decision *not* to grant an easement across the parkland for construction of the road, Stull introduced a bill asking the legislature to supersede the decision of the Commission.

The question of need was put to the Assemblyman four or five times during the interview (rephrased each time). Each question received an evasive or irrelevant answer. Stull appeared to be saying that "the people" of Borrego Springs wanted the road, and that that was sufficient need. When pressed for specific names of "the people," the Assemblyman answered that the Borrego Springs Chamber of Commerce had flown him over the proposed route of the road—once in a helicopter and again in a private plane— and that *he* had then made the decision that the road was necessary. Under further pressure, the Assemblyman offered the file of letters which he had received for and against his bill. A perusal of the list proved astounding. Stull had received letters and petitions from 867 voters opposed to his bill, and only 14 signatures in favor! Of the 867 opposed, 484 were voters within his own district; and of the 14 in favor, 10 were his own constituents.* When asked how he justified the introduction and continued support of a bill which was both a local issue and opposed by the majority of his constituents, Stull replied,

* A similar polling of the mail received by Assemblyman E. Richard Barnes, who also represents a San Diego district, showed 100% opposition to Stull's bill. A Sierra Club survey concluded that not one citizens' group in western San Diego County favored the road.

"To hell with the people. If they don't like what I'm doing, they can vote me out. I stand for election every two years."

Sub rosa support from the local Chamber of Commerce, the Southern California First National Bank (whose local branch manager wrote a letter of support to Stull), the Inter-Mountain Property Owners Association, and the big land developers suggests that Assemblyman Stull will probably not be defeated.

In an interview with Mr. H. M. Taylor, Assistant County Engineer, and Mr. R. J. Massman, it was pointed out that the State Division of Highways considered the road to be of extremely low priority. Mr. Massman admitted that the County Engineer's office also considered it low priority.

The engineers admitted that no ecological expertise had been included in their study (and ultimate route proposal) other than collaboration with the local park rangers. The Parks Commission, the Division of Parks and Recreation, and the Department of Fish and Wildlife opposed the project.

According to the county engineers, a total of thirteen private landowners had donated easements across their property for the construction of the road. At least one, Mr. Gilbert G. Mahlmeister, a licensed real estate agent in Inglewood, said that he has never been approached by anyone concerning an easement across his property but that if he were, he would not hesitate to grant it. Asked why an access road through the canyon might be needed, he could think of no other reason than to accommodate the interests of developers in the area. When questioned further as to whether one can justify the use of taxpayers' funds for the benefit of a few large developers, Mr. Mahlmeister replied, "I got you figured out. You're a socialist with all that environment and pollution stuff."

Also listed as having donated an easement for the road was the Coyote Creek Corporation, which has extensive land holdings in the area. A check of the certificate of incorporation showed the directors to be the present Federal District Judge for the Southern District, Howard B. Turrentine; the ex-secretary of his law practice, Mrs. Dorothy Kenney; and another legal secretary in San Diego, Geraldine F. Dickie. Judge Turrentine reluctantly confirmed in a telephone interview that he was the lawyer who incorporated the Coyote Creek Corporation, and that these names were filed as dummy directors at the time of incorporation. When asked who assumed the directorship when he resigned, he replied in a surprising fit of temper, "I don't know anything about it, and I don't give a goddamn." Judge Turrentine recently rendered an important decision favoring large landowners—refusing to apply 160-acre limits on federal water-project subsidies.

Other large holders of land who donated easements across their property include A. A. Burnand, who is reported to have been trying to develop his holdings in the desert for many years, and Title Insurance and Trust Company, apparently holding the land for some unknown individuals. (Insurance companies are prohibited by law from investing in unproductive land for speculation purposes— see Chapter 1.) The rest of the list of donators was unavailable for comment.

It is general knowledge that James A. Copley (publisher of a large newspaper syndicate), the DiGiorgio Corporation (an agricultural family turned real estate developers), and the Federated Mortgage Company own substantial holdings in the area which they plan to develop. In the Copley newspaper *Borrego Sun,* an editorial entitled "Coyote Canyon Road Vital to Future" stresses that "if Borrego Springs is to enjoy an *economically* healthy future," the road through the canyon is necessary (emphasis added). The editorial says nothing specific about the need for the road or about the costs of the road in terms of aesthetic or recreational losses.

The few who stand to benefit from the Coyote Canyon Road are wealthy and influential people who make major campaign contributions in San Diego County. County Supervisor Jack Walsh was reminded of this fact after his vote opposing the Board's endorsement of Stull's bill to supersede the Parks Commission. Walsh was told (anonymously) that a "war chest" was being accumulated for the cause of "good planning." He said, "I have been told that these monies will be used to back those interested in 'legitimate growth,' that people who have supported my campaigns in the past may have to oppose my reelection if I keep pressing." The *San Diego Magazine,* July, 1970, noted that Walsh "is . . . unpopular with San Diego County land-developers because of his proposals for acquiring open space, and advocacy of a slowdown in urban sprawl by requiring subdividers to pay the entire costs of

services in outlying areas, thus greatly increasing development expense on otherwise cheap hinterland property."

The Anza-Borrego county road through Coyote Canyon
is temporarily dormant because of the State Parks Commission refusal to grant access across the parkland, and the
legislature's refusal to set the precedent of superseding the
agency's judgment as Assemblyman Stull would have had
them do.

But the issue is far from dead. Ideas and proposals for
a road through the desert parkland have resurfaced many
times during the past twenty years, and this latest effort by
the local developers and the Chamber of Commerce has
been the strongest yet. A Borrego Springs developer,
George J. Kuhrts, of Golden Sands, wrote to the County
Director of Planning:

> By way of introduction, the writer and his family *along
> with DiGiorgio Corporation* of San Francisco own ex-
> tensive holdings in the Borrego Valley area. Also, we have
> constructed a shopping center, condominium complex and
> a deluxe mobile home park, all in the last few years, at an
> expenditure exceeding $3,000,000.
>
> The refusal of the Division of Beaches and Parks [*sic*]
> to grant a right-of-way to the County of San Diego for
> the road proposed through Coyote Canyon, opening up
> the State Park and Borrego to the flow of northern traffic,
> was a *stinging blow to our development plans* in Borrego
> Springs. *However, we have not given up all hope of this
> road being constructed at some point in the future* (em-
> phasis added).

As usual, the proposal for a highway is not based on
present traffic needs, but on the needs of a few men who
cannot make their speculative investments profitable until
the taxpayer provides them with this subsidy.

The Malibu-Whitnall Freeway

Malibu is a picturesque, deep canyon through which the
only remaining wild stream in the whole coastal area of Los
Angeles flows. Malibu Creek winds its way out of the steep
canyon and fills Malibu Lagoon, which has long been the
feeding and resting ground for a variety of waterfowl along
the Pacific Flyway. Its rich tidal pools provide food for the
waterfowl and contain many forms of marine life unique to
the southern California coast. The fresh water marsh adjoining the lagoon shelters a host of birds.

Both the State Department of Parks and Recreation and Los Angeles County have proposed that the lagoon be designated a waterfowl sanctuary. International and local conservation groups have pleaded with the various "planning" agencies and developers to preserve the precarious balance of nature in the canyon. However, Malibu Lagoon may soon be the site of a massive freeway interchange.

The proposed Malibu-Whitnall Freeway through the canyon is to be eight lanes wide. The right-of-way will be from 300 feet wide in some places to 700 feet in others. The freeway will consume an area of land as *wide* as the length of two football fields. For every mile of freeway, eighty acres will go under concrete. Construction easements will extend the swath cuts on the sides of the canyon to as much as a total of 1,000 feet. Overall land condemnations for right-of-way, swath cuts, and other construction easements will amount to as much as two miles on either side of the freeway.

The design requires cutting innumerable slopes, filling gullies, and leveling the canyon floor. Malibu Creek will be diverted to a man-made, cemented creekbed for almost half the length of the canyon.

For the moment a stalemate exists between the concerned citizens and the proponents of the freeway. The former have succeeded in deferring immediate, major development in the area, but the local developers are powerful, influential, and far from defeated.

The planning started with the master plan of proposed freeways approved by legislative mandate in 1959. Although even the Division of Highways does not foresee the "need" for the freeway for at least another fifteen years, route and design plans are all but complete today. At the public design hearing the DOH admitted that their premature planning was at the request of the land companies who wanted to know what was in store for the future of their speculations.

The Malibu-Whitnall Freeway proposal is only one segment of an area-wide freeway plan which also includes a segment from Oxnard to Winter Flats, one from Winter Flats to Malibu Canyon, and another from Malibu Canyon to Santa Monica, all three of which comprise one stretch with which the canyon route will intersect. Such segmental planning is indicative of the divisive tactic of the DOH. Freeway development does not confront all of the area's population at the same time, and the DOH is able to avoid the intricacies and expenditures of a study which considers the effect upon a *whole* area. Once the Malibu Canyon link of the freeway complex is completed, it will be too late for citizens in the adjoining areas to protest.

Despite opposition at the time of the route hearing, the Highway Commission approved the project and the DOH proceeded to design the freeway. In February, 1970, the Division held the required design hearings for both the freeway and the major interchange with Pacific Coast Highway. An overflow crowd of more than 500 people attended the hearings. The DOH justified the need for the freeway from population projection figures which assumed that the freeway was already constructed. They claimed that they did not know the amount of earth-moving involved though citizens later discovered that twenty-five million cubic yards would be moved. They denied they knew of a three-dimensional mockup of the freeway and instead displayed a map with a thin line grossly under the scale of the rest of the map. During the five and a half hours of hearings, not a single person or organization testified in favor of the freeway. The insensitivity of the DOH during this hearing encouraged the formation of the local Save Malibu Canyon Committee which then joined the Sierra Club, the Statewide Planning and Conservation League, and the Friends of the Santa Monica Mountain Park in one of the few truly widespread and relatively effective movements in opposition to DOH judgment.

There are numerous planning agencies which should be involved in the routing and design of such freeways. The Environmental Quality Study Council noted in their report on Malibu that the area's development was indicative of too much planning rather than too little; however, "excessive" planning has been both uncoordinated and limited in scope.

The DOH argues that the freeway is needed to get people from the eastern slopes of the Santa Monica Mountains over to the beaches. But only six of the twenty-six miles of shoreline in the area are public beaches, and that area is already overcrowded; parking areas are far too small to accommodate the existing sunbathers, and no attempt has been made to coordinate the plans for this new access with the various agencies entrusted with the management of the beaches.

Indeed, the EQSC Progress Report to the governor noted that "during the Malibu hearing, a dozen public officials were heard from. . . . It became evident that they shared no common concept of how Malibu should grow. Each agency pursues its own narrow objectives, as required by law, which, as we have seen, generally fail to consider environmental quality." These agencies are:

The State Division of Highways
The State Division of Beaches and Parks
The Los Angeles County Regional Planning Commission
The Los Angeles County Engineer
The Los Angeles County Road Department
The Los Angeles County Flood Control District
The Los Angeles County Waterworks District No. 29
The Los Angeles County Sanitation District
The Los Angeles County Department of Parks and Recreation
The Los Angeles County Department of Beaches
The Los Angeles County Department of Health
The Las Virgenes Municipal Water District

The effects of this lack of coordination will be disastrous. The excellent climate and the "infinite growth" philosophy in the greater Los Angeles area have resulted in temperature inversion layers sealing smog-filled air into the Los Angeles Basin. Malibu Canyon has been referred to as the vital "lung" of the polluted basin because it serves as an airshed for the whole region. Cool air currents off the Pacific Ocean flow through and around the canyon, feeding fresh air into the smog-ridden atmosphere to the north, east, and south. If the canyon becomes another source of auto pollution, it will deprive the surrounding area of the few breaths of clean air now available, and add to the heavy concentration of smog which air currents presently push to the eastern slopes of the basin.

The Los Angeles County Arboretum has determined that Malibu's lush vegetation serves to remove pollutants and to restore the oxygen content of the atmosphere. The onslaught of local automobiles will greatly reduce the scope of this activity.

Recently the Los Angeles county planning staff issued an "Environmental Guide" imploring the Commission to endorse a policy aimed at reversing growth in the Los Angeles Basin, and noting that "[A] long-standing accumulation of mistakes in environmental planning and development has led to serious negative consequences—blight, congestion, pollution, economic decline and explosive social unrest." As the EQSC concluded from its study of Malibu, "the continued existence of such unique areas as productive health, recreational, and agricultural resources is frightfully fragile." Whether the Regional Planning Commission will heed these warnings from the experts remains to be seen.

Mineral King Highway

Mineral King is a 15,000-acre oasis of land at the top of California's Sierra Nevada, surrounded on the north, west, and east by Sequoia National Park and on the south by Sequoia National Forest. Because the oasis forms a natural drainage basin that attracts wildlife from the surrounding parklands, it has been designated a national game refuge under the jurisdiction of the Department of Agriculture's Forest Service.

Walt Disney Productions has proposed to build a $35 million recreational area in the Mineral King Valley (see discussion in Chapter 4); and a state highway (276) has been proposed to connect Disney's recreation area to State Highway 198. The Forest Service has indicated that construction of the recreation area is contingent upon the building of a new access road into the valley.

Route 276 was added to the State Highway System by the 1965 legislature; and the 1966 legislature, via Senate Concurrent Resolution No. 19, urged the Highway Commission and the Division of Highways to undertake all steps necessary to construct the route. Acceptance by the legislature was without questions and no hearing was held on the Senate Resolution.

Approval by the National Park Service and the Department of the Interior was more difficult to obtain. Since the road cuts across nine miles of Sequoia National Park, it has to be approved by the Department of the Interior. But the Forest Service did not seek or obtain that approval before issuing its prospectus: the Service directed private developers bidding on the project to make arrangements for a new access road *before* it obtained the Interior Department's approval. The developers were thus expected to plan for a recreational complex with no assurances that the road to the area would be approved by the Department of the Interior, or that any construction would occur. They were then induced to lobby with the state legislature and the Department of the Interior for acceptance of a road into

Mineral King; they were successful—approval to cross the National Park was granted by then Secretary of the Interior Stewart L. Udall.

The Division of Highways estimated that the 20.4-mile-long, twenty-eight-foot-wide, two-lane highway would cost a total of $22 million for construction and $400,000 for right-of-way. In calculating this cost the Division tallied only the right-of-way expenditures for acquisition of private lands. The road, however, is located primarily within National Park Service, Forest Service, and Bureau of Land Management acreage. Even assuming that the public lands are equal in value to private lands (and in fact they are probably more valuable), the total right-of-way value would be $4 million.

Peripheral costs of the Mineral King Highway include annual snow removal expenses, slide cleanup expenditures, and funds for improvement of connecting roads. One source [37] estimates that the annual snow-removal costs will be $1 million and also points to the tendency of the geologic patterns in the Kaweah River area to "fold," causing slides which have blocked existing Route 198 during the annual "slide season." Costs of slide prevention and clearing must be added to the annual maintenance figures. Access to the start of the Mineral King Highway is over existing State Route 198, the improvement of which is not accounted for in the Mineral King estimate. Such factors as damage to giant sequoias, various forms of pollution, and hillside scarring should also be included in any cost analysis. Clearly, such an analysis would show a much higher projected cost than the Division figure of $22,400,000.

Use of the highway in winter may be especially hazardous. Snow-removal equipment will compete for space with both moving vehicles and autos stopped to attach chains. During the ski season there will be very heavy traffic at the beginning and end of each skiing day, with most traffic occurring with a few hours. Serious questions have been raised about the adequacy of the proposed two-lane road.[38]

Even if the Forest Service is able to control future expansion in the Mineral King Valley, the present Disney project may attract more customers than the highway can hold. The original Disney proposal estimated annual attendance at the resort to be 2.5 million visitors—60% of whom were to use the facilities in the summer. This estimate was later reduced to 1.7 million, and then to 980,000—from which

present traffic projections were drawn. The varying estimates were due in part to elimination of various types of
camping in the valley. However, they also have to do with
Walt Disney Productions' desire to estimate traffic conservatively in order to facilitate construction of a two-lane
highway which could later be expanded to four lanes. The
Forest Service, through Regional Forester J. W. Deinema,
indicated in a letter to the Superintendent of the Sequoia-
Kings Canyon National Park on July 24, 1968, that "We
cannot envision any need to have more than a well-desig-
nated, scenic, safe two-lane highway. . . ." [39] The Krueper
report has since cast doubts on the adequacy of the two-lane
highway, especially in winter months; any additional usage
may force the state to choose between expanding the highway through this wilderness area or allowing an unsafe road
to claim additional accident victims.

Walt Disney Productions alone stands to profit from this
road. In essence the state is building a $23 million driveway
for a private corporation. The $35 million recreational
complex will not attract enough visitors to be profitable
without a new road. But if Disney were to pay for the road
and charge its users a toll, it would so discourage use as
to again make the complex unprofitable. Only by using state
funds to build the road—forcing California taxpayers to
subsidize the private Disney Corporation for at least two-
fifths of its initial costs—can the Mineral King recreation
area be made profitable to Walt Disney Productions.

There is more than private enrichment involved in the
Disney road. Discrimination guarantees that benefits go to
Disney specifically. For example, owners of nearby land
have been told that their development opportunity will be
limited until construction of the two-lane road. In other
words, Disney, with a thirty-five year lease of Forest
Service land, is allowed to spend $35 million; but other
land owners owning their land in fee simple are prevented
from developing.

Perhaps the most unsettling aspect of the Mineral King
project is the behavior of a government supposedly accountable to the citizens and general taxpayer. Government
agencies understated the cost, refused to demand contribution from Disney or others, and have used the lower cost
of a two-lane highway to aid Disney in obtaining the four-
lane road that all anticipate. They have announced intentions to exclude from expansion others who have greater

legal and equitable title to the land. They have lobbied for the road in private and in public, even though the road explicitly violated federal standards.

Government

The critical agency of control over the Division of Highways and road policy on the state level is provided by the California Highway Commission (CHC). The Commission has been granted substantial responsibilities and powers by the legislature. In fact, because highway location can be such a politically charged issue, the legislature retained only the power to determine the terminuses of highways. It gave the CHC primary responsibility for route selection and allocation of funds for construction. To achieve a degree of impartiality, the legislature provided that the Commissioners not be selected to represent any particular section of the state, but rather the state as a whole. The intent was to create a public-interest input to freeway construction.

The Commission consists of seven laymen appointed by the governor to serve staggered terms of four years each. The private business and special interests of the members of the Commission preclude a representation of broader community interests.

The chairman of the Commission, Fred C. Jennings, is the president of a real estate development corporation (Sun Gold, Incorporated). As our case studies indicated, the real estate and development interests tend to support the construction of freeways, since a highway increases the value of land and is a prerequisite for a large residential development. From 1946 until 1958, Mr. Jennings operated an automobile agency. He is presently a member of the advisory board of the Automobile Club of Southern California, and is the past president of the Riverside Chamber of Commerce.

The "Highway Complex" is clearly well represented in the Commission. Four of the seven members are active in the Chamber of Commerce; two are affiliated with automobile and transportation organizations; and the occupational propensities of the seven members include trucking warehouses, trucking firms, produce warehouses, real estate development, auto dealerships, county road construction, and general contractors.

Conservation and environmental groups are virtually

ignored, as are urbanologists, county and municipal governments and representatives of other modes of transportation.

In addition to supplying the Division's membership, the "Highway Complex" lobbies extensively to and through the Division. The lobbyists include such moneyed industries as the petroleum industry, auto makers and dealers, the trucking industry, the auto clubs (especially the AAA), heavy-equipment manufacturers, concrete producers, rock and aggregate producers, contractors, and the lumber industry.

One example of the wealth of these interests is the freeway-promotion campaign sponsored by the State Chamber of Commerce. The Chamber of Commerce entered into a $15 million contract with Spencer-Roberts public-relations firm to "promote freeways." A front organization called "Citizens for Freeways and Highways" was created, and enormous sums were invested in colorful brochures, booklets, and propaganda sheets. The Chamber of Commerce has obtained the aid of the DOH itself, and the brightly colored, glossy booklets can be found in the information racks of Regional Offices and on display in the Information Office of the DOH in Sacramento.

We also found in the DOH Information Office a booklet published by a group called "California Highway Users Conference." Its officers, board of directors, and participating organizations are simply a list of the industries comprising the "Highway Complex," plus produce growers, dealers, brokers, auto insurance companies, auto and truck rental companies, auto tire manufacturers, etc.

The way in which freeways are financed also facilitates irrational construction, and is a second bond between the "Highway Complex" and public government. The DOH does not depend upon yearly appropriations by the legislature from the General Fund. It is assured of almost $1 billion a year primarily from state user taxes, motor vehicle fees, and federal aid, and another $500 million spent by cities and counties on roads and highways. Constitutional provisions and federal statutes require that this money be spent for highway purposes only. Hence, legislative control of the purse strings is totally absent.

The DOH is probably the single most powerful administrative agency in California government. Its power is derived from a combination of financial and statutory autonomy, comprehensive statutory mandate, a highly esoteric and competent professional staff, ineffective hearing and appeal procedures, a co-opted citizen input and control commission, and wealthy, well-organized private lobbying forces. It is subject to no outside control by the legislature, other affected agencies, the localities concerned, or the general public.

In 1959, the legislature designated about two-thirds of the State Highway System (over 10,000 miles of roadway) as part of the California Freeway and Expressway System. This system is subject to review by the legislature every four years, but so far the proliferation of freeways has not been controlled, nor is the Master Plan responsive to changing transportation needs.

In theory, a comprehensive program makes sense. It eliminates ad hoc freeway construction not coordinated with other lines, limits the amount of political influence in highway planning, and provides for more efficient expenditures of funds. But the way transportation master planning is conducted by the DOH negates all its advantages while providing for insulation from legislative scrutiny.

The Master Plan is not coordinated with development of other modes of transportation. And because the DOH is operating under the mandate of the Master Plan, it has been able to wash its hands of responsibility for serious blunders in the plan (e.g., freeways through the redwood forest or wildlife areas such as Malibu Canyon). It proceeds with its bulldozing with the rationale that "we are only carrying out the mandate of the legislature."

There is no long-range planning of land uses or environmental and social impacts. Such consideration must be introduced through special corrective legislation, which is much more difficult to pass than preventive or cautionary legislation. Any legislator asked by his constituency to get a local freeway deleted from the Master Plan must take a stand against an entrenched, autonomous, and powerful bureaucracy, and against the wealthiest lobby groups (and campaign contributors) in the state. He must also mobilize majority legislative support for what many other legislators will view as merely a local issue, support for which could jeopardize their own campaign funds.

The most avid supporter of DOH interests in the legislature is Senator Randolph Collier; the Highway Complex lobbyists are often referred to informally as "Randy's Rats."

During the late 1930s, when much of California had only dirt roads, Collier spearheaded the movement for a modern, efficient road system for the state. Over the years, however, the Senator became committed to freeways qua freeways. His contributors, contacts, and friends come from the Highway Complex and dominate his attention. Tunnels and DOH roadside parks have been named after him and he has long been lionized at conventions. As Transportation Committee chairman, he squelched bills with a tart "I don't like that idea" and a whack of his gavel. A former consultant told us that he is still willing to testify enthusiastically for projects "that even the industry's most avid lobbyists would refuse to push aggressively out of shame."

The procedures for adoption of a freeway location are contained in the California Administrative Code. Prior to any route-location studies, the DOH is directed to confer with local officials to determine "the most logical limits to be studied for route selection." At the initiation of the studies, written notice must be sent to the local governments, public agencies, and legislators connected with the districts affected. Upon commencement of the studies, the DOH is directed to confer "from time to time" with the local government bodies and public agencies. And when the study has progressed sufficiently to "permit intelligent discussion," the DOH must hold as many public meetings

> as may be reasonably necessary to acquaint interested individuals, officials and civic or other groups with the studies being made and the information developed, and to obtain their views with respect thereto.

The Code further provides that all such hearings are to be conducted in an informal manner with the objective that all interested persons be heard "as time will permit."

At this point in the freeway-proposal process, the DOH generally proposes several alternate routes, and thus divides the local opposition against itself. The public hearing appears to be a democratic process, but the specific routing and designs are so vague that the opposition is too confused and divided to mount an effective citizens' challenge.

The transcript of these hearings, the route location studies, and any other reports covering meetings and conferences with local officials are then filtered up the bureaucracy to the California Highway Commission. The

Commission notifies the local governments of its intention to consider the location of the freeway, whereupon the "local legislative body" can within thirty days of its next regular meeting request the Commission itself to hold another hearing on route adoption. If no such hearing is requested, the Commission proceeds to its conclusion— which is invariably to approve the DOH route proposal.

Once the location and design stages have been completed and routinely approved by the Highway Commission, the Right of Way Department of DOH commences condemnation and acquisition proceedings. Whereas the federal constitution and the laws of the state generally require elaborate administrative procedures to protect individual property against confiscation, the rubric of "public use" with reference to freeways excuses a considerably relaxed procedure and provides a rationale for the acquisition of property. The ony constitutional limits of the powers of eminent domain are requirements that the taking be for a "public use," and that the private owner receive "just compensation." The California Code of Civil Procedure (Section 1241) further requires: (1) that the proposed public improvement be a necessary one; (2) that the property acquired be necessary for the improvement; and (3) that the project be located in a manner most compatible with the greatest public benefit and the least private injury.

In practice, however, the DOH and the Legal Division of the DPW have extraordinary powers of eminent domain and are virtually immune to local challenge (see the full Report). Only when an occasional conservation group is mobilized or where there is need for approval from another powerful government agency at the state or federal level might the Division's mandate be questioned.

And when a local attorney faces the highly specialized DPW attorneys in court, he possesses neither the time, resources, nor experience to make the adversary hearing fair and meaningful. DPW lawyers point out that only 2.5% of their condemnation cases ever go to trial. Statutes and court opinions have granted conclusive presumptions in favor of the DOH on such issues as "necessity," and have shifted the burden of persuasion to the individual citizen suing on the issue of "public use." With courts, statutes, and legal staff bearing so heavily against the private property owner, his attorney is usually limited to utilizing what legal skills he can bring to bear to negotiate the best compensation possible. Even in the negotiation stage the DOH has statutory powers which operate coercively to prevent private challenge.

The most effective input to the allocation of funds comes from various regional committees of the State Chamber of Commerce. These regional committees submit requests to the State Chamber of Commerce, which organizes and compiles them and submits a proposal to its members on the Commission. The request includes a "suggested" allocation of funds and an overall request for specific amounts to be allocated to new highway construction. The sole engineering expertise provided the allegedly citizen-oriented California Highway Commission is from the DOH itself, and the financial expertise comes from the DOH and the State Chamber of Commerce.

Internal checks on the Division itself on behalf of other interests are precluded via the natural attrition of those who question policy, the momentum of the Master Plan and independent financing, and from the three pressures described above: the auto-highway complex, financial (tax) structures, and local speculators.

But the DOH is also endowed with a highly esoteric and professional staff of engineers. The whole Division is administered by the State Highway Engineer with a headquarters staff of engineer-technocrats; eleven district engineers administer the highway districts into which the state is divided. They are immune to criticism or effective control. Most laymen are too willing to concede that freeway placement and design is the exclusive domain of civil and structural engineering.

But in the face of congestion, smog, and increasing doubt that engineers possess all of the expertise necessary, the DOH has acted to ameliorate possible criticism. The DOH now requires every regional office have at least one environmental expert. In virtually every regional office the response has been to change the designation of one of their resident engineers to the title of "environmental planner."

11

Transportation: The Palmdale Airport

Air travel is popular and convenient in California. A traveler in the Golden State can fly from San Francisco to Los Angeles or from San Diego to San Francisco for less than it costs to fly between any other equidistant points in the country.

The number and location of airports affect land use in several ways: subsidization of airports vis-a-vis competing modes, national (CAB-FAA) regulation, and intrastate transportation regulation (the California Public Utilities Commission) significantly affect consumer behavior, traffic flow, and development pressures; air travel reduces demand on the highway for the traveler going over 100 miles; airports stimulate new development.

Development surrounding airports is generally regarded as more efficient and cohesive than the sprawling strip development encouraged by a single road. But the areas adjacent to an airport are often noisy, congested, and polluted, and most new airports now under construction must be built some distance from the centers they serve because of land-acquisition problems, displacement of development, noise, etc.; and the roads leading from these airports to population centers encourage strip development. Airport location must therefore be coordinated with road and rail transport and with land-use planning schemes.

On August 21, 1968, the Los Angeles Department of Airports announced that Palmdale had been chosen as the site of an enormous new intercontinental airport to serve the Los Angeles Basin. About seventy road-miles from the existing Los Angeles International Airport, at the high desert altitude of 2,500 feet and immediately northeast of the Palmdale urban area, the new facility would be built contiguous to an existing military airfield, Air Force Plant 42. Construction of the jetport was expected to start in 1971 and be completed in 1977, with total costs running to $900 million. The Palmdale facility would be designed to handle the coming generation of jet aircraft—jumbo jets and the SST—and, in the words of a Department of Airports official, would be "a center which will serve up to and including the Third Millenium."

The scale of the Palmdale project is immense. The site, covering some 17,000 acres, or twenty-seven square miles, is almost six times as large as Los Angeles International Airport (LAX). When Plant 42 is included in the calculation, the total area amounts to some 23,000 acres. According to airport planners, the facility is "intended to achieve a capacity of one hundred million passengers a year with an indicated capacity of 200 operations per hour," or a million flight operations annually. In terms of passengers moved, the Palmdale airport would exceed present levels at LAX by a factor of four to five. In the judgment of Welton Becket and Associates, a private firm which may be hired to do planning at the Palmdale site, a facility of this size "not only creates massive ground traffic volumes, but is also a major employment center. It will generate a residual population equal in size to a major city." Population-growth projections have run as high as two to three million for the Palmdale-Lancaster area, compared to the present population of 60,000.*

Plans for the gigantic intercontinental jetport began sometime in the early 1960s. A handful of officials within the Los Angeles Department of Airports made the site selection and developed virtually all of the plans for the airport without the knowledge of the Southern California Area Governments (SCAG), which was conducting a $700,000 long-range study of transportation in southern California. There is no mention of such a facility in the County Master Plan for 1961.

In 1966, the California legislature passed a joint resolution encouraging cooperative civilian-military use of the

---

* There are 120,000 in the entire 2,500-square-mile Antelope Valley.

experimental Air Force facility, Plant 42, in Palmdale. In March, 1967, the Los Angeles Department of Airports resolved to join with Palmdale in the commercial development of a small airport in that town. And in December, 1967, the Army Corps of Engineers agreed to lease fifty-four acres of government-owned land to Palmdale for the development of a municipal airport. The plan as presented to the legislature and as understood by the public was for a municipal terminal which would be another satellite airport to serve the northern part of the county, thereby relieving some of the pressure on LAX.

On August 21, 1968, an official map for the airport was submitted to the Airport Commission for approval. This was the first public record on the matter. It was also disclosed at this time that two local planners had recently made highly suspect land purchases in the Palmdale area, and stood to gain as much as 500% profits as a result of the airport.

Seven months later, the State Department of Aeronautics held hearings prior to giving their approval of the site and the plans. By this time, substantial opposition to the airport had developed around the issues of noise pollution and absence of environmental planning. The State Department of Aeronautics refused to consider such matters, claiming that its statutory obligation was to consider safety factors only. The agency approved the airport in August of 1969 and recommended that the governor also approve it.

In November, 1969, the Noise Abatement Committee of the governor's Environmental Quality Study Council convened hearings in Palmdale. The result was a recommendation to the governor that the construction of the airport be delayed until a comprehensive study of the environmental impact could be conducted. A few months later, a number of affidavits were presented to the governor by Assistant Attorney General Nicholas Yost. They contained expert testimony warning of such diverse problems as water shortages, dangers to air safety due to desert conditions and mountain obstructions to radar, and severe noise pollution. Yost also informed the governor that as of November, 1969, the State Department of Aeronautics possessed the statutory power to consider the environmental impact of proposed airports. Despite the powers of the state agency and the pleas of his own environmental experts, Reagan approved the airport site.

Once the state had approved the site and plan for the airport, federal agencies rubber-stamped it. None of these agencies, including the Department of Transportation, conducted the investigation required by the National Environmental Policy Act of 1969.* Instead, they knowingly issued false reports.

The Los Angeles Department of Airports

In March, 1970, when public pressure was mounting against the Palmdale project, Bert Lockwood, assistant general manager of the Department of Airports, wrote to an FAA official that the Palmdale airport is "mandatory to meet the traffic demands" of the state's air transportation system. This assessment was official. The letter, said Lockwood, was to be made part of the Department's Site Report, which would form the basis for federal scrutiny. The major premise of the airport promoters' argument was that one could not afford to be overscrupulous about unfortunate side effects on people and the environment.

This critical assumption about the overriding need for a one hundred million passenger airport was never challenged by the many officials who sat to approve or disapprove the Palmdale project. Many times, in documents and testimony, Department authorities claimed that "studies" had shown the total air-passenger demand in the Los Angeles area would exceed 200 million per year in the 1980s, and that all existing airports—including LAX—have a total capacity of 100 million. The Los Angeles area, with a population of around eight million, currently generates about twenty-five million passengers a year. LAX itself now serves some 87% of the air carrier passenger demand. The Department's staggering assumption is that in a decade or two, when LAX will be operating at its capacity of forty million, the demand will be eight or ten times as great as today, and a new 100 million passenger airport, four times the size of the present LAX, will be "mandatory." The studies referred to were never presented for critical review. It is true that

* The NEPA requires federal agencies to compile environmental-impact reports concerning the policies and decisions. The report must include a consideration of alternatives in relation to environmental damage.

passenger movements at LAX have increased dramatically
in the last fifteen years. In 1956, there were four million
passengers at LAX, and the Department foresaw only thirteen million passengers in 1970; by 1968, there were over
twenty million. And LAX, like other major jetports, is
congested, though the congestion is greater on the freeways
getting to the airport than on the runways or in the air.
But the airport managers do not pretend that the Palmdale
facility would reduce present levels of congestion or noise
at LAX. "It is apparent," an Interior Department investigator has concluded, that "operations will continue to
increase at L.A. International," and that "noise will not be
reduced because of the Palmdale airport."

The Department was well aware that the Southern California Association of Government was conducting an extensive study of the regional air transport system. The
SCAG study forecasts of air-traffic demands do not justify
the Department's "200 million passengers" argument. At
LAX today, less than one in ten flight operations is intercontinental. LAX is third in the world in terms of passenger volume, but ranks twenty-third as an international
airport. More than half of the total number of flights
are between locations 500 miles apart or less. How this
kind of traffic is served in the next two or three decades
depends on the prospects for high-speed, city-center-to-
city-center ground transport links. "Traffic demands" of
this nature do not necessarily justify an enormous investment in airport facilities, but questions as to the need for
air service over other modes of transportation were never
asked as the Palmdale project rolled through officialdom;
nor was there ever discussion of a more subtle and modest
plan of expanding some airports, dispersing the short-haul
traffic, and building new satellite airports if necessary. The
Department of Airports played its part as a single-purpose
agency, representing the "traffic demands" of a relatively
affluent minority of the traveling public, unconcerned about
whether its plans make sense in terms of broader urban or
interurban transportation needs, and doggedly promoting
narrow aviation interests at the expense of other claims to
public resources.

The Department is formally an operating agency of the
Los Angeles city government. However, the City Council
has only limited authority over the Board of Airport Commissioners, the Department's governors; functionally, the

Department is autonomous. A Los Angeles City Councilman who is concerned with city and regional planning reported that the City Planning Department and the City Council itself simply "can't find out" what sort of environmental planning the Department of Airports has done in connection with its Palmdale project.

The Department has consistently claimed that Palmdale is the only "technically feasible location" for a major new jetport. The technical case for the Palmdale project is complicated and difficult for the layman to assess. It turns on matters of airspace availability for a 100 million passenger facility and aircraft performance and flight safety under particular meteorological and terrain conditions; and it involves comparison of the Palmdale site with other possible locations. The Department has used its technical case and its own claim to special expertise to justify the paucity of environmental planning or consultation with planning agencies in the site-selection process. In the Department's view, as Mr. Lockwood says, "There's only one group around this town with the expertise of planning an airport."

The Department's claim to have considered all reasonable alternative locations and possibilities, and to have found everywhere drawbacks that were lacking at Palmdale, is patently false, according to the Department of the Interior:

> As to consideration given to environmental factors and alternate sites, we agree that there is little or no evidence that these factors were given early consideration. On the contrary, the Los Angeles Department of Airports testified at State Department of Aeronautics hearings . . . that no study (in the sense of a systematically compiled catalogue) of alternative sites is available.

When asked about the particular environmental studies undertaken by the Department prior to August 1968, Bert Lockwood acknowledged that there's "not a hell of a lot to look at." When queried about the Department's pre-announcement analysis of ground access problems, availability of water to support the airport, effects of the airport on desert ecology, land-use planning around the airport, and problems of rapid urbanization, Lockwood's response was a reference to the Site Report filed with the FAA in 1969: "It's all there." But the Report was filed almost a year *after* the project was announced, and does not represent so much the "planning" that went into selection of the Palmdale site as a post hoc attempt to justify the project. The fact is that the Department has nothing to show because virtually nothing was done prior to August, 1968, about environmental problems—by the Department's staff, or independent consultants, or anyone else. Lockwood's own ecological study was simplicity itself. As he told us, he got in an airplane, flew over the proposed site, and looked down. He saw "not a damn thing out there."

The Department claims that the Antelope Valley (and Palmdale in particular) is the "only area in Southern California where the volume of flight operations required for a new major jetport can readily be obtained," and that it is the only location in which so much airspace is available that the traffic of other airports will not be hampered. Even Air Force Plant 42, the large flight-test center immediately adjacent to the Palmdale site, will be able to continue "completely independent operation."

These optimistic assertions are completely unrealistic. The one independent airspace study commissioned by the Department, from the consulting firm of Peat, Marwick, Livingston and Company, was completed in June of 1969, almost a year *after* the Department had chosen the Palmdale site. The Peat, Marwick study noted that airspace availability at Palmdale is limited by mountainous terrain reaching elevations in excess of 5,000 feet within ten miles of Palmdale to the south and west, and that the eastern approaches to Palmdale are severely cramped because of two airspace areas reserved for military use. The two "create a throat through which passes a large portion of the traffic into the Los Angeles Basin." Given the restrictions, a Palmdale airport with arrivals and easterly departures coming through the twenty-mile throat could not operate at the capacity the Department seeks. An FAA memo of October 1, 1969, *never made public,* states that arrival routes to Palmdale would "adversely affect" operations at other airports, constituting "a potential hazard"; that "operation of Plant 42 would become impossible" when Palmdale traffic reached any appreciable level; and that the proximity of military-controlled airspace alone ought to condemn the Palmdale project because "the level of activity anticipated . . . demands that air traffic control must not be restricted to any significant extent."

Airspace problems at Palmdale are not absolutely insuperable. Airspace patterns are made by man and can be altered, and some joint use of military airspace in connection with the Palmdale project remains possible. The point is that the Department's "technical case" for the Palmdale site was not above question. The Department was well aware of these problems, but never admitted to them. The result was that public officials and citizen groups concerned about the Palmdale project were confronted with a deceptive unanimity on the part of airport-planning experts.

And there are serious doubts from other sources about likely aircraft performance at the Palmdale site. Palmdale sits in the Mojave Desert at an elevation of some 2,500 feet, north of the San Gabriel mountains which define the Los Angeles Basin. High altitudes and temperatures mean reduction of jet aircraft thrust; given less thrust, aircraft must have less total weight aboard in order to meet minimum climb gradients at takeoff ("second segment climb"). For example, the Boeing 707-300B would suffer a "weight penalty" at Palmdale when temperatures rose above 43° F., while the same jet at LAX would not suffer a penalty until temperatures rose above 89° F.—and temperatures in the desert at Palmdale are considerably higher than by the ocean at LAX. The Department's own Peat, Marwick study considered the problems of aircraft performance at the high temperatures and altitude of Palmdale, concluding that long-range international flights, and all-cargo flights which need to operate at or near maximum structural weight, will be "affected substantially": many intercontinental flights and some flights to Hawaii or across the continent simply wouldn't be able to take off at Palmdale during the day in the summer.

The suppressed FAA memo of October 1, 1969, reported that "heavily loaded long-range flights . . . will require excessive climb rate restrictions (which they may be unable to make on hot days) or excessive off-course routing to take advantage of lower terrain." The memo noted that the high terrain ignored by Peat, Marwick "will adversely affect the control of air traffic," and concluded that the resulting situation "cannot well be tolerated by Air Traffic Control at a very high-level airport." Though neither the Department nor the FAA revealed its pessimistic analysis to the public, to planning agencies, or to elected representatives, the problems were brought out at public hearings. The Professional Air Traffic Controllers organization went on record as opposed to the "killer port." After canvassing safety and air traffic handling problems arising from crowded airspace, nearby mountains, and summertime takeoff conditions, an Airline Pilots Association representative commented that "planning for . . . one of the greatest concentrations of air service in the world . . . should not be based on real estate promotions."

The Department at first justified its failure to consult with other concerned agencies during site selection on the grounds that an open decision-making process would have caused land prices at the Palmdale site to rise prohibitively. Low land-acquisition costs were indeed consistently cited as a reason in favor of the Palmdale site. Pre-August 1968 planning was done "very, very quietly," says Lockwood, "and it had to be, because of your land prices. Not even the secretaries knew."

The claim that secrecy was imperative because of rising land prices was little more than a bureaucratic dodge to turn aside valid criticism of the Department's planning failures. The main reason for secrecy was the Department's wish to preserve its own power unchecked by agencies with less constricted views of the public interest.

The prospect of a major jetport at Palmdale was well known in land-speculating circles long before planning and operating agencies were informed about it. As early as 1964, the county supervisor whose district includes Palmdale was calling for a new major airport in the Antelope Valley. In January, 1967, the *Ledger-Gazette,* one of two Palmdale area newspapers, reported a speech by the chief of Air Force Plant 42 before the Antelope Valley Board of Trade, under the headline, "International Airport at Palmdale Seen as Possibility in 4 or 5 Years." In June, 1968, the *Los Angeles Times* real estate editor wrote that land prices in the Palmdale area "were moving about $200 an acre in 1960 and are 'moving well' at $11,000 an acre today. . . ." "Valleyites," he said, "are fully aware of the possibility" that the Palmdale airport might be expanded to become the western intercontinental air center. And no wonder. On January 20, 1968, Francis Fox, then general manager of the Department of Airports, told the Palmdale Chamber of Commerce: "I will make a prediction to you

that the intercontinental center of western air travel . . .
is going to be in your Palmdale area." Fox regaled his
audience with stories of speculative profit on land sales
around LAX, and assured his listeners that "you are going
to have the most amazing population explosion related to
air transportation . . . that I think has ever been seen in
California."

Thus, it is strange to hear the president of the Los
Angeles City Planning Commission, John J. Pollon, chime
in with Department of Airports spokesmen and declare the
Palmdale project to be "one of the best-kept secrets of all
time." Just prior to the formal announcement of the Palmdale project in August, 1968, Pollon, along with Calvin S.
Hamilton, Los Angeles City Planning Director, purchased
acreage that turned out to be within the 17,000-acre Palmdale site. When the deal was uncovered, the two city-plan-
ning officials insisted that they had known nothing of the
Department of Airports' plans, and had made the purchases solely because of other economic developments in
the area (joint use of Plant 42 and the decision to locate a
Lockheed plant). The Planning Commission of the Los
Angeles City Council called for the two men to resign,
finding that they had had an opportunity to know that
imminent action of a city department would affect the
value of their holdings. The full City Council by a lopsided
vote decided *not* to press the point. One of the majority
did comment somewhat foggily in regard to Pollon that "I
just can't understand why he would want to be on the Planning Commission when he invests so heavily in real estate,"
but the majority had little doubt that the Pollon-Hamilton
cause was just. The investigation was called a "lynching,"
"witch hunt," "kangaroo court," "star chamber." According to one councilman, the two planning officials were "just
using common horse sense that the city was going to grow.
It's too bad they didn't let me know about this. I would've
bought some land, too." Both men remain in office.

After the formal public announcement on August 21,
1968, land prices at the site went right on rising. Between
the summer of 1968, when Hamilton and Pollon purchased
their bonanza, and December, 1969, when the *Times* uncovered the transaction, the value of the planners' acreage
had increased by 500%. The Department of Airports' stock
argument—that low land-acquisition costs made Palmdale
a preferred site—had been knocked into a cocked hat.

State and Federal Review

The California State Department of Aeronautics is responsible for bringing state policy to bear on the process of
airport-site selection. In the case of the Palmdale project,
the state agency construed its mandate narrowly indeed.
On certain technical aviation matters, it deferred to the
FAA; on others, it tiptoed in silence past the extravagant
claims of the Los Angeles Department of Airports. The
highest state aviation authority never questioned the "need"
for the Palmdale facility nor its relation to the state transportation system as a whole.

The Department of Aeronautics held public hearings in
March and April, 1969, to give critics a chance to state
their case on the problem of noise; but no attempt was
made to ensure that the project's environmental impacts
were considered or evaluated. On the contrary, according
to the Interior Department investigator, counsel for the
Department of Aeronautics was "more interested in preventing testimony pertaining to environmental conditions
than . . . in admitting it for the enlightenment of the
Department."

Shortly after the Department of Aeronautics approved
the Palmdale site, Joseph R. Crotti, California Director of
Aeronautics, stated the Department's goals in an address
before the Supporters of the Palmdale Intercontinental Airport: "Encouraging the development of . . . air transportation" and the "flow of private capital," and "establishing regulations in order that persons may engage in
every phase of aeronautics with the least possible restriction." The Department of Aeronautics did not question
the "need" for the Palmdale project because, as Crotti
claimed, economic life in California "is geared to air travel."

The FAA was well aware of the technical problems
afflicting the Palmdale project—problems of airspace availability, performance of aircraft at high altitude and temperatures, air-traffic control, and flight safety. Its staff explored
these matters independently, and they were aired by representatives of the military, Airline Pilots Association, and
Professional Air Traffic Controllers at the FAA's public
hearing. FAA files and memoranda express grave doubts
about the Palmdale site, suggest that the site should *not*

be approved, and offer an alternate and "significantly better site" two miles to the north. An FAA document dated October 27, 1969, concludes: "[In light of] the tremendous investment involved" and the availability of a "more suitable area," the Palmdale site is inadequate.

But the file documents were never released to the public, and in the end the FAA decided to approve the Palmdale site. The agency's official statement of approval, issued July 1, 1970, glosses over the airspace snarls which had earlier prompted its experts to urge that the Palmdale site be rejected, and remarks that reduced aircraft performance at Palmdale is "a matter for airline management to consider in deciding whether to operate from this airport." With regard to problems of air-traffic handling and safety, the official statement asserts that "our study . . . found no evidence to substantiate" PATCO's view—an assertion flatly contradicted by FAA file documents themselves.

Why had the FAA capitulated? The FAA's official statement of approval is a thinly veiled digest of the Department of Airports' arguments, themselves unaltered since the project's kickoff announcement in August, 1968. It is possible that the FAA was reluctant to reject a site which by early 1970 had been finally approved by the California State Department of Aeronautics. Many observers felt at the time that state approval made a federal green light virtually certain. This would be ironic indeed, for Department of Aeronautics approval was expressly made conditional on the FAA's assessment of technical aviation questions.

Noise

Airport noise is an environmental problem which even aviation-oriented agencies with the narrowest concerns cannot ignore. The noise problem at Palmdale is apparent to the most casual observer, since the site is in the center of the Antelope Valley's largest and densest population center.

Testimony at FAA and Department of Aeronautics public hearings emphasized that the need for greater thrust owing to high temperatures and elevation at Palmdale will increase noise at takeoff; noise attenuation will be less in clear, dry desert air than at sea level in moist air; the acoustically "hard" mountain backdrop at Palmdale provides an excellent reflector for an echo-chamber effect; noise abatement flight procedures may be useless owing to airspace snarls around the Palmdale site. In response to such criticism of its noise contours, the Department of Airports has claimed that Palmdale-area residents are uniquely accustomed to airport noise, because they have lived with Plant 42. This argument verges on the absurd. Plant 42 and the massive new jetport are not equivalent noise sources, but noise complaints and lawsuits are often directed at Plant 42 flight activity.

The Department has argued that the noise impact at Palmdale will be minimized by the existence of a "buffer" around the site zoned for nonresidential uses. During the public hearings, critics of the Palmdale project submitted noise contours which flatly contradict both the noise-containment and the buffer-zone claims. Alexander Cohen, Chief of the National Noise Study, HEW, estimated that half the city of Palmdale will fall in a noise exposure area where individual complaints are virtually inevitable and in which no schools, theaters, offices, residences, or churches should be situated without extensive sound control. A careful study by Paul H. Veneklasen and Associates, consulting acousticians, concluded that "the acoustical facts alone show that there will be a major deterioration of the noise environment which will threaten the livability of the area." The Department of Airports had claimed that "objectionable noise"—i.e., levels of ninety PndB (perceived decibels) or above—would be contained within the airport boundaries. (At ninety-five PndB, one must get six inches from a listener's ear and shout to be heard.) Dr. Veneklasen testified at the state hearing that the entire city would be blanketed by outside noise of ninety PndB and up, given an airport at Palmdale of the magnitude envisioned. He argued that it was "completely unrealistic" to plan an airport today in the hope of significant aircraft noise reduction sometime in the future.

But the FAA refused to act in the public interest. FAA files contain an astounding confidential document labeled a "Briefing Sheet" and dated March 24, 1969. The Sheet states that Senator Cranston had inquired about the noise problem at Palmdale, and that the FAA's reply may be introduced in evidence at the coming State Department of Aeronautics Hearing by the Senator or a constituent. Thus the answer is "very critical." The Sheet says there are three "answer choices" for the FAA:

1. We can be noncommittal on the basis that we have received no formal . . . airspace application. . . . [handwritten in margin: "Yes we have"] 2. We can agree that the noise impact could be serious. Six of the seven schools parallel the departure course . . . the departing aircraft will be abeam the nearest school at 800 feet. . . . 3. We can clarify FAA's legal limitations in controlling the ground environment . . . we have elected the third choice.

The Sheet goes on: "At present, it appears that the State is passing the buck to the FAA; and the DOA definitely succeeded in planting the impression . . . that FAA's airspace determination would encompass the noise issue." The Sheet concluded: "[The FAA area office is] insistent that noise problems will not influence the final FAA determination."

FAA airspace approval was announced in a letter of July 1, 1970. The announcement adopts the Department of Airports' noise arguments as the findings of the FAA, noting that noise is "a matter of vital concern to the FAA."

Environment

Although all three agencies directly involved in the site selection and review process—the Los Angeles Department of Airports, the State Department of Aeronautics, and the FAA—have all claimed, in response to public criticism, that important environmental impacts of the proposed Palmdale facility were given full and serious consideration, no serious study of the various environmental issues has been conducted.

The Department's own gestures in the direction of "environmental planning" are contained in its Site Report, filed with the FAA. The Department failed to present any serious analysis of ground access, water, and other utilities, failed to commission any study by independent consultants before they had announced their site, and failed even to check with the relevant state and local agencies to hear their views. There is nothing whatever in the Report concerning the problem of jet pollution, or pollution to be created by the airport metropolis of the future.

Two examples of the Department's planning failure are worthy of particular notice. Department documents claim that a major consideration in site selection was whether the area chosen could support a facility of the size envisioned. Two central questions, then, are whether there is adequate ground transportation to the site from the area served, and whether necessary utilities such as water are available to support the facility and the resulting urbanization around the site.

A glance at a map shows the ground access problem to be substantial. As the crow flies, the Palmdale site is forty-three miles northwest of Los Angeles city center and fifty-three miles northwest of LAX. But the San Gabriel mountains stand between the site and the Los Angeles metropolitan area, and by existing freeways, the distance from city center to the site is sixty miles. When the airport is fully operational, some 100 million passengers plus visitors and cargo vehicles will drive the roads through the mountains. "A thirty-two-lane freeway with vehicles bumper to bumper would not accommodate the traffic," noted an official of the Regional Planning Council. The Department must have recognized the dimensions of the problem at a very early stage in the site-selection process, for congested ground-access routes to LAX mean that that facility can never handle more than half the passenger capacity of the airfield itself. But the Department never analyzed the problem, and never tried to calculate the cost of providing adequate access to Palmdale; in its Site Report, the Department merely remarked, "We anticipate freeway completion will keep pace" so that the airport "will have adequate freeway access."

On June 4, 1970, federal approval for the Palmdale site finally was announced. On June 5, the Department of Transportation (DOT) announced a $300,000 federal grant to the Department of Airports to finance a preliminary study looking to the construction of a sixty-six-mile high-speed transit line using "tracked air cushioned vehicles," from LAX to the San Fernando Valley and then on to Palmdale, at an estimated cost of $330 million. An airport feeder of this type was originally slated to run from the Everglades airport to downtown Miami; when the Everglades project was killed on environmental grounds, Palmdale apparently fell heir to DOT's TACV bauble.

The grant was negotiated by the Department behind the backs of the Los Angeles City Planning Commission and the Southern California Rapid Transit District (RTD), and for good reason. This bizarre, airport-to-airport scheme has little or no relevance to the mass transit needs of the Los Angeles metropolitan area. Based on DOT's announcement, the system would initially have an hourly capacity many times less than a *single* freeway lane, and vastly less than a single rapid-transit track of the type planned by the RTD. The projected system's high speeds (50 mph from LAX to the San Fernando Valley stop, 250–300 mph on to Palmdale) would be lost with multiple stops necessary for urban service, and the airport-to-airport link avoids the more populated metropolitan areas where rapid transit service is needed most.

The Department's approach to the utilities problem also reveals its cavalier attitude toward any concern other than its own narrow self-interest. The Palmdale installation is expected to create 35,000 airport jobs and 300,000 airport-related jobs. Some estimates project a resultant population as high as three million for Palmdale, compared to 120,000 for the entire 2,500-square-mile Antelope Valley today. The Department's Site Report says that all major utilities, including water, power, gas, and electricity, can be made available in adequate quantities and at moderate cost, but no serious study or analysis was offered to support this assertion. In the case of water, a valuable commodity in a desert area, the Department's Site Report makes optimistic claims based on the Palmdale Irrigation District (PID) public-relations material; it shows the *route* of the California Aqueduct (through the Palmdale area), and promises that the Feather River project will make available by early 1972 "unlimited new water supplies . . . to support new urbanization development."

According to a director of the PID, using all available water resources, including the District's entitlement of 17,300 acre-feet of Feather River supplemental water, "under optimum conditions the District could support [80,000] to 100,000 people." (It now serves about 20,000.) An RPC official has cautioned that "if the population of Antelope Valley reaches one-half million by 1990, the last 200,000 will have to carry their water with them." The water simply isn't available. The Department knows, despite a legislative trend against supplemental water development, and despite valid criticism of the Feather River project as a whole, that water will somehow come to Palmdale once the airport and the people are there. As in the case of the TACV scheme, the Department is unconcerned about possible distortions in the state and regional water system which would result. It never tried to calculate the direct or indirect social costs. Needless to say, the Department did not consult the PID, the RPC, or state water authorities during the site selection process.

On the broadest environmental issues—the impact of the proposed facility on Antelope Valley ecology and urbanization—the Report makes two contributions to assuage obvious fears. First, the Report notes that state and county parks officials were asked whether public parks or wildlife sanctuaries within a twenty-mile radius would be damaged by the airport; the answers were negative. This kind of "ecological planning" is calculated to screen out only the most egregious siting disasters, and has nothing to do with the airport's impact on agricultural uses of land or the importance of preserving open spaces from airport-induced urbanization. Second, the Site Report does not view the prospect of massive and abrupt urbanization in Palmdale as a problem. The Report does assert that local and regional planning agencies have approved the Palmdale site as compatible with area-planning guidelines. Planning agencies did not in any way participate in the pre-August 1968 site-selection process, and did not have direct responsibility to review the site in the manner of the FAA and the State Department of Aeronautics. The Palmdale site was presented to the planning agencies as a virtual fait accompli.

The complete failure of environmental planning did not go unchallenged. The Noise Abatement Subcommittee of the Environmental Quality Study Council, a state investigative agency, held a hearing concerning the Palmdale project on November 12, 1969, and found no indication of "adequate consideration of environmental quality problems" relating to wildlife, open spaces, agriculture, clean air, and noise. The full EQSC concluded that available evidence "strongly suggests that severe environmental quality problems" may result from the Palmdale project—impacts that "might be disastrous to California's environment"—and the Council urged that the Reagan administration set aside the Department of Aeronautics' clearance so that new hearings might be focused on environmental problems and possible corrective measures. Council members objected to the failure of the aviation-oriented agencies to seriously consider environmental and ecological studies in connection with the Palmdale project, and to the "appalling lack of coordination" among concerned agencies from the inception of the project. According to one Council member, without careful planning the project's approval "would be a disgraceful and abhorrent surrender of the state's police power to economic interests in and around the City of Palmdale."

The Regional Planning Association of Southern California emphasized that the Antelope Valley is a major agricultural sector of Los Angeles County and the "only remaining" year-round area of open space for recreation near the Los Angeles Basin.

But in March of 1970 the Reagan cabinet rejected the EQSC's recommendation that state hearings on the Palmdale project be reopened, and Lieutenant Governor Ed Reinecke, former Congressman for the Antelope Valley, claimed for perhaps the first time that the Department of Aeronautics had thoroughly canvassed environmental quality matters.

The "detailed statement" on the environmental impact of and alternatives to the Palmdale airport, required by the National Environmental Policy Act of 1969, was received (a month after it was requested) by Deputy Attorney General Nicholas C. Yost from the Department of Transportation. It was an inch-thick compilation of correspondence and data relating to the Palmdale airport. A seven-page "Summary" is stapled to the front of the "Appendices," and the whole compilation is entitled, "Findings of the Secretary of Transportation Relative to the Environmental Impact of the Proposed Palmdale International Airport." This Report is little more than a hurried scanning of the existent files on Palmdale, Xeroxed and summarized. As Yost noted in his analysis of the Report:

> While containing a mish-mash of documents, neither the whole report nor any part of it could be called a thorough analysis of the ecological consequences of the proposed airport. The report does however include quotes from a public official and newspaper editorials critical of the one state agency that disputed approval of the airport—the Environmental Quality Study Council.

Yost's comments about the Report were supported by an editorial in the *Los Angeles Times* on August 11, 1970:

> The report submitted to federal officials didn't give environmental considerations anything more than a fast once-over—even though the National Environmental Policy Act of 1969 requires a detailed statement of such impact of any proposed major federal action.

The Report illustrates exactly how the FAA and the Department of Transportation interpret their responsibility under the Environmental Policy Act. Its conclusions were preconceived; it seriously misrepresents and obfuscates facts and data; and most of its information comes from proponents of the airport. The Report fails to meet the requirements of the National Environmental Policy Act: it is not a "detailed statement" of environmental impact, and it does not study or develop appropriate alternatives. Finally, in light of consistent statements contrary to FAA staff research and conclusions, the Report raises serious questions of information suppression and public fraud. (Appendix 11A analyzes the Report in detail.)

Recommendations

Specific reforms of the air and auto transportation systems, to guarantee external checks by the state legislature and local governments, are implicit in the commentary above. In addition, the following basic changes are essential for meaningful, statewide reform.

There is clearly a need for a single comprehensive Transportation Agency, which would coordinate and regulate air, rail, water, and road transportation.

Separate from this Agency should be a Board empowered to review and revise the Agency's detailed plans. The Board should be independent of affected special-interest groups, should have a large staff including economists, biologists, and land-use experts, and should not possess eminent-domain authority over parkland. The reforms of Chapter 12 concerning conflicts of interest should be strictly applied to the Agency and Board.

Changes in condemnation rules and the zoning-up fee and/or capital gains tax reforms suggested in Chapter 9 should minimize unjust enrichment and hence excessive and distorting pressure from local speculators and localities. Two other possibilities also exist for minimizing unjust enrichment from public expenditures: (1) The state could condemn land within a certain area of proposed highway interchanges or airports and sell or lease it back to developers after the facility is built, realizing for the public the profit from the land's increased value. Special taxes could be imposed on the land that is benefited (these could be imposed when the property is sold).

A single undifferentiated fund should be created for administration by the Transportation Agency. Monies should be collected from users of all modes, whether by taxing fuel, collecting tickets, or other revenue. Money should be allocated to the mode and to the projects which are, all costs considered, most efficient for a new need, rather than to the mode collecting the most revenue as a result of the largest (because most heavily subsidized) *prior* use.

The subsidy imbalance over the past several decades has been so great that we are out of touch with consumer needs and demands and have seen little development of mass transit or innovative systems. The state should commit large sums to research and development of alternative systems of transportation. These should be given first access to construction funds allocated over the next decade. Bond flotations can be used for leverage with federal programs.

The state should work for an end to the tax money ransom principle. Those who pay for projects should pay for what they receive, not be compelled to receive because they have already paid 90% of the cost.

12

Power Politics

Nineteen-seventy was billed as the "Year of the Environment." In the California legislature that year conservationists introduced 300 bills, 50 of which they considered "highly important" and 14 "vital to California's health and welfare." The legislature passed only two of the "vital" laws: AB 493, the weaker of the two bills (it requires subdividers to provide some access to the coast for the public), and SCA 18, allowing up to 25% of gas tax revenues to be used for air-pollution research and mass transit if the voters of a county so approve by special vote. This latter bill was then nullified in the defeat of Proposition 18.

The governor's official record on "the environment," according to his Secretary of Resources, Norman Livermore, is "excellent"—"112 major environmental bills passed." When asked for specifics, Mr. Livermore cites a bill to control outdoor burning of leaves; money for conservation education; a small appropriation for air-pollution research; increased penalties for litterbugs; and several normal bond issues for sewage treatment plants. These measures, although useful, hardly stand out as "major," nor do they threaten any important problem with solution. Approximately 40% of Reagan's 112 bills dealt with routine state activities, such as minor park development and the renaming of administrative agencies.

Conservationists did manage to defeat a bill which would have given utilities carte blanche for power-plant siting, and they did persuade the state at least to study the merits of building another bridge across San Francisco Bay.

State Legislature

There are several ways in which land interests influence governmental land-use decisions, and chief among them is direct or indirect influence of the state legislature.

The trade associations and large corporations enumerated in Chapter 1 have literally hundreds of lobbyists in the state capital. These interests provide much or all of the information available to the government for its land-use decision-making, and often control the "experts" who interpret this information. By helping meet the increasing financial needs of political candidacy, land interests establish great influence over individual public officials. And a great many individuals with personal stakes in land-use issues are themselves members of the legislature.

Lobbying

"The cobblestones in the courtyard of the Firehouse shone damp and polished in the rain of early spring that March evening of 1967 when California's political leaders met for dinner with the lobbyists. . . . The lobbyists knew all the legislators and the legislators knew them. It had been that way ever since the days of the old Southern Pacific. . . . They were experienced men, these lobbyists, and they represented clients who mattered. . . . They know how to put on a dinner . . . The waiters brought seven kinds of vintage wine and turtle soup with sherry . . . Californians have always cared for important men and men of economic influence." *

The activities of lobbyists in the first session of the California legislature at San Jose in 1850 led it to be called the "legislature of a thousand drinks." In the next century, lobbying in California became virtually synonymous in the public mind with bribery. Between 1900 and 1914 during legislative sessions the chief counsel of the Southern Pacific saw to it each week that a weekend round-trip ticket to San Francisco was left on the desk of each member. The correspondence of Collis P. Huntington, one of the "big four" who ran the railroad, contains long lists of corruptible officeholders and discusses frankly the costs of obtaining favorable legislation. The nefarious lobbying activities of the Southern Pacific largely provoked the reform

* Lou Cannon, *Ronnie and Jesse* (New York, Doubleday, 1969), p. 44.

regime of Hiram Johnson, but in the 1940s the Sacramento scene was much the same. Governor Warren admitted that the liquor lobbyist, Artie Samish, had more power than he. As Samish boasted, "I'm the governor of the legislature. To hell with the governor of the state." While Samish ultimately went to jail, an investigation of his activities revealed that "some of his clients undoubtedly paid more in fees to Mr. Samish than they paid in taxes for the support of all legitimate functions of state government." Many of the laws these fees bought remain on the books.

While lobbyists deal extensively with the governor and the various administrative agencies, they focus mainly on the Senate and Assembly, for that is where state policy is set. In this forum, the land-interest lobbyist has three major concerns—killing unfriendly legislation, amending what he cannot kill, and placing new legislation on the books. These activities require considerable manpower—to prepare arguments for or against proposals, and to draft alternative legislation. Normally, since the lobbyist himself has neither the time nor the skill to do these things, he must draw on a considerable back-up force. The California Retailers Association, with three registered lobbyists in the 1970 session, bolstered its manpower by drawing heavily on the attorneys of its clients. J. C. Penney, Montgomery Ward, and the May Company, often volunteer their counsel—often a large law firm—to help draft legislation, work out legislative compromises, or assist in other ways. The member pays for its lawyer's services to the Association, yet these lawyers rarely register as lobbyists. Roughly estimated, this activity doubles the actual lobbyist work force.

Today, nearly 500 *registered* "legislative advocates" (as lobbyists are now called in California) attest to the thoroughness of lobbying in the state. New legislators are given lavish "tours" of the state by powerful lobbyists. The Sutter Club, the Derby Club, and other exclusive social clubs provide the setting for discussion. Many of the clubs (e.g., the Sutter) automatically grant membership to high public officials. A review of membership lists reveals the prevalence of land-interest representation, particularly of construction and development executives.

The land-interest lobbyists in Sacramento during the legislative session spend huge sums of money entertaining the legislature, in spite of the fact that public-interest (nonprofit) organizations cannot maintain their tax-exempt status and at the same time "attempt to influence legislation" (e.g., lobby). Trade-association members usually deduct dues or fees which finance them as "business expenses." In fiscal 1970, the land interests alone had 235 lobbyists (see Table 12a) who reported total expenditures of over $3.6 million (see Table 12b), averaging $30,681 per legislator. California law requires lobbyists to file monthly expense statements, and these often run to several thousand dollars for food and drink alone: one lobbyist filed an item of $2,000 for "deerhunting—general goodwill." Since these expenditures are not dispersed equally among all legislators, but concentrated on important figures like committee chairmen, the actual sums spent on key people are staggering. In contrast, all lobbying adverse to land-interest goals is done by two lobbyists (both representing conservation organizations) who spend less than 2% of the money spent by land power.

But lobbyists do not obtain their advantages from money alone. Perhaps their biggest advantage is friendship. Three of the senators most hostile to environmental measures over the years and most capable of making their hostility stick, retiring Senators Hugh Burns, Richard Dolwig, and John McCarthy, formed a notoriously tight camp with

Table 12a

LOBBYISTS—BREAKDOWN BY INTEREST GROUP

Interest Group	Number of Organizations	Number of Full- and Part-Time Lobbyists
Financial	32	45
Transportation	26	38
Resource Extraction	21	18
Agricultural	17	24
Local	24	44
Construction (housing)	16	18
Water	18	22
Utilities	14	21
Landholders	5	5
	173	235[a]
Misc. Groups[b]	6	6
Conservation[c]	2	2

[a] Several of the contract lobbyists represent more than one interest group.
[b] CRLA, Cal. Roadside Council, Friends Committee, Traffic Safety, and two Homeowners Associations.
[c] Planning and Conservation League and California Wildlife Federation.

Table 12b

LOBBYING MONEY SPENT BY INTEREST GROUP

Interest Group	January 1970	February 1970	March 1970	April 1970	May 1970	June 1, 1969 to May 31, 1970	Salaries June 1, 1969 to May 31, 1970
			Expenses				
Financial	$11,600	$15,400	$ 17,700	$ 21,400	$ 23,800	$150,400	$ 458,700
Transportation	8,700	9,900	11,700	13,700	11,700	121,500	427,500
Resource Extraction	11,100	13,700	14,500	16,900	13,800	123,000	289,100
Agricultural	3,300	4,100	13,400	6,800	5,200	51,300	224,500
Local	19,500	24,300	23,300	23,900	23,300	189,000	651,500
Construction	5,500	5,700	6,500	5,800	5,800	59,500	267,100
Water	3,200	3,300	3,000	3,000	3,900	29,200	157,400
Utilities	12,700	15,000	11,900	15,800	16,200	122,000	293,100
Landholding	600	600	700	1,000	1,200	11,900	55,000
TOTAL	$76,200	$92,000	$102,700	$108,300	$104,900	$857,800	$2,823,900
Misc. People's Groups	$ 1,200	$ 1,200	$ 1,800	$ 2,500	$ 2,400	$ 11,500	$ 45,300
Conservation	1,000	1,400	1,100	1,200	900	10,800	34,000

"legislative advocates" James Garibaldi, Daniel Creedon, and Jefferson Peyser. Senator Randolph Collier, formerly chairman of the Transportation Committee and also hostile to environmental legislation, has long been a close friend of "advocates," and recently toured Europe with his friend Bert Trask, a lobbyist for the California Trucking Association. Assemblyman William Bagley, chairman of the Revenue and Taxation Committee, shared an apartment with Richard Ratcliff: Ratcliff is a contact "advocate," representing California Bankers and PG&E, for which Bagley's law firm does legal work. PG&E has not suffered at the hands of Bagley's committee.

Many lobbyists are former legislators and politicians who quite naturally remain friendly with their colleagues. Daniel Creedon—who currently is the "advocate" for beer, the Highway Patrol, funeral directors, and others—quit his legislative seat at the beginning of the 1955 session to "take over the duties of the deposed Artie Samish with the malt beverage industry." Gordon Carland, who currently represents the California Water Association and the Golden Gate Bridge Highway and Transportation District, was speaker of the Assembly thirty years ago. Kent Redwine, representing automobiles, mobile homes, and motion picture producers, was an assemblyman. J. D. Garibaldi, a powerful lobbyist who represents clients on contract, served with Redwine. Over the past eight years, at least seventeen former legislators and seven former directors of state departments have become full-time lobbyists. The lawmaker who may eventually want a lobbying job is not likely to vote against those who have money to hire him.

The numerous land-interest lobbyists are thus able to influence governmental decisions without reference to the merits of a given issue. Of course, the two conservation lobbyists have some of the same advantages. But land-interest groups and lobbyists outnumber conservation representatives by more than a hundred to one, and outspend them by about the same ratio.

The structure of the legislature adds to the informal influence of lobbyists. The Speaker of the Assembly and President Pro Tempore of the Senate help assign bills to particular committees, often determining the fate of legislation. The chairmen of the key committees are also extremely powerful; and any *one* of them can effectively kill any measure. Since land interests have flourished and are flourishing under existing legislation, they need only make sure that no new legislation of any real significance is passed. The fact that few committee votes are ever formally recorded guarantees that few legislators will be held accountable by any broad constituency.

As outmanned and outfinanced as the conservation lobbyists are, part of their weakness has to do with their own lobbying efforts. Many of their campaigns are poorly organized and waged against the wrong opponents. Within the environmental-protection movement there are small, narrow-interest and splinter groups that have arisen in response to various parochial or ideological crises. They usually don't know what their counterparts in the next city or county are doing. Even within the Sierra Club, by far the largest conservation organization in the state (and country), such factionalism and lack of coordination abounds. The Club is divided in California into twelve chapters, each sometimes absurdly jealous of its "prerogatives." The chapters have formed a Northern and a Southern California Regional Conservation Committee to coordinate their activities, but these have failed to work together very well. As a result, even on matters important to the Sierra Club, the mobilization of membership has been sporadic and largely ineffective.

The Planning and Conservation League, originally planned as a kind of umbrella lobbyist for environmentalists, lost a great deal of potential effectiveness through disorganization and internal power struggles. Its hired lobbyist, former legislator John Zierold, quit at the end of the 1970 legislative session and now works for the Sierra Club. There are mad scrambles for credit whenever success occurs, and conservationists have generally failed to seek out other allies.

For example, we found virtually no effort by the Sierra Club, PCL, or anyone else to persuade labor unions and consumer groups to support their positions. A labor-union representative, when informed that a critical piece of environmental legislation was killed by two votes in committee, told us that his union could have delivered those two votes if the conservationists had approached him. He further claimed that the leaders of his and other unions were philosophically committed to the preservation of the environment, and could deliver many votes if informed of the need for them. Some union leaders have actually been rebuffed when they attempted to approach environmentalists. Unfortunately, conservationists are virtually the only group organized to oppose land interests in Sacramento.

The law regulating lobbying in California defines it officially as "legislative advocacy," and by law, "lobbying" is the attempt to influence the vote of a member of the legislature by bribery, promise of reward, intimidation, or other dishonest means, declared by Article IV, Section 35 of the Constitution to be a felony. Under the same section, any member of the legislature who is influenced in his vote or action on any matter pending before the legislature by any reward, or promise of future reward, or who asks for or receives or agrees to receive a bribe, on the understanding that his official vote or action will be influenced thereby, is also guilty of a felony. Although this is the only law that regulates lobbying, it is poorly drafted, unenforced, and ignored.

The forms for expenses tend to be filled out perfunctorily and inaccurately. A lobbyist will often file exactly the same expenses month after month, even for such unpredictables as food and drink. Lobbyists generally ignore the requirement that they itemize campaign contributions beyond twenty-five dollars. Appendix 12A includes a brief survey of such violations, with the violators named and illustrative examples given. This Appendix also presents a critique of the law and suggestions for its reform.

None of our recommendations suggest the abolition of "advocacy." The submission of information and arguments is not only constitutionally guaranteed, but fulfills a useful function. The use of sources of influence *other* than information and argument is a matter of concern, however, as is the bias in information available to legislators. Tax laws favoring corporate lobbying and the allowance of powerful trade associations have created an imbalance inhibiting equitable judgments.

Control of Information and Expertise

Anyone who personally knows many politicians is aware that, despite all the pressures from organized interests, some will resist these interests on behalf of the general, unorganized public if given half a chance. But to do so, they must have some idea of what wise and just public policy would be. Such wisdom requires knowledge of economics, engineering, law, forestry, ecology, and other technical subjects which the legislator does not have. Knowledge of these subjects does not guarantee wise decision-making, but it helps.

Domination of expertise by one or a few private groups is fatal to wise legislation, for the power to define issues, frame alternatives, and amass factual support is effective power over public policy.

At present in California even the heads of comparatively specialized agencies find themselves at the mercy of their experts. The decison-maker is only as good as the expert he believes.

To an alarming extent, land interests control the experts. In a fairly recent reform engineered by Jesse Unruh, the state attempted to reduce its dependence on the information supplied by lobbyists by employing consultants for the committees of the legislature, for each party, and for additional research offices. Although many agree that consultants do have a salutary effect, one established and respected consultant claims that consultants are not effective countervailing forces to lobbyists, but merely make lobbyists work harder. What seems to determine the consultant's effectiveness is the size of the issue at stake. On a small issue, a strong consultant can pose for the legislator the relevant considerations, illuminating the designs of the bill, but on larger issues he lacks resources.

Furthermore, there are so few consultants (approximately two per committee) that they cannot possibly provide the same kind of information and research as the special interests. The average committee will process in excess of 200 bills each year. The consultant usually finds himself caught up in the logistics of hearings and procedure. Rarely is independent, detailed research possible. And turnover is high. As of the middle of 1970 over one-half of the legislature's consultants had been on the job for less than one and one-half years, over one-third for less than six months. The appointing of consultants thus does not at present really change the legislature's dependence on outside expertise or lobbying advocacy.

A great deal of the information needed for a government decision comes from industry. If the state wants to consider banning the internal combustion engine because it creates too much smog, it asks industry how much smog such an engine creates with the best control devices, what the technological alternatives are, and what the economic effect of such a ban would be. When the federal government decided to lease oil properties in the Gulf of Santa Barbara, it had to decide how valuable the property was, and what the environmental risks of drilling would be. Both decisions depended largely on geological information. The oil companies, in that case, not only supplied the information but refused to allow the government to inspect the basic data; the companies merely presented conclusions.

Even when the government hires its own experts, it faces some difficulty obtaining truly independent judgments. There are three sources of employment for most experts: government, industry, and the academic world. Many who achieve eminence shuttle back and forth between them.

What badly exacerbates this problem is that many of the government agencies which hire these experts do very much the same thing that industry does, and similarly depend for their continuation and prosperity on more of the same type of work. The State Department of Water Resources builds water projects, and its employees have the same prejudices in favor of such construction as the private firms with which it contracts, or which receive the benefits of the projects. The Department of Highways builds roads, and lobbies just as hard for continued road-building as any business does. Even the agencies which merely regulate owe their continued existence and importance to the continued existence and importance of whatever they supposedly regulate.

Bureaucratic sympathies are heightened by the extremely high rate of job interchange between government and private industry. This interchange can predispose government "experts," for purely selfish reasons, to favor the interests of the industry, and creates strong and subtle ties in terms of outlook, or "consciousness." In general, "experts" who depend on industry for a significant part of their work tend to adopt the rationalizations and points of view which members of that industry use (at times sincerely, at times cynically) to justify their activities. This view of reality makes their activities and desires seem perfectly consistent with the overall public good to which everyone nominally subscribes.

The problems of expert bias are no secret, and governments have come more and more to rely on so-called "independent consulting firms" like Arthur D. Little, the Stanford Research Institute, or individuals and firms with no direct financial connection to the particular problem under consideration. When the state was considering the California State Water Project, it hired a succession of independent consultants to make independent studies or check the work of the Department of Water Resources. These included the Bechtel Corporation (a San Francisco engineering firm), and the Stanford Research Institute in 1955; a Board of Consultants in 1957; another one in 1958; and, in 1960, assessments by Charles T. Main and Dillon, Read, eastern engineering and financial firms, respectively.

But in reality these consultants have little more independence than anyone else. They compete to get hired, and if they don't please their employer, they won't be hired again.

One might think, despite these factors, that the objective nature of professional disciplines would keep the expert from venting his prejudices. In economics, a project either is or is not feasible; in municipal finance, the city's tax base either is or is not raised; in engineering, a dam either can or cannot be built for the money offered; in law, the rule either does or does not require certain activity; in accounting, an activity is either profitable or not profitable. So experts constantly claim.

In fact, however, the "principles" of the expert's discipline are so flexible that he can choose his results while applying professionally justifiable techniques. As the engineer cited in Chapter 3 told us, "You tell me what benefit-cost ratio you want for a project, and I'll get it for you without straining my conscience." The most widely debated instance of this flexibility occurs in accounting, where presently "generally accepted accounting principles" cover such a multitude of approaches that one accountant can certify a corporation as showing a large profit while another, using equally acceptable techniques and the same "data," can show a huge loss. But the same problem holds for other disciplines.

The failure of various disciplines to choose standard techniques is due to the inherent complexity and difficulty of their subjects. There is simply too much the individual "expert" doesn't know: his "facts" are often guesses, such as the "fact" of how much water exists in underground basins in southern California, or how quickly a clear-cut area will regenerate itself.

Under these circumstances, it is easy to see how expertise

becomes subject to a form of Gresham's Law—the bad drives out the good. If an interest group wants something, and the state hires an expert to evaluate it from a broad, public perspective, and the expert's discipline permits him to come up with any answer he wants, and the expert himself both sympathizes with the interest group and feels some pressures to make a favorable finding, his answer is not hard to predict. Even if the expert doesn't feel able to give the desired answer, he can retreat behind the impenetrable barrier of his professional language, either saying nothing usable, or saying what his client wants to hear while making the necessary professional reservations in jargon that no one will read or understand.

Value judgments on public issues are extremely important in a democracy and are supposed to be made by politicians and, ultimately, the public. Yet experts attempting to maintain influence often cloak value judgments in the seemingly objective dress of statistics, specialized jargon, and technique. The result is what Philip Selznick has called "the retreat to technology"—an effort to make judgments which are heavily value-laden and problematical appear to be *compelled* by objective and technical criteria which seem beyond dispute. The public, craving "certainty" in the face of difficult value choices, often acquiesces to this deception.

Campaign Contributions

Campaign contributions are the most direct tools available to influence politicians. A lobbyist's expenditures on food and drink may ingratiate him to an officeholder, but the campaign contribution delivers the vote. Campaigns are increasingly expensive: in 1968, the average cost of a seat in the California Senate was $39,340.78, while an Assembly seat cost, on the average, $26,411.99. These figures don't tell the whole story, for they include such disparate campaigns as those of Donald Grunsky, who spent only $1,566 to win his seat in the Senate, and Nicholas Petris, State Senator from Oakland, who spent $115,154. Average campaign costs for Senate seats are over three times what they were in 1960, and Assembly costs have almost kept pace.

The costs of statewide candidacy are even more remarkable. Merely to win the Democratic primary for Secretary of State, Edmund G. Brown, Jr. spent $52,600! Charles O'Brien became the Democratic candidate for Attorney

General in the same 1970 election for $51,800. Ed Reinecke spent $79,100 to become Governor Reagan's "Team '70" partner as Republican candidate for Lieutenant Governor. Even the shoo-in candidates spent enormous sums of money. Jesse Unruh paid out $320,000 against Los Angeles Mayor Sam Yorty's token opposition to become the Democratic candidate for Governor (Unruh received only $302,100 in contributions, but drew on an $81,300 bank balance from "former dinners, receptions, and other fund-raising programs"). The innumerable committees representing Ronald Reagan, running unopposed for renomination as the Republican gubernatorial candidate, gathered about $1,632,500 and spent $800,300. These are all costs in the *primary* election alone. In 1966, Reagan spent altogether about $4 million, some of which went to help other Republicans.* Appendix 12B presents comparative campaign costs for each winning candidate in 1960 and 1968.

With these costs, politicians need the favors of campaign contributors. The more important an office, the more big money dominates the process by which the office is filled. In the 1970 primary, Jesse Unruh received 69% of his contributions, in a notably populist-oriented campaign, in checks of $500 or more from individuals and corporations. We stopped counting Governor Reagan's $500 contributions, but 58% of his money came in chunks of $1,000 or more from individuals and corporations, $2,500 and $5,000 being the standard donations. The domination of big money is even greater than these figures suggest, because political committee contributions, which are aggregates of unitemized individual contributions, are not included in the tabulations. One of Governor Reagan's PR men, William Roberts, has estimated that 75% of Governor Reagan's $4 million in 1966 had come in units of $5,000 or more.

Lieutenant Governor Reinecke's political career offers a good illustration of how large interests come to dominate campaign contributions as a "comer" moves up in political office. In the 1966 primary, Ed Reinecke was an underdog

---

* This amounts to almost 15% of the amount spent nationwide by the National Republican Committee for the Nixon-Agnew ticket in 1968. Because of loopholes in reporting requirements, actual costs for all of the campaigns listed above are probably a great deal more than the reported expenditures presented here.

candidate for the Republican nomination in the 27th Congressional District. Although he received about $5,600 in unitemized contributions from two Republican committees, the big money was not pouring in as it has for proven winners, nor was "Good Government" money. Consequently, Reinecke accepted a $27,000 loan from Robert McGee and Associates, an advertising firm, and proceeded to spend $34,080 winning the nomination.

The general election was a different story. As the Republican candidate in a Republican district, Reinecke received more attention. The number of committees contributing rose to eleven, supplying $30,370. Several "Good Politics" and "Education" committees also appeared for the first time. More visibly, Reinecke received contributions from Union Oil, Northrop, Hughes, Southern California Gas, General Telephone, the Fluor Corporation, Life Underwriters, and so forth. In all, Reinecke accumulated $41,200 in this campaign, which allowed him to repay $11,000 of his debt to McGee. But he reported a further deficit of $5,300 in the successful campaign.

By 1970, Reinecke had become Lieutenant Governor and was running for reelection. His contributors in the primary campaign paralleled those of Governor Reagan. Replacing the scattered committee support of previous campaigns was $45,000 from the Reagan Dinner Committee. Although a Reagan-Reinecke team fund gathered lots of money, it apparently didn't spend any on Reinecke. Altogether, Reinecke's records show a deficit of $12,740 from this race, giving him a total debt since 1966 of $35,060 on his campaign statements. We have no idea how these debts have been covered. Incumbents rarely report deficits. Challengers are usually forced to pay up out of their own pockets, but one of the rules of California politics seems to be that once a man gains office, people more willingly become his creditors.

Who pays the major costs? We surveyed fifty primary campaigns in 1970. Most of the identifiable contributions in 1970 came from big business, big labor, and big non-labor organizations. These groups have a definite preference for incumbents, rarely, if ever, helping challengers; and, except for labor, they tended to favor Republicans. Their lobbyists comprised between 5% and 10% of all the names appearing on lists of contributors. Since most of the several thousand names on these lists gave less than

$25, and lobbyists generally give more than that, lobbyists actually had a greater financial presence than the 5% to 10% figure would indicate. Futher, the greater power a legislator has, the more lobbyists one will find contributing. Thus, the recent President Pro Tem of the Senate, Jack Schrade, received over 35% of his contributions in the 1968 general election from lobbyists.

In addition to these sources, a few trusts, such as the H-P Trust, the C-B Trust, and the RR-CG (Ronald Reagan-California Governor?) Trust contributed regularly and substantially to nearly half the candidates in this survey. The trusts also had a Republican preference and a definite aversion to challengers. While the labor unions contributed almost exclusively to Democrats, they had counterparts in the Public Relations and Education Fund, the Committee for Government Improvement, the Good Government Club, the Public Vision League (not associated with optometrists), United for California, the Genteel Government Club, and other organizations of similar nomenclature, representing similarly unknown memberships and interests.

Land interests predominate among the big campaign contributors. At least two-thirds of those contributing $1,000 to Governor Reagan's 1970 primary campaign were corporations and individuals with a strong interest in land exploitation: lobbyists, major shareholders, officers, and such corporations as Southern Pacific, Tenneco, Tejon Ranch, Irvine Ranch, Kaiser Industries, PG&E, PT&T, Wells Fargo Bank, Bank of America, Standard Oil, Union Oil, Transamerica Title Insurance Company, etc. The two-thirds land-interest figure for Governor Reagan is duplicated in the case of the chairmen of key Senate and Assembly committees.* Most chairmen receive at least 40% to 50% of their financing from large land interests.

* Women were not included in this figure because we had no way of telling whether or not female contributors were related to corporate directors and presidents, although many had the same last names, and others could be identified with land interests in their own right. Appendix 12C lists the names of Governor Reagan's contributors, their connection with land interests, and the amount of their contribution for the 1970 primary. In total, land individuals and corporations contributed $462,000; $261,000 came from all other sources, excluding women and "front groups." Front groups, chiefly the "Committee for a Greater California" which gave the huge unidentified chunk of $123,000, are generally as land-connected as the individuals.

The present campaign-financing process provides land interests with several paths to influence. In California today, candidates are totally unaccountable for their expenditures. Under these circumstances, as the case of Senator Thomas Dodd illustrates on a national level, a contribution paid at the right time and place can be marked as a perfectly legal campaign contribution even though it ends up in the candidate's "private" pocket or goes to help a political friend of the candidate. In this way moneyed interests not only buy individual politicians but purchase power and influence for those politicians as well.

The ways in which politicians can accumulate patronage via these useful surpluses are many. One of the most widely used seems to be the "no opposition-big expense" primary campaign. For example, Lawrence Walsh, Republican and chairman of the Senate Select Committee on Urban Affairs, recorded primary campaign receipts of $42,600 and expenditures of $30,500 against two opponents who each spent about $4,000. The Senator's advantage was even more lopsided because as an incumbent, the state paid for his newsletters. In the election, Walsh faced a Democratic opponent who had gathered one-seventh as many votes as he did in the primary. On the other side of the aisle, Ralph Dills, Democrat and chairman of the Senate Public Utilities and Corporations Committee, received $39,300 in contributions and spent $42,900 in the primary, fighting off a challenger who spent $1,560. His opponent got more votes per dollar than Dills, but Dills still got through with a six-to-one margin. To aid him in this struggle, Dills hired two of his brothers for $6,700, and paid lobbyist Ken Ross $9,820 for printing advertisements.

California has few laws concerning campaign expenditures. It forbids bribery, of course, but since politicians can keep any money not spent on their campaigns, it is fairly simple to get away with calling a bribe a "campaign contribution." The major provisions directed at campaign financing call for disclosure. Candidates must list contributors of more than $20, identify contributions of more than $500 by name of the donor, and itemize their expenditures. Failure to comply can void the election, and possibly subject the candidate to perjury charges as well. Appendix 12D summarizes the law and includes copies of the reporting forms. The theory behind disclosure is that it permits the public to judge for itself the influences operating on the candidate. While tacitly acknowledging that politicians respond to the dollar as well as to the ballot, the disclosure law supposedly assures that the ballot has the last say.

For all candidates participating in the primary and general elections in California, "campaign statement" forms must be filed with the Secretary of State's office before the Secretary issues nomination papers or certificates of election. Secretary of State H. P. Sullivan indicated that inspection of campaign statements and subsequent enforcement is negligible. If a candidate does not submit a list of his contributions and expenditures by the date required, the Secretary of State has the power to request a court order extending the due date. These court orders are granted automatically and for any reason.

Most candidates (the proportion increases with the importance of the office to which they aspire) personally file forms indicating that *they* have received no money and have spent little or no money in the course of their campaign. Some of these candidates expand their disclaimer by stating that there are committees not under their control or direction that perform these functions for them. The "got nothing—spent nothing" forms are *absolutely* all the disclosure required under the present law, regardless of the number of committees that a candidate has. If a candidate is allowed to disavow responsibility for any funds collected or expended on his behalf, application of the present sanctions is bound to be difficult.

Even if a candidate does file a complete record of contributions in his own name, there is no guarantee that he can be held responsible for omissions and errors which might occur in these forms. The perjury clause at the bottom of the campaign statements is the main control device over the accuracy of the contents therein. However, the perjury clause, while present on the *primary* form, is mysteriously deleted from those forms used for the *general* elections. The forms are otherwise identical. According to Secretary of State Sullivan, all the participants in the *general* election are "good clean kids." In 1968, Mr. Sullivan suggested to the Assembly Committee on Elections that they include the perjury clause in the general election forms as well. Mr. Sullivan stated that his serious request was "literally laughed off" with a remark to the effect that "we're all good friends here." This system seems specifically designed to allow unequal policing of "outsiders" and to enable incumbents who run largely unopposed in the primaries and thus require relatively few primary contributions to bring in unlimited amounts secretly with complete immunity.

Mr. Sullivan stated that personally he must process the contribution and expense statements for over 1,000 candidates in a short period of time. Under these circumstances he can only perform such routine clerical duties as determining that all the blanks on the forms are completed and that the form is signed.

But even if enforced—with a perjury clause—the law can be directly circumvented. One obvious way to avoid disclosure is for donors to give less than $500 at a time. For example, in 1966, one incumbent received contributions from twenty-three individuals, including several lobbyists. None of the donors had a specific contribution attached to his name. However, the sum of these twenty-three contributions amounted to $10,500, or $457 per donor.

Another type of avoidance involves the use of "campaign committees." The law requires each such committee to furnish statements in accordance with the requirement for the candidate himself. By contributing to several such committees, a donor can conceal the total amount of his contribution. About $274,000 out of the $963,200 total of big-money contributions to the 1970 Reagan primary came from multiple givers like Tenneco (Kern County Land Company), which gave $2,500 five times, or Southern Pacific, which gave seven times for a total of $15,000. Perhaps the major avoidance, one we could not document for obvious reasons, is simple failure to report.

Donors can and do take other measures to avoid detection as contributors. We have been told by more than one source that middle- and upper-level employees of corporations, especially public utilities, have received pay increases with the understanding that a certain portion was to be contributed to designated candidates and parties. Airline companies, advertising firms, and any others who perform services for candidates on credit may make an indirect and unlisted contribution by forgetting the campaign debt—after the final statement of deficit has been submitted.

In Senate and Assembly races particularly, important contributors often hide behind the facades of local political committees or groups. The "Committee for a Greater Cali-

Table 12c

PERCENTAGE OF CONTRIBUTIONS REQUIRING FURTHER IDENTIFICATION
(1970 PRIMARY—SELECTED CANDIDATES)

Candidate	Party	Dist.	Total Contrib.	No. Disguised	Percent of Money Disguised
Fred W. Marler	Dem.	SD#2	$12,600	1	40%
Alan Short	Dem.	SD#6	41,300	2	2
Walter W. Stiern	Dem.	SD#18	6,300	1	39
William E. Coombs	Rep.	SD#20	26,940	2	4
Tom Carrel	Dem.	SD#22	3,600	1	28
Robert J. Lagomarsino	Rep.	SD#24	10,290	4	88
Anthony Bielenson	Dem.	SD#26	3,890	0	0
Lawrence Walsh	Dem.	SD#30	42,590	1	7
Ralph C. Dills	Dem.	SD#32	39,860	4	80
William T. Bagley	Rep.	AD#7	1,570	0	0

Walter W. Powers	Dem.	AD #8	12,370	0	32–40
Edwin Z'Berg	Dem.	AD #9	1,640	0	0
John T. Knox	Dem.	AD #11	4,280	1	94
Robert Monagan	Rep.	AD #12	15,980	2	98
Gordon W. Duffey	Rep.	AD #21	18,300	2	94
John Foran	Dem.	AD #23	13,700	0	0
William Ketchum	Rep.	AD #29	3,970	1	17
W. D. MacGilvray	Rep.	AD #36	16,520	8	67–73
Randolph Siple	Rep.	AD #37	14,520	8	36–54
Carley V. Porter	Dem.	AD #38	3,150	2	32
Robert Beverly	Rep.	AD #46	4,480	2	22
Frank Lanterman	Rep.	AD #47	–0–	0	0
Peter Schabarum	Rep.	AD #49	4,810	1	94
Robert Badham	Rep.	AD #71	11,720	2	36
John P. Quimby	Dem.	AD #72	8,530	1	69
Pete Wilson	Rep.	AD #76	28,710	2	3

fornia," for example, is the Los Angeles brainchild of the former director of the Merchants and Manufacturers Association. Mr. Shellenberger now works as a full-time fund-raiser who wants legislators to "approach situations involving the business climate realistically." In determining its donations, the Committee confers with the State Chamber of Commerce and the California Taxpayers Association (i.e., industry). In 1970, its anonymous members contributed $123,400 to Ronald Reagan's primary campaign. Such disguised contributions are widespread, as shown in the Table from our own survey.

The use of "anonymous" contributions has also been increasing. The "cashier" check device is the most common means of accomplishing this direct dodge—with bank, committee, and candidate knowing full well who the contributor is. If the candidate himself is kept academically in the dark, he is sure to discover who the contributor is while in office.

The present disclosure laws work to the extent that persistent investigators can compile a statistical picture of the election process, and perhaps even find some flagrant examples of abuse. But the public's chance of identifying the backers of any particular candidate or officeholder are slim—especially if the candidate or donors have any reason to conceal the relationship.

Conflicts of Interest

A conflict of interest exists whenever a public official's duty to evaluate measures with impartiality and a view to the public interest is jeopardized by the existence of a personal interest on his part in the fate of any measure.

The very notion of conflict of interest is premised on the exclusivity of the public official's duty to the public. Such a conflict frequently exists, therefore, *whether or not* the official actually succumbs to his selfish interest.* It is enough that he is placed in a position in which it is difficult or inconvenient for him to discharge his duty to the public. The special relationship of trust and confidence between public and official requires that he be above suspi-

---

* Clearly, the personal interests of legislators do not always determine votes. Legislators do sometimes vote against personal interests, sometimes do not care about, or may even be unaware of, their personal stakes. Sometimes a legislator who honestly votes for a given policy will attract the attention and support of interests benefiting from that policy only afterwards.

cion, for even the appearance of wrongdoing can poison this vital relationship.

Most government officials had jobs before they gained election or appointment, and many retain strong ties to their former jobs. Most legislators, for example, quietly continue outside employment, despite the $19,200 legislative salary, the highest in the nation. They justify such continued employment because $19,200, for many, is considerably less than they had been earning. In addition, expenses of office-holding are tremendous and the work is part time (the legislative session runs about eight months of the year). Actually, legislators receive more than $19,200.* The recent increase in legislative salaries (in 1966 the figure was $16,000) was made to encourage more full-time, independent legislation, but has failed to do so. In fact, campaign expenses have increased so much during this period that even legislators with heavy land-interest backing face overwhelming debts unless they seek other sources of income.

Over one-half of the members of the legislature are *currently* receiving sums from the ownership or development of land. About one-quarter are attorneys representing these interests. Many others own and operate their own real estate or construction firms or have their own large landholdings. Table 12d presents the totals according to our count. Appendix 12E sets forth the results by legislator.

After our initial survey of biographies and legal directories, a group of some twenty-nine attorney-legislators remained who were not included in the Martindale-Hubbell (M-H) Directory. Since this Directory is a major advertising resource in the legal profession, those legislators not listed therein are relatively unlikely to be active in soliciting new business. We therefore used this group as a sample for a survey. Identifying ourselves as an investment firm engaging in land investment, speculation, and development, we called the legislative offices of those legislators *not* listed in the M-H Directory and asked for the number of the legislator's law firm. Almost every office knew the number immediately. We then called the law office and spoke to the

---

* Each receives an expense allowance while the legislature is in session, a mileage allowance for limited travel, death benefits, and pension provisions. Those serving on interim committees receive per diem fees and expenses. And newsletter and similar "semi-campaign" costs are paid by the state.

Table 12d
OCCUPATIONAL CONFLICTS OF INTEREST
REGARDING LAND IN STATE LEGISLATURE

	Senate		Assembly	
	No.	%	No.	%
Known Present Conflicts	22	55	48	60
Known Past Conflicts Only	3	7½	7	8¾
Unknown	9	22½	4	5
Full-time Legislator without Past or Present Conflicts	6	15	21	26¼
Total	40	100%	80	100%

legislator's secretary, or more often, to his partners. We stated that we were an investment firm in land speculation and development and we wanted some "help." We contacted the offices of fifteen assemblymen and ten senators—once again those least openly connected with land law. Of ten law firms associated with senators, seven were willing to handle our case and "regularly handle" such cases. Of fifteen assemblymen's firms, eleven were willing to take our case and handle such cases regularly. When we asked if the assemblyman could "personally" handle our case, *eleven* said yes! Two of the senators would personally handle our case, two others expressed willingness but declined because of other work. The offices of only two assemblymen and three senators mentioned conflict-of-interest possibilities or worries. Most of these tied their hesitation to handling our case in their home district. Assemblyman Sieroty's law office seemed the most scrupulous in its refusal to take our business, since land matters were, the office felt, too related to his duties as a legislator for him or it to accept any such business anywhere.

Mr. Sieroty's position was unique among those we called. Appendix 12E includes summaries of the answers we received by legislators in addition to those with publicly listed (and advertised) conflicts.

Many legislators also have extensive conflicts of interest through financial holdings and investments. Lack of subpoena power precluded our taking a detailed survey of conflicts in this area.

California's laws against conflict of interest are weak. One law forbids members of the legislature and officers of the state, counties, special districts, judicial districts, and cities from having a financial interest in any contract they make or participate in making, or from buying or selling at any sale involving them in their official capacity (Government Code Sections 1090 to 1097). The 1966 legislature passed a Code of Ethics which proscribes activities that are in substantial conflict with the proper discharge of duties in the public interest, and employment of legislators in cases where there are reasons to believe this will impair their independence of judgment or breach official confidences. Upon adopting the Code, the legislature established a Joint Ethics Committee to hold hearings on charges of impropriety. This committee has never held a public hearing, despite serious charges of conflict in the past. Informal and secret "preliminary investigations" have disposed of these embarrassments.

The California statutes described above do not prohibit conflicting employment or receipt of gifts, services, loans, favors, or additional compensation from nonstate sources for executive officials * and employees. Executive officials are not prohibited from assisting or representing others in transactions with the state, from private sales to or purchases from firms regulated or licensed by the state, or from personal interests in business regulated or licensed by the state. A lawyer who is an executive official may appear before a state agency and is not disqualified or prohibited from participating in official actions. State legislative and executive officials are not required to divest themselves of conflicting interests.

Assemblywoman Pauline Davis purchased land at a fraction of its market value from Republican rancher Charles Carmichael (former vice-president of the California Cattlemen's Association) because, in Carmichael's words, "I wanted to show my appreciation for what she has done. . . ." According to the *Sacramento Bee,* Assemblyman L. E. Townsend is allegedly involved in a similar favor. And the millionaire governor of the state has accepted his house as a gift from oil and developments interests.

In recognition of California's poor conflict-of-interest laws, the 1969 legislature enacted, under Jesse Unruh's prodding, a fairly stiff financial-disclosure law which would at least have required public officials and candidates to

* There are limited and scattered requirements in some of the substantive codes (Education, Agriculture, etc.) for disclosure of investment conflicts by some executive departments.

disclose their investments and those of their immediate
families. Apparently, Unruh obtained passage of this law
only by making a big public issue out of it and forcing a
public floor vote. Considerable pressures built up around
the state to nullify the law. And the California Supreme
Court obligingly did so, holding last year that its provisions
were too broad and invaded privacy without proper discrimination. Although the Court's objections could be circumvented by proper redrafting, we were told frankly that the
"powers" within and without the legislature wanted the
matter dropped.

State Executive Branch

Power politics within the executive department are difficult
to summarize. The State Office of Planning, the State Board
of Equalization, the State Environmental Quality Study
Council, the Business and Transportation Agency with its
public works, real estate, and other divisions, the Resources
Agency with its many relevant boards and departments, and
others all have their separate modes of response to political
pressures, their own procedures and methods. The preceding text has covered many of these agencies individually.
However, there are several areas in which inordinate land-
interest influence cripples the enforcement of existing laws,
spawning special exceptions and token sanctions.

First, especially under the Reagan administration, land
interests almost completely dominate the appointment
process. The governor often appoints direct representatives
of the land interests to regulate or investigate their own
businesses. (The water attorney for the Kern County Land
Company was appointed to chair a water resources task
force; a past president of the California Real Estate Association and director of the National Association of Real Estate Boards was chosen as State Real Estate Commissioner;
a drayage (trucking) firm owner, president of a county
truck-owners' association and member of the California
Truck Owners' Association board of governors, was selected as a State Highway Commissioner; a savings and
loan consultant was appointed to the State Savings and
Loan Commission, and so on.) If he does not appoint
them, land interests often successfully pressure for their
choices. Industrial "advisory groups" attached to the executive branch help with this appointment process, and

exert considerable direct influence on the decision-making as well. Land interests regulate themselves as a matter of legal requirement: the Real Estate Commissioner, State Board of Agriculture, District Oil and Gas Commissions, State Forestry Board, and Regional Water Quality Control Boards consist primarily of a realtor, farmers, drillers, loggers, and polluters, respectively. Even where required preferential access is "advisory," it is extremely powerful since it engenders personal friendship, facilitates job offers and other informal sources of influence, and allows an input at the middle levels of bureaucracy—where policy is most malleable.

In some areas land interests directly finance their own regulation, as with pesticide registration controls, or the oil and gas regulators. The forces mentioned above—lobbying, information control, and occupational and investment conflicts of interest—are also applicable to executive officials. The dearth of conflict-of-interest laws applying to executive officials makes their conflicts legal and, to them, legitimate.

Another factor of considerable importance is the capacity of land interests to block real attempts at enforcement through litigation. Laws today permit lawyers to delay almost any governmental enforcement action interminably through discovery procedures and other delaying tactics. By contributing this bit of "reality" to the agency decision-making process, land interests can generally force agencies to opt for weak enforcement by "persuasion," even if the agency is initially inclined otherwise. The state's administrative behavior is characterized by nonenforcement of provisions designed to curb self-seeking land interests in cases of water pollution law nonenforcement, illegal oil revenue, state land giveaways, and nonprosecution for fraud. What enforcement there is goes not against the most important instances of white-collar crime but against political enemies or smaller and less influential violators to beef up statistical pictures.

Where publicity occasionally compels enforcement activity, it is almost always without sanction. Land interests currently have no fear of financial or prison penalty for past fraud, damage, or corruption. The concept of deterrence, of greatest efficiency and use when dealing with relatively rational entities like corporations, is nonexistent.

Hitting the leading violators hard would put a check on the activities of others as each corporation calculated real risks. For effective deterrence, prosecution must be successful and penalties must be more than merely the denial of fraudulently obtained profits and more than the cost of repairing environmental damage or economic misallocation.

Law and order in the executive branch takes the form of secret "accommodations," requests to stop or moderate, and abject surrender. Most energy is devoted to protecting the violator from public scrutiny and exposure and sometimes to issuing complimentary public-relations propaganda concerning the industry's progress in serving the public interest (which naturally reflects well on those regulating it).

The state's executive branch rarely seeks adequate authority or manpower to fulfill effectively the purposes for which it was created. In the area of manpower the state is in its usual budget crisis. But before taxpayers cringe at the expense of an effective government they should remember two things. First, deterrence costs relatively little. Second, filling the myriad tax loopholes now depriving the state of revenue and ending vast public subsidies for the corporate rich could impose the discipline of the market on beneficiaries of public favors and could cut most individuals' taxes substantially. The market could then allocate resources more efficiently.

Local Government

Since California has delegated most land-use authority to local agencies, such offices are important sources of positive favors for land interests. Thus, there is less defensive, behind-the-scenes elimination of possible legislation and more aggressive solicitation of positive governmental actions (e.g., rezonings, variances, etc.). Land interests are greatly aided in their endeavors by the fragmented structure of local government, which usually precludes effective public surveillance (see Chapter 9).

Two means of influence in particular are, campaign contributions and personal conflicts of interest.

In California, local offices are nonpartisan, which means that candidates cannot count on party money, but must raise every cent themselves. Local offices may be more significant than assembly or senate positions, and require commensurate expenditures: serious candidates for county supervisors in developed counties usually spend between $60,000 and $120,000! Moreover, unlike senate and assembly positions, which carry decent salaries, most local offices pay little, if anything, making corruption and conflicts of interest even more likely on that level.

By general consensus, San Francisco is the "cleanest" county in the state, with a tradition of widespread campaign contributions from ordinary citizens and a 1964 bribery scandal to boost "good government" efforts. A picture of its 1969 campaign should therefore provide a comparatively rosy view of local California politics.

One supervisor, Jack Morrison, showed a pattern of true grass-roots support. In spending $65,926, he received no contribution exceeding $1,100, and very few over $500. More than 1,200 individuals donated, but he received virtually no support from developers or even corporations. But Morrison, who lost in 1970, is atypical, even for San Francisco. While most of the other candidates did not include the amounts given by each contributor, but merely listed them, they obviously received much of their support from land interests. For example, Dorothy Von Beroldingen, who spent $69,000, listed over twenty-five developers, realtors, or financiers as contributors. John Barbagelata, who spent $33,329, collected from such sources as: Earl Realty, Lois Harper Realty, Saxe Realty, Cal Realty, Wm. Nadell Realty, Roman Realty, et al. Some of the contributors to the campaign of Peter Tamaras are listed below.*

About half of the major candidates were funded mainly by development interests, many of whom do indeed "expect to influence" (an element of the crime of bribery under

---

* Anchor Realty, Balliet Bros. Construction Co., Islais Creek Corp., B&D Properties, J. J. Castle and Co., Cal-Steam Supplies, Cutler & Co., Delis Ranch, Macco Corp. (a major developer), Gallagher Realty Co., Plumbing, Heating and Cooling Contractors of S.F., Keil Real Estate, Mac's Loan Co., Rosano Construction, Orange Land, Allied Properties, Union Oil Co., Stoneson Development Corp., Western Plumbing and Heating, Olympia Federal Saving, M. V. Construction, Wells Fargo Bank, S.F. Electrical Contractors Ass'n., Cahill Construction Co., Davis Realty Co., Crocker Citizens National Bank, Standard Oil of California, et al. PLUS "City and County of San Francisco Department of Public Works."

California law) and give for that purpose. All but one candidate had substantial support from these sources.

The Tax Assessor, despite San Francisco's "cleanness," is also deeply indebted to these interests. Assessor Tinney spent $18,531 in his campaign. Twenty-five of his large contributors are developers or holders of high-value land. Having the large taxpayers decide who shall assess their property has grave consequences for the tax bills of ordinary citizens. The same situation exists on the state level for the Board of Equalization. George Reilly received contributions from, among others, thirteen hotels and six realty firms, to foot his campaign bill of $17,070.

Direct bribery has become comparatively minor on the state level, but appears to be flourishing locally. The bribery indictments and convictions of Los Angeles Councilman Shepard, Harbor Commissioner Gibson, Assessor Watson, and others in past years are not isolated examples. More recently, practically the entire government of San Diego, including four City Councilmen, Mayor Frank Curran (president of the National League of Cities), two County Supervisors, and an Assemblyman were all indicted for bribery. In Riverside County, Supervisor Norman Davis, the Greatamerica Land Company, and its attorney Michael Rafferty (Reagan's Riverside County campaign manager) were all indicted for bribery to rezone an area. (The rezoning still stands.) In the northern part of the state, the San Francisco Assessor's scandal of the mid-sixties sent the County Assessor to prison for taking bribes from the city's largest and most "respectable" firms in exchange for low assessments. More recently, the City Attorney, after intense citizen pressure, reluctantly brought suit against these firms for the millions of dollars in taxes owed, and has announced an out-of-court settlement, for a fraction of the debt. The bribers paid no other penalty. In Stockton, a Municipal Judge has been indicted for bribery, and in Carson City, two City Councilmen (including the former mayor), the former deputy district attorney, the president of the Carson City Jaycees, a member of the city's Environmental Control Commission, and a former member of the city's Park and Recreation Commission have all been indicted for bribery to rezone an area for a $45 million shopping center and industrial park. They were also accused of accepting bribes to grant specific variances, as for a motorcycle park. In

Ventura County, County Supervisor H. F. Robinson has been convicted by a jury for accepting $3,000 in bribes for land-related favors.*

Indictment is not equivalent to guilt. And the conviction of these and others who may be guilty is by no means certain. Lacking any meaningful state conflict-of-interest law, the Attorney General has the exceedingly difficult task of proving "intent to influence" and "intent to be influenced," under bribery law.

When local government is made up of people with land interests, "influence" and the use of public policy for private profit is particularly clear. We surveyed the Supervisors in nineteen counties, obtaining biographical data for eighty-nine of them. Nearly half (forty-two) are large landowners or own their own real estate, development, or construction firms. Another sixteen are lawyers or financiers representing development interests. Only 35% have businesses or professions relatively unconnected with land development.

The results in 1970 leave the public with little hope for any real success in any future year. Powerful organized interests, identified in Chapter 1 and described throughout this work, can ensure these results because they have effective control of much of California's government. They use its power to protect themselves from the rigors of the marketplace; to extract subsidies and special privileges from taxpayers; and to prevent the enforcement of existing law or the enactment of new law which might threaten their profits—environmental and other social costs notwithstanding. While individual land interests do not control the state in the sense that they always succeed in winning affirmative favors, their power over the intricate and largely invisible day-to-day operations of government assures that public decisions affecting their vital interests are to a great extent fashioned by them or by those with a personal stake in their welfare. Government intervention is usually justified in our society only when a self-regulating system has failed. In the area of land use, the self-regulating market fails to take into account many significant long-range social or

---

* For those who are curious, it appears that the going rate for an unpopular rezoning or favorable vote varies from $500 to $3,500. Only the $45 million Carson City shopping center accusation involved substantially more money—$100,000, allegedly split among four officials.

environmental costs. Government must, therefore, intervene on behalf of the general public to regulate directly and assess total costs.

The control of government by those the public expects government to control—the coalition of private economic power unrestrained by effective competition and public law unrestrained by a vigilant citizenry—precludes the effective functioning of America's system of checks and balances. It approaches a form of socialism in which the state does not control the means of production but the means of production control the state.

Recommendations

The control of California's government by powerful private interests will continue until there are enforceable and enforced state laws requiring the following:

(1) The provision of proper resources for information from a public-interest perspective through enlarged independent legislative staffs and experts, independent consumer counsel for executive agencies, stricter control of special-interest lobbying, and state-facilitated support for public lobbying through tax-law changes and a volunteer voucher system.

(2) The provision of campaign funds by the state with maximum expenditures delineated to reduce special-interest impact.

(3) Full-time legislators, executive officials, and major local office holders with no alternative sources of income as a condition of public office.

(4) Not merely complete disclosure of investment conflicts, but divestiture of all nonpersonal assets by major office holders into blind trust or fund arrangements while holding office.

(5) Prohibition against the acceptance of any remuneration or employment by any interest affected by an official's activities for at least five years after leaving office.

(6) Widespread attention to openly disclosed votes in legislative committees.

(7) At the local level, a unified and visible multipurpose government covering a defined geographical area.

Lobbying Reforms

The government couldn't possibly function without the inputs provided by skilled advocacy of special interests, be they industrial or otherwise. However, those with clearly defined economic stakes in government action are far more capable and willing to finance such activity than those whose only care is for beauty, justice, or some other public good of little economic benefit to themselves. Thus, industry's lobbyists and trade associations will always be more plentiful and better equipped than the assortment of public-interest lobbies. However, governmental dependence on "legislative advocacy" can be greatly reduced.

An important step would be to go further in the use of legislative consultants by increasing manpower approximately fivefold in the legislative research offices and the offices of legislative counsel and legislative analyst, as well as by hiring many more committee and party consultants.

Certain of the specific steps recommended in some of the chapters of this book would also help. For example, when facing public-works projects, the state need not depend either on ad hoc "evaluations" cooked up by "experts" on the spot according to their professional standards, or on the evaluations of the state agency waiting to build the project. The state must have an evaluation agency with no task other than evaluating these projects according to the standard guidelines of independent experts.

Several other measures might be taken to redress directly the balance of public and private interests.

One would be revision of current tax laws which penalize organizations such as conservation groups for lobbying, while awarding valuable tax deductions to businessmen for the same activity.

A somewhat more unusual way to redress the balance would be a state-financed voucher system for lobbying. Every citizen of voting age would receive a voucher which he could dedicate to any cause he chose. The recipient of the voucher would redeem it for cash at the state treasury in order to finance its lobbying activities.

The strict application of current antitrust doctrine, bolstered by additional legislation, could be used to break up the state's trade associations. Trade associations make it possible for firms within an industry to engage in institutionalized conspiracy not only to fix prices but to fix and limit product characteristics and to formulate common courses of action.

To end improper personal influence, it might be wise to outlaw lobbying by former legislators, and to prohibit the acceptance of "wining-dining" favors and personal gifts beyond certain reasonable and specific limits. At present the law ties illegality to "intent to influence and be influenced" with regard to a specific piece of legislation. The law should set up the rebuttable presumption that valuable favors and offers are presented to officials with "an intent to influence." Current difficulties in proving "intent," even where large sums of cash change hands (presumably for "campaign contributions") makes conviction extremely difficult.

Campaign Financing

In 1938, H. R. Philbrick recommended "enactment of a statute requiring all contributors to political candidates or campaigns to file a detailed statement of contributions with the Secretary of State." If an *aggregate* minimum of $500 were required before this statute were to take effect, the statements would reveal those individuals and organizations that were making many separate $400 contributions—information that is now virtually unobtainable. A statute requiring that the aggregate of all *debts* and *profits* incurred in previous campaigns be recorded on a candidate's most recent campaign statement should also be enacted. Alternatively, all bank balances of committees' and candidates' campaign funds could be made public record.

Loopholes allowing many "anonymous" donations or donations through "fronts" must be closed. Reasonable enforcement provisions must be enacted which (1) make the candidate himself directly responsible for compliance with the law, and (2) set forth sanctions that work. Denying an office outright is impractical. However, an election could be nullified if a noncomplying candidate won—with restitution to be made upon compliance. More moderate measures include the use of fines. It might be possible to require that monies illegally hidden be donated to the candidate's next general election opponent for whatever office he next seeks.

The timing and publicity of campaign contribution

sources could also be improved. The position and employer of contributors (including those holding directorships) could be required. (Candidates generally know this information about their large contributors anyway.) The publicizing of contributions could be facilitated through compilation and publication by the state. Keeping one musty copy of 300 pages scattered loose-leaf fashion through various manila envelopes in an obscure office hardly encourages the active divulgence of candidate indebtedness. Very few examine these records over the years, either at state or local levels. Publishing this information in pamphlet form for immediate distribution at cost should be an easy task.

The basic objection to unlimited campaign contributions is that they inhibit a legislator from doing his duty impartially by giving disproportionate influence to powerful economic interests. Disclosure laws, even if fully enforced, cannot dispel this influence. The state could outlaw direct participation by these groups in campaign financing; yet such efforts have met with only limited success.

The federal Corrupt Practices Act excludes corporations and labor unions from the financing of campaigns. The "enforcement" of this law has resulted in twenty-one convictions and two acquittals. Of the seven reported decisions under the Act, all but two cases dealt primarily with political advertising by unions and resulting constitutional clashes with the right of free speech. In these cases, some doubt was cast on the constitutionality of the statute. Although a law probably cannot outlaw all union and corporate electoral activity, a state legislature certainly can impose some restraints.*

Violations of the federal Act appear to include loaning money and personnel, paying for tickets to fund-raising dinners for federal candidates, buying advertising space, and contributing to cover a deficit. There is a growing body of evidence that some corporations have evaded these prohibitions by augmenting salaries of contributing executives

---

* Under the federal law, unions are permitted to use funds "voluntarily" contributed for political purposes, but the uses to which these funds may be put are limited to advertising candidates' records and advertising not designed to affect the results of elections directly, as opposed to active electioneering.

and by "burying" (e.g., claiming these expenditures were payment for "legal" services).

If corporate and union money were in fact kept out of campaigns, the resulting reduction in available money could be ameliorated by making limited free TV time available to all candidates. Even if corporate and union contributions were not prohibited in campaigns, limited free TV time would serve to lessen the need for this kind of money and would thereby serve to limit the indebtedness which plagues virtually all campaigns.

The campaign base of officials could be broadened by granting tax deductions or credit for contributions to political candidates or parties.* The disadvantage here is that it associates contribution sources with those who pay state income tax—thus excluding the poor. Nevertheless, the base of financial support for candidates would be considerably broadened.

The simplest and most direct solution to the present financing problem is to limit the amount of money that can be spent in a campaign. Such a limit, coupled with requiring allotments of TV and radio time to candidates, would be fairly easy to enforce, since any expenditures would be highly visible and easy enough to calculate. A campaign-practices committee could be created, with bipartisan membership to initiate actions against violators.

A more involved approach would be some form of state financing. One suggestion has been for the state to provide each voter with a voucher which he could give to any candidate, redeemable for money with the state by the candidate. Such a system would not be very expensive for the state. Assuming four primary candidates for each Assembly seat and two in the general election; five primary candidates for each Senate seat and two in the general election; $10,000 per Assembly primary candidate and $12,000 for the general election candidates; and $15,000 per Senate primary candidate and $20,000 for the general election, the total cost would be only $3,710,000 per year—a small price to pay for the gains involved. The six major statewide offices would cost another $793,000 per year, assuming five candidates in all primaries and two for all general elections, and expenses consistent with present levels. The

* AB 958 provides for a one-dollar contribution to a political party of choice from state personal income tax liability for each citizen who so designates.

total cost of such a system would be well under one-tenth of one percent of the state's budget,* amounting to about twenty-five cents per Californian per year.

Or the state could simply provide financing up to a legal maximum to any candidate officially nominated by a party polling more than five percent of the vote in the previous election, or for any candidate with a petition of nomination signed by one percent, for example, of the previous vote for that office. The percentages could be set to guarantee four to five diverse candidates. If local government were reformed to include visible and fewer elected officials, the system could be extended to them. The total cost with free television would be trivial. The gain in independent public policy would be enormous.

Elimination of Conflicts of Interest

The state clearly needs a total revision of its conflict-of-interest and financial-disclosure laws.** At present, the only prosecutable conflict of interest is direct bribery. And bribery, as one Deputy Attorney General assured us, "is about the most difficult crime to prove."

Revision and reenactment of a disclosure law similar to the recent Unruh bill would be useful. Extending existing law into the executive branch (as have many other states, including Kentucky, Georgia, New York, and Massachusetts) is advisable. But the explicit legal requirement of full-time public service without alternative sources of income while in public office is essential. Salaries of legislators should be raised to whatever level will make this requirement reasonable. The closing of any one of a dozen unjustifiable tax loopholes presented in this work would easily provide the necessary revenue. This requirement

---

* Including federal subventions, etc.

** Some eight bills dealing with conflict of interest were introduced during the legislature's 1970 session. Five would further weaken the law, establishing exemptions, or extensions of time for compliance with current law (e.g., campaign expenditure reporting). The other three, while far from adequate, would bring some improvement. These include SB 274 and AB 430, which would extend some legislative conflict provisions to the executive branch, create an ethics commission, prohibit state employees from appearing before the old agency for two years after leaving, and require various investment disclosures; and AB 989, which requires disclosure of numbered bank account investments outside of California, where the law requires investment disclosure. None of these measures has passed.

should include the entire legislature, major staff, the entire executive branch, and important local officials. The non-personal investments of these officials would ideally be divested by law into standard blind trusts for the term of office. Where public responsibilities are narrow, disclosure on public records would be sufficient.

Afterword

I. Covering Up in California[*]
by Bob Kuttner

Nearly all of Ralph Nader's reports are released in Washington, where much of the press corps shares his gusto for taking on the bureaucracy and journalists regard him as a comrade-in-arms. Moreover, because of Nader's reputation for accuracy, the Washington press accords his reports the kind of credibility elsewhere reserved for official sources. Thus, it is almost always the pained denials of the Federal targets that are taken with skepticism, rarely the Nader allegations. In his most important foray outside the capital, however, these relationships were precisely reversed. The California press treatment of Nader's recent *Power and Land in California,* his most ambitious and comprehensive undertaking to date, was so hostile that it left most Californians thinking that Ralph Nader had, in the words of a San Francisco McGovern organizer, "finally screwed up."

Did he? Or does the indictment more properly belong to the California press, which seemed to react in chorus, "My State, Right or Wrong." The California report took twenty-five researchers fourteen months of investigation. It was directed by Robert Fellmeth, one of Nader's original and most careful raiders, an alumnus of a Los Altos grade school and Stanford University, member of the California bar, and co-author of the acclaimed Nader studies of the Interstate Commerce and Federal Trade Commissions. The report is a sophisticated and well-documented treatise on how wealth is translated into political power for the perpetuation of wealth, on the control of the regulators by the regulated, on the perversion of tax incentives for unearned private gain by land speculators, on the social and environ-

* Bob Kuttner's article, "Covering Up in California," is reprinted with the permission of [MORE:] A JOURNALISM REVIEW, where it originally appeared in November, 1971. Copyright © 1971 by Rosebud Associates, Inc. The author's references are to the full Report, POWER AND LAND IN CALIFORNIA, available from the Center for Study of Responsive Law, P.O. Box 919367, Washington, D.C. 20036.

mental costs of California land usage and on the fragmentation and manipulation of local government. Charts show
who literally owns California. Several case studies pinion
abuses by get-rich-quick land developers and inaction by
regulators. The politics of subsidized water is compre-
hensively analyzed, as is water pollution and the failure of
authorities at all levels to enforce existing standards. There
is a detailed study of Santa Clara County, with some
generalized conclusions about zoning mis-incentives. New
material is put on the record: on the transportation lobby
and on the near-monopoly of information flow by Sacramento special interest lobbyists generally. There are also
dozens of pages of recommendations for structured reform.
Some of the information has appeared in bits and pieces
elsewhere, but a great deal is new. In short, the report
provides enough raw data for months of follow-up investigation by a conscientious local press. Instead, the California
papers seized upon a few scattered references to personalities, which took up perhaps ten pages of the 2,000-page
report. In story after patronizing story, reporters made it
plain that they viewed the Nader group as green outsiders
who could not possibly know as much about the state as
the resident press.

Part I of the report was released in Washington on Fri-
day, August 20, [1971] for Sunday A.M. publication. It
dealt with "Who Owns California" and the politics of water
and large-scale agriculture. The initial stories, written by
Washington bureaus, were descriptive and fair. Corre-
spondents for the *Los Angeles Times,* the three Ridder
papers in California and the respected McClatchy papers in
Sacramento, Fresno and Modesto did a thorough job of
summarizing Part I. Copley's *San Diego Union* also gave
the story extensive play on the basis of its Washington
analysis.

Five days after the Washington release, Parts II and III,
1,600 pages in all, were given to the California press, and
coverage changed markedly. Typical was the *Times* story
on Part II, which concerns wild areas and new development. The page-one piece by Philip Fradkin and Paul
Houston was headlined NADER TEAM ACCUSES BROWN, BUT
ITS METHODS ARE QUESTIONED. Most of the story dealt with
Nader's allegations that the former California chief deputy
attorney general has quashed a report recommending prosecution of a land speculator and had taken a contribution

from another developer's attorney, and that former governor Pat Brown's law firm represents land interests, including Boise Cascade, the state's largest developer. All of this occupies a tiny portion of the 315-page Part II. But the reader had to wade past 47 paragraphs of copy implying that undocumented personal attacks are Nader's main point to discover, in the second jump on page 29, that "observers believe that despite the questions raised about some parts of the study, other parts appeared to be well-documented." This was followed by nine paragraphs of one-sentence summaries of everything else in Part II.

The *Times* is not without some vested interest in this matter. The report identifies the *Times* as the owner of several hundred thousand acres of Southern California land directly benefiting from subsidized water. The 348,000-acre Tejon Ranch, in which the *Times* has a substantial share, is the fourth largest private holding in the state. The *Times* Washington bureau had been directed by the paper's managing editor, Frank P. Haven, to note all references to the Times-Mirror Company's land holdings. These references were forwarded to company lawyers. Franklin, Houston and the three other reporters who handled the story in Los Angeles knew that management had requested the information. They also knew that *Times* publisher Otis Chandler, as a beneficiary and long-time booster of the California Water Project, was not favorably disposed to the Nader report.

On September 3, after giving the five reporters another week to work on interpretive features, the *Times* ran three stories and a profile of the study group, taking up almost a page-and-a-half. The treatment illustrates how California reporters reinforced the local public's disposition to dismiss the Nader report as an Eastern broadside directed at the Golden State itself. The report's lengthy sections on urban sprawl, land-use mis-incentives, freeway strangulation, etc., were taken as another of those put-downs of the California way of life. This is how *Times* reporter Ray Hebert began the lead piece in the paper's assessment, entitled THE NADER REPORT: HOW CONCLUSIONS STACK UP:

> When consumer advocate Ralph Nader's task force was deep in its study of California land usage last summer, Robert Fellmeth, the project's director explained:
> "We're sticking our nose into everyone else's business."
> Now that the report has been released, it's clear what

Fellmeth meant. He was referring to the twenty million
people in California. Few have come off untouched by the
denunciation of California's land-use practices. The report points a finger at most Californians—either directly,
by association, by implication through their own ignorance
or by the plain fact that they are residents of the state.

In other words, it is not really the landowners, the corrupt
politicians, the utilities, or the system of tax incentives that
Nader is attacking, gentle reader, it is you and me. The
rest of the story suggests that just about everything in the
report is either old-hat, obvious or wrong. Hebert notes
the report's finding that California has more cars than
licensed drivers to operate them, adding: ". . . but the
report does not explain that this situation is not unique
. . . Experts say the same balance exists in other well-to-do
states." In fact, according to Nader's documentation, the
California ratio of cars to drivers far surpasses that of
other states. Hebert also implies that anything useful in the
Nader report has already come out in the press, using
phrases like "little new material" and "who could argue
with the thesis that . . . ?" Like many other reporters who
covered the story, Hebert took denials at face value. He
quoted officials who insisted that a Nader charge was "pure
fabrication," and on the basis of that unchecked denial
termed the charge "unfortunate."

Philip Fradkin's September 3 piece paralleled Hebert's.
Its headline read: MONIED INTERESTS HELD REAL VILLAIN,
BUT REPORT LACKS NITTY-GRITTY CONSERVATION DATA, CON-
CLUSIONS. Whatever the weakness of the Nader report, the
most cursory reading shows that it does not lack data or
specific recommendations. To much of the press, Nader's
institutional or systematic analysis was "tarring with a
broad brush." Fradkin contrasted Nader's "broad brush"
with the wisdom of local conservationists, who, unlike
Nader, have the good sense "to use reasoned arguments in
hopes that they will influence specific decisions . . ." Two-
thirds of the way through the piece, Fradkin has some
grudging praise for the report's critique of regulatory
agencies.

The third *Times* interpretive piece, THE RAIDERS' LOOK
AT LAND LOBBYISTS: NO NEW INFORMATION, continues the
defensive theme. Reporter Bill Boyarsky argued that the
influence of Sacramento lobbyists "has been disclosed be-

fore. This newspaper and others have written about it for years . . ." In another place, he wrote: "Despite their manpower, the Nader investigators failed to dig into potentially fertile areas and ignored previously published information about abuses." Thus, he criticized the report both for using old material and for not using old material. Boyarsky also cited "factual errors," which were seized on by most papers in the state as ammunition for shooting down the report.

One such error concerned whether Assemblyman William Bagley, chairman of the Revenue and Taxation Committee, shared an apartment in Sacramento with Richard Ratcliff, lobbyist for the Pacific Gas and Electric Company. It turns out that at the time, Bagley was the ranking Republican on another, but related committee, and that Ratcliff is a contract lobbyist with several clients whose interests involved committee actions. Reporter Boyarsky quoted Bagley: "Dick had left P.G. & E. and had private accounts," neatly proving Nader's point. This "error," treated at length in the press, occupied two sentences in the report.

A second widely repeated error hinged on whether Lt. Gov. Ed Reinecke was a member of the State Lands Commission at a time when he took a contribution from the Leslie Salt Company, which benefited from commission rulings. The "error" is that the favorable rulings pre-date Reinecke's tenure on the commission. In fact, the Leslie Salt Company benefits from a continuing commission preference, which Reinecke shows no sign of reversing now that he is a commission member.

Other California papers without landholdings played the story much as the *Times* did. The McClatchy papers have been the state's most vehement defenders of the California Water Project, which the Nader report sharply criticized as a boondoggle for the rich, whose true cost to taxpayers has been consistently understated. As in the *Times,* the initial coverage from the McClatchy Washington bureau was solid. However, many stories written in California contained the same generalized attacks on the report, the same categorical faith in official denials, and the same preoccupation with personalities. Richard Rodda, the *Sacramento Bee's* liberal and well-connected political editor, wrote a front-page interpretive piece on how the report was being roundly denounced in political circles. In a follow-up piece, Rodda observed that there "is not enough evidence in the hundreds of pages of charges and insinuations to convict anyone of misappropriating so much as a state-owned paper clip." Which totally misses the point. Nader's California report was not written primarily as an exposé of misconduct in high places. Institutionalized conflict of interest—not individual wrong-doings—is at the heart of Nader's report. This basic thrust is underscored by a recent California Supreme Court ruling that the State Forestry Board—nominally a regulatory agency whose enabling legislation requires that it be industry-dominated—is in reality just that, an industry body, and therefore may not be accorded the status of a governmental agency. According to the report, the same is true of most environmental regulatory bodies in California.

Indeed it is. But it would be a mistake to center blame on nervous publishers eager to discredit embarrassing news. Doubtless this played some role, especially in the *Times'* coverage. But the principal reasons for the media's failure to give the report thoughtful scrutiny are more subtle and fundamental to the weaknesses of American journalism.

Almost instinctively, the press expects critics like Nader to go after the familiar conservative whipping boys. Yet here he was taking on liberals like Pat Brown, who, after all, had given California the nation's first office of consumer counsel. The point here is that the report, quite properly, is less concerned with whether Brown is a white hat or a black hat than with the fact that advocacy by a former governor on behalf of the state's largest land developer is accepted as normal. Here were outsiders saying that the liberal establishment—of which most of the press is, of course, a part—had failed. Significantly, Nader's one previous roasting came when he appeared to be attacking a liberal politician. In the context of a lengthy report on *Vanishing Air* last year, he devoted a few pages to how Senator Muskie, sponsor of the already weak 1967 Air Quality Act, had failed to hold follow-up hearings on its inadequate enforcement. For this "unwarranted attack" on a good guy, Nader was lambasted in the liberal press. (Ironically, Muskie now takes the position that gets Nader in so much trouble. "The blunt truth," he said in a recent address, "is that liberals have achieved virtually no fundamental change in our society since the end of the New

Deal.") Equally important, reporters dealt with the California story in terms of charge and counter-charge, a hopelessly anachronistic concept of journalism. Most reporters seemed unable to handle the difficult issues, to examine Nader's analysis of the role of institutional power. And once viewed in terms of charges and personalities, the report did, indeed, seem to be attacking everybody, which only served to reinforce the sense that it could not possibly be fair.

In the end, the message was clear. Outside of Washington, where Nader's integrity is taken for granted and he is valued as an alternative to official information, Nader's Raiders remain highly suspect. When a state rather than an industry is the target there is no general press to offset a hostile trade press. The dailies *are* the trade press, and many reporters in the Golden State clearly are Californians first and journalists second.

In San Jose, the Ridders' *Mercury* and *News* also eagerly put down the report. Santa Clara County, the object of a major section of the report, is home turf for the *Mercury* and *News*. In another example of a front-page interpretive piece by a political editor, Harry Farrell devoted most of his space to quoting categorical denials. Headlined *NADER HIT BY CITY OFFICIALS,* the piece approvingly includes such quotes as "I don't think Nader knows what he's talking about" and a reference to the Nader study group as "half-baked kids out of law school." Again, there was little apparent effort by the writer to weigh independently the official disclaimers against the Nader contentions. The *News* also cut three paragraphs from a column by its Washington correspondent, Lou Cannon. Although favorable material was retained, Cannon's description of the report as possibly "the best thing that's happened to the state in years" did not get into print in San Jose.*

---

* The excluded section stated:
. . . Shows a courage and a devotion to documentation that have simply been missing from most of the efforts that have gone before it.

Instead of nibbling around the edges of the environmentally destructive state water plan, for instance, the report goes right to the heart of its funny-money economics with an indictment that ought to stop the project once and for all.

The report also performs a useful service by publishing the long-suppressed attorney general's report on California City, which serves as a focal point for a devastating chapter on the ruin caused

In more extreme cases, the combination of unchecked official disclaimers and slanted headlines produced absurd results. The Nader report's case study of the proposed new Los Angeles airport at Palmdale is devastating. It was prepared by the number one and two men of the Harvard Law School class of 1970, who now clerk for U.S. Supreme Court Justices Potter Stewart and Thurgood Marshall, respectively. The account documents how Palmdale, a development fallen on hard times, lured the new airport plans through boosterism and cronyism, and how the location is environmentally hazardous and of dubious safety for air traffic. The site, sixty miles from central Los Angeles, was chosen in violation of Federal Environmental Policy Act procedures. The *Los Angeles Herald Examiner* story on August 26 was headlined: L.A. REFUTES NADER ON PALMDALE. Not rebuts, but refutes; not L.A. officials, but L.A. The story was a series of routine denials, which were not themselves checked. The *Times'* Paul Houston, who has written on Palmdale and criticized other portions of the Nader report, says that he regards the Palmdale section as one of the best in the study.

In San Francisco, the *Chronicle,* which delights in spicy stories about North Beach hookers and is generally bored by state politics, gave the report scant coverage. In fairness, however, it was the only major California paper that gave as much coverage to the report's findings as it did to generalized denials. Two major pieces ran on August 26, the release date for Part II, both leading with factual information on the report's findings. The *Chronicle,* which has editorially opposed the State Water Project, also ran two stories on the positive response to the report by Congressman Jerome Waldie, a gubernatorial aspirant.

Whether reporters took their cues from editors or vice versa, the public received a grossly misleading view of the Nader study. And editorials only magnified the distortions. The *Oakland Tribune* used such words as "egocentric" and "self-serving" to dismiss the Nader study group. The *San*

---

the California wilderness by recreational subdivisions. And there are valuable observations on the gap between practice and propaganda in reforestation and wild land management.

This is the stuff of which crusades are made, or, better yet, lawsuits. One doesn't have to buy Nader's moralistic view of California to believe that his report may be the best thing that's happened to the state in years.

Diego Union observed that most members of the study group were outsiders. (The opening line of the Nader press release begins, "Most of us are native Californians.") The *Union* wondered where the group got its money. (Page one of the report thanks the three foundations that paid for it.) A McClatchy editorial called the report "an intemperate, reckless and unwarranted blemishing of men dedicated to public service." The *Times* stated flatly: "Nader's group has failed to come up with new material," accusing the study of making "reckless charges . . . for which there is no evidence." Even the *Chronicle,* which at least provided balanced play in its news columns, editorially had the most categorical indictment of all: "It could be said of this report that there is much that is new and much that is true, but what's true isn't new, and what's new isn't true." Nearly all of the editorial criticism was generalized. The few specifics dealt with the same trivial "errors." Liberal Republican Norton Simon was so annoyed by the performance of the press that he was moved to call a news conference on September 15 to urge more serious consideration of the report, expressing shock at "the nitpicking negativism" of the newspapers. "The media itself," said Simon, "is very much on trial."

II. The Press and the Politics of Land

The report on Power and Land in California received widespread attention in the media and editorial support for many of its conclusions and recommendations. But the issues it raised persist far beyond the few days of reportage devoted to them. The investigative and evaluative followthrough by the media of these and related issues, highlighted by other citizen efforts, require a stamina of purpose that is often lacking. So it is worthwhile to make additional observations about the media's treatment of the report, the rebuttals it published, and other responses to the findings of our study.

The press and other news media are prime conveyors of information. Without them democracy is impossible. The Constitutional guarantees behind the media must therefore be exceptionally strong to ensure the carrying out of its public responsibilities with freedom, courage, and skill. It has been an unfortunate trend that, along with the inhibitions that flow from advertising considerations, further restraints on free expression are due to the fact that much of the news media is interlocking through networks, chains, ownership, etc. Moreover, the companies that own the media have engaged in acquisitions and other business investments that are far removed from communications.

Such is the case among several important media companies in California who reach millions of readers, viewers, and listeners daily. There can be little doubt that in some important respects, such a "conglomeratization" of the communications media increases their vulnerability to compromises with the independence of judgment and objectivity of coverage that are essential to their public trust. Nowhere is this more true than in the conflicts of allegiance implicit in those media companies with substantial operating interests in California land and land resources.

The major newspapers in California's three largest cities —Los Angeles, San Francisco, and San Diego—along with their radio and television counterparts, have been long-standing and substantial investors in timberland and logging, agricultural and ranch land, and recreational developments. The Tejon Ranch is partly owned by the *L.A. Times*'s parent conglomerate, together with timber holdings; the Hearst chain, which controls the other L.A. paper, the *Herald Tribune,* and the *S.F. Examiner,* and enormous developments and timberland holdings; Scott Newhall, until recently controlling the *S.F. Chronicle,* has huge holdings; the Copley chain, controlling both San Diego papers, has diverse holdings. The total involved in these holdings, as a reading of the appendices reveals, approaches 2 million acres of California. Together, they or related subsidiaries receive ample and documented benefits from Williamson Act subsidies, unnecessary roads, unrestrained logging policies, lax real estate laws and even laxer enforcement, tax loopholes, the State Water Project, and other public works. Their stake is by no means academic, but critical to the comfortable wealth of their owners, who hire and promote the news and editorial staffs. Such conflicts of interest should be seen as intolerable by more enlightened owners and by the Antitrust Division of the U.S. Department of Justice.

When the California report was released, the California press responded by and large with outrage, ignoring the difficult issues while accusing the report of everything from typographical errors to being a conspiracy of "outsiders."

The *L.A. Times,* for example, owner of several hundred thousand acres of land in southern California, accused the report of rhetorical overkill, citing the Palmdale critique which, according to the *Times,* makes "sweeping generalizations without a shred of documentation." Palmdale backers, now confronted by some of this alleged nonexistent documentation in court, would hardly agree.*

Richard Rodda (the *Sacramento Bee*) followed with a front-page article alleging that the Report accused all legislators with land holdings of "corruption" because they all vote according to their personal interests and then presented the voting records of two legislators with some land connections as 100% conservationist. The report had not alleged that *all* legislators voted for personal gain, specifically mentioning that many did not (see above).

Both the *Sacramento Bee* and the *San Diego Union* ran stories stating, "The California report asserts [former Governor Pat] Brown deliberately had a $2 billion bond issue for the water project placed on the ballot. . . . In fact, Brown said, the bond issue was for $1,750,000,000." The report (see above) nowhere makes the error attributed to it. In both stories the report's arguments against the water project were replaced with fabricated or mistaken allegations.** The San Jose papers went even further and accused the report of advocating the dismantling of already built water projects serving Santa Clara County. Both Los Angeles and Sacramento papers did not print letters we sent them to rebut criticism of the water project section.

The *Bee* and radio stations widely repeated the allegations of Ralph Brody, manager of the Westlands Water District, that the report was "just plain silly" because there is a 160-acre limitation per person on land holdings which receive federally subsidized waters—this breaks up large

---

* Supporters of the Palmdale site, upon review of the evidence against the site (almost all of it presented in the report), have admitted non-compliance with the National Environmental Policy Act and are at least forced to delay construction pending a bona fide impact study.

** For example, we are quoted as saying in both papers that the total cost of the water project was $2.8 billion but the Governor set it as $2 billion. The *Tulare Advance Register* and other papers then accused us of deception for failing to take inflation into account which would make up this difference. In fact, as the text reveals, we argued that the cost of the Project is closer to $10 billion and our figures take inflation into account.

landholding just as we say should be done. But the report does not deny the existence of the 160-acre limitation, it documents the gross violation, loopholing, and nonenforcement of the limitation.

The *San Francisco Chronicle* and other papers widely quoted Jerome Gilbert, executive director of the State Water Quality Control Board: "the report is clearly mistaken in reporting only 7 cease and desist orders in the first 5½ months of the . . . Act's existence." One paper went on, "He brought out tabulations indicating that the *regional boards* issued 55 such orders in the first six months" (emphasis added). The report actually states: "the *State* Board issued only 7 cease and desist orders," which is both the correct and relevant figure, as Board officials have subsequently admitted in correspondence with project co-authors.

Lt. Governor Reinecke issued a statement denying that he had a campaign debt as alleged and cited a typographical error before concluding that "there are so many errors it is funny." The report noted that Reinecke probably did *not* have a campaign debt since electoral victors have no trouble finding creditors, but that his campaign records show a campaign debt. The point of the report is that the records do not show the disposition of campaign surpluses or the identities of those who pay off campaign debts. Reinecke further buttressed our point by neatly failing to disclose who had paid off his apparent debt while admitting that *someone* had (since it no longer existed).

The judgments of former governor Pat Brown—that the report is "inaccurate," "sensational," and "shallow"—were widely quoted in the press and on television.* Rarely did a story mention that Brown's law firm represents substantial land interests, including Boise Cascade, the largest developer in the state. Nor did they mention that, as he

---

* On KABG-TV in Los Angeles, August 21, 1971, the former Governor expressed his critique of the report's views of the Water Project: "Now it's true that some farmers will benefit from the water, but so be it. We need the farmers in California, they're the largest exporters that we have, and they're paying for the water, and they're paying a good price for the water, and it's simply—the report is simply, absolutely inaccurate. . . ." While the former Governor is asserting that the farmers will pay for their water, Water Project supporters are agreeing that although farmers will not be paying fully for the water, they should not have to. The *Sacramento Bee* quoted Brown as follows: "The report tends to be sensational; it is a shallow report . . . I don't think it's been thought through."

told one of our researchers, he had not read the report. Typically, the media followed a pattern of publicizing the emotional quotes and denunciations of California "patriots and politicians" while failing to examine or take issue with the report's evidence or its analysis of institutional power.

Governor Reagan responded to the report primarily by making "flat world" assertions: the Task Force consists of "flat worlders" who would have called Columbus back into harbor because of safety lapses. The Governor's appointments secretary, Ned Hutchinson, announced in response to the report that appointees are required by the Governor to sell—or put into trust—anything that would raise a question of possible conflict of interest.

This is nonsense. As the text documents, the Governor's appointees are generally from the industries regulated, and many of them maintain positions in industry before, while, and after holding positions of public trust. Indeed, Mr. Hutchinson is referring only to the "investments" of some appointees. Investments would appear to be a moot point when the industry regulated is an official's private legal client, his employer, or even quite literally himself. As for questionable investments, there has been no public disclosure of this alleged divestiture order by the Governor, nor has there been any notable enforcement of it.

The local media, with some exceptions, also repeated at great length what was the brunt of the attack directed against the report—an *ad hominem* characterization of the researchers as zealous "outsiders" carpetbagging into California and inaccurately criticizing everything and everyone in the state.* The nature of the attack was pure assertion. "Irresponsible juvenile delinquents," "young zealots," youth with an "inbred dislike of the establishment." This last characterization from the Western Developers' Conference statement is accompanied by references to the "drug oriented, free-loading youth culture." The L.A. Department of Airports stated that the researchers "are trying to prove pre-conceived ideas. This is an attempt to mislead the

---

* For example, in an article repeating an incorrect criticism of State Controller Houston Fluorney, the *San Jose News* headlines of August 26, 1971 read: *State Broadside Fired at Nader,* elevating Mr. Fluorney's status to spokesmen for 20 million. Or, there is the *Bee* headline of August 24 "Nader indicts 3 Governors, People . . ." or the *L.A. Times* of August 27 "Most of California Hit in Nader Report Wrap Up."

public and as a result they have lost all credibility." The
Metropolitan Water District similarly announced in a press
release handed out before receiving a copy of the report:

> Unfortunately the Nader report can only be termed a
> highly irresponsible and slapdash compilation of inaccu-
> racies, untruths, malicious rumors, unsupported charges,
> distortions and headline-hunting generalizations.

The remarks of former Assemblyman and Democratic
gubernatorial candidate Jesse Unruh were given the widest
circulation. He was quoted via radio and television as follows: "Unruh says that inaccuracies hurt the Nader Report
on California land use. Today, Mr. Unruh described the
report as only about eighty percent accurate." What Unruh,
who now represents Mendelsohn, the developer of California City, actually said was that in his judgment the
report was "eighty percent accurate, which is better than
most reports."

From the Western White House at San Clemente, the
President's Communications Director, Herb Klein, responded to the report before he saw it, remarking that
easterner Nader "might contribute more by concentrating
on his own environment."*

At his press conference, attorney "legislative advocate"
Whiting of the Western Developers' Conference issued
further assertions, and based his criticism on the lack of
knowledge by the report's researchers of development laws
or of the subtle field of construction. The *Independent
Journal* of August 26 describes Mr. Whiting as then noting
that

> *he* was familiar with state laws governing developers be-
> cause he had "worked closely with the legislature and real
> estate commissioner's office" on writing and enforcing the
> laws.

Actually, 18 of the report's 25 researchers in California
are natives of the state. And the group includes 9 attorneys
(one of whom has spent several years with a firm representing major developers such as Boise Cascade), a Ph.D.
in economics, one in agricultural economics, one in biology,
and one in city planning. But it is true that expertise gen-

* See the *San Francisco Sunday Examiner & Chronicle,* August
22, 1971.

erally is not essential. Citizens can, in a matter of months of intensive study, master concepts and vocabulary enough to contribute solidly to public discussion—that, at least, is the basis of the theory of democratic government.

There were exceptions to such one-sided publicity. The *San Jose News,* after three days of blasting* chapter VI of the report (now Chapter 9), which focuses on San Jose and Santa Clara County, finally discovered that, editorially, they in fact agreed with part of it. In an editorial entitled "Nugget of Reason in Nader Exposé" the paper lauds at least *one* good point about about chapter VI: its critique of local government fragmentation. The editorial quotes from the report and mentions the paper's own long concern with this problem. It is somewhat ironic, however, that it was described as a "nugget." For the issue of fragmentation was not a nugget of chapter VI, it *was* chapter VI. Witness the subheadings: "economic fragmentation," "political fragmentation," "geographical fragmentation," etc.

Furthermore, *The Analyst, The American Society of Planning Officials,* and numerous conservation groups backed the report. Industrialist and Republican senatorial candidate Norton Simon called a press conference to back the report after reading it and publicly declared that the "media" was "on trial." His remarks, however, were not widely quoted.

Most recently, Paul Houston, a reporter for the especially critical *L.A. Times,* was asked by Ralph Nader to get specifics on errors and criticisms and to suggest changes based on the judgments of the five *Times* reporters assigned the task by management of "evaluating" the report. In a letter to the Project Director, Houston notes that none of those he asked could give him any suggestions for correction or improvement. One reporter specifically told him that he had reviewed a chapter carefully and had found no errors, but had written nothing because several articles had already been written on the subject. The letter-writer himself suggested revisions that amount to about one page.

Perhaps the most disturbing point about the nature of the

---

* Most of the front page critique consisted of the quoted polemics of officials stung by criticism. Hence, State Senator Alquist is quoted as doubting Nader's allegiance to democracy because of the report's criticism of local government fragmentation, mixed with "who does he think he is" outrage.

news coverage of the report was not the distortion or in-
accuracy or parochialism of it, but the fact that the report's
content lies substantially unreported in California. Reacting
to a complex report by getting quick hostile quotes meant
that political commentators read at most isolated sentences
of the report before making judgment and reply. They were
not confronted with any of the details or evidence of the
report nor obliged to respond with specificity. Except for
the report itself, Californians have no way of learning about
the details of the following major reports and documents:
The ignored report by the Frauds Division of the Attorney
General's office on the $102 million California City swindle;
internal FAA and other file documents recommending
against the Palmdale Airport site; State Department of
Public Health reports revealing violation of sewage and
water quality standards; unreleased reports by State Public
Health showing violation of pesticide regulations and resulting sickness and deaths; survey data demonstrating
enormous concentration in land ownership; surveys showing the Williamson Act benefitting a few conglomerate
holders of wasteland not intended to be covered; assessment
data and surveys indicating general violation of the law;
the Governor's letter asking the President not to enforce
federal water pollution law; evidence of general nonenforcement of the State Porter-Cologne water pollution
act; fish kill data from the State Department of Fish and
Game; general election campaign record forms excluding
the perjury statement necessary to enforce it.

Events since the release of the report in August of 1971
have now substantiated many of its findings and themes.
The recent decision of the California Supreme Court declaring the school financing scheme of the state unconstitutional—by virtue of its violation of Fourteenth Amendment equal protection standards—repeats the findings and
arguments of chapter VI (now 9). In *Bayside Timber Co.,
Inc.* v. *San Mateo County Board of Supervisors,** the California Court of Appeals decided that the State Forest
Practices Act (see chapter 4) does not constitute state
regulation because industry controls the act's administration. Hence, San Mateo County may enforce its own regulations since there is no legitimate preemption in the area

---

* California Court of Appeals, September 16, 1971.

by the State. Judge Elkington, who presided over the case, wrote:

> As pointed out, the legislature has delegated to timber owners and operators the exclusive power to formulate forest practice rules which, when adopted, have the force and effect of law. The combination of forest practice committees, and timber ownership, in their absolute discretion, are free to formulate, or not formulate, rules tending to prevent erosion, to lessen flooding, to protect wildlife, to preserve natural beauty, or otherwise to serve the public interest.
>
> It is an age-old principle of our law that no man should judge or otherwise officially preside over disputed matters in which he has a pecuniary interest. California's Constitution, Article IV, Section 5, notices the same concept by providing that the legislature shall enact laws to prohibit its members "from engaging in activities or having interests which conflict with the proper discharge of their duties and responsibilities. . . ."

The mantle of state action on industry cartels is by this ruling removed by the court. In the regulation of oil and gas drilling, water pollution, real estate, and in other areas, the ruling could equally apply, although there are no petitions with standing able to extend it.

Other suits may affirm by court order what the report has argued should be policy. Dr. Ben Yellen, a long-time crusader for enforcement of the 1902 Federal Reclamation Act, won a major round in one of his suits against the Department of the Interior on November 22, 1971. In a partial summary judgment, Federal District Judge William Murray, citing legislative sources, noted that "from its very inception reclamation policy has been to make [federally financed] benefits available to the largest number of people. The 1902 Act contained a 160-acre limitation, required that users [of federally provided water] be bona fide residents . . . and provided that rights to the water be limited to beneficial use." The loopholing and nonenforcement of these provisions is described in chapter 2, above, but Judge Murray notes that "The fact that residency has not been required by the Department of Interior for over 55 years cannot influence the outcome of this decision . . . failing to apply the requirement is contrary to any reasonable interpretation of the reclamation law. . . ." An end to conglomerate enrichment from taxpayer-financed projects would mean divestiture of many of California's largest holdings. Yet the *New York Times* carried the story of the decision in greater detail than did California's major papers.

Sierra Club suits against specific roads, Mineral King, the State Water Project, and the Palmdale Airport are now pending. David Daar, a leading class action attorney, has brought suit against the Metropolitan Water District to test the "rumors" and "unsupported generalizations," as the District describes the report. He has been joined by a former director of the District. In addition, several grand juries have sought out the report and are investigating several of its specific case studies. The new Republican Attorney General's Office is prosecuting Boise Cascade. The State Board of Equalization has completed a study on the Williamson Act which explicitly backs the report's data and conclusions—and has discovered some additional evidence since the report's release. The Bureau of Reclamation issued a 1972 paper that verified much of the report's case study of Lake Berryessa.

Hearings in California by Senator Fred Harris (D.-Okla.) into agricultural subsidies and land monopoly in March of 1972 have produced additional evidence supporting much of the report's chapter 2.*

These, however, are moral victories. And being right is, unfortunately, not enough to stop the Water Project, the Palmdale Airport, wasteful road construction, the Williamson Act, damaging and often fraudulent speculative subdivisions, unnecessary agricultural subsidies, or harmful pesticide practices. Water pollution laws are unenforced, logging is unrestricted, open spaces and parks are not reserved or preserved, tax subsidies for land speculators continue, local government fragmentation grows more confusing and damaging, conflict-of-interest relations are prevalent within executive and legislative branches, and the list continues.

Clearly, much work is ahead. And in this area of private wealth and enormous profit at public expense, the institutional allies will not be many. Assuredly, we cannot rely on politicians trapped by campaign needs and their own private interests, for whom political survival is tantamount

---

* See *Congressional Record,* May 17, 1972, E5391-5429.

to financial aggrandizement. Nor, it would seem, can we rely on the media.

Several co-authors of the report helped to start "Clear Creek," an environmental publication. Others have begun to work with California Action, a San Francisco-based lobbying group which is trying to mobilize local citizens, conservation groups, and organized labor behind the report. Student Public Interest Research Groups (PIRGs) are now striving to fund full-time action arms in Sacramento, and similar efforts are in progress elsewhere in the state.

To understand the obstacles to these efforts, citizens have but to view the ability of Ronald Reagan to campaign successfully for Governor in 1970. In ad after ad Reagan was portrayed as the enforcer of the "toughest water pollution control law in the history of the world," "$6,000 a day in fines and the cost of cleaning up their own mess . . . we've hit them so hard they don't dare pollute." In fact, not a cent* in fines had been assessed against any polluter, although two-thirds of the dischargers in the allegedly "best" region of California are in open defiance of the state pollution law. And year after year, propositions that would protect California's environment have been kept off the legislature due to campaign efforts of the public relations firm of Whittaker and Baxter. Hired by the secretive oil and land interests, Whittaker and Baxter use the "big lie" technique in billboard ads, radio and television spots, and ads. Proposition 18 in 1970 for mass transit would "raise taxes" and lead to "toll roads." Proposition 9 in 1972 would mean a 1929 depression, more pollution, and perhaps an outbreak of cholera. Private wealth and public deceit have set much policy in California. Even the most absurd claim, if repeated enough without response, eventually appears truthful. Clearly, there is no other area where citizen involvement is more needed.

—Robert C. Fellmeth

* The State levied a $12,000 fine against U.S. Steel, an illegal polluter since 1964, about one week before the August 1971 release of the California report. The fine is being called a "contribution" and can be deducted as an "ordinary business expense" for tax purposes.

Appendices

Appendix 1A
Major Private Landowners and Holdings in California—Data List *

PRIMARILY AGRICULTURE

Name	Acreage	Comments
200,000+ acres		
Newhall Land and Farming	1,600,000	
Tenneco Inc.	362,843	+53,584 leased in California and over one million acres owned in other states, mostly through Kern County Land Co. subsidiary.
Tejon Ranch Co.	348,000	50% owned by L.A. Times Mirror Corp.
So. Pacific Co.	2,411,000	394,000— approx. rt. of way and trans. acreage; 163,000 agricultural; 674,000 grazing; 468,000 timber. Rest is idle and held for investment.
		179,023—Siskiyou Co. survey; 17,500—Butte Co.; 60,294.84—Nevada Co.; 28,852—Sierra Co.; 197,160—Trinity Co.; 156,400—Shasta Co.; 111,256—Fresno Co. (D. Survey).
		2,017,000 nontrans. holdings verified by owner.
Standard Oil of California, Inc.	306,000	Mostly agricultural—also for oilfield operations, refining, marketing, pipelines, grazing and development. Verified by owner.
80,000–200,000 acres		
Irvine Co.	101,600	Row and field crops—25,837; Pasture and grazing—49,016; Develop.—15,747; 10,000 in Imperial County. Verified by owner.
J.G. Boswell	108,000	Includes Boston Ranch Inc.— verified by owner.
Miller & Lux, Inc.	93,058	Includes Buena Vista Farms (26,766 acres), Bowles Farming Co., Santiago Ranch.
Newhall Land and Farming	152,000	50,000 in agriculture, numerous ranches.
Kaiser-Aetna	118,000	Rancho California (98,000 acres) and Rancho Ventura (10,000 acres).

* As of January, 1971. See text for general sources. "Verified by owner" means owner responded to our survey, supplying the acreage figure. "Metsker's" refers to "Metsker's Map." "Danielson Survey" refers to the assessor survey of the State Senator in cooperation with our Task Force (see Chapter 2.) "Studies" or "surveys" of individual counties refers to our separate survey of assessors (note forms in Appendix 1B and in text).

Name	Acreage	Comments
	40,000–80,000 acres	
Giffen Inc.	60,000	52,410 in Westlands Water District.
San Diego Water Co.	46,000	Pre-1960 records.
Sutter Basin Corp.	41,922	Pre-1960 records.
Anderson, Clayton & Co. (ACCO)	52,000	(Vista del Llano) 30,738 in Westlands Water District.
Rancho Mission Viejo Co.	50,000	Orange Co.
Wm. G. Henshaw	60,000	San Diego Co.
Cammatti Ranch	40,000	Shandon, San Luis Obispo Co.—both cultivated and range land.
R.E. Jack Co.	60,000	Cholane, San Luis Obispo Co.—both cultivated and range land.
Twisselman Estate	45,000	Cholane, San Luis Obispo Co.—ranch, cultivated, and orchard land.
Dibles Estate Co.	46,000	Santa Barbara Co.
Jesus Marina Rancho Co.	47,000	Santa Barbara Co.
H. & W. Pierce	47,000	Santa Barbara Co.
Edwin L. Stanton	50,000	Santa Cruz Island, Santa Barbara Co.—range land.
Vailt Vickers	52,000	Santa Rosa Island, Santa Barbara Co.—range land.
Hearst Ranch	50,000	San Simeon, San Luis Obispo Co.—range land.
K. Walker et al.	51,200	
Getty Oil	62,000	Danielson Survey, Kern Co.—12,000 development, 48,000 agricultural.
Bangor-Punta Corp.	54,000	54,000 acres in Southlake Farms—conglomerate.
	20,000–40,000 acres	
Purex Corp.	30,000	Major subsidiaries: Brock Ranches, Fresh Pick. Others include: Valley Packing Co., Wilco Produce Co., Gonzales Potato Co., George Russ Co. (Col.), Assoc. Produce Distributors, Cochran Co., Ferry Morse Seed Co., John Jacobs Farms (Ark.), Oceanview Farms. Most land in vegetable production. Purex is being told to divest by FTC.
River Farms Co.	31,000	

Name	Acreage	Comments
Di Giorgio Corp.	27,000	
Del Monte Corp.	21,220	Formerly *Del Monte*
Colt Ranch Inc.	24,500	6,500 agriculture; 1,800 recreation; 6,252 in Westlands Water District. Verified by owner.
Will Gill & Sons	29,926	
Tidewater Assoc. Oil Co.	25,551	
Von Glahn Lands	21,553	
Blackwell Land Co.	25,000	Owned by Lazard Freres.
Samuel S. Vener	28,000	
Sisquoi Ranch	38,000	Owned by James Flood; Santa Barbara Co.
Moulton Co.	21,500	El Toro Orange Co.—range, orchard, cultivated land.
C.W. Clark Co.	20,000	Shandon, San Luis Obispo Co.—range land.
Grayson Owens Co.	35,000	Carrisa, San Luis Obispo Co.—range and cultivated land.
Santa Margarita Ranch	26,000	Santa Margarita, San Luis Obispo Co.—cultivated and range land.
Claude Arnold	20,000	Carrisa, San Luis Obispo Co.—cultivated and range land.
La Panza	30,000	Carrisa, San Luis Obispo Co.—cultivated and range land.
Sinton Bros.	25,000	Shandon, San Luis Obispo Co.—range land.
Pike	30,000	Stewarts Pt., Sonoma Co.—range land.
I.G. Zumwalt	30,000	Colusa, California—cultivated, orchard, and range land.
Wendell Payne	20,000	Woodland, Colusa Co.—range land.
J.E. Mitchell	28,000	Colusa Co.—range land.
Wm. Sites	20,000	Colusa Co.—range land.
French Co.	27,000	Willows, Glenn Co.—range land.
Grenoc Ranch	22,000	Middletown, Lake Co.—range and cultivated land.
Hewlett Packard Co.	22,828	San Felipe Ranch, Danielson Survey, Santa Clara Co.
Adobe Ranch	22,000	Madera Co.—range land.
Flournoy Bros.	25,820	13,540 Modoc Co.—cultivated and range land; 12,280 Fassen Co.—Metsker's.
Nels Monroe & Son	25,000	Modoc Co.—cultivated and range land.
Broome Ranch	24,000	Camarillo, Ventura Co.—range land.

Name	Acreage	Comments
L. Doheny	22,000	Ventura, Santa Barbara Co.
Lewis Family	20,000	Carrisa, San Luis Obispo Co.
Belridge Oil Co.	24,000	Through Belridge Land Co.
Roger Jessup Farms	21,700	18,500 Modoc Co.—Metsker's '58; 3,200 Trinity Co.—Metsker's '59.
Anderson, Clayton	30,738	In Westlands Water District.
L. McConnel	20,480	Shasta Co.—Metsker's '59.
Wm. Smith	34,960	25,760—Humboldt Co.; 9,200—Lassen Co.
Salyer Land Co.	34,000	Danielson Survey, Kings Co.
Westlake Farms	24,250	Danielson Survey, Kings Co.
California Land & Cattle	31,370	Danielson Survey, Monterey Co.
Galvin Trust	30,057	Danielson Survey, Monterey Co.

10,000–20,000 acres

Name	Acreage	Comments
Dow Chemical	16,940	15,000 for Bud Antle Lettuce land; 1,158 more for agriculture; 782 for industrial—some is in Arizona.
Giumarra Vineyards Corp.	12,459	Including some leases.
Spreckels Sugar Co.	14,800	
Union Sugar Co.	11,200	Verified by owner.
San Emidio Rancho	15,660	
J.F. Gibson	12,517	
Kings Co. Devel. Co.	11,371	
Sayler, William Jr.	10,240	
General Petroleum Co.	12,296	
South Dawn— McCarthy Farms	14,000	
Bruce Church Inc.	14,000	
M.J. Yoder	15,000	Hemet, Riverside Co.—cultivated land.
Searl Bros.	15,000	Hemet, Riverside Co.—cultivated land.
Martin Bloom & Co.	18,000	San Diego Co.
Jean Cazaurang	16,000	San Diego Co.
P.J. Connolly	12,000	Tracy, San Joaquin Co.—range land.
White Ranch Co.	10,000	Shandon, San Luis Obispo Co.—cultivated and range land.

Name	Acreage	Comments
Heilmann Bros.	15,000	Atascadero, San Luis Obispo Co.—cultivated and range land.
Miller & Hanson	12,000	Shandon, San Luis Obispo Co.—range land.
Asa Porter	15,000	Arroyo Islands, San Luis Obispo Co.—cultivated and range land.
Elmer King	10,000	Carrisa, San Luis Obispo Co.—cultivated land.
Rice Ranch	10,000	Nipomo, San Luis Obispo Co.
Guy Arnold	10,000	Pozo, San Luis Obispo Co.
Goodwin Ranch	10,000	Carrisa, San Luis Obispo Co.
Howard Sumner	10,000	Carrisa, San Luis Obispo Co.
Howard Iverson	15,000	Cholane, San Luis Obispo Co.—cultivated and range land.
Iver Hansen	10,000	Paso Robles, San Luis Obispo Co.—cultivated and orchard land.
J.R. Ranches	15,000	Paso Robles, San Luis Obispo Co.—cultivated and range land.
Fields Ranch	10,000	San Luis Obispo—range land.
Marre Land & Cattle Co.	15,000	San Luis Obispo—range land.
Tar Springs Ranch	10,000	Arroyo Grande—range land.
Buck Horn Ranch	10,000	Carrisa, San Luis Obispo Co.—cultivated and range land.
R.T. Buell	16,000	Santa Barbara Co.
Orena family	18,000	Santa Barbara Co.
J.E. Cebrian	19,000	Santa Barbara Co.
Patterson Bros.	11,000	Livermore, Alameda Co.—range land
George Walker	15,000	Livermore, Alameda Co.—range land.
E.L. Adams	10,000	Nelson, Butte Co.—cultivated land.
Chester Tiscornia	17,000	San Andreas, Calaveras Co.—range land.
J.L. Browning	10,000	Colusa—cultivated land.
Howell Davis	10,000	Colusa—cultivated land.
Bacchi Ranch	15,000	Lotus, El Dorado Co.—range land.
Todd Wheeler	14,000	Orland, Glenn Co.—range land.
Holmes Livestock Co.	17,000	Willows, Glenn Co.—range land.
Ernest Michael	14,000	Artois, Glenn Co.—range land.
Sherman Thomas	11,000	Madera Co.—cultivated land.
H.C. Cattle Co.	19,000	Modoc Co.—cultivated and range land; 3,000—Lassen Co.
W.S. Orvies & Son	10,000	Northern Stanislaus Co.—cultivated land.
Dickerson Ranch	12,000	Patterson, Stanislaus Co.—range land.
George Covert	12,000	Coast range, Stanislaus Co.—range land.

Name	Acreage	Comments
George Covell	10,000	Patterson, Stanislaus Co.—cultivated land.
Sutter Basin Corp.	12,000	Robbins, Sutter Co.—cultivated land.
River Farms	13,500	Knights Landing, Yolo Co.—cultivated land.
American Crystal Sugar Co.	12,000	
Meiss Ranch, Inc.	13,323	Siskiyou Co. assessor.
Porterfield Bros., Inc.	12,852	Siskiyou Co. assessor.
Roy Naftzger	13,794	Danielson Survey, Santa Clara Co.
Mills Ranch	10,532	Siskiyou Co. Assessor.
Redfern Ranches	13,017	Danielson Co., Santa Clara Co.
John Gill et al.	10,383	Sacramento Co. assessor.
Bar Seventy-One	10,385	Danielson Survey, Santa Clara Co.
Nora Henderlong-Wickersham Ranch	11,883	Danielson Survey, Sonoma Co.
Soper Wheeler Co.	10,120	Butte Co. Survey.
5-D Ranch (Douglass)	11,359	Danielson Survey, Stanislaus Co.
Taylor, Augustus Jr.	10,100.11	Nevada Survey, Stanislaus Co.
Hansen Cattle Co.	12,020	Lassen Co.—Metsker's '58.
W.H. Raupp et al.	13,040	" "
G.R. Heath	11,520	" "
T.E. Connolly	13,400	" "
W.H. Hunt, Est. Co.	14,440	" "
J.W. Mapes	13,400	" "
S.S. Jaksick	17,680	" "
Dean Witter Jr. et al.	18,040	Trinity Co.—Metsker's '55.
R.G. & E. Jameson	10,920	" "
Wm. C. McCulloch	10,600	" "
P. & J. McAuliffe	11,520	Shasta Co.—Metsker's '59.
Tooby & Prior	13,000	Humboldt Co.— "
Calif. Barrel Co.	11,680	" "
Hill-Davis Co.	18,325	" "
Jos. & S.A. Russ	10,000	" "
Merillon & D'Oultremont	13,240	" "
Gamble	13,970	Danielson Survey, Napa Co.
R. Hunter	19,640	Humboldt Co.—Metsker's.

Name	Acreage	Comments
Stimson & Miller	14,400	Del Norte Co.—Metsker's '59
Westgate-California Corp.	17,000	14,000 acres agricultural in San Joaquin Valley; rest is development.
West Haven Farming Co.	10,273	Bureau of Reclamation—Excess Land Ownership Study 12/68.
N-3 Cattle Co.	16,112	Danielson Survey, Alameda County.
W.J. Deal Co. Ltd.	10,555	Danielson Survey, Fresno Co.
Noble, Wm. H.	18,197	" "
Nickel, George	15,770	Danielson Survey, Kings Co.
Mouren Farming Co.	12,120	" "
Elsie Buchanan	17,354	" Madera Co.
George A. Pope, Jr.	15,543	Danielson Survey, Madera Co.
Albert Hansen	18,619	" Monterey Co.
Walti & Pearson Ranch, Inc.	11,136	" "
Raymond F. Reynolds et al.	10,146	" "
Laurette Echeberria et al.	11,109	" "
William Luton	13,131	" Santa Barbara Co.
Cowell Estate	at least 15,000	Davis, Yolo Co.—over 10,000 acres range land.
Santa Margarita Ranch	at least 15,000	San Juan Capistrano, Orange Co. —over 10,000 acres cultivated land.
Starr Ranch	at least 15,000	San Juan Capistrano, Orange Co. —over 10,000 acres cultivated land.
Bryant Ranch	at least 10,000	Olive, Orange Co.—over 10,000 acres range land.
Rudnick & Mendiboro	at least 15,000	Kern Co.—range over 10,000, cultivated over 5,000.
A. Brown Co.	at least 15,000	Weldon, Kern Co.—over 10,000 acres range land.
Carver-Bowen Ranch	at least 15,000	Glennville, Kern Co.—over 10,000 acres range land.
Carl I. Carver	at least 10,000	Delano, Fresno Co.—over 10,000 acres range land.
Crofton Ranches	at least 10,000	Keene, Kern Co.—over 10,000 acres range land.
Jameson Ranch	at least 10,000	Tehachapi, Kern Co.—over 10,000 acres range land.
Mrs. W.D. Joughin & Sons	at least 10,000	Isabella, Kern Co.—over 10,000 acres range land.
Leroy Rankin	at least 10,000	Walker Basin, Kern Co.—over 10,000 acres range land.

Name	Acreage	Comments
Russell Bros.	at least 10,000	Maricopa, Kern Co.—over 10,000 acres range land.
Sneddon Land Cattle Co.	at least 10,000	Maricopa, Kern Co.—over 10,000 acres range land.
Carl Tweisselman	at least 10,000	McKittrick, Kern Co.—over 10,-000 acres range land.
Sheldon Potter	at least 10,000	Mendocino Co.—over 10,000 acres range land.
Buttes Gas & Oil	13,800+	Includes Tree Crop Co., Jasmin Groves, and Schenley Subsidiaries.
Vener Brothers	15,100	Tomatoes.

5,000–10,000 acres

Name	Acreage	Comments
Frank C. Trosi	7,473	
P.J. Divizich	5,500	Bankrupt—in process of selling land.
Zaninovich Family	8,200	Zaninovich brothers compete against each other. They are: A. & N. Zaninovich—2,283; Marko Zaninovich—3,686; V.B. Zaninovich—2,157.
Donald Ramelli	8,280	
Daniel Russell	7,893	Verified by owner.
Schramm Ranches, Inc.	5,500	Verified by owner.
M.J. & R.S. Allen	9,000	Directors of Producer's Cotton Oil; verified by owner.
Sam Hamburg Farms	6,000	Verified by owner.
Comfort Farms, Inc.	6,000	Verified by owner.
Superior Oil Co.	7,500	Verified by owner.
Frank Lanterman	6,000	La Canada Ranch.
Hammond Ranch	5,102	
Chanseer Canfield	5,000	
Midway Oil Co.	9,435	
Frank Diener	7,000+	Fresno Co.
Simon Newman Co.	9,813	
Kerman Cattle Co.	7,971	
Bragg, T.T. & Vera	6,079	
Boston Invest. Co.	5,916	
Karpe, A.H.	5,950	
Ray Flanagan	5,665	
Terra Bella, J.D.	5,839	
National Distillers and Carl J. Maggio	5,000	

Name	Acreage	Comments
Temescal Water Co.	7,500	
Motte Bros.	5,000	Perris, Riverside Co.—cultivated land.
California Vegetable Growers	5,000	Blythe, Riverside Co.—cultivated land.
Adolph Miller	6,000	Blythe, Riverside Co.—cultivated land.
Delta Lands	8,700	San Joaquin Co.—cultivated land.
Ogden Corp.	5,000	Isleton, San Joaquin Co.—cultivated land conglomerate.
Staten Island	5,000	Lodi, San Joaquin Co.—cultivated land.
R.W. Cooper	5,600	Carrisa, San Luis Obispo Co.—cultivated land.
Nels Beck & Sons	6,000	Carrisa, San Luis Obispo Co.—cultivated land.
Earl Cavanaugh	5,000	Carrisa, San Luis Obispo Co.
El Chicote Ranch	5,550	" "
Pinole Land & Cattle Co.	7,000	" "
Clarence Wreden	8,000	" "
Filos & Walters	6,000	" "
Dewey Werling	5,000	" "
Jack Pond	5,000	" "
Fred Traver	5,000	" "
Wm. Washburn	5,000	Carrisa, San Luis Obispo Co.—cultivated land.
Painted Rock Ranch	6,000	Carrisa, San Luis Obispo Co.—cultivated land.
M.T., Inc.	8,000	Chico, Butte Co.—cultivated land.
H. Balsdon	8,000	Arbuckle, Colusa Co.—cultivated land.
Fred Schultz	8,000	Arbuckle, Colusa Co.—cultivated land.
Chas. Welch	7,000	Colusa—cultivated land.
Terhel Farms	6,000	" "
Butte Creek Farms	5,000	" "
Hotchkiss Estate Co.	7,550	Fresno Co.—cultivated land.
Finch Bros.	5,000	Orland, Glenn Co.—cultivated land.
R.M. Montz & Sons	7,000	Willows, Glenn Co.—cultivated land.
Baher Bros.	7,000	Artois, Glenn Co.—cultivated land.
Frank Reimann	5,000	Artois, Glenn Co.—cultivated land.
John Elmoie	5,000	Westley, Stanislaus Co.—cultivated land.
Wm. Cox & Son	8,000	Westley, Stanislaus Co.—cultivated land.

Name	Acreage	Comments
Louie & Sons	8,824	Siskiyou Co. assessor.
Criss Bros., Inc.	6,920	" "
Scott, Glen	9,058	" "
Friden, Stan	7,389	" "
Dennis, Jeff	9,948	" "
Rodden, Wm.L., et al.	5,104.92	Sacramento Co. assessor.
Schneider, John, et al.	7,557.896	" "
Elna Schore	7,830	Butte Co. survey.
John N. Graham	5,700	" "
Nathan Thomasson	5,600	" "
Mabel Safford	5,100	" "
William Austin Co.	6,170.78	Nevada Co. top twenty.
May, W.	6,340.73	" "
Lloyd S. Whaler	7,000	Lassen Co.—Metsker's '58.
C.F. Stone & J.T. Bath	8,940	" "
A.R. Hughes et al.	7,000	" "
N.H. Monroe	9,720	" "
McClean Ranch Co.	7,680	" "
Herbert E. Bell, Jr.	7,500	Modoc Co.—Metsker's '58.
Floyd S. Whaley	7,000	" "
Wm. H. Hunt, Est. Co.	9,280	" "
Stanley Johnson	5,000	" "
Fee Ranch, Inc.	7,200	" "
George Doms	8,200	Modoc Co.—Metsker's '58.
Univ. Hill Foundation	9,480	Trinity Co.—Metsker's '55.
E. Blodgett	5,760	Shasta Co.—Metsker's '59.
W. Hunt Estate	9,960	" "
Crone Hereford Ranch	5,760	" "
C. Cransford	8,400	" "
Foundation Stock Plants Inc.	5,846	" "
McKay & Co.	7,040	Humboldt Co.—Metsker's.
Western Livestock Co.	6,400	" "
A.W. Mather & H.A. Truslow	7,680	" "
Lamb Bros. Co.	5,200	" "
D. & O. Bohanon et al.	9,600	" "
D.T. Harville	6,400	" "
C.R. Barnum	7,680	" "
Airway Farms, Inc.	6,381	Bureau of Reclamation—Excess Land Ownership Study 12/31/68

Name	Acreage	Comments
W.J. Deal & Co., Inc.	9,852	Bureau of Reclamation—Excess Land Ownership Study 12/31/68
Mt. Whitney Farms Inc.	8,380	Bureau of Reclamation—Excess Land Ownership Study 12/31/68
Gerald K. Hoyt et al.	8,570	Bureau of Reclamation—Excess Land Ownership Study 12/31/68
H.C. and Irene Reece	5,098	Bureau of Reclamation—Excess Land Ownership Study 12/31/68
Raymond Thomas, Inc.	5,279	Bureau of Reclamation—Excess Land Ownership Study 12/31/68
Vernon L. Thomas, Inc.	7,151	Bureau of Reclamation—Excess Land Ownership Study 12/31/68
Albert Lewallen	7,410	Danielson Survey—Calaveras Co.
Ginochio Family	6,753	Danielson Survey—Contra Costa Co.
Van Vleck	9,950	Danielson Survey—Amador, Sacramento, and El Dorado Co.
Farley Lassotovitch	7,990	Danielson Survey—Fresno Co.
R. Keithly	5,000	Danielson Survey—Lake Co.
Will Gill & Sons	9,794	Danielson Survey—Madera Co.
Clay Daulton	7,289	" "
Sherman Thomas	5,099	" "
Dolcini, et al.	8,434	Danielson Survey—Marin Co.
G.P. Bradford	8,790	Danielson Survey—Mendocino Co.
Herb Funn	6,233	Danielson Survey—Napa Co.
Daley Corp.	8,320	Danielson Survey—San Diego Co.
D.B. & J. Bonnheim	5,307	Danielson Survey—San Luis Obispo Co.
Crawford Estate (San Lucas Ranch)	9,028	Danielson Survey—Santa Barbara Co.
Louis Hanson	7,129	Danielson Survey—Santa Barbara Co.
Fenton O'Connell	7,822	Danielson Survey—Santa Clara Co.
Walter Aldridge	5,144	Danielson Survey—Shasta Co.
John Foster	5,535	Danielson Survey—Siskiyou Co.
Peterson Estate Co.	5,939	Danielson Survey—Solano Co.
Tom Baxter	7,217	Danielson Survey—Sonoma Co.
Harold F. Richardson	6,500	" "
Lewis Norton	6,380	" "
Cooley Ranch Inc.	6,159	" "
Butler Noble	7,621	Danielson Survey—Stanislaus Co.
Paul Gerber	6,882	" "
George Brichetto	5,414	" "
Frank Elliot et al.	9,672	Danielson Survey—Tulare Co.
R.E.S. & Frank Hesse	8,832	" "

Name	Acreage	Comments
J. Guthrie	8,326	Danielson Survey—Tulare Co.
L.B. Hyde & Sons	7,644	" "
Louis Price	8,108	Danielson Survey—Tuolumne Co.
Eleanor Hughes	5,663	" "
Hershey Estate	at least 5,000	Yolo Co.—5,000 cultivated.
Earl Wallace	at least 5,000	Knights Landing, Yolo Co.—over 5,000 cultivated.
Woodland Farms, Inc. (Heidrich Bros.)	at least 5,000	Woodland, Yolo Co.—over 5,000 acres each—cultivated.
Lilley Bemmerly	at least 5,000	Zamora, Yolo Co.—over 5,000 cultivated acres.
Fred Hamblet	at least 5,000	Esparato, Yolo Co.—over 5,000 cultivated acres.
T.S. Glide	at least 5,000	Davis, Yolo Co.—over 5,000 cultivated acres.
Bruce Mace	at least 5,000	Davis, Yolo Co.—over 5,000.
Bernal Giffen	at least 5,000	Fresno—over 5,000 cultivated acres.
J.E.O. Neill	at least 5,000	Burrell, Fresno Co.—over 5,000 cultivated acres.
Jess Goforth	at least 5,000	Mojave, Kern Co.—over 5,000 cultivated acres.
Maricopa Farms	at least 5,000	Kern Co.—over 5,000 cultivated acres.
Floribel Ranch	at least 5,000	Hanford, Kings Co.—over 5,000 cultivated acres.
Ralph Gilkey	at least 5,000	Corcoran, Kings Co.—over 5,000 cultivated acres.
Heck Bros.	at least 5,000	Corcoran, Kings Co.—over 5,000 cultivated acres.

1,000–5,000 acres

Name	Acreage	Comments
Limonera Ranch Co.	2,300	
Jack Harris, Inc.	3,000	
W.B. Camp	4,908	
D.M. Steele	4,187	
Hugh Hudson Ranches	3,624	Verified by owner.
D.M. Bryant, Jr.	2,980	
Roberts Farm Inc.	1,835	Cal. Mission Orchards—owned by Prudential Ins. Co. & Roberts Farms.
J.H. Benson Ranches, Inc.	2,800	
Bliss Ranch	2,650	
Meyer Farms	3,000	
Brookside Vine-yards	2,160	

Name	Acreage	Comments
Distillers Corp.— Seagram Ltd.	2,500	Through subsidiary, Paul Masson Vineyards.
Mont LaSalle Vineyards	2,000	Christian Bros.
Elmco Vineyards	3,610	
Pandol & Sons	2,288	
John Hancock Life Insurance Co.	1,500	Through subsidiary, J.H. Realty Development Corp. & M.B. Mc-Farland & Sons.
Mann Packing Co.	4,000	
D'Arrigo Bros. Co. of California	4,000	
Griffith Bros. Inc.	1,700	
J.D. Martin Ranch	2,000	
James Mills Orchards	1,500	
Vereschagin Family	2,000	
V.P. Baker Ranch	4,100	
Corona Foothills Lemon Co.	2,200	
Robert Draper	3,300	Butte Co. survey.
R. Lund family	3,260	"
Peter L. Ahart	2,900	"
Joie Osgood	2,800	"
John F. Henning	2,500	"
Ella Cooper	2,400	"
Jon Bechtel	2,500	"
Kommoorian, Arika	4,575	Nevada Co. top twenty.
Casper & Pane— Rancho Ca-pornicas	1,915	"
McAlister	1,953	"
Bancroft, J.R.	1,987	"
Coughlan, M.J.	2,007	"
Robinson & Sons	2,385.16	"
Adamson, P.	2,400	"
Peacock, J.C.	2,504.13	"
Vicia, A.	2,882.24	
Webber, G.D. & E.	3,626	Sierra Co. Assoc.
Johnson, Clifton O.	2,942	"
Roivley, Sterling H.	2,496	Sierra Co. Assoc.
Turner, Frank	1,937	"
Genasci, A.R.	1,853	"
Torri, Kenneth	1,800	"
Vanetti, Alice	1,558	"
McPherrin, Anastasia	1,482	"
E.G. Babcock	2,000	Lassen Co.—Metsker's '58.
L.W. Kramer	4,000	" "

Name	Acreage	Comments
A.S. Walton Family	4,480	Lassen Co.—Metsker's '58.
Holland Livestock Ranch Co.	3,000	" "
Pierre Mendiboure	4,160	" "
Johnson Stock Co.	4,500	Modoc Co.—Metsker's '58.
N.H. Monroe	2,640	" "
Stephen Takacs	4,500	" "
North Fork Cattle Co.	3,200	" "
David J. Bayne et al.	3,200	" "
M. Tyson et al.	1,600	Trinity Co.—Metsker's '55.
First Nat'l Finance	3,500	
Paramount Citrus Assoc.	1,875	
Rancho Sespe	4,300	Owned by Cal. Tech.
S.E.J. Ranch	3,000	
Ventura Coastal	1,800	
Venus Citrus Ranches	1,800	
Porter Estate Co.—El Solyo Ranch	4,500	
Richardson Mineral Springs	4,000	Butte Co. survey.
G & M Ranches	3,798	"
George Roney	3,700	"
Alma Hugge	3,600	"
Hazel D. Gianella	3,400	"
J.M. Gainer	3,340	"
Oscar O. Davis	1,000	Trinity Co.—Metsker's '55.
S.F.C.B. Mitchell	1,800	" "
John A. Shaw	1,500	" "
Frank M. Crawford	2,240	" "
S.E. Underwood	4,320	" "
George Dear	1,000	" "
Consolidated Farms	1,987	San Mateo Co. assessor.
Emma Muzzi	1,788	" "
Joseph Cabral	1,659	" "
Rudolph W. Svisiol	1,464	" "
A.L. Powrie	4,800	Del Norte Co.—Metsker's '50.
Rust Estate	3,200	" "
Pacific Oil & Gas Development Corp.	2,000	Used for grazing, farming, or idle.
C. Foley	4,937	Danielson Survey—Alameda Co.
Patterson Ranch	4,767	" "

Name	Acreage	Comments
M. Rowell	4,264	Danielson Survey—Alameda Co.
Jean Applegate	2,692	" "
Frank Boskovich	2,462	" "
James Busi	2,388	" "
Greilich Bros.	1,790	" "
Harry Bosse	3,527	Danielson Survey—Calaveras Co.
Flower Winston	3,876	" "
L.M. Hunt	2,611	" "
Garamendi, Raymond	2,296	" "
Elworthy Family	2,566	Danielson Survey—Contra Costa Co.
Becker Family	2,383	Danielson Survey—Contra Costa Co.
Ruth Bosley	1,969	Danielson Survey—Contra Costa Co.
Nissen Family	1,822	Danielson Survey—Contra Costa Co.
W.H. Payne	1,855	Danielson Survey—Lake Co.
O. Holdenried	1,011	Danielson Survey—Lake Co.
T. Nures, et al.	2,824	Danielson Survey—Marin Co.
R. Hill et al.	2,454	" "
Vedanta Society	2,136	" "
George Chalfant	2,149	Danielson Survey—Mendocino Co.
Reta Land Co., Inc.	2,001	" "
Howard Twining	1,872	" "
Nohl Ranch	2,359	Danielson Survey—Orange Co.
Domenigoni, Francis	3,211	Danielson Survey—Riverside Co.
Latter Day Saints Church	1,486	" "
John Coudures	1,090	" "
Jack Garner	2,405	" "
Campbell Ranch Co.	1,249	" "
George and Bertha Wilson	3,919	Danielson Survey—Sacramento Co.
Aqua Tibia Ranch	1,282	Danielson Survey—San Diego Co.
Blythe, H.E.	4,987	Danielson Survey—San Luis Obispo Co.
Di Collelmo, U.&M.M.	1,798	Danielson Survey—San Luis Obispo Co.
Carver Ranch	2,258	Danielson Survey—San Mateo Co.
Consolidated Farms	1,987	" "
Mattei-Filber	1,726	" "
E.J. Cabral	1,659	" "
F. Jensen	1,329	Danielson Survey—Shasta Co.
Cruikshank	1,230	" "
Pasero, Maderal	4,296	Danielson Survey—Siskiyou Co.

Name	Acreage	Comments
Merle, Ed	3,900	Danielson Survey—Siskiyou Co.
Timberhitch	2,111	" "
Lawler Ranches, et al.	3,626	Danielson Survey—Solano Co.
Olin H. Timm	3,273	" "
H.E. McCure Co.	2,160	" "
Gordon Anderson et al.	1,843	" "
Frank Draghi	4,965	Danielson Survey—Stanislaus Co.
Christine Bloss	4,872	Danielson Survey—Tuolumne Co.
Richard Rosasco	4,410	" "
U.A. Rodden	3,303	" "
Edwards Farming Group	1,047	Danielson Survey—Ventura Co.
American Agronomics Corp.	2,800+	From *Investment Dealer's Digest,* September 22, 1970, p. 19.
United Packing Co.	3,000	

Acreages unknown

S.A. Camp Farms Co.,[1] United Fruit,[2] Williams Austin Co., Coello Farms,[3] Shuklian Bros. Inc., McKittrick Ranch Inc., G.W. Nickel, Jr.,[4] H.B. Murphy Co.,[5] Harger Corp. Ltd., Liberty Farms Co., Gilkey Farms Inc., J.G. Stone Land Co., Riverview Farm & Cattle, Timco,[6] Houchin Bros. Farming Co.,[7] Gragnani Bros., Rideside Farms, C.J. Vignola, W.F. Young & W.E. Young, Jr.,[8] Maggie Farms,[9] Summer Peck Ranch Inc., Bedart Bros.,[10] Clarence Matheson, Twen Farms, Borba Bros., Joe Mendibura, Berman Leasing (Black Watch Farms), Bogett Farming, R.A. Rowan & Co., Coberly West Co.,[11] Red Fern Ranches, George B. Willoughby, Jack Elmore, D.K. Ranch, Reynold M. Mettler, V.C. Britton Co., Wolfson Land & Cattle, Marion Harris, Em. H. Mettler & Sons,[12] Hacienda Ranch, Antelope Ranch, Deepwell Ranch, Las Yeguas Ranch, Rio Bravo Ranch, Chimineas Ranch, Wells Ranch, Conner, Bonita Ranch, Laguna Seca Ranch, Chounet Ranch, Chaney Ranch, Tres Picos Farms, Tillis Ranch, Domengine Ranch, Rancho Mirage, Warners Ranch, Cholame Ranch, Howard Ranch, Turner Ranch, Henry Doelger,[13] El Rico Ranch, Butler Valley Ranch,[14] Rindge Family, E. & J. Gallo Winery, Harden Farms of California, Jane Macchiaroli Fruit Co., Blue Goose Growers, Church Rancho,[15] L.M. & V. Jacks [16]

PRIMARILY TIMBERLAND

Name	Acreage	Comments
100,000 acres +		
Boise Cascade Corp.	303,000	8,000 Nevada Co.; 77,000 acres in development and repeated there. Major subsidiaries here are Sonoma Timber Co., Unco Lumber Co. Verified by owner.

Appendices

Name	Acreage	Comments
Georgia Pacific Corp.	278,500	Verified by owner.
Shasta Forest Co.	479,196	151,445.84 Modoc Co. (supplied by assessor); 264,000 Lassen Co. (Metsker's); 53,751 Siskiyou Co.
Sunkist Corp.	192,000	Through Fruit Growers Supply Co. subsidiary—192,000 for timber, Xmas trees (68,219 Siskiyou, 45,560 Lassen Co., 74,760 Shasta Co.). Verified by owner.
Masonite Corp.	110,000	Verified by owner.
Fibreboard Corp.	155,000	65,000 in Pickering Lumber Corp.; 25,000 in development and repeated there through Trimont Land Co., a subsidiary; 80,000 Hobart Mills, Nevada Co.; 28,978 Sierra Co. (verified by owner).
The Pacific Lumber Co.	171,062	Includes 5,062 acres of agricultural land in Yolo, Sutter and Yuba Counties (rice and tomatoes) and 10,000 acres of grazing land in Humboldt (verified by owner); 140,000 timber in Humboldt Co.; 3,480 San Mateo Co. (verified by owner).
The Times Mirror Corp.	145,000	White Mountain Lumber Co. is major subsidiary.
American Forest Production	150,000+	American Box Corp. of California, Pine Logging Co. of California, Calaveras Land and Timber Corp. (49,000), & Winton Co. are major subsidiaries or timber acquisitions. See Siskiyou Co. assessor survey and Danielson Surveys—El Dorado and Placer Counties.
International Paper Co.	103,547	Siskiyou Co. survey.
Hammond Lumber Co.	119,840	Humboldt Co.—Metsker's.
Diamond International Corp.	100,000	Mostly Butte Co., 10,900 in Shasta Co.

Under 100,000 acres

Name	Acreage	Comments
Weyerhaeuser Corp.	27,174.98	For growing, managing and harvesting forests—Modoc County survey (22,080 Modoc County), verified by owner.
Collins Lumber Co.	80,000	Chester, Plumas Co.

Name	Acreage	Comments
Feather River Pine Mills	60,000	Feather Falls, Butte Co.
Northern Redwood Lumber Co.	32,000	26,960 in Humboldt and Del Norte Co.
Empire Redwood Co.	26,000	Sonoma and Mendocino Co.
Hearst Corps.	66,614	21,814 Siskiyou Co. survey; 44,800 Shasta Co.
Kimberly Clark Co.	51,158	Siskiyou Co. survey.
Soda Creek Forest	10,206	Siskiyou Co. survey.
U.S. Plywood Champion Corp.	87,852	71,332 Siskiyou Co. survey, 14,510 Shasta Co., 2,000 Trinity Co.
Di Giorgio Lumber Co.	2,176	Sierra Co. survey.
Yuba River Lumber Co.	2,101	Sierra Co. survey.
Northern Calif. Lumber Co.	3,620	Trinity Co.—Metsker's.
Calif.-Oregon Lumber Co.	1,960	Trinity Co.—Metsker's.
Trinity Alps Lumber Co.	760	Trinity Co.—Metsker's.
Shasta Box Co.	19,200	Trinity Co.—Metsker's '55.
Mt. Shasta Pine Mfg. Co.	3,840	Trinity Co.—Metsker's '55.
R.L. Smith	63,885	Shasta Co.—Metsker's '55.
Scott Lumber Co.	12,040	" "
McCloud River Lumber Co.	16,900	" "
Trinity Logging Co.	3,520	" "
Elk River Mill & Timber Co.	8,220	Humboldt Co.—Metsker's.
Solbeer & Carson Timber Co.	12,500	" "
Arrow Mill Co.	6,120	" "
Arcata Redwood Co.	1,920	" "
Sage Ind. & Lumber Co.	37,280	34,080 Humboldt Co.; 3,200 Del Norte Co.
Ward Redwood Co.	8,720	3,520 Humboldt Co.—Metsker's. 5,200 Del Norte Co.—Metsker's '50.
Simpson Timber Co.	19,440	5,200 Del Norte Co.—Metsker's '50.
Westmoreland Pacific Lumber Co.	5,120	Del Norte Co.—Metsker's '50.
Santa Cruz Lumber Co.	5,000	San Mateo Co. assessor.

Name	Acreage	Comments
Michigan-California Lumber Co.	71,733	Danielson Survey—El Dorado Co.
Georgetown Lumber Co.	10,876	" "
North Fork Assoc., Inc.	4,836	" Placer Co.
J.F. Moore	2,529	" "
F. Bonnifield	2,366	" "
Pomfret Estates, Inc.	2,326	" "
R.G. Watts & Assoc.	19,520	Shasta Co. survey.

Acreages Unknown

Cyprus Mines Corp., Fall River Lumber Co.,[17] Union Lumber Co.,[18] D.E. Ayer,[19] Walker Forest, Willits Redwood Products Co., Crane Mills Co., Michigan-California Lumber Co., Red River Lumber Co., R.G. Watt & Assoc.

DEVELOPMENT
(INCLUDING HOUSING, INDUSTRIAL, AND MINERAL)

Name	Acreage	Comments
50,000 acres +		
Norris Oil Co.	50,000	
Occidental Petroleum Co.	200,000	Occidental Petroleum Land Co.; also Deane Bros. Co., major subsidiary in real estate development operations.
Kaiser Industries	111,000	12,000 acres development through Kaiser Steel, 88,000 in Rancho California, and 11,200 presently in agriculture in Madera and Tweimore.
Boise Cascade	84,000*	In eighteen separate developments through many subsidiaries total acreage owned in California is 303,000.
Leslie Salt	59,000	4,400 acres in Redwood City in a planned community known as Redwood Shores—rest are salt flats; 9,000 acres in Alameda Co., 50,000 verified by owner.
Union Oil of California	52,000	Verified by owner.
P.G. & E.	250,000	83,600 miles electric lines; 22,480 Shasta Co.; 1,406 Sierra Co. (verified by owner).

* Included in timberland total above

Name	Acreage	Comments
Penn Central Co.	120,000	Through three subsidiaries: Arvida Corp., Macco Corp., and Great Southwest Corp.; 30,000 acres are devoted to development. A Macco subsidiary, Vail and Porter Ranches, has 90,000 acres.
Standard Oil Co.	**	

20,000–50,000 acres

Name	Acreage	Comments
Monolith Portland Cement	45,000	Verified by owner, Mojave Desert —25,469; mineral deposits— 3,040; agriculture—1,380; Tehachapi City, Valley and Mountains—15,340
Magma Power Co.	46,000	Through Magma Energy Inc., subsidiary.
Fibreboard	25,000	Development "Northstar"; see timberland for total amount. This figure is included in that total.
Dart Industries	26,000	Charter member of Western Developer's Conference.
Kaufman & Broad, Inc. (Leisure Industries, Inc.)	30,000	
Standard Pacific Corp.	22,000	Primarily through Beauchamp and Brown Properties Co. and three other subsidiaries.
Crocker Land Co.	20,000	Verified by owner.
Larwin Developments, Inc.	20,000	Paradise Pine.
San Diego County Water Co.	46,000	From "Landholdings in California," 1937.
Sutter Basin Corp.	41,922	From "Landholdings in California," 1937.
Parrott Investment Co.	21,870	Butte Co.
So. Calif. Edison Co.	40,000	Through Associated Southern Investment Co. and Calabasas Park Co., approximately 4,000 acres; rest for electrical generation, transmission, and distribution, recreation, agriculture and timber. Verified by owner.
Appleton Ind. & Water Co.	30,000	San Bernardino Co.
Murdock Land Co.	22,000	Willows, Glenn Co.
Wm. Wrigley	48,000	Catalina Is. Resort, L.A. Co.

** So much of Standard Oil land is in agriculture that its figure is given above, in that category

Name	Acreage	Comments
Sierra Pacific Power Co.	45,380	For development and grazing, 30,000-acre mountain resort through lands of Sierra; also 27,300 miles of gas mains, 418 miles of water mains, 5,100 miles of electric lines.
Texaco	23,723	14,800 for agriculture, 8,000 for producing feed, verified by county.

10,000–20,000 acres

Name	Acreage	Comments
Signal Companies	10,000	Verified by owner—includes developments through Signal Properties, Inc., a subsidiary, plus property through Shattuck and McHone, a 1969 acquisition now called Signal Landmark as a fully owned subsidiary; 10,000 are residential—S. Cal. devel.
Great Basins Petroleum Co.	12,500	Lease land.
Castle & Cooke	16,000	Oceanic Properties Inc., 5,000 acres Sea Ranch through a subsidiary; another 11,000 acre development imminent S. of San Jose, verified by owner.
Allied Properties	15,000	Taylor Ranch and Rindge Island developments are major factors. In addition, 44,500 acres leased from r.r. and 2,000,000 from public domain for grazing.
Westbay Community Assessor	10,152	San Mateo Co.—assessor's survey.
Citizen's National Trust and Savings Bank of California	11,600	Modoc Co.—Metsker's '58.
Rocky Hill, Inc.	14,920	Lassen Co.—Metsker's '58.
Hudson-Whitney Corp.	16,000	Nevada Co. (top twenty-eight).
Aerojet General Corp.	12,382	Sacramento Co.—assessor's survey.
Crocker Anglo National Bank	12,908	Sacramento Co.—assessor's survey—presently in agriculture.
Beverly Enterprises	14,000	Siskiyou Co.—assessor's survey.
Christiana Oil Co.	18,000	Through Huntington Harbour Corp., a subsidiary now developing land; Christiana Community Builders Inc.; and 15,000 acres in desert lands in Yacco Valley for "Pioneer Town."

Name	Acreage	Comments
Shasta Acres	12,000	Verified by owner.
American Hawaiian Land Co.	11,500	Westlake Village, subsidiary.
John Hancock Life Insurance Co.	10,000	El Dorado Hills through subsidiary firm, Sierra Pacific Properties.
Shell Oil Co.	17,860	
Atlantic Richfield Co.	10,718	Palomar Land Co., subsidiary of Richfield Oil, purchased 2,651 acres from Rancho California.
Shoreland Corp.	13,000	
Yuba Consolidated Goldfields	18,211	
Chino Land, Water Co.	17,000	San Bernardino Co.
Kings County Development Co.	11,300	Kings Co.
Getty Oil Co.	12,000*	

5,000–10,000 acres

Name	Acreage	Comments
Fortuna Devel. Co.	7,680	Humboldt Co.—Metsker's.
Ogletree Land Co.	9,540	" "
Deane & Deane, Inc.	8,000	San Mateo Co.—assessor's survey.
Ideal Cement Co.	6,113	" "
Monarch Investment Co.	5,717	Sierra Co.—assessor's survey.
Hobert & Co.	9,000	Nevada Co.—subsidiary Tahoe Northland.
M & T Inc.	5,870	Butte Co.
Zita Corp.	5,281	Sacramento Co.—assessor's survey.
Reserve Oil & Gas	9,500	Long Beach Dock and Terminal and other subsidiaries.
New Idria Mining and Chemical Corp.	8,000	
Budget Industries	8,000	Subdivided in S. California through El Chicote Properties Ltd., subsidiary.
Lone Star Cement	9,300	Through Pacific Cement & Aggregates, a subsidiary, verified by owner.
Utah Mining and Construction Co.	8,300	Verified by owner.
Dillingham Corp.	5,700	
Del Monte Properties Co.	8,200	

* Included above in Getty agriculture total

Name	Acreage	Comments
Laguna Niguel Corp.	5,700	For land development.
JKM Industries, Inc.	7,000	
World-Wide Realty and Investing Corp.	5,000	
Property Research, Inc.	6,000	Through RPS Investments, Inc., a subsidiary.
Lakeworld Development Corp.	9,000	Prosser View Estates, a subsidiary, charter member of Western Developers Conference.
Spring Valley Co., Ltd.	8,870	
Sutter Buttes Land Co.	8,512	
Santa Fe Ry. Co.	8,750	San Diego Co.
John K. Assoc.	9,000	Formerly the Strathearn Ranch.

Under 5,000 acres

Name	Acreage	Comments
Portland Mfg. & J.A. Malarkey	2,500	Del Norte Co.—Metsker's '50.
Mitchell—Dorr Realty Co.	3,200	Humboldt Co.—Metsker's.
Wagner Corp.	2,560	" "
Bollibokka Land Co.	4,140	Shasta Co.—Metsker's '59.
U.S. Smelting Refining Man. Co.	3,000	" "
Theodore Char, Inc.	4,319	San Mateo Co.—assessor's survey.
Purisima Canyon Associates	2,513	" "
Crummer Corp.	4,350	" "
Ax Mountain	2,012	" "
Ainsley Corp.	1,826	" "
California Water Ser. Co.	1,471	" "
Nielson Motor Co.	1,500	Trinity Co.—Metsker's '59.
Favell-Utley Realty Co.	4,320	" "
Sierraville Properties	4,520	Sierra Co.—assessor's survey.
Sierra Pacific Power	3,430	Sierra Co.—assessor's survey.
Graegle Land, Water	2,054	" "
San Juan Gold Co.	2,243.84	Nevada Co. (top twenty).
Spring Valley Land Co., Grass Valley Land Co.	2,155	" "

Name	Acreage	Comments
Gorrill Land Co.	2,800	Butte Co.
Chico Moulding Co.	2,400	"
Riverlands Development Co.	2,300	"
Sacramento Municipal Utility Dis.	2,400	Sacramento—assessor's survey.
Pension Trust Fund Oper. Engin.	3,534.9	" "
McDonell-Douglas Aircraft Inc.	3,958	" "
California Portland Cement	1,000	For industrial development, verified by owner.
Natomas Co.	3,500	Verified by owner.
Exeter Oil Co.	1,000	
The Colwell Co.	500	Verified by owner.
Pacific Clay Products	2,600	Also leases 6,200 acres.
E.I. duPont de Nemours & Co. Inc.	600	Bonadette Co., subsidiary, reports they own 600+ acres for manufacturing and warehousing.
Western Pacific R.R. Co.	3,000	Standard Realty and Development Co., subsidiary, has a S.F. industrial park development; also agricultural and investment, and approximately 1,500 track mileage.
Garden Land Co., Ltd.	2,500	Through Don the Beachcomber Enterprises.
Angeles Crest Development Co., Inc.	1,000	
Pauley Petroleum Inc.	2,500	
General American Development Corp.	4,000	
J.P. Edmondson Co.	2,200+	Through Garner Ranch and subsidiary, Great American Land Co.
Jules Berman	3,600	El Capitan Ranch.
Union Pacific	1,000	
Great Lakes Development Co., Inc.	4,800	Charter member, Western Developer's Conference—Copper Cove at Lake Tullock.
Land Tec. Sales Co., Inc.	3,400	Auburn Lake Trails.
T. Jack Foster	2,600	Foster City.
A.W. Sweet	3,000	Pt. Reyes.
Marblehead Land Corp.	3,000	

Name	Acreage	Comments
Weyl-Zuckerman Co.	2,704	
San Jose Water Works	3,000	Watershed land, plus 1,655 miles of mains.
So. Calif. Water Co.	100	170 miles electric lines, 1,722 miles of water mains; say "own" app. 100 acres for water-storage tanks and wells.
Trans Union Corp.	3,000+	Lang Ranch, Walnut, and West Covina properties through subsidiary, Trans Union Land Development Co.

Acreages Unknown

Pacific Telephone and Telegraph, Lenkurt Electric, S.F. Water Department, King Resources Co., U.S. Steel, Transland Co., La Jolla Properties, Del E. Webb Corp., Century Properties, California Pines, EMCO Companies, Levitt & Sons of California, Rolling International, Inc., Great Western Cities, Inc.,[20] Tidewater Oil, Gulf Oil, Mobil Oil Corp., Phillips Petroleum, Texaco Inc., TransAmerica Development Co.,* City Investing Corp.,*[21] American Standard Corp.,*[22] Corona Land Co.,* American Forest Properties,* Santa Fe Industries, Inc., California-Pacific Utilities Co.,[23] California Water Service Co.,[24] General Telephone Co. of California, Pacific Lighting Service Co.,[25] Pacific Power & Light Co.,[26] San Diego Gas & Electric,[27] Southwest Gas Corp., El Rico Land Co.,[28] Fritz Burns, Twentieth Century Fox, Continental Heritage Corp.,* Landtec, Southern California Financial Corp.,* George McKeon and Co., American Standard, Inc.,* Auland Development Co.,* Benguet of California,* Boston & Maine Industries,[29] Metropolitan Development Corp.,[30] Pit River Recreation Est.,[31] California Enterprises, Southern California Land Development Corp.

Notes Appendix 1A

1. Cultivated over 5,000 acres, Kern County.
2. Acquired Nunes Bros. of California, Inc., Earl Myers Co., Peter A. Stolich Co., Jerome Kantro Co., Salinas Valley Vegetable Exchange, Consolidated Growers, Inc.—told to divest by F.L.C. —much of land is leased.
3. Fresno Co.
4. Connected to Miller & Lux.
5. Farms at least 10,000 acres in Imperial Co. (including leases).
6. Fresno.
7. Cultivated over 5,000 acres.
8. Imperial Co.
9. Kern Co.
10. Cultivated over 5,000 acres, Kern County.
11. Cultivated over 5,000 acres.
12. Cultivated over 5,000 acres.
13. San Mateo Co.
14. Near Maple Creek, Humboldt Co.

* Charter member, Western Developer's Conference

15. Salinas, Monterey Co.
16. Salinas, Monterey Co.
17. Fall River Mills, Shasta Co. (over 10,000).
18. Ft. Bragg, Mendocino Co. (over 10,000).
19. Tehama Co.
20. California City.
21. So. California—Finance Co. subsidiary.
22. Subsidiary William Lejon Corp.
23. 3,430 miles electric lines, 890 miles gas; water and telephone are minor.
24. 3,000 miles of mains.
25. Includes So. California Gas Co.; technically not considered a utility—operates 903 miles of gas lines.
26. Controlled by A.T. & T.
27. 7,500 miles electric lines; 3,324 miles gas mains.
28. Corcoran, Kings Co.
29. Through United Construction Development Corp., subsidiary.
30. Controlled by Mark Boyar.
31. Modoc Co.

Appendix 1B
Land Ownership Concentration in Selected,
Less Concentrated Counties

COUNTY OF BUTTE *

Total Acreage 1,067,520
Private Acreage 847,371

THE TWENTY LARGEST PRIVATE
LANDOWNERS IN COUNTY BY ACREAGE

Owner	No. of Acres	Cumulative Percentage of Total Private Acreage
1. Diamond International Corp.	85,000	10.0%
2. Parrott Investment Co.	21,870	12.7
3. Georgia Pacific Corp.	21,759	15.2
4. Southern Pacific Corp.	17,500	17.3
5. Newhall Land & Farming Co.	12,570	18.7
6. Soper Wheeler Co.	10,120	19.9
7. Elna Schore	7,830	
8. M & T Inc.	5,870	
9. John N. Graham	5,700	
10. Nathan Thomasson	5,600	
11. Mabel Safford	5,100	
12. Leah Gunn	4,760	
13. Jack Meline	4,400	
14. Richardson Mineral Springs	4,000	
15. G & M Ranches	3,798	
16. George Roney	3,700	
17. Alma Hugge	3,600	
18. Hazel D. Gianella	3,400	
19. J.M. Gainer	3,340	
20. Robert Draper	3,300	27.5

* Source: Henry Maps Survey, 1969

542

COUNTY OF SISKIYOU *

Total Acreage 4,008,960
Private Acreage 1,452,667

THE TWENTY LARGEST PRIVATE
LANDOWNERS IN COUNTY BY ACREAGE

Owner	No. of Acres	Cumulative Percentage of Total Private Acreage
1. Southern Pacific Land Co.	179,023	12.3%
2. International Paper Co.	103,547	19.5
3. U.S. Plywood Corp.	71,332	24.4
4. Fruit Growers Supply Co.	68,219	29.1
5. Shasta Forests Co.	53,751	32.8
6. Kimberly Clark Corp.	51,158	
7. Hearst Corp.	21,814	
8. American Forest Products	20,987	
9. Beverly Enterprises	14,000	
10. Meiss Ranch Inc.	13,323	
11. Porterfield Bros., Inc.	12,852	
12. Mills Ranch	10,532	
13. Soda Creek Forest	10,206	
14. Dennis, Jeff	9,948	
15. Ed Hart, et al.	9,674	
16. Scott, Glen	9,058	
17. Louie & Sons	8,824	
18. Frieden, Stan	7,389	
19. Criss Bros., Inc.	6,920	
20. Kel-Del Ranch	1,138	47.4

* Source: Assessor's survey, 1970

COUNTY OF SHASTA *

Total Acreage 2,427,520
Private Acreage 1,439,491

THE TWENTY LARGEST PRIVATE
LANDOWNERS IN COUNTY BY ACREAGE

Owner	*No. of Acres*	*Cumulative Percentage of Total Private Acreage*
1. Southern Pacific Land Co.	156,400	10.8%
2. Fruit Growers Supply Co.	74,760	16.1
3. R.L. Smith Lumber Co.	63,885	20.5
4. K. Walker et al.	51,200	24.1
5. Hearst Corp.	44,800	27.9
6. P.G. & E.	22,480	
7. L. McConnel	20,480	
8. R.G. Watt	19,520	
9. McCloud River Lumber Co.	16,900	
10. U.S. Plywood Corp.	14,520	
11. Scott Lumber	12,040	
12. P. & J. McAuliffe	11,520	
13. Diamond Match Co.	10,880	
14. W. Hunt Estate	9,960	
15. C. Cransford	8,400	
16. E. Blodgett	5,760	
17. Crone Hereford Ranch	5,760	
18. Welch & Welch	4,480	
19. Bollibukka Land Co.	4,140	
20. Foundation Stock Plants Inc.	3,840	39.1

* Source: Metsker's Map Survey (1959 records)

COUNTY OF SIERRA *

Total Acreage 612,480
Private Acreage 229,278

THE TWENTY LARGEST PRIVATE
LANDOWNERS IN COUNTY BY ACREAGE

Owner	No. of Acres	Cumulative Percentage of Total Private Acreage
1. Fibreboard Corp.	28,978	12.7%
2. Southern Pacific Land Co.	25,852	23.9
3. Ramelli, Donald	8,280	27.5
4. Russell, Daniel (dir. of So. Pac. & Tenneco)	7,893	31.0
5. Trosi, Frank C.	7,473	34.3
6. Monarch Investment Company	5,717	
7. Sierraville Properties	4,520	
8. Webber, G.D. & E.	3,626	
9. Sierra Pacific Power	3,430	
10. Johnson, Clifton O.	2,942	
11. Roivley, Sterling H.	2,496	
12. Di Giorgio Lumber Co.	2,176	
13. Yuba River Lumber Co.	2,101	
14. Graegle Land & Water	2,054	
15. Turner, Frank	1,937	
16. Genasci, A.R.	1,853	
17. Torri, Kenneth	1,800	
18. Vanetti, Alice	1,558	
19. McPherrin, Anastasia	1,482	
20. P.G. & E.	1,406	48.9

* Source: Survey by John Elam et al., U.C. Davis, 1970

COUNTY OF NEVADA *

Total Acreage 624,000
Private Acreage 438,483

THE TWENTY LARGEST PRIVATE
LANDOWNERS IN COUNTY BY ACREAGE

Owner	No. of Acres	Cumulative Percentage of Total Private Acreage
1. Southern Pacific Land Co.	59,958	13.6%
2. Pacific Gas & Electric	12,750	16.5
3. Taylor, A., et al.	9,418	18.5
4. May, W.	7,213	20.2
5. William Austin Co.	6,247	21.5
6. Fibreboard Corp.	5,357	
7. Johnson, D.	4,897	
8. San Juan Gold	3,995	
9. Sierra Pacific Power Co.	3,905	
10. Hoffert Co.	3,840	
11. Walton, J.E., et al.	3,590	
12. Boise Cascade	3,269	
13. Peacock, J.C.	3,021	
14. Viscia, A.A.	2,882	
15. Robinson, Guy	2,484	
16. Nicholls Estate Co.	2,441	
17. Spring Valley Land Co.	2,155	
18. Graham, R.K.	2,081	
19. McAllister, J. et al.	1,954	
20. Bancroft, J., et al.	1,818	32.5

* Source: Assessor's Survey, 1970

COUNTY OF HUMBOLDT *

Total Acreage 2,295,040
Private Acreage 1,635,874

THE TWENTY LARGEST PRIVATE
LANDOWNERS IN COUNTY BY ACREAGE

Owner	No. of Acres	Cumulative Percentage of Total Private Acreage
1. Pacific Lumber Co.	140,000	8.8%
2. Hammond Lumber Co.	119,840	16.2
3. Sage Land & Lumber Co.	34,080	18.4
4. Northern Redwood Lumber Co.	26,960	20.1
5. William Smith	25,760	21.7
6. C.G. & L.W. Wiggins	23,680	
7. R. Hunter	19,640	
8. Hill-Davis Co.	18,325	
9. Merillon & D'Oultremont	13,240	
10. Tooby & Prior	13,000	
11. Dolbeer & Carson Lumber Co.	12,500	
12. California Barrel Co.	11,680	
13. Jos. & S.A. Russ	10,000	
14. D & O Bohanon et al.	9,600	
15. Ogletree Land Co.	9,540	
16. Elk River Mill & Lumber Co.	8,220	
17. C.R. Barnum	7,680	
18. A.W. Mather & H.A. Truslow	7,680	
19. Fortuna Development Co.	7,680	
20. McKay and Co.	7,040	32.9

* Source: Metsker's Map Survey, 1958

COUNTY OF LASSEN *

Total Acreage 2,919,040
Private Acreage 1,113,804

THE TWENTY LARGEST PRIVATE
LANDOWNERS IN COUNTY BY ACREAGE

Owner	No. of Acres	Cumulative Percentage of Total Private Acreage
1. Shasta Forests Co.	264,000	24.0%
2. Fruit Growers Supply Co.	45,560	28.1
3. Rocky Hill Inc.	14,920	29.5
4. W.H. Hunt Est. Co.	14,440	30.8
5. T.E. Connoly	13,400	32.0
6. J.W. Mapes	13,400	
7. W.H. Roupp et al.	13,040	
8. Flournoy Bros.	12,280	
9. Hansen Cattle Co.	12,020	
10. G.R. Heath	11,520	
11. N.H. Monroe	9,720	
12. W.M. Smith	9,200	
13. C.F. Stone & J.T. Bath	8,940	
14. McClean Ranch Co.	7,680	
15. A.R. Hughes et al.	7,000	
16. Lloyd S. Whaler	7,000	
17. S.S. Jaksick	5,000	
18. A.S. Walton Family	4,480	
19. Pierre Mendibourne	4,160	
20. L.W. Kramer	4,000	43.7

* Source: Metsker's Map Survey (1959 records)

COUNTY OF SAN MATEO *

Total Acreage 286,080
Private Acreage 259,467

THE TWENTY LARGEST PRIVATE
LANDOWNERS IN COUNTY BY ACREAGE

Owner	No. of Acres	Cumulative Percentage of Total Private Acreage
1. Westbay Community Associates	10,152	3.9%
2. Deane & Deane, Inc.	8,000	6.9
3. Leslie Salt Co.	7,343	9.8
4. Ideal Cement Co.	6,113	12.1
5. Santa Cruz Lumber Co.	4,976	14.0
6. Theodore Char, et al.	4,319	
7. Pacific Lumber Co.	3,480	
8. Crocker Land Co.	3,082	
9. Purisima Canyon Assoc.	2,513	
10. Leland Stanford Jr. University	2,478	
11. Carver Ranch	2,258	
12. R.E. Crummer, et al.	2,225	
13. Crummer Corp.	2,125	
14. Ox Mountain	2,012	
15. Consolidated Farms	1,987	
16. Ainsley Corp.	1,826	
17. Emma Muzzi	1,788	
18. Joseph Cabral	1,659	
19. California Water Service Co.	1,471	
20. Rudolph W. Driscol	1,464	27.4

* Source: Survey of Assessors, 1970

COUNTY OF VENTURA *

Total Acreage 1,192,320
Private Acreage 538,164

THE TWENTY LARGEST PRIVATE
LANDOWNERS IN COUNTY BY ACREAGE

Owner	No. of Acres	Cumulative Percentage of Total Private Acreage
1. Getty Oil	17,679	3.3%
2. Newhall Land and Farming	15,443	6.1
3. Adrian Woods	12,504	8.5
4. Union Oil Company	9,744	10.3
5. Kay Investment Company	8,899	11.9
6. Danielson, Richard E. Jr.	7,115	
7. American Hawaiian Steamship Co.	7,078	
8. Rancho Guadalasca (J. Broome et al.)	6,785	
9. Bob Hope	6,466	
10. Adams Canyon	5,818	
11. Fred Smith	4,621	
12. Rancho Sespe	4,246	
13. Flying "H" Ranchos	2,899	
14. Kaiser Aetna	2,610	
15. Moreland Investment Co.	2,421	
16. Elstree Ltd.	1,913	
17. Lang Ranch	1,788	
18. Camulos Ranch	1,770	
19. Limoneira	1,726	
20. North American Aviation	1,360	22.8

* Source: Survey of Assessors, 1970

COUNTY OF SACRAMENTO *

Total Acreage 624,000
Private Acreage 567,215

THE TWENTY LARGEST PRIVATE
LANDOWNERS IN COUNTY BY ACREAGE

Owner	No. of Acres	Cumulative Percentage of Total Private Acreage
1. Crocker Anglo National Bank	12,908	2.3%
2. Aerojet General Corporation	12,382	4.5
3. Gill, John S. et al.	10,383	6.3
4. Schneider, John et al.	7,557	7.6
5. Zita Corp.	5,281	8.5
6. Rodden, William L., et al.	5,104	
7. Valensin/Valensin Trust of	4,989	
8. Van Vleck, Stanley	4,384	
9. Gau, Louis	4,066	
10. McDonnell-Douglas Aircraft Inc.	3,958	
11. Willson, George & Bertha	3,919	
12. Pension Trust Fund Operating Engin.	3,534	
13. Hamel, Richard H.	3,000	
14. Upham, Charles E. & Joseph E.	2,998	
15. Silva, Faustino Sr.	2,960	
16. SMUD (Sacto. Municipal Utility Dist.)	2,400	
17. Simas, Antonio	2,200	
18. Ledbetter, Lester C.	2,025	
19. Elrod, Margaret, & Finn, Eleanor	1,922	
20. Cavitt, S.H.	1,908	17.3

* Source: Survey of Assessors, 1970

COUNTY OF TRINITY *

Total Acreage 2,042,880
Private Acreage 571,081

THE TWENTY LARGEST PRIVATE
LANDOWNERS IN COUNTY BY ACREAGE

Owner	No. of Acres	Cumulative Percentage of Total Private Acreage
1. Southern Pacific Land Co.	197,160	34.5%
2. Shasta Box Co.	19,200	37.9
3. Dean Witter, Jr. et al.	18,040	41.0
4. R.G. & E. Jameson	10,920	43.0
5. William C. McCulloch	10,600	44.7
6. University Hill Foundation	9,480	
7. Favell-Utley Realty Co.	4,320	
8. S.E. Underwood	4,320	
9. Mt. Shasta Pine Mfg. Co.	3,840	
10. N. Calif. Lumber Co.	3,620	
11. Roger Jessup Farms	3,200	
12. Frank M. Crawford	2,240	
13. U.S. Plywood Corp.	2,000	
14. California-Oregon Lumber Co.	1,960	
15. S.F. & C.B. Mitchell	1,800	
16. M. Tyson et al.	1,600	
17. John A. Shaw	1,500	
18. Nielson Motor Co.	1,500	
19. George Dear	1,000	
20. Oscar O. Davis	1,000	52.5

* Source: Metsker's Map Survey, 1955

Appendix 1C
Landownership Concentration by Value Analysis

1. CONCENTRATION BY ASSESSED VALUATION IN SELECTED COUNTIES

County of Siskiyou
   Total Assessed Valuation $91,025,000

Owner	Appraised Valuation *
International Paper	$18,775,000
S.P. Land Co.	14,000,000
U.S. Plywood	14,142,000
Fruit Growers	9,633,000
Kimberly Clark	2,149,000
Total	$58,699,000

Top five landowners own 16% of land by dollar value.

County of Sacramento
   Total Assessed Valuation $1,207,000,000

Owner	Assessed Valuation
Texaco	$6,246,000
Standard Oil	4,476,000
S.P. Land Co.	4,392,000
Amerada	3,940,000
Aero Jet	1,732,000
Total	$20,784,000

Top five landowners own 2% of land by dollar value.

* Siskiyou amounts are given as appraised at full market value, which is approximately 4 times assessed valuation. Therefore the total appraised valuation must be divided by 4 to approximate the assessed valuation and the percentage thereof.

The concentration figures by property value reveal far less concentration than by acreage. The table above presents the data for the top five landowners by assessed value in two sample counties, one rural (Siskiyou) and one urban (Sacramento). The much lower concentration in ownership of land by value in urban Sacramento helps to explain why concentration by land value is so much lower than concentration by acreage. As a county becomes urbanized, the high value land is sold off by the large landowners. The profit is taken off land ownership at the disposition-for-intense-development stage. Thus, as urbanization proceeds, more small parcels of land have higher value.

Another explanation for the lower concentration figures by land value is the nature of the assessment criteria behind these "value" figures. Almost by definition, the large landowners own large but low valued tracts of raw land. As parcels are assessed higher, landowners are forced either to sell or to continue to pay high taxes. Since they often lack the capital necessary for development which would bring returns to justify holding, they sell. Further, these assessed value figures include value attributable to structures as well as that attributable to land per se. Here again, urban land is valued highly, which distorts the concentration figures. At the point where there is a structure, the speculative profits from the land have probably already been taken.

The tables below present the basic data for all of the four urban and three rural counties answering our survey forms.

2. TEN LARGEST TAXPAYERS IN SELECTED COUNTIES

Urban Counties
County of Sacramento

Corporation or Individual	Property Tax Paid (Inc. Imp. and P.P.)	Value of Land
1. Pacific Telephone	$7,758,425.16	978,290
2. Aero Jet	1,857,904.42	1,731,633
3. P.G. & E.	2,514,646.60	22,980
4. Southern Pacific	1,788,363.90	4,391,890
5. Western Pacific	436,709.84	1,209,010
6. Texaco	391,268.68	6,246,353
7. Standard Oil	216,491.08	4,473,861
8. Amerada	234,074.02	3,939,698
9. Citizens Utility	212,635.40	7,710
10. Roseville Telephone	195,689.50	8,030

County of Ventura

Corporation or Individual	Property Tax Paid	Appraisal of Property
1. So. Calif. Edison	$2,160,828.19	Multiple
2. Shell Oil Co. and Shell Chemical	936,321.29	"
3. General Telephone Co.	858,460.96	"
4. Pacific Telephone Co.	672,581.86	"
5. American-Hawaiian Land Co.	514,548.16	"
6. Getty Oil Co.	443,257.02	"
7. Kaiser Aetna	361,620.86	"
8. So. Counties Gas Co.	359,687.59	"
9. Union Oil Co.	319,204.18	"
10. North American Aviation Inc.	291,499.92	"

County of San Mateo

Corporation or Individual	Property Tax Paid	Appraisal of Property
1. Pacific Tel. & Tel.	$4,140,781.34	*
2. Pacific Gas & Electric	3,730,151.90	
3. T. Jack Foster & Co.	3,287,438.10	
4. Leslie Salt	1,701,376.00	
5. Crocker Land	1,483,544.92	
6. Southern Pacific	1,201,484.94	
7. Henry Doelger	972,538.96	
8. Lenkurt Electric	635,695.38	
9. San Fran. Water Dept.	586,871.16	
10. Calif. Water Service	529,083.18	

County of San Francisco

Corporation or Individual	Property Tax Paid	Assessed Value	Acreage Owned
1. Pacific Tel. & Tel.	$7,784,819	60,724,020	24.722
2. Pacific Gas & Elec.	7,046,032	54,961,250	100.045±
3. Bank of America	3,254,458	25,385,789	3.2575
4. Metropolitan Life Ins.	1,859,082	14,501,420	145.5085
5. So. Pac. Trans Co.	1,598,360	12,467,710	335±
6. Stoneson Dev. Corp.	1,057,992	8,252,675	66.0578
7. Golden Gateway Center	1,042,378	8,130,875	8.9037
8. Hilton Hotels Corp.	1,012,780	7,900,000	1.9602
9. Wells Fargo Bk. Bldg.	929,450	7,250,000	.5136
10. Fairmont Hotel	783,747	6,113,475	2.6041

Rural Counties
County of Siskiyou

Corporation or Individual	Property Tax Paid	Appraisal of Property	Acreage Owned
1. American Forest Prod.		1,980,250	20,987
2. Fruit Growers		9,632,670	68,219
3. Hearst Corp.		1,757,255	21,814
4. International Paper		18,775,655	103,547
5. Kimberly Clark Corp.		2,149,100	51,158
6. Shasta Forests Co.		973,920	53,751
7. S.P. Land Co.		14,000,060	179,023
8. U.S. Plywood Corp.		14,142,915	71,332
9. Frieden		1,012,000	7,389
10. Meiss Ranch		1,069,000	13,323

County of Nevada

Corporation or Individual	Property Tax Paid	Appraisal of Property	Acreage Owned
1. Pacific Gas & Elec.	$580,000	$8,279,000	12,750
2. Pacific Telephone	266,000	3,802,000	13 (approx.)
3. So. Pacific Land	154,000	2,196,000	59,958
4. Boise Cascade	75,000	1,074,000	3,269
5. Sierra Pacific Power	71,000	1,013,000	3,905
6. So. Pacific Rail	65,000	930,000	1,200 (approx.)
7. Fibreboard Corp.	35,000	496,000	5,357
8. May, W.	31,000	440,000	7,213
9. Southern Pacific Pipe Line—SPR r/w	25,000	362,000	utilizes SPR right-of-way
10. Spring Valley Land	20,000	279,000	2,155

County of Modoc

Corporation or Individual	Property Tax Paid	Appraisal of Property	Acreage Owned
1. Weyerhaeuser Co.	$51,363.78	$690,245	27,174.98
2. Shasta Forest Co.	35,091.37	509,320	151,445.84
3. Leisure Ind., Inc.	27,164.40	388,385	19,522.55
4. McKinley & Unruh	25,818.00	335,000	10,976.92
5. Calandor Pine Corp.	20,037.77	261,365	804.90
6. Grace, Willoughby T.	18,595.31	249,640	25,045.37
7. Flournoy, D.F.	12,277.65	159,450	3,434.51
8. H.C. Cattle Co.	10,480.34	136,245	6,965.41
9. Cockrells, Inc.	10,419.94	142,200	4,804.29
10. Stewart, Walter	10,194.71	135,325	8,986.28

Appendix 1D
Financial Industry Interests in Land Use

The interests of the financial industry in maximum land development include insurance, banking, and the savings and loan associations. In a direct sense, insurance company profits depend upon the number and value of insured properties. Direct premiums totaling $183,742,000 were written in 1969 for fire and earthquake coverage in an increase from $169,435,000 in 1968. Multiple peril premiums including property damage for California homeowners is up from $203,056,000 in 1968 to $223,240,000 in 1969. Multiple peril commercial premiums are up from 1968 levels of $134,300,000 to $154,203,000.

Title insurance firms will also profit in this direct sense from land sales transactions. There are nine California domiciled real estate title insurers that conduct over 95% of the business in the state.* These firms took in $69,055,000 in premiums in 1969. They paid out a total of $2,997,000 in claims. This is an incredibly low loss ratio of $4.34 for every $100 in premiums collected. This compares to about $65 paid out in claims for every $100 in premiums for all of California's more numerous (and more competitive) fire, marine, and casualty insurance companies. Nor do title search expenditures or other "unique" expenses explain this immense profit.** The small number of firms in California, and their strong trade association might explain their rates. Price-fixing suspicions have already interested Congressional investigators from Senator Hart's antitrust and monopoly subcommittee. Whatever their findings, it is clear that this branch of the insurance industry stands to profit handsomely indeed from land transactions and development.

One important interest in land is provided by loans to agriculture. Farmers depend on two types of credit: short-range, to finance this year's crop, and long-range, to pay for machinery, land, and other capital items. They need the short-term credit because farming, with its once or twice a year crop, presents a cash flow problem; the farmer gets paid only at rare intervals. Meanwhile, he must plant, pay his men, and meet other daily expenses. A similar reason explains the need for long-term credit: purchase of a major capital item requires paying a large sum at one time, which is difficult for most farmers.

Thus, California agriculture finds itself heavily dependent on financing. Its potential financial sources include the federal govern-

---

* First America Title Insurance Company, Land Title Insurance Company, Northern Counties Title Insurance Company, Pioneer National Title Insurance Company, Security Title Insurance Company, Southern Counties Title Insurance Company, Title Insurance and Trust Committee, Transamerica Title Insurance Company, Western Ttitle Insurance Company.

** The purpose of the insurance is to protect the mortgage lender and homeowner against challenge to land title because of prior claims, back taxes or the return of claimants. Thus, investigations are often conducted into deeds, court records, etc. But other types of insurance have similar expenses —actuarial tables, individual tailoring, investigation into false or fraudulent claims, etc. which title insurance does not require. The federal General Accounting Office checked title searchers on one set of 9,000 FHA-insured properties in 1966. It found the cost of correcting title defects and searches to be less than $1,000; the FHA had paid $687,000 for title insurance.

ment, through the Soil Conservation & Stabilizations Service; commercial banks; and recently, insurance companies (savings and loans deal only in mortgages). The SCSC money, for soil improvements such as irrigation ditches, comes in very small amounts and is not significant over all. The bank loans seem to be clearly divided among two groups of banks—those lending short-term, and those lending long-term. Recently, insurance companies have begun to compete for long-term loans. Each group, while specialized, is also small. Indeed, for reasons too complex to discuss here, one bank, the Bank of America, handles over a billion dollars worth of farm loans by itself, a substantial portion of the total. The Bank once owned, through foreclosure, several hundred thousand acres of California farmland.

One of the more direct connections between all branches of the financial community and land development is provided through the lending of money for industrial, commercial and housing projects. In the case of commercial building, banks lend for the construction of offices and other large structures. This loan is called the "interim" loan and must be bought out for long term by another lender, the "taker-out" lender, after the completion of construction. This second, long-term loan is to be repaid from the project's revenues over a twenty year period or more. Insurance companies have become the major investors in these latter arrangements. The reason for such heavy financial participation in development (a participation which may be less necessary in developments undertaken by such huge corporations as Kaiser and Boise Cascade) is that the developer generally operates with very little capital of his own; his assets, or skills, lie in his ability as a go-between for the builder, the buyer, and the financier. This arrangement also has the "advantage" that fly-by-night developers cannot be sued for very much since they themselves (i.e., their *corporations*) have little capital, while the financial heavies, such as the banks, hide behind legal rules limiting their liability—even from fraud of the developers. In the same way, they escape "liability" for the environmental damage wrought by the developers they keep in business. Changes in both rules of liability is the critical precursor to the enforcement of common rules of equity against fraud, environmental damage, etc.

Table 1D-1 presents the amount and trend of California bank commitment to various kinds of enterprise. Commercial, industrial and real estate loans dominate. Savings and loans and insurance companies also devote portions of their resources to the direct financing of apartments, office buildings, industrial parks, etc.

After agriculture and development, the third activity in the real estate lending area is financing home purchases by individuals. Here the banks compete with savings and loan associations, and since the return on the projects is not as generous as on other types of loans, banks prefer to avoid these loans in favor of some other types of construction.

As a group, savings and loan associations are the largest lenders financing real property in the state. Estimates of real estate activity based on trust deeds recorded are no longer available. Estimates of institutionally held mortgage debt outstanding in California are shown in Table 1D-2. These estimates cover all types of real property; therefore, they include raw land, commercial and industrial properties as well as residential properties. On the other hand, the mortgage debt held by pension funds, conglomerates and other corporations not normally involved in real estate financing are not included, nor are mortgages held by individuals. Therefore, the total amount of mortgage debt is probably understated in the estimates for both California and the United States. Since 1962, savings and loan associations in California have supplied roughly half the

Table 1D-1
LOANS BY SELECTED CATEGORIES OF ALL INSURED
COMMERCIAL BANKS, CALIFORNIA, 1950–68
(In millions)

Year	Residential real estate		Other real estate	Commercial and industrial loans	Automobile installment loans	Single-payment consumer loans
	FHA-insured	Not FHA-or VA-insured				
1950	n.a.*	n.a.*	$ 366	$ 1,791	$ 422	$ 153
1955	$1,631	$1,040	592	2,968	819	275
1960	2,030	1,625	1,045	4,762	1,142	618
1961	1,980	1,843	1,120	5,122	1,190	687
1962	2,047	2,286	1,451	5,668	1,407	775
1963	2,111	2,727	1,838	6,009	1,633	891
1964	2,035	3,111	2,072	7,081	1,899	1,040
1965	1,989	3,390	2,309	8,284	2,081	1,155
1966	1,934	3,651	2,399	9,318	2,170	1,197
1967	2,030	3,731	2,372	10,112	2,133	1,302
1968	2,165	4,145	2,485	11,631	2,329	1,456

* Not available.
Source: Reports of Call of the Federal Deposit Insurance Corporation.

funds for real estate financing, compared to less than forty percent throughout the nation. Table 1D-3 presents the type of construction and purchase loans made by California Savings and Loans.* Insurance companies (most of which are headquartered outside the state) are the next largest lenders.** Commercial banks headquartered in California closely follow insurance companies. California has long been relatively capital short: a large portion of the funds to support real estate financing has come from outside the state. Table 1D-4 presents the breakdown of out-of-state funds by institutional source.

* Note that California Savings and Loans generally hold mortgage loans approximately 85% of their total assets. (In 1967, 265 associations had 28 billion in assets and held 23.6 billion in mortgage loans.)
** Note that insurance firms in California also wrote $956,000 in premiums in 1969 for mortgage guarantees. (This is up from $779,000 in 1968 and is another increasing source of insurance revenue deriving from development.)

Table 1D-2

ESTIMATED MORTGAGE DEBT OUTSTANDING HELD BY MAJOR INSTITUTIONAL LENDERS

Secured by Real Property Located in California [a]

(In Billions of Dollars)

Year	Savings and Loan		Mutual Savings Banks	Commercial Banks	Life Insurance Companies	U.S. Govt. Agencies	Total
		% of Total					
1969	$26.8	50.3%	$5.0	$55.8	$70.9	$26.8	$365.8
1968	25.2	50.2	4.7	53.5	65.7	21.7	341.7
1967	23.6	49.9	4.5	50.5	59.0	18.4	317.2
1966	22.5	49.9	4.3	47.3	54.4	15.8	296.5
1965	22.2	51.5	3.9	44.6	49.7	12.4	277.0
1964	20.5	51.8	3.4	40.6	44.0	11.4	252.5
1963	17.7	50.7	2.8	36.2	39.4	11.2	228.2
1962	13.9	47.0	2.2	32.3	34.5	12.2	204.7
1961	11.2	44.1	1.9	29.1	30.4	11.8	184.3
1960	9.1	40.6	1.6	26.9	28.8	11.2	168.8

[a] Sources: Federal Home Loan Bank Board, *Selected Financial Data;* National Association of Mutual Savings Banks, *Mutual Savings Bank Fact Book;* Federal Deposit Insurance Corporation, Reports of Call; Federal National Mortgage Association; Institute of Life Insurance

Table 1D-2 (Cont'd)
Secured by Real Property Located Throughout the United States [b]
(In Billions of Dollars)

Year	Savings and Loan % of Total	Mutual Savings Banks	Commercial Banks	Life Insurance Companies	U.S. Govt. Agencies	Total
1969	$140.2	38.3%	$55.8	$5.0	$9.8	$2.2	$53.3
1968	130.8	38.3	53.5	4.7	9.6	1.5	50.2
1967	121.8	38.4	50.5	4.5	9.4	1.3	47.3
1966	114.4	38.6	47.3	4.3	9.0	1.0	45.1
1965	110.3	39.8	44.6	3.9	8.3	0.7	43.1
1964	101.3	40.1	40.6	3.4	7.5	0.7	39.6
1963	90.9	39.8	36.2	2.8	6.7	0.7	34.9
1962	78.8	38.5	32.3	2.2	6.2	1.1	29.6
1961	68.8	37.3	29.1	1.9	5.8	1.1	25.4
1960	60.1	35.6	26.9	1.6	5.5	1.0	22.4

[b] Source: Economic Report of the President, 1970, page 247

In 1970, partly to overcome the capital shortage in California and partly to satisfy the extraordinary demands on real estate developers participating in the California land boom at the end of the sixties, banks seized upon an organization with special tax features for attracting new capital. The Real Estate Investment Trust (REIT) is a trust that qualifies under sections 856–858 of the Internal Revenue Code. The advantage a qualifying organization enjoys is that it is not subject to federal income tax with respect to income distributed to its shareholders. The management and investment policies of the trust are not currently supervised or regulated by a federal or state authority or regulatory agency. The trust is established to invest in a diversified portfolio of related property investments. The authority over the management of the trust and the conduct of its affairs is exclusively vested in the trustees of the trust, which usually are officers of the bank sponsoring the trust. The trust invests in construction loans, development loans and permanent and intermediate-term interests, which generally are first mortgages and which may or may not be guaranteed or otherwise backed by a governmental agency. It also invests in equities and other investments related to real property. The trust contracts with the sponsoring bank for advice. A bank is the advisor of the trust and proposes to the Trustees a continuing and suitable investment program, and, through its relationship with its customers, "seeks out and presents to the Trustees investment opportunities." The trust also derives investment funds through borrowings evidenced by short-term obligations of the trust and by establishing lines of credit with banks. Table 1D-5, etc., present the proposed instruments and returns of various California banks.

Certainly REIT has surmounted the tight credit restrictions designed in part to restrain speculation in land. The infusion of capital to the three major California lenders amounts to $175 million. With this capital, banks are permitted to promote most directly development activities.

Banks themselves are prohibited by section 750 of the Financial Code from owning real estate * for purposes other than location of banking houses. Insurance firms have similar restrictions. Nevertheless, loopholes and the holding company device have permitted more than the financing of development. There has been, despite the law, ownership and development of land.

Thirty years ago, the Bank of America owned over .5 million acres (mostly directly through foreclosures). Despite the laws designed to keep their immense financial power from dominating land development, banks still own directly much of California. The Crocker Anglo Bank is the largest landowner in Sacramento County. More interesting is the involvement in development and ownership directly through subsidiaries of newly formed holding companies. Although the state government refuses to compile or release information regarding the scope and nature of land activities through this dodge, it is known to be immense. John Hancock Life Insurance Company, for example, has formed a parent holding company and

---

* Note that § 1220 (b) limits obligations secured by real property to fifteen percent of the capital and surplus of a commercial bank. See §750 *et. seq.* for specifications concerning real property ownership limitations.

Table 1D-3

REAL ESTATE LOANS MADE BY PURPOSE,
INSURED CALIFORNIA SAVINGS ASSOCIATIONS
(In Millions of Dollars)

Year	Total	Construction			Home Purchase		All Other Imp. R.E.	Refinancing	Other Purposes[a]
		1–4 Family Homes	Multiples 5 or More Units	All Other Structures	1–4 Family Homes	Multiples 5 or More Units			
1969	$3,845	$ 604	$329	$91	$2,157	$182	$63	$300	$ 119
1968	3,912	606	209	58	2,230	206	43	448	112
1967	3,641	526	138	65	1,841	179	36	679	177
1966	2,954	464	87	46	1,387	110	43	679	138
1965	5,825	1,273	na	na	2,454	na	na	na	2,098
1964	7,137	1,951	na	na	2,684	na	na	na	2,502
1963	7,691	2,486	na	na	2,594	na	na	na	2,611
1962	5,590	1,856	na	na	1,847	na	na	na	1,887
1961	4,147	1,442	na	na	1,324	na	na	na	1,381
1960	2,952	1,246	na	na	926	na	na	na	780

[a] Prior to January, 1966, construction loans on multiples of 5 or more units and other structures; purchase loans on multiples of 5 or more units and other improved real estate; and refinancing loans were included in "other purposes."

Source: Federal Home Loan Board, Washington, D.C.

Table 1D-4

SOURCES OF ESTIMATED OUT-OF-STATE FUNDS SECURED
BY REAL PROPERTY IN CALIFORNIA
(In Billions of Dollars)

Year	Mutual Savings Banks	Life Insurance Co.	U.S. Govt. Agencies	California Savings and Loans — FHLB Advances and Other Borrowed Money	California Savings and Loans — Out-of-State Savings	Total Out-of-State — Amount	Total Out-of-State — % of Total Debt Outstanding	Total R.E. Debt Outstanding
1969	$5.0	$9.8	$2.2	$3.7	$3.5	$24.2	45.4%	$53.3
1968	4.7	9.6	1.5	2.3	4.6	22.7	45.2	50.2
1967	4.5	9.4	1.3	1.8	4.9	21.9	46.3	47.3
1966	4.3	9.0	1.0	2.9	4.6	21.8	48.3	45.1
1965	3.9	8.3	0.7	2.2	5.0	20.1	46.6	43.1
1964	3.4	7.5	0.7	1.9	4.2	17.7	44.7	39.6
1963	2.8	6.7	0.7	1.4	3.3	14.9	42.7	34.9
1962	2.2	6.2	1.1	1.0	2.3	12.8	43.2	29.6
1961	1.9	5.8	1.1	0.9	1.7	11.4	44.9	25.4
1960	1.6	5.5	1.0	0.6	1.2	9.9	44.2	22.4

Sources: National Association of Mutual Savings Banks, Mutual Savings Bank Fact Book; Institute of Life Insurance; Federal Deposit Insurance Corporation, Reports of Call; Federal Home Loan Bank Board, Selected Financial Data; Estimates by Federal Home Loan Bank of San Francisco and the Department of Savings and Loan.

Table 1D-5
WELLS FARGO MORTGAGE INVESTORS

Type of Project	Location	Total Amount of Loan	Amount of Trust's Participation	Stated Interest Rate	Yield to Trust [a]	Due Date of Loan	Permanent Financing
Apartments	San Diego, California	$ 1,700,000	$ 1,500,000	9.5%	10.0%	7/24/71	Life Insurance Company
Apartments	Mt. View, California	2,500,000	2,375,000	10.0%	10.0%	15 mos. from closing	GNMA
Office Building	Honolulu, Hawaii	17,000,000	2,000,000	10.0% [b]	11.7%	10/22/72	Pension Fund
General Hospital	Houston, Texas	1,300,000	1,200,000	10.0%	11.7%	9/ 1/71	Savings and Loan Association
Office Building	New York, New York	25,000,000	3,000,000	13.5% [b]	13.5%	9/ 1/72	None
Hotel	San Francisco, California	31,000,000	4,500,000	8.75% [b]	10.0%	2 yrs. from closing	Life Insurance Company
Mobile Home Park	Anoka County, Minnesota	728,400	728,400	8.0%	18.0%	9/30/70	FNMA
Office Building	Portland, Oregon	8,000,000	2,160,000	10.0%	10.0%	6/30/71	Insurance Company
Motel	Sacramento, California	900,000	800,000	10.0%	10.0%	7/15/71	Life Insurance Company

Apartments	San Mateo, California	2,700,000	2,430,000	9.5%	10.0%	2/28/71	Life Insurance Company
Industrial	Palo Alto, California	1,950,000	1,755,000	9.5%	10.0%	5/ 1/71	Life Insurance Company
Convalescent Hospital	Daly City, California	1,100,000	900,000	10.0%	10.0%	10/25/70	Life Insurance Company
Apartments	Fremont, California	972,000	874,800	9.5%	10.0%	10/31/70	Life Insurance Company
Hotel, Garage and Department Store	Honolulu, Hawaii	9,500,000	2,565,000	9.25%	9.25%	7/ 1/71	Life Insurance Company
Factory	Madera, California	5,000,000	2,000,000	9.50%	10.0%	11/15/71	Life Insurance Company
Office Building	San Francisco, California	25,000,000	7,000,000	9.50%	10.0%	3 yrs. from closing	Insurance Company
Office Building	Buffalo, New York	40,000,000	5,000,000	9.0% [b]	9.0%	7/ 1/72	Commercial Bank
Office Building	New York, New York	91,000,000	3,000,000	9.0% [b]	9.0%	12/31/72	None
Office Building	New Orleans, Louisiana	14,000,000	5,000,000	10.0% [b]	12.1%	2/ 1/71	Life Insurance Company
Total			$48,788,200				

[a] Including fees receivable by the trust and assuming that an average of 60% of the commitment would be outstanding during the life of commitment.

[b] Floating rate subject to change with changes in the prime rate.

Table 1D-6
UNIONAMERICA MORTGAGE AND EQUITY TRUST

Location of Property	Trust's Amount of Participation	Total Principal Amount of Loan	Expiration Date of the Trust's Investment	The Trust's Current Effective Interest Rate	Type of Property	Nature of Institution(s) Issuing Permanent Loan Commitment
Phoenix, Arizona	$ 650,000	$ 7,100,000	3-15-71	10½ %	Apartments	Life Insurance Company
Cerritos, California	381,411	1,171,300	1- 1-70	10 %	Single-Family Development	Mortgage Banker
Concord, California	1,200,000	1,883,472	4- 1-70	10 %	Single-Family Development	Mortgage Banker
Encino, California	4,000,000	5,500,000	1-16-71	10 %	Office Building	Life Insurance Company
Fountain Valley, Calif.	865,000	1,375,509	5- 1-70	10 %	Single-Family Development	Mortgage Banker
Fremont, California	1,150,000	2,850,000	10- 2-70	11 %	Apartments	Life Insurance Company
Huntington Beach, Calif.	1,600,000	2,755,415	6- 1-70	10¼ %	Single-Family Development	Mortgage Banker
Huntington Beach, Calif.	1,000,000	2,452,810	5- 1-70	10 %	Single-Family Development	Mortgage Banker
San Jose, California	700,000	929,645	4- 1-70	10 %	Single-Family Development	Mortgage Banker
Thousand Oaks, Calif.	1,400,000	1,759,121	8- 1-70	10½ %	Single-Family Development	Mortgage Banker
Honolulu, Hawaii	2,200,000	7,000,000	3-15-71	10 %	Shopping Center	Life Insurance Company
Mishawaka, Indiana	600,000	665,000	4-18-70	11 %	Post Office	Commercial Bank
Houma, Louisiana	500,000	1,090,000	5- 1-70	10 %	Apartments	Life Insurance Company
Ardmore, Oklahoma	640,000	880,000	5-15-70	10 %	Apartments	Life Insurance Company
Dallas, Texas	1,575,000	1,800,000	8-15-70	10 %	Apartments	Life Insurance Company
Dallas, Texas	240,000	370,000	8- 1-70	10 %	Apartments	Life Insurance Company
Waxahachie, Texas	690,000	1,300,000	5- 1-70	10 %	Shopping Center	Life Insurance Company
	$19,391,411	$40,882,272				

is deeply involved in development through Sierra Pacific Properties, owning 10,000 acres at least.*

One final interconnection between land development and the financial industry is the latter's investments. All branches of the financial industry invest heavily in oil and mineral development, in the construction industry, and so on. Fire, marine, casualty, and miscellaneous insurance firms made an investment gain of $2,224,752 in 1969. California firms made $130,420. These gains, of course, are but a part of the total monies invested. A brief survey of insurance company annual report forms which we were able to obtain from Department of Insurance sources, for example, reveals that insurance company investment portfolios include many firms committed to and dependent upon increased land development along current lines.

---

* California is reputedly a leading state in the regulation of holding companies, particularly insurance holding companies. The Insurance Holding Company System Regulatory Act, effective November 10, 1969, was heralded as a progressive step in monitoring these entities. And indeed, within certain limits, this Act can be quite useful if strictly and properly enforced—a dubious possibility given the evidence presented throughout this book. But even though it does require the registration of holding company systems, its powers over holding company activity are limited to the disapproval of outside acquisition offers and of extraordinary dividend disbursements. The California Department of Insurance rarely disapproves of any request from any part of the insurance industry and spends much of its time maintaining in questionable secrecy data that state law requires it to obtain from insurance firms.

The powers which the Department exercises under the 1969 Holding Company Act are primarily designed to prevent misuse of insurance assets or gross mismanagements which might result in failures. But there is no power to regulate misuse of the vast economic power available to these firms to mobilize massive resources in order to dominate a market. The Registration Statement that is required under the Act is made on a "Form B." Item V of Form B asks the holding company system to describe agreements, investments, loans, transfer of securities, etc., between the involved affiliates. Although there is no authority to do anything of importance with this information, it is collected. It is not, however, divulged. As we shall see, the secrecy which pervades the many and increasing relationships between those owning, developing, and financing the land raises serious dangers of conflict of interest in governmental decision-making.

Table 1D-7
BANK AMERICA REALTY INVESTORS

Location of Property	Type of Property	Amount of Participation	Amount of Loan	Loan Maturity	Stated Interest Rate	Nature of Institution(s) Issuing Permanent Loan Commitment
Atlanta, Ga.	Motel	$ 2,227,500	$ 2,250,000	11/6/70	9.00%[a]	Insurance Company
San Francisco, Calif.	Garden Apartments	3,861,000	3,900,000	9/15/70	9.75	Insurance Company
San Diego, Calif.	Motel	2,227,500	2,250,000	10/1/70	9.00[a]	Pension Fund
Los Angeles, Calif.	Office Bldg. & Warehouse	2,598,750	2,625,000	4/3/72	9.50	Bank of America
Modesto, Calif.	Apartment Building	346,500	350,000	10/25/70	8.25	Savings & Loan Assn.
Stockton, Calif.	Apartment Building	965,250	975,000	11/6/71	9.00[a]	Savings & Loan Assn.
Burlingame, Calif.	Office Building	509,600	1,040,000	2/1/71	10.00	Insurance Company
Mountain View, Calif.	Apartment Building	787,185	1,606,500	7/9/71	10.00	Insurance Company
Portland, Oregon	Motel	2,534,400	2,560,000	5/11/71	9.00[a]	Bank of America
San Mateo, Calif.	Office Building	3,465,000	3,500,000	6/19/71	8.75	Bank of America
Monterey, Calif.	Apartment Building	227,700	230,000	10/1/70	8.75	Insurance Company
Palo Alto, Calif.	Office Building	1,683,000	1,700,000	11/30/70	10.00	Insurance Company
Union City, Calif.	Warehouse	460,350	465,000	4/15/71	8.75	Insurance Company
San Jose, Calif.	Commercial Bldg.	633,600	640,000	4/20/71	9.50	Bank of America
San Francisco, Calif.	Hospital	495,000	500,000	7/1/72	9.00	Bank of America

Location	Property Type	Amount	Date	Rate	Lender
San Francisco, Calif.	Parking Garage	1,188,000	1,200,000	7/1/72	8.25	Bank of America
San Francisco, Calif.	Apartment Building	594,000	600,000	9/1/70	9.00[a]	Insurance Company
Palo Alto, Calif.	Apartment Building	12,177,000	12,300,000	1/24/71	9.00[a]	Insurance Company
Oakland, Calif.	Office Building	2,467,500	3,500,000	7/1/71	9.00[a]	Insurance Company
Stockton, Calif.	Apartment Building	262,350	265,000	3/4/71	9.00[a]	Savings & Loan Assn.
Stockton, Calif.	Apartment Building	598,950	605,000	6/9/71	9.50	Savings & Loan Assn.
Stockton, Calif.	Office Building	544,500	550,000	11/1/70	9.00[a]	Pension Fund[b]
Orange, Calif.	Apartment Building	2,168,958 / 381,101	7,026,322	8/31/70 / 1/31/71	9.00	Insurance Company
Orange, Calif.	Commercial Development	3,330,000	35,200,000	4/15/73	9.00	Insurance Company
San Diego, Calif.	Apartment Building	380,160	384,000	11/11/70	9.50	Insurance Company
Los Angeles, Calif.	Office Building	9,600,000	10,000,000	10/1/70	8.00	Insurance Company
Riverside, Calif.	Regional Shopping Center	4,900,500	9,900,000	6/30/71	9.50	Insurance Company
Santa Ana, Calif.	Office Building	5,445,000	5,500,000	11/30/70	8.00	Insurance Company
Mountain View, Calif.	Apartment Building	990,000	1,000,000	8/30/71	10.00	Mutual Savings Bank
San Francisco, Calif.	Office Bldg. & Warehouse	766,755	774,500	10/8/70	9.50	Insurance Company
Hollywood, Calif.	Show Room & Service Bldg.	841,500	850,000	9/15/70	9.50	Bank of America
		$69,658,609	$114,246,322			

[a] Floating rate subject to changes with changes in the prime rate.
[b] Bank of America is trustee of the pension fund.

Appendix 2A
Williamson Act Statewide Survey:

A Summary of All Forms Returned, with a Sampling of Counties with over 150,000 Acres under the Act

WILLIAMSON ACT SUMMARY

County	Date Rec'd.	Date of Report	Total Acres under the Act	Total Prime	Total Non-Prime	Decr. Assessed Val.	Decr. Tax Revenue
Alameda	9-10-70	6-30-70	103,491.98	1,474.90	102,017.08	$ 12,167,675	$ 1,222,850
Alpine	9-28-70	9-25-70	None	0	0	0	0
Amador	10-8-70	10-7-70	47,582	964.91	46,617.09	2,500,000	125,000
Butte	9-24-70	9-23-70	66,356	14,020	52,336		a
Calaveras	10-9-70	5-16-70	68,026.21	134	67,892.21	664,635	39,878
Colusa	10-1-70	9-30-70	None	0	0	0	0
Contra Costa	9-17-70	6-30-70	35,258	218	35,040	2,894,830	297,807
Del Norte	9-4-70		None	0	0	0	0
El Dorado	9-16-70	9-14-70	156,028.52	5,000	151,028.52	8,517,500	681,400
Fresno	9-14-70	7-1-70	843,258.61	485,655	357,603.61	30,189,438	2,514,780
Glenn	9-21-70	6-30-70	None	0	0	0	0
Humboldt	9-4-70	9-3-70	None	0	0	0	0
Imperial	9-8-70	6-30-70	None	0	0	0	0
Inyo	10-2-70	6-30-70	None	0	0	0	0
Kern	10-8-70	10-5-70	1,127,563.91	464,103	663,460.91	36,022,760	2,880,000
Kings	9-4-70	7-1-70	320,304.75	178,436.08	141,868.67	15,751,664	1,417,650
Lake	9-14-70	7-1-70	24,549	756	23,793	453,600	28,123
Lassen	10-1-70	6-30-70	None	0	0	0	0
Los Angeles	9-15-70	6-30-70	None	0	0	0	0
Madera	9-11-70	3-1-70	172,499.50	41,913.77	130,585.73	3,297,910	267,760
Marin	9-14-70	6-30-70	92,499	9,518	82,981	7,127,316	655,713

a Dollar values for Butte County have not been set forth; see Butte County data received by us on September 24, 1970, which seems to indicate a reduction of $3,200,630.00 in "appraised values," which would be about $800,157 in "assessed" values, if we understand it correctly.

WILLIAMSON ACT SUMMARY (Cont'd)

County	Date Rec'd.	Date of Report	Total Acres under the Act	Total Prime	Total Non-Prime	Decr. Assessed Val.	Decr. Tax Revenue
Mariposa	9-4-70	6-30-70	None	0	0	0	0
Mendocino	10-6-70	6-30-70	29,316.59	159.47	29,157.12	693,690	60,700
Merced	9-8-70	9-3-70	None	0	0	0	0
Modoc	9-10-70	9-8-70	None	0	0	0	0
Mono	9-4-70	9-3-70	None	0	0	0	0
Monterey	9-15-70	9-1-70	364,331.56	22,901.81	341,429.75	$ 3,008,055	$ 240,640
Napa	9-4-70	6-30-70	60,680	4,396	56,284	2,027,670	180,784.46
Nevada	9-4-70		None	0	0	0	0
Orange	9-22-70	6-30-70	80,837	8,280	72,557	21,659,430	1,816,898
Placer	10-1-70	5-15-70	76,474	6,579	69,895	4,707,660	367,200
Plumas	9-11-70	7-1-70	None	0	0	0	0
Riverside	9-8-70	6-30-70	29,848.54	16,227.90	13,620.64	2,927,767	203,493
Sacramento	9-18-70	6-30-70	102,105.254	18,101.28	84,003.974	3,343,019	300,871
San Benito							
San Bernardino	9-14-70	6-30-70	6,585.36	None	6,585.36	3,444,870	344,480
San Diego	9-11-70	6-30-70	13,098.35	2,694.40	10,403.95	2,989,975	260,472
San Francisco	9-17-70	6-30-70	None	0	0	0	0
San Joaquin							
San Luis Obispo	9-8-70	6-30-70	26,056	2,100	23,956	669,910	60,292

County						
San Mateo	9-21-70	7-1-70	34,342.596	1,355.354	32,987.242	4,811,760	475,500
Santa Barbara	9-16-70	3-1-70	228,349.35	12,323	216,026.35	11,690,000	935,200
Santa Clara	9-22-70	6-30-70	198,097.88	9,503.38	188,594.50	11,589,145	200,000
Santa Cruz	10-23-70	6-30-70	2,849	1,442	1,407	161,470	13,360
Shasta	9-8-70	6-30-70	11,790	775±	11,015	300,800	20,400
Sierra	9-8-70	6-30-70	None	0	0	0	0
Siskiyou	9-10-70	7-1-70	44,698	8,570	36,128	81,520	6,300
Solano	9-15-70	5-25-70	164,559	71,059	93,500	7,860,680	628,854
Sonoma	9-21-70	6-30-70	198,760.21	3,388.09	195,372.12	8,903,852	890,000
Stanislaus	9-16-70	3-1-70	161,521.107	4,439.061	157,082.046	4,726,000	508,500
Sutter	9-4-70	9-3-70	None	0	0	0	0
Tehama							
Trinity	9-15-70	9-14-70	None	0	0	0	1,440,406.77
Tulare	9-8-70	5-15-70	365,653.62	110,708.78	254,944.84	16,945,962	Offset by higher taxes 439,268.72
Tuolumne	9-11-70	6-30-70	123,656	None	123,656	5,490,859	
Ventura[b]	9-11-70	3-1-68	10,536.99	10,536.99	None		
	9-11-70	7-1-70	10,536.99	10,536.99	None	28,724,460	2,442,000
Yolo							
Yuba	9-4-70	6-30-70	None	0	0	0	0
Total			5,391,563.87	1,517,734.17	3,821,493.70	$264,372,082.00	$21,966,580.95

[b] Ventura County supplied figures for both 1968 and 1970; We have used only the 1970 figure. See Ventura County letter of Sept. 9, 1970.

Data Relating To
CALIFORNIA LAND CONSERVATION ACT OF 1965
(Williamson Act)

El Dorado County

As Of September 14, 1970

(1) COUNTY-WIDE DATA:

| Total Acres Under Act | Acres Prime | Acres Within Distance From Cities | | | Number Notices of Non-Renewal | Number Petitions for Cancellation | Number Approved | Acres Cancelled |
		0–1 Miles	1–2 Miles	2–3 Miles				
156,028.52	5000 Est.	460	None	600 Est.	None	One	None	None

Decrease in Assessed Valuations in County as a Result of Act $8,517,500
(please estimate if not known)

Decrease in Tax Revenue in County as a Result of Act $681,400 Est.
(please estimate if not known)

(2) INDIVIDUAL DATA: FIVE LARGEST PARTICIPANTS

(All close estimate)

Name	Total Acres	Acres Prime	Decrease in (estimate if not known) Assessed Valuation	Tax Revenue
1. Michigan Calif. Lumber Co.	71,733.72	None	$3,883,000	$310,640
2. American Forest Products Co.	30,272.70	None	$1,289,400	$104,150
3. Georgetown Lumber Co.	10,876.58	None	$ 691,000	$ 55,280
4. Bacchi Family	9,485.41	None	$ 412,300	$ 33,000
5. Van Vleck	2,592.00	None	$ 50,900	$ 4,072

Data Relating To
CALIFORNIA LAND CONSERVATION ACT OF 1965
(Williamson Act)
Fresno County
As Of July 1, 1970

(1) COUNTY-WIDE DATA:

Total Acres Under Act	Acres Prime	Acres Within Distance From Cities			Number Notices of Non-Renewal	Number Petitions for Cancellation	Number Approved	Acres Cancelled
		0–1 Miles	1–2 Miles	2–3 Miles				
843,258.61	485,655	Estimated 98% of all acres under act are more than 3 miles from cities.			4	1	0	0

Decrease in Assessed Valuations in County as a Result of Act $30,189,438
(please estimate if not known)

Decrease in Tax Revenue in County as a Result of Act   * $ 2,514,780
(please estimate if not known)

(2) INDIVIDUAL DATA: FIVE LARGEST PARTICIPANTS

Name	Total Acres	Acres Prime	Decrease in (estimate if not known) Assessed Valuation	* Tax Revenue
1. Giffen Inc.	51,133	48,576	$2,207,144	$183,855
2. Southern Pacific	111,256	100,130	$4,165,784	$347,010
3. W. J. Deal Co. Inc.	10,555	10,555	$ 532,191	$ 44,331
4. Noble, Wm. H.	18,197	16,377	$1,377,163	$114,717
5. Lassotovitch, Farley R.	7,990	0	$ 172,141	$ 14,339

* Tax revenue estimated with the use of 1969–70 average tax rate for open-space parcels in the amount of $8.33/100 of A.V.

Data Relating To
CALIFORNIA LAND CONSERVATION ACT OF 1965
(Williamson Act)

Kern County

As of October 5, 1970

(1) COUNTY-WIDE DATA:

Total Acres Under Act	Acres Prime	Acres Within Distance From Cities			Number Notices of Non-Renewal	Number Petitions for Cancellation	Number Approved	Acres Cancelled
		0–1 Miles	1–2 Miles	2–3 Miles				
1,127,563.91	464,103	Not available—see attached letter			1	1	0	0

Decreased in Assessed Valuations in County as a Result of Act (for the 1970–71 Tax Year) $36,022,760
(please estimate if not known)

Decrease in Tax Revenue in County as a Result of Act (for the 1970–71 tax year) $ 2,880,000
(please estimate if not known) Estimated using a $8.00/100 tax rate

(2) INDIVIDUAL DATA: FIVE LARGEST PARTICIPANTS

Name	Total Acres	Estimated Acres Prime	Decrease in Assessed Valuation	(estimate if not known) Tax Revenue
1. Tejon Land Co.	200,000	0	$	$ Not available—
2. Kern County Land Co.	138,143	135,266	$	$ See attached letter
3. Getty Oil Co.	48,655	33,655	$	$
4. Standard Oil Co.	63,000	33,000	$	$
5. Buena Vista Farms	26,766	16,766	$	$

Data Relating To
CALIFORNIA LAND CONSERVATION ACT OF 1965
(Williamson Act)

Kings County

As of July 1, 1970

(1) COUNTY-WIDE DATA:

Total Acres Under Act	Acres Prime	Acres Within Distance From Cities 0–1 Miles	1–2 Miles	2–3 Miles	Number Notices of Non-Renewal	Number Petitions for Cancellation	Number Approved	Acres Cancelled
320,304.75	178,436.08	1,962	not available	not available	none	none	none	none

Decrease in Assessed Valuations in County as a Result of Act — $15,751,664
(please estimate if not known)

Decrease in Tax Revenue in County as a Result of Act (based on $9.00 tax rate) — $ 1,417,650
(please estimate if not known)

(2) INDIVIDUAL DATA: FIVE LARGEST PARTICIPANTS—Estimate only

Name	Total Acres	Acres Prime	Decrease in (estimate if not known) Assessed Valuation	Tax Revenue
1. Boswell Company, J. G.	65,650	not available	$3,313,500	$298,300
2. Salyer Land Company	34,000	not available	$1,335,500	$120,200
3. Westlake Farms	24,250	not available	$1,018,200	$ 91,600
4. Nickel, George W.	15,770	not available	$ 144,500	$ 13,000
5. Mouren Farming Company	12,120	not available	$ 52,400	$ 4,700

Data Relating To
CALIFORNIA LAND CONSERVATION ACT OF 1965
(Williamson Act)
Monterey County
As of September 1, 1970

(1) COUNTY-WIDE DATA:

Total Acres Under Act	Acres Prime	Acres Within Distance From Cities			Number Notices of Non-Renewal	Number Petitions for Cancellation	Number Approved	Acres Cancelled
		0–1 Miles	1–2 Miles	2–3 Miles				
364,331.56	22,901.81				0	0		0

Decrease in Assessed Valuations in County as a Result of Act
(please estimate if not known) — $3,008,055

Decrease in Tax Revenue in County as Result of Act estimate based on $8.00 av. rate
(please estimate if not known) — $240,640

(2) INDIVIDUAL DATA: FIVE LARGEST PARTICIPANTS

Name	Total Acres	Acres Prime	Decrease in (estimate if not known) Assessed Valuation	Tax Revenue
1. Calif. Land & Cattle Co. 68-107(3)	31,370.63	0	$ 16,495 @ 6.827 99,052 @ 6.488	$ 1,126.11 6,426.49
2. Albert Hansen	18,619.07	0	$178,770 @ 7.178 28,915 @ 8.543	$12,832.11 2,470.21
3. Walti & Pearson Ranch, Inc.	11,136.32	0	$ 58,825 @ 5.497	$ 3,233.61
4. Raymond F. Reynolds, et al.	10,146.85	0	$ 2,375 @ 6.572 35,755 @ 5.497 17,250 @ 6.488	$ 156.08 1,965.45 1,119.18
5. Echeberria, Laurette, et al.	11,109.29	0	$ 64,065 @ 6.572 17,705 @ 5.497	$ 4,210.35 973.24

Data Relating To
CALIFORNIA LAND CONSERVATION ACT OF 1965
(Williamson Act)

Santa Barbara County

As of March 1, 1970

(1) COUNTY-WIDE DATA:

Total Acres Under Act	Acres Prime	Acres Within Distance From Cities 0–1 Miles	1–2 Miles	2–3 Miles	Number Notices of Non-Renewal	Number Petitions for Cancellation	Number Approved	Acres Cancelled
228,349.35	12,323.0	118.58	1,452.31	713.50	None	None	None	None

Decrease in Assessed Valuations in County as a Result of Act
(please estimate if not known)   Estimated $11,690,000

Decrease in Tax Revenue in County as a Result of Act
(please estimate if not known)   Estimated 2% $ 935,200

(2) INDIVIDUAL DATA: FIVE LARGEST PARTICIPANTS

Name	Total Acres	Acres Prime	Decrease in (estimate if not known) Assessed Valuation	Tax Revenue
1. James Flood Ro Sisquoc	36,836.93	170.2	$ 780,000	$62,000
2. Galvin Trust Ro San Fernando Ray	30,057.66	27.0	$1,048,000	$78,600
3. Wm. Luton Ro San Juan	13,130.85	0	$ 630,000	$52,000
4. Crawford Estate San Lucas Ranch	9,028.36	112.0	$ 346,000	$26,000
5. Louis Hansen Ro Los Llanitos	7,129.52	29.0	$ 417,000	$32,000

Data Relating To
CALIFORNIA LAND CONSERVATION ACT OF 1965
(Williamson Act)

Santa Clara County

As of June 30, 1970

(1) COUNTY-WIDE DATA:

Total Acres Under Act	Acres Prime	Acres Within Distance From Cities			Number Notices of Non-Renewal	Number Petitions for Cancellation	Number Approved	Acres Cancelled
		0–1 Miles	1–2 Miles	2–3 Miles				
198,097.88	9,503.38	This information may be available at a later date.			3	1	1 Pending	None

Decrease in Assessed Valuations in County as a Result of Act $11,589,145
(please estimate if not known)

Decrease in Tax Revenue in County as a Result of Act $ None *
(please estimate if not known)

* There is no loss in revenue as the tax burden is shifted to the rest of the taxpayers when the budget is divided by the assessed value.

(2) INDIVIDUAL DATA: FIVE LARGEST PARTICIPANTS

Name	Total Acres	Acres Prime	Decrease in (estimate if not known) Assessed Valuation	Tax Revenue
1. Hewlett-Packard (San Felipe Ranch)	22,828.49	81.00	$778,960	$ None
2. Naftzger, Roy E.	13,794.67	None	$150,370	$ None
3. Redfern Ranches	13,017.68	None	$233,670	$ None
4. Bar Seventy One	10,385.42	None	$121,990	$ None
5. O'Connell, Fenton	7,822.33	121.00	$216,750	$ None

Data Relating To

CALIFORNIA LAND CONSERVATION ACT OF 1965

(Williamson Act)

Solano County

As of May 25, 1970

(1) COUNTY-WIDE DATA:

Total Acres Under Act	Acres Prime	Acres Within Distance From Cities			Number Notices of Non-Renewal	Number Petitions for Cancellation	Number Approved	Acres Cancelled
		0–1 Miles	1–2 Miles	2–3 Miles				
164,559	71,059				0	0	671	0

Decrease in Assessed Valuations in County as a Result of Act $7,860,680
(please estimate if not known)

Decrease in Tax Revenue in County as a Result of Act $ 628,854
(please estimate if not known)

(2) INDIVIDUAL DATA: FIVE LARGEST PARTICIPANTS

Name	Total Acres	Acres Prime	Decrease in (estimate if not known) Assessed Valuation	Tax Revenue
1. Peterson Estate Co.	5939	1232	$ 71,520	$ 5,722
2. Lawler Ranches, et al.	3626		$103,780	$ 8,302
3. Olin H. Timm	3273		$ 77,050	$ 6,164
4. H. E. McCune Co.	2160	1316	$178,450	$14,276
5. Gordon Anderson, et al.	1843		$ 26,660	$ 2,133

Data Relating To

CALIFORNIA LAND CONSERVATION ACT OF 1965
(Williamson Act)

Stanislaus County

As of March 1, 1970

(1) COUNTY-WIDE DATA:

| Total Acres Under Act | Acres Prime | Acres Within Distance From Cities | | | Number Notices of Non-Renewal | Number Petitions for Cancellation | Number Approved | Acres Cancelled |
		0–1 Miles	1–2 Miles	2–3 Miles				
161,521.107	4,439.061	200	150	300	0	0	192	0

Decrease in Assessed Valuations in County as a Result of Act $4,726,000
(please estimate if not known)

Decrease in Tax Revenue in County as a Result of Act $ 508,500
(please estimate if not known)

(2) INDIVIDUAL DATA: FIVE LARGEST PARTICIPANTS

Name	Total Acres	Acres Prime	Decrease in (estimate if not known) Assessed Valuation	Tax Revenue
1. 5-D Ranch (Douglass)	11,359.88	0	$108,350	$12,150
2. Butler Noble	7,621.64	0	$204,500	$22,080
3. Paul Gerber	6,882.82	0	$ 68,650	$ 7,550
4. George Brichetto	5,414.19	0	$202,300	$21,201
5. Frank Draghi	4,965.87	0	$ 48,380	$ 4,988

Data Relating To
CALIFORNIA LAND CONSERVATION ACT OF 1965
(Williamson Act)

Sonoma County

As of June 30, 1970
(Includes 70–71 Roll)

(1) COUNTY-WIDE DATA:

Total Acres Under Act	Acres Prime	Acres Within Distance From Cities			Number Notices of Non-Renewal	Number Petitions for Cancellation	Number Approved	Acres Cancelled
		0–1 Miles	1–2 Miles	2–3 Miles				
198,760.21	3,388.09	10,956.98	unknown	unknown	15 parcels	0	0	0

Decrease in Assessed Valuations in County as a Result of Act (On 1970–71 Roll—Assessed) $8,903,852
(please estimate if not known)

Decrease in Tax Revenue in County as a Result of Act (Estimated in 1970–71) $ 890,000
(please estimate if not known)

(2) INDIVIDUAL DATA: FIVE LARGEST PARTICIPANTS

Name	Total Acres	Acres Prime	Decrease in (estimate if not known) Assessed Valuation	Tax Revenue
1. Nora Henderlong-Wickersham Ranch	11,883.69	0	$223,020	$18,750
2. Tom Baxter	7,217.09	0	$101,615	$ 8,550
3. Harold F. Richardson	6,560.18	0	$244,145	$19,000
4. Lewis Norton	6,380.28	0	$ 83,235	$ 6,050
5. Cooley Ranch, Inc.	6,159.95	0	$122,555	$10,400

Data Relating To
CALIFORNIA LAND CONSERVATION ACT OF 1965
(Williamson Act)

Tulare County

As of May 15, 1970

(1) COUNTY-WIDE DATA:

Total Acres Under Act	Acres Prime	Acres Within Distance From Cities			Number Notices of Non-Renewal	Number Petitions for Cancellation	Number Approved	Acres Cancelled
		0–1 Miles	1–2 Miles	2–3 Miles				
365,653.62	110,708.78	5,840	17,200	22,400	0	0	0	0

Decrease in Assessed Valuations in County as a Result of Act $16,945,962
   (please estimate if not known)

Decrease in Tax Revenue in County as a Result of Act. Higher Tax Rates offset reduced assessments in all but districts
with fixed rates such as schools. $

(2) INDIVIDUAL DATA: FIVE LARGEST PARTICIPANTS

Name	Total Acres	Acres Prime	Decrease in (estimate if not known) Assessed Valuation	Tax Revenue
1. Boston Ranch Company	30,004	0	$205,077	$
2. Frank T. Ellitt, et al.	9,672	0	$ 43,495	$
3. R.E.S. & Frank J. Hesse	8,832	0	$109,860	$
4. J. Guthrie	8,326	406.5	$155,620	$
5. L.B. Hyde & Sons	7,644	0	$ 51,030	$

Appendix 2B
Summary of U.S. Agricultural Subsidy Programs

1. PARITY

Essential to all federal programs is the concept of "parity," the supposed fair return for a farmer's investment on a par with returns elsewhere in the economy. The USDA calculates parity starting with farmers' returns during the last boom years of agriculture, 1910 to 1914, and adjusting for subsequent increases in costs. Since the USDA does not adjust to any extent for the change in the *pattern* of costs, especially the increased mechanization etc., parity prices usually come out distorted and unrealistically high. As a study of parity prices concluded:

. . . parity, like Topsy, just growed; and whatever economic justification can be found for it in its present form may be considered largely a rationalization.[1]

Nonetheless, the USDA still strives to support at least that part of the crop marketed domestically at or near parity.

2. FEDERAL COMMODITY PROGRAMS

The federal Commodity programs cover first of all the "mandatory basic commodities"—cotton, rice, tobacco, peanuts, wheat, and corn—and the "mandatory or non-basic commodities"—oats, rye, barley and grain sorghum (all four tied to corn as "feedgrains")—as well as tung nuts, which produce a drying oil for paint; honey, milk and butterfat; wool and mohair. In addition, at the discretion of the Secretary of Agriculture, cottonseed, flaxseed, soybeans, and dry edible beans may also receive support—and do. Sugar has its own special program under the Sugar Act, as do wool and mohair under the National Wool Act. While the economic importance of some commodities like cotton and wheat may make them obvious candidates for special attention, other commodities seem to have been included more for reasons of politics than logic. For example, almost every agricultural expert we talked to muttered darkly about peanuts being a boondoggle to the South.

The USDA's Agricultural Stabilization and Conservation Service (ASCS) operates the commodity programs for each county. Elected representatives of the growers, three per county, have nominal charge of the program in their county, but in fact influence policy very little. In California, there are approximately thirty-six such ASCS offices with a total staff of 198 and a budget in fiscal 1970 of $2,415,000. The biggest office in Fresno County has a staff of fourteen plus a director.

3. PRICE SUPPORT "LOANS"

While the exact details of the price support programs vary from commodity to commodity, all the commodities receive primary support through the Commodity Credit Corporation (CCC). The CCC, a nonprofit (to say the least), government-owned corporation, was established in 1933. In 1939 it became part of the Department of Agriculture. Today it has a capitalization of $100,000,000 and authority to borrow up to $14.5 billion. Annual appropriations replace its multibillion dollar annual deficits, a little over $4 billion for fiscal 1970.

CCC was originally designed simply to "stabilize" farm prices. Under pressure from the farm lobby, this authority gradually came to be interpreted as "stabilize upwards." The CCC stabilizes prices as follows:

When crops flood onto the market at harvest time, the market price usually drops sharply, frequently below the official support price, which the ASCS announced the year before as a percentage, say 80%, of the parity price. When this happens, a farmer may "borrow" from the CCC the support price value of his crop, putting the crop into CCC-approved storage as collateral, with a CCC loan to cover the cost of storage. If the market price of the crop rises above the support price during a set period (usually eight months) thereafter, he may redeem the crop for the support value plus thirty cents per $100 a month (3.5% per year) interest, and sell it on the open market for the higher price.

In this case, the CCC subsidizes the farmer only for the difference between the 3.5% interest charge and the commercial bank interest rate for such a risky loan (anywhere from 7 to 12%). Meanwhile since the harvest-time price of crops usually is lowest, the CCC has allowed the farmer to get his money in advance without having to sell his crop cheaply. Since most farmers use the CCC, the price and supply of a crop therefore tend to even out through the year.

If, on the other hand, the market price of the crop fails to rise above the support price, the CCC receives the crop. In this case the CCC subsidizes the farmer by the difference between the market and support prices, plus the commercial interest on that amount, plus the cost of storing and disposing of the crop. The CCC may sell the crops in the domestic market but usually does not, as that would depress the price further. Or, to avoid the cost of storage, the CCC may give away the crops to the poor, to school lunch programs, and to disaster areas. Most likely, however, it will try to "dump" the crops abroad at cut prices under PL 480 and other export programs. In fiscal 1967, "export payments"—the difference between the support price and the world market price—totalled $224.7 million.[2] What the CCC cannot dispose of immediately it continues to store at enormous expense, although in recent years better production controls have greatly reduced the disastrous surpluses it accumulated in the 1950s and early 1960s.

Possibly the CCC loan program benefits consumers as well as farmers in thus stabilizing prices and supplies. Whether the public pays too high a price for this stability in terms of higher taxes and higher prices is not a question we could answer here.*

4. DIRECT PAYMENTS

Commodity Credit Corporation price-support "loans" are only the beginning. The CCC, through the Agricultural Stabilization and Conservation Service, also gives growers of some commodities direct cash payments proportional to that part of their produce marketed in the United States. Thus, cotton receives a *loan support* at about twenty cents per pound and on top of this a *direct payment* to the grower of sixteen cents per pound. In 1969, California cotton growers received direct payments totalling $80,189,133, growers of feed grains (corn, oats, rye, barley, and grain sorghum) received $12,588,

---

* However, when it comes to income maintenance, CCC price supports obviously help big growers proportionally more than small, since big growers produce more.

532, and wheat growers received $6,244,342.[3] Direct payments to California sugar-beet growers under the Sugar Act amounted to $11,533,000 in 1969. Finally, sheep raisers in California received $4,138,524 in 1969 for regular wool and $9,354 for mohair—"incentive payments" to keep national production of wool at 300 million pounds per year. (In the National Wool Act of 1954, Congress found this level of production necessary "as a measure for our national security and in promotion of the general economic welfare."[4] "After all," said one ASCS official, "otherwise we would have to depend on Australia for wool.")

It is these payments that Senator Williams complains about, yet in fact *they* are only a part of the subsidy. Boswell, Giffen, and the others also receive a tidy sum indirectly through price supports and other programs.

5. PRODUCTION CONTROLS

Since price support of any sort inevitably stimulates farmers to produce more, worsening overproduction, the Agricultural Stabilization and Conservation Service also administers a variety of programs designed to reduce production. Only the tobacco program, however, controls production directly by limiting the actual pounds of tobacco a grower produces; the other programs attempt to control production by reducing acreage.

The principal acreage reduction or "allotment" program is tied directly to the subsidies. Every grower of a given commodity has a certain "base acreage," e.g., for cotton a grower's base acreage is the average amount of land he had planted to cotton from 1951 to 1953. Each year USDA economists calculate how much of a crop can be grown so that only a small amount winds up in CCC storage at the supported price. They then figure out what fraction of the total base acreage will produce. Then to qualify for price support loans and direct payments, the grower must plant only his individual allotment of 80% of his base acreage. The rest of his base acreage must lie fallow, or be limited to a restricted list of unsupported crops, like alfalfa. Formerly farmers received payments for keeping this land out of production, and still do for cotton. They do get paid, however, for taking out additional land up to a certain limit, usually 20% more, and small farmers may receive payments to take all their land out. These payments have generated a considerable outcry about "paying farmers to grow nothing," especially since farmers who grow the most nothing get the biggest payments.

The ASCS also pays farmers to grow nothing under a variety of "conservation" programs designed to take land out of production for longer than a year, and perhaps permanently.

---

[1] E. W. Grove, "The Concept of Income Parity for Agriculture," *Studies on Income and Wealth*, National Bureau of Economic Research, Vol. 6, New York, 1943, quoted in *Organization and Competition in the Fruit and Vegetable Industry*, Technical Study No. 4, National Commission on Food Marketing (June 1966), p. 315.

[2] ASCS BI No. 2, p. 3.

[3] ASCS Fact Sheet.

[4] ASCS BI No. 21, p. 1.

Appendix 2C
California State Board of Agriculture

Name and Address *	*Term Expires*	*Represents*
Allan Grant, President 2855 Telegraph Avenue Berkeley, CA 94705	1/15/71	Milk production, cotton and hay
Paul Ames 82-674 Highway 111 Indio, CA 92201	1/15/71	Farm management
Francisco Bravo, M.D. 735 South Soto Street Los Angeles, CA 90023	1/15/71	Hogs, hay, cattle, produce, and horses
C. Brunel Christensen P.O. Box 43 Likely, CA 96116	1/15/73	Cattle
Athalie Clarke, Mrs. 4633 Brighton Road Corona Del Mar, CA 92625	1/15/71	Oranges, walnuts, sugar beets, cotton, and alfalfa
John M. Garabedian 3104 E. Huntington Blvd. Fresno, CA 93702	1/15/72	Grapes and deciduous fruits
James B. Kendrick, Jr. University of California Berkeley, CA 94720	1/15/72	University
Howard H. Leach P.O. Box 2157 Salinas, CA 93901	1/15/74	Vegetables
E.C. (Bill) Mazzie 5263 Kent Drive Bakersfield, CA 93306	1/15/73	Potatoes, grain, cotton, field crops, and cantaloupes
Carl G. Samuelson 1225 Fairview Court Ojai, CA 93023	1/15/72	Citrus
Wesley N. Sawyer 600 Roberts Ferry Waterford, CA 95386	1/15/73	Dairy and walnuts
Alfred Tisch Mills Orchard Hamilton City, CA 95951	1/15/74	Citrus, deciduous fruits, and field and truck crops
Harold O. Wilson Calif. State Polytechnic College San Luis Obispo, CA 93401	1/15/71	State College

Donald A. Weinland
Executive Secretary
California Department of Agriculture
1220 N Street
Sacramento, CA 95814
Telephone-916-445-7730

* Mailing address
Revised 2/9/70

STATE BOARD OF AGRICULTURE
(BIOGRAPHY)

1. ALLAN GRANT—President, State Board of Agriculture—ex-officio member of the Board of Regents of the University of California —eighth year as President of the California Farm Bureau Federation. Has traveled extensively throughout the U.S., Japan, India, Mexico, and the Caribbean area seeking to develop international relations and expand trade—dairy farmer in the San Joaquin Valley for many years.

2. PAUL AMES (new member)—lives in Indio—owner of the Paul Ames Management Service—member of a pioneer Coachella Valley ranching family—member Citrus Research Committee of the University of California—past president of the Coachella Valley Farm Bureau.

3. FRANCISCO BRAVO—Doctor of medicine—owns farming properties in Los Angeles, Riverside, and Imperial counties—Vice-Chairman of the Agricultural Committee of the Greater Los Angeles Chamber of Commerce—organized the first and only Mexican-American National Bank in the U.S.

4. C. BRUNEL CHRISTENSEN—A cattle rancher in Modoc County—former president of the California Cattlemen's Association and served as director of the American National Cattlemen's Assn. from 1959–66—former chairman of the Western Regional Beef Council.

5. MRS. ATHALIE CLARKE—Native of Los Angeles—owns farms in Tulare and in Los Angeles County, and an interest in the Irvine Ranch in Orange County—Trustee of the Los Angeles County Museum of Science and Industry.

6. JOHN M. GARABEDIAN—a fruit and vegetable farmer-shipper in the San Joaquin and Coachella valleys for three decades—past director of the Calif. Grape and Tree Fruit League—member of the Council of California Farmers—resides in Fresno.

7. JAMES B. KENDRICK JR.—Vice President for Agricultural Sciences, University of California, Berkeley—worked his way up through the ranks beginning as a plant pathologist at Riverside in 1947.

8. HOWARD H. LEACH (new member)—President of Fresh Pict Foods, Inc.—chairman of the Traffic Committee of the Grower Shipper Vegetable Association at Salinas and is a director of the Monterey Boy Scout Council.

9. E. C. (BILL) MAZZIE—is a director of the Western Growers' Association of Calif. and Arizona, the Potato Growers' Association and the National Potato Council—operates a grower-shipper organization doing business throughout the U.S. and Canada—lives in Bakersfield.

10. CARL G. SAMUELSON—co-owner and manager of the Ventura-Pacific Company of Montalvo, a lemon packing and shipping firm—President of the Council of California Growers—is an alternate director of Sunkist Growers, Inc. and a director of the Agricultural Producers Labor Committee—served as a Ventura City Councilman—resides in Ojai.

11. WESLEY N. SAWYER—is a Waterford dairy farmer—is President of the California Milk Producers' Association—director of the Memorial Hospital Assn. of Stanislaus County and a member of the Stanislaus County Farm Bureau and Grange.

12. ALFRED TISCH (new member)—resides in Chico and is a managing partner of James Mills Orchards Company—a member of the Governor's Advisory Committee on Agricultural Foreign Trade since 1967—served as a member of President Eisenhower's Latin American Agricultural Trade Mission.

13. HAROLD O. WILSON—Executive Vice President, California State Polytechnic College, San Luis Obispo—native of Kings County —graduate of U. of Calif. at Davis, with a B.S. in agriculture —did graduate work at U.C. Berkeley and Los Angeles.

DONALD A. WEINLAND—Executive Secretary and Assistant Director California Department of Agriculture—Department Legislative Representative.

MRS. CLEDITH FORBES—Secretary to Mr. Weinland.

Appendix 3A
Wildlife Kills
Details—1969
California Department of Fish and Game

County	Location	Specific Cause	Ref. No. or Date	Species Killed
Region 1				
Tehama	Salt Creek (3 mi. SE of Red Bluff)	Toxaphene & DDT	7/21	250 Bass 25 Sunfish 250 Rough fish
Shasta	Olney Creek (Anderson Cottonwood Irrigation District)	Aqualin	7/23	55 Salmonids
Humboldt	Mill Creek	Pentachlorophenate	1/7	27 Salmonids 19 Unknown
Shasta	Sacramento River below Keswick Dam	Copper-laden waters	1/69	1,620 Salmon (yearling and adult king)
Shasta	Olney Creek (Acid Canal area)	Aqualin	8/69	200 Steelhead trout
Siskiyou	Indian Creek (Luther Gulch area)	Acid mine water		2,430 King salmon fingerlings 7,414 Juvenile steelhead 125 Adult steelhead
Siskiyou	Dwinnel Reservoir	Dissolved oxygen	10/6	600,000 Pond smelt 15,000 Largemouth bass 1,500 Rainbow trout 5,000 Brown bullhead 12,000 Green sunfish 3,750 Klamath sucker 750 Tui chub
Region 2				
El Dorado	Indian Creek on Bob Ranch, Shingle Springs	Herbicide—Weed killer	69-11	250 Bluegill 250 Catfish

County	Location	Cause	No.	Fish
Glenn	Capay Creek on Richard Rold prop.	Toxaphene, DDT, & Disyston	69-14	10,000+ Carp 250 Catfish 250 Bluegill 250 Perch
San Joaquin	Duck Creek Hwy 4 to ¼ mi. east of Hollenbeck Rd.*	Thiodon	69-8	250 Bluegill 250 Catfish 750 Carp
San Joaquin	½ mi. east of Paradise Rd. alongside of Tom Payne Slough in small pond near Banta	Thiodon	69-7	1,000+ Bluegill 250 Sacramento pike 75 Crappie 25 Catfish 25 Striped Bass
Solano	Horse Creek between Byrnes Rd. and Leisuretown Rd.	Xylene herbicide	69-12	750 Carp 750 Hitch 25 Crayfish
San Joaquin	Victoria Island, ½ mi. east of Old River on Hwy 4	Thiodon	7/21	1,000+ Carp 25 Bluegill
San Joaquin	Mormon Slough near Stockton	Unknown	69-2	500 Carp
Solano	Leisuretown Rd. and Lewis Rd. 7½ miles	Herbicide—Standard weed oil	69-1	(over 10,000 fish) 95% Carp 4% Hitch 0.5% Sunfish & Mosquitofish
Colusa	Letts Lake—17 mi. west of Stonyford	Ice? winter kill	69-6	1,000+ Frogs 25 Trout
San Joaquin	Telephone Cut	Cow manure & liquid dairy waste	69-10	500+ Carp 6 Black bass

County	Location	Specific Cause	Ref. No. or Date	Species Killed
San Joaquin	South of Guild Winery next to Bear Creek south of Bear Creek Rd.	Possible pollution	69-9	75 Carp
San Joaquin	Diverting Canal—500 yds. east of freeway south side of canal	Possible pollution from chemical company	69-3	75 Perch 250 Carp
San Joaquin	Mormon Slough—½ mi. before entering turning basin of Port of Sotckton	Pollution	69-4	1,000+ Threadfin shad 250 Catfish 250 Striped bass
Solano	Irrigation Canal on Petersen Estate—7 mi. N of Rio Vista & 1 mi. W of Liberty Island Rd.	Fish stranded—Canal being drained—low dissolved oxygen	69-5	250 Perch 25 Striped bass
Butte	Pine Creek, 8 mi. west of Chico	Toxaphene & DDT	69-15	1,000+ Carp 1,000+ Chub 400 Black bass 300 Bluegill 300 Perch
Sacramento	East Natomas Main Drain —Silver Eagle Rd. downstream to Sacramento River about 3 miles	Possibly low dissolved oxygen due to excessive algae blooms & high water temperature	69-16	10,000+ Carp 250 Catfish
Sacramento	Sherman Island. West side near 3 mile Slough & San Joaquin River	Stranding, low dissolved oxygen	69-17	10,000+ Striped bass

County	Location	Cause	No.	Kill
San Joaquin	Yosemite Lake at east end of Smith Canal	Low dissolved oxygen	69-18	10,000+ Threadfin shad 25 Catfish 25 Bluegill 250 Black bass
San Joaquin	¼ mi. E of S. Manteca Rd. at Stanislaus River	Pollution—plant algae	69-19	
San Joaquin	Live Oak Canal at Live Oak Rd.	Unknown—Pollution	69-20 10/22	25 Green sunfish 75 Carp
Region 3				
Contra Costa Alameda	Lake Lafayette Alameda Beach—San Francisco Bay	Copper sulfate (herbicide) Pesticide	7/24 6/3	1,000 Black crappie 2 Striped bass
Contra Costa	Port Chicago & Martinez	Unknown (fish decomposed)	7/19	3 Spiny dog shark 75 Striped bass 12 Catfish 2 Shad
Lake Santa Cruz	Clear Lake Manressa Beach—Rio Del Mar, Sunset Beach	Unknown Unknown—heavy fresh water runoff	5/28 2/8	500+ White catfish 10,000+ Soft-shell clams 250 Basket cockles 250 Red crabs 250 Slender-leg crabs
Alameda Alameda	Near dam—Lake Chabot Estuary near Coast Guard Govt. Island	Paint Unknown	6/12 6/14	12 Trout 6 Striped bass
Marin	Bel Marin Keys near Novato	Unknown	6/11	15 Carp 6 Striped bass
San Mateo	San Gregorio Beach	Oil	3/3	40 Murres 3 Sea lions

County	Location	Specific Cause	Ref. No. or Date	Species Killed
Lake	All areas of Clear Lake	Unknown	9/27	20,000 Carp 7 White catfish 5 Suckers
Solano	Westerly off Crawford Slough for .4 mi. (area adjacent to Grizzly Island Wildlife Area on Pintail Ranch)	Unknown (low dissolved oxygen?)	10/23	450 Striped bass 1 Sucker 1 Perch
Santa Clara	Alamitos Creek, 21350 Almaden Rd., San Jose	Chlorine from commercial swimming pool	10/27	25+ Trout 250+ Stickleback 250+ Suckers
Marin	Larkspur Lagoon, Marina Lagoon of Greenbrae Properties	Pollution	8/21	25+ Black bass 25 Striped bass
Marin	Bolinas Bay, between Duxbury & mouth of Bolinas Lagoon	Unknown	8/21	40 Striped bass 2 Sand shark
Lake	Clear Lake	Unknown	8/28	1 Grebe 1,000+ Carp 800 Blackfish 100 Hitch 100 Bluegill, crappie & white catfish
San Mateo	Los Trancos Creek, tributary of San Francisquito Creek (Portola Valley area)	Low dissolved oxygen	9/8	150 Rough fish

County	Location	Cause	Date	Fish
Alameda	Aquatic Park Lagoon Berkeley	Oxygen depletion	9/10 & 9/12	1,000+ Needlefish 1,000+ Stickleback 2,725 Striped bass
Solano	Sears Point Rd.—Second Leslie Salt Co. Pond, west of Sears Point Bridge	Lack of oxygen	9/1	2,500 Striped bass
Santa Cruz	Bean Creek near Dufor private fish farm, near Felton	Pollution from Santa Cruz Aggregates Co., settling ponds	10/6	6,000 Steelhead & rainbow trout
Santa Cruz	Newell Creek—Rancho Rio Subdivision at Hart La. in Ben Lomand T 10s R2W Sec. 3	Siltation	10/3	750 Rainbow trout
San Luis Obispo	San Luis Obispo Creek foot of Cuesta Grade, Hwy 101, 2 mi. north of City of San Luis Obispo	Diesel fuel (tanker overturned)	11/7	750 Steelhead & rainbow trout 1,000 Dace & stickleback
San Luis Obispo	San Luis Obispo Creek at City Sewage plant	Raw sewage (overflow from treatment plant); float & pump failure	11/8 & 11/9	100 Rainbow trout 500 Stickleback
San Luis Obispo	San Luis Obispo Creek	Pollution—solvent type whitish-oily color with scum	11/12	1,000 Rainbow trout 2,000 Dace
Region 4 Stanislaus	Laird Park Inlet—Pond Outlet to San Joaquin River	Unknown (possible pollution)	7/24	3 Striped bass 21 Catfish 3 Black bass 75 Carp

County	Location	Specific Cause	Ref. No. or Date	Species Killed
Stanislaus	Tuolumne River, 1-6 mi. below Modesto Sewage Farm	Sewage	69-16	20,000+ Hardheads 5,000+ Perch 10,000 Catfish 20,000 Carp
Merced	Santa Fe Drive—½ mi. south of East Ave., Power Ranch Stock Pond	Unknown	69-10	75 Black bass 250 Crappie 250 Perch
Fresno	P. Heinrich Ranch, Parkfield Rd.	Possibly 1080	69-8	19 Scrub jay 1 Quail 2 Rabbits
Fresno	Cotton field at SE corner of Adams & Ohio Avenues	Azodrin	69-17	2 Pheasants
Fresno	SE corner Belmont & Hayes Avenues	Azodrin	69-18	2 Meadowlarks
Fresno	Rocha Ranch, Highland & Clarkson Ave.	Azodrin	69-19	1 Dove
Fresno	Teilman Ranch	Azodrin	69-20	1 Barn owl 20 Sparrows (adult)
Fresno	Frietas Ranch	Azodrin	69-21	1 Meadowlark
Fresno	Russell Ranch	Azodrin	69-22	1 Cottontail
Fresno	Efrid Ranch	Azodrin	69-23	1 Dove 1 Pheasant
Fresno	Mason Ranch	Azodrin	69-24	1 Blackbird
Fresno	Gragnani Ranch	Azodrin	69-26	1 Blackbird 1 Dove
Fresno	Wood Ranch	Azodrin	69-25	1 Pheasant 1 Pheasant 6 Sparrows

County	Location	Cause	No.	Species
Fresno	Barcelus Ranch	Azodrin	69-27	1 Sparrow hawk (affected)
Tulare	Kaweah River below Power-house 2	Copper sulfate	69-28	1 Pheasant (dead), 3 affected
Kings	Lemoore Sportsmen's Pond	Unknown, perhaps spray	69-29	1,000 Rainbow trout, suckers, and smallmouth bass; 2,000 Bluegill; 2,000 Bass; 50 Black crappie; 50 Bullfrogs
Tuolumne	Lockhart Ranch near Columbia	Unknown	69-1	1 Deer (yearling)
Fresno	Delta Mendota Canal, between Hwy 33 & Fairfax	Unknown	69-30	25 Striped bass
Madera	Martin & Sons (farmed by R. Mortimer) Ave. 14, Rd. 20-½	Azodrin	69-31	1 Pheasant (sick)
Tulare	Corner of Rd. 48, Avenue 394	Azodrin	69-32	1 Valley quail; 5 Juvenile quail
Imperial	Elmore Duck Club	Unknown	9/3, 69-1	50 Pintail Duck; 300 G.W. Teal Duck; 1 Shoveller
Los Angeles	Hollenbeck Park	Crude Oil	69-2	12 Mallards
Riverside	Sunset Ranch, Mecca	Botulism	69-5	25 Mallards
Orange	Newport Bay	Possible disease	7/69	? Spotted bass
Orange	Newport Bay	Possible disease	9/6	25 Gulls
Riverside	Fairmont Park	Possible oil	69-4, 4/8	15 Largemouth bass; 10 Crappie; 10 Bullhead
Imperial	Vail Canal, near F-2 Section of Federal Wildlife Refuge Area	DDT and parathion	11/9/69, 69-7	25 Carp

Appendix 3B
State Water Plan Finance

Typical of the Congressman's inaccurate statements are his charges that the State Water Project will supply subsidized agricultural water to San Joaquin Valley farmers. The Congressman simply doesn't know what he is talking about because the State does not subsidize its water deliveries. San Joaquin Valley ranchers will pay in full for every drop of water they receive from the State Water Project.

—Assemblyman Kent Stacey of Kern County, Vice-Chairman of the Assembly Water Committee, Press release, July 29, 1970

The most basic problem with the DWR's cost figure arises from its definition of the word "cost." The common and economic idea of "cost" is represented well enough by the dictionary definition: "the amount of money, time, labor, etc. required to get a thing; price; expenditure." But, as Harvey Banks put it, "engineering cost" represents something entirely different. It represents the amount of money which must be granted or borrowed to build a project—the capital expenditures. It omits the single largest expense of any major construction project—the expense of obtaining this capital. As a statement of what the public understands as cost, therefore, the DWR's figures are about as accurate as though it assumed the materials would be donated, or labor contributed for free; actually, since the cost of money is considerably higher than either of these, the DWR's figures are even more deceptive.

The State Water Project will obtain its money in four ways. By issuing bonds, it will borrow from the capital market approximately $1.95 billion—$1.75 billion in the General Obligation Bonds authorized by the 1960 referendum, and $245 million in Oroville Revenue Bonds (*Bulletin 132-69*, Table 19). It also expects to borrow $1.194 billion from the state's Tidelands oil and gas revenues, which have been placed for that purpose in a fund called the California Water Fund. The third source of money will be direct grants from the state and federal governments for so-called general public benefits provided by the Project, such as flood control, recreation, and wildlife habitat improvement. In addition, the state before 1960 had spent about $100 million on the Project in various ways which will not be repaid. The total amount obtained from these grants will be $475 million. The fourth source will be revenues generated through the Project's sale of water and power.

The cost of the money which the state obtains in these ways is stupendous, and totally unaccounted for in its official cost estimates —although one can find most in the Department's admirably detailed bulletins, if one has time and patience.

1. THE BONDS

Using a 4% interest rate, the state expects to pay $2.9333 billion in interest on its $1.75 billion General Obligation bond borrowing. (*Bull. 132-70*, Table 17) This undoubtedly represents a serious understatement since the average interest on the $1.15 billion worth of bonds sold by June 1970 had already reached four percent. The rest of the bonds will be sold at higher interest rates, ranging up to seven percent and perhaps beyond. This will raise the interest which must be paid on general obligation bonds by several hundred million dollars. In addition to this interest, the state will pay $460 million interest on the $245 million of revenue bonds it sells. (*Bull. 132-69*, Table 19) Thus, interest on the bonds alone comes to $3.399 billion —and even that sum is, as noted, seriously understated.

2. THE STATE LOAN

The state is expected to loan $1.194 billion to the Project, not to mention the loan of its credit (which Legislative Analyst A. Alan Post recently estimated has cost the state about one percent of interest on all other borrowings since the Report) for the General Obligation bonds. The loan will be interest free; that is, the Project must repay only the amount of the loan over the repayment period (which lasts until 2035). It is difficult to calculate the cost to the state of such a loan, because that cost depends on the rapidity with which it will be repaid. There can be no doubt that such a cost is real, however. The funds to be loaned would have been available for other use or for investment. Actually, some of the money now earmarked for the interest-free loan had originally been placed in a fund for school expenditures. If one assumes that the cost of the interest-free loan is the amount lost because the state did not invest it at present investment rates (approximately 9%), the cost, under almost any conceivable repayment plan, is astronomical. It is so high that the Task Force presents it with trepidation, for it seems unbelievable; yet, it represents what *in fact* the state would be receiving over the repayment period from investing its present Tidelands receipts. If one assumes a repayment schedule for the state loan identical to that for the General Obligation Bonds, it comes out to $4.1 *billion*.* Even assuming only the General Obligation Bond interest rate, the cost comes to $2 billion. Both estimates are actually low because the repayment period for the state loan will probably be longer than for the General Obligation Bonds, or at least a greater percentage of the state's loan will be repaid later. The reason is that repaying the state is only the Project's third priority, after repaying the General Obligation and Revenue bonds.

3. THE GRANTS

The projected state and federal contributions alone account for $475 million, or nearly twenty percent of the DWR's estimated project costs. It is therefore difficult to see how the Department could under any circumstance claim that taxpayers will pay less than ten percent of the costs. The reader may wonder why a "loan" from the state has a greater cost attached to it than an outright grant. The reason is that the interest on a loan is charged to the borrower—in this case, the Project. Thus, the cost of the loan is a cost to the Project. Since the Project does not actually repay the loan, its cost is found by looking at what the money would be earning if it weren't loaned. But the Project need not repay a grant, and so the grant is no cost to it. Naturally, one *could* calculate alternate

* G.O. Bond Interest : G.O. Bonds at 4% = state interest : state loan at 9%

$$\$2.9 : \$1.75 \,(.04) = \text{state interest} : \$1.1 \,(.09)$$

$$\frac{\$2.9 \times \$1.75 \,(.04)}{\$1.1 \,(.09)} = \text{state interest} = \$4.1$$

revenues to the state from the amount granted, and call this the "cost" of the grant over the repayment period, but this is not done in conventional accounting.

4. REPAYMENT FROM PROJECT REVENUES

DWR expects Project revenues to pay not only enough to cover the interest on borrowings, but to finance additions to the Project as well.

The results of the above are summarized in the table below.

INCOME STATEMENT FOR THE SWP TO 2035
(IN BILLIONS OF DOLLARS)

	Amount	Source of Estimate
Costs		
1. Construction Expenses [a]	3.517	132-70, Table 14(1)
2. Operating Expenses [b]	3.612	132-70, Table 11(10)
3. General Obligation Bond Service [c]	2.933	132-70, Table 17
4. Revenue Bond Service [d]	.460	132-69, Table 19
5. Cal. Water Fund Loan, estimated service [e]	2.000	Assumes same interest as G.O. Bonds
6. Direct Project Costs	12.522	
7. Future Projects Reserve [f]	1.785	132-70, Figure 8, p. 69
8. Total Costs	14.307	
Revenues		
9. Water Contractor Payments [g]	10.542	132-70, Table 13(5)
10. U.S. San Luis Operating Payments [h]	.119	132-70, Table 13(7)
11. U.S. Flood Control, etc. [i]	.073	132-70, Table 15(3)
12. Miscellaneous and Oroville Income [j]	1.009	132-70, Table 13(9) plus 132-69, Table 19
13. State Payments		
i) Amounts Paid pre-1960	.100	132-70, Table 8
ii) Rec., Fish, Wildlife	.302	132-70, Table 10(3) & 12(5)
iii) Cal. Water Fund Service (State Taxpayer Contribution)	2.000	See item 5
14. Davis-Grunsky Loan Repaymt [k]	.044	132-70, Table 13(6)
15. Extra Water Contractor Paymts not otherwise noted	.118	132-70, Table 15(4) & (5)
16. Total Revenues	14.307	

[a] Construction expenses include the actual construction costs—labor, materials, management, etc. These are broken down in a number of ways in *Bulletin 132–70:* project purpose, function, and facilities.

A. PROJECT PURPOSE

1. Davis-Grunsky Program, planning for features now deleted, unassigned costs: $ 140 million
2. San Joaquin Drain—agricultural waste water disposal: 6
3. Recreation, Fish & Wildlife Enhancement 153
4. Flood Control 75
5. Water Supply and Power Generation: Conservation Facilities: 1,504
6. Water Supply and Power Generation: Transportation Facilities: 1,640
   3,518

B. FUNCTION

1. Surveys and engineering studies 41
2. Preliminary and final design 135
3. Rights of way and relocations 206
4. Construction contracts and supervision 1,968
5. Operating costs during construction 76
6. Davis-Grunsky loan and grant programs 130
7. Payments to U.S. for San Luis ($282 million) and Eel rivers 962
   3,518

C. FACILITIES

1. Davis-Grunsky Projects 130
2. San Joaquin Drain 6
3. Upper Feather River Facilities (five small dams) 27
4. Oroville Division (dam, powerhouse, etc.) 504
5. Peripheral Canal 150
6. Upper Eel (Dos Rios) 842
7. California Aqueduct 1,760
8. North Bay Aqueduct 19
9. South Bay Aqueduct 69
10. Unassigned Costs 9
    3,516

N.B.: These expenses do not include the federal share of the San Luis unit; totals may vary because of rounding off.

b Operating expenses include salaries and expenses of the DWR and personnel required to operate the facilities, the cost of power for pumping, and costs of related supplies and equipment.

c Interest that will be paid on the $1.75 billion bond issue authorized by the Burns-Porter Act and ratified by the voters in the November 1960 referendum. The present Project interest rate is slightly over 4%.

d Interest that will be paid on the $245 million Central Valley Project Revenue Bonds issued to finance construction of Oroville (anna. *Bill 132–6, Bull. 132–6*, Table 19).

e Calculated simply by assuming the same ratio of interest to loan as obtains for the Burns-Porter Bonds. The Water Fund will loan a total of $1.194 billion (*Bull. 132–70*, Table 14(7)).

f The amount returned during the Project repayment period in excess of expense will be placed, apparently, in a reserve for future projects. This is counted, in accounting, as a "cost."

g This figure includes all payments from water contractors—the thirty-one local water agencies buying water from the DWR. These are expected to include $7.204 billion in capital-cost payments, and $3.336 billion in operating costs. (The remaining $256 million in operating costs will be met by power user payments).

h Under its contract with the Bureau of Reclamation, the DWR will operate the joint San Luis Project facilities. The federal payment will cover the federal share of the operating costs. The DWR accounts differently for the federal share of the construction costs. Since the U.S. was responsible for

These figures may be reconciled with the DWR's own public statements that the cost will be $2.8 billion if the reader remembers that the DWR is referring in such a statement solely to the amount of "outside" money needed. It reaches its $2.83 billion figure by adding the net receipts for the following "outside" sources: (from p. 52–3, and Table 14, *Bull. 132-70*)

General Obligation Bonds	$1.728
Revenue Bonds	.213
California Water Fund	.514
Miscellaneous Receipts	.382
	$2.837

The $2.8 billion figure does not include an expected $680 million loan from the Water Fund for the Eel River facilities, to be paid out between 1985 and 2035; adding this to the DWR's figures yields the Task Force's total "construction cost" of $3.517 billion, as well as the total Water Fund loan of $1.194 billion.

As to the amounts contributed toward these costs by various groups, the Task Force has frankly been unable to learn how the DWR arrived at its estimates. Clearly it includes neither the cost of the state's interest-free loan, which the state taxpayers bear, nor any allowance for the amount of "water user payments" actually paid through local property tax assessments by the water agencies buying state water. But even then, it appears that state and federal taxpayers would contribute $475 million of the DWR's estimated $2.8 billion cost, or 17%—not the 7% allowed by the DWR for BOTH taxpayer and power user receipts. In any event, the Task Force's own calculations follow.

From the income statement, it appears that the Project's capital costs will total $8.910 billion—Item 6 minus Item 2. The state and federal share of payments, Items 11 and 13, comes to $2.475 billion, or 28%. Total power revenues will be the amount required to retire the revenue bonds, $705 million (*Bull. 132-69,* Table 19), plus the net income from power operations, $99 million (*Bull. 132-69,* Table 14(11)), for a total of $804 million, which is 9% of the capital costs.

The remaining capital payments, 63% of the total, come from water contractors, who thus pay $5.631 billion. Of this amount, two

---

construction, the state share of the capital or construction costs appears as payment to the U.S. (see note a above).

i Includes federal payments for flood control benefits from Oroville, plus a small amount for open-space protection.

j This figure comes from two sources. *Bull. 132–69,* Table 19, shows that $245 million of revenue bonds will be issued, with total interest payments, before they are repaid of $460 million. *Bull. 132–70,* Table 13(9), estimates that revenues from Oroville power *after* the bonds have been paid off, plus miscellaneous income such as short-term interest on funds temporarily invested, will amount to $304 million. Of these funds, *Bull. 132–69,* Table 13(9), tells that $99 million will be power profits.

k The Burns-Porter Act sets aside $130 million of the funds raised for the SWP to fund the Davis-Grunsky Act. This Act provides for state assistance to small projects, and was made part of the Burns-Porter Act as a political concession to the northern counties—a payoff in return for their votes. Some of the Grunsky-Davis money will be granted, some will be loaned.

agencies pay $4.373 billion, or 78%. These are the Kern County Water Agency, $963 million, and the MWD of Southern California, $3.410 billion (computed from Tables B-19 and B-20, *Bull. 132-70*). In 1970, Kern County taxpayers paid 33% of the state water charge (see Kern County section). There is no indication that they will pay any less a share during the rest of the repayment period—indeed, the agency was formed for precisely the purpose of providing a subsidy. Thus, it can be assumed that Kern County taxpayers will ultimately pay $320 million of the capital costs, or 3.5%.

The taxpayer share of MWD payments is harder to estimate. Taxpayers presently pay over 50% of the District's costs, and will continue to do so through at least 1972. Under a policy adopted in 1960, however, the District will strive to reduce taxpayer payments; it has recently predicted a gradual reduction of taxpayer payments to one eighth of the total by 1990 (MWD Statement, p. 58). Nevertheless, past District policies make such a forecast unreliable, to say the least. Should MWD taxpayers continue to foot half the bill, they would end up paying $1.705 billion, or 19% of the capital costs. Should their share of costs decline steadily to one-eighth in 1990 and remain at that level thereafter, they would pay a total of about $632 million,* or 7%. Actually, both are low figures since the member districts of the MWD meet some of their water payments through taxes as well. These results are summarized below.

Item	Amount	% of Cost
Capital Cost	8.910	100
State Contribution	2.402	27
Federal Contribution [a]	.073	1
Power Revenues	.804	9
Water Contractor Payments	5.631	63
MWD Capital Payments	3.410	39
KCWA " "	.963	11
Others	1.258	13
Tax Share of KCWA	.320	3.5
Tax Share of MWD		
Fifty percent Assumption	1.705	19
Declining Share	.632	7

[a] Does not include several hundred million dollars of capital costs borne by the U.S. for the state's share of the San Luis unit.

If one assumes that the remaining water agencies meet 10% of their total payments from tax revenues, then the total taxpayer share of the water costs will be a minimum of $3.552 billion, and a maximum of $4.604 billion, or 40% minimum, 51% maximum. Power users will pay an additional 9%. Thus, *at the very most*, water users will

* Total $= \frac{1}{2} \ (T + D)'_{68-'73} + \sum_{\frac{1}{2}}^{\frac{1}{8}} (T + D)'_{74-'90} + \frac{1}{8} \ (T + D)'_{91-2035}$

        where $T =$ Capital Cost component of Transportation charge, Table B-19; and where $D =$ Capital Cost component of Delta water charge, $8.20 \times$ entitlement for the year; and where the years are indicated by the subnumerals.

        $= \frac{1}{2} \ (172 + 3) + 244 + 39 + \frac{1}{8} \ (1349 + 742)$

        $= \$632$ million

pay only 51% of the Project's cost, while they may pay as little as 40%

The DWR's false financial calculations have, of course, been crucial to public acceptance of the Project. In 1959, Governor Brown demanded a project "costing" less than $2 billion because he didn't think anything more would be acceptable, and even then, despite vastly greater publicity expenditures by Project promoters, the state accepted the bond issue by only the narrowest margin.

Actually, the analysis here does not reveal the full deception practiced in 1960, for the DWR has subsequently corrected several "errors" it made at that time. The most significant of these errors was a failure to include in the statement of costs any allowance for inflation—although the Department had itself calculated that cost at over a quarter billion dollars, at 1959 inflation rates! (Senate Water Committee Report #2, *State Water Project Financing*, 1968, Appendix I, "Summary History of Financing of the State Water Project," p. 30) Harvey Banks, the Department's director at the time, explained that Governor Brown had ordered him not to include this cost, and he, being a "good German," obeyed. Of course, there was a more genteel way of saying "omit the cost" than saying it directly; Governor Brown requested that Project costs be stated "in terms of 1959 prices." Naturally, any citizen was free to calculate for himself what the inflation cost would be, when armed with this information. The Department omitted another $100 million of costs in 1960 by somehow forgetting about interest charges during the construction period. Mr. Banks admitted that this was just a plain mistake on the Department's part.

CAPITAL COSTS OF THE STATE WATER PROJECT

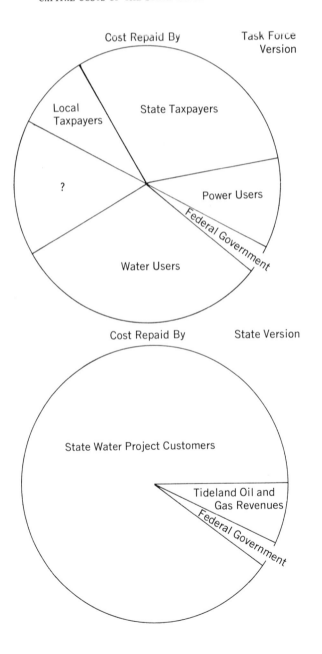

Cost Repaid By   Task Force
                        Version

State Taxpayers

Local
Taxpayers

?

Power Users

Federal Government

Water Users

Cost Repaid By   State Version

State Water Project Customers

Tideland Oil and
Gas Revenues

Federal Government

Appendix 3C
History, Partisans, and Details Benefits and Costs

Economic analyses of the feasibility . . . [of the State Water Project] were generally made after the Department and the State legislature had become committed to supporting construction . . . of the Project. Thus they were made in a setting where objective appraisal was difficult to obtain . . . Under these conditions, it is not surprising that some rather bizarre expedients were employed to arrive at estimates of benefits high enough to "justify" the project on economic grounds.

—Bain, Caves and Margolis,
Northern California's Water
Industry, op. cit., pp. 720–21

The planning and evaluation of the State Water Project encompassed several steps. The original idea, even as presented to the legislature in 1951, was basically a vague sketch. To push this idea to reality, the Department had first to obtain a rough estimate of what it would cost. Then, it had to progressively refine its notions of the need for the Project, the physical nature of the Project, and its cost. By 1957, it had prepared a fairly specific Project proposal, known at the time as the Feather River Project because the first feature would be the Oroville Dam on the Feather River. However, the Department had not yet chosen the exact route for the California Aqueduct, and a quarrel had developed with the Metropolitan Water District of Southern California over whether the water should be pumped over the Tehachapi Mountains, or around them along the coast. Furthermore, additional refinement of cost and financing was necessary. As a 1957 Board of Consultants said, "no specific project [should] be authorized for construction prior to detailed investigation of its engineering feasibility, *economic* justification, and financial feasibility (emphasis added)." (Quoted by Ackerman, p. 1.)

To determine the proper route, and make the necessary financial and economic studies, the Department assigned an engineer, Robert Edmonston, and a huge staff to provide a final report. Edmonston came to the assignment not merely as a DWR engineer, but also as the son of the state's former Chief Engineer, whose dream and design the Project had been back in 1951. Apart from Edmonston's personal commitments, much was riding on this study. To water engineers throughout the nation, the California State Water Project was an undertaking to be conjured with, a pinnacle of engineering achievement and audacity rivaling, even surpassing, such monuments to engineering daring and imagination as the Hoover Dam, the Central Valley Project, or Grand Coulee. As boosters of the Project liked to boast, it would be one of the "seven engineering wonders of the world."

The report they produced, prosaically entitled *Bulletin 78,* "Alternative Routes—Feather River—Southern California Aqueduct," was issued in a preliminary version in the spring of 1959. Although a Board of Consultants hired to check the report and lend credence to it had not yet considered this preliminary version, it served as the basis for the legislature enacting the Burns-Porter Act authorizing the Project. The final version, together with the consultants' reports, was released in 1960. *Bulletin 78* serves as the Department's final and authoritative justification for the Project.

Based on this report, the DWR told the legislature and the people of California that the Project would return benefits of $2.50 for every dollar of cost, and that the total cost would amount to only $1.9 billion. To reach these rosy conclusions, the Bulletin systematically understated costs, inflated benefits, and ignored alternatives. The Department then shaved even the Bulletin's final cost estimates. A 1967 review of the Project's financing history says, "Although future escalation of construction costs through inflation had been estimated by the department at $268,474,000 . . . , allowance for such escalation was not included." (Senate Water Committee, State Water Project Financing, Appendix I, p. 30 (1968)) According to Harvey Banks, who was Director of the DWR at the time, failure to include the inflation cost "was a political decision by the governor." (Telephone interview, September 8, 1970).

It also appears that the Department was aware of the deception inherent in the Bulletin's inflated estimates of benefits in excess of cost. The Bulletin was speaking only of benefits and costs incurred *south* of the Delta—although major Project *costs*, such as Oroville Dam, would occur *north* of the Delta as well. According to Bain, Caves and Margolis, the Bulletin "produced for the aqueduct system a fantastic benefit-cost ratio in excess of 2.5 [$2.50 in benefits for every dollar of cost]. Subsequently the Department . . . prepared for internal use, *but did not make public,* three editions of an office report which arrived at an estimated benefit-cost ratio for the *entire* Feather River Project. This ratio, again derived from very questionable estimates of urban water demand, was placed at *1.3*. . . (emphasis added)." (Appendix D, p. 721.)

It is worth exploring a few of the more important mistakes in *Bulletin 78*.

One of the most significant errors in *Bulletin 78* was its use of a 3.5% interest rate for the purpose of "discounting" (reducing to present values) future costs and benefits. The difference between this and a higher rate is critical. At 3.5%, the Bulletin estimates that water in Los Angeles would cost $60 an acre-foot. At 5%, it would cost $83 (Hirshleiffer, Milliman and DeHaven, *Water Supply,* 1967, Table 49, p. 342); and at 10% it would cost *$287* an acre-foot! (*Ibid.,* p. 341).

It is difficult to say just what the proper rate for a Project should be. The Department's 3.5% was a fairly low approximation of what it would, in fact, have to pay in interest on borrowed money (bonds sold through 1969 carried an interest rate of just over four percent). But California pays much lower interest than private borrowers pay, because its bonds are tax exempt. That is, one who buys a California bond and receives interest on it pays no federal tax on that interest. Naturally, investors can accept much lower yield bonds when they carry that exemption. Thus, while the DWR was using 3.5% as a discount rate, the state could have invested money to receive a somewhat higher return—at least 5%. Most economists maintain that a discount rate, to represent the true cost, must reflect the real market rate, not anything less. They say, look at the state as an investor. If it could be earning 5% on its money in the market (by purchasing the bonds of private borrowers), the cost of investing that money in the State Water Project cannot be calculated as anything less.

Many economists, however, would insist that the discount rate should be even higher than the market borrowing rate. They look at it this way. They agree with all other economists that the discount rate measures the cost of spending money to build the Project. But they say, don't look at the state as an investor—look at it as a borrower. If the market rate is 5%, what does that mean? It means that borrowers, like the state, take that money and use it so productively that they can return the lender's 5%, and also make themselves a profit. The actual cost of using money for the Water Project, then, represents not merely the market rate, but an additional amount which the state could have earned through its investments. That additional amount is called the opportunity cost.

But, whether economists would use 5% or 10% or something in between as the discount rate, one thing is clear. All who have studied the State Water Project, and other water projects using similar discount rates, unanimously agree that 3.5% is far too low, and economically and intellectually unjustifiable. Indeed, in a recent interview, Harvey Banks agreed that 3.5% was much too low, but tried lamely to justify it on the grounds that its use was standard operating procedure. The Bureau of Reclamation used it, and indeed continues to use a low discount rate, he noted. He also added that economists can't agree on any one other rate. But the Bureau hardly represents a sparkling professional standard, while economists *do* agree on one thing; that the minimum defensible discount rate is at least 5%. But that would have raised costs more than 33%, giving the overall project an unfavorable benefit-cost ratio.

In determining the Project's benefits, the authors of *Bulletin 78* similarly abandoned economics. Although they predicted water would cost $60 an acre-foot in southern California, they assumed the level of demand would be the same as if the water cost only half as much, $30 an acre-foot, which was the historical price. Thus abandoning elementary economic logic, they simply extrapolated existing population and water trends to determine southern California's total "requirements" in the future. To meet these quite imaginary "requirements," they then assigned a wholly arbitrary value (the cost of the next most costly method of meeting them), and termed the result the "benefit" of the Project! A similar procedure was used for other areas to be served by the Project.

Economists have long reviled the engineering practice of disregarding price in predicting water demand. As the engineers always learn when they try to sell the water, price has a substantial effect on the amount people use: generally, the higher the price, the less they use. By assuming that state water supplies would cost $30 an acre-foot, when in fact they would cost $60 or more, the DWR artificially inflated the amount of water that would be "needed." As Professor Hirshleifer and his colleagues comment in their critical Rand Corp. review of the Project, "There is a shortage of water at $20 an acre-foot in just the same sense that there is a shortage of new Cadillacs at a price of $500, except that desires for Cadillacs are usually not dignified by the term 'needs' or 'requirements.' " (p. 347)

As to the "benefit" that supplying this inflated amount of water would confer, the Bulletin used equally unfortunate calculations. Ordinarily, the benefit—the value—of water supplied can be measured very easily by the amount people will pay for it. But *Bulletin 78* has already discarded price in measuring the amount of water that would be "needed"; it could hardly turn around and apply that same price to measure benefit. So a new measure had to be used. This, the engineers decided, was the cost of the next cheapest alternative, at least for urban water. Of course, as Hirshleiffer et al. say, "Such a method of estimating benefits permits justification of any project, so long as a still worse one can be found and declared to be the least costly alternative source." (p. 350) Still, as Harvey Banks pointed out, this method is standard operating procedure in the engineering profession.

In the case of the SWP, however, the authors of *Bulletin 78* had yet another embarrassment to overcome. It seems that several of the "next cheapest alternatives," such as reclaiming waste water, buying agricultural water, and making more efficient use of existing canals, were actually considerably cheaper than the SWP.* To use them would never do, because then the benefits wouldn't add up to the costs. So the Bulletin blithely disregards these other alternative sources, on grounds that they are politically impractical, or don't provide enough water to meet the total "requirement." (Which is like discarding Willie Mays, Hank Aaron, and Juan Marichal from your team because they don't make a *whole* baseball team.)

So the next cheapest alternative the Bulletin chose to use was desalinization. According to Bain et al., the costs of desalinization assumed in the Bulletin were 50% higher than the best estimates at the time suggested they would be. (Bain, et al., p. 403, n. 93) Ironically, the discrepancy between the DWR's estimates and realistic estimates would not be so great today, since the DWR's research into desalinization virtually halted after approval of the SWP, while federal research never amounted to much anyway.

In calculating the value of water to agricultural users, the DWR made additional errors. The value was to be the net additional crop income, at existing market prices, which the water would make available. There are two major faults with this approach. First, present market prices for the major commodities float on a margin of federal price supports, so measuring general "benefit" by those prices produces inflated results. As Bain et al. show, the world price for crops provides a more accurate measure of the benefit conferred by state water, and yields a much lower total than that claimed by the DWR. The second problem is that the calculation assumes that Project water will have no effect on price. But the state water is bringing vast new acreages into production, severely lowering prices in a number of important crops. As Chapter 2 explains more fully, these lower prices not only drastically curtail expected benefits from the Project, they promise to drive thousands of small farmers from the land.

In concluding this section, it is worth noting that a Project may be deemed desirable, or undesirable, on other grounds than economics. But ordinary citizens can evaluate these other reasons as well as specialists can. Only the Project's *economic* value is a matter of technical judgment for which the public relies on specialists like

---

* Bain, Caves, and Margolis comment that refusing to consider agricultural water "resulted at the extreme in valuing Project-supplied urban water in a desert area at $150 per acre-foot . . . when abundant irrigation water in the area could be transferred to urban use at . . . cost of no more than $30 per acre-foot without significantly affecting the supply of irrigation water." (p. 721)

the DWR. In this light, the fairly obvious errors reviewed here amount to a breach of public trust. These were not errors on matters of discretion, about which reasonable men can differ; they were genuine mistakes beyond the pale of intellectual excuse. The justifications advanced for such practices by Mr. Banks do not exonerate the Department; they merely indict the engineering profession as a whole.

By contrast to the Department's rosy view of the Project, independent economists have uniformly castigated it, in 1959 and subsequently. According to Erwin Cooper, author of the best history of California water:

> [In 1959] a startling dissent from the gospel that the Feather River Project was the only thing that could keep California whole was the antibond resolution endorsed by more than fifty professors of economics, business, and engineering . . . As members of the Western Economics Association, the professors charged that the project was premature and involved vast expenditures "in violation of sound engineering, economics, and financial practices." [Cooper, *Aqueduct Empire*, 1968, p. 236]

Hirshleiffer, Milliman and DeHaven concluded in 1967 "that the South Coastal Area is a region where water rates that understate . . . costs have led to profligate use of water, thus creating an apparent 'need' for new supplies when what is more urgently needed is economical use of existing supplies." (pp. 309–10)

Bain, writing in 1966, concluded that the Project "rates slightly worse, in terms of efficiency, than the basic features of the Central Valley Project," a project which he and many others thoroughly condemn.

CONSULTING ENGINEERS: QUIS CUSTODIET CUSTODIES?

As the SWP took shape in the fifties, numerous independent consulting engineers escorted it along the way to public acceptance. These consultants were chosen for their credibility—large, dignified, and reputable professional firms, individuals of high personal attainment, and academicians with impressive credentials. Their prestige and their financial independence from the project at hand made them seem ideal as independent checks on the DWR.

In 1956, the Bechtel Corp., a leading San Francisco engineering firm, was asked to prepare a report on the Project's feasibility as it had developed to that date. Bechtel subcontracted the economic analysis to the Stanford Research Institute. In 1957, the Department appointed another group of consultants, a Board of Consulting Engineers, under the Chairmanship of Ralph Tudor, another top San Francisco engineer. This Board succeeded another, equally prestigious board which offered an inconclusive report in 1957 and disbanded. Then, after the legislature had approved the Project in 1959, but before the public voted on the bond issue in 1960, two new consultants were hired: the Charles T. Main Co., a Boston-based engineering firm, to report on the Project's economic feasibility; and Dillon, Read & Co., a New York investment house, to report on financing.

Considering the prestige of these firms, their positions of trust and responsibility, and their presumed financial independence from the state, their collective performance on the SWP is unfortunate at best. We believe that it raises serious questions about the role of such consultants in the arena of public decision-making.

The first consultant, Bechtel Corp., was called in after the DWR's predecessor department issued *Bulletin No. 2,* a massive report detailing the areas to be served by a State Water Plan. As Mc-Gauhey and Ehrlich write, "*Bulletin No. 2* had not explained the way in which service areas were determined, nor did it consider the ability of water users to pay . . . When the Bechtel Corporation found that scheduled sale of water was not based on economic studies of the proposed service areas it called upon the Stanford Research Institute to evaluate potential water demand from an economic point of view." (pp. 68–70) In its own conclusions, Bechtel mainly called for more studies. Stanford Research Institute concluded that, first, in the Central Valley, 584,000 acres would be suitable for development IF water prices remained at about present levels; and, second, in the Mojave Desert area, agricultural development was not feasible. Since it was obvious that state water could *not* be delivered to the Central Valley at existing local prices, the SRI's conclusion would seem to weigh heavily against the Project. But, note that SRI didn't put it that way; it made the positive statement that lots of acreage would be suitable for development, save only the improbable "if." By stating the "unpalatable truth" in this form, SRI and Bechtel, which were responsible for the overall report, rendered it obscure and easily hidden by politicians and a Department eager to get on with the Project.

However, these early consultants were not being asked for final judgments about the Project, and the public did not rely heavily on their word at the time. A more serious case involved the Board of Consulting Engineers appointed to oversee preparation of *Bulletin 78,* the basic document justifying the Project. The Board's final report was such that one member, Professor Adolph Ackerman, took the unprecedented and personally costly step of dissenting, and then toured the state to speak against the Project.

Ackerman, then a professor of engineering at the University of Wisconsin, issued a clear and stinging dissent from the Board's report, the gist of which was that

> No conventional demonstration has been made of the financial feasibility or justification for the project, and no clearly engineered concept has been presented which may be considered as valid and in the public interest. Any inference at this stage that the project has had the benefit of a complete engineering study and represents the best product of the engineering profession in which the public can repose its full confidence is, in my opinion, wholly unwarranted. [Comments on the Final Report of the Board of Consulting Engineers, "Feather River-Southern California Aqueduct," December 31, 1959, Assembly Journal, March 8, 1960, p. 268.]

Strangely enough, the details of Ackerman's criticisms were corroborated by the Board's own report. The basis for his dissent was not techincal disagreement, therefore, but the manner of statement. For the Board, while agreeing with Ackerman that the Project's desirability remained, at best, unproved, nevertheless issued its report in such a form that the public could and did believe it supported the Department's recommendations. By a subtle manipulation of words and definitions, therefore, the Board misled the public which relied on its expertise.

To understand what the distinguished chairman, Ralph Tudor, and his colleagues did, the reader must remember that *Bulletin 78.*

the subject of the Board's deliberations, was designed to perform two separate functions. One was to select the Aqueduct's final route —a function chiefly of technical interest to the MWD of Southern California. The MWD hardly needed the Board of Consulting Engineers to help it assess the Bulletin's job in selecting this route. The other function, however, was entirely a matter of public interest: namely, a determination of the Project's economic and financial desirability. For this, both the public and potential investors in Water Project bonds relied wholly on the consultants as their independent check. As Ackerman said,

> both the stature of the engineering profession as well as the public confidence in the profession are under severe test. It may well be said that never before in engineering history have such great responsibilities been entrusted to a board of consulting engineers. With respect to the planning of public works, a board of professional engineers has the primary obligation of safeguarding the public interest. The public has developed a great trust and faith in the integrity of the engineering profession and this serves as a powerful challenge to merit such confidence in the future. [p. 259]

But in its report, the Board chose to emphasize the first function —selection of routes—to the virtual exclusion of commentary about the Department's performance of the far more critical second function—evaluation of the Project. Thus, in the Introduction, it states twice that selection of the best route is the basic problem (pp. 234–5, *Assembly Journal*). It then adds:

> The basic conclusions of *Bulletin 78* are, first, that no individual route will serve adequately . . . and, second, that a combination of routes . . . will be the most effective and favorable combination for the conveyance of water to the various areas of water-need. We concur in these basic conclusions. [p. 235]

Only when the reader gets beyond the Introduction into the dense body of the technical report does he find that the Board considered the second aspect of *Bulletin 78,* an evaluation of the Project. With respect to that attempt, the Board says something about the need for "intensive additional studies of various kinds—engineering, geological, economic, and financial," and makes various critical comments about the DWR's benefit-cost calculations. (p. 239)

The Board of Consulting Engineers followed the same approach as the Stanford Research Institue before it, and the Charles T. Main Co. after it. At the risk of repetition, it is important to mark that pattern. First, it clearly and forthrightly declares its support for the Project—by virtue of defining its task to include only those aspects which it can clearly and forthrightly support. But to maintain a punctilious and technical kind of honesty, the Board later admits, in convoluted and highly unquotable phrases, that the Project has serious problems. While remaining technically accurate, therefore, the Board does everything in its considerable power to promote a Project which it actually believes highly questionable. Of all the consultants the state hired to examine the Project, only one had the integrity and courage to tell the public in clear language what he really thought of the Project, and what the public *hired* him to find out. That was Adolph Ackerman.

Promoters of the SWP naturally made excellent use of the Board's abuse of trust. To cite only one prominent example, Governor Brown used the Board's statements to refute the *San Francisco*

Chronicle's critical comments. The *Chronicle* had asked, "Is there any justification for building a State water system that may not be fully needed for sixty years?" Brown wrote back that the Project would be fully used very shortly, and cited the Board's conclusion that "In our opinion, the projections portray the trends of growth and water demands as realistically as possible." (Brown, Letter to *S.F. Chronicle,* April 6, 1960) What Brown did not bother to say was that the Board's approval related to projections as used for route selection, not as used for justifying the Project economically, so that in fact the Board's language did not support the Governor's point at all.

The final batch of consultants was hired as a result of Ackerman's charges against *Bulletin 78.* The legislature had passed the Burns-Porter Act setting up the Project, but the public still had to approve the bond issue in November 1960, and opponents of the Project were raising hell over its dubious economic justifications. So the DWR hired the Charles T. Main Co. to show that the Project was economically justified, and the Dillon, Read Co. to prove that the state could handle it financially. Neither firm had ties to California, and both seemed eminently respectable and trustworthy. Unfortunately, the public never did learn that the Charles T. Main Co., a Boston engineering outfit, had never studied a water project before (Harvey Banks interview). The result of their studies has already been described in the main text. Essentially, Charles T. Main claimed the Project was economically justifiable after defining economic justifiability in a contrived way, and then salved its conscience by hedging all bets in the jargonized body of the report. Dillon, Read likewise proclaimed the Project financially feasible, and then so hedged its forthright declaration as to make it meaningless.

After studying the performance of "independent consultants" on the State Water Project, it is impossible to again hold the illusion that their nominal independence makes them a trustworthy check on calculations purporting to justify public works. If one asks why independent consultants are so untrustworthy, various reasons are advanced. Those suggested to us are as follows:

—Some consultants, like Charles T. Main, don't know what they're doing, and fall easy prey to those with more obvious vested interests.

—Many consultants make their living by pleasing clients. If they don't provide the desired answers, someone else will. And reputations for intractability get around. Employees of the Stanford Research Institute have suggested that a substantial number of that firm's "studies" have predetermined results, and that other consultants are even worse.

—In the professional community of engineers, a consultant asked to judge another engineer's work has a natural reluctance to embarrass the other by criticizing his work plainly or vigorously.

—Some "independent" consultants aren't quite as independent as they seem. Bechtel, Ralph Tudor, SRI, and various other consultants do considerable work for the State of California, and even for public and private water agencies.

POLITICS: THE BABY IN THE BATHWATER

Water is a political football . . . Coalitions of pressure groups, bureaucracies, legislators, and executives form to se-

cure approval of projects within a process in which project
evaluations are flexible instruments of questionable validity.
                                                          [Bain et al., p. 658]
    In recent years the DWR has been under great political pres-
sure to formulate a Water Plan and policies which would be
acceptable to the State Administration. As a consequence,
there has been a gradual drift towards the exploitation of professional disciplines to serve political ends.
                                        [Ackerman, *Feather River-*
                                        Southern California Aqueduct,
                                        Final Report, p. 3, October 20, 1960]

Conventional wisdom blames politicians for bad public decisions.
After all, they make them. Particularly do the "objective" experts
vilify the politicians for exerting all sorts of illicit pressures, disregarding advice, responding to special interests, and behaving in a
generally unpredictable way. But the case of the SWP shows politicians in a quite different role. While neither saints nor villains,
their mistakes were largely consistent with the rules of the political
game, while in many respects the SWP represents a masterpiece of
the politician's art. While with the aid of hindsight we can see that
the Project is an enormous disaster for the public, and that the experts had reason to know that even in 1960, most of the politicians
who supported the Project in 1959–60 could honestly have believed
otherwise. And, given that belief, their work in putting the Project
together has many creditable features.

In 1958, Edmund G. Brown, a Beverly Hills lawyer, was elected
governor of California, the first Democrat to hold that office since
Culbert Olsen in 1942. Brown had pledged to make the SWP a
reality, and he made this his first goal in office. From his perspective,
this made sense. While clearly beneficial to important interests in
the San Joaquin Valley and southern California, the Project was,
according to the water experts, vital to the state's welfare as a whole.
In one swoop, therefore, he could gain the support, or at least neutrality, of the special interests while working for the public welfare.
As he saw it, the problem was one of reconciling contending political
factions and reaching an acceptable compromise among them
which would free the Project; not one of deciding whether the Project would be beneficial or not. As his special water assistant, Ralph
Brody, told the Task Force, "we never considered" the underlying
economic justification for the Project; "we just assumed that had all
been taken care of." So did most politicians, even some who today
bitterly oppose the Project and the "water interests."

Of course, it is fair to say the politicians *should* have known
better. They should have understood the vested interests held by
the various water agencies which recommended the Project, and
they should have realized that even "independent consultants"
weren't completely trustworthy. They should have developed their
own independent assessments of the Project, especially after they
became aware—as they did in 1959—of the serious academic criticisms levelled at the Project's justifications. Neither Governor Brown
nor the Assembly and Senate Water Committees had the staff or
expertise to do this, and neither made any effort to obtain it. Governor Brown's Special Water Assistant, Ralph Brody, was hired
solely to ramrod a project through the legislature and the people,
and Brody's background was hardly calculated to inspire him to
blow the whistle on the Department. A former Bureau of Reclama-

tion lawyer, he had served as a lobbyist for private water interests in Sacramento, and upon leaving Governor Brown's staff, became the director of the Westlands Water District, considered by many the most outrageous single water boondoggle in history. As for the Senate and Assembly Water Committees, they were firmly dominated by long-time water boosters who probably had every confidence in the self-serving calculations of their friends, the water engineers. But, however negligent the politicians may have been, there is no reason to assume they were deliberately hiding the truth from themselves or the public, as did the engineers.

Believing the Project to be a good thing, the politicians nevertheless faced some real problems in getting it accepted. In 1959, the State Senate had not yet been reapportioned, and rural interests held a veto over any legislation. They opposed the Project because they feared a "water grab" by southern California. When Los Angeles built its Owens River Aqueduct in 1904, it took the water rights to what was then a prosperous farming valley, turning it into a virtual desert, destroying our towns and driving out its population. The Owens Valley became a battleground. "Heavily armed guards from the city of Los Angeles were to patrol its precious aqueducts. Machine guns were to be mounted at strategic posts along the waterway. Legal battles were to rage in the courts. Again and again the sound of high explosives would be heard as pipes, siphons, and spillways were blasted." (Dasmann, *The Destruction of California*, (Paperback, 1970), p. 128.) Memory of this incident cast a shadow over plans for the SWP.

In addition, northerners feared that once southern California started using northern water, it would never let go of it. Under California water law, the first to appropriate water from a stream has a right to as much as he uses for as long as he uses it. While the northerners didn't need the water in 1959, their Chambers of Commerce had dreams for the future which a permanent loss of water would thwart.

On the other hand, promoters of the Project wanted it quickly. Not only did the water engineers threaten imminent tragedy if it weren't built, they feared that the same water law would deprive them of northern water if someone else got there first. And agencies like the U.S. Bureau of Reclamation were making ominous sounds. In addition, the San Joaquin agribusinesses, whose money and whose influence with the rural Senate were critical to the Project's prospects, would abandon the Project if it were not approved quickly. Their water tables were sinking rapidly, raising pumping costs to unprofitable levels and carrying the risk of contamination by bad water. If the state did not move quickly, they would be forced to turn to the Federal Bureau of Reclamation for irrigation water, despite the acreage limitations attached to federal water (see text). So the coalition favoring the Project threatened to fall apart, unless action came quickly.

The conflict between northern and southern desires appeared total. Northerners would not let the south take their water permanently. But southerners would not accept a mere contract for the water because the State Supreme Court had ruled that the state, as sovereign, could not be bound by its own contracts.

In this situation, Governor Brown proposed a brilliant compromise. Brody discovered that, although the state could not be bound by its contracts, it *could* be bound by the terms of its bond commitments. If repayment of the bonds was based on contracts with southern California, the state could not renege on those contracts. The trick was to make the repayment period long enough to satisfy southern Californians. This broke the obstacle, and the rest was just a matter of negotiation. Since the northerners still controlled the Senate, southern California had to meet their price in terms of public works projects and the like for northern counties. As one observer commented, Governor Brown's people "just started trading and counting, and stopped when they reached twenty-one."

The Burns-Porter Act was the writing which embodied this series of compromises. It authorized a State Water Project, specified its features, stipulated that the state would borrow $1.75 billion on its general credit and would repay the loan from Project revenues over a sixty-five year period (1970–2035) from water contracts. The package further provided a $100 million "local projects fund" from the bond issue, to be used under a companion law, the Davis-Grunsky Act, for "local projects," meaning northern boondoggles. While this fund was the chief bribe offered northern senators, a few additional goodies were built in. For instance, among the specified features of the Project are three little lakes in Placer County. Otherwise useless, they provide a recreational attraction to enhance the income of powerful Assemblywoman Pauline Davis's constituents, and have come to be known as "Pauline's puddles."

As part of the political compromising, the Act pointedly omits reference to some of the thornier problems raised by the Project. For example, "public interest" opponents were concerned that the Project would enable San Joaquin agribusinesses to obtain water without the 160-acre limitation provided under federal projects, thereby subsidizing them in proportion to their acreage. Governor Brown promised repeatedly that he would take care of the limitation, but the promise doesn't appear in the Act. Likewise, the Act omits any mention of the terms of repayment or the allocation of payment between various customers such as water and power, north and south, agriculture and residential. All of this was left to the governor's and the DWR's administrative discretion, rather than handled legislatively as it should have been.

Once the legislature accepted Brown's compromise, he and other politicians turned to selling the Project to the people, since California's constitution required their approval before it could sell General Obligation Bonds. In this sales effort, it is clear that the politicians were often less than candid with the public. Governor Brown's decision to shave over a quarter billion dollars in costs by deceptively stating the Project's cost without any allowance for inflation is only the most blatant example. Throughout the state, politicians used hyperbole, scare tactics, and vituperation to cow the opposition and gain public support.

We could not, at a ten year remove, trace the web of more personal and selfish ties which undoubtedly had a part in motivating politicians like Edmund Brown to work for the Project. Brown has recently admitted, "I knew some of the large corporate interests would gain," but added, "that's part of the capitalist system." (KFRC, "Focus," 70, July 13, 1970) Obviously, as Chapter 12 shows, the interests to be helped by the Project—construction firms, developers, agribusiness, major landowners, etc.—are politically potent.

We could not pin it down, but some knowledgeable observers have commented that Governor Brown was consciously trading his support for the Water Project for the neutrality in 1962 of such traditionally Republican forces as the *Los Angeles Times* (Tejon Ranch), Kern County Land Co., Southern Pacific Railroad, and others. It is a fact that Richard Nixon received a surprisingly lukewarm reception from these interests in that race. As to other politicians with local bases, such as the chairman of the Assembly Water Committee, Carley V. Porter of Riverside County, their interests were, and are, obvious. As the political system stands, it takes a rather unusual politician to do other than represent the sectional interests of the community which elects him. For Carley Porter, and many others, it seemed that the Project would help at home.

The politicians, then, played a mixed role. Many obviously fought skillfully and well for what they could honestly believe was a good Project. At the same time, however, it was clear that significant benefits would go to special interests; important responsibilities to the public were ignored in the compromising to obtain a viable Project; the politicians labored in something of a self-created vacuum of ignorance about the economic defects of the Project; and the effort to promote the Project with the public had important overtones of dishonesty. The main difference between the politicians and the experts was this: given the context of their work, and public reliance and expectations, the politicians did not stray seriously beyond the bounds of expected behavior; the experts did. Naturally, as Chapter 12 stresses, the context of political work in California requires radical change. But with respect to the SWP, the public use of expertise requires even more urgent and radical change.

WATER INTERESTS

The role of economic interests in water development is simple and straightforward. Those who can benefit from the water seek to obtain it; those who can prevent them from obtaining it seek the largest possible payoff for their compliance. One may hope that in the clash of self-interests, the public interest will be served. But that happens only fortuitously, since none of the water interests feels any obligation to befriend the public interest for its own sake. In 1960, the clash of interests did not, in fact, produce much service for the public, since the conflicting interests—northern counties and southern water users—basically agreed that the Project was good, and were just haggling over the price. On the other hand, opposition to the Project since 1960, emanating from landowners and industries in the Sacramento Delta, has served the public by revealing serious ecological questions about the Project's plan to reduce fresh water inflow to the Delta. In that case, the Delta's selfish concern to preserve the existing inflow coincides with a public interest in preserving the ecology.

The most active promoters of the SWP were the large landholders of the southwestern San Joaquin Valley. As Erwin Cooper, former chief of publicity for the DWR, writes, the Project "began as the brainchild of the big San Joaquin Valley landowners: the corporate farms, land management firms, railroads with huge acreages . . .

The men who controlled them, along with much else in California, were unanimously dedicated to the proposition that the only way to beat the Bureau of Reclamation's 160-acre limitation on water for farmers was to have the State, rather than the federal government, operate a water distribution system." (p. 201) The most prominent of these, and the most virulent in its opposition to the 160-acre limitation, was and is the Southern Pacific. Interestingly enough, the SP obtained nearly all its Central Valley land by outright fraud —a fraud which has not yet been corrected. The federal government gave the land for building a railroad; Southern Pacific has never built that railroad. Yet, as of 1956, it owned approximately 10% of the land served by water from the State Aqueduct—nearly 200,000 acres. (See Chapter 1 for additional large landholdings in the state service area accumulated by fraud, e.g., Miller and Lux.)

The present concentration of ownership in the San Joaquin Valley is remarkable. According to a 1959 study, about 100 owners hold 2,755,713 out of four million acres in the state service area, or 69%. Of the remaining 31% a substantial but undetermined portion is owned by state, county, or local governments for roads, schools, and the like. Even more amazing is the fact that four land companies, Standard Oil, and three or four smaller oil companies own fully 36% of all this land, or 2.43 million acres.

These landowners had long sought to obtain water from the U.S. Bureau of Reclamation. The Bureau was all too willing to supply it, but under a provision written into the 1902 Reclamation Act—the 160-acre limitation—the Bureau could supply water to only 160 acres per owner; if it supplied water to more land, the owner had to sell the excess within ten years, at present pre-water prices. Since firms like Southern Pacific had no desire to dismantle their holdings at desert prices, the San Joaquin landowners fought long and hard to escape the limitation. The Central Valley Project, which might have served them, was originally conceived as a state project, but the Depression delivered it into the hands of the Bureau and its embarrassing limitation. In 1940, the landowners sought to have the state buy the Project back from the government. The ever-compliant state was willing, but Harold Ickes, President Roosevelt's Secretary of the Interior and the Bureau's boss, said the limitation would still apply. This cooled the state's ardor.

At various times, the landowners have also fought to exempt the Central Valley Project, or other Bureau projects, from the limitation. The latest such attempt was a bill introduced by Senator George Murphy for his friends in 1965, just after he assumed office, and resubmitted frequently thereafter. These have all proved unsuccessful to date, however—largely because of the economic conflict between southern agricultural areas and the western areas that benefit from reclamation.

Frustrated in their efforts to avoid the limitation, and feeling a growing need for imported water supplies as they stupidly depleted their ground-water reserves, the large landholders formed the Feather River Project Association in 1951 to promote the state project. It would serve little purpose to discuss here who specifically was involved or what their methods were, for the FRPA was a standard lobby-pressure group, and acted like any other well-financed effort of the sort. They beat the drums, contacted legislators, feasted politicians and personages, drafted bills, financed campaigns, and all the rest of it.

While the FRPA was the special tool of the landowners, other lobbying organizations chipped in as well. The state's hundreds of irrigation districts were organized into the Irrigation Districts Association, a lobbying organization similar to the League of California Cities, or the League of County Supervisors. The Districts, however, are governmental merely in form. In fact, they operate as private utilities, formed and controlled by the landowners they serve, in proportion to the land owned and the water supplied. Their "governmental" nature is merely a device to avoid taxes and borrow money more cheaply. Consequently, their trade association acted, and continues to act, as a straightforward booster of the Project. It publishes the *Western Water News,* a journal remarkable for the colorful emphasis it gives to the views of its owners.

The story of nonagricultural interests is less clear-cut. One firm is worth special note, however, for its power and its connections with the large landowners. The Bank of America does more than a billion dollars worth of business with the large landowners of the Central Valley. It is the most important agricultural bank in the world. It itself controls, through foreclosures, trusts, and the like, a substantial amount of land at any given time. Its key importance to San Joaquin Valley agriculture, and the importance of that agriculture to it, gives it an enormous interest in the SWP.

The Bank's involvement with agriculture stems from the plight of even the richest farmers. They receive money only when they harvest the crop, but they must spend money throughout the year. Moreover, farming has become increasingly mechanized, and the most important building on any major San Joaquin Valley farm is now the garage, which houses a fabulous array of specialized and expensive machines. To keep up with the mounting capital costs of their business, plus daily expenses, farmers must borrow. Moreover, once they have obtained machines, they must usually buy new land, which means more borrowing. They buy the land to maximize the machines' efficiency. Thus they develop a symbiotic relationship with banks, of which, for historical reasons, the Bank of America is far and away the most important.

Major farmers, like J. G. Boswell, sit on the Bank's Board of Directors. The Bank's Vice President in charge of agriculture is Robert Long, formerly an officer of the 88,000-acre Irvine Ranch. The State Secretary of Agriculture, until fairly recently, was also a Bank of America officer. The Bank's other ties to agriculture are too innumerable to mention.

The Bank contributed substantially to the lobbying for the SWP. The Bank has performed perhaps a more important service for the Project by underwriting the Bonds. Although the initial sales of bonds were perhaps not too difficult, more recently the state has run into substantial difficulties in financing, and the Bank has advanced massive aid in the form of advice, market influence, and purchases on its own account. The Bank is, in fact, the major holder of SWP bonds.

As to southern California interests, many obviously believe that the Project aids them substantially. Whether or not their belief is well based, their organizations and firms give the Project important support. The Los Angeles Chamber of Commerce, and local politicians tributary to it, were vociferous in support, as were innumerable businessmen's civic groups and the like.

The most important individual contributors to organizations lobbying for the Project were, of course, construction firms and real estate developers, including utilities. In June, 1970, the state had to hold a referendum to raise the interest rates on SWP bonds so that the rest could be sold. The referendum became a contest over the Project, although Governor Reagan, a strong supporter of the Project, managed to muddy the waters by including other bonds, such as school bonds, in the referendum vote. Among the largest contributors to the pro-Project side, as listed with the Secretary of State, are the major utilities like Southern California Edison, PG & E, and Pacific Telephone and Telegraph; natural gas companies like El Paso Natural Gas and Trans-western Pipeline Co.; banks and savings and loan associations; and such developers as the Macco Corp., Penn-Central's landowning subsidiary.

In addition to these, of course, southern California has certain large water-using firms which, as described in the text, benefit from the Project's early construction. They receive huge water subsidies. The table below suggests the extent of these.

SUBSIDIES TO SOME SO. CAL. WATER USERS

Firm *	Water Used/Year (Acre-Feet)	Surplus	Tax	Total
Irvine Ranch	150,000	$3 mil.	$ 8.25m	11.25m
Flintkote Co.	2,567	51,340	141,185	192,525
Swift & Co.	2,047	40,940	112,585	153,525
Richfield Oil Corp.	4,428	88,560	243,540	332,100
Shell Oil Co.	4,516	90,220	248,380	338,600
Texaco Oil Co.	3,432	68,640	188,760	257,400
Union Oil Co.	2,670	53,400	146,850	200,250
Standard Oil Co.	4,542	90,790	249,810	340,600

* All of these users pump approximately the amounts listed from underground water basins. These basins are "replenished" with surplus water sold for $20 an acre-foot less than regular water prices charged by the MWD. In addition, the 1969–70 tax collections by the MWD accounted for $55 of the cost of each acre-foot sold by the District. The total subsidy here overstates the actual benefit received by the firms, of course, since it is based on the cost of supplying the benefit; for most, which could cheaply convert to less profligate water-using processes, the benefit is undoubtedly less than the listed cost of supplying the subsidy. Furthermore, the listed cost subtracts nothing for water payments made by these firms through taxes. Such payments, while undoubtedly substantial, would probably not reduce the $55 tax subsidy by a great deal, and would not at all affect the surplus water subsidy, which early development of the State Water Project makes possible to continue.

In addition to water users benefitting from the Project, and of course the DWR, one must not overlook construction interests. They wield extraordinary political influence; as noted in the power chapter, over half of all state legislators have connections with developers in one way or another, particularly through campaign contributions. Builders also contributed heavily to the pro-bond side in the referendum campaign.

The most heavily involved opponents of the Project were the northern counties and the State Federation of Labor. The northerners simply wanted to obtain the best trade they could for their water. They got a fairly good deal. In addition to Pauline's Puddles (obtained in blatant violation of the most elementary ethics), it would seem, since these lakes benefit only a few of her constituents—a majority voted against the Project (Cooper). Northerners obtained the Davis-Grunsky Act, authorizing loans and grants for "small projects"—a euphemism for northern recreational lakes. The Act was to be financed by the SWP bond issue to the tune of $130 million. In addition, they obtained a provision setting aside bond money for "future projects"—another euphemism for northern recreation—to the extent that other state money was spent on the Project. Since reapportionment, this set-off provision has been interpreted to mean money for future SWP projects, and in 1959 was effectively abrogated. But its author claims the original intent was to further bribe the northerners (Brody interview).

Labor had no particular ax to grind, but was the only group in the state both aware of and concerned about the enormous specialized benefits the Project would bring. Campaign expenditure statements filed with the secretary of state after the 1960 bond campaign showed that all the funds spent by opponents came from labor —the AFL-CIO and Los Angeles County COPE. As a measure of relative strengths, the campaign expenditure seems accurate: labor spent $37,800 against the Project, the promoters spent $224,800 for it, not counting the state resources which Governor Brown threw into the fight on the side of the proponents.

More recently, labor's opposition has somewhat abated, and conservationists have taken over. Although the Sierra Club—the largest California conservation group—sat on its hands in 1960, it took a leading role in opposing the 1970 referendum campaign. The most spectacular single instance of conservation attack on the Project was the effort to stop Dos Rios. According to the DWR's plans, the Project will take additional fresh water supplies from the north by damming the Eel River at a site called Dos Rios and transferring the stored water through the coast mountains to the Sacramento, and thence south. Since a dam at Dos Rios would have marginal flood-control uses, the Army Corps of Engineers took responsibility for planning it, and unveiled its plan for this monstrosity in 1968. A dam at Dos Rios would destroy much of the Eel River, one of the last few free-flowing streams in California, and a run for salmon and steelhead; it would destroy one of the loveliest valleys in creation, Round Valley, and by doing so it would violate a treaty with the Indians who now live in Round Valley. Conservationists, headed by a wealthy Round Valley rancher, Richard Wilson, attacked the Corps's calculations and sensibilities, and raised such a fuss that Governor Reagan has postponed any decision on the project.

That fight probably awakened conservationists to the threat inherent in the SWP, which stands poised to take the water of every stream between San Francisco and Amchitka. They have since fought another proposed extension, the Peripheral Canal, on grounds that it would stop most of the fresh water flowing to the Delta and destroy that important estuary. And they have formed a group—the

Committee of 2 Million—to fight for the northern rivers. They are nonpartisan, although their class background gives them a somewhat Republican cast. But it seems clear at this point that the SWP has always been a strictly bipartisan effort.

The other important opponents to the Project in recent years have been landowners and water users in the Sacramento-San Joaquin Delta. The SWP will take so much of the fresh water flow through the Delta that the DWR has admitted that over 100,000 acres in the western part of the Delta will be ruined by salt water intrusions. Furthermore, the reduced flow through the Delta will make it necessary for many of these interests to stop dumping sewage into the water, since the small flow will make the sewage more apparent. There may also be a legal reason for objecting. At present, Delta water users draw on the fresh water supply for all their needs, and should their needs expand, they can draw as much more water as they want. As owners of land abutting the water, this is their legal right, and for free. But the state has rights as well. It can only exercise them if it builds the Project and, in particular, the Peripheral Canal. But if it can exercise its rights, they limit those of the Delta users. Consequently, Delta water users might find themselves unable to expand their present free use of Delta water. An even greater worry for them is the fact that, with a Peripheral Canal, the DWR will have de facto control over their water, even that to which they have a right. There are enough uncertainties about the nature of legal rights in water that, should the DWR cut off Delta supplies wrongfully, as the Canal would give it power to do, it might take the Delta owners a very long time to get it back. As Congressman Jerome Waldie, who has spearheaded the Delta fight, put it:

> We fear that almost the entire flow of the Sacramento River will be diverted southward and that once the tap is turned on for Southern California, we in the Bay and Delta areas will not be able to turn it off—with tragic consequences to the Bay-Delta area. ["The Rape of Northern Waters," Cong. Record, March 20, 1969, p. 16401]

At the moment, the main forum for the dispute is a hearing room of the State Water Resources Control Board. There, the Delta interests contend they "use," and therefore have a right to, nearly all the enormous flow of fresh water through the Delta and into San Francisco Bay. The DWR claims the Delta needs considerably less. The Water Resources Control Board must decide how much the Delta legally "uses," which determines how much it has a right to. The remaining fresh water flow, under California laws, would belong to the federal Bureau of Reclamation and the DWR.* Under this law, there is no legal right to "use" the water for environmental purposes; however, the Board has included the question of water quality and effect on the Delta in its hearings, since it also sits as the state's watchdog over water pollution.

Congressman Waldie believes the legal battle is somewhat one-

---

* This is a highly simplified account of the legal situation, based on various interviews and an unpublished paper by William Atwater, "Analysis of Legal Problems in the Delta," written while Mr. Atwater was an attorney for the DWR. Mr. Atwater is presently an attorney for the Water Resources Control Board, around a corridor corner from his old offices. He does not work on the Delta case.

sided. The Board lives in the same building, on the same floors, as the DWR, one of the contending parties. As William Atwater's case suggests, most of its staff is drawn from the DWR, or the Bureau of Reclamation, or other water agencies. The state has already invested billions of dollars in its water system, and much of that investment depends on the Board's approval of the DWR's requests for Sacramento River water. It seems virtually inconceivable that a state agency would rule against the DWR under these circumstances. In addition, many of the Board's members are hardly inimical to water development. To quote Congressman Waldie:

> There is no administrative or quasi-judicial body, commission or agency in California that allocates water or adjudicates water controversies, that is not carefully contrived to arrive at predetermined judgments advancing the overall plan to export Delta water to the South. . . .
> As an example of this contention, [consider] the State Water Resources Control Board . . . The single most important agency for resolving disputes as to the allocation of the State's water resources is no longer impartial—and we have learned from repeated experiences before that Board that a non-customer of the State cannot expect to get a fair shake before it if his dispute involves a water customer of the state.
> In my opinion, one only has to look at the background of the men who comprise this Board to see the built-in conflicts of interests that must result.

Waldie then points out that Chairman Kerry W. Mulligan's "complete allegiance to the water export policies of the Department is very well known." Member Dibble, he notes, was manager of the San Gorgonio Pass Water Agency when appointed—a southern California customer of the Project—and held the same position with the San Bernardino Valley Water Conservation District, slated to receive state water. A third member, William Alexander, has worked for the DWR, Bureau of Reclamation, and Corps of Engineers, as well as various water districts in the San Joaquin Valley.

While Waldie's suspicions about the Board's final decision may prove correct, the Board has held extensive hearings over several years on the water rights question. These hearings have permitted the development of materials documenting the ecological perils of the Peripheral Canal, and have given Project opponents time to build public pressure. On the other hand, the Board's hearings have not been lengthy for solely altruistic motives. Its final ruling is bound to be appealed to the courts, and it would hardly like to repeat the process for failure to adequately consider all sides. And there is a deeper threat.

For many years, the state's water users have quailed at one grisly specter which has loomed on the horizon since the state began extensive water development at the turn of the century. This was the specter, or threat, of the Ultimate Water Rights Lawsuit. As Walter M. Gleason, attorney for the California Water Development Council in 1958, explained:

> Due to the "open-ended" and unadjudicated nature of the vast multitude of water rights along the Sacramento and San Joaquin river systems (including the Delta), an incredibly complex and unsettled water right situation existed even before the construction of the Central Valley Project [in 1951].
> With the advent of the CVP, this Central Valley water right situation became even more complex and confusing . . .

If the [State Water Project] is superimposed upon this already extremely complicated water right situation now existing
in the Central Valley, involving as it will the making of huge
and irrevocable export allocations from the "Delta Pool" to
the South, this will, in my opinion, inevitably require and bring
about *a complete adjudication of all water rights along all parts
of the Central Valley stream systems* [Gleason's emphasis].

Litigation of the nature described above would, in the opin-
ion of competent water experts, require decades to complete.
[Gleason, Memorandum to Mr. Gordon Garland, Executive
Director, California Water Development Council, "Re: The
California Water Plan—the Two Roads Ahead and their 'liti-
gation potential.'" December 31, 1958.]

Gleason's memo was, essentially, a brief for people advocating a
different variety of Project from the one adopted. But his warnings
of a "legal Frankenstein" were serious and realistic. The Water Resources Control Board must find a solution which avoids this nightmare. Thus, it has very good reasons for holding prolonged hearings, and the Delta interests have a powerful club in their litigous
hands if they want it.

Appendix 9A
Regressivity and Slums: Taxation and the Poor *

There are three facts about current local, state, and federal tax systems of relevance to the poor. Tax systems associated with land are extremely regressive, assessing the poor a larger percentage of their income than the rich. The systems also often discourage the construction or improvement of low-cost housing. And the systems act to deprive the poor of services, as we have described with schools above, as boundaries are drawn reserving revenue sources for the middle and upper classes.

The regressivity of local taxes is well known. The sales tax is a consumption tax. The poor must pay a greater share in relation to their income since a larger portion of their income is spent on consumptive needs, as opposed to land or securities investment. But the property tax is even more regressive. It is inherently regressive because it taxes the value of housing. Since the poor tend to devote a larger percentage of their income to the necessary provision of housing than do the wealthy, they pay a higher percentage of their income in taxes, usually in the form of high rents.

But in California, the regressivity of the property tax is especially great because of three additional forces, each one of which independently and significantly increases regressivity yet more. First, there is the time lag between assessments. A piece of land and its structures are assessed, for example, in 1967. On the average, the next assessment will not occur for three years, probably not until after the 1970 taxes are paid. Property A is located in the ghetto and is assessed at $25,000 in 1967. Property B is located in the newly built suburbs and is also assessed at $25,000 that same year. But the house in the suburbs appreciates in value while the house in the ghetto depreciates. Assuming a mere 4% appreciation in the suburbs and a mere 3% depreciation in the ghetto per annum (both very conservative), by 1970 the suburban property is worth $28,120 and the ghetto property $22,722. If both were taxed at 10% their value each year from 1967 through 1970, the suburban resident will pay 8.9% on the actual current value of his property while the ghetto dweller will pay 11.1%. This is what happens, although the disparity is usually larger because the appreciation and depreciation rates are low in the above example. And, of course, the fact that the ghetto dweller is assessed a higher percentage of his actual property value excludes the fact that his tax rate to begin with is liable to be 15% instead of the wealthy suburbanite's 10% because of the lack of high value property and new industry in his political jurisdiction, as the National Commission on Urban Problems has documented in their 1968 report, *Building the American City*. Some economists have expressed the view that the inherent regressivity of the local tax structure nullifies the progressivity of income taxes.**

The second source of inequity is the overassessment of the *cur-*

* Of 20 million Californians, approximately 2 million are Mexican-American and 1.4 million are Negroes. When referring to "poor," we mean that sector earning less than $3,000 annually. According to recent studies, this amounts to about 16.6 percent of the population or 3.3 million persons. Those earning $3,000 to $5,000 per year constitute another 11.1 percent or 2.2 million.

** See page 416 of *Building the American City* for data on state and local tax regressivity and the partial nullification of federal tax progressivity.

rent value (when assessed) of ghetto property and the underassessment of suburban property. We surveyed data on all land sales in San Diego County for one year, as described above. As part of our analysis, we took the 200 most overassessed and the 200 most underassessed properties and attempted to determine their location. We found thirty-three of the overassessed properties in model cities or known slum areas. We found five of the underassessed properties in the same neighborhoods. The variation is enormous; the overassessed property is assessed at between 26% and 29% of its market value and the underassessed property at one-third this level, from 7% to 11% of its market value. As mentioned above, most of these assessments occurred the same year and immediately *following* the land sales.

The third independent source of regressivity is the homeowner's exemption discussed above. The poor are much more likely to rent than are the wealthy.* The figures in the poorer communities indicate five to ten times the percentage of renters as in the wealthier communities. As economist Dick Netzer, the National Commission on Urban Problems and others have pointed out, this does not help the poor with regard to property tax regressivity, since the taxes are passed along through the rents. But it does mean that renters do not receive benefits from California's homeowner's exemption. Those who pay indirectly through rent and are thus not as aware of the tax are not aware of the exemption. A break for renters has been enacted, but it is very limited and acts as a deduction to state income tax, and only middle- and upper-level renters can take full advantage of it.

A final miscellaneous source of regressivity from property tax comes from the fact that property tax on business is passed on through the price of consumer goods, including medicine, food and other necessities that, as with the sales tax, affect a greater percentage of the income of the poor than of the wealthy. The overassessment of utilities adds to this.

It seems clear that property taxes should be ended, certainly as presently applied. The federal income tax system makes matters worse by allowing homeowners to deduct both property taxes and mortgage interest from income in figuring federal income tax. It then taxes capital gains (e.g. from the sale of land) at one-half the rate as other income. Finally, those who own their homes do not have to pay tax on the imputed rent which is in fact a very real form of income they derive as landlords.

A detailed study of the bias in the federal tax system was conducted by Henry Aaron (to be published in the *American Economic Review*). It presents data gathered from a representative sample of 86,610 federal returns in the Brookings Institution file for 1966. The calculations indicate that a renter with an income of $10,000 will have a federal tax liability of $1,304 while an owner with the same income and all else identical will have a tax liability of $962, twenty-six percent less. On Monday, March 3, 1969, Professor Roger F. Miller presented to Congress alternative provisions which would eliminate most of the current discrimination against renters. They were not adopted.

* Tables from Henry Aaron's study record homeownership at forty percent for those making up to $2,999. The percentage climbs through each bracket to 96% at $100,000+.

Aside from the above, the federal income tax laws have for many years provided for preferential treatment for certain kinds of real estate: commercial and industrial buildings, hotels and motels, shopping centers, office buildings, and rental housing operators. The breaks have consisted of highly favorable accelerated tax depreciation allowances enhanced by little equity financing and then reduced or deferred taxation of gains at time of sale. In other words, one could borrow a great deal of money for a commercial real estate enterprise, say a department store, contributing merely $50,000 to $60,000 personally. Then, as operations begin, one could deduct interest on the loan and take enormous deductions for the "depreciation" of the building on the theory that most items depreciate the most during the first several years of use. In fact, however, the building has probably increased in value. When Mr. X sells, he pays tax at only one-half the normal rate for his profit. If it turns out that he lied, that there has been no depreciation, but that, in fact, the building is worth more, he does not have to pay *any* taxes on all of the "depreciation" loss he alleged to avoid paying taxes over past years. If X reinvests under certain conditions or dies, the tax at one-half the normal rate may even be avoided.

These arrangements are often referred to by attorneys in one combination or another as the "real estate tax shelter." Through this device, taxpayers indirectly handed large real estate interests a gift of approximately $1 billion in 1967. Only a portion went to *housing* and virtually none to low-income housing. In 1969, a Tax Reform Act was passed which allegedly tightens somewhat these recapture provisions. Furthermore, it provided certain exemptions to stimulate just low-income housing. There appears to be much of the shelter left in industrial and commercial construction, and the exemptions tend to result in the stimulation of middle-income rather than low-income housing.*

Unfortunately, however, local tax systems have more than compensated for any effort by the federal government to encourage new low-cost housing and slum rehabilitation. Local property taxes discourage the rehabilitation of slum apartments which would cause substantial increases in assessments and in taxation for the owner. Removing structures from assessment would tend to reduce this effect, as we have suggested above. More indirectly, the stimulation of sprawl, fragmentation of local government and subsidization of land speculation, all discussed in chapters above, remove land from the market and raise the price of land to discourage new low-income housing.

Why does a society put a consumptive tax on the value of housing,

---

* There is little doubt that the real-estate shelter encouraged all construction qua construction. But the nature of the tax system, the industry, and market has meant that the diverted activity is going toward commercial and high-income housing construction. Professor Surrey of Harvard has noted (class mats., p. 443, 1970):

> The "trickle down" supply effect for the lower income rental housing market is apparently slow and uncertain in a growing general housing market.
>
> Capital and other resource demands engendered by the existing tax stimuli probably tend to expand luxury housing, commercial, office, motel, shopping center, and other forms of more glamorous investment, *squeezing out lower income housing* (emphasis added).

a necessity, when it generally seeks to exempt necessities such as food or medicine from sales tax? It seems more puzzling that housing is singled out to carry such an enormous burden. Economist Dick Netzer has estimated that if it were expressed as a sales tax, nationwide average property tax rates would be about eighteen percent. California has higher property tax rates than does the nation as a whole. But it seems to reach the preposterous when political boundaries are drawn around neighborhoods dependent upon this source of revenue (see below for analysis of consequences). The addition of the sales use tax does not improve matters. A community's need for or right to services may have very little correlation with the sales volume of the local Safeway store. The end result of all of this is the need for the poorer communities, as we have seen, to charge higher tax rates within their jurisdiction. This then drives commercial enterprise and the mobile high-income groups out of the neighborhood, increasing the need for a yet higher tax rate and completing a vicious circle. The National Commission cited above found the burden of local taxes to average 7.6% of personal income in central cities and 5.6% for residents outside central cities. Nor is it merely a matter of percentages. The National Commission (Id.) found that in 1965, the per person *non*educational expenses were 78% higher for the residents of the nation's thirty-seven largest central cities than for their suburban counterparts. Things have not improved since 1965.

Appendix 10A
Billboards: A Case Study of the Amelioration of
One Land-Use Cost of Highways

Primary reliance on a sprawling highway complex creates many additional miscellaneous costs. One of these is the diminution of beauty for those travelling via the mode. Garbage dumps, unimaginative design and inadequate landscaping, litter and billboards often proliferate over a wide area required for this mode's right of way. In many of these areas California has taken some action to minimize the impact on the aesthetics of land use for motor transport. Laws have been passed to deal with all of the above named problems. Their effect has been generally minimal. As one example, we shall consider briefly the one area that has witnessed the most laws and the most self-congratulatory publicity, the control of billboards.

The drive to eliminate or control billboards began in 1958 with federal legislation. The early law provided a bonus of federal aid highway funds to those states enacting expanded controls over outdoor advertising along the interstate system. This led to California's passage of the Collier-Z'Berg Act of 1964. This law had no great impact on the presence or nature of signs anywhere in the state. It is widely described as "establishing the principle of expanded control of outdoor advertising." * Its real purpose was to ostensibly comply with federal law to qualify for more federal money. California thus received an additional eight million dollars annually in federal funds.

In 1965 the Congress passed the Highway Beautification Act of 1965, sometimes called "Lady Bird's Bill." In 1966 California passed a junkyard control law to qualify the state for an additional $10 million annually for incentives written into the 1965 federal law. In 1967 California updated its billboard control laws in a much vaunted Outdoor Advertising Act. The federal law of 1965 and the state law of 1967 determine the fate of California's 30,000 poster structures, 5,000 nonstandard signs and 3,000 painted bulletins. The 15,000 billboards along highways, the interstate system, and outside incorporated cities are especially affected.

The 1965 Act authorized use of federal funds to pay 75% of the state's costs in controlling (e.g., purchase, removal) billboards along the interstate system *and* along the state's own primary (intercity) highway system. Owners of existing billboards were to receive "just compensation" with the help of this federal aid, but virtually all the billboards allegedly were to be removed by July 1, 1970, five years from the enactment. On July 2, 1970, a few people noticed that the billboards were still up. Despite the law, not one had come down anywhere.

A 1969 Senate Report contains one of the reasons for this failure. Of the $42 million authorized for the program, less than $3 million had been appropriated and only $1.9 million expended. Most of this was expended to count the number of billboards up. One of the Outdoor Advertising lobby's early "compromises" in the bill was to take the money for this program from the General Fund, instead of from gas tax trust fund revenues. Although it was obvious that the program would have to compete with health and defense programs coming from the General Fund, the lobbyists argued that there was a very severe shortage in gas tax revenues for highway

* See Report of the Assembly Committee on Natural Resources, January 1967, p. 9.

purposes—a common argument of the freeway complex at both federal and state levels. As of late 1970 there had grown an unspent surplus of $2.3 billion in the trust fund.

Under the 1965 Act, 10% of a state's highway-building aid from the trust fund could be withheld if the state failed to comply with billboard restrictions. But because the federal government did not provide the $42 million authorized for "just compensation," the 10% penalty was suspended. Hence, not a single sign has come down. The notion of penalties to deprive a state of large amounts of revenue is rarely as successful as a system of positive incentives (take away 10% from everyone and give it back to those who comply).

The 1965 Act also had other flaws. Loopholes are rampant, with "business areas" excepted. First, a buffer zone one fifth of a mile on either side of a "business area" is tacked on. A "business area" is almost anywhere where there is business. Second, if there is advertising of the business or service rendered on the premises, the sign is excepted. A number of enterprises thus keep their Marlboro ads by either selling a few packs or by adding in some obscure corner of the sign that these premises "belong to X."

Third, the law is directed primarily at *new* signs put up, and within 660 feet of an interstate or primary highway. A jumbo lighted action spectacular 670 feet away is allowable under the law.

Nor are signs in these limited areas prohibited—not even new signs. There are "restrictions" limiting size, height, nature and spacing. These are hardly ambitious. Signs cannot be higher than *twenty-five* feet or longer than *sixty* feet. They cannot interfere with traffic signals. They must be 500 feet apart on freeways and 300 feet apart on primary highways. They must be 500 feet from an interchange. As most California highway travelers will attest, even these minimums are regularly violated. The state Department of Public Works has admitted to us that over 1,000 billboards, *not* compensable, violate federal law as of 1971.

The state law of 1967 repeats all of the inadequacies of the federal version. It exempts all displays in existence before 1967 and duplicates federal loopholes. It has added one possibly useful section dealing with "protected bonus areas." These are limited areas 660 feet from interstate highways only. Once again we have incorporated, commercial and other exceptions, including "Class 3 Signs" allowing billboard advertising for activities within twelve miles of the sign. Slightly stricter spacing, size and animation standards are imposed. Nevertheless, we can count on large billboards nearly every 335 yards. As loose as things are, another 4,000 to 5,000 billboards violate state standards but are compensable. As with the federal law, money has not been appropriated for compensation. The law stands, as do all the state's billboards, but is unenforced.

At the state level, AB 1252 (Milias) to phase out billboards merely on designated scenic highways, was defeated in Senate Committee in 1970, as was AB 481 (Scharabum) to substitute discreet highway information panels for certain high-rise signs. At the federal level, President Nixon has proposed the scrapping of the 1965 Act and offered a completely new start with a more realistic incentive system, a "line of sight" (not 660 feet) test and gas tax revenue (trust fund) use. Private individuals, such as advertising executive Douglas T. Snarr, have proposed removal arrangements with a far greater chance of success. Perhaps for this very reason these proposals are destined for the same fate as the state proposals described above.

Unfortunately, government nonfeasance turns into malfeasance upon even closer examination. Refusal to draft and enforce a law to accomplish the gushing public relations promises is not as surprising as the actual subsidization of outdoor advertising by public agencies. In a little known, little circulated publication by the Urban Property Research Company, conducted for the Business and Transportation Agency (especially the Department of Public Works, Division of Highways) and the federal Department of Transportation, researchers collected records on rents charged advertisers for placing signs on public land regulated by federal and state agencies.

On page fourteen of *Valuation of Outdoor Advertising Sites* (November, 1969), the report reveals that

> Public agencies generally have a set price for sign leases; however these generally bring only a nominal rental. One federal agency contacted indicated their annual charge was $0.20 per square foot of advertising surface. For a 12' x 25' poster board, this would yield only $60 per year. A regional agency having extensive land holdings on two major state routes indicated they lease signs at $0.20 per square foot annually with a minimum rate of $5.00 per year.

In contrast, the study in Table A, page 7, found that private land for 12' x 25' poster board displays was rented for from $100 to $2,500 per year, depending upon location and lighting, for the 8,000 signs located on Southern Pacific Co. land.* On page 6 the authors quietly observe that

> Some public agencies have permitted signs at very nominal rates and have presented the advertising companies with windfall profits from the use of their lands.

This is hardly discouraging, much less removing, billboards.

---

* The special interests operating at the state level are reviewed in Chapter 12. Briefly, there are two trade associations and several direct lobbyists. In addition, it should be noted that Southern Pacific Company receives over $3 million in annual revenue from the 8,000 signs on its property. Further, a large percentage of the remaining signs sit on land owned by major oil firms.

Appendix 11A
Substantive Analysis of DOT's Public Report
as Written on Palmdale Airport Site

After briefly considering the natural and recreational environment in terms of the conclusory affidavits from the state and the county, and the illogical conclusions of the Department of the Interior study, the Report switches to consideration of the "Urban Environment." Once again, this section of the Report is filled with inconsistencies, incomplete data, unsound conclusions, and statements which prove to be serious misrepresentations when one carefully reads the cited appendices.

First, an attempt is made to discount the seriousness of the noise pollution by stating:

> To a large extent, the area to be impacted is the same area as is presently noise impacted by jet aircraft utilizing Runway 4/22 at Plant 42.

Reference is then made to an appendix of maps showing noise contours for the proposed airport and for Plant 42. The significant difference that is not mentioned is the fact that the frequency of flights to and from the "transcontinental airport will exceed the present occurrence of test flights from Plant 42 to such an extent that disruptive and psychological effects of the noise is incomparable." Today the residents are disturbed by an occasional jet flight over their homes: in the future the noise will be a constant roar as jets take off and land at a rate of one per minute, twenty-four hours a day. The attempt to compare the noise level of Plant 42 test flights and an "intercontinental" facility is both deceptive and misleading, as described earlier.

The next paragraph talks about the noise damage to the seven schools in the area, citing at one point the state Dept. of Aeronautics hearings, but applying in the next sentence findings of noise damage which are grossly out of line with the conclusions of these hearings. To appreciate fully the manner and extent that the Report misrepresents its cited authority, some elaborations of the Dept. of Aeronautics findings must be understood.*

The Dept. of Aeronautics report drew from the studies of Veneklasen and Associates which had divided the noise effect into three "zones," each progressively more deleterious to the schools. The zones were evaluated as follows:

PNL (PnDB)	Zone	Description of Response
Less than 90	1	Essentially no complaints . . . noise may however interfere occasionally with certain activites of the residents.
90 to 105	2	Individuals may complain, perhaps vigorously. Concerted group action is possible.
Greater than 105	3	Individual reaction would likely include repeated, vigorous complaints. Concerted group action may be expected.

* Recall that the Dept. of Aeronautics took testimony on the issue of noise damage to Palmdale, and, while including such testimony in its report, it refused to include those findings in arriving at its decision, claiming (correctly at the time) that it was empowered to evaluate the airport construction only to the extent that it might affect "safety."

Using these standards of evaluation and the findings of the Veneklasen study, the Dept. of Aeronautics hearing officer determined
that:

> Based on the new location of the runways and using the per-
> ceived noise level now expected for the supersonic transport,*
> three of the schools would be in Zone 3, one would be on the
> line separating Zone 2 and Zone 3, and three would be com-
> pletely in Zone 2.

and that

> Based on the new location of the runways and using the per-
> ceived noise level of four engine turbojet aircraft, three of the
> seven schools would be in Zone 2, part of one would be in Zone
> 2 with most of it being in Zone 1, and three would be com-
> pletely in Zone 1.

The Department of Transportation Report cites the Dept. of Aeronautics hearings, but then proceeds to measure noise levels in un-
conventional and obfuscating units which they call "Composite
Noise Ratings (CNR)" ** Contrary to anything faintly resembling
the Dept. of Aeronautics hearings and findings, the Report claims
that "of the 8 existing schools in the Palmdale area, 7 lie within
Zone 1 and one lies within Zone 2." It then reverts without explanation of the last quoted sentence to testimony from the state hearing
to claim that buildings damaged by noise can either be modified "by
reworking the school's roof structures plus the addition of a suspended ceiling," or that "alternatively it should be relocated."

By drawing from testimony of the state hearing to substantiate
the feasibility of structural modifications to attenuate the damage to
the schools, the Report leaves the reader to conclude by implication
that the alleged extent of the noise damage was also obtained from
the state hearing. The above quotes of the findings of the Dept. of
Aeronautics hearing officer, however, indicate that four rather than
one school will be damaged by noise. It was also disclosed at the
Dept. of Aeronautics hearings—but not mentioned in this Report—
that because of original construction, the necessary structural modifications of the four schools would probably be unfeasible and/or
uneconomic.

There is no citation in the Report for the claim that only one
school would be affected by noise. The sentence making that claim is
couched between statements of findings from the State Dept. of
Aeronautics hearing.

In a paragraph dealing with the condemnation of buildings for
the construction of the airport, the Report notes that the airport
"will require condemnation of a total of 113 dwelling units, 13 of
which have been permanently abandoned." The next sentence quotes
from a city survey indicating that 80 "units" contain under 1,000
square feet of floor space, 60 "units" are unmaintained with tar-paper
exteriors, 30 "units" are "poorly maintained" wood-stucco structures valued under $2,000, and that only 10 structures are "large
and well maintained farm type homes with a probable value in excess of $20,000 each."

* Recall that Veneklasen later determined that his earlier estimates of SST
noise generation were at least three decibels low.
** The Dept. of Aeronautics' recent publication "Prosped Noise Standards" recognizes a number of measures of noise, none of which is the CNR
measure used in the Report. One suspects that the measure was obtained
from the Los Angeles City Dept. of Airports.

Reading the two sentences in context, one might understandably conclude that the buildings being condemned are not of much value. But a closer analysis shows the information to be quite deceptive: The total number of "units" cited in the city's survey exceeds the 113 "dwelling units" referred to in the preceeding sentence. Thus, when the city survey refers to the number of tar paper shacks and low-valued stucco-wood structures, it must be including more than the "113 dwelling units" of the preceding sentence. But the report's reference to "dwelling units" followed immediately by the unexplained city survey would lead the casual reader to conclude that both sentences refer to the same structures, and that many of these are merely tar-paper shacks, "poorly maintained" or low-value units.

It should also be noted that no accounting is given as to how many of the units fall into the value category between $2,000 and $20,000. The references are limited to a few large farmhouses and many tarpaper shacks. The implication is that all buildings being condemned are accounted for in the city survey, however it is clear that that survey does not coincide with the rest of the data in the Report. For whatever reason, the Report is very unclear as to how many homes will be condemned and families displaced by the airport.

Also in this section of the Report is an interesting recognition that the residents with the lowest standard of living are the ones who will suffer most from the noise pollution.

> It is estimated that about 950 residences lie within projected noise-exposure Zone 2. . . . The predominant portion of the dwellings are of frame/stucco construction and tend to be quite old. . . . The involved newer residences appear to be of substantially better construction quality and tend to lie more distant from the airport's boundary.

In an attempt to polish over the issue of damages to these residences, the Report says that "most of the closer-in units are now subjected to a comparable degree of noise" from the existing Plant 42. As discussed earlier, any attempt to compare the noise of Plant 42 with that which will be produced by an intercontinental facility is misleading and erroneous. In a rare moment of candor the Report admits,

> . . . it would appear desirable to apply reasonable sound attenuation techniques to effect interior noise level reductions in these close-in residences of frame or conventional construction. *No such program is presently contemplated* [emphasis added].

The Report's "Finding of Facts" as to "Site Selection" indicates that the FAA (DOT) knew very little about the actual decision-making process, and that they attempted to pad the Report to hide this ignorance. It is stated that "the enabling ground work for the new airport was laid by the California State Legislature when it jointly resolved to seek joint civil-military usage of Air Force Plant 42" in 1966. The implication is that even the state legislature concurred in the construction of the intercontinental airport. In fact, the legislature knew nothing about the incipient plans of the Los Angeles Department of Airports to construct such a gigantic facility. At the time that the joint resolution was passed, Palmdale was being considered as a small, contiguous airport to serve the northern part of the county. Given the lack of coordinated planning and the extensive controversy which has arisen since the disclosure that the airport would be of intercontinental dimensions, it is highly questionable that the legislature would be willing to endorse the project.

The Report also claims that

selection of the Palmdale site . . . followed three years of intensive study of all possible locations throughout the entirety of southern California.

No such study exists. Burt Lockwood of the L.A. Dept. of Airports admitted at the state hearings that alternative sites were not considered. As noted earlier, SCAG—the one agency which was conducting a comprehensive, long-range study of transportation in southern California—was never consulted by the Department of Airports during the "planning" for an intercontinental airport. The progress of the SCAG study suffered a significant setback by the disclosure that a major air facility would be constructed at Palmdale. SCAG now has resigned itself to continue its broad transportation study with the airport as a "given" fact.

While the Report asserts that there was such an "intensive study of all possible locations," it does not include any citation for the claim. Indeed, the only appendix to the whole fact-finding section on site selection is the contents of a letter written by Supporters of the Palmdale Intercontinental Airport (SPIA) to the Dept. of Aeronautics on June 6, 1969. (Recall that SPIA is the organization which collaborated with the Antelope Valley Board of Trade and others to demean the members of the EQSC Noise Abatement Committee.) In its letter of support for the airport, SPIA included a number of resolutions from local realtors and merchants who also support the airport. Citing "Appendix 2" the Report claims that "most all of the directly involved state and local governments," as well as . . . several civic improvement organizations" have passed supporting resolutions. Apparently the writers were confident that Secretary Volpe would not take the time to read the appendix, for the "civil improvement organizations" are nothing more or less than the local realtors and businessmen who will personally gain from the new airport:

Antelope Valley Board of Realtors
Palmdale Board of Realtors
Antelope Valley Board of Trade
Palmdale Chamber of Commerce
Lancaster Chamber of Commerce
Quartz Hill Chamber of Commerce

Recalling the 500% profit which the President of the L.A. Planning Commission and the Director of Planning have already reaped from their land speculations in Palmdale, it is not difficult to understand why the realtors favor the airport. And, given the expected population increase from the present 8,200 to over half a million by 1990, the support of the local merchants is also understandable. It is incomprehensible, however, that the FAA Report would use these biased interests to allude to a conclusion that widespread support exists for the airport.

The third major part of the Report deals with the hearings by the FAA, the Department of Aeronautics and the EQSC Noise Abatement Committee. The EQSC hearing was the only one which considered the environmental impact of the airport, and, not by mere coincidence, it was also the only agency which recommended a delay in construction pending further studies and planning of the full effect of the airport upon the surrounding community and countryside. Interestingly, the EQSC hearing is also the only hearing which the Report does not discuss in any detail. The excuse given is that a written transcript was not available. While acknowledging that tape recordings of the hearing were available, the Report claims that the identity of the persons testifying could not be established from the tapes. However, the appendix of the Report which is referred to in this same paragraph lists the names of all who testified in the order that they gave their testimony. Virtually every speaker either identified himself before speaking, or was identified by a member of the Committee.

Moreover, a simple request to the Committee would have produced both the written copies of testimony which many speakers submitted to the panel when they testified, and a copy of the very detailed report of the hearings by Nicholas Yost, the Deputy Attorney General assigned to the EQSC. The combination of the taped transcript, Yost's detailed notes, and the written copies of testimony which many of the speakers submitted at the time they spoke, could have provided as much if not more information about the hearing than could be obtained from a stenographic transcript. It becomes clear that the Dept. of Transportation was simply groping for an excuse for not including a discussion of the one hearing which reached a conclusion contrary to their own. This is especially interesting given the fact that the Report purports to be an inquiry into the "environmental impact" of the airport.

While the writers of the Report refuse to consider the extensive information available from the EQSC hearing, they do not hesitate to comment that "in character the hearing was volatile and emotional," and that "newspaper editorials appear to confirm the existence of an unproductive atmosphere. . . ." Curiously, the absence of a stenographic transcript is no impediment to a judgment about the "character" of the hearing; and, the earlier qualms about the use of second-hand accounts of the EQSC hearing seem not to apply to the inclusion and endorsement of admittedly "editorial" accounts by the *Antelope Valley Press* and the *Lancaster Daily Ledger-Gazette*. While the *Los Angeles Times*—the largest and most cosmopolitan newspaper in southern California—supported the EQSC, none of its articles or editorials are mentioned in the Report. The only editorials included in the appendix were from the two local, pro-airport newspapers which have everything to gain from an undelayed influx of five hundred thousand people.

On the basis of information which permitted the derogatory judgment of the character of the hearing but not consideration of the hearing's content, the Report concludes that "the hearing *apparently* provided the council with the basis for its recommendations to Governor Reagan . . . (emphasis added)" One can truly question the basis for the Report's own conclusions. On the one hand, it is claimed that the EQSC hearing cannot be discussed for lack of a stenographic transcript; and on the other hand, a discussion and conclusion of the "character" of the hearing follows from editorials in two pro-airport newspapers. The reasoning is indeed difficult to follow.

The final section of Findings of Fact purports to consider the alleged environmental protective actions executed by the planners of the airport. It is claimed that the Dept. of Airports "carefully studied" the noise problem and "as the result" planned for sizable buffer zones and runway orientations to minimize the noise. In fact, the noise studies were conducted by the independent firm of Veneklasen & Associates for the Palmdale School District; and the creation of buffer zones by reorienting the runways was a pre-emptive and embarrassing change occurring during the state Dept. of Aeronautics hearings and under pressure of the devastating testimony of Paul Veneklasen. The Department of Airports does not deserve credit for either the studies or the resultant buffer zones (which were subsequently determined to be insufficient).

The Report claims that the runway shift "was motivated by the desire to minimize noise exposure to existing schools within the Palmdale school district." In fact, the planners were deaf to the pleas of the school district and the residents of the area surrounding the airport. These citizens' groups had to solicit the expert opinion of a private acoustical engineering firm, and the resulting runway shift by the Dept. of Airports was motivated more by a desire to dis-arm the opposition's study.

The Report further claims that "comprehensive planning actions are being, or soon will be pursued. . . ." In characteristic "bureaucratese," the statement neither tells the reader whether comprehensive plans are presently being pursued, or whether they are merely anticipated at some future date. Certainly we have not been able to find any comprehensive plan (other than the SCAG study which was flouted by the airport planners), or any commitment greater than the above-type evasive statement that such planning "soon will be" forthcoming.

Under claim of "Positive Land Controls," the Report says that the city of Palmdale has annexed land to the north of the airport and has zoned it for industrial use, and that the city plans to annex more land to the south. Nothing is mentioned of the residential land to the west—which the Report has already admitted will be damaged by noise. Nor are any "positive controls" indicated for the rest of the city which will generally be impacted by the airport development.

The conclusions of the Report are no different in style and claim from the "Findings of Fact." The first conclusion is that "the environmental impacts of the Palmdale project have been totally identified and considered."

However, as indicated by the letters of experts compiled by Nicholas Yost, the agencies have not identified many of the potential problems. And, even if it were assumed that they were aware of the full range of implications of the airport, there is still no comprehensive study which can provide substantiation to having "considered" the problem.

Another claim in the conclusion is that

the involved local, state and Federal agencies . . . agree that the resulting imposition is an acceptable adversity when weighed in precedence to the project's enhancement of the greater metropolitan area's long-term productivity.

In fact, the only governmental agency which seriously considered the environmental impact concluded that the level of adversity may not be acceptable, and that further plans for the airport should be delayed until a comprehensive study and plan can be completed.

Given the arbitrary exclusion of the EQSC's hearing information earlier in the Report, one can only conclude that the FAA and the Dept. of Transportation do not consider the governor's Environmental Advisory Commission a relevant or "involved" agency. Without the information from the EQSC hearing, one wonders what information from what source is being "weighed" against the advantages of having a new airport to serve the metropolitan area.

This alleged Report on "environmental impact" closes with a recommendation from John H. Shaffer, FAA Administrator, "that the Secretary of Transportation concur with the findings of the Administrator . . ." As we have seen, however, the "findings" of the FAA Administrator amount to a "mish-mash of documents" which misrepresent many issues and facts, which show an unconcealed bias for pro-airport factions and documents, which claim substantiations that are not to be found in the appendices, and which generally are not addressed to the question of environmental impact.

Indeed, the omissions of environmental data are almost as conspicuous as the irrelevancies and misrepresentations which are included. The Report does not consider the serious problem of a potential water shortage. Nor is there any consideration of the possible smog problems, the temperature effect on fuel consumption, wind turbulences, mountain obstacles to radar; and landing clearances, and the numerous ecological ramifications of developments contingent to the airport, e.g., highways, industry, and residential development.

The National Environmental Policy Act of 1969 requires a "detailed statement" of the project's impact upon the surrounding area, and, a consideration of alternative sites which may not adversely effect the environment to the same extent. Neither of these legal requirements is met by the FAA Report. Perhaps the only way to force the needed delay and study of the comprehensive impact of the airport is to obtain in federal court an injunction against continued construction until the requirements of the federal law are satisfied.

Appendix 11B: Analysis of the "Findings of the Secretary of Transportation Relative to the Environmental Impact of the Proposed Palmdale International Airport"

The Report is best analyzed in terms of the "Statement of Findings" which comprise the first seven pages. The remainder of the Report is a compilation which allegedly substantiates these findings. References to these appendices throughout the analysis will prove that often they say things quite different from what is alleged, and often they do not relate to the conclusions drawn from them.

In the mere two sentences devoted to a description of the surrounding countryside, the Report is quick to note that Antelope Valley is a "semi-arid desert":

> Flora and fauna in the site vicinity are typical of local desert areas with the fauna chiefly consisting of jack rabbits, pack rats, kangaroo rats and snakes.

The implication is clearly that Antelope Valley is a wasteland on the fringe of a metropolitan area. The Report makes no mention of the varieties of desert lizards, insects, tortoises, toads, birds, gophers, foxes, coyotes, cats, skunks, and moles which also inhabit the desert. Nor does the Report ever mention any of the myriad desert flora, except for a parenthetical reference to one of the state parks in the area ("Joshua Tree—4,240 acres"). One can only conclude that the writer was either uninformed or unconcerned as to the variety and importance of the wildlife. Certainly one cannot conclusively presume that the natural habitat of the desert will be unaffected by jet noise, air pollution, concrete roadways, new housing developments and diverted water supplies.

Later in the Report, three paragraphs are devoted to "Natural and Recreational Environment." Two of these paragraphs describe the procedure by which the FAA requested an inventory of all parks within a twenty-mile radius of the site. Absolutely nothing is said about the natural environment or the recreational environment beyond the impacting on the publicly maintained park areas. And, as the appendices indicate, the polling of the parks in the area was merely perfunctory.

The appendix labeled "Approval by Public Owners of Parks, Recreational Areas, Sanctuaries, Etc." contains only three affidavits which hardly address themselves to any serious study of the environmental impact of the airport. The first "affidavit" is a Xeroxed copy of a telegram from the Director of California Parks and Recreation, William Penn Mott, Jr., declaring that the Department "finds that there is no interference with park and recreational value" of Joshua Tree State Park. Mott indicates that there is a letter to follow the telegram, but that letter—which presumably would elaborate the Parks and Recreation findings—has not been included in the Report.

Another letter, dated February 4, 1970, from the Los Angeles County Department of Parks and Recreation, indicates that the Department "does not project any significant interference in any of these areas . . ." Again, there is no evidence that any type of a study was undertaken, or that the conclusion was anything more than a visceral reaction by the county director, N. S. Johnson. Indeed, one month later, in an interview with a Department of the Interior investigator, Johnson claimed that the city and county were merely at the discussion stages of beginning a study of the environment, transportation and the econonomy of Palmdale. He said that the study would not begin before "mid-year."

The tone and composition of the Johnson letter indicated that environmental impact was a secondary concern. For the most part, the letter elaborates a wholly separate and distinct interest of the County Parks and Recreation Department, viz., the possibility of obtaining land for a golf course in the Palmdale-Lancaster vicinity:

> It seems entirely feasible that your interests and ours could be jointly served on the perimeter or buffer properties of the airport.

Johnson then requests that the Department of Airports (to whom the letter is addressed) consider providing sufficient property to his Department for the construction of their golf course.

That is not to say that the buffer area ought not to be used for a golf course, or that Johnson should not have made the request for consideration of his Department's interest at that time. It simply illustrates that the issue of the airport's impact on the environment of the county parks and recreational areas was a rather minor consideration in the letter which is used by the FAA as a substantiating affidavit.

The final document which the FAA included in its appendix as evidence of no serious environmental impact to natural and recreational areas is nothing more than a list of fourteen wildflower and wildlife sanctuaries and thirteen local parks. There is no accompanying letter or statement by anyone concerning the environmental impact on these areas. Yet the FAA proclaims in the fact-finding section of the Report that it has received evidence that the airport's existence will not adversely affect these sanctuaries and parks, and that statement is allegedly substantiated by reference to the appendix. A reader not prepared to make the tedious investigation of the cited appendices would take the FAA Report at its word. Presumably, that is what was hoped, and what did in fact happen when the Report was considered by the reviewing bureaucrats and the Secretary of Transportation.

A final item of note in this same appendix is a cover letter which accompanied the Mott telegram and the Johnson letter to the Washington office of FAA.* The letter was written by Arvin O. Basnight, the Western Regional Director of the FAA, and the same official who had earlier disclaimed any responsibility for environmental effects of the airport in the letter (above) to Congressman Brown. Dated February 6, 1970, the letter indicates that the Mott and Johnson letters are attached, and concludes with the following plea:

> As you know, the pressure for decision of FAA airspace clearance of this airport continues to build. The *Los Angeles Times* specifically is planning a major news release for Sunday, 15 February, on the status of the airport project, and your support for a decision on the ecology and environment in light of this data will be very much appreciated.

---

* The fact that this letter was even included in the Report suggests that someone in Washington quickly and indiscriminately took a whole file-drawer on "Palmdale," Xeroxed every document and correspondence and titled it "Report on the Environmental Impact . . ."

For Basnight, the outcome of the "environmental study" is a foregone conclusion. He is not asking the FAA to expedite the evaluation of the environmental impact of the airport. He is asking them to rubber stamp their "support," and thus help stave off the mounting opposition.

The Report at this stage turns to the "Urban Environment." It is filled with clippings from the pro-airport *Antelope Valley Press* white omitting all *L.A. Times* coverage which was extensive and occasionally critical. It distorts the record on noise pollution danger, misrepresenting its own cited authority. It makes inconsistent claims about minor building condemnation. It seeks to imply that the state legislature approved the site; it did not. It claimed deference to "intensive study" by the local Department of Airports which did not exist. It claims the support of most all of the state and local governments, as well as ". . . several civic improvement organizations." These latter consist of two boards of realtors, one board of trade, and two chambers of commerce.

The Report's claim of public support is particularly illustrative: "[the] PTA (Palmdale Taxpayers Association) conducted a mail survey . . . and *determined* that about 78% thereof favored the airport . . . (emphasis added)." The PTA is a pro-airport group, of which the authors are well aware. The "poll," stated as evidence of support, was a fraud. Less than one-half of those polled returned questionnaires. Moreover, those opposing the airport would be less likely to answer an inquiry from the PTA, particularly when the cover letter states:

> It is obvious to everyone that a billion dollar industry will provide increased property values and create many jobs. Aside from these clearly obvious facts, there is the matter of "how you feel about it."

The poll questions themselves are even more biased:

> 5. Property tax base supporting our schools amounts to almost $200 million. When completed, the Palmdale International Airport will add almost five times this amount or an estimated 1 billion dollars. This indicates that the local school tax (about 60% of your present tax bill) can be reduced to a very small amount. *With this in mind,* do you favor the IDEA of the International Airport?
>
> 7. Due to this proposed industry locating in Palmdale, your home and all property has increased in value. Real Estate leaders predict as much as "doubling" of home values within the next two years. *Does this fact* incline you to support the proposed Airport?
>
> 8. Some people favor economic growth in the Antelope Valley. Others prefer to keep the desert rural in appearance and came here for the semi-isolation which they enjoy. *Do you favor economic growth?*
>
> 10. If the issue of the Palmdale International Airport were placed on a ballot, would you vote FOR or AGAINST it? *

* These questions were clearly meant to imply that *all* homes were going to double in value; that the additional $1 billion tax revenues would eliminate 60% of the present tax bill of *every* private homeowner; and that all people who like the open spaces of the desert are necessarily opposed to economic growth. The PTA questionnaire does not tell the voters that residential properties within about a seven-mile radius of the airport will decrease in value because of the intolerable noise from jet aircraft overhead. Nor does PTA inform the voter that while the airport may bring an addi-

The Report then omits discussion of the problems raised at the three public hearings, glossing over them to imply unanimous assent. The Report states that preparatory urban planning "soon will be forthcoming" when there is no evidence that this will occur. The Report completely fails to mention whatsoever: serious problems of water shortage, possible smog problems, temperature effect on fuel consumption, altitude, wind turbulence, mountain obstacles for radar, landing clearances or the numerous environmental impacts of the airport and contingent development. Nevertheless, the Report makes its first conclusion from the Findings of Fact: "The environmental impacts of the Palmdale project have been totally identified and considered."

Those portions of the DOT study allegedly satisfying the National Environmental Policy Act of 1969 were conducted by the Department of the Interior. In early February, 1970, Oscar Gray, Acting Director of the Office of Environmental and Urban Research, Department of Transportation, requested the Department of the Interior to conduct a "quick check" of the environmental impact of the Palmdale Airport. The resulting study, by an Interior investigator named J. Eichstedt, was completed on March 10, 1970.

Eichstedt, working alone, was the deputy regional director of Interior's Bureau of Outdoor Recreation. As the *Los Angeles Times* points out, that "bureau is concerned with the preservation of public recreation and wildlife areas, not with problems of urban noise, smog, and land use . . . Other Interior agencies concerned with air and water pollution did not make an investigation." One deputy director, with a narrow range of expertise and responsibility, obviously could not undertake the ambitious environmental study called for. That was particularly true in view of the fact that he was instructed to make a "quick check" of the matter, not a "detailed" analysis. The eighteen-day investigation consisted of phone calls and visits to all interested parties, including the Department of Airports, the City Planning Commission and SCAG. To the official's credit, he did at least talk briefly with some opponents of the airport in the Palmdale Homeowners Association.

Considering the inadequate, restricted nature of the investigation, the information gathered is remarkably complete. However, the conclusions reached in the report are in striking contrast to the weight of the evidence set forth therein. The result is eight pages of evidence showing blunders and machinations throughout the planning of the airport, followed by the conclusion that it has been approved by all local and state agencies, and therefore the Department of the Interior should not withhold its approval.

---

tional $1 billion tax revenues, it will also bring over 500,000 additional people who will need schools for their children, fire and police protection, garbage collection, street maintenance, and various other community services which absorb tax revenues very quickly. The contention that the added revenues from the airport will decrease the tax bill of the homeowner by 60% is utter conjecture.

And finally, the presumption that desert conservation and economic growth are mutually incompatible is a gross over-simplification of the issue. The real issue is whether economic growth should proceed totally oblivious of land-use planning and environmental considerations. Those people and organizations opposing the present, unplanned and incompatible airport construction are arguing that true economic growth cannot be extracted from the broader societal interests.

A summary of the adverse findings of the investigator are quite enlightening:

—That HUD considered its $22,500 planning grant to the City of Palmdale wasted because an airport was not even mentioned in the report released thirteen months after the facility became a matter of public record.

—That "the L.A. Department of Airports proceeded with very little substantive cooperation or consultation with other planning or operating agencies," and that "when they presented the airport, the site had already been decided upon for all practical purposes."

—That cross-examination of the Assistant General Manager of the L.A. Department of Airports, Burt Lockwood, at the State Department of Aeronautics hearing, disclosed "that there had been no systematic environmental study or study of alternative airport sites."

—That during the same hearing, the L.A. Department of Airports attempted to "dampen" expert testimony of serious noise pollution in Palmdale by changing the configuration of proposed runways on their demonstration map.

—That despite the pre-emptory changes in runway alignment, "there was very little change in noise to any of the existing schools."

—That "none of the sound contour diagrams supplied . . . by the Department of Airports projected community growth under the flight patterns, or sound contours for supersonic jets."

—That "both Department of Airports and Department of Aeronautics personnel seem to have relied considerably on improved technology for reduction of noise levels," but that "it remains to be seen whether supersonic jets can, indeed, be made as quiet as the FAA standards would require."

—That "counsel for the Department of Aeronautics was more interested in preventing testimony pertaining to environmental considerations than he was in admitting it for the enlightenment of the Department."

—That Joseph R. Crotti, Director of the Department of Aeronautics, maintained that the EQSC Noise Abatement Committee was "politically motivated," but that "after talking with the three subcommittee members, I am inclined to discount the allegation . . ."

—That airport planners conceded that the problem of transportation between Los Angeles and the airport has not been solved, and that the solution will be very expensive.

—That on April 30, 1969, the Los Angeles City Council authorized the Department of Airports to hire an environmental planner, but that as of March 10, 1970, they still had not hired one; and that "in any event, April 30, 1969, was too late for such an individual to have had any effect on the site selection."

These findings should be kept in mind as the conclusions of the investigation are discussed below. While the amount of information gathered in the short time available is both conscientious and praiseworthy, the conclusions which follow are so grossly out of line that one cannot help but think that they were dictated by higher bureaucrats in spite of the findings.

Even within the conclusion itself there are unexplainable conflicts and contradictions. For example, one sentence reads: "There is no federally designed recreation area or wildlife area which will be adversely affected by the development . . ." while the following sentence says, "this does not mean that development of the airport . . . may not make them less desirable as parks and recreation areas." It would seem that the potential smog problem, the inevitably high noise pollution, and the construction of highways and new developments cannot help but substantially and adversely impact the atmosphere of the parks and recreational areas in the vicinity of the airport.

The author of the Interior Report further evades the issue of environmental impact by concluding that "there are no unique outstanding values that I could recognize as worthy of taking precedence to locating a new airport outside of the Los Angeles Basin." In fact, the issue never has been the limited alternative of either Palmdale or somewhere within the Los Angeles Basin. Moreover, while locating an airport outside the Los Angeles Basin may be a positive good, it simply is not the issue under investigation, which is whether this particular site at Palmdale is the most appropriate of all feasible sites outside the Basin. As the Assistant Manager of the L.A. Department of Airports admitted at the State Department of Aeronautics hearings, alternative sites were never studied. And, as this investigator for the Department of the Interior indicated in his findings, not even SCAG was consulted during site selection process albeit it was general knowledge that SCAG was in the process of an ambitious study of a comprehensive transportation plan for southern California. However, it is not mentioned in the conclusion of the Report that no other sites outside the Basin were ever considered, or that there might have been an alternative site somewhere to the south of Los Angeles (e.g., between El Toro and Pendleton Marine Bases) where recreational and wildlife areas might not have been "adversely affected" to the same extent as in Antelope Valley.

As already noted, the investigator acknowledged the fact that no environmental or land-use plan preceded the site selection or construction plans for the airport. However, the author concludes that this is no case for alarm:

> Arguments that an ecological study should precede site selection are theoretically logical and acceptable. However, the valley is in such a disturbed state already that it is doubtful whether such a study would turn up any additional useful information.

No basis for such a statement exists. There is virtually no air pollution; the only noise is from the limited number of flights at Plant 42; there is sufficient water to meet the present needs of Palmdale; the recently constructed freeway is sufficient to accommodate the present population; the desert is still wild, serene, and awesome, and the small communities in Antelope Valley conduct their day-to-day business at a typical small-town pace.

In light of the findings of fact noted earlier, the last paragraph of the Department of the Interior Report provides the only plausible justification for the conclusion to support the construction of the airport:

> Approval of the site by the Department of the Interior would be consistent with actions by the Department of Housing and Urban Development (and) with the Governor's position . . .

HUD never conducted a study of the site or plans, and the governor's decision was based on the advice of the Director of Aeronautics, Joseph R. Crotti, whose pronouncements were discounted by this same investigator for the Department of the Interior. It seems that Interior does not want to assume the task of exposing the malfeasance which other state and federal agencies have likewise brushed over. Nor does Interior want the burden of opposing a site development for which support has already been railroaded from state and county politicians.

Eichstedt's study and conclusion was accepted by the Regional Director, Frank E. Sylvester, and then by the Director of Interior. It is clear, however, that Sylvester had reached his conclusion even before the result of the Eichstedt study reached his desk. While the Eichstedt study is dated March 10, 1970, Sylvester writes to the Director of Interior that the study "confirms *our memorandum of March 6, 1970, in which we concluded that there is no Section 4(f) problem* in connection with the proposed Palmdale airport site (emphasis added)." On May 4, 1970, Secretary of the Interior Walter Hickel wrote a memo to John Volpe, Secretary of Transportation, indicating that Interior would "interpose no objection to the development of this project." Signed, "Wally, Secretary of the Interior."

Appendix 12A
Lobby Laws—Weakness and Violations
An Ambiguous and Weak Law

The California law regulating lobbying, or "legislative advocacy," was modeled after the federal Regulation of Lobbying Act. Section 9906 requires the filing of certain information by paid lobbyists with the Clerk of the Assembly and the Secretary of the Senate. The lobbyist must include in required forms his name, address, authorization from his employer, duration of employment, how much he is paid in salary and by whom. He must then file monthly reports, recording all money he has received in "carrying on his work" and an itemization of all expenditures over $25. He must identify the legislation he is using his expenditures to influence, where the expenditures are going, identify articles or stories written for publications in the furtherance of his advocacy. Section 9906 also provides that the above information is to be printed in the journals of each house (on a monthly basis). The Section requires a lobbyist who employs (or causes his employer to employ) a legislator or state official, to file a statement with the Clerk of the Assembly and Secretary of the Senate, revealing the name of the official, nature of employment and consideration paid. The Section prohibits the payment of a lobbyist contingent upon the passage or defeat of a piece of legislation. The Section exempts from registration mere hearing witnesses, public officials, church officials and journalists.

Sections 9901, 9902, and 9903 deal with soliciting money for lobbying purposes. People who solicit or receive money for lobbying must keep itemized accounts for at least two years identifying the names and addresses of all contributors of over $100 and of all expenditures of over $25 (e.g., in soliciting money for lobbying). Monthly statements must be filed by those soliciting (or receiving) money to finance lobbying with the Clerk and Secretary, as above. These statements are not published, but are open to public inspection.

Section 9909 gives committees of each house the power (and duty) to grant, revoke, and suspend the certificates of registration of lobbyists, or require explanations of those who fail to register or report violations of the law to "appropriate law enforcement officers." Section 9910 sets forth some standards for the exercise of the revocation or suspension powers of §9909. A lobbyist is not allowed to put any legislator under personal obligation, to deceive a legislator, to create a false impression of public support or hostility for a measure, to represent interests adverse to his employer, to retain books and records required by other provisions for two years, and to represent an ability to control votes of legislators.

Finally, Section 9908 makes violation of the above provisions a misdemeanor punishable by a maximum fine of $5,000, a maximum prison term of one year, or both, and prohibition from lobbying for three years. Failure to observe the prohibition is then a felony.

At first reading the law appears strong, clear, and reasonably complete. The information specified relates to all sorts of abuses which may jeopardize legislative impartiality, the standards seem reasonable and the sanctions perhaps adequate. But the law has serious weaknesses. Some of its ambiguities were pointed out in 38 Cal. L.R. 486-491. The authors noted among other ambiguities:

The major difficulty is to determine to whom Sections 9901 to 9903 apply. Section 9905 states that the "provisions of Section

9901 to 9903, inclusive, shall apply to any person, except a political committee, who . . . solicits, collects, or receives money . . . to be used principally to aid, or the principal purpose of which person is to aid, in the accomplishment of . . . the passage or defeat of any legislation." It therefore becomes vital to determine what the words "principally" and "principal" mean. Organizations not wishing to comply with the federal act claimed that the word "principal" means "primary" or "major." This interpretation is aided by the fact that the statute expressly says "*the* principal purpose" and not "a principal purpose." Such an interpretation would exempt a wide variety of organizations which lobby; for example labor groups, farm organizations and veteran organizations.

There is considerable doubt as to the application of Section 9906. It requires "any person who shall engage himself for pay or for any consideration for the purpose of lobbying to register, exempting a person who "merely appears" before a committee. Many persons will be uncertain as to their status. For example, a corporation officer who is sent to Sacramento to lobby might contend that he did not engage himself for the purpose of lobbying. A member of a labor organization lobbying on a pending measure, but only reimbursed for out of pocket expenses, would appear to be exempt since he has not engaged himself for pay or consideration. The section is too vague generally to apprise such persons if their registration is contemplated.

As the act is written, it is even difficult to ascertain what records a lobbyist or employer must keep and file. The lobbyist for compensation appears to be within the scope of Sections 9901, 9902, 9903 and 9906, which would necessitate his keeping four types of records and filing two different monthly reports of his financial transactions. He may be a person who solicits or receives contributions under Section 9901, who receives contributions under Section 9902, who receives contributions and expends money under Section 9902 and who engages himself for pay or consideration under Section 9906. Section 9906 limits reports to money received and expended in "carrying on his work," but Section 9903 seems to require a report of all contributions and expenditures whether for lobbying or not. Proper reporting under the chapter seems not only to impose an excessive burden, but also to create a danger of concealment by overexposure. The lobby can file so many reports that no one could possibly examine the conglomeration, much less ascertain violations.

But the wording of the Act is far more troubling than these criticisms indicate. For example, the Section 9906 provision requiring certain information where a lobbyist hires or "causes his employer" to hire a legislator or state official. How does a lobbyist "cause his employer" to pay this official? How does one prove that the lobbyist was the cause of the hiring? When the coverage of the Act is somewhat ambiguous, and the criteria for enforcement based on virtually unprovable relations, then there is hesitation in applying the law. The burden of the law is continually wrong in that there should be specified behavior which is prima facie illegal (e.g., the hiring of a public official). Once the behavior is proven, the burden should then be shifted to the violator to show that the intentions or relations were such that there is no violation.

The Act also suffers from two other deficiencies which outweigh all of the above. First, the Act is essentially a disclosure statute, with sanctions primarily directed at enforcing disclosure. But dis-

650   APPENDICES

closure requirements have limitations. They can easily be circumvented by vague wording or by the use of large categories of expense.
They are of little effect unless the public pays close scrutiny to them,
even if precise and in a useful form. With hundreds of lobbyists,
such attention is doubtful. In fact, despite the journal printing requirements and despite the possibility of press coverage, there has
been virtually no detailed attention given to these records. During
our research in Sacramento, we were the only persons to go through
the records in detail. Second, the Act is without any specific enforcement agency. This fact alone strips the Act of any deterrent effect.

ACTUAL NONENFORCEMENT

Some progress would surely result from enforcing this existing
law regulating lobbyists. Enforcement of the laws initially trans-
lates into policing of the form which must be filed regularly by the
lobbyists. Currently, enforcement is the responsibility of the Office
of the Legislative Analyst; however, this responsibility is given the
lowest priority. If a well known lobbyist does not file an annual
registration form, he is warned by this office that he will not be
permitted to remain a practicing advocate if he continues to flaunt
the statute. The only disbarment in the history of enforcement of
the law occurred in the first year of its existence. Seven lobbyists
were barred by the Legislative Analyst from advocacy shortly after
the registration legislation was passed. However, since then, there
have been no further disbarments because the lobbyists have discovered that the registration requirement imposes no real burden on
them: both annual and monthly forms can be circumvented with
vague, uninformative answers.

Today, the enforcement efforts of this office consist only of insisting that all required documents be submitted by lobbyists. No official concern over the contents of these forms was ever encountered.*

Given a little manpower for the policing of the entries, the state
could easily uncover a number of irregularities. The apparent violations described below were not difficult to detect and are testimony
to the fact that policing of these records could be productive. Further, subpoena power of the state and courts (which we are not
able to use) could explore these discrepancies which suggest a
desire not to reveal where expense money is actually going. After
the existing laws are enforced, or even while this policy change is
taking place, the following changes in the letter and/or interpretation of the law should be made:

(1) Lobbyists who work for more than one client should be required to list their monthly expenditures separately by client. They
sometimes do this themselves and it would not impose a hardship on
them.

(2) A lobbyist should be required to list the total salary paid to
him by his clients as well as the portion which he considers to be
applicable to his duties as an advocate.

(3) A lobbyist should be required to list all campaign contribu-

* The secretary in the office where these forms were kept on several occasions was overheard quizzing state employees about possible $1.50 discrep-
ancies on their travel accounts while innumerable thousandfold discrepancies
of a much more suspicious nature existed in the lobbyists' forms ten feet
away. The duty of policing the files was not her duty, nor was it anybody's
duty.

tions of $25 or more as lobbying expenses regardless of where the money initially came from.

(4) A lobbyist should be required to list by bill number all legislation which he is actively opposing or supporting, which client he is representing in so doing and whether he is advocating a "yes" or a "no" vote.

(5) A lobbyist should not be allowed to practice advocacy on measures for which he has not registered as per (4).

(6) All trade organizations and lobbying associations in general should be required to indicate the names of their supporting members and the level of financial support that these members provide for lobbying.

In addition to these measures, there are numerous others implicit in the critique above.*

INCONSISTENCIES AND ACTUAL VIOLATIONS

The law does not produce uniform recording by lobbyists. Some lobbyists report their hotel bills (up to $2,500 a month in several cases!) on the monthly expense forms which they are required by law to file, while others, frequently those who have a full time residence in Sacramento, do not report their normal living expenses. Similar ambiguous recording situations exist for the reporting of office costs, secretarial help, etc. Reporting practices in this area reflect personal judgments on the question of where one draws the line on "attempted influence of legislation."

Lobbyists submit their monthly expenses on a single page form provided by the state. The expenses declared on forms submitted by some lobbyists do not vary in their composition and totals over long periods of time. This regularity and standardization bespeaks a contempt for the whole recording and policing system. A big spending example of this category is Ken Ross (representing contractors, horse racing, cement companies, and his own computer-printing outfit). His monthly expense account is always $6,999.66, which is composed of standard, large-figure, general-category expenses. When one realizes that Ross employs and pays the expenses of two other individuals, who must obviously have expenses that also vary from month to month, one realizes how much license the "standard" form really gives.

Some lobbyists do not itemize expenses at all. This in itself is not illegal, for only single-item expenses in excess of $25 need to be itemized. Some lobbyists have unitemized balances of $500 to $1,000 per month while other equally big spenders itemize all but $100.

Some forms present flagrant violations of the lobbying regulations. The expense account of Vincent D. Kennedy (Leslie Salt) for April was an exact duplicate of his January form to the penny. His expenses included many restaurant bills and other nonstandard, nonpredictable items, all of which were also identical. His February and March accounts were also *exact* duplicates of each other. It is a well known practice of another lobbyist to check weekly with the legislative analyst's office, where advocates are required to register, if it is time to file his monthly report. If the end of the month has passed, he is informed that the proper time has arrived. He then scrib-

* See the test for more substantive reforms to remedy the present imbalance in representation between the contending interests and to eliminate improper and excessive influence by individual lobbyists.

bles a copy of the previous month's report, exact to the inexact detail and submits the report. Certainly lobbyists' records do not deserve to be taken any more seriously than the lobbyists take them. Nor is it a question of bookkeeping difficulty. All lobbyists keep personal records of disbursements for tax and other purposes.

One common practice of lobbyists constitutes a direct violation of Sections 9903 and 9906 of the Government Code. With infrequent exception, no lobbyist records on his monthly statement contributions given by him in excess of $25 for the purpose of electing legislators and other government officials, as required by the aforementioned sections of the Government Code.

A very limited check of the candidates' and committee chairmen's contributions receipts revealed that a large number of lobbyists were contributing to the campaign funds of the gubernatorial and legislative candidates. In a check of all the 1970 expenditure records of the lobbyists against these campaign statements, the following lobbyists were found to have failed to record on their monthly statements contributions of $25 or more which were recorded in their names in the records of various candidates:

Daniel J. Creedon, Gordon Garland, J. E. Howe, Leslie D. Howe, R. D. Innis, Anthony Kennedy, Fred A. McCanlies, Jefferson E. Peyser, Robert Shillito.

The following lobbyists were listed on campaign contribution statements as contributors of amounts under $500. If their contributions are in excess of $25, they too are in violation of the statute:

Clive Bradford, R. Brown, A. Burdick, D. Burns, W. Cannon, Lawrence Chandler, K. Corkhill, Bruce Denebeim, James D. Garibaldi, Joseph Farber, Gordon Fleury, E. Frank, T. Giammugani, Donald A. Jensen, W. Keese, Paul Lunardi, LeRoy Lyon, J. P. McFarland, R. L. McNitt, M. Mahoney, J. Mahoney, A. Oppmen, Kent Redwine, J. Reidy, R. Reynolds, Kenneth A. Ross, D. Shields, Ed Soderberg, M. Stravers, R. Thigpen, R. E. Thompson, D. Trolio, J. Wells.

Before it is possible to ascertain whether a lobbyist is actually in violation of the requirement of recording contributions over $25, it is necessary to require that all contributions over $25 (instead of $500 in the present case) received by campaign committees be listed by contributor.

Comparative Campaign Expenditure Data,[a] 1960–1968

Name	Party	District	Amount Spent in 1968	1962 Candidates' Amounts
U.S. Senate—				
SIX-YEAR TERM				
Max Rafferty	R	——	$2,870,554	$ 392,563
Alan Cranston	D	——	1,374,611	243,482
Total			$4,245,165	$ 636,045

Name	Party	District	Amount Spent in 1968	Amount Spent By Winner In 1960
Congress—				
TWO-YEAR TERM				
*Don H. Clausen	R	1st	$ 46,705.33	$ 38,159.98
*Harold T. "Bizz" Johnson	D	2nd	23,591.92	14,882.07
*John E. Moss	D	3rd	32,089.31	1,135.30
*Robert L. Leggett	D	4th	59,205.63	37,966.69
*Phillip Burton	D	5th	30,696.97	33,228.34
*William S. Mailliard	R	6th	50,896.52	34,675.03
*Jeffery Cohelan	D	7th	51,145.71	23,497.71
*George P. Miller	D	8th	10,776.10	6,742.23
*Don Edwards	D	9th	43,507.20	32,245.21
*Charles S. Gubser	R	10th	24,235.10	42,245.93
*Paul N. "Pete" McCloskey, Jr.	R	11th	81,131.02	8,679.58
*Burt L. Talcott	R	12th	11,420.13	5,524.01
*Charles M. Teague	R	13th	61,446.67	41,207.98
*Jerome R. Waldie	D	14th	35,141.59	14,027.64
*John J. McFall	D	15th	31,549.76	44,779.62
*B. F. Sisk	D	16th	44,672.68	82,126.91
Glenn M. Anderson	D	17th	68,878.13	6,581.00
*Robert B. "Bob" Mathias	R	18th	75,901.25	55,663.74
*Chet Holifield	D	19th	13,563.28	3,853.75
*H. Allen Smith	R	20th	39,628.75	22,893.41
*Augustus F. "Gus" Hawkins	D	21st	13,525.88	77,268.57
*James C. Corman	D	22nd	79,914.76	62,031.43
*Del Clawson	R	23rd	48,196.46	9,030.91
*Glenard P. Lipscomb	R	24th	22,893.29	30,255.49
*Charles E. Wiggins	R	25th	27,846.36	68,662.19
*Thomas M. Rees	D	26th	29,521.00	13,880.55
*Ed Reinecke[2]	R	27th	75,133.09	9,920.01
*Alphonzo Bell	R	28th	28,513.74	43,344.74
*George E. Brown, Jr.	D	29th	86,452.21	9,468.96
*Edward R. Roybal	D	30th	28,143.67	53,628.52
*Charles H. Wilson	D	31st	43,759.44	——
*Craig Hosmer	R	32nd	29,693.02	——
*Jerry L. Pettis	R	33rd	69,515.73	——
*Richard I. Hanna	D	34th	66,391.00	——

a We are grateful to Pacific Telephone and Telegraph for gathering and presenting this information—even if at the expense of California's taxpayers.

Name	Party	District	Amount Spent in 1968	Amount Spent By Winner In 1960
*James B. Utt	R	35th	49,320.15	——
*Bob Wilson	R	36th	39,565.00	——
*Lionel Van Deerlin	D	37th	57,787.15	——
*John V. Tunney	D	38th	86,007.83	——
Total			$1,718,362.73	$ 927,607.50
Average			$ 45,220.07	$ 30,920.25

State Senate—
FOUR-YEAR TERM

Name	Party	District	Amount Spent in 1968	Amount Spent By Winner In 1960
*Randolph Collier	D	1st	$ 41,079.45	$ 3,161.34
*Stephen P. Teale	D	3rd	30,224.62	9,654.18
*Albert S. Rodda	D	5th	13,437.09	174.62
*George Miller, Jr.[2]	D	7th	27,388.94	5,916.41
*Milton Marks	R	9th	106,177.06	7,890.44
*Nicholas C. Petris	D	11th	115,154.60	11,621.95
*Alfred E. Alquist	D	13th	26,313.19	11,828.90
*Howard Way	R	15th	63,913.18	12,715.89
*Donald L. Grunsky	R	17th	1,566.26	9,733.32
*H. L. "Bill" Richardson	R	19th	26,532.71	11,140.75
*John L. Harmer	R	21st	33,482.50	24,894.59
*Lou Cusanovich	R	23rd	26,132.88	13,880.11
*Robert S. Stevens	R	25th	24,270.65	21,015.23
*George E. Danielson	D	27th	44,934.48	5,211.26
*Mervyn M. Dymally	D	29th	31,550.99	10,666.84
*James Q. Wedworth	D	31st	29,134.53	15,396.69
*Joseph M. Kennick	D	33rd	41,125.45	3,666.31
*James E. Whetmore	R	35th	25,520.17	18,406.65
*George Deukmejian	R	37th	8,084.29	15,043.81
*Jack Schrade	R	39th	70,792.48	7,970.44
Total			$ 786,815.52	$ 219,989.73
Average			$ 39,340.78	$ 10,999.49

State Assembly—
TWO-YEAR TERM

Name	Party	District	Amount Spent in 1968	Amount Spent By Winner In 1960
*Pauline L. Davis	D	1st	$ 18,717.10	$ 12,707.67
*Frank P. Belotti	R	2nd	11,581.40	6,970.00
*Leroy F. Greene	D	3rd	29,862.74	1,026.44
*Ray E. Johnson	R	4th	13,294.28	8,556.05
*John F. Dunlap	D	5th	14,138.28	15,460.70
*Eugene A. Chappie	R	6th	19,734.66	6,589.30
*William T. Bagley	R	7th	8,492.06	20,360.78
*Walter W. Powers	D	8th	15,163.50	11,667.79
*Edwin L. Z'berg	D	9th	30,521.28	7,324.95
*James W. Dent	R	10th	23,957.11	11,854.72
*John T. Knox	D	11th	26,864.94	7,526.35
*Robert T. "Bob" Monagan	R	12th	20,760.91	17,284.84
*Carlos Bee	D	13th	9,232.19	3,814.41
*Robert W. Crown	D	14th	19,560.11	8,820.52
*March K. Fong	D	15th	22,232.46	7,012.93

Name	Party	District	Amount Spent in 1968	Amount Spent By Winner In 1960
Don Mulford	R	16th	64,944.63	5,608.29
*John J. Miller	D	17th	26,484.87	1,204.77
*Willie L. Brown, Jr.	D	18th	33,993.91	19,969.10
Leo T. McCarthy	D	19th	32,113.08	7,485.82
*John L. Burton	D	20th	15,735.08	6,048.99
*Gordon W. Duffy	R	21st	22,362.43	2,331.20
*George W. Milias	R	22nd	15,707.09	6,532.86
*John F. Foran	D	23rd	44,962.88	3,139.98
*John Vasconcellos	D	24th	22,171.05	6,798.89
*Earle P. Crandall	R	25th	50,008.82	11,772.31
*Carl A. Britschgi	R	26th	17,801.89	6,298.29
*Leo J. Ryan	D	27th	7,721.49	3,322.68
*Kent H. Stacey	R	28th	32,098.73	9,606.54
*William M. Ketchum	R	29th	29,636.82	18,394.43
*John G. Veneman[2]	R	30th	14,185.62	7,277.88
*Frank Murphy, Jr.	R	31st	25,990.52	6,740.02
*George N. Zenovich	D	32nd	11,292.78	2,410.75
*Ernest N. Mobley	R	33rd	23,761.59	8,656.51
*Alan G. Pattee[2]	R	34th	6,696.35	10,526.37
*John V. Briggs	R	35th	23,452.41	6,702.06
W. Don MacGillivray	R	36th	80,624.42	17,992.35
*Ken MacDonald	D	37th	22,496.42	5,259.11
*Carley V. Porter	D	38th	15,087.69	4,854.76
*James A. Hayes	R	39th	11,242.84	4,157.65
Alex P. Garcia	D	40th	17,064.68	4,032.32
Henry "Hank" Arklin	R	41st	86,482.51	10,402.97
*Bob Moretti	D	42nd	25,520.15	15,361.49
*Carlos J. Moorhead	R	43rd	12,430.38	10,287.35
*Mike Cullen	D	44th	49,793.91	17,643.59
*Walter Karabian	D	45th	48,865.66	8,302.47
*Robert G. Beverly	R	46th	16,373.28	25,520.15
*Frank Lanterman	R	47th	5,220.89	7,123.97
*David A. Roberti	D	48th	34,236.70	7,357.70
*Peter F. Schabarum	R	49th	19,791.56	15,951.57
*William "Bill" Campbell	R	50th	62,945.31	17,997.36
*Jack R. Fenton	D	51st	19,610.49	11,025.94
*Floyd L. Wakefield	R	52nd	45,985.11	6,386.03
*Bill Greene	D	53rd	19,583.01	9,425.13
*John L. E. Collier	R	54th	3,302.92	11,267.73
*Leon Ralph	D	55th	15,951.79	3,484.53
*Charles Warren	D	56th	11,028.90	17,425.55
*Charles J. Conrad	R	57th	15,873.34	20,925.14
*Harvey Johnson	D	58th	54,054.67	10,477.32
*Alan Sieroty	D	59th	11,636.51	19,270.19
*Paul Priolo	R	60th	23,111.01	8,985.16
Henry A. Waxman	D	61st	13,805.32	8,265.00
*Newton R. Russell	R	62nd	24,160.35	5,901.65
*Yvonne W. Brathwaite	D	63rd	22,900.73	13,606.58
*Patrick D. McGee	R	64th	13,905.03	17,440.60

Name	Party	District	Amount Spent in 1968	Amount Spent By Winner In 1960
*Jesse M. Unruh	D	65th	53,767.00	6,142.19
*Joe A. Gonsalves	D	66th	37,113.50	12,343.39
*L.E. "Larry" Townsend	D	67th	43,142.51	3,140.11
*Vincent Thomas	D	68th	14,861.57	4,292.92
*Kenneth Cory	D	69th	70,862.46	4,828.94
*Robert H. Burke	R	70th	12,568.62	20,459.22
*Robert E. Badham	R	71st	6,367.29	11,096.47
*John P. Quimby	D	72nd	30,011.46	5,544.69
Jerry Lewis	R	73rd	47,038.32	7,658.31
*W. Craig Biddle	R	74th	17,546.98	8,781.61
*Victor V. Veysey	R	75th	18,495.80	25,079.01
*Pete Wilson	R	76th	24,596.41	5,611.68
*Wadie P. Deddeh	D	77th	36,047.28	17,534.24
*E. Richard Barnes	R	78th	20,763.88	15,190.88
Tom Hom	R	79th	44,196.65	10,955.48
*John Stull	R	80th	27,258.68	20,696.85
Total			$2,112,959.08	$ 813,292.54
Average			$ 26,411.99	$ 10,166.16

		Grand Total, Campaigning Costs	1968	1960
		(In both Primary and General Election)[3]	$8,863,301.33	$2,596,934.77

* Incumbent.

[1] Only 30 Congressional Districts existed in 1960, so there are no comparative figures for Districts 31–38. Based on the 1960 Census, the Districts were reapportioned in 1961 from 30 to a total of 38.

[2] No longer in office due to death or resignation.

[3] This figure represents the total amount spent by winning candidates only in the races for the House of Representatives, State Senate and State Assembly. The amount spent by the losing candidates is not included, except in the race for U.S. Senate.

Appendix 12C
Ronald Reagan—1970 Primary Contributors *

LAND-CONNECTED CORPORATIONS

Name	Amount
Adam Associates	$ 1,000
American Pine & Construction Co. (water)	$ 2,500
American Forest Prods. Corp.	$ 1,200
Bell Petroleum Co.	$ 5,000
Bechtel Corp.	$ 2,500
Beverly Lincoln-Mercury Inc.	$ 2,500
Beneficial Std. Life Ins. Co.	$ 1,000
Carnation Company	$ 7,500
Challenge-Cook Bros.	$10,000
Coberly-West Co.	$ 2,100
Coberly Ford	$ 2,500
Consolidated Rock Prods. Co.	$ 1,000
Central Industrial Engineering	$ 2,500
Cypress Management Co. (mining)	$ 1,000
California Cotton Oil Corp.	$ 1,500
California Liquid Fertilizer Co.	$ 1,000
Crocker National Corporation	$ 2,500
California Savings & Loan League	$ 2,500
Crown-Zellerbach Corp.	$ 2,500
California Canners & Growers	$ 1,500
Dart Industries Inc. (developers)	$ 5,300
Dunn Properties Corp.	$ 2,500
Dean Witter & Co. (owners)	$ 6,600
Engineering & Grading Contrs. Assn.	$ 7,500
E. & J. Gallo Winery	$10,000
Financial Federation Inc.	$ 2,500
Fireman's Fund Ins. Co.	$ 2,500
FMC Corp.	$ 5,000
Ferguson & Bosworth	$ 800
Gibson, Dunn & Crutcher	$ 2,500
Great Western Financial Corp.	$ 2,500
Gelco Developments	$ 1,000
George D. Hart, Inc.	$ 5,000
Hughes Active Citizenship Campaign	$ 2,500
Holmes Tuttle Ford	$ 2,500
Henry Sutcliffe Co.	$ 2,500
Hospital Pharmacies Inc.	$ 1,000
Imperial Bank	$ 1,000
Islais Creek Corp.	$ 1,500
Johnson & Higgins	$ 2,500
Kern County Land Co.	$12,500
Knudsen Corp.	$ 3,500
Lincoln-Manchester Properties	$ 3,000

* The Governor is not atypical in the nature of his campaign financiers. He has been selected not to single him out, but because he is an important example. The lists for other candidates, particularly for committee chairmen, are similar in nature, though not as long.

Note: A brief survey of recently submitted 1970 general election fund campaign contributors reveals that the same groups and individuals gave additional moneys in the same approximate proportion as in the primary.

Name	Amount
Latham & Watkins	$ 1,000
Lou Ehlers Cadillac	$ 2,500
Lurie Co., The	$ 2,500
McKee & Co.	$ 1,000
Macco Corp. (developer)	$ 2,500
Mission Viejo Co.	$ 1,000
Occidental Life	$ 1,000
Pacific Telephone Citizenship Plan	$ 2,500
Pan American Underwriters	$ 2,500
Property Research Financial Corp.	$ 2,500
Pacific Employers Ins. Co.	$ 2,500
Pinehurst Financial, Inc.	$ 2,500
Pacific Mutual Life Ins. Co.	$ 2,500
Pillsbury, Madison & Sutro	$ 5,000
Rifkind & Sterling	$ 1,000
Ralph M. Parsons Co., The	$ 2,500
Schneider Investments	$ 1,000
Southwest Savings & Loan	$ 1,000
Santa Fe Intl. Corp.	$ 8,500
Seaboard Finance Co.	$ 2,500
Santa Monica Bank	$ 1,000
Southern Pacific Co.	$ 7,000
Standard Realty & Development Co.	$ 1,000
Snider Lumber Prods. Co.	$ 1,000
Safeway Stores, Inc.	$ 1,000
Tishman Realty & Constr. Co.	$ 2,500
T.R.W. Good Government Program	$ 2,500
225 California Corp.	$ 2,500
Transamerica Corp.	$ 2,500
Twentieth Century Fox	$ 2,500
Union Bank	$ 1,500
United Financial	$ 1,000
U.S. Leasing International	$ 1,000
Western Airlines	$ 1,000
Warren King & Assoc., Inc.	$ 1,000
World Airways, Inc.	$ 2,500
Yosemite Insurance Co.	$ 1,000

LAND-CONNECTED INDIVIDUALS *

Name	Amount
AWES, GERALD A.—Chain-store executive; Chm. of Bd. & Chief Exec. officer of Lucky Stores, Inc.	$ 2,300
HAZELTINE, HERBERT S.—(of Adams, Duque & Hazeltine) Sec., Hoffman Electronics Corp., President of La Bolsa Tile Co.; Director of Norris Industries (Developers)	$ 2,500
DE BRETTEVILLE, CHARLES—banker; Pres. & Dir. of Spreckles Sugar Co. from 1951–'62; now Pres. & Chm. of Bd. of Dir. of Bank of California; also Dir. of P.G.&E., Shell Oil Co., Western Union, Safeway Stores	$ 800

* Sources: Who's Who, Standard and Poor's Directories, and Funk and Scott's Index to Trade Periodicals

Name	Amount
ASHBY, JACK L.—Steel Executive—President, Kaiser Steel in 1959; now V. Chmn. & Chief Exec. Officer & Dir. of Kaiser Industries Corp., Hamersley Iron, Meyers Drum Co., American Iron & Steel Ind., & National Industrial Conference Board	$ 2,500
BURNS, FRITZ B.—Real Estate Developer; has worked with Kaiser in developing communities; Chm. & Chief Exec. of Fritz B. Burns, Assoc., Santa Clara Indus. Park, Airport-Marina Hotel, Lincoln-Manchester Properties, Inc., Hawaiian Develop. Co.; President of Burns-Wilshire Corp., Panorama City Shopping Center, Kaiser Community Homes, Plaza Del Rey Development Corp., Hilton-Burns Holding Company; V.Chm., Bd. Dir. of Hilton Hotels Corp., Dominguez Water Corp.	$ 2,500
BECHTEL, K.K.—Chrm. & Dir., Industrial Indemnity Co., Dir., Wells Fargo Bank, Bechtel Corp.	$ 2,500
BECHTEL, STEPHEN S.—Sr. Dir., Bechtel Corp.; Dir., Indus. Indem. Corp.; Lakeside Corp.—Pres. & Dir.; So. Pacific Co., Dir.; Stanford Research Inst., Trustee; Ford Foundation, Trustee; Morgan Guaranty Trust Co. of N.Y., Dir.	$ 1,000
BARLOW, SYDNEY R.—V. Chm., Gibraltar Savings & Loan of Beverly Hills; Dir., Beverly Hills Nat. Bank	$ 5,000
CHANDLER, NORMAN—Chm. & Chief Exec. Off. of Times Mirror Co.; Chm., Emmett & Chandler; Dir., Buffms'; Dir., Tejon Ranch Co. & V.P.; Dir., Chandis Securities; Dir., Dresser Indus.; Dir., Security First Nat. Bnk., L.A.; Dir., Safeway Stores; Dir., Kaiser Steel; Dir., Pan Am. World Air.; Dir., Atchison, Topeka & Santa Fe Ry.; Pres. & Dir., Pacific Western Ind.; Advisory Bd. American Mutual Fund.	$ 2,500
COBERLY, C.—Pres. & Dir., Kobe Inc.; V-P & Dir., Wulff Acetylene Co., Dir., Baker Transworld Inc.	$ 2,400
COBERLY, WM. B., JR.—Pres. & Dir., Calif. Cotton Oil Corp.; Dir. of So. Calif. Edison; Dir., Kobe Co.; Pres. & Dir., Coberly-West; Dir., Forest Lawn; Dir., Amer. Sec. & Fidelity Corp.	$ 1,600
COOK, JOHN BROWN—Chm., Whitney Blake Co.; Chm., Reliable Electric Co.; Dir., Bradley Semi-Conductor; Pres. & Dir., Koiled Kords; Dir., Mich. Ave. National Bank of Chicago	$ 1,500
CROCKER, ROY—Crocker & Steelman (attorneys); Chrm., Lincoln Savings & Loan; Chrm., First Lincoln Finan. Corp.	$ 2,000
CALL, ASA—Dir., Auto. Club of So. Calif.; Dir., West. Bancorporation; Dir., Cypress Mines; Dir., United Calif. Bnk; Dir., Ass. So. Invest. Co.; Dir., Newhall Land & Farming Co.; Dir., Pacific Mutual Life Ins.; Dir., Calif. Portland Cement; Chm., Music Center Operating Co.	$ 2,500
CHICKERING, SHERMAN—(Chickering & Gregory, Att.); V-P, San Diego Gas & Elec.; Dir., San Luis Mining Co.	$ 1,000

Name	Amount
CHAMBERS, FRANK G.—Pres. & Dir., Continental Capitol Corp.; Dir., Data Products Co.; Dir., Guardian Packaging Co.; Dir., S. F. Life Ins. Co.; Dir., Western Operations; Dir., James Dole Engr.	$ 1,000
CARLSON, GEORGE—Dir., Odgers Drillings, Inc.	$ 1,200
DISNEY, ROY—Chm., Walt Disney Prod. (developer)	$ 9,600
DUQUE, GABRIEL C.—Dir., Security First Nat. Bank	$ 2,500
DE GUIGNE, CHRISTIAN—Chm. & Dir., Stauffer Chem. Co.; Dir., Bank of Calif.; Dir., Pacific Tel. & Tel.	$ 2,500
ENGLAND, A.E.—Pres. & Treas., A. E. England Pontiac, Inc.	$ 2,000
EDGERTON, HOWARD—Pres. & Dir., Calif. Savings & Loan	$ 2,200
EVANS, HUGH—Chm., West. Federal Savings & Loan Assn.	$ 2,500
FOGELSON, E.E.—Dir., Dr. Pepper; Dir., Mercantile Security Co.; Dir., Lone Star Exploration, Inc.	$ 6,000
FIRESTONE, LEONARD—Pres., Firestone Rubber & Tire; Dir., Wells Fargo Bank	$ 2,500
FOLLIS, F.G.—Dir., Crocker Citizens Nat. Bnk., & Crocker Nat. Corp.; Dir., Emporium Capwell Co.; Dir., Del Monte Corp.; Dir., Fund America; Dir., Fireman's Fund Ins.	$ 1,000
FLETCHER, KIM—Pres. & Dir., Home Federal Savings & Loan; Dir., First Fed. Savings & Loan; Calif. Savings & Loan League	$ 1,000
GRAY, DAVID—V-P, Continental Ins. Co., plus 13 other insurance companies and banks	$ 1,200
GRIFFITH, JOHN S.—Dir., John S. Griffith Properties; Dir., Norris Ind.; Dir., Buena Park Center; Dir., Calif. Inst. of Tech.; Dir., City Securities Co.; Dir., State Mutual Savings & Loan; Dir., Far West Finan. Corp.	$ 2,500
HARVEY, L.A.—Chm., Harvey Aluminum; Pres. & Dir., Consolidated Pacific Invest. Co.; Pres., Harcraft Co.; Chrm., Signal Ins. Co.	$ 2,000
HIBBARD, R. G.—Prs. & Dir., Calif. Shopping Centers, Inc.	$ 2,000
HOPE, FRANK—Dir., Home Fed. Savings & Loan; Pres., 6th Ave. Bldg. Corp.; V-P, Hope & Witheroe	$ 1,000
HOFFMAN, H. LESLIE—Hoffman Electronics, Chm.; Dir., Norris Indus.; Dir., Hollywood Turf Club; Dir., Pacific Lighting Corp.; Dir., AMFAC, Inc.	?
HARRISON, GREGORY—Pacific Power & Light Co., Dir.; Thermal Power Co., Dir.	$ 7,500
HAYNES, H. J.—Pres. & Dir., Standard Oil	$ 5,000
HEFFERNAN, PATRICK—Sunspiced Veg., Inc., Dir.	$ 2,500
HELLMAN, MARCO—Sr. Ptnr., J. Barth & Co.; Dir., Thermal Power Co.; Dir., Reserve Oil & Gas Co.; Dir., Coleman Co.; Dir., Fargo Oils; Dir. D.N. & E. Walter Co.	$ 5,000
JORGENSEN, EARLE—Earle M. Jorgensen Co., Chm.; Dir., Rheem Mfg. Co.; Dir., Northrop Corp.; Dir., Trans-	

Name	Amount

america Corp.; Dir., Kerr McGee Corp.; Trustee, Calif. State Col. | $ 2,500

JONES, FLETCHER—Chm. & Pres., Computer Sciences Corp.; Century City; Computax Corp. | $ 2,500

JEWETT, G. F.—Corp. V-P, Potlatch Forests; Dir., Rock Island Cir. | $ 2,000

KEITH, WILLIARD W.—Dir., Lockheed Aircraft; Hilton Hotels; Inv. Co. of America; Marineland of the Pacific; Amer.-Haw. S.S. Co.; Norris Industries; Marsh & Mc-Lennan; Colonial S & L | $ 8,200

KAISER, EDGAR—Kaiser Industries | $ 1,500

KAISER, L. M.—Mutual Broadcasting Corp.; Kaiser Ind. | $ 2,500

KENDRICK, CHARLES—Chrm., Schlage Lock Co. | $ 1,000

LINKLETTER, ART—A. Linkletter Oil Enterprise; World Wide Ventures; Bailer-Zoyer Ins.; Western Airlines; Royal Ind.; Neotec, Inc.; Harrell Corp. | $ 1,000

LEAVEY, THOMAS—Chm., Farmers Ins. Ex.; Truck Ins. Ex.; Mid-Century Inc., etc. | $ 1,000

LEE, RAYMOND E.—Lerner Stores; Hogan Faximile Corp.; Telautograph Corp.; Faberge, Inc.; Blue Cross | $ 5,100

LUNDBORG, LOUIS—Chm., Bank of America; Dir., Getty Oil | $ 2,500

MUDD, SEELEY W.—Cypress Mines Co.; Harvey Mudd College | $ 1,000

MACKAY, A. CAULDER—Pendleton Tool Ind.; Pacific Empl. Insurance Co. | $ 2,000

MILLER, ROBERT W.—Chm., Pacific Lighting Co.; Wells Fargo Bank; American Airlines; Caterpillar Tractor; Fiberboard Paper Prd. | $ 2,500

MILLER, OTTO N.—Chm., Standard Oil; Amer. Petroleum Ins.; Chamber of Commerce | $10,000

METCALF, J. R.—V-P, Alexander & Alexander, Inc. | $ 1,500

MURRAY, JAMES G.—Western Union International | $ 2,500

NIVEN, R. F.—Sec., Union Oil; Community Tel. of S. Cal. | $ 2,500

NORRIS, KENNETH—Chm., Norris Industries | $ 2,500

O'MELVENEY, JOHN—O'Melveney & Meyers; Crosby Invest. Co.; Security First Nat. Bank; Northrop Aircraft; Summit Lake Co.; Lerds Land; Denmar; Bing Crosby Land | $ 2,500

PIKE, ROBERT M.—Sec., Crocker Citizens Bank | $ 2,500

POWELL, STANLEY—B. of Cal. Int. Corp.; Matson Research Corp.; Matson Terminals; Oceanic Steamship; Bank of Calif.; Pacific National Life Ins.; First Hawaiian Bank | $ 5,000

PAGANINI, FRANK L.—Diamond Int'l Corp. V-P; First Western Bank, Dir. | $ 2,500

REYNOLDS, ROBERT O.—L. A. Rams Co.; Pacific Indemnity Co.; Air West Co., Inc.; Chubb Corp.; etc. | $ 1,000

Name	Amount
REED, CHARLES H.—Owner of Reed's; First National Bank of New Jersey, Dir.	$ 2,500
READY, THOMAS J.—Pres., Kaiser Alum. & Chem.; Dir., James Booth Alum., etc.	$ 1,000
ROBERTS,WILLIAM E.—Chm., Ampex; Dir., Wells Fargo; Dir., Raychem Corp.; Dir., R.R. Donnelly & Sons	$ 1,000
SALVATORI, HENRY—Chm., Western Geophysical; Dir., Litton Ind.; Transamerica Corp.; Grant Oil Tool Co.	$ 5,000
SIX, ROBERT F.—President, Continental Airlines; Dir., U.S. National Bank, etc.	$ 2,400
SHUMWAY, FORREST—President, The Signal Co.; Dir., Garret Corp.; Dir., Mack Trucks; Dir., Standard Insurance; Dir., Magnavox, etc.	$ 2,500
SIMPSON, W. A.—William Simpson Construction Co.	$ 2,500
SMITH, H. RUSSELL—President, Avery Prods.; Dir., Unitek Corp.; Dir., Title Ins. & Trust, etc.	$ 1,000
SESNON, PORTER—Director of: Fibreboard Corp., Calif. State Auto. Assn., Cypress Lawn Cemetery, Porter Estate Co., P.G.&E., Watkins-Johnson Co., Air California Co., etc.	$ 2,500
STARKEY, HAROLD—Chairman, First Fed. Savings & Loan; Southern Mortgage Co.; Starkey Investment; Fidelity & Guaranty Co.; Financial Realty, etc.	$ 1,000
TREFETHEN, EUGENE E., JR.—President & Dir., Kaiser Industries; Dir. of 11 Kaiser Companies; V. Chmn. of National Steel & Shipbuilding Co.	$ 1,000
WARD, MURRAY—Sr. Consultant, E. F. Hutton & Co.; Dir., Ducommun Realty; Ducommun, Inc.	$ 2,500
WITHERSPOON, WILLIAM D.—V-P, Bateman Eichler, Hill Richards Inc.; Dir., Associated Transport; Dir., Ralphs Grocery Co.; Dir., Witherspoon & Co.	$ 2,000
WOODRUFF, ROBERT W.—Chmn., Finance Comm. & Dir. of Coca-Cola; Dir., Southern Railway	$ 1,000
WILSON, W.A.—President & Dir., Pit & Quarry Publ.	$ 1,500
WRATHER, J.D., JR.—Chm. & Pres., Wrather Co. (owns and operates Disneyland Hotels); Dir., Transcontinental T.V. Corp.; Dir., Wrather Oil Co., Tele Prompter Corp., Capitol Records; General T.V., Pres. & Dir.; Balboa Bay Club, Inc., Pres. & Dir.; A. C. Gilbert Co.; Chm. & Dir. of Neotoc Corp.	$ 2,500
WILKIE, LEIGHTON A.—Chm., Doall Co. (sawing machines and tools); Chm., Continental Machines, Contour Saws, Fourth Northwestern Nat'l Bank, Director	$ 1,000
WIBLE, LEWIS A.—Chm. & Pres., Union Elec. Steel Corp.	$ 1,000
WATTIS, PAUL L.—Dir., Utah Construction Co.; Pres. & Dir. Wattis & Co.; Lakeview Mining Co.; Marsh & McLennan, Inc., V-P; Wattis Construction Co., V-P & Dir.	$ 2,500

Name	Amount
WHITE, WILLIAM G.—Chm. & Pres., Consolidated Freightways, Inc.	$ 1,200
WARD, STANLEY—V-P, Tenneco, Inc. (land use, oil, paper, real estate)	$ 1,200

Also:

SCHREIBER, T.	$ 2,500
LIVERMORE, N.	$ 2,500
IRVINE, S.	$ 2,500
CREEDON, DANIEL	$ 1,000
GOSLINE, J.E.	$ 2,500

Others: (Major Landowners or Known Development Investors)

ANNENBERG, WALTER H.	$ 5,000
HOPE, BOB	$10,000
FLEISHHACKER, MORTIMER	$ 2,500
GETCHELL, C.W.	$12,000
SESNON, W.T., JR.	$ 5,000
TROUSDALE, PAUL	$ 5,000

FRONTS (SOURCE NOT DETERMINABLE, BUT KNOWN GENERALLY TO BE SAME SOURCE AS INDIVIDUALS ABOVE)

Name	Amount
Anonymous	$ 2,000
A.F.C.	600
Committee for a Greater California	123,400
Californians for Truth in Campaigning	7,500
Citizenship Plan	2,500
General Telephone Government Club	2,500
Good Government Committee (Marin Co.)	3,500
Maritime Committee for Reagan	12,600
W. F. C. Committee	5,000

WOMEN (SOURCE NOT DETERMINED BUT MANY KNOWN LANDED INTERESTS, WIVES OR SISTERS)

Name	Amount
Appleby, Irene C.	$ 2,500
Autry, Jan	2,500
Alles, Mary Pope	5,000
Boyd, Mrs. Katherine E.	2,500
Browne, Mrs. Margaret Gray	2,000
Coberly, Victoria N.	800
Corbett, Margaret J.	1,000
Crocker, Ruth C.	2,500
Frawley, Geraldine Ann	3,000
Goldwyn, Frances	2,000
Hoffman, H. Leslie	2,500
Hume, Jacqueline H.	2,000

Name	Amount
Hamilton, Harriett	1,000
Hanna, Mrs. Howard	3,000
Kaiser, Sue Mead	1,500
Ledbetter, Mrs. F.W.	2,000
May, Mrs. Tom	8,000
Marvin, Elsie M.	1,000
Morse, Mrs. Maurine Church	2,500
Mudd, Mrs. Dorothy D.	1,000
Murphy, Gwendolyn Castle	1,000
Smith, Iris W.	700
Seaver, Mrs. Frank R.	14,500
Shumway, Agnes M.	2,500
Trugens, Lillian Disney	2,500
Up de Graff, Dorthy G.	1,000

GENERAL CORPORATIONS (NOT DIRECTLY LAND CONNECTED)

Name	Amount
Broadway-Hale Stores, Inc.	$ 5,000
Bloomingdale	5,000
Computer Science Corp.	15,500
California Retail Liquor Dealers Inst.	2,500
Emporium-Capwell Co.	1,000
Hospital Pharmacies Inc.	1,000
Lear-Siegler, Inc.	2,500
Max Factor & Co.	2,500
McCann-Erickson, Inc.	2,600
Northrop Good Citizenship Comm.	2,500
Reliable Electric Co.	1,500
Stauffer Chemical Co.	7,500
St. Francis Hotel	1,000
Virco Manufacturing Co.	2,500
Wood, James T., Jr.	1,000

UNLISTED PERSONS (LAND CONNECTION UNKNOWN)

Name	Amount
Afton, Frank H.	$ 800
Brennan, Bernard	1,000
Brandstedt, William	5,000
Bancroft, Phillip, Sr.	1,000
Bacciocco, Edward	1,500
Banks, Gerald	6,800
Brokate, George	1,000
Broidy, Steve	1,200
Coffey, Bertram C.	1,000
Chow, David	2,500
Cravens, Malcolm	1,000
Chasin, George & Eileen	1,000
Coghlan, John Phillip	1,000
Clausen, A.W.	2,500
Campbell, Dr. E. E.	1,000
Christensen, Mr. & Mrs. Charles	1,000

Name	Amount
Crean, Harry	1,000
Deutsch, Armand S.	2,500
Davis, Dr. Loyal	1,000
Davis, W. Thomas & Elizabeth Lloyd	1,500
Davis, Ralph K.	5,000
Davis, Paul L., Jr.	2,500
Doheny, William H.	2,500
Doccommun, Charles	2,500
Dutton, C.W.	500
Ester, Eddy B.	1,000
Evans, Lee & Goldie	1,000
Fisher, Montgomery R.	1,200
Finkelstein, Lester	1,200
Fasken, Davis	2,500
Glanville, Donald C.	1,000
Griffin, Z. Wayne	2,500
Gauer, Edward H.	1,000
Hughes, R.P.	1,000
Handler, Elliot	1,000
Henderson, G.B.	5,000
Hope, Charles B.	1,000
Hudson, Fred G.	1,000
Hartfield, Leo	1,000
Hahn, Ernest W.	2,500
Hilliard, H.T.	1,000
Hartunian, Mr. & Mrs. Albert	1,000
Jensen, J. Wilmar	1,000
Jenkins, Carey K.	1,000
Juda, Felix	1,000
Jagels, George D.	2,500
Jacobs, Clyde E.	1,000
Johnson, Gordon N.	1,000
Jennings, Fred	1,000
Ketchum, S.M.	1,000
Kerr, R.W.	2,000
Lowery, Edward E.	2,500
Landon, William	5,000
Lusk, John D.	1,000
Lund, William S. & Sharon D.	2,500
Lolli, Andrew R.	1,000
Lahanier, W.A.	1,000
Lundy, Mr. & Mrs. Victor	1,000
Middleton, J.D.	1,000
Morris, R.B.	1,000
MacLeod, John	800
Mortensen, Mr. & Mrs. William S.	2,500
Moe, Stanley A.	2,500
Miller, Ronald W. & Diane D.	2,500
Miller, Robert	1,000
Mott, G.M.	2,000
Moore, Joseph A., Jr.	1,000
Moore, Joseph G.	1,000
Metcalf, Lawrence V.	1,000

Name	Amount
McGuffin, M.S. (Custodian)	2,500
McBean, Peter	1,000
Ohrbach, Jerome K.	2,500
Parrin, A.B.	2,500
Pontius, H. Jack	1,100
Park, A.L.	1,000
Prentice, Mr. Spelman	2,500
Pereira, William L.	2,500
Peck, G.L.	1,000
Porter, Albert S.	1,800
Pardee, Douglas	2,000
Ross, N. Joseph	2,000
Robinson, J.D.	1,500
Sinclair, Harold J.	5,000
Slusser, Willis S.	1,500
Shumway, Douglas M.	2,500
Schmidt, M.M.	2,500
Sprague, Norman F., Jr.	1,000
Stillwell, Charley	2,500
Stearns, T.L.	1,000
Sparlis, Albert A.	2,500
Singleton, Henry E.	2,500
Shapiro, Marvin	5,000
Seipp, Edwin A., Jr.	5,000
Schilling, August H.	1,000
Swartz, Stanley	1,000
Sickles, Mr. & Mrs. Christopher	1,000
Sansone, O.O.	2,000
Tarble, Newton E.	1,000
Trammell, George W., Jr.	1,000
Timmermann, Ed	1,000
Thompson, George M.	1,000
Title, Sidney R.	2,500
Treathway, John A.	2,000
Tweeter, Clifford H.	2,500
Tully, Jasper W.	2,500
Virtue, Julian A.	2,500
Warner, J.L.	2,500
Welk, Robert	1,000
Washburn, Gene M.	2,500
Walker, G.A.	1,000
Wright, Cycil & Jane	2,200
Wittier, Mrs. Helen P.	2,500
Walker, Robert W.	1,000
Wunderlich, Martin	1,500
Weir, M. Brock	2,500

Appendix 12D
Campaign Contribution Law Summary

Section 11503 of the Electors Code compels disclosure of receipts and expenditures made by or on behalf of candidates for public office. Section 11504 limits the purposes for which such expenditures may be made. In Sections 11805 and 11834, parallel provisions exist for receipts and expenditures on behalf of propositions on the ballot. Under Section 11530, each campaign committee must appoint a treasurer to receive, disburse, and keep a true account of all money contributed and disbursed for campaign purposes. Candidates must file these accounts as statements for primary and other elections, and the statement filed in the primary must contain a verification stating that the candidate or treasurer has used all reasonable diligence in its preparation, and that it is true and as full and as explicit as he is able to make it. The statement requirement of Section 11560 applies where more than $200 is received or spent. Under Section 11504, the statement must show all money contributed to the candidate, all money expended by him, directly or indirectly, through himself or any other person, the names of all persons who furnish such money, the names of the persons to whom such money was paid, the specific nature of each item, any services performed, by whom they were performed, and the purposes for which the money was expended. The lawful expenses are restricted to the candidate's official filing fee, preparing, printing, circulating and verifying nomination papers, personal traveling expenses, rent and expenses of maintaining headquarters, halls and rooms for public meetings, payment of certain campaign personnel, advertising and office supplies, canvassing voters, conveying voters to and from the polls, and supervising registration of voters. In 1969, the provisions relating to political contributions were strengthened by an amendment sponsored by Assemblyman Unruh, making it mandatory to identify each donor with his specific contribution. For noncompliance with the disclosure requirements, an association and each treasurer is liable for $1,000, to be recovered in a civil suit brought by a citizen. Use of fraud, bribery, coercion or intimidation in election are felonies. All of these provisions are virtually without any history of enforcement.

Appendix 12E
Legislators' Occupation

ASSEMBLY

Name, District, Party, Committee Chairmen	Occupation	Clients of Firm or Area of Business
Arklin, Henry Dis. 41 (R)	Presently a general contractor	"Member of the Building Industry of America, and of the California Builders Council"; also large real Estate investor *
Badham, Robert Dis. 71 (R) Commerce & Public Utilities	Presently wholesale hardware and building material executive	Hoffman Hardware Company *
Bagley, William Dis. 7 (R) Revenue & Taxation	Presently an attorney	with Bagley, Bianchi & Sheeks; clients include: Calif. Western Gas Co., Allstate Insurance Co., Cal.-Marin Title Co., P.G. & E., Redwood National Bank, The Frouge Corp., Gulf Oil Corp., et al.**
Barnes, Richard Dis. 78 (R)	Legislator, formerly clergyman and Navy chaplain *	
Bee, Carlos Dis. 13 (D)	Legislator, formerly a teacher *	
Belotti, Frank Dis. 2 (R)	Farmer *	
Berryhill, Clare Dis. 30 (R)	Presently a rancher *	
Beverly, Robert Dis. 46 (R) Finance & Insurance	Presently an attorney	with Richards, Watson & Hemmerling; clients unknown, but specialize in "corporation, anti-trust, municipal, bank securities, mining, oil and gas, and real estate law . . . public utilities and public lands matters."**

* *Members of the California Legislature*, the *Sacramento Newsletter*, 1969; or the legislator's own biography.
** Martindale Hubbell Directory, 1969.

Name, District, Party, Committee Chairmen	Occupation	Clients of Firm or Area of Business
Biddle, Craig Dis. 74 (R)	Presently an attorney	with Badger, Biddle, & Ensign; clients include: Golden Valley Groves, Riverside Shopping Center, Inc., Totman Construction Co., et al.**
Braithwaite, Yvonne Dis. 63 (D)	Attorney	Private practice, clients unknown, but mostly civil rights; has represented Negro real estate brokers in the S.W. Realty Board Case*
Briggs, John Dis. 35 (R)	Presently an insurance broker	Owner of John Briggs Insurance Group*
Britshgi, Carl Dis. 26 (R) Government Adm.	Presently a farmer and realtor*	
Brown, Willie Dis. 18 (D)	Attorney	with Brown & Dearman; clients unknown—Brown will handle "redevelopment" cases according to office, but does not specialize in real property at all***
Burke, Robert Dis. 70 (R)	Presently owns building and construction blueprinting service. Formerly an engineer in oil and drilling production for a "major Orange Co. oil company"*	
Burton, John Dis. 20 (D)	Attorney	with Burton, Blumenthal & Burton; clients unknown but office and partner admit that they "have handled" development, zoning change, etc., matters***

*** Personal inquiries of office, legislator, or partners as prospective land developers seeking rezoning (asked only of attorneys where clients unknown).

Campbell, William
Dis. 50 (R) — Legislator, formerly school administrator *

Chappie, Eugene
Dis. 6 (R)
Rules — Presently a rancher (cattle) and fruitgrower *

Collier, John
Dis. 54 (R) — Businessman *

Conrad, Charles
Dis. 57 (R) — Presently in motion pictures and television *

Cory, Kenneth
Dis. 69 (D) — Presently businessman and insurance man — V.P. of Cornet Insurance Counselors Inc.*

Crandall, Earle
Dis. 25 (R) — Legislator, formerly school administrator *

Crown, Robert
Dis. 14 (D) — Attorney * — Private practice; clients unknown

Cullen, Mike
Dis. 44 (D) — Attorney — with firm of James H. Ackerman; clients unknown, but does specialize in real property law, office offers Cullen's personal services ***

Davis, Pauline
Dis. 1 (D) — Legislator *

Deddeh, Wadie
Dis. 77 (D) — Legislator, formerly teacher *

Dent, James W.
Dis. 10 (R) — Legislator, formerly educator *

Duffy, Gordon
Dis. 21 (R) — Legislator, formerly optometrist *

Dunlap, John
Dis. 5 (D)
Health & Welfare — Presently an attorney — with Coombs, Dunlap, & Dunlap; clients include: Napa Savings & Loan Assoc., Pacific Indemnity Co., City of Napa, and Southern Pacific Co. **

Name, District, Party, Committee Chairmen	Occupation	Clients of Firm or Area of Business
Fenton, Jack Dis. 51 (D)	Presently an attorney	with Diamond & Fenton; clients unknown, but do *not* specialize in real property law. They would, however, take a development or land case, offer Fenton's services ***
Fong, March Dis. 15 (D)	Legislator, formerly an educational consultant *	
Foran, John Dis. 23 (D) Transportation	Presently an attorney	with Leonoudakis, Kleines, Foran & McCarthy; clients unknown, but specializes in "property law" **
Garcia, Alex Dis. 40 (D)	Legislator *	
Gonsalves, Joe Dis. 66 (D)	Legislator, formerly a dairy farmer *	
Greene, Bill Dis. 53 (D)	Legislator *	
Greene, Leroy F. Dis. 3 (D)	Presently a civil engineer in highway and bridge design, etc.	Leroy F. Greene & Associates (consulting engineers). "While designing bridges he also serves as public member of the qualifications appraisal panel for Civil Service positions in the Calif. Bridge Department." *
Hayes, James F. Dis. 39 (R)	Attorney	with Blakey and Hayes; clients unknown, but do specialize in real property, offer Hayes' services ***
Hom, Tom Dis. 79 (R)	Presently a businessman	President of David Produce Co., Inc. (large San Diego produce company) *
Johnson, Harvey Dis. 58 (D)	Attorney *	with Wolford, Johnson, Pike and Wilson

Johnson, Ray E. Dis. 4 (R)	Presently in real estate and development, formerly in agriculture, petroleum, and forest industries *
Karabian, Walter Dis. 45 (D)	Presently an attorney; with Karns & Karabian; clients unknown, but "frequently handle matters in real estate," offer Karabian's services ***
Ketchum, William Dis. 29 (R) Agriculture	Presently a farmer; Works over 3,000 acres in northern San Luis Obispo County growing grain, beets, and alfalfa *
Knox, John T. Dis. 11 (D) Local Govern. Comm. Ways & Means	Presently an attorney; with Knox & Herron; clients unknown but "do a great deal of rezoning, etc.," offer Knox's services ***
Lanterman, Frank Dis. 47 (R)	Presently a land developer; Manages Lanterman Estate Properties, which includes 6,000 acre Spanish land grant, Rancho La Canada, inherited from his grandfather *
Lewis, Jerry Dis. 73 (R)	Insurance *
MacDonald, Ken Dis. 37 (D)	Legislator, formerly with the automobile industry*
MacGillivray, Don Dis. 36 (R)	Presently a general contractor *
McCarthy, Leo Dis. 19 (D)	Presently an attorney; with Leonoudakis, Kleines, Foran & McCarthy; clients unknown, but specialization includes property law **
McGee, Patrick Dis. 64 (R)	Deceased
Milias, George Dis. 22 (R) Select Comm. on Environmental Quality	Legislator, formerly a rancher *

Name, District, Party, Committee Chairmen	Occupation	Clients of Firm or Area of Business
Miller, John Dis. 17 (D)	Presently an attorney	with Miller, George & White; clients unknown but "have handled rezoning matters in the past," offer Miller's services ***
Mobley, Earnest Dis. 33 (R)	Presently a rancher *	
Monagan, Bob Dis. 12 (R) SPEAKER	Presently in insurance	Partner in Monagan-Miller Agency and member of the California Real Estate Association *
Moorhead, Carlos Dis. 43 (R)	Presently an attorney	Private practice; clients unknown, but practice includes "probate, corporation, business, real property . . ." **
Moretti, Bob Dis. 42 (D) Government Organization	Legislator, formerly staff of Assembly Comm. on elections and reapportionment; worked for manufacturing firms in Glendale *	
Mulford, Don Dis. 16 (R)	Presently in insurance	Partner in firm of Mulford, Poulton & Orr in Oakland *
Murphy, Frank Dis. 31 (R)	Presently an attorney	with Murphy, Murphy & Black; clients include: Big Creek Lumber Co., Fox Rents & Sells, E.P. Madigan & Son, Inc.; Da Pont Construction Co., et al.**
Porter, Carley Dis. 38 (D)	Legislator *	
Powers, Walter Dis. 8 (D)	Attorney	Private practice; clients unknown, but "has handled zoning and development matters." Powers might not be able to handle case because of "conflict," but only if in Sacramento ***

Priolo, Paul
Dis. 60 (R)
Presently in retail sales

Quimby, John
Dis. 72 (D)
Presently radio announcer & master of ceremonies *

Ralph, Leon
Dis. 55 (D)
Legislator *

Roberti, David
Dis. 48 (D)
Attorney but not practicing at this time (legislator) with Gelfand, Bergreen & Feinberg; clients unknown but does not specialize in real property; Roberti is not active ***

Russell, Newton
Dis. 62 (R)
Legislator, formerly in insurance *

Ryan, Leo
Dis. 27 (D)
Legislator, formerly teacher *

Schabarum, Peter
Dis. 49 (R)
Presently in realty and development President and owner of own real estate investment and development company *

Sieroty, Alan
Dis. 59 (D)
Attorney, but not practicing at this time (legislator) Neiman, Sieroty & Neiman; clients unknown but Sieroty not active and partners refuse to handle any case of this type because of possible conflict of interest ***

Stacy, Kent
Dis. 28 (R)
Legislator, formerly a pharmacist *

Stull, John
Dis. 80 (R)
Legislator, retired Navy Commander *

Thomas, Vincent
Dis. 68 (D)
Attorney "Although he represents the commercial fishermen, he has served on the Assembly Fish & Game Comm., and was Vice-Chairman for many years." *

Townsend, L.E.
Dis. 67 (D)
Formerly union representative and San Diego Gas & Electric Co. employee *

Unruh, Jesse
Dis. 65 (D)
Legislator *

Name, District, Party, Committee Chairmen	Occupation	Clients of Firm or Area of Business
Vasconcellos, John Dis. 24 (D)	Presently an attorney	with Ruffo & Oneto; clients include: Del Webb Corp. (developers), San Martin Vineyards Co., A.J. Raisch Paving Co., San Felipe Cattle Co., Doud Lumber Co., Santa Clara Sand & Gravel Corp., San Jose Lettuce Dist., Trans America Title Ins. Co., O'Neill & Ellis Lumber Co., et al.**
Veysey, Victor Dis. 75 (R)	Presently rancher and farmer, formerly worked for General Tire & Rubber	Raises, among other things, sugar-beets on 1,000 acres *
Wakefield, Floyd Dis. 52 (R)	Retail businessman *	
Warren, Charles Dis. 56 (D)	Presently an attorney	with Warren, Odell & Miller; clients include: Eastern Columbia Inc., various unions, the Montebello Meat Co., etc.**
Waxman, Henry Dis. 61 (D)	Presently an attorney	with Valenci, Rose & Gerstensled; clients unknown, but handles cases in development, real property, offer Waxman's services *** Waxman claims that he does not handle cases
Wilson, Pete Dis. 76 (R) Urban Affairs & Housing	Attorney, but not now practicing law; member of San Diego Realty Board	with Davies & Burch; clients unknown, but do handle real estate and zoning matters ***
Wood, Bob Dis. 34 (R)	Farmer *	
Z'Berg, Edwin Dis. 9 (D)	Presently an attorney	Private practice; clients unknown, but "does handle development and rezoning, etc., cases often, offer Z'Berg's services ***

Name, District, Party, Committee Chairman	Occupation	Clients of Firm or Area of Business
Zenovich, George Dis. 32 (D)	Presently an attorney	Private practice; clients unknown, but "has worked with development in the past," offers Zenovich's services ***

SENATE

Name, District, Party, Committee Chairman	Occupation	Clients of Firm or Area of Business
Alquist, Alfred Dis. 13 (D) Select Comm. on Rapid Transit	Legislator, formerly Trans. Supervisor for So. Pacific R.R. and former lobbyist	
Bielenson, Anthony Dis. 26 (D) Health & Welfare	Attorney, but hasn't practiced for several years (legislator) ***	with Bielenson & Leavey; clients unknown
Bradley, Clark Dis. 14 (R)	Attorney *	Private practice; clients unknown
Burgener, Clair Dis. 38 (R)	Presently a realtor	Real estate (member of Calif. Real Estate Assoc. and the Nat'l Assoc. of Real Estate Boards) *
Burns, Hugh Dis. 16 (D)	Presently in insurance and savings & loan	Chm. of the Bd. of Sequoia Savings & Loan Assoc.*
Carrell, Tom Dis. 22 (D) Select Comm. on Environmental Control	Businessman	Interests unlisted and unknown, member of Chamber of Commerce *
Collier, Randolph Dis. 1 (D) Transportation	Presently in title business (real estate)	Directs Siskiyou County Title Co.*

Name, District, Party, Committee Chairman	Occupation	Clients of Firm or Area of Business
Cologne, Gordon Dis. 1 (D) Transportation	Presently an attorney	with March, Moore & Cologne in Indio; clients include: Valley Sanitary District, I.K.I. Farms, Security Title Insurance Co., Thermal Sanitary District, Coachella Valley Recreation & Park District, Hartford Accident & Indemnity, et al.**
Coombs, William Dis. 20 (R) Water Resources	Attorney, formerly a CPA and an executive in the construction industry	with Coombs & Friel; clients unknown, but have handled and will handle real property, zoning, development cases. Coombs will not handle such matters "while in Senate," partner will handle ***
Cusanovich, Lou Dis. 23 (R)	Legislator, formerly owned and operated lumber business until his election, associated with Hammond Lumber Co. & E.K. Wood Lumber Co.*	
Danielson, George Dis. 27 (D)	Presently an attorney	with Danielson, Johnson & Burgard; clients include: Security First Nat'l Bank and United Calif. Bank, others unknown**
Deukmejian, George Dis. 37 (R)	Presently an attorney	with Lucas, Lucas & Deukmejian; clients unknown, but "specialize" in real property, development and zoning cases. Deukmejian will not personally handle all cases because of possible conflict ***
Dills, Ralph Dis. 32 (D)	Attorney, but not practicing at this time (legislator) *	Private practice, clients unknown

Dolwig, Richard Dis. 12 (R)	Presently an attorney	with Dolwig, Miller, Berlin and O'Grady, representing land interests. "Since 1946 he has been carving himself a career as a practicing lawyer in Redwood City and as a lawmaker in Sacramento." *
Dymally, Mervyn Dis. 29 (D)	Legislator, formerly teacher *	
Grunsky, Donald Dis. 17 (R) Finance	Presently an attorney	with Grunsky & Pybrum; clients include: P.G. & E., Allstate Insurance Co., Calif. State Auto Assoc., State Farm Mutual Auto Ins. Co., Pacific Greyhound Lines, Granite Construction Co., Lester Development Corp., Owen B. Cattle Co., et al.**
Harmer, John Dis. 21 (R)	Presently an attorney, formerly Program Director of Public Affairs for the National Assoc. of Manufacturers	with Harmer & Crane; clients unknown, but firm has handled development cases and will handle them, offers Harmer's personal services ***
Kennick, Joseph Dis. 33 (D)	Presently in insurance	"Since 1955 (he) has been an active representative for Insurance Securities Inc., a California trust fund." *
Lagomarsino, Robert Dis. 24 (R) Natural Resources & Wildlife	Presently in insurance	with Danch, Ferro, Lagomarsino & Cooper; clients include: Santa Clara Realty Co., Ventura Industrial Park, Westlands Savings and Loan Assoc., Crestview Mutual Water Co., Del Norte Municipal Water District, County Growers Supply Co., Beneficial Finance, La Vista Farms, et al.**
Marks, Milton Dis. 9 (R)	Presently an attorney	with Marks, Pederson & Frediani; clients unknown, but "have handled real estate, rezoning, etc., cases in past." Possible conflict of interest might preclude Marks handling case ***
Marler, Fred Dis. 2 (R)	Attorney *	Private practice; clients unknown

Name, District, Party, Committee Chairman	Occupation	Clients of Firm or Area of Business
McCarthy, John Dis. 4 (R) Insurance & Financial Institutions	Presently a contractor and developer	"He is Vice President and General Manager of the Robert McCarthy Company." *
Mills, James Dis. 40 (D)	Legislator, former teacher and historian *	
Moscone, George Dis. 10 (D)	Presently an attorney	with Morgan & Moscone; practice includes: "corporation, real property, and probate law" **
Nejedly, John Dis. 7 (R) Select Comm. on Salinity Intrusion in Agricultural Soils	Attorney, but not practicing law at this time (legislator) ***	Private practice, clients unknown
Petris, Nicholas Dis. 11 (D)	Presently an attorney	with FitzSimmons & Petris; clients unknown, but specialize in development law, handle such cases regularly, offer Petris's personal services ***
Richardson, H.L. Dis. 19 (R)	Presently in advertising	Owner of Richardson Advertising of Pasadena *
Rodda, Albert Dis. 5 (D)	Legislator,* formerly teacher *	
Schmitz, John Dis. 34 (R) Local Government	Legislator, formerly college instructor	Honored with awards from "Realtors of Orange County" *

Schrade, Jack
Dis. 39 (R)
Rules Committee

Presently a rancher-businessman

For twenty years the Director of Southland Savings & Loan; for twelve years Director, V.P., of Helix Irrigation District—"Winner of California Real Estate Citation . . . 'He prides himself on his ability to kill bad legislation.'"*

Sherman, Lewis
Dis. 8 (R)
Government Organization

Presently an attorney

with Sherman, Coward, MacDonald, Gonser; clients include: Lambert Properties, Ponderosa Paper Co., Graysix Corp., West Coast Steel Co., H.F. Walker Co., Nelson Vacuum Pump Co., Alasco Rubber & Plastic Co., Cal-Pride Co., et al.**

Short, Alan
Dis. 6 (D)

Presently an attorney *

with Short & Short; clients unknown, but does not specialize in property law

Song, Alfred
Dis. 28 (D)

Presently an attorney

with Song, Kell & Schwartz; clients unknown but have handled development cases, etc. Song is busy but otherwise might personally handle case ***

Stevens, Robert
Dis. 25 (R)

Attorney

Private practice; clients unknown but have handled development cases. Stevens might be too busy to personally handle the case, but it is not precluded ***

Stiern, Walter
Dis. 18 (D)
Revenue and Taxation

Legislator, formerly a veterinarian *

Teale, Stephen
Dis. 3 (D)

Legislator, formerly physician, surgeon

Walsh, Lawrence
Dis. 30 (D)
Select Comm. on Urban Affairs

Presently in construction

The Walsh Equipment Company "became the number one industrial dealer for Massey-Ferguson, Inc. in the U.S. and Canada."

Name, District, Party, Committee Chairman	Occupation	Clients of Firm or Area of Business
Way, Howard Dis. 15 (R)	Legislator, formerly a farmer *	
Wedworth, James Dis. 31 (D)	Businessman (retail sales) *	
Whetmore, James Dis. 35 (R)	Presently an attorney	with Roarke & Holbrook; clients include: Tustin Water Works, The Fund Insurance Co., Security Title Insurance Co., The Orange County Republican Central Comm., The Huntington Beach Co. (oil and land developers), W.T. Grant Co., et al.**

Notes

CHAPTER 1

1. Source: U.S. Department of Commerce, Bureau of the Census, *Area Measurement Reports, Areas of California: 1960*, Series GE-20 No. 6 (March, 1965).
2. *Ibid.*
3. From 1969 *California Statistical Abstract*.
4. From 1969 *California Statistical Abstract*.
5. *1939 Hearings: Violations of Free Speech and Rights of Labor* Landholdings in California, Exhibit 9589.
6. Includes survey of *Los Angeles Times* and *Sacramento Bee* over past several years and of trade press both through *Funk and Scott's Directory* and separate reviews of *Western Fruit Grower, Produce Marketing,* other leading agricultural press.
7. Including *Walker's Manual of Far Western Corporations* (1968), *Standard and Poor's, Moody's,* et al.
8. Including *Metsker's Atlases, Ballis's Map, Price's Map, Henry's Atlases, Real Estate Directory Inc. Atlases,* et al.
9. "A Statistical Profile of California Corporate Farms," December, 1970.
10. *Ibid.*, p. 1.
11. Source: Survey of Assessors, 1970.
12. Source: Survey by John Elam et al., U.C. Davis, 1970.
13. Source: Metsker's Maps Survey, 1958.
14. Source: Assessor's Survey, 1970.
15. See W. Reich's Analysis over San Francisco radio station KPFA, 1969 (transcript); see also Drapers, *Dirt on California;* see also Appendix 1D.
16. See *S.F. Chronicle*, February 21, 1969.
17. *Ibid.*
18. See Appendix 1B for a comparative listing of landholdings of these corporations and others. A list of Ronald Reagan contributors is presented in Appendix 12C and includes their individual directorate and executive positions.
19. *Land interest* is here defined as any party or association with a direct profit stake in a particular land use or in a public policy which subsidizes or enriches that use. This definition includes landowners and developers, farmers, loggers, miners, and drillers. It also includes the financiers who specialize in backing and profiting from these endeavors. Chapters 2 and 5, and the full Report, define these interests in greater detail and describe the nature and extent of land involvement of California's financial industry.

CHAPTER 2

1. Dr. Snyder, "Problems of Agricultural Land," testimony taken before a joint meeting of the Assembly Interim Committees on

Revenue and Taxation and Agriculture of the California State Legislature (Fresno, January 30, 1964), p. 6.

2. *Ibid.*, p. 7.
3. Hearings Before the Joint Committee on Open Space Lands, California Legislature (Sacramento, 1968), part 2, p. 5.
4. Livingston and Blainey recently attempted to compute the cost to Palo Alto of the development of the open spaces of its rolling foothills. Even without including the cost of open-space loss, their analysis concluded that net economic benefits of development would be less than the net benefits of leaving most of the land as open space.
5. Source: U.S. Bureau of the Census.
6. Report on the Williamson Act by the Joint Commitee on Open Space Land, 1969.
7. These lands are generally appraised (four times assessed value) at between $600 and $1400 per acre. However, actual value is often put at $1500 to $3000 (see *Calif. Crop and Livestock Reporting Service*, Sacramento, May 1970).
8. Assembly Committee on Agriculture, *California Farm Labor Force: A Profile* (April 1969), p. 12.
9. Sheldon L. Greene, *Immigration Law and Rural Poverty—The Problems of the Illegal Entrant*, Duke L.J. 487, 1969.
10. *Alberto Dias and Epitacio Rios et al. v. Kay-Dix Ranch et al.*, p. 15.
11. 20 CFR 602.20-22.
12. *L.A. Times*, March 3, 1959.
13. *S.F. Chronicle*, July 30, 1959.
14. Frank Valenzuela Affidavit, pp. 1–2.
15. C. Dirck Ditwiler, "Institutional Constraints and Economic Optima—A Basis for Management Decisions in Intraregional Water Transfer," *Land Economics*, Vol. XLIV, No. 2 (May 1968), Gianninni Foundation Paper No. 280, p. 183.
16. Bain et al., see Chapter III, p. 399.
17. Bain, "Water Resource Development," pp. 61–62.
18. Quoted in *Dirt*, p. 5, from September 1968 article, *Wall Street Journal*.
19. Sekler, p. 10.
20. Roy J. Smith, "The Lemon Pro-Rate in the Long Run," *Journal of Political Economy*, Vol. 69, No. 6 (December 1961), pp. 573–586.
21. John Jamison, "Marketing Orders, Cartels, and Cling Peaches," Food Research Institute Studies, Vol. VI, No. 2 (1966), p. 123.
22. E.W. Grove, "The Concept of Income Parity for Agriculture," quoted in *Organization and Competition in the Fruit and Vegetable Industry*, Technical Study No. 4, National Commission on Food Marketing (June 1966), p. 320.
23. Charles M. Hardin, "Agriculture in the Nation's Politics," *Readings in Agricultural Policy*, R.J. Hildreth, ed. (U. of Nebraska Press, 1968), p. 89.
24. See *Vanishing Air*, by John Esposito (Grossman, 1970).
25. This figure, from the 1970 *Pesticide Use Report* of the California Department of Agriculture, does not include many pesticide applications which growers perform themselves, instead of hiring a commercial applicator. Total pesticide application in

California has been estimated at 200 million pounds per year (*Public Health Report*).

26. See the alarming laboratory study, suppressed for many months, documenting teratogenic (birth-defect-causing) properties of 2,4,5-T, described in Thomas Whiteside, *Defoliation* (Ballantine, 1970).

27. Investigators are now checking the degree of dioxin contamination in 2,4-D.

28. Temperatures as high as 1500 degrees Fahrenheit do not destroy dioxins.

29. For a complete discussion of pesticide control, see *Sowing the Wind*, by Harrison Wellford (Grossman Publishers, 1972).

30. Most of the cases presented were collected from State Public Health files by Dr. Irma West, formerly a medical officer of the Bureau of Occupational Health and director of the Injury Control Project of the California State Department of Public Health.

31. Contract Report #19, California Community Studies on Pesticides, California Department of Public Health, files of Project Director, Robert C. Fellmeth.

CHAPTER 3

1. Ronald Reagan, Address to the California Legislature, Jan. 22, 1969.

2. California Water Code, §1320 (a).

3. California Water Code, §13207.

4. California Water Code, §13360.

5. California Water Code, §13320–13331.

6. California Water Code, §13050 (1); §13241; §13263 (a); §13000.

7. California Water Code, §13241 (d).

8. See Martindale-Hubbell Directory.

9. List of those supporting AB413, available from Assembly Water Committee.

10. Interview with Richard Bain, FWQA in Alameda, California.

11. California Water Code, §13350.

12. Final Report of the Study Panel, Appendix A, p. 21.

13. Final Report of the Study Panel, Foreword, p. ii.

14. Report of actions taken by the SWRCB and the nine California Regulation Water Quality Control Boards, January 1–May 15, 1970 (hereinafter Report of Actions Taken . . . January 1–August 15, 1970).

15. Ronald Robie, *Water Pollution: An Affirmative Response by the California Legislature*, 1 Pacific L.J.1, 29 (1970).

16. California Water Code, §13260 (a); see San Francisco Bay Regional Board, Status of Water Quality Control 4th Quarter 1969, p. 12. We were told that no marked change has occurred. No more recent report exists.

17. *Sacramento Bee*, August 6, 1970.

18. *Sacramento Bee*, July 30, 1970, p. 1 (reporting hearings of the U.S. Senate Environment Subcommittee); "Environmental Mercury Hazards," Sportfishing Institute Bulletin No. 215, June 1970 (reporting the testimony of Victor Lambou, Federal Water

Quality Administration, at U.S. Senate Commerce Committee hearings in early May, 1970).

19. San Francisco Regional Water Quality Control Board Resolution 68-27 (Union Oil Company Requirements), April 30, 1968, pp. 7–9.

20. San Francisco Regional Board, Report to the Public—"Water Quality In San Francisco Bay, Past-Present-Future" (incomplete edition, March 13, 1970) unnumbered page between p. 3 and p. 7.

21. San Francisco Regional Board, Resolution 68-27, *supra*. pp. 9–12.

22. *Id.*, p. 9.

23. *Id.*

24. *Id.*, p. 10.

25. Self-Monitoring Program and Schedule, *supra*. n. 1 p. 71.

26. Union Oil Company, "Water Quality Report for San Francisco Refinery, Summary of Compliance, 1970 Monthly Discharge Rating"—RWQCTB. July 14, 1970.

27. Untitled memo in Union Oil Refinery's file at the San Francisco Board, Oakland, California.

28. San Francisco Regional Water Quality Control Board, Status of Water Quality Control, 4th Quarter 1969, p. 18.

29. Report of a phone call from Neil O'Brien, Union Oil, February 3, 1970, in Union's file at the San Francisco Board.

30. *Id.*

31. *Id.*

32. *Id.*

33. Untitled memo in Union Oil's file at the San Francisco Board (same as note 2, p. 75).

34. *Id.*

35. California Water Code §13005 (West Supp. 1968).

36. The information in this section draws heavily from the article "Poisoning the Wells," *Environment*, January–February 1969, V. 1, No. 1, pp. 16–22.

37. Public Health Service, Drinking Water Standards, Revised 1962, U.S. Department of HEW, pp. 6 and 46–50.

38. Memo to City Council, City of Delano, January 23, 1967, from Louis Shepard, City Manager.

39. USDA, Crop Reporting Board, Statistical Reporting Service, Consumption of Commercial Fertilizers (November 28, 1969).

40. George R. Hawkes, Assistant National Manager—Agronomy, Chevron Chemical Company; quoted in *Agricultural Waste Waters*, Report No. 10 of the Water Resources Center, University of California, 1966.

41. *Delano Nitrate Investigation*, Department of Water Resources, Bulletin 143-6, August 1968.

42. State Department of Public Health, "POLICY FOR ADMINISTRATIVE PROCEDURES WHEN NITRATES IN PUBLIC WATER SUPPLIES EXCEED USPHS DRINKING WATER STANDARDS," March 1967, contained in Appendix to *Delano Nitrate*, investigation, *ibid.*, p. 42.

43. Article in *Ventura Star Free Press*, Ventura, California, July 8, 1970, "Farm Worker Health Laws Said Undermined By Pressures."

44. Letter from Robert Webster, Deputy Director, California De-

partment of Public Health, July 3, 1969 to Gerald Minford, City Manager of Delano.

45. Hearings Before the Subcommittee on Air and Water Pollution of the Senate Public Works Committee, 1968, pp. 975 et seq.

46. *Id.*

47. *Id.*, Albert Stevenson, pp. 1246–1947.

48. See Richard Curtis and Elizabeth Hogan, *Perils of the Peaceful Atom* (Ballantine, New York, 1969), pp. 193–194.

49. *Id.*

50. *Outdoor California*, (Department of Fish and Game, March–April 1970), p. 16.

51. Precise statistics available from the federal Environmental Protection Agency.

52. Professor Joseph Sax, *Casebook*, University of Michigan, p. 11.

53. One acre-foot is the amount of water which would cover one acre to a depth of one foot. It equals approximately 325,851 gallons.

54. According to A. Alan Post, the State's Legislative Analyst, California pays approximately ½% more interest on its borrowings because of the Water Project—a difference amounting to hundreds of millions of dollars for the towns, cities, school districts, and other governmental units that rely heavily on bond issues. The Project also may have totally prevented some areas from selling bonds.

55. Carey McWilliams, *California: The Great Exception*, 1948, p. 298.

56. James Milliman, "Economic Problems of the MWD of Southern California," 32nd Annual Conference of the Western Economic Association, *Proceedings*, (1957), p. 42.

57. *Ibid.*, p. 43.

58. Charles T. Main, Inc., Final Report, "General Evaluation of the Proposed Program for Financing and Constructing the State Water Resources Development System," October 1960.

59. 86th Congress, 1st Session, 1959, 105 Congressional Record, Part 6, p. 7670.

60. Bureau of Reclamation, "Feasibility Report on San Luis Units," (May 6, 1955), p. 89.

61. 38% of $24.

62. The actual supply will be one maf until 1979, and 783,000 acre-feet, adjustable up to 900,000 acre-feet thereafter.

63. Subcommittee on Irrigation and Reclamation, *Acreage Limitation Review*, 85 Cong. 2nd Session (1958), pp. 87–88.

64. Bain et al., p. 417.

65. *Ibid.*, p. 645.

66. *Ibid.*, p. 276.

67. *Ibid.*, p. 409.

CHAPTER 4

1. From an advertisement in *California Living*, the magazine of the Sunday *San Francisco Chronicle and Examiner*.

2. *The Last Frontier*—A Study of the Conservation and Development of the Resources of the Marine and Coastal Environment in California, prepared by the Subcommittee on Marine Resources

and the Subcommittee on Conservation of the Assembly Committee on Natural Resources.

CHAPTER 5

1. William H. Holmes, "The Small Timber Company—An Endangered Species," for the S.J. Hall Lectureship in Industrial Forestry, May 26, 1970.
2. *Ibid.*

CHAPTER 6

1. Kenneth Goldin, *Recreational Parks and Beaches . . .* , Research Report No. 16 (Institute of Governmental Affairs, U.C. Davis, 1970). Table 1.
2. Legislative Analyst, *op. cit.,* 1971–1972, p. 462.
3. *Ibid.*
4. Legislative Analyst, *op. cit.,* 1970–1971, p. 826.
5. Legislative Analyst, *op. cit.,* 1971–1972, p. 463.
6. *Ibid.,* p. 464.
7. *Ibid.,* p. 466.
8. *Ibid.*
9. *Ibid.*
10. Gordon Robinson, now Forestry Consultant for the Sierra Club, in a statement released on February 26, 1969.
11. Sam Wood, *Open Space: Problems and Programs* (1964), p. 7.

CHAPTER 7

1. Legislative Analyst, *op. cit.* (1970–1971), p. 31.
2. See Nader Report on Water Pollution, *Water Wasteland,* by David Zwick, et al., released in April of 1971.

CHAPTER 8

1. See the full Report for details.
2. "Draft for Discussion Purposes Only," *op. cit.*

CHAPTER 9

1. National Commission on Urban Problems, *Building the American City,* (U.S. Government Printing Office, 1968), p. 388.
2. Douglas Commission, *op. cit.,* p. 390.
3. Richard Netzer, *Economics of the Property Tax,* (Brookings Institute, Washington, D.C., 1966), p. 33.
4. *Ibid.*
5. *Ibid.*
6. Douglas Commission, *op. cit.,* p. 386.
7. State Office of Planning, *California State Development Plan Program,* 1968, p. 252.
8. *Building the American City,* pp. 325–326.
9. *Id.*
10. Bureau of the Census, *A Study of the Economy of Santa Clara County,* p. 31.
11. Brendan Lynch et al., San Jose Land Use Study (preliminary draft), pp. 57–58.
12. *Village of Euclid v. Ambler Realty Co.,* 272 U.S. 365, 47 S. Ct. 114 (1926).

13. The famous case of *Nectow v. Cambridge* moderated the *Euclid* decision.
14. "Let's Abolish the Planning Commissions," *Cry California*, Vol. II, No. 4 (Fall 1967), pp. 15–39.
15. Karl Belser, "The Planning Fiasco in California," Vol. II, No. 3 (Summer 1967), p. 13.
16. *Id.*
17. Lynch, et al., *op. cit.*, p. 29.
18. *Ibid.*, p. 16.
19. *Ibid.*
20. Belser, *op. cit.*, p. 13.
21. State Office of Planning, *op. cit.*, p. 110.
22. See especially the Statewide Public Policy Conference, the California State Development Plan Program (June 26 and 27, 1968), Sacramento.
23. State Office of Planning, *op. cit.*, p. 110.
24. Belser, *op. cit.*, p. 13.
25. Lynch et al., *op. cit.*, p. 2.
26. *Ibid.*, p. 1.

CHAPTER 10

1. *California Statistical Abstract*, 1969, p. 140.
2. See *The Environmental Handbook*, ed. by Garrett DeBell (Ballantine, New York, 1970), p. 204.
3. *The Potential for Bus Rapid Transit*, (Automobile Manufacturers Association, Inc., Detroit, February 1970), at 37.
4. Standard & Poor's *Standard Corporation Descriptions*, January 15, 1970, p. 4915.
5. *United States v. National City Lines*, (7th Circuit 1951) 186 F.2d 562, 565; *cert. den.* 71 S.Ct. 735.
6. *Ibid.*, pp. 565–566.
7. *Ibid.*, p. 566.
8. *Ibid.*, pp. 564–565.
9. *Ibid.*, p. 564.
10. *Ibid.*, p. 565.
11. Crump, Spencer, *Ride the Big Red Cars: How Trolleys Helped Build Southern California*, (Los Angeles, Crest Publications, 1962) at 94.
12. Moody's *Public Utility Manual*, 1950.
13. *Oakland Post-Enquiry*, May 15, 1946.
14. *Ibid.*
15. *United States v. National City Lines*, (7th Circuit 1951), 186 F.2d 562 at 564.
16. *Christian Science Monitor*, February 6, 1958.
17. See note 15, p. 569.
18. (7th Circuit 1951) 186 F.2d 562, rehearing denied January 31, 1951.
19. 71 S.Ct. 735.
20. *A.C. Transit Times*, September 1963, p. 29.
21. *Oakland Post-Enquirer*, August 22, 1950, p. 3.
22. *Christian Science Monitor*, February 6, 1958.
23. *Standard and Poor*, see note 2.
24. Moody's *Transportation Manual* 1969 at 1603.
25. *Id.*

26. *Id.*
27. Crump, *supra,* note 9 at 208.
28. *Oakland Post-Enquirer,* May 15, 1946 at 1.
29. The list is contained in Department of Public Works, *Southern Crossing, supra,* note 5, following p. 9.
30. *Southern Crossing, supra,* note 75, p. 3.
31. The following are excerpted from Table 7-2, *Id.,* p. 58.
32. Stokes, B.R., "Bay Area Rapid Transit," *Highway Research Board Special Report III,* Washington, 1970, p. 3.
33. *Oakland Tribune,* August 7, 1970.
34. Government Code §66509 (b).
35. Government Code §66514 (b).
36. Government Code §66518.
37. Letter from Harry J. Krueper to Albert Hill dated May 6, 1970.
38. *Id.,* p. 3.
39. Letter from J.W. Deinema to John F. McLaughlin dated July 24, 1968, p. 1.

Index